DICTIONARY OF
ICT

FOURTH EDITION

Also published by Bloomsbury Reference:

***Specialist dictionaries*:**

Dictionary of Accounting	0 7475 6991 6
Dictionary of Banking and Finance	0 7475 6685 2
Dictionary of Business	0 7475 6980 0
Dictionary of Computing	0 7475 6622 4
Dictionary of Economics	0 7475 6632 1
Dictionary of Environment and Ecology	0 7475 7201 1
Dictionary of Hotels, Tourism and Catering Management	1 9016 5999 2
Dictionary of Human Resources and Personnel Management	0 7475 6623 2
Dictionary of Law	0 7475 6636 4
Dictionary of Marketing	0 7475 6621 6
Dictionary of Medical Terms	0 7475 6987 8
Dictionary of Military Terms	0 7475 7477 4
Dictionary of Nursing	0 7475 6634 8
Dictionary of Politics and Government	0 7475 7220 8
Dictionary of Science and Technology	0 7475 6620 8

***Easier English™ titles*:**

Easier English Basic Dictionary	0 7475 6644 5
Easier English Basic Synonyms	0 7475 6979 7
Easier English Dictionary: Handy Pocket Edition	0 7475 6625 9
Easier English Intermediate Dictionary	0 7475 6989 4
Easier English Student Dictionary	0 7475 6624 0
English Study Dictionary	1 9016 5963 1
English Thesaurus for Students	1 9016 5931 3

Check Your English Vocabulary workbooks:

Business	0 7475 6626 7
Computing	1 9016 5928 3
Academic English	0 7475 6691 7
PET	0 7475 6627 5
IELTS	0 7475 6982 7
FCE +	0 7475 6981 9
TOEFL®	0 7475 6984 3

Visit our website for full details of all our books
www.bloomsbury.com/reference

DICTIONARY OF
ICT

FOURTH EDITION

S.M.H. Collin

BLOOMSBURY

A BLOOMSBURY REFERENCE BOOK
www.bloomsbury.com/reference

Originally published by Peter Collin Publishing
as *Dictionary of Information Technology*

First published 1987
Second edition published 1996
Third edition published 2002
Fourth edition published 2004

Bloomsbury Publishing Plc
38 Soho Square, London W1D 3HB

British Library Cataloguing-in-Publication Data
A catalogue record for this book is available from the British Library

ISBN 0 7475 6990 8

Editor
Steven Gregory
Lecturer, York College

Text Production and Proofreading
Katy McAdam, Heather Bateman, Emma Harris

All papers used by Bloomsbury Publishing are natural, recyclable
products made from wood grown in well-managed forests.
The manufacturing processes conform to the
environmental regulations of the country of origin.

Text processing and computer typesetting by Bloomsbury
Printed and bound in Great Britain by
CPI Antony Rowe, Chippenham and Eastbourne

Preface

This dictionary provides the user with a comprehensive up-to-date vocabulary used in information technology. It covers computers, programming, networks, communications, database design, the Internet, electronic mail, world wide web, electronics, music, graphics, multimedia, desktop publishing, and many other computer applications. In addition, the dictionary covers communications subjects including film, video, TV and radio.

The entries are each explained in clear and strightforward English. Examples are given to show how the words and phrases are used in context. General comments about particular items of interest, complex ideas or hardware or software applications are given in separate boxes. Quotations from a range of magazines and journals are given to show how the words are used in real text. The supplement at the back of the book provides extra information that would be useful for computing and communications studies.

A

A: used in some operating systems to denote the first disk drive on the system

A1 /ˌeɪ ˈwɒn/, **A2, A3, A4, A5** *noun* ISO recommended international standard sizes of paper or sizes of screen ○ *a standard 300 d.p.i. black and white A4 monitor* ○ *You must photocopy the spreadsheet on A3 paper.* ○ *We must order some more A4 headed notepaper.*

abandon /əˈbændən/ *verb* to clear a document, file or work from a computer's memory without saving it ○ *Once you have abandoned your spreadsheet, you cannot retrieve it again.*

abbreviation /əˌbriːviˈeɪʃ(ə)n/ *noun* a short form of a word, command or instruction ○ *Within the text, the abbreviation proc is used instead of processor.*

ABD *abbr* Apple Desktop Bus

abend /ˈæbend/ *noun* an unexpected stoppage of a program that is being run, caused by a fault, error or power failure ○ *An interrupt from a faulty printer caused an abend.* Also called **abnormal end, abnormal termination**

aberration /ˌæbəˈreɪʃ(ə)n/ *noun* **1.** distortion of a light beam or image caused by defects in the optical system **2.** distortion of a television picture caused by a corrupt signal or incorrect adjustment

ablation /əˈbleɪʃ(ə)n/ *noun* a method of writing data to an optical storage device in which a laser burns a hole or pit, representing digital bits of data, into the thin metal surface of the storage device

COMMENT: A laser burns a hole or pit (which represents digital bits of data) into the thin metal surface of the storage device.

abnormal /æbˈnɔːm(ə)l/ *adjective* not normal ○ *It's abnormal for two consecutive disk drives to break down.*

abnormal end /æbˌnɔːm(ə)l ˈend/ *noun* same as **abend**

abnormally /æbˈnɔːməli/ *adverb* not as normal or not as usual ○ *The signal is abnormally weak.*

abnormal termination /æbˌnɔːm(ə)l ˌtɜːmɪˈneɪʃ(ə)n/ *noun* same as **abend**

abort /əˈbɔːt/ *verb* to end a process in the event of a malfunction occurs by switching the computer off manually or by an internal feature ○ *The program was aborted by pressing the red button.*

About... /əˈbaʊt/ (*in the SAA CUA front end*) a menu selection that tells you who developed the program and gives copyright information

above-the-fold /əˌbʌv ðə ˈfəʊld/ *adjective* referring to the part of a webpage that is seen by all users who call up the page, because they do not have to scroll down to read it. Compare **below-the-fold**

above-the-line costs /əˌbʌv ðə ˌlaɪn ˈkɒsts/ *plural noun* variable costs involved in making TV films (such as scriptwriters, actors, sets, etc.) as opposed to below-the-line costs (film crew, technicians, etc.). Compare **below-the-line costs**

AB roll /ˌeɪ ˈbiː ˌrəʊl/ *noun* (*in a multimedia application*) a sequence of two video or music segments that are synchronised so that one fades as the second starts

absolute address /ˌæbsəluːt əˈdres/ *noun* a computer storage address that can only access one location. Also called **actual address, machine address**

absolute cell reference /ˌæbsəluːt sel ˈref(ə)rəns/ *noun* a spreadsheet reference that always refers to the same cell, even when copied to another location

absorb /əbˈzɔːb/ *verb* to take in light, liquid or a signal

absorptance /əbˈzɔːptəns/ *noun* a measure of how completely an object or substance absorbs radiant energy. Opposite **reflectance**

absorption /əbˈzɔːpʃən/ *noun* the power loss of a signal when travelling through a medium, due to its absorptance

abstract /ˈæbstrækt/ *noun* a short summary of a document ○ *It's quicker to search through the abstracts than the full text.*

abstracting and indexing /ˌæbstræktɪŋ ən ˈɪndeksɪŋ/ *verb* making summaries and indexes for articles and books

ac *abbr* academic organisation (NOTE: used in email and website addresses)

AC *abbr* alternating current

Academy The Academy of Motion Picture Arts and Sciences □ **Academy awards** the yearly presentation of the Oscar award by the Academy to artists and technicians for excellence in their area of the film world

ACAP /ˌeɪ siː eɪ ˈpiː/ *noun* an email system developed to work with the IMAP4 email protocol to provide extra features such as management of an address book. Full form **application configuration access protocol** (NOTE: It was originally termed IMSP (Interactive Mail Support Protocol).)

ACC /ˌeɪ siː ˈsiː/ *noun* the most important internal CPU storage register, containing the data word that is to be processed. Full form **accumulator**

accelerated graphics port /ək ˌseləreɪtɪd ˈɡræfɪks ˌpɔːt/ *noun* full form of **AGP**

accelerated motion /əkˌseləˌreɪtd ˈməʊʃ(ə)n/ *noun* a special (film) effect in which the camera is run at a slower frame rate than the standard 24 frames per second which gives the effect of faster-than-average motion

acceleration /əkˌseləˈreɪʃ(ə)n/ *noun* ◆ **mouse acceleration**

acceleration time /əkˌseləˈreɪʃ(ə)n taɪm/ *noun* the time taken for a disk drive to spin a disk at the correct speed, from rest ○ *Allow for acceleration time in the access time.*

accelerator /əkˈseləreɪtə/ *noun* ◆ **accelerator key**

accelerator board /əkˈseləˌreɪtə bɔːd/, **accelerator card** /əkˈseləˌreɪtə kɑːd/ *noun* a circuit board that carries a faster or more advanced version of the same processor that runs a computer. Adding an accelerator board to a computer makes it run faster.

accelerator key /əkˈseləˌreɪtə kiː/ *noun* a key that, when pressed together with another, carries out a function that would otherwise have to be selected from a menu using a mouse ○ *Instead of selecting the File menu then the Save option, use the accelerator keys Alt and S to do the same thing and save the file.*

accent /ˈæksənt/ *noun* a mark above a character to indicate a different pronunciation

accented /ˈæksəntɪd/ *adjective* (*of a letter*) with an accent on it

accept /əkˈsept/ *verb* **1.** to agree to do something ○ *He accepted the quoted price for printing.* **2.** to take something which is being offered **3.** to establish a session or connection with another computing device

acceptable /əkˈseptəb(ə)l/ *adjective* which can be accepted ○ *The error rate was very low, and is acceptable.*

acceptable use policy /əkˌseptəb(ə)l juːz ˈpɒlɪsi/ *noun* a set of rules that describe what a user can write or do on the Internet without offending other users. Abbr **AUP**

acceptance /əkˈseptəns/ *noun* the action of accepting something

acceptance test /əkˈseptəns test/ *noun* a test to check that a piece of equipment will perform as required or will reach required standards

acceptance testing /əkˌseptəns ˈtestɪŋ/ *noun* the performing of an acceptance test

access /ˈækses/ *noun* the fact of being allowed to use a computer and read or alter files stored in it. This is usually controlled by a security device such as a password. □ **to deny access** to refuse access to a circuit or system for reasons of workload or security

access authority /ˈækses ɔːˌθɒrəti/ *noun* permission to carry out a particular operation on data

access-barred /ˌækses ˈbɑːd/ *adjective* prevented from accessing particular data

access category /ˈækses ˌkætəɡ(ə)ri/ *noun* a category that defines which files or data a user can access and which he or she cannot

access code /ˈækses kəʊd/ *noun* a series of characters or symbols that must be entered to identify a user before access to a computer is permitted

access control /ˈækses kənˌtrəʊl/ *noun* a security device such as a password that only allows selected users to use a computer system or read files

access control list /ˌækses kənˈtrəʊl lɪst/ *noun* full form of **ACL**

access head /ˈækses hed/ *noun* the part of a disk drive that moves to the correct part of the disk's surface and reads information stored on the disk ■ *verb* to call up (data) which is stored in a computer; to obtain data from a storage device ○ *She accessed the employee's file stored on the computer.*

accessible /əkˈsesɪb(ə)l/ *adjective* which can be reached or accessed ○ *Details of customers are easily accessible from the main computer files.*

accession number /əkˈseʃ(ə)n ˌnʌmbə/ *noun* **1.** a number in a record that shows in which order each record was entered **2.** a serial number used in a library indexing system

accessions /əkˈseʃ(ə)nz/ *plural noun* new books which are added to a library

access log /ˈækses lɒɡ/ *noun* a file on a website server computer that contains a record of every visitor to the website, showing when a person visited and which pages he or she viewed ○ *The access log is invaluable – we produce graphs of the pages that are most popular using an access log analyser program.*

access method /ˈækses ˌmeθəd/ *noun* **1.** a means used for the internal transfer of data between memory and display or peripheral devices. Differences in the methods used are often the cause of compatibility problems. **2.** a set of rules that allows a device to send data onto a network. Token passing and CSMA/CD are two methods commonly used in a local area network.

accessor /ˈæksesə/ *noun* a person who accesses data

accessory /əkˈsesəri/ *noun* an extra, add-on device, e.g. a mouse or printer, that is attached to or used with a computer ○ *The printer comes with several accessories including a soundproof hood.* (NOTE: The plural is **accessories**.)

access privilege /ˈækses ˌprɪvɪlɪdʒ/ *noun* the status granted to a user that allows him or her to see, read or alter files

access provider /ˈækses prəˌvaɪdə/ *noun* same as **ISP**

access rights /ˈækses raɪts/ *plural noun* the rights of a particular user to access a particular file or data object

access time /ˈækses ˌtaɪm/ *noun* **1.** the total time that a storage device takes between the moment the data is requested and the return of the data ○ *The access time of this dynamic RAM chip is around 200nS – we have faster versions if your system clock is running faster.* **2.** the length of time required to find a file or program, either in main memory or a secondary memory source

accidental /ˌæksɪˈdent(ə)l/ *adjective* which happens by accident ○ *Always keep backup copies in case of accidental damage to the master file.*

accordion fold /əˈkɔːdiən fəʊld/, **accordion fanfold** *noun* method of folding continuous paper, one sheet in one direction, the next sheet in the opposite direction, allowing the paper to be fed into a printer continuously with no action on the part of the user. Also called **fanfold**

account /əˈkaʊnt/ *noun* (*in a network or online system*) a record of a user's name, password and rights to access a network or online system ○ *If you are a new user, you will have to ask the supervisor to create an account for you.* ■ *verb* to keep track of how much time and resources each user of a network or online system uses

accounting package /əˈkaʊntɪŋ ˌpækɪdʒ/ *noun* a piece of software that automates a business's accounting functions ○ *We now type in each transaction into the new accounting package rather than write it into a ledger.* Also called **accounts package**

account name /əˈkaʊnt neɪm/ *noun* the unique name of a user on a network or online system ○ *John Smith's account name is JSMITH.*

accounts package /əˈkaʊnts ˌpækɪdʒ/ *noun* same as **accounting package**

accumulate /əˈkjuːmjʊleɪt/ *verb* to gather several things together over a period of time ○ *We have gradually accumulated a large databank of names and addresses.* (NOTE: **accumulates – accumulating – accumulated**)

accumulator /əˈkjuːmjʊleɪtə/, **accumulator register** /ˌeɪ siː ˈsiː/ *noun* full form of **ACC** ○ *Store the two bytes of data in registers A and B and execute the add instruction – the answer will be in the accumulator.*

accuracy /ˈækjʊrəsi/ *noun* the total number of bits used to define a number in a computer (NOTE: The more bits allocated the greater the accuracy of the definition.)

accurate /ˈækjʊrət/ *adjective* correct; without any errors ○ *The printed bar code has to be accurate to within a thousandth of a micron.*

accurately /ˈækjʊrətli/ *adverb* correctly or with no errors ○ *The OCR had difficulty in reading the new font accurately.*

> COMMENT: Most high level languages allow numbers to be represented in a more accurate form by using two or more words to store the number.

ACD /ˌeɪ siː ˈdiː/ *noun* a specialised telephone system that can handle lots of incoming calls and direct them to a particular operator according to programmed instructions in a database. Full form **automatic call distribution**

ACE *noun* a 1000 watt spotlight (*film*)

ACES *noun* computer-operated camera movement system developed by Disney Studios which is designed to film repeatable camera moves on separate exposures. Full form **automatic camera effects system**

acetate /ˈæsɪteɪt/ *noun* a sheet of transparent plastic used for making overlays

acetate base /ˈæsɪteɪt beɪs/ *noun* plastic material used as the standard base for motion picture film

acetate tape /ˈæsɪteɪt teɪp/ *noun* audiotape consisting of acetate backing with magnetically sensitive oxide coating

acetone /ˈæsəˌtəʊn/ *noun* a clear, flammable liquid which is used to clean film print surfaces and splices and other editing and filming apparatus (*film*)

achromatic /ˌeɪkrəˈmætɪk/ *noun, adjective* (an optical device) that has been corrected for chromatic aberration

achromatic colour /ˌeɪkrəmætɪk ˈkʌlə/ *noun* a grey colour within the range between black and white displayed by a graphics adapter

ACK /ˌeɪ siː ˈkeɪ/ *noun* a signal that is sent from a receiver to indicate that a transmitted message has been received and that it is ready for the next one ○ *The printer generates an ACK signal when it has received data.* Full form **acknowledge**

acknowledge /əkˈnɒlɪdʒ/ *noun* full form of **ACK**

acknowledged mail /əkˌnɒlɪdʒd ˈmeɪl/ *noun* a function that signals to the sender when an electronic mail message has been read by the recipient

acknowledgements /əkˈnɒlɪdʒmənts/ *noun* text printed at the beginning of a book, where the author or publisher thanks people who have helped

ACL /ˌeɪ siː ˈel/ *noun* a security system that has a list of user names and passwords that is checked by the operating system to find out if a particular user is allowed to access or use a resource or feature of the shared computer or network. Full form **access control list**

acoustic /əˈkuːstɪk/ *adjective* referring to sound

acoustical feedback /əˌkuːstɪk(ə)l ˈfiːdbæk/ *noun* distortion in an audio signal, due to a part of an amplified signal being picked up by the microphone and amplified again until the amplifier is overloaded

acoustic coupler /əˌkuːstɪk ˈkʌplə/ *noun* a device that connects to a telephone handset, converting binary computer data into sound signals to allow it to be transmitted down a telephone line

COMMENT: The acoustic coupler also converts back from sound signals to digital signals when receiving messages. It is basically the same as a modem but uses a handset on which a loudspeaker is placed to send the signals rather than a direct connection to the phone line. It is portable and clips over both ends of a normal telephone handset. It can be used even in a public phone booth. The acoustic coupler has generally been replaced by a direct cable link from the computer's modem to the standard telephone socket.

acoustic hood /əˈkuːstɪk hʊd/ *noun* a soundproof cover put over a line printer to cut down its noise

acoustics /əˈkuːstɪks/ *noun* study and science of sound waves

acquisition /ˌækwɪˈzɪʃ(ə)n/ *noun* the accepting, capturing or collecting of information

ACR /ˌeɪ siː ˈɑː/ *noun* a type of videotape recorder

Acrobat ▸ **Adobe Acrobat**

acronym /ˈækrənɪm/ *noun* an abbreviation, formed from various letters, which makes up a word which can be pronounced ○ *The acronym FORTRAN means Formula Translator.*

actintic light /ˈæktɪntɪk ˌlaɪt/ *noun* light which is able to cause chemical change in a material, such as film

action /ˈækʃən/ *noun* **1.** something which has been done **2.** (*in an SAA CUA front end*) a user event **3.** movement **4.** the command to begin a performance, said by a director to an actor (*film*)

action bar /ˈækʃən bɑː/ *noun* a top line of the screen that displays the menu names

action bar pull-down /ˌækʃən bɑː ˈpʊl ˌdaʊn/ *noun* (*in an SAA CUA front end*) a feature whereby the full menu is displayed below the menu name when a user moves the cursor to a particular menu name on the action bar

activate /ˈæktɪˌveɪt/ *verb* to start a process or to make a device start working ○ *Pressing CR activates the printer.*

activated /ˈæktɪveɪtɪd/ *adjective* button or field in a screen layout that has a script attached to it; the script is executed when the user clicks on the button (NOTE: If the button or field is not activated, it is normally displayed greyed out and does not respond if a user selects it.)

active /ˈæktɪv/ *adjective* busy, working or being used

Active Document /ˌæktɪv ˈdɒkjʊmənt/ *noun* a standard Windows application that is accessed from within a web browser and controlled by special commands in the webpage

active file /ˌæktɪv ˈfaɪl/ *noun* a file that is currently being worked on

active pixel region /ˌæktɪv ˈpɪks(ə)l ˌriːdʒən/ *noun* an area of a computer screen that can display graphic image information

active printer /ˌæktɪv ˈprɪntə/ *noun* a printer that is currently connected to the computer's printer port

active program /ˌæktɪv ˈprəʊgræm/ *noun* (*in a multitasking system*) a program that is currently in control of the processor

active record /ˌæktɪv ˈrekɔːd/ *noun* a record that is being updated or accessed

Active Server Page /ˌæktɪv ˈsɜːvə peɪdʒ/ *noun* a webpage that is created only when accessed by a visitor, allowing the website to display up-to-date information or information from a database ○ *The database search results page is implemented as an Active Server Page.* Abbr **ASP**

active streaming format /ˌæktɪv ˈstriːmɪŋ ˌfɔːmæt/ *noun* full form of **ASF**

active video /ˌæktɪv ˈvɪdiəʊ/, **active video signal** /ˌæktɪv ˈvɪdiəʊ ˌsɪɡn(ə)l/ *noun* a part of a video signal that contains picture information

ActiveVRML /ˌæktɪv viː ɑː em ˈel/ *noun* ♦ **VRML**

active window /ˌæktɪv ˈwɪndəʊ/ *noun* **1.** an area of the display screen where the operator is currently working **2.** (*in a GUI or SAA CUA front end*) the window that is currently the focus of cursor movements and screen displays. ◊ **window**

ActiveX /ˌæktɪv ˈeks/ a trade name for a programming language and program definition used to create small applications designed to enhance the functionality of a webpage. ◊ **applet, Java, VBScript**

COMMENT: ActiveX applications, called applets, are often used to add database or multimedia effects to a website that cannot be supported with basic HTML commands. When a user visits the web page that uses the ActiveX applet, the program is automatically downloaded by the user's browser and run on the user's computer.

activity /ækˈtɪvɪti/ *noun* being active or busy

actual address /ˌæktʃuəl əˈdres/ *noun* same as **absolute address**

actual data transfer rate /ˌæktʃuəl ˌdeɪtə ˈtrænsfɜː ˌreɪt/ *noun* the average number of data bits transferred in a period of time

actuator /ˈæktʃʊeɪtə/ *noun* a mechanical device that can be controlled by an external signal, e.g. the read/write head in a disk drive

ACU /ˌeɪ siː ˈjuː/ *noun* a device that allows a computer to call stations or dial telephone numbers automatically. Full form **automatic calling unit**

acuity /əˈkjuːɪti/ *noun* ability of the ear to detect frequency or volume changes

acutance /əˈkjuːtəns/ *noun* the ability of a lens to produce clear edges

acute /əˈkjuːt/ *adjective* very sharp or clear

AD *noun* the person who carries out the director's instructions, oversees the work and whereabouts of the actors, technicians and rest of crew and works in close contact with the production unit (*film*) Full form **assistant director, associate director**

A/D *abbr* analog to digital

ADA /ˌeɪ diː ˈeɪ/ *noun* a high-level programming language that is used mainly in military, industrial and scientific fields of computing

adapt /əˈdæpt/ *verb* to change, adjust or modify something so that it fits ○ *Can this computer be adapted to take 5.25 inch disks?*

adaptation /ˌædæpˈteɪʃ(ə)n/ *noun* the ability of a device to adjust its sensitivity range according to various situations

adapter /əˈdæptə/, **adaptor** /əˈdæptə/ *noun* a device that allows two or more incompatible devices to be connected together ○ *The cable adapter allows attachment of the scanner to the SCSI interface.*

adaptive channel allocation /əˌdæptɪv ˈtʃæn(ə)l æləˌkeɪʃ(ə)n/ *noun* provision of communications channels according to demand rather than a fixed allocation

adaptive compression /əˌdæptɪv kəm ˈpreʃ(ə)n/ *noun* a data compression system that continuously monitors the data it is compressing and adjusts its own algorithm to provide the most efficient compression

adaptive differential pulse code modulation /əˌdæptɪv dɪfəˌrenʃ(ə)l ˈpʌls kəʊd mɒdjuˌleɪʃ(ə)n/ *noun* full form of **ADPCM**

adaptive interframe transform coding /əˌdæptɪv ˌɪntəfreɪm trænsˈfɔːm ˌkəʊdɪŋ/ *noun* a class of compression algorithms commonly used with video signals to reduce the data transmission rate

adaptive packet assembly /əˌdæptɪv ˈpækɪt əˌsembli/ *noun* a method used by the MNP error correcting protocol to adjust the size of data packets according to the quality of the telephone line. The better the line, the bigger the packet size.

adaptive routing /əˌdæptɪv ˈruːtɪŋ/ *noun* the ability of a system to change its communications routes in response to various events or situations such as line failure (NOTE: The messages are normally sent along the most cost-effective path unless there is a problem with that route, in which case they are automatically re-routed.)

adaptive system /əˌdæptɪv ˈsɪstəm/ *noun* a system that is able to alter its responses and processes according to inputs or situations

adaptor /əˈdæptə/ *noun* another spelling of **adapter**

ADB™ *abbr* Apple Desktop Bus

ADC /ˌeɪ diː ˈsiː/ *noun* an electronic device that converts an analog input signal to a digital form, which can be processed by a computer. Full form **analog to digital converter**

add /æd/ *verb* **1.** to put figures together to make a total ○ *In the spreadsheet each column should be added to make a subtotal.* **2.** to put things together to form a larger group ○ *The software house has added a new management package to its range of products.*

added entry /ˌædɪd ˈentri/ *noun* a secondary file entry in a library catalogue

addend /'ædend/ *noun* the number added to the augend in an addition

adder /'ædə/ *noun* a device or routine that provides the sum of two or more inputs, either digital or analog

COMMENT: A parallel adder takes one clock cycle to add two words, a serial adder takes a time equal to the number of bits in a word to add.

add-in /'æd ɪn/ *noun, adjective* something that is added to something else

additional /ə'dɪʃ(ə)nəl/ *adjective* added or extra ○ *Can we link three additional workstations to the network?*

additional dialogue replacement /əˌdɪʃ(ə)nəl ˌdaɪəlɒg rɪ'pleɪsmənt/ *noun* full form of **ADR**

additive colour mixing /ˌædɪtɪv ˌkʌlə 'mɪksɪŋ/ *verb* to mix different coloured lights to produce the colour which is wanted

add-on /'æd ɒn/ *adjective* added to a computer system to improve its performance ○ *The add-on hard disk will boost the computer's storage capabilities.* Opposite **built-in**

address /ə'dres/ *noun* **1.** a number allowing a central processing unit to reference a physical location in a storage medium in a computer system ○ *Each separate memory word has its own unique address.* **2.** a unique number that identifies a device on a network ○ *This is the address at which the data starts.* ■ *verb* to put the location data onto an address bus to identify which word in memory or storage device is to be accessed ○ *A larger address word increases the amount of memory a computer can address.*

'The world's largest open data network, the Internet, links more than 10,000 local networks and 3 million workstations in 50 countries. It has grown so fast that its address space is 'bust' and is being redesigned to allow further expansion.' [*Computing*]

addressability /əˌdresə'bɪlɪti/ *noun* the control available over pixels on screen

addressable /ə'dresəb(ə)l/ *adjective* which can be addressed ○ *With the new operating system, all of the 5MB of installed RAM is addressable.*

addressable point /əˌdresəb(ə)l 'pɔɪnt/ *noun* a point or pixel in a graphics system that can be directly addressed

address book /ə'dres bʊk/ *noun* **1.** (*in a network*) a list of node addresses **2.** (*in electronic mail*) a list of the network addresses of other users to which electronic mail can be sent

addressing /ə'dresɪŋ/ *noun* the process of accessing a location in memory

addressing machine /ə'dresɪŋ məˌʃiːn/ *noun* a machine which puts addresses on envelopes automatically

address resolution protocol /əˌdres ˌrezə'luːʃ(ə)n ˌprəʊtəkɒl/ *noun* full form of **ARP**

adjacent /ə'dʒeɪs(ə)nt/ *adjective* which is near or next to something ○ *The address is stored adjacent to the customer name field.*

adjunct register /ˌædʒʌŋkt 'redʒɪstə/ *noun* a 32-bit register in which the top 16 bits are used for control information and only the bottom 16 bits are available for use by a program

adjust /ə'dʒʌst/ *verb* to change something to fit new conditions or so that it works better ○ *You can adjust the brightness and contrast by turning a knob.*

adjustment /ə'dʒʌstmənt/ *noun* the making of a slight change made to something so that it works better, or a change made ○ *The brightness needs adjustment.*

administrator /əd'mɪnɪstreɪtə/ *noun* a person who is responsible for looking after a network, including installing, configuring and maintaining it

Adobe Acrobat /əˌdəʊbi 'ækrəbæt/ a trade name for a piece of software that converts documents and formatted pages into a file format that can be viewed on almost any computer platform or using a web browser on the Internet (NOTE: For example if you publish a newsletter, you could lay out the pages using a desktop publish system, print the pages for a paper version, and convert the files to Acrobat format allowing you to distribute the same formatted pages on CD-ROM or over the Internet.)

Adobe Systems /əˌdəʊbi 'sɪstəmz/ a software company that developed products including Acrobat, ATM, and PostScript

Adobe Type Manager /əˌdəʊbi taɪp 'mænɪdʒə/ a trade name for a standard for describing scalable fonts, used with Apple System 7 and Microsoft Windows to provide fonts that can be scaled to almost any point size, and printed on almost any printer. Abbr **ATM**

ADP /ˌeɪ diː 'piː/ *noun* data processing done by a computer. Full form **automatic data processing**

ADPCM /ˌeɪ diː piː siː 'em/ *noun* a CCITT standard that defines a method of converting a voice or analog signal into a compressed digital signal. Full form **adaptive differential pulse code modulation**

ADR *noun* the process of adding words or phrases to a section of film in post production; a continuous loop of film is shown to the artists in which the same scene is shown repeatedly to help them synchronise their speech with their filmed lip movements

ADSL /ˌeɪ diː es ˈel/ *noun* high-speed transmission standard that uses the same copper telephone wires as a normal telephone service, but is much faster than a standard modem or a digital system such as ISDN. Full form **Asymmetric Digital Subscriber Line** (NOTE: As well as the speed, ADSL provides a user with an 'always on' connection to the Internet – there is no need to dial an access number and no delay. Typically, companies provide ADSL for a fixed monthly rental; data is usually transferred from the Internet to the user's computer at 2Mbps but transferred from the user's computer to the Internet at a slower rate of 256Kbps.)

advance /ədˈvɑːns/ *verb* to move forward; to make something move forward ○ *The paper is advanced by turning this knob.*

advanced /ədˈvɑːnst/ *adjective* more complicated or more difficult to learn

Advanced Interactive Executive /əd ˌvɑːnst ˌɪntərˌæktɪv ɪɡˈzekjʊtɪv/ *noun* full form of **AIX**

Advanced Micro Devices /ədˌvɑːnst ˈmaɪkrəʊ dɪˌvaɪsɪz/ full form of **AMD**

advanced peer-to-peer networking /ədˌvɑːnst ˌpɪə tə ˌpɪə ˈnetwɜːkɪŋ/ *noun* full form of **APPN**

advanced power management /əd ˌvɑːnst ˌpaʊə ˈmænɪdʒmənt/ *noun* full form of **APM**

advanced program to program communications /ədˌvɑːnst ˌprəʊɡræm tə ˌprəʊɡræm kəˌmjuːnɪˈkeɪʃ(ə)nz/ *noun* full form of **APPC**

Advanced Research Projects Agency Network /ədˌvɑːnst ˌriːsɜːtʃ ˌprɒdʒekts ˌeɪdʒ(ə)nsi ˈnetwɜːk/ *noun* full form of **ARPANET**

advanced technology attachment /ədˌvɑːnst tekˌnɒlədʒi əˈtætʃmənt/ *noun* full form of **ATA**

Advanced Television Systems Committee /ədˌvɑːnst ˈtelɪvɪʒ(ə)n ˌsɪstəmz kəˌmɪti/ *noun* full form of **ATSC**

advanced version /ədˌvɑːnst ˈvɜːʃ(ə)n/ *noun* a program with more complex features for use by an experienced user

advisory lock /ədˈvaɪz(ə)ri lɒk/ *noun* (*in a multitasking system*) a lock placed on a region of a file by one process to prevent any other process accessing the same data

advisory system /ədˌvaɪz(ə)ri ˈsɪstəm/ *noun* an expert system that provides advice to a user

aerial /ˈeəriəl/ *noun* a device for receiving or sending radio transmissions by converting electromagnetic impulses into electrical signals and vice-versa ■ *adjective* in the air

aerial cable /ˈeəriəl ˌkeɪb(ə)l/ *noun* a wire stretched between poles which acts as an aerial

aerial perspective /ˌeəriəl pəˈspektɪv/ *noun* a view of a three-dimensional landscape as if the viewer is above the scene

aerial view /ˌeəriəl ˈvjuː/ *noun* a view from high above a scene

affect /əˈfekt/ *verb* to touch or to influence or to change something ○ *Changes in voltage will affect the way the computer functions.*

affiliate /əˈfɪlieɪt/ *verb* to connect or join with

affiliated /əˈfɪlieɪtɪd/ *adjective* connected with or owned by another company ○ *one of our affiliated companies*

affiliate marketing /əˈfɪliət ˌmɑːkɪtɪŋ/ *noun* a type of marketing that uses a central website to advertise and sell products and services from other sites

affirmative /əˈfɜːmətɪv/ *adjective* meaning 'yes'

AFIPS *abbr* American Federation of Information Processing Societies

AFNOR /ˈæfnɔː/ *noun* (*in France*) the French standards organisation. Full form **Association Française de Normalisation**

AFP /ˌeɪ ef ˈpiː/ a protocol used to communicate between workstations and servers in a network of Apple Macintosh computers. Full form **Appletalk Filing Protocol**

afterglow /ˈɑːftəɡləʊ/ *noun* ♦ **persistence**

after-image /ˌɑːftə ˈɪmɪdʒ/ *noun* a copy of a block of data that has been modified

AGC *noun* an electronic circuit that adjusts the level of an incoming signal so that it is suitable for the next part of the circuit. Full form **automatic gain control**

agenda /əˈdʒendə/ *noun* a list of tasks or appointments or activities that have to be carried out on a particular day

agent /ˈeɪdʒənt/ *noun* a series of commands or actions that are carried out automatically on a particular file or data

aggregate /ˈæɡrɪɡət/ *noun* a collection of data objects

AGP /ˌeɪ dʒiː ˈpiː/ *noun* a dedicated bus between a graphics controller and main memory that allows data to be transferred very quickly without using the main processor. Full form **accelerated graphics port** (NOTE: It is used with the Intel Pentium II processor to provide very high-speed three-dimensional graphics and video processing. This port does not replace a PCI bus but works with it.)

AI /ˌeɪ ˈaɪ/ *noun* the design and development of computer programs that attempt to imitate human intelligence and decision-making functions, providing basic reasoning and other human characteristics. Full form **artificial intelligence**. ◊ **IKBS**

aiming symbol /ˌeɪmɪŋ ˈsɪmbəl/, **aiming field** /fiːld/ *noun* a symbol displayed on screen which defines the area in which a light-pen can be detected

airbrush /ˈeəˌbrʌʃ/ *noun* (*in graphics software*) a painting tool that creates a diffuse pattern of dots, like an mechanical airbrush ○ *We used the airbrush to create the cloud effects in this image.*

air gap /ˈeə gæp/ *noun* a narrow gap between a recording or playback head and the magnetic medium

AIX a trade name for a version of UNIX produced by IBM to run on its range of PCs, minicomputers and mainframes. Full form **Advanced Interactive Executive**

ALC *abbr* automatic level control. ◊ **AGC**

alert /əˈlɜːt/ *noun* a warning message sent from software to warn a person or application that an error or problem has occurred

algebra /ˈældʒɪbrə/ *noun* the use of letters in certain mathematical operations to represent unknown numbers or a range of possible numbers

algebraic language /ˌældʒɪbreɪɪk ˈlæŋgwɪdʒ/ *noun* a context-free language

ALGOL /ˈælgɒl/ *noun* a high-level programming language using algorithmic methods for mathematical and technical applications. Full form **algorithmic language**

algorithm /ˈælgərɪð(ə)m/ *noun* a set of rules used to define or perform a specific task or to solve a specific problem

> '...image processing algorithms are step by step procedures for performing image processing operations' [*Byte*]

> '...the steps are: acquiring a digitized image, developing an algorithm to process it, processing the image, modifying the algorithm until you are satisfied with the result' [*Byte*]

algorithmic /ˌælgəˈrɪðmɪk/ *adjective* expressed using algorithms

algorithmic language /ˌælgərɪðmɪk ˈlæŋgwɪdʒ/ *noun* full form of **ALGOL**

alias /ˈeɪliəs/ *noun* **1.** a representative name given to a file, port, device or spreadsheet cell or range of cells ○ *The operating system uses the alias COM1 to represent the serial port address 3FCh.* **2.** an undesirable value within a digital sample – often because a very high input signal has exceeded the limits of the converter and is wrongly represented as a very low value ○ *The operating system uses the alias COM1 to represent the serial port address 3FCh.*

aliasing /ˈeɪliəsɪŋ/ *noun* jagged edges that appear along diagonal or curved lines displayed on a computer screen caused by the size of each pixel

alias name /ˈeɪliəs neɪm/ *noun* another name that is used on a network instead of the user name

alien /ˈeɪliən/ *adjective* not fitting the usual system

align /əˈlaɪn/ *verb* **1.** to make sure that the characters to be printed are spaced and levelled correctly, either vertically or horizontally **2.** to arrange numbers into a column with all figured lines up against the right hand side (**right-aligned**) or the left-hand side (**left-aligned**) **3.** to ensure that a read/write head is correctly positioned over the recording medium **4.** to tune two or more radio circuits together

aligner /əˈlaɪnə/ *noun* a device used to make sure that the paper is straight in a printer

aligning edge /əˈlaɪnɪŋ edʒ/ *noun* an edge of an optical character recognition system used to position a document

alignment /əˈlaɪnmənt/ *noun* the correct spacing and levelling of printed characters

allocate /ˈæləˌkeɪt/ *verb* to divide a period of time or a piece of work in various ways and share it out between users ○ *The operating system allocated most of main memory to the spreadsheet program.* (NOTE: **allocates – allocating – allocated**)

allocation /ˌæləˈkeɪʃ(ə)n/ *noun* the dividing of something such as memory, disk space, printer use, operating system time, or a program or device in various ways ○ *allocation of time* or *capital to a project*

allophone /ˈæləfəʊn/ *noun* the smallest unit of sound from which speech can be formed. ◊ **phoneme**

all points addressable mode /ˌɔːl ˌpɔɪnts əˈdresəb(ə)l ˌməʊd/ *noun* a graphics mode in which each pixel can be individually addressed and its colour and attributes defined. Also called **APA mode**

alpha /ˈælfə/ *noun* **1.** same as **alpha test** ○ *The new software is still in an alpha product stage.* **2.** an item of data that defines the properties of a pixel or part of an image

ALPHA /ˈælfə/ *noun* a 64-bit RISC processor chip developed by Digital Equipment Corporation

alphabet /ˈælfəˌbet/ *noun* the 26 letters used to make words

alpha beta technique /ˌælfə ˈbiːtə tek ˌniːk/ *noun* a free structure technique used in artificial intelligence for solving game and strategy problems

alphabetically /ˌælfəˈbetɪkli/ *adverb* in alphabetical order ○ *The files are arranged alphabetically under the customer's name.*

alphabetical order /ˌælfəbetɪk(ə)l ˈɔːdə/ *noun* the arrangement of records (such as files, index cards) in the order of the letters of the alphabet (A,B,C,D, etc.)

alphabetic character set /ˌælfəbetɪk ˈkærɪktə ˌset/ *noun* the set of characters, both capitals and small letters, that make up the alphabet

alphabetise /ˈælfəbetaɪz/, **alphabetize** *verb* to put items into alphabetical order ○ *Enter the bibliographical information and alphabetise it.* (NOTE: **alphabetises – alphabetising – alphabetised**)

alpha channel /ˈælfə ˌtʃæn(ə)l/ *noun* **1.** (*in 32-bit graphics systems*) the top eight bits that define the properties of a pixel (NOTE: The lower 24 bits define the pixel's colour.) **2.** a video channel, often used to hold mattes

alphageometric /ˌælfədʒiːəʊˈmetrɪk/ *adjective* referring to a set of codes that instruct a teletext terminal to display various graphics patterns or characters

alphamosaic /ˌælfəməʊˈzeɪɪk/ *adjective* (character set) used in teletext to provide alphanumeric and graphics characters

alphanumeric /ˌælfənjʊˈmerɪk/ *adjective* using the letters of the alphabet, the Arabic numerals and punctuation marks

alphanumeric data /ˌælfənjʊmerɪk ˈdeɪtə/ *noun* data that represents the letters of the alphabet and the Arabic numerals

alpha-particle /ˈælfə ˌpɑːtɪk(ə)l/ *noun* an emitted alpha radiation particle

alphaphotographic /ˌælfəfəʊtəʊ ˈɡræfɪk/ *adjective* which represents pictures using predefined graphics characters, for teletext services

alphasort /ˌælfəˈsɔːt/ *verb* to sort data into alphabetical order

alpha test /ˈælfə test/ *noun* the first working attempt of a computer product. Also called **alpha**. ◊ **beta test**

alpha wrap /ˈælfə ræp/ *noun* a method used for feeding tape into a helical scan video recorder to make sure the alignment is correct

alt /ɔːlt/ *noun* a type of newsgroup on the Internet that contains discussions about alternative subjects. ◊ **newsgroup** (NOTE: These are not official newsgroups and are not supported or monitored by any company, and any user can write just about anything that he or she wants to say. Some online service providers do not allow their subscribers to view all of the alt newsgroups because they may contain offensive and pornographic material.)

alter /ˈɔːltə/ *verb* to change ○ *to alter the terms of a contract*

alterable /ˈɔːtərəb(ə)l/ *adjective* which can be altered. ◊ **EAPROM, EAROM**

alteration /ˌɔːltəˈreɪʃ(ə)n/ *noun* a change which has been made ○ *The agreement was signed without any alterations.*

alternate *verb* /ˈɒltəneɪt/ to change from one state to another and back, over and over again (NOTE: **alternates – alternating – alternated**) ■ *adjective* /ɒlˈtɜːnət/ which change from one to another

alternately /ɔːlˈtɜːnətli/ *adverb* switching from one to the other

alternating current /ˌɔːltəneɪtɪŋ ˈkʌrənt/ *noun* an electrical current whose value varies with time in a regular sinusoidal way, changing direction of flow each half cycle. Abbr **AC**

> COMMENT: The mains electricity supply uses alternating current to minimise transmission power loss, with a frequency of 50 Hz in the UK, 60 Hz in the USA.

alternative /ɔːlˈtɜːnətɪv/ *noun* something which can be done instead of something else ○ *What is the alternative to re-keying all the data?* ■ *adjective* other or which can take the place of something

alternator /ˈɔːltəˌneɪtə/ *noun* a device which produces an alternating current

Alt key /ˈɔːlt kiː/ *noun* a special key on a PC's keyboard used to activate special functions in an application ○ *Press Alt and P at the same time to print your document.*

> COMMENT: The Alt key has become the standard method of activating a menu bar in any software running on a PC. For example, Alt-F normally displays the File menu of a program, Alt-X normally exits the program.

ALU /ˌeɪ el ˈjuː/ *noun* a section of the CPU that performs all arithmetic and logical functions. Full form **arithmetic logic unit**. Also called **arithmetic unit**. ◊ **CPU**

always on /ˈɔːlweɪz ɒn/ *adjective* referring to a feature of high-speed broadband communications devices such as cable modems and ADSL that link your computer to the Internet whereby your computer appears to be permanently connected to the net and you do not need to dial up a special number

AM *abbr* amplitude modulation

A-MAC /ˌeɪ ˌem eɪ ˈsiː/ *noun* a low bandwidth variation of MAC

ambient /ˈæmbiənt/ *adjective* referring to normal background conditions

ambiguous /æm'bɪgjuəs/ *adjective* which has two or more possible meanings

ambisonics /ˌæmbi'sɒnɪks/ *noun* the process of recording more than one audio signal to give the effect of being surrounded by sound

AMD a company that develops and produces processor components including a range of processors that are compatible with Intel processors and are used in many PCs. Full form **Advanced Micro Devices**

American National Standards Institute /əˌmerɪkən ˌnæʃ(ə)nəl 'stændədz ˌɪnstɪtjuːt/ *noun* full form of **ANSI**

American Standard Code for Information Interchange /əˌmerɪkən ˌstændəd kəʊd fər ˌɪnfəmeɪʃ(ə)n 'ɪntətʃeɪndʒ/ *noun* full form of **ASCII**

American Standards Association /ə ˌmerɪkən 'stændədz əˌsəʊsieɪʃ(ə)n/ *noun* an organisation that sets standards for the light sensitivity of photographic film emulsion – e.g., 100 ASA. The film is numbered in accordance to it's sensitivity to light; the higher the number, the higher the film's sensitivity. Abbr **ASA**

America Online /əˌmerɪkə 'ɒnlaɪn/ a company that is the largest Internet service provider in the world. Abbr **AOL**

AMM *noun* a multimeter that uses a graduated scale and a moving needle as a readout for voltage, current and impedance levels. Full form **analog multimeter**. Compare **DMM**

amount /ə'maʊnt/ *noun* the quantity of data or paper, etc. ○ *What is the largest amount of data which can be processed in one hour?*

amp /æmp/ *noun* same as **ampere** (NOTE: used with figures: **a 13-amp fuse**)

ampere /'æmpeə/ *noun* the base SI unit of electrical current, defined as the current flowing through an impedance of one ohm which has a voltage of one volt across it. Abbr **A**

ampersand /'æmpəˌsænd/ *noun* a printing sign (&) which means 'and'

amplification /ˌæmplɪfɪ'keɪʃ(ə)n/ *noun* the output-to-input signal strength ratio ○ *Increase the amplification of the input signal.*

amplifier /'æmplɪˌfaɪə/ *noun* an electronic circuit that magnifies the power of a signal

amplify /'æmplɪˌfaɪ/ *verb* to magnify a signal power or amplitude ○ *The received signal needs to be amplified before it can be processed.* (NOTE: **amplifies – amplifying – amplified**)

amplitude /'æmplɪˌtjuːd/ *noun* the strength or size of a signal

amplitude modulation /'æmplɪtjuːd mɒdjuˌleɪʃ(ə)n/ *noun* a method of carrying data by varying the size of a carrier signal of fixed frequency according to the data

analog /'ænəlɒg/, **analogue** /'æn(ə)lɒg/ *noun* the representation and measurement of numerical data by continuously variable physical quantities, as for the size of electrical voltages. Compare **digital**

analog display /ˌænəlɒg dɪ'spleɪ/ *noun* a display or monitor that can display an infinite range of colours or shades of grey, unlike a digital display that can only display a finite range of colours. VGA monitors are a form of analog display.

analog multimeter /ˌænəlɒg 'mʌlitmiːtə/ *noun* a piece of testing equipment which uses a moving needle to indicate voltage, current or impedance levels. Abbr **AMM**

analog to digital /ˌænəlɒg tə 'dɪdʒɪt(ə)l/ *adjective* referring to changing a signal from an analog form to a digitally coded form. Abbr **A/D, A to D**

analog to digital converter /ˌænəlɒg tə ˌdɪdʒɪt(ə)l kən'vɜːtə/ *noun* full form of **ADC**

analyse /'ænəlaɪz/, **analyze** *verb* to examine in detail ○ *to analyse a computer printout*

analyser /'ænəlaɪzə/ *noun* a piece of electronic test equipment that displays various features of a signal (NOTE: The US spelling is **analyzer**.)

analysis /ə'næləsɪs/ *noun* a detailed examination and report ○ *market analysis*

analyst /'ænəlɪst/ *noun* a person who carries out an analysis of a problem

analytical engine /ˌænəlɪtɪk(ə)l 'endʒɪn/ *noun* a mechanical calculating machine developed by Charles Babbage in 1833 that is generally considered the first general-purpose digital computer

anamorphic /ˌænə'mɔːfɪk/ *adjective* referring to an image that has unequal vertical and horizontal scaling, making it appear squashed or taller than the original

anamorphic image /ˌænəˌmɔːfɪk 'ɪmɪdʒ/ *noun* an image which has been distorted in one direction

anamorphic lens /ˌænə'mɔːfɪk lenz/ *noun* a motion picture camera lens which allows a wide picture to be compressed on to standard film. When in a projector, it lets the image expand to fill a wide screen. (*film*)

ANAPROP /'ænəprɒp/ *abbr* anomalous propagation ■ *noun* distortion of transmitted television signals due to atmospheric conditions

anastigmatic /ˌænəstɪg'mætɪk/ *noun* a lens or optical device that has been corrected for astigmatism

ancestral file /æn,sestrəl 'faɪl/ *noun* a system of backing up files based on a son to father to grandfather file, where the son is the current working file

anchor /'æŋkə/ *noun* the main presenter of a television programme who sets the style and tone of the show (*film*)

anchor cell /'æŋkə sel/ *noun* a cell in a spreadsheet program that defines the start of a range of cells

ancillary equipment /æn,sɪləri ɪ 'kwɪpmənt/ *noun* equipment which is used to make a task easier but which is not absolutely necessary

AND /ænd/ *noun* an operator, often used in searches, that matches text that contains both search words. Compare **OR** (NOTE: For example searching for 'cat AND dog' finds all entries that contain both the words 'cat' and 'dog')

AND circuit /'ænd ,sɜːkɪt/, **AND element** /'ænd ,elɪmənt/ *noun* same as **AND gate**

AND function /'ænd ,fʌŋkʃən/ *noun* a logical function whose output is true if both its inputs are true. Also called **coincidence function**

COMMENT: If both inputs are 1, results of the AND will be 1. If one of the input digits is 0, then AND will produce a 0.

AND gate /'ænd geɪt/ *noun* electronic gate that performs a logical AND function on electrical signals. Also called **AND circuit, AND element**. Compare **coincidence gate**

AND operation /'ænd ,ɒpəreɪʃ(ə)n/ *noun* the processing of two or more input signals, outputting their AND function

anechoic /,ænek'əʊɪk/ *adjective* (room) that produces no echoes, used for testing audio equipment

anechoic chamber /,ænekəʊɪk 'tʃeɪmbə/ *noun* a perfectly quiet room in which sound or radio waves do not reflect off the walls

ANG *abbr* Anglia Television (*film*)

angle /'æŋgəl/ *noun* a measure of the change in direction, usually as the distance turned from a reference line

angled line /,æŋgləd 'laɪn/ *noun* a line with three or more points, e.g. a zig-zag

Anglia Television /,æŋgliə 'telɪvɪʒ(ə)n/ *noun* an independent commercial TV company based in Norwich and serving the surrounding east coast areas

angstrom /'æŋstrɒm/ *noun* a unit of measurement equal to one thousand millionth of a metre

ANI /,eɪ en 'aɪ/ *noun* a telephone system which displays the telephone number of the caller. Full form **automatic number identification**

animate /'ænɪmeɪt/ *verb* to make a series of drawings which, when filmed, will create moving images

animated GIF /,ænɪ,meɪtɪd ,dʒiː aɪ 'ef/ *noun* a simple animation effect created by saving several small graphic images within one file so that they can be repeatedly displayed in sequence giving an impression of animation. It is often used to create animated buttons or other effects on a webpage. ◊ **transparent GIF**

animated graphics /,ænɪmeɪtɪd 'græfɪks/ *plural noun* images that move on the screen

animatic /,ænɪ'mætɪk/ *noun* a succession of drawings describing the story of a film, advertisement, animation or multimedia production before filming begins (*film*) ◊ **story board**

animation /,ænɪ'meɪʃ(ə)n/ *noun* **1.** the creation of the illusion of movement by displaying a series of slightly different images on screen very rapidly to give the effect of smooth movement. Also called **computer animation** **2.** the process of filming puppets or still drawings in sequence in order to give the appearance of movement **3.** the process of drawing images on film, especially using a computer to create moving graphical images, such as cartoons

ANN *noun* a voice over or a person on camera who gives information during a broadcast or who introduces and closes a radio or TV programme (*film*) Full form **announcer**

annotation /,ænə'teɪʃ(ə)n/ *noun* a comment or note in a program which explains how the program is to be used

announce /ə'naʊns/ *verb* to publicise a new or updated website by registering the domain name with the main search engines; (NOTE: **announces – announcing – announced**)

COMMENT: Each search engine allows a person to add a new website and enter a description and category. Because there are now several hundred search engines, special software utilities are available to automatically register the website with each engine.

announcer /ə'naʊnsə/ *noun* full form of **ANN**

annunciator /ə'nʌnsieɪtə/ *noun* a signal which can be heard or seen in order to attract attention

anode /'ænəʊd/ *noun* a positive electrical terminal of a device

anomalistic period /ə,nɒməlɪstɪk 'pɪəriəd/ *noun* the time taken for a satellite to travel between consecutive maximum points in its orbit

anomalous propagation /əˌnɒmələs ˌprɒpəˈgeɪʃ(ə)n/ *noun* distortion of transmitted television signals due to atmospheric conditions

anonymiser /əˈnɒnɪmaɪzə/, **anonymizer** *noun* a website that allows a person to browse the World Wide Web without leaving any traces of his or her identity

anonymous FTP /əˌnɒnɪməs ef tiː ˈpiː/ *noun* a method commonly used on the Internet that allows a user to connect to a remote computer using the FTP protocol and log in as a guest to download publicly accessible files. ◊ **FTP** (NOTE: If you are using the FTP protocol to connect to a remote computer and you are asked for a login name and password, you can normally gain access to the remote computer's public areas by entering 'anonymous' as the login user name and your full email address as the password.)

ANSI /ˈænsi/ *US* a US organisation which specifies computer and software standards, including those of high-level programming languages. Full form **American National Standards Institute**

ANSI screen control /ˌænsi ˈskriːn kənˌtrəʊl/ *noun* a set of standard codes developed by ANSI that control how colours and simple graphics are displayed on a computer screen

answer /ˈɑːnsə/ *noun* a reply or solution to a question ■ *verb* **1.** to reply or provide the solution to a question **2.** to reply to a signal and set up a communications link ○ *The first modem originates the call and the second answers it.*

answerphone /ˈɑːnsəfəʊn/ *noun* a cassette recorder attached to a telephone, which plays a prerecorded message and records messages from people dialling the number

answer print /ˈɑːnsə prɪnt/ *noun* the initial composite or graded print (copy) from an edited negative colour film which includes sound, music, titles (*film*)

antenna /ænˈtenə/ *noun* an aerial or device for receiving or sending radio transmissions by converting electromagnetic impulses into electrical signals and vice-versa

antenna array /ænˈtenə əˌreɪ/ *noun* a series of small transmitting or receiving elements connected in parallel, that make up a complex antenna

antenna gain /ænˈtenə geɪn/ *noun* the increase in transmitted signal power due to using a certain type of antenna

anthropomorphic software /ˌænθrəpəmɔːfɪk ˈsɒftweə/ *noun* artificial intelligence software that appears to react to what a user says

anti- /ænti/ *prefix* against

anti-aliasing /ˌænti ˈeɪliəsɪŋ/ *noun* **1.** a method of reducing the effects of jagged edges in graphics by using shades of grey to blend in along edges. Also called **dejagging** **2.** a method of adding sound signals between the sound samples to create a smoother sound

anti-virus program /ˌænti ˈvaɪrəs ˌprəʊgræm/ *noun* a software program that looks for virus software on a computer and destroys it before it can damage data or files

anti-virus software /ˌænti ˈvaɪrəs ˌsɒftweə/ *noun* software that removes a virus from a file

AOL *abbr* America Online

APA *abbr* all points addressable

APA mode /ˌeɪ piː ˈeɪ ˌməʊd/ *noun* same as **all points addressable mode**

APC *abbr* asynchronous procedure call

APD *abbr* avalanche photodiode

aperture /ˈæpətʃə/ *noun* **1.** a lens diaphragm that allows the amount of light that reaches the film to be regulated according to the user's wishes **2.** an opening in a device that allows a certain amount of light or a signal to pass through it

aperture illumination /ˌæpətʃə ɪˌluːmɪˈneɪʃ(ə)n/ *noun* a pattern generated from an aperture antenna

API /ˌeɪ piː ˈaɪ/ *noun* a set of standard program functions and commands that allow any programmer to interface a program with another application ○ *If I follow the published API for this system, my program will work properly.* Full form **application programming interface**

APL /ˌeɪ piː ˈel/ *noun* a high-level programming language used in scientific and mathematical work. Full form **A programming language**

APM /ˌeɪ piː ˈem/ *noun* a specification that allows an operating system such as older Windows to control the power management features of a computer. Full form **advanced power management** (NOTE: This standard has been replaced by the ACPI standard in Windows 98 and Windows NT 5.0.)

apochromatic lens /ˌæpəʊkrəmætɪk ˈlenz/ *noun* an optical lens that has been corrected for chromatic aberration

apogee /ˈæpədʒi/ *noun* the point in a satellite's orbit where it is at its maximum distance from the earth

apostrophe /əˈpɒstrəfi/ *noun* a printing sign ('), which generally indicates that a letter is missing or used in ('s), to indicate possession (NOTE: **computer's** can mean 'belonging to a computer' *or* 'the computer is': *The computer's casing is blue; The compu-*

ter's broken and has to be repaired. Note that this is different from **it's** = 'it is' as opposed to **its** = 'belonging to it': *It's easy to program; You cannot edit a disk when its write protect tag is closed.*)

APPC /ˌeɪ piː piː 'siː/ *noun* a set of protocols developed by IBM that allows peer-to-peer communication between workstations connected to an SNA network. Full form **advanced program to program communications.** ◊ **LU**

append /ə'pend/ *verb* **1.** to add data to an existing file or record ○ *If you enter the DOS command COPY A+B, the file B will be appended to the end of file A.* **2.** to add a file or data to the end of an existing file

appendix /ə'pendɪks/ *noun* a section at the back of a book, containing additional information ○ *For further details see the appendices.* (NOTE: The plural is **appendices.**)

Apple Computer Corporation /ˌæp(ə)l kəm'pjuːtə ˌkɔːpəreɪʃ(ə)n/ a company, formed in 1975, that has developed a range of personal computers including the Apple II, Apple Lisa and, more recently, the Apple Mac

> 'Apple Computer has fleshed out details of a migration path to the PowerPC RISC architecture for its 7 million Apple Macintosh users. Developments in the pipeline include PowerPC versions of the AppleTalk Remote Access networking protocol.' [*Computing*]

Apple Desktop Bus /ˌæp(ə)l ˌdesktɒp 'bʌs/ a trade name for a serial bus built into Apple Macs that allows low-speed devices, e.g. the keyboard and mouse, to communicate with the processor

Apple file exchange /ˌæp(ə)l 'faɪl ɪks ˌtʃeɪndʒ/ a trade name for a software program that runs on an Apple Mac allowing it to read disks from a PC

Apple filing protocol /ˌæp(ə)l 'faɪlɪŋ ˌprəʊtəkɒl/ a trade name for a protocol used to communicate between workstations and servers in a network of Apple Macintosh computers. Abbr **AFP**

Apple Key /'æp(ə)l kiː/ a trade name for a special key on the keyboard of an Apple Mac that, when pressed with another key, provides a short-cut to a menu selection

Apple Mac /'æp(ə)l mæk/, **Apple Macintosh computer** /ˌæp(ə)l ˌmækɪntɒʃ kəm 'pjuːtə/ a trade name for any of a range of personal computers developed by Apple Computer Corporation that has a graphical user interface and uses the 68000 family of processors

AppleScript /'æp(ə)lskrɪpt/ a trade name for a script language built into the operation system of an Apple Mac that allows a user to automate simple tasks

Appleshare /'æp(ə)lʃeə/ a trade name for software that allows Apple Macs to share files and printers using a file server

applet /'æplət/ *noun* **1.** a small utility within Microsoft Windows, originally any of the icons in the Control Panel window, but now any piece of software that is used to configure the computer ○ *There are applets to help format your disk and configure your keyboard.* **2.** a small applications on the Internet designed to enhance the functionality of a webpage. ◊ **ActiveX, Java, VBScript** (NOTE: For example if you want to add multimedia effects to your webpage, you cannot carry out these functions with standard HTML commands, but you could write a small ActiveX program, called an applet, that is automatically downloaded by the user's browser and run on the user's computer.)

AppleTalk™ /'æp(ə)ltɑːk/ a trade name for a communications protocol developed by the Apple Computer Corporation that carries data over network hardware between two or more Apple Macs and peripherals (NOTE: AppleTalk is similar to the seven-layer OSI protocol model. It can link up to 32 devices, uses a CSMA-CA design, and transmits data at 230Kbps.)

AppleTalk Filing Protocol /ˌæp(ə)ltɑːk 'faɪlɪŋ ˌprəʊtəkɒl/ full form of **AFP**

appliance /ə'plaɪəns/ *noun* a machine, especially one used in the home ○ *All electrical appliances should be properly earthed.*

appliance computer /əˌplaɪəns kəm 'pjuːtə/ *noun* a ready-to-run computer system that can be bought in a shop, taken home and used immediately for a particular purpose. ◊ **turnkey system**

applicant /'æplɪkənt/ *noun* a person who applies for something ○ *applicant for a job* or *job applicant* ○ *There were thousands of applicants for shares in the new company.*

application /ˌæplɪ'keɪʃ(ə)n/ *noun* **1.** asking for something, usually in writing ○ *application for an account on the system* **2.** a task which a computer performs or a problem which a computer solves

> 'How do users interact with a computer system? Via a terminal or PC. So what application layer OSI protocol do we need first? The Virtual Terminal. And what do we get? File Transfer Access and Maintenance.' [*Computing*]

application configuration access protocol /ˌæplɪkeɪʃ(ə)n kən ˌfɪgjʊreɪʃ(ə)n 'ækses ˌprəʊtəkɒl/ *noun* full form of **ACAP**

application icon /ˌæplɪ'keɪʃ(ə)n ˌaɪkɒn/ *noun* a small image or graphical symbol that represents an application program in a graphical user interface

application package /ˌæplɪˈkeɪʃ(ə)n ˌpækɪdʒ/ *noun* a set of computer programs and manuals that cover all aspects of a particular task, e.g. payroll, stock control or tax. Also called **applications package**

application program /ˌæplɪˈkeɪʃ(ə)n ˌprəʊɡræm/ *noun* a piece of application software ○ *The multi-window editor is used to create and edit applications programs.*

application programming interface /ˌæplɪkeɪʃ(ə)n ˈprəʊɡræmɪŋ ˌɪntəfeɪs/ *noun* full form of **API** ○ *If I follow the published API for this system, my program will work properly.*

application service provider /ˌæplɪkeɪʃ(ə)n ˈsɜːvɪs prəˌvaɪdə/ *noun* a specialist company that installs, configures and manages software on its own server and then allows any business to use the software via the Internet or a private network. Abbr **ASP** (NOTE: The user does not realise that the software is located on a distant server, and the business does not need to buy or support the software, just rent it.)

application software /ˌæplɪkeɪʃ(ə)n ˈsɒftweə/ *noun* software designed to make the computer do what is required and perform particular tasks ○ *The multi-window editor is used to create and edit applications programs.* Also called **applications software**

applications package /ˌæplɪˈkeɪʃ(ə)nz ˌpækɪdʒ/ *noun* same as **application package**

application specific integrated circuits /ˌæplɪkeɪʃ(ə)n spəˌsɪfɪk ˌɪntɪɡreɪtɪd ˈsɜːkɪts/ *noun* full form of **ASIC**

applications software /ˌæplɪˈkeɪʃ(ə)nz ˌsɒftweə/ *noun* same as **application software**

apply /əˈplaɪ/ *verb* **1.** to ask for something, usually in writing **2.** to affect or to touch ○ *This formula applies only to data received after the interrupt signal.*

APPN /ˌeɪ piː piː ˈen/ *noun* an extension to the IBM SNA protocol that allows workstations to share information on a peer-to-peer basis without the need for a central mainframe. Full form **advanced peer-to-peer networking** (NOTE: It is often used to route information around a network and dynamically adjusts the route if part of the network is damaged.)

appoint /əˈpɔɪnt/ *verb* to choose someone for a job ○ *to appoint James Smith (to the post of) manager* ○ *We have appointed a new computer services manager.* (NOTE: you appoint a person **to** a job)

appointee /əpɔɪnˈtiː/ *noun* a person who is appointed to a job

appointment /əˈpɔɪntmənt/ *noun* **1.** an arrangement to meet □ **appointments book** desk diary in which appointments are noted **2.** being appointed to a job □ **on his appointment as manager** when he was made manager □ **letter of appointment** letter in which someone is appointed to a job **3.** a job □ **staff appointment** job on the staff □ **computer appointments vacant** list (in a newspaper) of jobs which are available in the computer industry

approval /əˈpruːv(ə)l/ *noun* an agreement that something can be used ○ *A BABT approval is needed for modems.*

approve /əˈpruːv/ *verb* to agree to something ○ *to approve the terms of a contract*

approximate /əˈprɒksɪmət/ *adjective* not exact, but almost correct ○ *We have made an approximate calculation of the time needed for keyboarding.*

approximately /əˈprɒksɪmətli/ *adverb* almost correctly ○ *Processing time is approximately 10% lower than during the previous quarter.*

approximating /əˈprɒksɪmeɪtɪŋ/ *adjective* which is nearly correct

approximation /əˌprɒksɪˈmeɪʃ(ə)n/ *noun* a rough calculation ○ *approximation of keyboarding time*

A programming language /ˌeɪ ˈprəʊɡræmɪŋ ˌlæŋɡwɪdʒ/ *noun* full form of **APL**

APT /ˌeɪ piː ˈtiː/ *noun* a programming language used to control numerically controlled machines. Full form **automatically programmed tools**

arbitrator /ˈɑːbɪtreɪtə/ *noun* software that is responsible for allocating resources to devices, often used to manage the way Plug and Play adapters use other resources in a computer

arcade game /ɑːˈkeɪd ɡeɪm/ *noun* an adventure game played on a machine in a public place

archetype /ˈɑːkɪtaɪp/ *noun* a document or book that illustrates the styles of a particular time and subject

Archie /ˈɑːtʃiː/ *noun* a system of servers on the Internet that catalogue the public files available on the Internet

Archimedes /ˌɑːkɪˈmiːdiːz/ *noun* a personal computer developed by Acorn Computers; the Archimedes is based around a RISC central processor and is not compatible with either the IBM PC or Apple Macintosh

architecture /ˈɑːkɪtektʃə/ *noun* the layout and interconnection of a computer's internal hardware and the logical relationships between CPU, memory and I/O devices

'Software giant Microsoft is also interested in using Xerox' Glyph technology as part of its Microsoft At Work architecture that seeks to unite office computers with fax machines and copiers.' [*Computing*]

archival quality /ˈɑːkaɪv(ə)l ˌkwɒləti/ *noun* the length of time that a copy can be stored before it becomes illegible

archive /ˈɑːkaɪv/ *noun* storage of data over a long period ■ *verb* to put data in storage (NOTE: **archives – archiving – archived**)

archived copy /ˌɑːkaɪvd ˈkɒpi/ *noun* a copy kept in storage

archive file /ˈɑːkaɪv faɪl/ *noun* a file containing data which is out of date but which is kept for future reference

archive storage /ˌɑːkaɪv ˈstɔːrɪdʒ/ *noun* storage of data for a long period of time

area /ˈeəriə/ *noun* **1.** a measurement of the space taken up by something. calculated by multiplying the length by the width. ○ *The area of this office is 3,400 square feet.* **2.** a section of memory or code that is reserved for a certain purpose

area fill /ˈeəriə fɪl/ *noun* (*in graphics*) an instruction to fill an area of the screen or an enclosed pattern with a colour or pattern

area manager /ˌeəriə ˈmænɪdʒə/ *noun* a manager who deals with a certain part of the country

arg /ɑːg/ *noun* same as **argument**

argue /ˈɑːgjuː/ *verb* to discuss something about which you do not agree ○ *They argued over* or *about the design of the cover.* (NOTE: you argue **with** someone **about** *or* **over** something)

argument /ˈɑːgjʊmənt/ *noun* **1.** the process of discussing something without agreeing ○ *They got into an argument with the customs officials over the documents.* **2.** a variable acted upon by an operator or function ○ *If you enter the words 'MULTIPLY A, B', the processor will recognise the operator, MULTIPLY, and use it with the two arguments, A and B.* ◊ **operand**. Abbr **arg**

arithmetic /əˈrɪθmətɪk/ *noun* a science concerned with mathematical functions such as addition, subtraction, division and multiplication

arithmetic logic unit /ˌærɪθmetɪk ˈlɒdʒɪk ˌjuːnɪt/ *noun* full form of **ALU**

arithmetic unit /ˌærɪθmetɪk ˈjuːnɪt/ *noun* same as **ALU**

ARP /ˌeɪ ɑː ˈpiː/ *noun* a protocol within the TCP/IP standard that is used to determine whether the source and destination address in a packet are in the data-link control or Internet protocol format. Full form **address resolution protocol** (NOTE: Once the format of the address is known, the packet can be correctly routed over a network.)

ARPANET /ˈɑːpənet/ *noun* the original network of interconnected computers, linked by leased lines, that formed the first prototype for the current Internet. It was developed by the US Department of Defense. Full form **Advanced Research Projects Agency Network**

ARQ /ˌeɪ ɑː ˈkjuː/ *noun* an error correction system, used in some modems, which asks for data to be re-transmitted if it contains errors. Full form **automatic repeat request**

array /əˈreɪ/ *noun* an ordered structure containing individually accessible elements referenced by numbers, used to store tables or sets of related data

array processor /əˈreɪ ˌprəʊsesə/ *noun* a computer that can act upon several arrays of data simultaneously, for very fast mathematical applications ○ *The array processor allows the array that contains the screen image to be rotated with one simple command.*

arrow key /ˈærəʊ kiː/ *noun* each of a set of four keys on a keyboard that move the cursor or pointer around the screen, controlling movement up, down, left and right

arrow pointer /ˌærəʊ ˈpɔɪntə/ *noun* a small arrow on-screen that you can move using the mouse

art file /ˈɑːt faɪl/ *noun* a digital picture store which has extra graphic and painting facilities (*film*)

article /ˈɑːtɪk(ə)l/ *noun* **1.** one message in a newsgroup **2.** a section of a newspaper or magazine ○ *He wrote an article about the user group for the local newspaper.* **3.** a section of an agreement ○ *See article 8 of the contract.*

artifacts /ˈɑːtɪfækts/ *plural noun* very small errors in a digital version of an analog signal

artificial intelligence /ˌɑːtɪfɪʃ(ə)l ɪnˈtelɪdʒ(ə)ns/ *noun* full form of **AI**

artificial neural network /ˌɑːtɪfɪʃ(ə)l ˈnjʊərəl ˌnetwɜːk/ *noun* a system for processing information that is made up of interconnected elements that behave in a similar way to the neurons in the human nervous system and have the ability to learn through experience

artwork /ˈɑːtˌwɜːk/ *noun* graphical work or images

ASA *abbr* American Standards Association (*film*)

ascend /əˈsend/ *verb* to increase

ascender /əˈsendə/ *noun* a part of a character that rises above the main line of printed characters, e.g. the upward line of a 'b' or 'd'

ASCII /ˈæskiː/ *noun* a code which represents alphanumeric characters in binary code. Full form **American Standard Code for Information Interchange**

ASCII character /ˈæski ˌkærɪktə/ *noun* a character which is in the ASCII list of codes

ASCII file /ˈæski faɪl/ *noun* a stored file containing only ASCII coded character data ○ *Use a word processor* or *other program that generates a standard ASCII file.*

ASCII text /ˈæski tekst/ *noun* the set of letter and number characters with an ASCII code between 0 and 127

ASF /ˌeɪ es ˈef/ *noun* a multimedia delivery format developed by Microsoft for delivery over the Internet and used in its NetShow product. Full form **active streaming format**

ASIC /ˌeɪ es aɪ ˈsiː/ *plural noun* specially designed ICs for one particular function or to special specifications. Full form **application specific integrated circuits**

ASP *abbr* **1.** Active Server Page **2.** application service provider

aspect /ˈæspekt/ *noun* the way in which something appears

aspect ratio /ˌæspekt ˈreɪʃiəʊ/ *noun* the ratio of the width to the height of pixel shapes

ASR /ˌeɪ es ˈɑː/ *noun* a device or terminal that can transmit and receive information. Full form **automatic send/receive**. Compare **KSR**

COMMENT: An ASR terminal can input information via a keyboard or via a tape cassette or paper tape. It can receive information and store it in internal memory or on tape.

assemble /əˈsemb(ə)l/ *verb* **1.** to put a hardware or software product together from various smaller parts ○ *The parts for the disk drive are made in Japan and assembled in France.* (NOTE: **assembles – assembling – assembled**) **2.** to translate assembly code into machine code ○ *There is a short wait during which time the program is assembled into object code.*

assemble edit /əˌsemb(ə)l ˈedɪt/ *verb* adding new images, sounds, control tracks or timecodes to previous material on a videotape when in the process of editing (*film*)

assembler /əˈsemblə/ *noun* a program which converts a program written in assembly language into machine code. Also called **assembler program**

assembler program /əˈsemblə ˌprəʊɡræm/ *noun* same as **assembler**

assembly /əˈsembli/ *noun* **1.** the process of putting an item together from various parts ○ *There are no assembly instructions to show you how to put the computer together.* **2.** the process of converting a program into machine code

assertion /əˈsɜːʃ(ə)n/ *noun* a program statement of a fact or rule

assets /ˈæsets/ *plural noun* separate data elements such as video, audio and image that are used in a multimedia application

assign /əˈsaɪn/ *verb* **1.** to give a computer or person something to do ○ *He was assigned the job of checking the sales figures.* **2.** to set a variable equal to a string of characters or numbers **3.** to keep part of a computer system for use while a program is running

assigned numbers /əˌsaɪnd ˈnʌmbəz/ *plural noun* unique numbers that are each assigned to an Internet or network manufacturer's device, protocol or other resource (NOTE: Manufacturers apply for a unique ID number from the IANA organisation.)

assignment /əˈsaɪnmənt/ *noun* **1.** a particular job of work **2.** the process of setting a variable equal to a value or string or character **3.** the transfer of a property or of a right ○ *assignment of a copyright*

assignor /ˌæsaɪˈnɔː/ *noun* a person who assigns something to someone

assist /əˈsɪst/ *verb* to help ○ *Can you assist the stock controller in counting the stock?* ○ *He assists me with my income tax returns.* (NOTE: you assist someone **in** doing something or **with** something)

assistant cameraman /əˌsɪst(ə)nt ˈkæm(ə)rəmæn/ *noun* the person who carries out camera operations under the instruction of the director of photography

assistant director /əˌsɪst(ə)nt daɪˈrektə/ *noun* the person who carries out the director's instructions, oversees the work and whereabouts of the actors, technicians and rest of crew and works in close contact with the production unit. Also called **associate director**

associate /əˈsəʊsiət/ *adjective* linked ■ *noun* a person who works in the same business as someone ○ *She is a business associate of mine.*

associated document /əˌsəʊsieɪtɪd ˈdɒkjʊmənt/, **associated file** /faɪl/ *noun* a document or file that is linked to its originating application (NOTE: When you select the file, the operating system automatically starts the originating application.)

associate director /əˌsəʊsiət daɪˈrektə/ *noun* same as **assistant director**

associate producer /əˌsəʊsiət prəˈdjuːsə/ *noun* a personal assistant to the producer who is likely to have a particular understanding of the subject of the film or programme being made (*film*)

associational editing /əˌsəʊsieɪʃ(ə)nəl ˈedɪtɪŋ/ *noun* a way of editing a film or video so as to present together scenes which are similar to others

associative addressing /əˌsəʊsiətɪv əˈdresɪŋ/ *noun* the identification of a location by its contents rather than its address. Also called **content-addressable addressing**

associative processor /əˌsəʊsiətɪv ˈprəʊsesə/ *noun* a processor that uses associative memory

AST *noun* a system which permits broadcast quality videotape pictures to be broadcast at different speeds or frame rates (*film*) Full form **automatic scan tracking**

astable multivibrator /ˌeɪsteɪb(ə)l ˈmʌltivaɪbreɪtə/ *noun* an electronic current that repeatedly switches an output between two voltage levels

asterisk /ˈæstərɪsk/ *noun* a graphical symbol (*) used in programming as a sign for multiplication

astigmatism /əˈstɪgmətɪz(ə)m/ *noun* a camera lens defect which causes focal problems such as out-of-focus or blurred images (*film*)

Asymetrix™ /ˌeɪsɪˈmetrɪks/ *noun* a software company that publishes the ToolBook multimedia authoring software package

asymmetric compression /ˌæsɪˌmetrɪk kəmˈpreʃ(ə)n/ *noun* a method of reducing the space taken by data

Asymmetric Digital Subscriber Line /ˌæsɪˌmetrɪk ˌdɪdʒɪt(ə)l səbˈskraɪbə ˌlaɪn/ *noun* full form of **ADSL**

asymmetric system /ˌæsɪˌmetrɪk ˈsɪstəm/ *noun* a system that requires more equipment to compress the data than to decompress it

asymmetric transmission /eɪsɪˌmetrɪk trænzˈmɪʃ(ə)n/ *noun* a method of data transmission which has two different speeds for data received by the computer and data transmitted by the computer

asymmetric video compression /eɪsɪˌmetrɪk ˈvɪdiəʊ kəmˌpreʃ(ə)n/ *noun* the use of a powerful computer to compress video, allowing it to be played back on a less powerful computer

async /eɪˈsɪŋk/ *adjective* same as **asynchronous** (*informal*)

asynchronous /əˈsɪŋkrənəs/ *adjective* referring to serial data or equipment which does not depend on being synchronised with another piece of equipment

asynchronous cache /eɪˌsɪŋkrənəs ˈkæʃ/ *noun* a type of cache memory that provides the slowest performance and uses a type of SDRAM that is cheap but slow

asynchronous communication /eɪ ˌsɪŋkrənəs kəˌmjuːnɪˈkeɪʃ(ə)n/ *noun* data transmission between devices that is not synchronised to a clock, but is transmitted when ready

asynchronous procedure call /eɪ ˌsɪŋkrənəs prəˈsiːdʒə ˌkɔːl/ *noun* a program function that runs separately from the main program and will execute when a particular set of conditions exist. Abbr **APC**

asynchronous sound /eɪˌsɪŋkrənəs ˈsaʊnd/ *noun* sound which is not synchronised to each particular frame but is related to the general action (*film*)

asynchronous transfer mode /eɪ ˌsɪŋkrənəs ˈtrænsfɜː ˌməʊd/ *noun* full form of **ATM**

asynchronous transmission /eɪ ˌsɪŋkrənəs trænzˈmɪʃ(ə)n/ *noun* data transmission that uses handshaking signals rather than clock signals to synchronise data pulses

AT /ˌeɪ ˈtiː/ *noun* a trade name for a standard of PC originally developed by IBM that uses a 16-bit 80286 processor

COMMENT: AT originally meant IBM's Advanced Technology personal computer, but is now used to describe any IBM PC compatible that uses a 16-bit processor.

ATA /ˌeɪ tiː ˈeɪ/ *noun* hard disk drive technology in which the controller is part of the disk drive rather than being part of the main computer or located on the motherboard. Full form **advanced technology attachment**. Also called **AT attachment**

ATD /ˌeɪ tiː ˈdiː/ *noun* a standard command for compatible modems used to dial a telephone number; defined by Hayes Corporation. Full form **attention, dial**

ATM[1] /ˌeɪ tiː ˈem/ *abbr* Adobe Type Manager

ATM[2] /ˌeɪ tiː ˈem/ *noun* **1.** method of transferring data very rapidly, at up to 155 Mbps, across an ISDN link or network **2.** a CCITT and ANSI standard defining cell relay transmission ▶ full form **asynchronous transfer mode**

ATM[3] /ˌeɪ tiː ˈem/ *noun* electronic machine in a bank that dispenses cash when you insert a magnetic card. Full form **automated teller machine**

atmosphere /ˈætməsˌfɪə/ *noun* a gas which surrounds the earth

atmospheric interference /ˌætməsˌferɪk ˌɪntəˈfɪərəns/ *noun* electrical disturbances in the earth's atmosphere which cause hissing and crackling sounds on radio or TV channels

A to D /ˌeɪ tə ˈdiː/ *adjective* same as **analog to digital**

atom /'ætəm/ *noun* the smallest particle of an element that has the same properties as the element

atomic /ə'tɒmɪk/ *adjective* referring to atoms

ATSC /ˌeɪ tiː es 'siː/ *noun* a committee that defines the SDTV and HDTV standards for use in the USA. Full form **Advanced Television Systems Committee**

attach /ə'tætʃ/ *verb* to connect a node or login to a server on a network

attachment /ə'tætʃmənt/ *noun* **1.** a device which is attached to a machine for a special purpose ○ *There is a special single sheet feed attachment.* **2.** a named file which is transferred together with an electronic mail message ○ *There is an attachment with my last mail message – it contains the sales report.*

attack /ə'tæk/ *noun* the shape of the start of a sound signal over time

attended operation /əˌtendɪd ˌɒpə'reɪʃ(ə)n/ *noun* a process which has an operator standing by in case of problems

attend to /ə'tend tuː/ *verb* to give careful thought to (something) and deal with it ○ *The managing director will attend to your complaint himself.* ○ *We have brought in experts to attend to the problem of installing the new computer.*

attention, dial /əˌtenʃən 'daɪəl/ *noun* full form of **ATD**

attention code /ə'tenʃən kəʊd/ *noun* the two characters 'AT' that are used to preface a command to a Hayes-compatible modem (NOTE: For example 'ATD123' tells the modem to dial the number '123')

attenuate /ə'tenjueɪt/ *verb* to reduce the strength or size of peaks (of a signal)

attenuation /əˌtenju'eɪʃ(ə)n/ *noun* the difference between transmitted and received power measured in decibels ○ *If the cable is too long, the signal attenuation will start to cause data errors.* Opposite **gain**

attribute /'ætrɪbjuːt/ *noun* **1.** a piece of information concerning the display or presentation of information **2.** a set of control data stored with and controlling particular functions or aspects of the file in some operating systems such as DOS and OS/2 **3.** a single bit that defines whether the font has a particular characteristic, e.g., whether it is displayed in normal, bold or underlined

audible /'ɔːdɪb(ə)l/ *adjective* which can be heard ○ *The printer makes an audible signal when it runs out of paper.*

audience /'ɔːdiəns/ *noun* people who watch a TV programme or listen to a radio programme

audience rating /'ɔːdiəns ˌreɪtɪŋ/ *noun* the rating of a programme by calculating the number of people who have watched it

audio /'ɔːdiəʊ/ *adjective* referring to sound or to things which can be heard

audio file /'ɔːdiəʊ faɪl/ *noun* a digital sound sample stored on disk

audio range /'ɔːdiəʊ reɪndʒ/ *noun* the frequency range between 50–20,000 Hz that can be detected by a human ear

audiotape /'ɔːdiəʊteɪp/ *noun* tape treated with magnetisable metallic oxide in order to allow sound to be recorded (*film*)

audiotex /'ɔːdiəʊteks/ *noun* an interactive voice response over the telephone in which a computer asks the caller questions and the caller responds by pressing numbers on his telephone

audio/video interleaved /ˌɔːdiəʊ ˌvɪdiəʊ ˌɪntə'liːvd/ *noun* full form of **AVI**

audio-video support system /ˌɔːdiəʊ ˌvɪdiəʊ sə'pɔːt/ *noun* full form of **AVSS**

audiovisual /ˌɔːdiəʊ 'vɪʒuəl/ *adjective* which uses sound and images

audiovisual aids /ˌɔːdiəʊvɪʒuəl 'eɪdz/ *plural noun* equipment used in teaching, which includes both sound and pictures

audiovisual scripts /ˌɔːdiəʊvɪʒuəl 'eskrɪpts/ *plural noun* scripts that indicate and separate live and mechanical sources

audit /'ɔːdɪt/ *noun* the process of noting tasks carried out by a computer ■ *verb* to examine the state of a system and check that it is still secure or working properly

audit trail /'ɔːdɪt treɪl/ *noun* a record of details of the use made of a system by noting transactions carried out, used for checking on illegal use or malfunction

augend /'ɔːgend/ *noun* the number to which another number, the addend, is added to produce the sum

augment /ɔːg'ment/ *verb* to increase

augmenter /ˌɔːg'mentə/ *noun* a value added to another

AUI connector /ˌeɪ juː 'aɪ kəˌnektə/ *noun* a D-connector used to connect thick Ethernet cable to a network adapter

aural /'ɔːrəl/ *adjective* by ear

authentic /ɔː'θentɪk/ *adjective* which is true

authenticate /ɔː'θentɪˌkeɪt/ *verb* to say that something is true or genuine

authentication /ɔːˌθentɪ'keɪʃ(ə)n/ *noun* the process of making sure that something is authentic

authenticator /ɔː'θentɪkeɪtə/ *noun* a trustworthy company that provides authentication for digital signatures on the Internet (NOTE: This process is used by secure websites (shopping or payment sites) to prove to a visitor that the website has been created by the authorised publisher.)

author /'ɔːθə/ *noun* the person who wrote a program ■ *verb* to create a multimedia application by combining sound, video and images

'The authoring system is a software product that integrates text and fractally compressed images, using any wordprocessor line editor, to create an electronic book with hypertext links between different pages.' [*Computing*]

authoring language /ˌɔːθərɪŋ 'læŋgwɪdʒ/ *noun* a programming language used to write CAL and training programs

authoring software /ˌɔːθərɪŋ 'sɒftweə/, **authoring system** /ˌɔːθərɪŋ 'sɪstəm/ *noun* **1.** a special application that allows you to create multimedia titles. Authoring software lets you design the pages of the multimedia book and place video clips, images, text and sound on a page. (NOTE: Almost all multimedia developers use some type of authoring software rather than a traditional programming language because it's a much faster and easier way to create multimedia programs.) **2.** same as **webpage design software**

authorisation /ˌɔːθəraɪ'zeɪʃ(ə)n/, **authorization** *noun* the process of giving a user permission to access a system

authorisation code /ˌɔːθəraɪ'zeɪʃ(ə)n kəʊd/ *noun* a code used to restrict access to a computer system to authorised users only

authorised user /ˌɔːθəˌraɪzd 'juːzə/, **authorized user** *noun* person who is allowed to access a system

authority /ɔː'θɒrəti/ *noun* the power to do something ○ *He has no authority to delete your account.*

authorize /'ɔːθəˌraɪz/ *verb* **1.** to give permission for something to be done ○ *to authorise the purchase of a new computer system* **2.** to give someone the authority to do something

authorized /'ɔːθəraɪzd/ *adjective* permitted

author level /ˌɔːθə 'lev(ə)l/ *noun* the mode of an authoring software package that is used by the author to design the application (NOTE: The user uses the finished application at user level.)

auto /'ɔːtəʊ/ *adjective, prefix* automatic or which works without the user needing to act

'...expansion accessories include auto-dial and auto-answer' [*Electronic & Wireless Worlds*]

autocue /'ɔːtəʊkjuː/ *noun* a method that enables a person to read out a rolling text which is projected on to an angled mirror in front of the camera lens (*film*) ○ *Autocue enables a TV presenter to read a script without looking down.* ○ *An autocue operator controls the speed.*

AUTOEXEC.BAT /ˌɔːtəʊɪg'zek bæt/ *noun* (*in an IBM PC running the MS-DOS operating system*) a batch file that contains commands that are executed when the computer is first switched on or reset

autoflow /'ɔːtəʊfləʊ/ *noun* a feature of DTP or wordprocessing software that automatically flows text around a graphic image or from one page to the next

autofocus /'ɔːtəʊfəʊkəs/ *noun* an infrared sensors in cameras or camcorders that activate the focusing operation (*film*)

automate /'ɔːtəˌmeɪt/ *verb* to install machines to do work previously done by people

automated teller machine /ˌɔːtəmeɪtɪd 'telə məˌʃiːn/ *noun* full form of **ATM**

automatic /ˌɔːtə'mætɪk/ *adjective* which works by itself, without being worked by an operator

automatically /ˌɔːtə'mætɪkli/ *adverb* (machine) working without a person giving instructions ○ *The compiler automatically corrected the syntax errors.* ◊ **APT**

automatically programmed tools /ˌɔːtəmætɪkli ˌprəʊgræmd 'tuːlz/ *plural noun* full form of **APT**

automatic backup /ˌɔːtəmætɪk 'bækʌp/ *noun* same as **auto save**

automatic call distribution /ˌɔːtəmætɪk 'kɔːl ˌdɪstrɪbjuːʃ(ə)n/ *noun* full form of **ACD**

automatic calling unit /ˌɔːtəmætɪk 'kɔːlɪŋ ˌjuːnɪt/ *noun* full form of **ACU**

automatic camera effects system *noun* full form of **ACES**

automatic data processing /ˌɔːtəmætɪk 'deɪtə ˌprəʊsesɪŋ/ *noun* full form of **ADP**

automatic frequency switching /ˌɔːtəmætɪk 'friːkwənsi ˌswɪtʃɪŋ/ *noun* same as **automatic mode**

automatic gain /ˌɔːtəmætɪk 'geɪn/ *noun* an electronic circuit which automatically increases the volume when someone is speaking quietly and drops it when someone is speaking loudly

automatic gain control /ˌɔːtəmætɪk ˌgeɪn kən'trəʊl/ *noun* full form of **AGC**

automatic mailing list /ˌɔːtəmætɪk 'meɪlɪŋ ˌlɪst/ *noun* ♦ **listserv**

automatic mode /ˌɔːtə'mætɪk məʊd/ *noun* a feature of a monitor that can adjust its internal circuits to the different frequencies used by different video standards. Also called **automatic frequency switching**

automatic number identification /ˌɔːtəmætɪk ˈnʌmbə aɪˌdentɪfɪkeɪʃ(ə)n/ *noun* full form of **ANI**

automatic repeat request /ˌɔːtəmætɪk rɪˈpiːt rɪˌkwest/ *noun* full form of **ARQ**

automatic scan tracking *noun* full form of **AST**

automatic send/receive /ˌɔːtəmætɪk ˌsend rɪˈsiːv/ *noun* full form of **ASR**

automatic volume control /ˌɔːtəmætɪk ˈvɒljuːm kənˌtrəʊl/ *noun* full form of **AVC**

automation /ˌɔːtəˈmeɪʃ(ə)n/ *noun* the use of machines to do work with very little supervision by people

autopositive /ˌɔːtəʊˈpɒzɪtɪv/ *noun* a photographic process that produces a positive image without a negative stage

auto-reliable mode /ˌɔːtəʊ rɪˈlaɪəb(ə)l ˌməʊd/ *noun* a feature of a modem in which the modem will try and establish a reliable connection with another modem using error correction

auto save /ˈɔːtəʊ seɪv/ *noun* a feature of some application programs, e.g. word-processor or database software, that automatically saves the file being used every few minutes in case of a power failure or system crash. Also called **automatic backup**

auto scan /ˈɔːtəʊ skæn/ *noun* the ability of a monitor to maintain the same rectangular image size when changing from one resolution to another

autosizing /ˌɔːtəʊˈsaɪzɪŋ/ *noun* the ability of a monitor to maintain the same rectangular image size when changing from one resolution to another

auto trace /ˈɔːtəʊ treɪs/ *noun* a feature of some graphics programs that will transform a bit-mapped image into a vector image by automatically locating the edges of the shapes in the image and drawing lines around them

AUX /ˌeɪ juː ˈeks/ *noun* a serial communications port under the DOS operating system. Full form **auxiliary**

A/UX a trade name for a version of the Unix operating system for the Apple Mac range of computers

auxiliary /ɔːgˈzɪliəri/ *adjective* which helps ○ *The computer room has an auxiliary power supply in case there is a mains failure.* ■ *noun* full form of **AUX**

auxiliary device /ɔːgˌzɪliəri dɪˈvaɪs/ *noun* a piece of computer hardware that is not part of the central processing unit but is controlled by it, e.g. a printer or scanner. Same as **peripheral**

a/v *abbr* audiovisual

avalanche /ˈævəlɑːntʃ/ *noun* a sequence of actions in which each action starts another ○ *There was an avalanche of errors after I pressed the wrong key.*

avalanche photodiode *noun* full form of **APD**

avatar /ˈævətɑː/ *noun* **1.** the graphical image that is used to represent a real person in a cyberspace or three-dimensional system, e.g. the image of a person in a three-dimensional adventure game **2.** the name for the superuser account on a UNIX system. Also called **root**

AVC¹ /ˌeɪ viː ˈsiː/ *noun* an electronic circuit that maintains a constant sound level despite undesired differences in strength of the incoming signal. Full form **automatic volume control**

AVC² /ˌeɪ viː ˈsiː/ a trade name for multimedia software developed by IBM that works with its Audio Capture and Video Capture boards

AVI /ˌeɪ viː ˈaɪ/ *noun* a Windows multimedia video format developed by Microsoft. Full form **audio/video interleaved**

AVSS /ˌeɪ viː es ˈes/ *noun* a digital video system, originally for MS-DOS, used to play back video and audio files on a computer. Full form **audio-video support system**

A wind /ˈeɪ waɪnd/ *noun* a videotape wound onto a reel so that it winds in a clockwise direction; the oxide layer being on the inside (*film*)

axis /ˈæksɪs/ *noun* **1.** a line around which something turns ○ *The CAD package allows an axis to be placed anywhere.* (NOTE: The plural is **axes**.) **2.** a reference line which is the basis for coordinates on a graph

azerty keyboard /əˌzɜːti ˈkiːbɔːd/ *noun* a method of arranging the keys on a keyboard where the first line begins AZERTY, used mainly in Continental Europe. Compare **QWERTY keyboard**

azimuth /ˈæzɪməθ/ *noun* the angle of a tape head to a reference, e.g. a tape plane

B

b *abbr* bit

B¹ *abbr* byte

B² *symbol* the hexadecimal equivalent of the decimal number 11

B: used in personal computers to indicate the second disk drive, normally a floppy disk drive ○ *Copy the files from the hard drive, C:, to the floppy drive, B:.*

B2B /ˌbiː tə ˈbiː/ *adjective* referring to advertising or marketing that is aimed at other businesses rather than at consumers. Full form **business-to-business**

B2C /ˌbiː tə ˈsiː/ *adjective* referring to advertising or marketing that is aimed at consumers rather than at other businesses. Full form **business-to-consumer**

babble /ˈbæb(ə)l/ *noun* crosstalk or noise from other sources which interferes with a signal

BABT /ˌbiː eɪ biː ˈtiː/ *noun* an independent organisation that tests and certifies telecommunications equipment ○ *If you design a new modem, you must have BABT approval before you can sell it.* Full form **British Approvals Board for Telecommunications**

baby /ˈbeɪbi/ *noun* a spotlight with a 1000 watt bulb (*film*)

baby legs /ˈbeɪbi legz/, **tripod** /ˈtraɪpɒd/ *noun* a small tripod which is used when shooting low angle shots (*film*)

back /bæk/ *noun* the opposite side to the front ○ *There is a wide range of connectors at the back of the main unit.*

> 'The V3500 has on-board Ethernet and SCSI interfaces, up to 32Mb local DRAM, two programmable timers, a battery-backed real-time clock with 32Kb RAM and four serial ports.' [*Computing*]

backbone /ˈbækˌbəʊn/ *noun* a high-speed, high-capacity connection path that links smaller sub-networks, usually used to connect servers on a network ○ *We have linked the servers in each office using a high-speed backbone.* (NOTE: Smaller workgroups or networks are connected to the backbone as segments or ribs.)

back buffer /ˌbæk ˈbʌfə/ *noun* a section of memory used as a temporary storage for graphics before they are displayed on screen (NOTE: The image is built up in the back buffer memory area then transferred to the main video memory area for display.)

backdate /bækˈdeɪt/ *verb* to put an earlier date on a cheque or a document ○ *Backdate your cheque to April 1st.* ○ *The pay increase is backdated to January 1st.*

backdrop /ˈbækdrɒp/ *noun* a static background image in front of which are displayed actors or scenes

back-end network /ˌbæk end ˈnetwɜːk/ *noun* a connection between a mainframe computer and a high-speed mass storage device or file server

back-end server /ˌbæk end ˈsɜːvə/ *noun* a computer connected to a network that carries out tasks requested by client workstations

back focus /ˌbæk ˈfəʊkəs/ *noun* the distance between the electronic camera transducer (that converts light into electronic signals) and the rear part of a zoom lens; this gap is adjusted when the lens is set to its widest point to produce a sharp image (*film*)

background /ˈbækgraʊnd/ *noun* **1.** past work or experience ○ *His background is in the computer industry.* **2.** the part of a picture which is behind the main object of interest ○ *The new graphics processor chip can handle background, foreground and sprite movement independently.* **3.** a system in a computer where low-priority work can be done in the intervals when very important work is not being done

background colour /ˌbækgraʊnd ˈkʌlə/ *noun* the colour of a computer screen display, different from that of characters and graphics ○ *White background colour with black characters is less stressful for the eyes.*

background image /ˌbækgraʊnd ˈɪmɪdʒ/ *noun* an image displayed as a backdrop behind a program or windows of a GUI (NOTE: The background image does not move and does not interfere with any programs.)

background mode /ˈbækgraʊnd ˌməʊd/ *noun* in a computer system in which two modes for program execution are possible, the mode that is for housekeeping and other necessary system programs. Compare **foreground mode**

background plane /ˌbækgraʊnd ˈpleɪn/ *noun* ▶ **backdrop**

background processing /ˌbækgraʊnd ˈprəʊsesɪŋ/ *noun* **1.** the execution of a low-priority job when there are no higher priority activities for the computer to attend to **2.** a process which does not use the on-line capabilities of a system. Opposite **foreground**

background projection /ˌbækˌɡraʊnd prəˈdʒekʃən/ *noun* a special effect in which actors seem to be performing in front of an actual moving background when instead, they are acting in front of images being projected onto the back of a screen (*film*)

backing memory /ˌbækɪŋ ˈmem(ə)ri/ *noun* same as **backing store**

backing storage /ˈbækɪŋ ˌstɔːrɪdʒ/ *noun* same as **backing store**

backing store /ˈbækɪŋ stɔː/, **backing storage** /ˈbækɪŋ ˌstɔːrɪdʒ/, **backing memory** /ˌbækɪŋ ˈmem(ə)ri/ *noun* a permanent storage medium onto which data can be recorded before being processed by the computer or after processing for later retrieval ○ *By adding another disk drive, I will increase the backing store capabilities.*

backlash /ˈbæklæʃ/ *noun* a fault when slack film, caused by a fault in mechanics, is broken or damaged; common when using take-up or rewind wheels (*film*)

back-level /ˈbæk ˌlev(ə)l/ *noun* the earlier release of a product which may not support a current function

backlight /ˈbæklaɪt/ *noun* light behind a liquid crystal display unit that improves the contrast of characters on the screen and allows it to be read in dim light

backlit display /ˌbæklɪt dɪˈspleɪ/ *noun* a liquid crystal display unit that has a backlight fitted to improve the contrast of the display

backlog /ˈbækˌlɒɡ/ *noun* work or tasks that have yet to be processed ○ *The programmers can't deal with the backlog of programming work.*

back office /ˌbæk ˈɒfɪs/ *noun* a secure area of e-commerce software containing details of a company's store properties and products and tax tables ■ *adjective* relating to the internal administration of a business, not to its contacts with the public

backout /ˌbækˈaʊt/ *verb* to restore a file to its original condition before any changes were made

back pack /ˈbæk pæk/ *noun* lightweight television recording equipment which the cameraman carries on his back when filming (*film*)

back panel /ˌbæk ˈpæn(ə)l/ *noun* a panel at the rear of a computer which normally holds the connectors to peripherals such as keyboard, printer, video display unit and mouse

backplane /ˈbækpleɪn/ *noun* part of the body of a computer which holds the circuit boards, buses and expansion connectors (the backplane does not provide any processing functions). ◊ **motherboard, rack** (NOTE: The backplane does not provide any processing functions.)

back projection /ˌbæk prəˈdʒekʃ(ə)n/ *noun* the projection of an image from behind a screen (NOTE: It is often used in animation where the static scene is displayed with back projection, then the foreground characters are displayed and the composite scene photographed.)

backscatter /ˈbækskætə/ *noun* a reflected or scattered radio wave travelling in the opposite direction to the original signal

backslash /ˈbækslæʃ/ *noun* ASCII character 92, \, the sign which is used in MS-DOS to represent the root directory of a disk, such as C: or to separate subdirectories in a path, such as C:

backspace /ˈbækˌspeɪs/ *noun* a movement of a cursor or printhead left or back by one character

backspace key /ˈbækˌspeɪs kiː/ *noun* the key which moves the cursor left on the screen or back by one character ○ *If you make a mistake entering data, use the backspace key to correct it.*

backstage /bækˈsteɪdʒ/ *noun* the area behind a theatrical stage or film set which is not seen by the audience or camera (*film*)

backtab /ˈbæktæb/ *verb* (*in an SAA CUA front end*) to move the cursor back to the previous field (NOTE: **backtabbing – backtabbed**)

backtime /ˈbæktaɪm/ *noun* a method of timing the length of rewinding from a specific end point in material to establish a specific start point in order to permit the end point to occur at a precise time (*film*)

back up /ˈbæk ʌp/ *verb* **1.** to support something or help someone ○ *He brought along a file of documents to back up his claim.* **2.** to make a copy of a file or data or disk ○ *The company accounts were backed up on disk as a protection against fire damage.*

backup /ˈbækʌp/ *noun* **1.** the providing of help ○ *We offer a free backup service to customers.* **2.** a copy of a file or data or disk made as a security precaution. Also called **backup copy, backup version 3.** the process of making a copy of a file or data or disk as a security precaution

'...the previous version is retained, but its extension is changed to .BAK indicating that it's a back-up' [*Personal Computer World*]

backup copy /ˈbækʌp ˌkɒpi/ *noun* same as **backup 3**

backup disk /'bækʌp dɪsk/ *noun* a disk which contains a copy of the information from other disks, as a security precaution

backup file /'bækʌp faɪl/ *noun* a copy of a file, made as a security precaution

backup plan /'bækʌp plæn/ *noun* a set of rules that take effect when normal operation has gone wrong ○ *The normal UPS has gone wrong, so we will have to use our backup plan to try and restore power.*

backup procedure /ˌbækʌp prə'siːdʒə/ *noun* a method of making backup copies of files

backup server /ˌbækʌp 'sɜːvə/ *noun* a second computer on a network that contains duplicate files and up-to-date data in case of a problem with the main server

backward /'bækwəd/, **backwards** *adjective, /A/ adverb* towards the back or in the opposite direction

COMMENT: Backward recovery is carried out by passing the semi-processed data from the crashed computer through a routine that reverses the effects of the main program to return the original data.

backwards compatible /ˌbækwədz kəm'pætəb(ə)l/ *adjective* **1.** able to work with older versions or systems **2.** referring to a new piece of software that provides the same functions as the previous version and can read the files created in the previous version

BACS /bæks/ *noun* a system to transfer money between banks using computer linked via a secure network. Full form **Bankers Automated Clearing Services**

bacterium /bæk'tɪəriəm/ *noun* ◊ **virus**

bad break /ˌbæd 'breɪk/ *noun* a hyphen inserted in the wrong place within a word, a problem sometimes caused by the automatic hyphenation feature of word-processing software

bad copy /ˌbæd 'kɒpi/ *noun* an illegible or badly edited manuscript which the typesetter will not accept

badge reader /'bædʒ ˌriːdə/ *noun* a machine that reads data from an identification badge ○ *A badge reader makes sure that only authorised personnel can gain access to a computer room.*

bad sector /ˌbæd 'sektə/ *noun* a disk sector that has been wrongly formatted or which contains an error or fault and is unable to be correctly written to or read from ○ *You will probably receive error messages when you copy files that are stored on bad sectors on a disk.*

baffle /'bæf(ə)l/ *noun* a sound absorber and deflector which is a moveable unit used in recording studios and film and television sets

BAFTA /'bæftə/ *abbr* British Academy of Film and Television Arts (*film*)

BAK file extension /ˌbæk faɪl ɪg 'stenʃ(ə)n/ *noun* a standard three-letter file extension used in MS-DOS systems to signify a backup or copy of another file

balance /'bæləns/ *noun* **1.** the placing of text and graphics on a page in an attractive way ○ *The dtp package allows the user to see if the overall page balance is correct.* **2.** the positioning of musical instruments so that they may be recorded to their best advantage **3.** amplitude control of left and right audio signals in a stereo system **4.** the adjustment of the blue, green and red TV camera signals in order to create a neutral chart of tones ranging from black to white. This is done to enable the production of a true colour picture on television. **5.** lighting equal to that in other takes shot on the same set ■ *verb* **1.** to plan something so that two parts are equal **2.** to calculate the amount needed to make the two sides of an account equal ○ *I have finished balancing the accounts for March.*

band /bænd/ *noun* a range of frequencies between two limits

B and C /ˌbiː ən 'siː/ *noun, adjective* (videotape) ready for editing; the tape includes the timecode, control track and colour black signals (*film*) Full form **blacked and coded**

bandlimited /'bændlɪmɪtɪd/ *adjective* (signal) whose frequency range has been limited to one band

bandpass filter /'bændpɑːs ˌfɪltə/ *noun* an electronic filter that allows a range of frequencies to pass but attenuates all frequencies outside the specified range

bandwidth /'bændwɪdθ/ *noun* **1.** a range of frequencies **2.** a measure of the amount of data that can be transmitted along a cable or channel or other medium ○ *This fibre-optic cable has a greater bandwidth than the old copper cable and so it can carry data at higher speeds.*

bandwidth on demand /ˌbændˌwɪdθ ɒn dɪ'mɑːnd/ *noun* a system used with a switching service, e.g. ISDN, in a wide area network that allows a user to send as much information as he or she wants because the network will adjust to transmit this amount of information

bank /bæŋk/ *noun* a collection of similar devices ○ *A bank of minicomputers process all the raw data.*

COMMENT: Memory banks are used to expand the main memory of a CPU (often above the addressing range of the CPU) by having a number of memory chips arranged into banks. Each bank operates over the same address range but is selected independently by a special code.

Bankers Automated Clearing Services /ˌbæŋkəz ˌɔːtəmeɪtɪd 'klɪərɪŋ ˌsɜːvɪsɪz/ *noun* full form of **BACS**

bank Internet payment system /ˌbæŋk ˌɪntənet 'peɪmənt ˌsɪstəm/ *noun* a protocol that enables bank payments to be made over the Internet and gives each financial institution a unique identification number for the purposes of Internet transactions. Abbr **BIPS**

banner /'bænə/, **banner advertisement** /ˌbænə əd'vɜːtɪsmənt/, **banner ad** /'bænə æd/ *noun* **1.** an image that carries an advertising slogan, logo or message and is displayed on a web page **2.** a heading or title extending to the width of a page

COMMENT: A long, narrow strip is now the unofficial standard format for advertisements that appear on almost every commercial website on the Internet. Some banner ads are images, others include animation to attract the viewer's attention. If you click on a banner ad, you will usually jump to the advertiser's own site. If you would rather not see banner advertisements when you surf, you can install special software that blocks them. Websites normally charge advertisers according either to the number of times the banner ad is displayed (called the number of impressions) or the number of times that a user clicks on the ad (called the click-through rate).

bar /bɑː/ *noun* a thick line or block of colour ■ *verb* to stop someone from doing something

bar chart /'bɑː tʃɑːt/ *noun* a graph on which values are represented as vertical or horizontal bars. Also called **bar graph**

bar code /'bɑː kəʊd/ *noun* data represented as a series of printed stripes of varying widths

COMMENT: Bar codes are found on most goods and their packages; the width and position of the stripes is sensed by a light pen or optical wand and provides information about the goods such as price and stock quantities.

bar code reader /'bɑː kəʊd ˌriːdə/ *noun* an optical device that reads data from a bar code

bar graph /'bɑː grɑːf/ *noun* same as **bar chart**

bar graphics /'bɑː ˌgræfɪks/ *noun US* same as **bar code**

barndoor /bɑːn'dɔː/ *noun* hinged metal shutters at the front of a studio spotlight used to shield or direct the light (*film*)

barney /'bɑːni/ *noun* a piece of heavy cloth which is put over a film camera when recording sound in order to help prevent the noise of the camera being heard (*film*)

barrel /'bærəl/ *noun* a conducting post in a terminal

barrel distortion /ˌbærəl dɪ'stɔːʃ(ə)n/ *noun* an optical lens distortion causing sides of objects to appear curved

barrel printer /ˌbærəl 'prɪntə/ *noun* a type of printer where characters are located around a rotating barrel

barrier box /'bæriə bɒks/ *noun* a device that electrically isolates equipment from a telephone line to prevent damage

baryta paper /bə'raɪtə ˌpeɪpə/ *noun* a coated matt paper used to produce final high quality proofs before printing

base /beɪs/ *noun* **1.** the lowest or first position **2.** a collection of files used as a reference. ◊ **database 3.** a place where a company has its main office or factory or a place where a businessman has his office ○ *The company has its base in London and branches in all European countries.* **4.** an initial or original position **5.** notation referring to a number system ■ *verb* **1.** to start to calculate something from a position ○ *We based our calculations on the basic keyboarding rate.* **2.** to set up a company or a person in a place ○ *The European manager is based in our London office.* (NOTE: **bases – basing – based**)

base 2 /'beɪs tuː/ *noun* the binary number system, using the two digits 0 and 1

base 8 /'beɪs eɪt/ *noun* the octal number system, using the eight digits 0 – 7

base 10 /ˌbeɪs 'ten/ *noun* the decimal number system, using the ten digits 0 – 9

base 16 /ˌbeɪs sɪks'tiːn/ *noun* the hexadecimal number system, using the ten digits 0 – 9 and the six letters A – F

baseband /'beɪsbænd/, **base band** /'beɪs bænd/ *noun* **1.** the frequency range of a signal before it is processed or transmitted ○ *Voice baseband ranges from 20 Hz to 15 KHz.* **2.** digital signals transmitted without modulation **3.** information modulated with a single carrier frequency

base film /'beɪs fɪlm/ *noun* transparent material which bears the light sensitive emulsion of a film or the magnetic oxide of magnetic recording tape (*film*)

base hardware /ˌbeɪs 'hɑːdweə/ *noun* the minimum hardware requirements that a particular software package needs in order to run

base level synthesizer /ˌbeɪs ˌlev(ə)l 'sɪŋθesaɪzə/ *noun* (*on a sound card*) a synthesiser that supports three melodic instruments and can play six notes simultaneously

basic /'beɪsɪk/ *adjective* normal or from which everything starts ○ *The basic architecture is the same for all models in this range.*

BASIC /ˈbeɪsɪk/ *noun* a high-level programming language for developing programs in a conversational way, providing an easy introduction to computer programming. Full form **beginner's all-purpose symbolic instruction code**

basically /ˈbeɪsɪkli/ *adverb* seen from the point from which everything starts ○ *The acoustic coupler is basically the same as a modem.*

basic control system satellite /ˌbeɪsɪk kənˌtrəʊl ˌsɪstəm ˈsætəlaɪt/ *noun* a system that runs dedicated programs or tasks for a central computer. It is controlled by using interrupt signals. Abbr **BCS**

basic encoding rules /ˌbeɪsɪk ɪn ˈkəʊdɪŋ ˌruːlz/ *plural noun* full form of **BER**

basic input/output operating system /ˌbeɪsɪk ˌɪnpʊt ˌaʊtpʊt ˈɒpəreɪtɪŋ ˌsɪstəm/ *noun* full form of **BIOS**

basic rate access /ˌbeɪsɪk reɪt ˈækses/ *noun* full form of **BRA**

basis /ˈbeɪsɪs/ *noun* the point or number from which calculations are made ○ *We calculated keyboarding costs on the basis of 5,500 keystrokes per hour.*

bass /beɪs/ *noun, adjective* low range of audible frequencies that make up a sound

batch /bætʃ/ *noun* **1.** a group of items which are made at one time ○ *The last batch of disk drives are faulty.* **2.** a group of documents which are processed at the same time ○ *today's batch of orders* **3.** a group of tasks or amount of data to be processed as a single unit ○ *We deal with the orders in batches of fifty.* ■ *verb* **1.** to put data or tasks together in groups **2.** to put items together in groups

batch mode /ˈbætʃ məʊd/ *noun* a method of operating in which several tasks are specified in advance and run without user intervention. Compare **conversational mode**

batch number /ˈbætʃ ˌnʌmbə/ *noun* a reference number attached to a batch

batch processing /ˈbætʃ ˌprəʊsesɪŋ/ *noun* a system of data processing where information is collected into batches before being processed by the computer in one machine run

COMMENT: Batch processing is the opposite of interactive processing, where the user gives instructions and receives an immediate response.

BAT file extension /ˌbæt faɪl ɪk ˈstenʃən/ *noun* a standard three-letter file extension used in MS-DOS systems to signify a batch file

battery /ˈbæt(ə)ri/ *noun* a chemical device that produces electrical current

battery backup /ˌbæt(ə)ri ˈbækʌp/ *noun* a battery to provide power to volatile storage devices to retain data after a computer has been switched off

baud rate /ˈbɔːd reɪt/ *noun* a measure of the number of signal changes transmitted per second ○ *The baud rate of the binary signal was 300 bits per second.*

COMMENT: Baud rate is often considered the same as bits per second, but in fact it depends on the protocol used and the error checking (300 baud is roughly equivalent to 30 characters per second using standard error checking).

bay /beɪ/ *noun* a space within a computer's casing where a disk drive is fitted. Also called **drive bay**

bazooka /bəˈzuːkə/ *noun* an adjustable pole used as a camera support in restricted locations where a tripod is too big (*film*)

BBC *abbr* British Broadcasting Corporation (*film*)

BBS /ˌbiː biː ˈes/ *noun* an information and message database accessible by modem and computer link. Full form **bulletin board system**

bcc *noun* a feature of many electronic mail programs that allows a user to send one message to several users at a time but does not display this list to the recipients. Full form **blind carbon copy**. Also called **blind copy receipt**

BCC[1] /ˌbiː siː ˈsiː/ *noun* an error detection method for blocks of transmitted data. Full form **block character check**

BCC[2] /ˌbiː siː ˈsiː/ *abbr* Broadcasting Complaints Commission

BCD /ˌbiː siː ˈdiː/ *noun* a representation of single decimal digits as a pattern of four binary digits ○ *The BCD representation of decimal 8 is 1000.* Full form **binary coded decimal**

BCNF /ˌbiː siː en ˈef/ *noun* ➧ **normal form**

BCPL /ˌbiː siː piː ˈel/ *noun* a high level programming language

BCS *abbr* **1.** British Computer Society **2.** basic control system satellite

BCU *noun* a camera shot that is so close it only reveals part of the subject in the picture frame (*film*) Full form **big close up**

beacon /ˈbiːkən/ *verb* a signal transmitted repeatedly by a device that is malfunctioning on a network

beacon frame /ˈbiːkən freɪm/ *noun* a special frame within the FDDI protocol that is sent after a network break has occurred

bead /biːd/ *noun* a small section of a program that is used for a single task

beam /biːm/ *noun* a narrow set of light or electron rays ○ *A beam of laser light is used in this printer to produce high-resolution graphics.*

beam diversity /ˈbiːm daɪˌvɜːsɪti/ *noun* the process of using a single frequency communications band for two different sets of data

beam splitter /ˈbiːm ˌsplɪtə/ *noun* an optical device to redirect part of a light beam

beard /bɪəd/ *noun* a blank section between bottom of a character and the type face limit

bearding /ˈbɪərdɪŋ/ *noun* a fault that occurs when the electronic limits of a television system have been exceeded and is visible with marks between the horizontally adjacent light and dark areas of a television picture (*film*)

Beaulieu /ˈbjuːli/ *noun* a lightweight motion picture camera that is popular with people making documentaries or news programmes (*film*)

beep /biːp/ *noun* an audible warning noise ○ *The printer will make a beep when it runs out of paper.* ■ *verb* to make a beep ○ *The computer beeped when the wrong key was hit.* ◊ **bleep**

begin /bɪˈɡɪn/ *verb* to start ○ *The company began to lose its market share.* ○ *He began to keyboard the changes to the customer address file.* (NOTE: you begin something *or* begin **to do** something *or* begin **with** something. Note also: **beginning – began – has begun**)

beginner's all-purpose symbolic instruction code /bɪˌɡɪnəz ɔːl ˌpɜːpəs sɪm ˌbɒlɪk ɪnˈstrʌkʃən ˌkəʊd/ *noun* full form of **BASIC**

beginning /bɪˈɡɪnɪŋ/ *noun* the first part of something

beginning of file /bɪˌɡɪnɪŋ əv ˈfaɪl/ *noun* a character or symbol that shows the start of a valid section of data. Abbr **bof**

beginning of information mark /bɪ ˌɡɪnɪŋ əv ˌɪnfəˈmeɪʃ(ə)n ˌmɑːk/ *noun* full form of **BIM**

behind-the-lens filter /bɪˌhaɪnd ðɪ lenz ˈfɪltə/ *noun* a gelatin filter which is able to cut out chosen colours when placed behind the camera lens and in front of the film (*film*)

bel /bel/ *noun* a unit used when expressing ratio of signal power in logarithmic form (P bels = Log (A/B) where A and B are signal power)

BEL *noun* bell character (equivalent to ASCII code 7)

bell character /ˈbel ˌkærɪktə/, **BEL** *noun* a control code that causes a machine to produce an audible signal, equivalent to ASCII code 7

Bell-compatible modem /ˌbel kəm ˌpætɪb(ə)l ˈməʊdem/ *noun* a modem that operates according to standards set down by AT&T

bells and whistles /ˌbelz ənd ˈwɪs(ə)lz/ *plural noun* advanced features or added extras to an application or peripheral ○ *This word-processor has all the bells and whistles you would expect – including page preview.*

below-the-fold /bɪˌləʊ ðə ˈfəʊld/ *adjective* referring to the lower part of a webpage that is seen only by a user who scrolls down the page and that is therefore less commercially valuable. Compare **above-the-fold**

below-the-line costs /bɪˌləʊ ðə laɪn ˈkɒsts/ *plural noun* costs of crew and technicians used in making a TV programme (as opposed to scriptwriters, actors, etc., who are above-the-line costs)

benchmark /ˈbentʃmɑːk/ *noun* **1.** a point in an index which is important, and can be used to compare with other figures **2.** a program used to test the performance of software or hardware or a system ○ *The magazine gave the new program's benchmark test results.*

benchmarking /ˈbentʃmɑːkɪŋ/ *noun* the testing of a system or program with a benchmark

bending /ˈbendɪŋ/ *noun* distortion in videotape playback which is a result of defects in the tape or in the video machine itself (*film*)

BER /ˌbiː iː ˈɑː/ *noun* a standard method of encoding data that is stored in the ASN language, often used in libraries and other Internet data sites. Full form **basic encoding rules**

Berkeley UNIX /ˌbɜːkli ˈjuːnɪks/ *noun* a version of the UNIX operating system developed by the University of California, Berkeley

bespoke software /bɪˌspəʊk ˈsɒftweə/ *noun* software that has been written especially for a customer's particular requirements

best boy /ˌbest ˈbɔɪ/ *noun* the second in command on the electrical team on a film set

best fit /ˌbest ˈfɪt/ *noun* **1.** something which is the nearest match to a requirement **2.** a function that selects the smallest free space in main memory for a requested virtual page

Betacam™ /ˈbiːtəkæm/ *noun* a standard developed for video player and cameras

Betacam SP /ˌbiːtəkæm es ˈpiː/ *noun* a more accurate and sharper version of the Betacam system (*film*) Full form **Betacam superior performance**

beta site /ˈbiːtə saɪt/ *noun* a company or person that tests new software before it is released in a real environment to make sure it works correctly

beta software /ˈbiːtə ˌsɒf(t)weə/ *noun* software that has not finished all its testing before release and so may still contain bugs

beta test /ˈbiːtə ˌtest/ *noun* a second stage of tests performed on new software just before it is due to be released ○ *The application has passed the alpha tests and is just entering the beta test phase.*

'The client was so eager to get his hands on the product that the managing director bypassed internal testing and decided to let it go straight out to beta test.' [*Computing*]

beta version /ˈbiːtə ˌvɜːʒn/ *noun* a version of a software application that is almost ready to be released ○ *We'll try out the beta version on as many different PCs as possible to try and find all the bugs.*

bezel /ˈbez(ə)l/ *noun* the front cover of a computer's casing or disk drive unit

Bézier curve /ˈbezieɪ kɜːv/ *noun* a geometric curve with the overall shape defined by two midpoints, called control handles

COMMENT: Bézier curves are a feature of many high-end design software packages. They allow a designer to create smooth curves by defining a number of points. The PostScript page description language uses Bézier curves to define the shapes of characters during printing.

BFI *abbr* British Film Institute

BGP /ˌbiː dʒiː ˈpiː/ *noun* a protocol that allows routers to share routing information to allow each router to calculate the most efficient path for information. Full form **border gateway protocol** (NOTE: This protocol is most often used between routers installed at Internet Service Providers (ISPs).)

bias /ˈbaɪəs/ *noun* **1.** an electrical reference level **2.** the deviation of statistical results from a reference level **3.** a high frequency signal added to recorded information to minimise noise and distortion (the high frequency is removed on playback)

biased /ˈbaɪəst/ *adjective* which has a bias

bibliographic /ˌbɪbliəˈɡræfɪk(ə)l/, **bibliographical** *adjective* referring to books or to bibliographies

bibliography /ˌbɪbliˈɒɡrəfi/ *noun* **1.** a list of documents and books which are relevant to a certain subject ○ *He printed a bibliography at the end of each chapter.* **2.** a catalogue of books

bid /bɪd/ *verb* (*of a computer*) to gain control of a network in order to transmit data ○ *The terminal had to bid three times before there was a gap in transmissions on the network.*

bi-directional /ˌbaɪ daɪˈrekʃ(ə)n(ə)l/ *adjective* (operation or process) that can occur in forward and reverse directions ○ *bi-directional file transfer*

bifurcation /ˌbaɪfəˈkeɪʃ(ə)n/ *noun* a system where there are only two possible results ○ *The result of a binary multiplication is a bifurcation: the result is either 1 or 0.*

big close up /ˌbɪɡ ˈkləʊs ˌʌp/ *noun* full form of **BCU**

bilinear filtering /baɪˌlɪniə ˈfɪltərɪŋ/ *noun* a method of removing unwanted image defects, particularly on a texture-mapped object, by looking at the four adjacent pixels that surround each pixel to check that there is no sudden change in colour

billion /ˈbɪljən/ *noun* a number equal to one thousand million. Abbr **bn**

BIM /ˌbiː aɪ ˈem/ *noun* a symbol indicating the start of a data stream stored on a disk drive. Full form **beginning of information mark**

bin /bɪn/ *noun* a tray used to hold a supply of paper ready to be fed into a printer

binary /ˈbaɪnəri/ *adjective* referring to the number notation system which uses only the digits 0 and 1 ■ *noun* same as **binary digit**

binary bit /ˈbaɪnəri bɪt/ *noun* same as **binary digit**

binary chop /ˈbaɪnəri tʃɒp/ *noun* same as **binary search**

binary coded decimal /ˌbaɪnəri ˌkəʊdɪd ˈdesɪm(ə)l/ *noun* full form of **BCD**

binary digit /ˌbaɪnəri ˈdɪdʒɪt/ *noun* smallest single unit in binary notation, either a 0 or a 1. Also called **binary, binary bit, binary number, bit**

binary field /ˈbaɪnəri fiːld/ *noun* a field in a database record that contains binary digits, often one capable of holding any information, including data, text, graphics images, voice and video

binary large object /ˌbaɪnəri lɑːdʒ ˈɒbdʒekt/ *noun* a field in a database record that can contain a large quantity of binary data, normally a bitmap image. Full form of **blob**

binary look-up /ˌbaɪnəri ˈlʊk ʌp/ *noun* same as **binary search**

binary number /ˌbaɪnəri ˈnʌmbə/ *noun* same as **binary digit**

binary search /ˈbaɪnəri sɜːtʃ/ *noun* a search method for use on ordered lists of data. Also called **binary chop, binary look-up** (NOTE: The search key is compared with the data in the middle of the list and one half is discarded. This is repeated with the remaining half until only the required data item is left.)

binary system /ˈbaɪnəri ˌsɪstəm/ *noun* the use of binary digits, or the data system that operates with binary digits

binary tree /ˈbaɪnəri triː/ *noun* a data system where each item of data or node has only two branches. Also called **btree**

binaural /baɪnˈɔːrəl/ *adjective* method of recording two audio channels

binaural sound /baɪnˈɔːrl saʊnd/ *noun* a method of recording sound so that it gives the impression of stereophony when played back. ◊ **Dolby Digital™**

bind /baɪnd/ *verb* to glue or attach sheets of paper along their spine to form a book

binder /ˈbaɪndə/ *noun* **1.** a program that converts object code into a form that can be executed **2.** a company which specialises in binding books **3.** a substance used to join the metallic oxide particles together and to the base film (*film*)

Bindery /ˈbaɪndəri/ *noun* a special database used in a Novell NetWare network operating system to store user account, access and security details

binding /ˈbaɪndɪŋ/ *noun* **1.** the action of putting a cover on a book **2.** the cover of a book

binding offset /ˌbaɪndɪŋ ˈɒfset/ *noun* an extra wide margin on the inside of a printed page to prevent text being hidden during binding (NOTE: It is the left margin on a right hand page, the right margin on a left hand page.)

BIOS /ˈbaɪɒs/ *noun* a set of system routines that interface between high-level program instructions and the system peripherals to control the input and output to various standard devices. Full form **basic input/output operating system** (NOTE: This often includes controlling the screen, keyboard, and disk drives.)

biosensor /ˈbaɪəʊˌsensə/ *noun* a device that allows electrical impulses from an organism to be recorded ○ *The nerve activity can be measured by attaching a biosensor to your arm.*

bipack /ˈbaɪpæk/ *noun* (*film*) **1.** two sections of film that are run in contact through a motion picture camera in order to be printed as one **2.** the camera which is used for this method of filming

biphase /ˈbaɪfeɪz/ *noun* an electronic signal that gives information about film speed and direction (*film*)

bipolar /baɪˈpəʊlə/ *adjective* with two levels

BIPS *abbr* bank Internet payment system

birdseye /ˈbɜːdzeɪ/ *noun* a reflector type of spotlight (*film*)

bis *adjective* used to describe an extension of the V-standards that cover the features of modems providing error detection and correction. ◊ **CCITT, V series**

B-ISDN /ˌbiː ˌaɪ es diː ˈen/ *abbr* broadband ISDN

bistable /baɪˈsteɪb(ə)l/ *adjective* referring to a device or circuit that has two possible states, on and off

bit /bɪt/ *noun* **1.** same as **binary digit** **2.** the smallest unit of data that a system can handle

bit blit /ˈbɪt blɪt/ *noun* same as **blit**

bit block transfer /ˌbɪt blɒk ˈtrænsfɜː/ *noun* full form of **blit**

BITC *abbr* burned-in time code

bit image /ˈbɪt ˌɪmɪdʒ/ *noun* a collection of bits that represent the pixels that make up an image on screen or on a printer

bitmap /ˈbɪtmæp/ *noun* **1.** an image whose individual pixels can be controlled by changing the value of its stored bit ○ *In Windows, every icon picture is stored as a small bitmap image.* (NOTE: One is on, zero is off. In colour displays, more than one bit is used to provide control for the three colours red, green and blue.) **2.** a binary representation in which each bit or set of bits corresponds to some object such as an image or font or to some condition **3.** a file format for storing images in which data in the file represents the value of each pixel. Compare **vector**. Abbr **bitmp**

> '...microcomputers invariably use raster-scan cathode ray tube displays, and frequently use a bit-map to store graphic images' [*Soft*]

bit-map /ˈbɪt mæp/, **bitmap** /ˈbɪtmæp/ *verb* to define events or data using an array of single bits, which can be, e.g., an image or graphics or a table of devices in us (NOTE: **bitmapping – bitmapped**)

> '...the expansion cards fit into the PC's expansion slot and convert bit-mapped screen images to video signals' [*Publish*]

bit-mapped font /ˌbɪt mæpt ˈfɒnt/ *noun* a font whose characters are made up of patterns of pixels

bit-mapped graphics /ˌbɪt mæpt ˈgræfɪks/ *plural noun* images whose individual pixels can be controlled by changing the value of stored bits (NOTE: One is on, zero is off. In colour displays, more than one bit is used to provide control for the three colours red, green and blue.)

bit-mapped register /ˌbɪt mæpt ˈredʒɪstə/ *noun* a memory location that holds configuration information in a processor in which each separate bit within the location has a different use or meaning (NOTE: For example a register that refers to a mouse might be one byte (eight bits) wide and each bit could indicate whether a mouse button is up or down.)

bitmp /ˈbɪtmæp/ *abbr* bit-map

BitNet /ˈbɪtnet/ *noun* a network used to connect mostly academic sites and computers and allows transfer of electronic mail and listserver application (NOTE: BitNet is similar to the Internet and is connected to allow the transfer of electronic mail to and from academic users to other users on the Internet.)

bit rate /'bɪt reɪt/ *noun* a measure of the number of bits transmitted per second

bits per inch /ˌbɪts pɜː 'ɪntʃ/ *noun* full form of **BPI**

bits per pixel /ˌbɪts pɜː 'pɪks(ə)l/ *noun* full form of **BPP**

bits per second /ˌbɪts pɜː 'sekənd/ *noun* a measure of the number of binary digits transmitted every second. Abbr **bps**

bit stream /'bɪt striːm/ *noun* a binary data sequence that does not consist of separate, distinct character codes or groups

biz /bɪz/ *noun* a type of newsgroup that contains business discussions and opportunities (NOTE: For example 'biz.opportunities' contains messages from users that are offering ways of making money. Only the biz series of newsgroups are supposed to discuss commercial aspects: the rest of the newsgroups are for technical or academic discussion.)

black and white /ˌblæk ən 'waɪt/ *noun* **1.** the use of shades of grey to represent colours on a monitor or display **2.** an image in which each pixel is either black or white with no shades of grey

black level /'blæk ˌlev(ə)l/ *noun* a level of a video signal that represents absolutely no light: total blackness

black list /'blæk lɪst/ *noun* a list of goods or people or companies which have been blacked

blacklist /'blæklɪst/ *verb* to put goods or people or a company on a black list ○ *His firm was blacklisted by the government.*

blackout /'blækaʊt/, **black-out** /'blæk aʊt/ *noun* a complete loss of electrical power. Compare **brown-out**

black writer /'blæk ˌraɪtə/ *noun* a printer in which toner sticks to the points hit by the laser beam when the image drum is scanned ○ *A black writer produces sharp edges and graphics, but large areas of black are muddy.*

blank /blæŋk/ *adjective* empty or with nothing written on it ■ *noun* a space on a form which has to be completed ○ *Fill in the blanks and insert the form into the OCR.*

blanking[1] /'blæŋkɪŋ/ *noun* the process of preventing a television signal from reaching the scanning beam on its return trace

blanking[2] /'blæŋkɪŋ/ *noun* **1.** a state in which a screen displays nothing, in between two images or during the picture beam flyback **2.** the short period of time when the picture beam in a television picture either moves from right to left after each line (horizontal blanking) or from bottom to top after each field (vertical blanking) (*film*)

blanking interval /'blæŋkɪŋ ˌɪntəvəl/ *noun* the period during which a screen displays nothing, in between two images or during the picture beam flyback ■ the time taken for the scanning beam in a TV to return from the end of a picture at the bottom right of the screen to top left

blanking pulse /'blæŋkɪŋ pʌls/ *noun* the electrical signal used to start the blanking of a TV signal

blast-through alphanumerics /ˌblɑːst θruː ˌælfənjuː'merɪks/ *plural noun* characters that can be displayed on a videotext terminal when it is in graphics mode

bleed /bliːd/ *noun* **1.** a line of printing that runs off the edge of the paper **2.** a badly adjusted colour monitor in which colours of adjoining pixels blend

bleep /bliːp/ *noun* an audible warning noise ○ *The printer will make a bleep when it runs out of paper.* ■ *verb* to make a bleep. ◊ **beep**

bleeper /'bliːpə/ *noun* a device which bleeps (often used to mean radio pager) ○ *The doctor's bleeper began to ring, and he went to the telephone.* ○ *He is in the factory somewhere – we'll try to find him on his bleeper.*

blessed folder /ˌblesɪd 'fəʊldə/ *noun* the Apple Mac System Folder that contains files loaded automatically when the Mac is switched on

blimp /blɪmp/ *noun* a soundproofed film camera case which prevents camera noise being detected by the microphone (*film*)

blind carbon copy /ˌblaɪnd ˌkɑːbən 'kɒpi/ *noun* full form of **bcc**

blind certificate /ˌblaɪnd sə'tɪfɪkət/ *noun* a means of tracking visitors to websites that identifies the user's system but not his or her name

blind copy receipt /ˌblaɪnd ˌkɒpɪ rɪ'siːt/ *noun* same as **bcc**

blind dialling /ˌblaɪnd 'daɪəlɪŋ/ *noun* the ability of a modem to dial out even if the line appears dead, used on certain private lines

blink /blɪŋk/ *noun* the way a cursor flashes on and off to show you where you are positioned on the screen or in a document

blinking /'blɪŋkɪŋ/ *noun* a flashing effect caused by varying the intensity of a displayed character

blip /blɪp/ *noun* a small mark on a tape or film counted to determine the position

blister pack /'blɪstə pæk/ *noun* a type of packing where the item for sale is covered with a thin plastic sheet sealed to a card backing

blit /blɪt/ *verb* (*in computer graphics*) the act of moving a block of bits from one memory location to another. Full form **bit block transfer**. Also called **bit blit**

blitter /ˈblɪtə/ *noun* an electronic component designed to process or move a bit-mapped image from one area of memory to another ○ *The new blitter chip speeds up the graphics display.*

blob /blɒb/ *noun* a field in a database record that can contain a large quantity of binary data, usually a bitmap image. Full form **binary large object**

block /blɒk/ *noun* **1.** a series of items grouped together **2.** a number of stored records treated as a single unit **3.** a wide printed bar **4.** a piece of metal from which a halftone or line drawing is printed ■ *verb* to stop something taking place ○ *The system manager blocked his request for more CPU time.*

block capitals /ˌblɒk ˈkæpɪt(ə)lz/ *plural noun* capital letters, e.g. A,B,C ○ *Write your name and address in block letters.* Also called **block letters**

block character check /ˌblɒk ˈkærɪktə tʃek/ *noun* full form of **BCC**[1]

blocking factor /ˈblɒkɪŋ ˌfæktə/ *noun* the number of records in a block

block letters /ˌblɒk ˈletəz/ *plural noun* same as **block capitals**

blogging /ˈblɒgɪŋ/ *noun* the act of creating or maintaining a weblog

> 'Over the past year, blogging has grown, in both importance and size. The original hardcore blogging community is still there, and still vociferous. But every month, thousands of others are trying their hand at this unique publishing form.' [*The Guardian*]

blond /blɒnd/ *noun* a film business name for a 20000 watt variable-beam floodlight (*film*)

blooding /ˈblʊdɪŋ/ *noun* (*film*) **1.** the application of a particular opaque ink, paint or tape **2.** the process of using a triangular opaque patch when dealing with a photographic sound-track to cover up noise caused by a join

bloom /bluːm/ *noun* a bright spot on the screen of a faulty television

blooming /ˈbluːmɪŋ/ *noun* distortion of a picture on television due to a too high brightness control setting

bloop /bluːp/ *verb* to pass a magnet over a tape to erase signals which are not needed

blow /bləʊ/ *verb* to program a PROM device with data. Also called **burn** (NOTE: **blew – blown**)

blow-up /ˈbləʊ ʌp/ *noun* the enlargement of a picture from a 16mm to a 35mm film (*film*)

blue packing shot /ˌbluː ˈpækɪŋ ˌʃɒt/ *noun* a foreground action shot in front of a blue background in order to enable the director to mix the scene with another using a travelling matte or chroma key processes; the final picture appears with the blue background replaced (*film*)

Bluetooth /ˈbluːtuːθ/ a trade name for a short-range radio communications system that is designed to provide a simple way for computer, Internet and input devices to communicate (NOTE: For example a palm-top computer could transfer information to a mobile phone using a Bluetooth link. The technology was developed by a group of computer and telecommunications companies that included Ericsson, IBM, Intel, Nokia and Toshiba.)

blur /blɜː/ *noun* an image in which the edges or colours are not clear ■ *verb* to make the edges or colours of an image fuzzy ○ *The image becomes blurred when you turn the focus knob.* (NOTE: **blurring – blurred**)

BMP /ˌbiː em ˈpiː/ *noun* a three-letter extension to a filename that indicates that the file contains a bitmapped graphics image ○ *This paint package lets you import BMP files.* ◊ **GIF, JPEG, TIFF**

bn /ˈbɪljən/ *abbr* billion

BNC connector /ˌbiː en ˈsiː kəˌnektə/ *noun* a cylindrical metal connector with a copper core that is at the end of coaxial cable and is used to connect cables together (NOTE: It attaches by pushing and twisting the outer cylinder onto two locking pins.)

BNC T-piece connector /ˌbiː en ˌsiː ˈtiː piːs kəˌnektə/ *noun* a T-shaped metal connector used to connect an adapter card to the ends of two sections of RG-58 'thin' coaxial cable, used in many Ethernet network installations

board /bɔːd/ *noun* a flat insulation material on which electronic components are mounted and connected

body /ˈbɒdi/ *noun* **1.** the main section of text in a document **2.** the main part of a program

bof, BOF *abbr* beginning of file

boilerplate /ˈbɔɪləpleɪt/ *noun* a final document that has been put together using standard sections of text held in a word-processor

boilerplating /ˈbɔɪləpleɪtɪŋ/ *noun* the putting together of a final document out of various standard sections of text

bold face /ˈbəʊld feɪs/ *noun* a thicker and darker form of a typeface

bomb /bɒm/ *noun* a routine in a program designed to crash the system or destroy data at a particular time ■ *verb* (*of software*) to fail (*informal*) ○ *The program bombed, and we lost all the data.*

bond paper /ˈbɒnd ˌpeɪpə/ *noun* a heavy grade writing paper

book /bʊk/ *noun* **1.** a multimedia title. ◊ **ebook** (NOTE: The name comes from the fact that most multimedia titles are arranged as a series of different pages, which together form a book.) **2.** a set of sheets of paper attached together ○ *They can print books up to 96 pages.* ○ *The book is available in paperback and hard cover.*

booklet /ˈbʊklət/ *noun* a small book with a paper cover

bookmark /ˈbʊkmɑːk/ *noun* a code inserted at a particular point in a document that allows the user to move straight to that point at a later date

book palette /ˈbʊk ˌpælət/ *noun* a set of colours that is used in a particular multimedia application (NOTE: Two different applications could use different palettes, and each must load its own palette otherwise the colours will appear corrupted.)

Boolean algebra /ˌbuːliən ˈældʒɪbrə/ *noun* a set of rules that define, simplify and manipulate logical functions, based on statements which are true or false. ◊ **AND, NOT function, OR**. Also called **Boolean logic**

Boolean logic /ˌbuːliən ˈlɒdʒɪk/ *noun* same as **Boolean algebra**

boom /buːm/ *noun* a long metal arm that allows the operator to position a microphone close to the sound source; also used to position a video camera

boost /buːst/ *verb* to make something increase ○ *The extra hard disk will boost our storage capacity by 25MB.*

boot /buːt/ *verb* to execute a set of instructions automatically in order to reach a required state

boot block /ˈbuːt blɒk/ *noun* the first track, track 0, on a boot disk of an IBM-compatible floppy disk. Also called **boot record**

boot disk /ˈbuːt dɪsk/ *noun* a special disk that contains a bootstrap program and the operating system software ○ *After you switch on the computer, insert the boot disk.*

booting /ˈbuːtɪŋ/ *noun* same as **boot up**

bootleg /ˈbuːtˌleg/ *noun* an illegal copy of recorded material

BOOTP /ˌbiː əʊ əʊ tiː ˈpiː/ *noun* an Internet protocol used by a diskless workstation to find out its IP address, then load its operating system from a central server. Full form **bootstrap protocol**. ◊ **IP** (NOTE: This protocol allows a workstation to start up and load all its software over the network: Ordinarily, a workstation would load its operating system and software from an internal floppy or hard disk drive.)

boot partition /ˌbuːt pɑːˈtɪʃ(ə)n/ *noun* a partition on a hard disk that contains the bootstrap and operating system

boot record /ˈbuːt ˌrekɔːd/ *noun* same as **boot block**

bootstrap, bootstrap loader *noun* a set of instructions that are executed by the computer before a program is loaded, usually to load the operating system once the computer is switched on. Compare **loader**

bootstrap protocol /ˌbuːtstræp ˈprəʊtəkɒl/ *noun* full form of **BOOTP**

boot up /ˌbuːt ˈʌp/ *noun* automatic execution of a set of instructions usually held in ROM when a computer is switched on. Also called **booting**

border /ˈbɔːdə/ *noun* **1.** an area around printed or displayed text **2.** a thin boundary line around a button or field or a graphic image

border style /ˈbɔːdə ˌstaɪl/ *noun* an attribute that determines the type of border around a button or field, e.g. a single line, a shadow or a double line

Borland™ a software company which has developed a wide range of programming languages, database management systems and spreadsheet applications, including Turbo C++, Paradox, and QuatroPro

borrow /ˈbɒrəʊ/ *noun* an operation in certain arithmetic processes such as subtraction from a smaller number

bot /bɒt/ *noun* a robot utility program that helps a user or another application carry out a particular task – e.g. a search bot will help a user search the Internet by submitting the query to several engines at once; a link bot will check that all the hyperlinks on a website are correct

bottom /ˈbɒtəm/ *noun* the lowest part or point of something □ **bottom price** lowest price □ **bottom line** last line on a balance sheet indicating profit *or* loss □ **the boss is interested only in the bottom line** he is only interested in the final profit □ **bottom space** blank lines at the bottom of a page of printed text

bottom space /ˌbɒtəm ˈspeɪs/ *noun* blank lines at the bottom of a page of printed text

bottom up method /ˌbɒtəm ʌp ˈmeθəd/, **bottom up programming** /ˈprəʊgræmɪŋ/ *noun* a method in which low-level instructions are combined to form a high-level instruction, which can then be further combined

bounce /baʊns/ *noun* **1.** a multiple key contact caused by a faulty switch **2.** an electronic mail message that could not be correctly delivered and is returned to the sender **3.** vertical film image distortion when being projected

boundary /ˈbaʊnd(ə)ri/ *noun* a line or marker that indicates the limits of something

bounding box /ˈbaʊndɪŋ bɒks/ *noun* a rectangle that determines the shape and position of an image that has been placed in a document or on screen

box /bɒks/ *noun* **1.** a cardboard or wood or plastic container **2.** a square of ruled lines round a text or illustration ○ *The comments and quotations are printed in boxes.*

boxed /bɒkst/ *adjective* put in a box or sold in a box

box in /ˌbɒks ˈɪn/ *verb* to surround a section of text with ruled lines

Boyce-Codd normal form /ˌbɔɪs kɒd ˈnɔːməl ˌfɔːm/ *noun* ♦ **normal form**. Abbr **BCNF**

bozo bit /ˈbəʊzəʊ bɪt/ *noun* (*in an Apple Macintosh system*) an attribute bit that prevents a file being copied or moved

BPI, bpi *noun* the number of bits that can be recorded per inch of recording medium. Full form **bits per inch**

BPP /ˌbiː piː ˈpiː/ *noun* the number of bits assigned to store the colour of each pixel. One bit provides black or white, four bits give 16 colour combinations, eight bits give 256 colour combinations. Full form **bits per pixel**

bps /ˌbiː piː ˈes/ *abbr* bits per second ○ *Their transmission rate is 60,000 bits per second (bps) through a parallel connection.*

Bps /ˌbiː piː ˈes/ *abbr* bytes per second

bps rate /ˌbiː piː ˈes reɪt/ *noun* the rate at which information is sent, equal to the number of bits transmitted or received per second

BRA /ˌbiː ɑː ˈeɪ/ *noun* a basic ISDN service that provides two data channels capable of carrying data at a rate of 64Kbps together with a signalling channel used to carry control signals at 16Kbps. Full form **basic rate access**

braces /ˈbreɪsɪz/ *plural noun* curly bracket characters ({}) used in some programming languages to enclose a routine

bracket /ˈbrækɪt/ *noun* a printing sign to show that an instruction or operation is to be processed separately

bracketed /ˈbrækɪtɪd/ *adjective* (characters) joined together with small lines between serif and main part

bracketing /ˈbrækɪtɪŋ/ *noun* the process of photographing the same scene with different exposures to make sure there is one good picture

Braille /breɪl/ *noun* a system of writing using raised dots on the paper to indicate letters, which allows a blind person to read by passing his fingers over the page □ **Braille marks** raised patterns on equipment *or* in books to permit identification by touch

branch /brɑːntʃ/ *noun* **1.** a possible path or jump from one instruction to another **2.** a line linking one or more devices to the main network ○ *The faulty station is on this branch.* ■ *verb* to jump from one section of a program to another, often using a test or decision with two or more possible results that lead to two different points in the program

COMMENT: In BASIC, the instruction GOTO makes the system jump to the line indicated; this is an unconditional branch. The instruction IF...THEN is a conditional branch, because the jump will only take place if the condition is met.

branching /ˈbrɑːntʃɪŋ/ *noun* a decision with two or more possible results that lead to two different points in the program

brand /brænd/ *noun* a make of product, which can be recognised by a name or by a design ○ *the number one brand of software*

brand new /ˌbrænd ˈnjuː/ *adjective* quite new or very new

breach /briːtʃ/ *noun* a failure to carry out the terms of an agreement

breach of warranty /ˌbriːtʃ əv ˈwɒrənti/ *noun* the act of failing to do something which is a part of a contract

breadboard /ˈbredbɔːd/ *noun* a device that allows prototype electronic circuits to be constructed easily without permanent connections or soldering

break /breɪk/ *noun* an action performed, or a key pressed, to stop the execution of a program ■ *verb* to decipher a difficult code ○ *He finally broke the cipher system.*

break down /ˌbreɪk ˈdaʊn/ *verb* to stop working because of mechanical failure ○ *The modem has broken down.*

breakdown /ˈbreɪkˌdaʊn/ *noun* the process of stopping work because of mechanical failure ○ *We cannot communicate with our New York office because of the breakdown of the telex lines.*

breakout box /ˈbreɪkaʊt bɒks/ *noun* a device that displays the status of lines within an interface, cable or connector ○ *The serial interface doesn't seem to be working – use the breakout box to see which signals are present.*

breakpoint /ˈbreɪkpɔɪnt/ *noun* a symbol inserted into a program which stops its execution at that point to allow registers, variables and memory locations to be examined (NOTE: Breakpoints are often used when debugging a program.)

breathing /ˈbriːðɪŋ/ *noun* a fault in which the image on screen continually comes in and out of focus; caused by buckling of the film during exposure or during high intensity projection (*film*)

breezeway /ˈbriːzweɪ/ *noun* a signal used to separate the colour information from the horizontal synchronising pulse in a television signal

bricks-and-mortar /ˌbrɪks ən ˈmɔːtə/ *adjective* referring to businesses that operate using buildings such as shops and warehouses, as opposed to operating only or mainly via the Internet. Compare **clicks-and-mortar**

bridge /brɪdʒ/ *verb* to use bridgeware to help transfer programs and data files to another system (NOTE: A bridging product is available for companies with both generations of machines.) ■ *noun* **1.** a device that connects two networks together and allow information to flow between them. ◊ **router, brouter** (NOTE: Bridges function at the data link layer of the OSI network model.) **2.** a process of ensuring that pieces of computer equipment match, so that power losses between them are kept to a minimum **3.** hardware or software that allows parts of an old system to be used on a new system ○ *A bridging product is available for companies with both generations of machines.*

> 'Lotus Development and IMRS are jointly developing a bridge linking their respective spreadsheet and client server reporting tools. It will allow users of IMRS' Hyperion reporting tool to manipulate live data from Lotus Improv.' [*Computing*]

bridgeware /ˈbrɪdʒweə/ *noun* hardware or software used to make the transfer from one computer system to another easier, by changing e.g. file format and translation

Briefcase utility /ˈbriːfkeɪs juːˌtɪlɪti/ *noun* (*in Windows*) a special utility that allows you to keep files stored on a laptop and a desktop PC up to date

brightness /ˈbraɪtnəs/ *noun* the intensity of the light emitted by an image on a screen ○ *A control knob allows you to adjust brightness and contrast.*

brightness range /ˈbraɪtnəs reɪndʒ/ *noun* the variation in the intensity of the light emitted by something

brightness setting /ˈbraɪtnəs ˌsetɪŋ/ *noun* TV brightness control position

brilliance /ˈbrɪljəns/ *noun* the luminance of an object as seen in a picture

brilliant /ˈbrɪljənt/ *adjective* (*of light or colour*) very bright and shining

bring up /ˌbrɪŋ ˈʌp/ *verb* to start a computer system

British Approvals Board for Telecommunications /ˌbrɪtɪʃ əˌpruːvəlz bɔːd fɔː ˌtelikəmkjuːnɪˈkeɪʃ(ə)nz/ *noun* full form of **BABT**

British Standards Institute /ˌbrɪtɪʃ ˈstændədz ˌɪnstɪtjuːt/ *noun* full form of **BSI** (*UK*)

broad /brɔːd/ *noun* a wide-angled floodlight (*film*)

broadband /ˈbrɔːdbænd/ *noun* (*in local area networks or communications*) a transmission method that combines several channels of data onto a carrier signal and can carry the data over long distances. Compare **baseband**. Also called **wideband**

> COMMENT: The three most popular broadband communication devices are ISDN, cable modems and ADSL, which is part of the wider DSL standard. Each country has different prevalent standards and pricing models. For example, ISDN provides a digital link that can transfer data at the rate of 64Kbps; it dials an access number and provides a link when required. ADSL, in contrast, provides a direct connection that appears to be 'always on' using a network adapter to link the computer to the Internet provider. ADSL normally supports a transfer speed of up to 2Mbps.

broadband communication device /ˌbrɔːdbænd kəˌmjuːnɪˈkeɪʃ(ə)n dɪˌvaɪs/ *noun* a communication channel and device that allow a computer to connect to the Internet at a very high speed, often several thousand times faster than a dial-up modem connected to a telephone line

broadband ISDN /ˌbrɔːdbænd ˌaɪ es diː ˈen/ *noun* a high-speed data transfer service that allows data and voice to be transmitted over a wide area network. Abbr **B-ISDN**

broadcast /ˈbrɔːdkɑːst/ *noun* **1.** (*in radio communications*) a data transmission to many receivers **2.** (*in a network*) a message or data sent to a group of users ■ *verb* to distribute information over a wide area or to a large audience ○ *He broadcast the latest news over the WAN.* (NOTE: **broadcasts – broadcasting – broadcast**)

broadcast message /ˌbrɔːdkɑːst ˈmesɪdʒ/ *noun* a message sent to everyone on a network ○ *Five minutes before we shut down the LAN, we send a broadcast message to all users.*

broadcast network /ˌbrɔːdkɑːst ˈnetwɜːk/ *noun* a network for sending data to a number of receivers

broadcast quality /ˌbrɔːdkɑːst ˈkwɒlɪti/ *noun* a quality of video image or signal that is the same as that used by professional television stations ○ *We can use your multimedia presentation as the advert on TV if it's of broadcast quality.*

broadsheet /ˈbrɔːdʃiːt/ *noun* an uncut sheet of paper or paper which has printing on one side only

broadside /ˈbrɔːdsaɪd/ *noun US* a publicity leaflet

brochure /ˈbrəʊʃə/ *noun* a publicity booklet ○ *We sent off for a brochure about holidays in Greece* or *about maintenance services.*

brochure site /ˈbrəʊʃə saɪt/ *noun* a simple, often one-page, website that advertises a company's products and gives its contact details

bromide /ˈbrəʊmaɪd/, **bromide print** /ˈbrəʊmaɪd prɪnt/ *noun* **1.** a positive photographic print from a negative or the finished product from a phototypesetting machine ○ *In 24 hours we had bromides ready to film.* **2.** a lithographic plate used for proofing

brouter /ˈbruːtə/ *noun* a device that combines the functions of a router and bridge to connect networks together ○ *The brouter provides dynamic routing and can bridge two local area networks.* ◊ **bridge, router**

brown-out /ˈbraʊn aʊt/ *noun* a power failure caused by a low voltage level rather than no voltage level

browse /braʊz/ *verb* **1.** to view data in a database or online system **2.** to search through and access database material without permission

browse mode /ˈbraʊz məʊd/ *noun* a mode of operation in multimedia software that allows a user to move between pages in no fixed order

browser /ˈbraʊzə/ *noun* a software program that is used to navigate through webpages stored on the Internet. A browser program asks the Internet server to send it a page of information, stores, decodes and displays the page, and will jump to other pages if you click on hyperlinks. ◊ **HTML, Netscape, IE**

COMMENT: A browser program asks the Internet server (called the HTTP server) to send it a page of information; this page is stored in the HTML layout language that is decoded by the browser and displayed on screen. The browser displays any hotspots and will jump to another page if the user clicks on a hyperlink.

brush /brʌʃ/ *noun* a tool in paint package software that draws pixels on screen ○ *The paint package lets you vary the width of the brush (in pixels) and the colour it produces.*

brush style /ˈbrʌʃ staɪl/ *noun* the width and shape of the brush tool in a paint package ○ *To fill in a big area, I select a wide, square brush style.*

brute /bruːt/ *noun* a large 10,000 watt spotlight, generally an arc lamp (*film*)

brute force method /ˌbruːt fɔːs ˈmeθəd/ *noun* a problem-solving method which depends on computer power rather than elegant programming techniques

BS *abbr* backspace

BSI /ˌbiː es ˈaɪ/ *noun* an organisation that monitors design and safety standards in the UK. Full form **British Standards Institute**

BTL filter /ˌbiː tiː ˈel ˌfɪltə/ *noun* same as **behind-the-lens filter** (*film*)

btree /ˈbiː triː/ *noun* same as **binary tree**

bubble jet printer /ˌbʌb(ə)l dʒet ˈprɪntə/ *noun* ♦ **ink-jet printer**

bubble memory /ˌbʌb(ə)l ˈmem(ə)ri/ *noun* a method of storing binary data using the magnetic properties of certain materials, allowing very large amounts of data to be stored in primary memory

bubble pack /ˈbʌb(ə)l pæk/ *noun* same as **blister pack**

bubble sort /ˈbʌb(ə)l sɔːt/ *noun* a sorting method which repeatedly exchanges various pairs of data items until they are in order

bucket /ˈbʌkɪt/ *noun* a storage area containing data for an application

buckle switch /ˈbʌk(ə)l swɪtʃ/ *noun* an automatic circuit breaker in a film camera which is activated by a film jam and shuts off the motor to prevent the film tearing or buckling (*film*)

buckling /ˈbʌklɪŋ/ *noun* the distortion and bending of a film due to heat or dryness

buffer /ˈbʌfə/ *noun* **1.** a circuit that isolates and protects a system from damaging inputs from driven circuits or peripherals. ◊ **driver 2.** a temporary storage area for data waiting to be processed ■ *verb* to use a temporary storage area to hold data until the processor or device is ready to deal with it

COMMENT: Buffers allow two parts of a computer system to work at different speeds, e.g. a high-speed central processing unit and a slower line printer.

bug /bʌg/ *noun* an error in a computer program which makes it run incorrectly (*informal*)

buggy /ˈbʌgi/ *noun* a small computer-controlled vehicle (NOTE: The plural is **buggies**.)

build /bɪld/ *noun* a particular version of a program ○ *This is the latest build of the new software.*

building block /ˈbɪldɪŋ blɒk/ *noun* a self-contained unit that can be joined to others to form a system

buildup /ˈbɪldʌp/ *noun* a blank tape inserted into a videotape or film sequence in order to leave spaces for scenes that have not yet been filmed (*film*)

built-in /ˌbɪlt ˈɪn/ *adjective* already included in a system ○ *The built-in adapter card makes it fully IBM compatible.* Opposite **add-on**

built into /ˌbɪlt ˈɪntə/ *adjective* (feature) that is already a physical part of a system ○ *There are communications ports built into all modems.*

bulk /bʌlk/ *noun* a large quantity of something

bulk eraser /ˌbʌlk ɪˈreɪzə/ *noun* the removal of recorded material on a magnetic tape or film by the repositioning of all iron dioxide molecules (*film*)

bulk update terminal /ˌbʌlk ˈʌpdeɪt ˌtɜːmɪn(ə)l/ *noun* a device used by an information provider to prepare videotext pages off-line, then transmit them rapidly to the main computer

bullet /ˈbʊlɪt/ *noun* a symbol, often a filled circle ● or square ■, placed in front of a line of text and used to draw attention to a particular line in a list

'For a bullet chart use four to six bullet points and no more than six to eight words each' [*Computing*]

bulleted /ˈbʊlɪtɪd/ *adjective* marked with a bullet in front of the line of text ○ *a bulleted list*

bulletin board system /ˌbʊltɪn bɔːd ˈsɪstəm/ *noun* full form of **BBS**

'The Council of European Professional Informatics Societies has instituted an experimental Bulletin Board System based at the University of Wageningen.' [*Computing*]

bullets /ˈbʊlɪts/ *noun* **1.** a solid area of typeset tone indicating the required image intensity **2.** a method of indicating an important section of text by the use of large dots on the page

bundle /ˈbʌnd(ə)l/ *noun* **1.** a number of optic fibres gathered together **2.** a package containing a computer together with software or accessories offered at a special price ○ *The bundle now includes a PC with CD-rewriter, digital camera and scanner for just £599.* ■ *verb* to market at a special price a package that contains a computer together with a range of software or accessories

bundled software /ˌbʌnd(ə)ld ˈsɒftweə/ *noun* software included in the price of a computer system

bureau /ˈbjʊərəʊ/ *noun* **1.** an office that specialises in keyboarding data or processing batches of data for other small companies ○ *The company offers a number of bureau services, such as printing and data collection.* **2.** a company that specialises in typesetting from disks or outputting DTP or graphics files to bromide or film

'IMC has a colour output bureau that puts images onto the uncommon CD-ROM XA format.' [*Computing*]

burn /bɜːn/ *verb* same as **blow**

burned-in time code /ˌbɜːnd ɪn ˈtaɪm ˌkəʊd/ *noun* time code information included in the video signal as an image that is visible on any TV or monitor. Abbr **BITC**

burner /ˈbɜːnə/ *noun* a device which burns in programs onto PROM chips or CD

burn in /ˌbɜːn ˈɪn/ *verb* **1.** to mark a television or monitor screen after displaying a high-brightness image for too long **2.** to write data into a PROM chip **3.** to increase the exposure for a part of a photographic image

burn-in /ˈbɜːn ɪn/ *noun* **1.** a heat test for electronic components **2.** the addition of an image or title over the projected action (*film*)

burn out /ˌbɜːn ˈaʊt/ *noun* excess heat or incorrect use that causes an electronic circuit or device to fail

burst /bɜːst/ *noun* a short isolated sequence of transmitted signals

burster /ˈbɜːstə/ *noun* a machine used to separate the sheets of continuous fanfold paper

bus /bʌs/ *noun* **1.** a communication link consisting of a set of leads or wires which connects different parts of a computer hardware system, and over which data is transmitted and received by various circuits in the system. Also called **highway 2.** a central source of information that supplies several devices

business computer /ˈbɪznɪs kəm ˌpjuːtə/ *noun* a powerful small computer which is programmed for special business tasks

business package /ˈbɪznɪs ˌpækɪdʒ/ *noun* same as **business system**

business system /ˈbɪznɪs ˌsɪstəm/ *noun* a set of programs adapted for business use, comprising e.g. payroll, invoicing and customers file

business-to-business /ˌbɪznɪs tə ˈbɪznɪs/ *adjective* full form of **B2B**

business-to-consumer /ˌbɪznɪs tə kən ˈsjuːmə/ *adjective* full form of **B2C**

bus network /ˈbʌs ˌnetwɜːk/ *noun* a network of computers where the machines are connected to a central bus unit which transmits the messages it receives

busy /ˈbɪzi/ *adjective* **1.** occupied in doing something or in working ○ *When the busy line goes low, the printer will accept more data.* **2.** (*of a signal*) indicating that a device is not ready to receive data **3.** distracting or detailed (background to a film shot)

button /ˈbʌt(ə)n/ *noun* **1.** a switch on a mouse or joystick that carries out an action ○ *Use the mouse to move the cursor to the icon and start the application by pressing the mouse button.* **2.** a square shape displayed that will carry out a particular action if selected with a pointer or keyboard ○ *There are two buttons at the bottom of the status window, select the left button to cancel the operation* or *the right to continue.*

button bar /ˈbʌt(ə)n bɑː/ *noun* a line of small buttons along the top of the screen, just below the menu bar, in many applications such as Microsoft Word, Works and Excel. Each button on the bar contains an icon that helps describe its function and is equipped with bubble-help.

butt splice /ˈbʌt splaɪs/ *noun* a join in film or tape which has been taped together with the edges touching in order to prevent overlapping (*film*)

buzz /bʌz/ *noun* a sound like a loud hum ■ *verb* to make a loud hum

buzzer /ˈbʌzə/ *noun* an electrical device which makes a loud hum

buzz track /ˈbʌz træk/ *noun* the sound track of a test film which is used to position correctly the visual film in an optical sound reproduction system (*film*)

buzzword /ˈbʌzwɜːd/ *noun* a word which is popular among a certain group of people (*informal*)

BVA *abbr* British Videogram Association (*film*)

B/W, B and W *abbr* black-and-white

bypass /ˈbaɪˌpɑːs/ *noun* an alternative route around a component or device, usually a faulty one, so that it is not used ○ *There is an automatic bypass around any faulty equipment.*

byte /baɪt/ *noun* a group of usually eight bits or binary digits that a computer operates on as a single unit

bytes per second /ˌbaɪts pɜː ˈsekənd/ *noun* the number of bytes that can be transmitted per second. Abbr **Bps**

C

C[1] *symbol* the hexadecimal number equivalent to decimal 12

C[2] *noun* a high level programming language developed mainly for writing structured systems programs (NOTE: The C language was originally developed for and with the UNIX operating system.)

C++ /ˌsiː plʌs ˈplʌs/ *noun* a high-level programming language based on its predecessor, C, but providing object-oriented programming functions

cable /ˈkeɪb(ə)l/ *noun* a flexible conducting electrical or optical link ○ *The cable has the wrong connector for this printer.*

cable modem /ˌkeɪb(ə)l ˈməʊdem/ *noun* a device that links a computer to the Internet via an existing cable television line. This system provides high speed access to the Internet by sharing the coaxial cable that is used to distribute cable television signals.

cabling /ˈkeɪblɪŋ/ *noun* cable as a material ○ *Using high-quality cabling will allow the user to achieve very high data transfer rates.*

> 'It has won a £500,000 contract to supply a structured voice and data cabling system to the bank and its stockbrocking subsidiary.' [*Computing*]

cache /kæʃ/ *noun* a section of memory used to store a temporary copy of selected data for faster access. Also called **cache memory** ■ *verb* to file or store in a cache ○ *This CPU caches instructions so improves performance by 15 percent.*

cache memory /ˈkæʃ ˌmem(ə)ri/ *noun* same as **cache**

CAD /kæd/ *noun* the use of a computer and graphics terminal to help a designer in his work ○ *All our engineers design on CAD workstations.* Full form **computer-aided design, computer-assisted design**

> 'John Smith of CAD supplier CAD/CAM Limited has moved into sales with responsibilities for the North of England. He was previously a technical support specialist.' [*Computing*]

CAD/CAM *noun* interaction between computers used for designing and those for manufacturing a product

caddy /ˈkædi/ *noun* ➧ **CD caddy**

CAE /ˌsiː eɪ ˈiː/ *noun* the use of a computer to help an engineer solve problems or calculate design or product specifications. Full form **computer-aided engineering, computer-assisted engineering**

CAI /ˌsiː eɪ ˈaɪ/ *noun* the use of a computer to assist in teaching a subject. Full form **computer-aided instruction, computer-assisted instruction**

CAL /ˌsiː eɪ ˈel/ *noun* the use of a computer to assist pupils to learn a subject. Full form **computer-aided learning, computer-assisted learning**

calculate /ˈkælkjʊˌleɪt/ *verb* **1.** to find the answer to a problem using numbers ○ *The DP manager calculated the rate for keyboarding.* **2.** to estimate ○ *I calculate that we have six months' stock left.*

calculating machine /ˈkælkjʊleɪtɪŋ məˌʃiːn/ *noun* a machine which calculates

calculation /ˌkælkjʊˈleɪʃ(ə)n/ *noun* the answer to a problem in mathematics

calculator /ˈkælkjʊˌleɪtə/ *noun* an electronic machine which works out the answers to numerical problems ○ *My pocket calculator needs a new battery.*

Calculator /ˈkælkjʊˌleɪtə/ a software utility that is supplied with Windows, works just like a normal calculator and is started by double-clicking on the Calculator icon in the Accessories group

calibrate /ˈkælɪbreɪt/ *verb* to adjust a monitor or joystick so that it is responding correctly and accurately to the signals or movements

call /kɔːl/ *noun* a conversation (between people or machines) on the telephone ■ *verb* to transfer control from a main program to a separate program or routine

callback /ˈkɔːlbæk/ *noun* a security system that is used to reduce the risk of any unauthorised user connecting to a computer if dial-in networking is installed. With callback, the communications software and modem are used to dial the remote computer and enter a name and password. The remote computer then hangs up the telephone line and calls back on a preset telephone number. Abbr **CB**

call discrimination /ˌkɔːl dɪˌskrɪmɪˈneɪʃ(ə)n/ *noun* a feature of a modem that allows it to check if an incoming telephone call is from a fax machine, another computer with a modem or from a person

call diverter /ˈkɔː daɪˌvɜːtə/ *noun* a device which, on receiving a telephone call, contacts another point and re-routes the call

caller /ˈkɔːlə/ *noun* a person who telephones or requests a call

call handler /ˈkɔːl ˌhændlə/ *noun* ♦ **handler**

callier effect /ˈkæliə ɪˌfekt/ *noun* the scattering of light as it passes through one or more lenses

calligraphy /kəˈlɪgrəfi/ *noun* the art of handwriting

call in /ˌkɔːl ˈɪn/ *verb* to telephone to make contact ○ *We ask the representatives to call in every Friday to report the weeks' sales.*

call logger /ˈkɔːl ˌlɒgə/ *noun* a device which keeps a record of telephone calls

call scheduling /ˈkɔːl ˌʃedjuːlɪŋ/ *noun* (*in a fax server*) the process of arranging calls so that long-distance calls are made at off-peak times

call up /ˌkɔːl ˈʌp/ *verb* to ask for information from a backing store to be displayed ○ *All the customers addresses were called up.*

CAM /ˌsiː eɪ ˈem/ *noun* the use of a computer to control machinery or assist in a manufacturing process. Full form **computer-aided manufacture, computer-assisted manufacturing**

Cambridge ring /ˌkeɪmbridʒ ˈrɪŋ/ *noun* a local area networking standard used for connecting several devices and computers together in a ring with simple cable links

camcorder /ˈkæmkɔːdə/ *noun* a compact, portable video camera with built-in video cassette recorder and microphone; records onto VHS, S-VHS or Hi-8 format cassettes (*film*)

cameo /ˈkæmiəʊ/ *noun* **1.** reverse characters, that is, white on a black background **2.** a front-lit subject filmed in front of a dark background

camera /ˈkæm(ə)rə/ *noun* **1.** a photographic device that transfers a scene onto a piece of film, usually via a lens **2.** a device that transforms a scene into electronic signals that can be displayed on a television

camera chain /ˈkæm(ə)rə tʃeɪn/ *noun* the pieces of equipment necessary to operate a television camera

camera crew /ˈkæm(ə)rə kruː/ *noun* a group of people who man a TV camera

camera exposure sheets /ˌkæm(ə)rə ɪkˈspəʊʒə ˌʃiːts/ *plural noun* in animation photography, the frame by frame instruction sheet for the camera operator

camera operator /ˈkæm(ə)rə ˌɒpəreɪtə/ *noun* the main camera technician who is in charge of the lighting and photography of a shot

camera original /ˌkæm(ə)rə əˈrɪdʒɪnəl/ *noun* the original film in the camera which was used to photograph a scene

camera ready copy /ˌkæm(ə)rə ˈredi ˌkɒpi/ *noun* the final text or graphics ready to be photographed before printing. Abbr **CRC**

camera script /ˈkæm(ə)rə skrɪpt/ *noun* the script on which information of shots, lighting and sound are listed

camera speed /ˈkæm(ə)rə spiːd/ *noun* the speed with which film moves through camera; rate is measured by frames per second, in feet, or metres per minute

campus environment /ˌkæmpəs ɪn ˈvaɪrənmənt/ *noun* a large area or location that has lots of users connected by several networks, such as a university or hospital

campus network /ˌkæmpəs ˈnetwɜːk/ *noun* a network that connects together the smaller local area networks in each department within a building or university site

cancel /ˈkænsəl/ *verb* to stop a process or instruction before it has been fully executed

cancellation /ˌkænsəˈleɪʃ(ə)n/ *noun* the action of stopping a process which has been started

candela /kænˈdiːlə/ *noun* the SI unit of measurement of light intensity

canonical schema /kəˌnɒnɪkl ˈskiːmə/ *noun* a model of a database that is independent of hardware or software available

cans /kænz/ *plural noun* headphones (*film*)

capability /ˌkeɪpəˈbɪləti/ *noun* being able to do something ○ *resolution capabilities*

capable /ˈkeɪpəb(ə)l/ *adjective* able to do something ○ *That is the highest speed that this printer is capable of.* (NOTE: a device is capable **of** something)

capacitance /kæˈpæsɪtəns/ *noun* the ability of a component to store electrical charge

capacitor /kəˈpæsɪtə/ *noun* an electronic component that can store charge

capacity /kəˈpæsɪti/ *noun* **1.** the amount which can be produced or amount of work which can be done ○ *industrial* or *manufacturing* or *production capacity* **2.** the amount of storage space available in a system or on a disk

capitalisation /ˌkæpɪt(ə)laɪˈzeɪʃ(ə)n/, **capitalization** *noun* function of a word-processor to convert a line or block of text into capitals

capitals /ˈkæpɪt(ə)lz/, **caps** *plural noun* letters in their large form, A,B,C,D, etc., as opposed to lower-case letters, a,b,c,d, etc. ○ *The word BASIC is always written in caps.*

caps lock /ˈkæps lɒk/ *noun* a key on a keyboard that allows all characters to be entered as capitals ○ *The LED lights up when caps lock is pressed.*

capstan /ˈkæpstən/ *noun* a spindle of a tape player or tape backup unit that keeps the tape pressed against the magnetic read/write head or pinch roller

caption /ˈkæpʃən/ *noun* a descriptive text that appears at the top of a window, in white text on a blue background

caption generator /ˈkæpʃən ˌdʒenəreɪtə/ *noun* a computer or electronic device that allows a user to add titles or captions to a video sequence

capture /ˈkæptʃə/ *verb* **1.** to take data into a computer system **2.** (*in a Token-Ring network*) to remove a token from the network in order to transmit data across the network. ◊ **Token Ring network 3.** to store the image currently displayed on screen in a file; useful when creating manuals about a software product ○ *The software allows captured images to be edited.* ○ *Scanners usually capture images at a resolution of 300 dots per inch (dpi).*

carbon /ˈkɑːbən/ *noun* **1.** carbon paper ○ *You forgot to put a carbon in the typewriter.* **2.** a carbon copy, a copy made with carbon paper ○ *Give me the original, and file the carbon copy.* ◊ **NCR paper**

carbon copy /ˌkɑːbən ˈkɒpi/ *noun* full form of **cc**

carbonless /ˈkɑːbənləs/ *adjective* which makes a copy without using carbon paper □ **carbonless paper** paper that transfers writing without carbon paper

carbon microphone /ˌkɑːbən ˈmaɪkrəfəʊn/ *noun* a microphone that uses changes of resistance in carbon granules due to sound pressure to produce a signal

carbon paper /ˈkɑːbən ˌpeɪpə/ *noun* thin paper with a coating of ink on one side, used to make copies in a typewriter or printer

carbon ribbon /ˌkɑːbən ˈrɪbən/ *noun* a thin plastic ribbon, coated with black ink, used in printers. Compare **fibre ribbon**

carbon set /ˈkɑːbən set/ *noun* forms with carbon paper attached

carbon tissue /ˌkɑːbən ˈtɪʃuː/ *noun* light sensitive material used to transfer an image to the printing plate of a photogravure process

card /kɑːd/ *noun* **1.** a small piece of stiff paper or plastic **2.** a punched card **3.** a sheet of insulating material on which electronic components can be mounted **4.** a single page within a HyperCard program; each card can have text, images, sound, video and buttons on it

'A smart card carries an encryption chip, which codifies your ID and password prior to their being transmitted across a network.' [*Computing*]

CardBus /ˈkɑːdbʌs/ a high-speed, up to 33MHz, version of the original PCMCIA PC Card standard that allows 32-bits of data to be transferred in one operation compared to the 16-bit capability of the original PC Card standard

cardinal number /ˌkɑːdɪn(ə)l ˈnʌmbə/ *noun* a positive whole number ○ *13, 19 and 27 are cardinal numbers, –2.3 and 7.45 are not.*

cardioid response /ˌkɑːdiɔɪd rɪˈspɒns/ *noun* the heart-shaped response curve of an antenna or microphone when a signal source is moved around it

cardoid microphone /ˌkɑːdɔɪd ˈmaɪkrəfəʊn/ *noun* a highly sensitive microphone which is used to pick up sound in a specific area. It is not used for general noise recording. (*film*)

card reader /ˈkɑːd ˌriːdə/ *noun* a device which reads data from the magnetic strip on the back of a identity or credit card

caret /ˈkærət/ *noun* symbol '^' that is often used to mean the Control key

caret mark /ˈkærət mɑːk/, **caret sign** /ˈkærɪt ˈsaɪn/ *noun* a proofreading symbol to indicate that something has to be inserted in the text

carpal tunnel syndrome /ˌkɑːp(ə)l ˈtʌn(ə)l ˌsɪndrəʊm/ *noun* same as **repetitive strain injury**

carriage /ˈkærɪdʒ/ *noun* the mechanical section of a printer that correctly feeds or moves the paper that is being printed

carriage return /ˌkærɪdʒ rɪˈtɜːn/ *noun* a code or key to indicate the end of an input line and to move the cursor to the start of the next line. Abbr **CR**

carriage return key /ˌkærɪdʒ rɪˈtɜːn ˌkiː/ *noun* a key that moves a cursor or printhead to the beginning of the next line on screen or in printing

carrier /ˈkæriə/ *noun* **1.** a device that holds a section of microfilm **2.** a continuous high-frequency waveform that can be modulated by a signal **3.** a substance that holds the ink for photocopying or printing processes

carrier sense multiple access-collision avoidance /ˌkæriə sens ˌmʌltip(ə)l ˌækses kəˈlɪʒ(ə)n əˌvɔɪdəns/ *noun* full form of **CSMA-CA**

carrier sense multiple access-collision detection /ˌkæriə sens ˌmʌltip(ə)l ˌækses kəˈlɪʒ(ə)n dɪˌtekʃ(ə)n/ *noun* full form of **CSMA-CD**

carrier telegraphy /ˌkæriə təˈlegrəfi/ *noun* a system of transmitting telegraph signals via a carrier signal

carrier wave /ˈkæriə weɪv/ *noun* a waveform used as a carrier

carry /ˈkæri/ *verb* to move (something) from one place to another ○ *The fibre optic link carried all the data.*

cartridge /ˈkɑːtrɪdʒ/ *noun* a removable cassette, containing a disk or tape or program or data, usually stored in ROM

cartridge paper /ˈkɑːtrɪdʒ ˌpeɪpə/ *noun* good quality white paper for drawing or printing

CAS /ˌsiː eɪ ˈes/ *noun* a standard developed by Intel and DCA to allow communication software to control a fax modems. Full form **communicating applications specification**

cascading menu /kæˌskeɪdɪŋ ˈmenjuː/ *noun* a secondary menu that is displayed to the side of the main pull-down menu

cascading style sheet /kæˌskeɪdɪŋ ˈstaɪl ˌʃiːt/ *noun* a method of describing the font, spacing and colour of text within a webpage and storing this information in a style sheet that can be applied to any text within the page. Abbr **CSS**

cascading windows /kæˌskeɪdɪŋ ˈwɪndəʊz/ *plural noun* (*in a GUI*) multiple windows that are displayed overlapping so that only the title bar at the top of each window is showing

case /keɪs/ *noun* **1.** a protective container for a device or circuit **2.** a programming command that jumps to various points in a program depending on the result of a test

case sensitive /ˌkeɪs ˈsensətɪv/ *adjective* referring to a command or operation that will only work when the characters are entered in a particular case ○ *The password is case sensitive.*

case sensitive search /ˌkeɪs ˌsensətɪv ˈsɜːtʃ/ *noun* a search function that succeeds only if both the search word and the case of the characters in the search word match

casing /ˈkeɪsɪŋ/ *noun* a solid protective box in which a computer or delicate equipment is housed

cassette /kəˈset/ *noun* a hard container used to store and protect magnetic tape

cassette recorder /kəˈset rɪˌkɔːdə/ *noun* a machine to transfer audio signals onto magnetic tape

cassette tape /kəˈset teɪp/ *noun* narrow reel of magnetic tape housed in a solid case for protection (NOTE: Using cassette tape allows data to be stored for future retrieval. It is used instead of a disk system on small computers or as a slow, serial access, high-capacity back-up medium for large systems.)

cast /kɑːst/ *noun* **1.** (*in a programming language*) an instruction that converts data from one type to another ○ *To convert the variable from an integer to a character type, use the cast command.* **2.** (*in a multimedia presentation or animation*) each individual part of a multimedia presentation or animation. The members of a cast can be individual images, sound clips or text.

cast-based animation /ˌkɑːst beɪs ˌænɪˈmeɪʃ(ə)n/ *noun* a type of animation in which everything is an object and has its defined movement, colour and shape, and the actions of each object are controlled by a script

caster machine /ˌkɑːstə məˈʃiːn/ *noun* a machine that produces metal type

casting agent /ˌkɑːstɪŋ ˈeɪdʒənt/ *noun* a person who chooses the performers for a film or television production (*film*)

casting off /ˈkɑːstɪŋ ɒf/ *noun* the process of calculating the amount of space required to print text in a certain font

cast member /ˈkɑːst ˌmembə/ *noun* a single object, e.g. text, an image or an animated object, within a cast used in a presentation

cast off /ˌkɑːst ˈɒf/ *noun* the amount of space required to print a text in a certain font ■ *verb* to calculate the amount of space needed to print a text in a certain font

CAT /kæt/ *noun* **1.** the use of a computer to demonstrate to and assist pupils in learning a skill. Full form **computer-aided training, computer-assisted training 2.** the use of a computer to test equipment or programs to find any faults. Full form **computer-aided testing, computer-assisted testing**

catadiatropic lens /ˌkætədaɪətrɒpɪk ˈlenz/ *noun* a telephoto lens incorporating mirrors which are used to diminish the lens size (*film*)

catalogue /ˈkæt(ə)lɒg/ *noun* a list of contents or items in order ■ *verb* to make a catalogue of items stored ○ *All the terminals were catalogued, with their location, call sign and attribute table.*

cataloguer /ˈkætəlɒgə/ *noun* a person who makes a catalogue

catastrophe /kəˈtæstrəfi/ *noun* a serious fault, error or breakdown of equipment, usually leading to serious damage and shutdown of a system

catastrophic error /ˌkætəstrɒfɪk ˈerə/ *noun* an error that causes a program to crash or files to be accidentally erased

catastrophic failure /ˌkætəstrɒfɪk ˈfeɪljə/ *noun* a complete system failure or crash

cathode /ˈkæθəʊd/ *noun* the negative electrical terminal of a device or battery. Opposite **anode**

cathode ray tube /ˌkæθəʊd ˈreɪ tjuːb/ *noun* full form of **CRT**

COMMENT: Cathode ray tubes are used in traditional-style television sets, computer monitors and VDUs. A CRT consists of a vacuum tube, one end of which is flat and coated with phosphor, while the other end contains an electron beam source. Characters or graphics are visible when the controllable electron beam strikes the phosphor, causing it to glow.

cathode-ray tube storage /ˌkæθəʊd reɪ ˌtjuːb ˈstɔːrɪdʒ/ *noun* a cathode ray tube with a long-persistence phosphor screen coating that retains an image for a long time

CATV *noun* a cable television system using a single aerial to pick up television signals and then distribute them over a wide area via cable. Full form **community antenna television**

CAV /ˌsiː eɪ ˈviː/ *noun* a CD-ROM that spins at a constant speed. The size of each data frame on the disc varies so as to maintain a regular data throughput of one frame per second. Full form **constant angular velocity**

CB¹ *noun* a cheap popular system of radio communications, usually between vehicles. Full form **citizens band radio**

CB² *abbr* callback

C band /ˈsiː bænd/ *noun* a microwave communications frequency range of 3.9 – 6.2GHz

CBI /n/ *abbr* computer-based instruction

CBL /ˌsiː biː ˈel/ *noun* education or learning using special programs running on a computer. Full form **computer-based learning**

CBMS /ˌsiː biː em ˈes/ *noun* the use of a computer system to allow users to send and receive messages from other users, usually in-house. Full form **computer-based message system**. ◊ **BBS**

CBT /ˌsiː biː ˈtiː/ *noun* the use of a computer system to train students. Full form **computer-based training**

CBX *abbr* computerised branch exchange

cc /ˌsiː ˈsiː/ *noun* a feature of electronic mail software that allows you to send a copy of a message to another user. Full form **carbon copy**. ◊ **bcc**

CCD *abbr* charge-coupled device

CCIR 601 /ˌsiː siː aɪ ɑː ˌsɪks əʊ ˈwʌn/ *noun* a recommended standard for defining digital video

CCITT /ˌsiː siː aɪ tiː ˈtiː/ *noun* an international committee that defines communications protocols and standards. Full form **Comité Consultatif International Téléphonique et Télégraphique**

CCR *abbr* camera cassette recorder. ◊ **camcorder**

CCTV /ˌsiː siː tiː ˈviː/ *abbr* closed circuit television

CCU *abbr* communications control unit

CD¹ /ˌsiːˈdiː/ *noun* a system instruction in MS-DOS and UNIX that moves you around a directory structure ○ *Type in CD DOCS to move into the DOCS subdirectory.* Also called **CHDIR**. Full form **change directory**

CD² /ˌsiːˈdiː/ *abbr* compact disc

CD32 /ˌsiː diː ˌθɜːti ˈtuː/ *noun* a unit with a processor and CD-ROM drive developed by Commodore that uses its Amiga computer

CD-audio /ˌsiː ˌdiː ˈɔːdiəʊ/ *noun* a standard that defines how music can be stored in digital form, i.e. as a series of numbers, on a compact disc

CD-bridge /ˌsiː ˈdiː brɪdʒ/ *noun* an extension to the CD-ROM XA standard that allows extra data to be added so that the disc can be read on a CD-i player

CD caddy /ˌsiː ˈdiː ˌkædi/ *noun* a flat plastic container that is used to hold a compact disc

CD-DA /ˌsiː ˌdiː ˌdiː ˈeɪ/ *abbr* compact disc-digital audio (NOTE: also called **Red Book audio**)

CD-E /ˌsiː ˈdiː iː/ *noun* a format that allows data to be saved to and erased from a compact disc

CD+G /ˌsiː diː plʌs ˈdʒiː/, **CD+Graphics** /ˌsiː diː plʌs ˈgræfɪks/ *noun* a CD format that adds a text track to an audio disc – used to store song title information

CD-i /ˌsiː diː ˈaɪ/ *noun* hardware and software standards that combine sound, data, video and text onto a compact disc and allow a user to interact with the software stored on a CD-ROM. The standard defines encoding, compression and display functions.

CD-I /ˌsiː ˈdiː aɪ/ *noun* set of enhancements to the normal CD-ROM standard, developed by Philips, and aimed for home use. The system uses its own special hardware console with speakers, joystick and a connection to a television screen to display the images. The special feature of CD-I is that it allows you to interact with what you see on the television screen and choose options or respond to questions or a game.

CD-i digital audio /ˌsiː diː aɪ ˌdɪdʒɪt(ə)l ˈɔːdiəʊ/ *noun* a format that enables a CD-i disc to record audio in digital format in one of four ways, either mono or stereo and at two different sample rates

CD-i digital imaging /ˌsiː diː aɪ ˌdɪdʒɪt(ə)l ˈɪmɪdʒɪŋ/ *plural noun* the compression method used to store images and video frames on a CD-i disc

CD-i sector /ˌsiː diː ˈaɪ ˌsektə/ *noun* a unit of storage on a CD-i disc that can store 2352 bytes

CD Player /ˌsiː ˈdiː ˌpleɪə/ *noun* a utility supplied with Windows that allows a user to play back audio CDs in the PC's CD-ROM drive

CD quality /ˌsiː ˈdiː ˌkwɒlɪti/ *adjective* able to provide recording quality similar to a compact disc. The term normally refers to equipment that can store 16-bit samples at a sample rate of over 44,000 samples per second. ○ *A sound card in a computer might have several modes of operation: low-quality for general use that does not use up too much memory and CD quality recording mode for final recordings.*

CD-R /ˌsiː diː ˈɑː/ *noun* technology that allows a user to write data to and read from a CD-R disc. Full form **compact disc recordable**

CD real time operating system /ˌsiːdiː ˌrɪəl taɪm ˈɒpəreɪtɪŋ ˌsɪstəm/ *noun* full form of **CDRTOS**

C: drive /ˈsiː draɪv/ *noun* the main hard disk drive, denoted by the letter C in many operating systems, including DOS, Windows and OS/2. ◊ **floppy disk, hard disk**

COMMENT: Usually, a PC has two or three disk drives within its casing. The convention is to provide one floppy disk, called 'A': and one hard disk called 'C':. If you have a second floppy disk, this is called 'B': and a CD-ROM drive is usually 'D':. When talking about the different disk drives, you say 'Drive A' for the floppy drive, but usually write 'A':. If you are using DOS, when your PC starts up it will usually show what's called the C-prompt (which looks like 'C:\> your screen); this means you are currently looking at the hard disk. If you want to change to drive A to read data from a floppy disk, enter 'A': and press return.

CD-ROM /ˌsiː diː ˈrɒm/ *noun* a small plastic disc that is used as a high capacity ROM storage device that can store 650Mb of data; data is stored in binary form as holes etched on the surface which are then read by a laser

"Customers' images will be captured, digitised, and stored on optical disk or CD-ROM, and produced if queries arise about responsibility for ATM transactions." [*Computing*]

CD-ROM drive /ˌsiː ˈdiː rɒm/ *noun* a mechanical device that spins a compact disc and reads data stored on the surface of the disc using a tiny laser beam

CD-ROM Extended Architecture /ˌsiː ˌdiː rɒm ɪkˌstendɪd ˈɑːkɪtektʃə/ *noun* an extended CD-ROM format that defines how audio, images and data are stored on a CD-ROM disc. Abbr **CD-ROM/XA**

CD-ROM Extensions /ˌsiː ˈdiː rɒm/ *plural noun* the software required to allow an operating system to access a CD-ROM drive

CD-ROM mode 1 /ˌsiː ˈdiː rɒm məʊd/ *noun* the standard, original method of storing data in the High Sierra file format

CD-ROM mode 2 /ˌsiː ˈdiː rɒm məʊd/ *noun* the higher-capacity storage format that stores data in the space used in mode 1 for error correction

CD-ROM player /ˌsiː ˈdiː rɒm/ *noun* a disc drive that allows a computer to read data stored on a CD-ROM; the player uses a laser beam to read etched patterns on the surface of the CD-ROM that represent data bits

CD-ROM Re-Writable /ˌsiː ˈdiː rɒm reɪ/ *noun* a disc technology that can read a standard CD-ROM, write to a CD-R or write data many times to the same CD-R

CD-ROM/XA *abbr* CD-ROM Extended Architecture

CDRTOS /ˌsiː diː ɑː tiː əʊ ˈes/ *noun* an operating system used to run a CD-i hardware platform

CD-RW /ˌsiː diː ɑː ˈdʌb(ə)ljuː/ *noun* a compact disc that can have its contents erased and something else recorded onto it many times

CDS *noun* digital sound recorded on a film track (*film*) Full form **cinema digital sound**

CDTV /ˌsiː diː tiː ˈviː/ *noun* a CD-ROM standard developed by Commodore that combines audio, graphics and text. This standard is mainly intended as an interactive system for home use, with the player connected to a television and also able to play music CDs.

CD-V /ˌsiː ˈdiː viː/ *noun* a format, now no longer used, for storing 5 minutes of video data on a 3-inch disc in analog form

CD-video /ˌsiː diː ˈvɪdiəʊ/ *noun* a compact disc used to store and play back video images

CD-WO /ˌsiː ˌdʌb(ə)l juː ˈəʊ/ *noun* a CD-ROM disc and drive technology that allows a user to write data to the disc once only. It is useful for storing archived documents or for testing a CD-ROM before it is duplicated.

cel /sel/ *noun* a single frame in an animation sequence

cell /sel/ *noun* **1.** a single function or number in a spreadsheet program **2.** a single memory location, capable of storing a data word, accessed by an individual address

cell address /ˈsel əˌdres/ *noun* (*in a spreadsheet*) a code that identifies the position of a cell by row and column. The rows are normally numbered and the columns use the letters of the alphabet.

cell phone /ˌməʊbaɪl ˈfəʊn/ *noun US* a small, portable device that lets someone make and receive telephone calls. Same as **mobile phone**

COMMENT: Older cell phone standards transmitted the user's voice as an analog radio signal; current phones convert the voice to digital data and transmit this via a radio signal. New cell phones provide data and messaging services as well as basic telephone functions: some include built-in modems to provide dial-up access to the Internet, many allow text messages to be transmitted to other phone users and some incorporate an electronic diary, organiser and address book. Current cell phones transmit information using the GSM, PCS or GPRS standard and can provide basic Internet access using WAP and GPRS.

cellular /ˈseljʊlə/ *adjective* clear plastic sheet used for animation and for overhead projectors

cellular phone /ˌseljʊlə ˈfəʊn/ *noun* same as **mobile phone**

celluloid /ˈseljʊlɔɪd/ *noun* cellulose nitrate which was used as a film base in the past (*film*) ◊ **acetate**

centering /ˈsentərɪŋ/ *noun* the action of putting text in the centre of the screen ○ *Centering of headings is easily done, using this function key.*

centi- /senti/ *prefix* meaning one hundred or one hundredth

centimetre /ˈsentɪmiːtə/ *noun* one hundredth of a metre

central /ˈsentrəl/ *adjective* in the middle

centralized /ˈsentrəlaɪzd/ *adjective* which is located in a central position

central memory /ˌsentrəl ˈmem(ə)ri/ *noun* full form of **CM**

central processing unit /ˌsentrəl ˌprəʊsesɪŋ ˈjuːnɪt/, **central processor** /ˌsentrəl ˌprəʊˈsesə/ *noun* full form of **CPU**

centre /ˈsentə/ *noun* the point in the middle of something ■ *verb* **1.** to align the read/write head correctly on a magnetic disk or tape **2.** to place a piece of text in the centre of the paper or display screen ○ *Which key do you press to centre the heading?*

centre text /ˌsentə ˈtekst/ *noun* an option in a word-processing or DTP package that changes the formatting of a line of text so that is in the centre of the page or frame

Centronics interface /senˈtrɒnɪks ˌɪntəfeɪs/ *noun* a parallel printer interface devised by Centronics Inc

Centronics port /senˈtrɒnɪks ˌpɔːt/ *noun* a standard that defines the way in which a parallel printer port on a PC operates

CEPT standard *noun* a videotex character standard defined by the Conference of European Post Telephone and Telegraph

ceramic /səˈræmɪk/ *adjective* made from baked clay. ◊ **capacitor**

CERN /sɜːn/ *noun* the research laboratory in Switzerland where the world wide web was originally invented. Full form **Conseil Européen pour la Recherche Nucléaire**

certificate /səˈtɪfɪkət/ *noun* a unique set of numbers that identifies a person or company and is used to prove the person's identity during network transmissions

COMMENT: A certificate is normally used to provide security over the Internet for secure e-mail or secure website transactions. A trusted company, such as VeriSign (www.verisign.com) or Thawte (www.thawte.com) issues the certificate once it is satisfied that the person or company is legitimate, authentic, and who they claim to be. The company can now use this certificate to prove its identity, create secure messages, or setup a secure website to accept payments online.

certificate authority /səˈtɪfɪkət ɔː ˌθɒrɪti/ *noun* an independent server or company on the Internet that supplies or validates a special digital certificate to prove that another company is genuine (NOTE: The certificate authority issues a special encrypted number that complies with the X.509 standard and is encrypted with a public-key encryption system.)

certificate of approval /səˌtɪfɪkət əv ə ˈpruːv(ə)l/ *noun* a document showing that an item has been approved officially

C-format /ˈsiː ˌfɔːmæt/ *noun* a popular, broadcast-quality videotape format that uses 1-inch magnetic tape to store analog video recordings; often used before conversion to digital format (*film*)

CGI /ˌsiː dʒiː ˈaɪ/ *noun* a standard that defines how a webpage can call programs or scripts stored on an Internet server to carry out functions and exchange information with the program, e.g., to provide a search function. Full form **common gateway interface.** ◊ **Perl**

CGM /ˌsiː dʒiː ˈem/ *noun* a device-independent file format that provides one method of storing an image as objects. Full form **computer graphics metafile**

chad /tʃæd/ *noun* a waste material produced from holes punched in tape or card

chain /tʃeɪn/ *noun* **1.** a series of files or data items linked sequentially **2.** a series of instructions to be executed sequentially

chaining /ˈtʃeɪnɪŋ/ *noun* the execution of a very large program by executing small segments of it at a time. This allows programs larger than memory capacity to be run.

change /tʃeɪndʒ/ *verb* to make something different; to use one thing instead of another

change directory /ˈtʃeɪndʒ daɪˌrekt(ə)ri/ *noun* full form of **CD, CHDIR**

changeover cue /ˈtʃeɪndʒˌəʊvə kjuː/ *noun* visual warnings, usually circles or dots, towards the end of a reel of film to warn the operator to change from one projector to the other (*film*)

changer /ˈtʃeɪndʒə/ *noun* a device which changes one thing for another

channel /ˈtʃæn(ə)l/ *noun* **1.** a physical connection between two points that allows data to be transmitted, e.g. a link between a CPU and a peripheral **2.** a way in which information or goods are passed from one place to another **3.** a signal path for transporting information between two points (*communications*) **4.** a term used to refer to an individual plane within an image that can store a matte or special effect or one part of the final picture **5.** a method of identifying individual tracks or instruments in a MIDI setup. There are 16 channel numbers and an instrument can be set to respond to the instructions on one particular channel; each channel also has a patch associated with it that defines the sound that is played. **6.** a method of organising cast members in a presentation. Each channel can hold a cast member, background or a special effect according to time – these are played back together to create the final presentation. ■ *verb* to send signals or data via a particular path

channelling /ˈtʃænəlɪŋ/ *noun* a protective pipe containing cables or wires

chapter /ˈtʃæptə/ *noun* **1.** a sequence of frames on a videodisc **2.** a section of a book or document

char /tʃɑː/ *noun* (*in programming*) a data type which defines a variable as containing data that represents a character using the ASCII code

character /ˈkærɪktə/ *noun* a graphical symbol which appears as a printed or displayed mark such as one of the letters of the alphabet, a number or a punctuation mark

characteristic /ˌkærɪktəˈrɪstɪk/ *noun* **1.** the value of exponent in a floating point number ○ *The floating point number 1.345 x* 10^3*, has a characteristic of 3.* **2.** a measurement or property of a component ■ *adjective* which is typical or special ○ *This fault is characteristic of this make and model of personal computer.*

character set /ˈkærɪktə set/ *noun* a list of all the characters that can be displayed or printed

characters per inch /ˌkærɪktəz pɜː ˈɪntʃ/ *plural noun* the number of printed characters that fit within the space of one inch ○ *You can select 10* or *12 cpi with the green button.* Abbr **cpi**

characters per second /ˌkærɪktəz pə ˈsekənd/ *noun* the number of characters that are transmitted or printed per second

charge /tʃɑːdʒ/ *noun* **1.** a quantity of electricity **2.** the number of, excess of or lack of electrons in a material or component ■ *verb* to supply a device with an electric charge

chargeable /ˈtʃɑːdʒəb(ə)l/ *adjective* which can be charged

> 'Compaq Computer and Duracell are developing a new type of standard-size re-chargeable battery for portable computers that lasts 40% longer than those now available.' [*Computing*]

charge-coupled device /ˌtʃɑːdʒ ˌkʌp(ə)ld dɪˈvaɪs/ *noun* an electronic device operated by charge. Abbr **CCD**

chart /tʃɑːt/ *noun* a diagram showing information as a series of lines or blocks

chassis /ˈʃæsi/ *noun* a metal frame that houses the circuit boards together with the wiring and sockets required in a computer system or other equipment. ◊ **rack**

chat /tʃæt/ *verb* to send and receive messages, in real time, with other users on the Internet

chat group /ˈtʃæt gruːp/ *noun* a group of people, often with a common interest, who exchange messages online

chat room /ˈtʃæt ruːm/ *noun* an area of a website where visitors can exchange messages with other visitors in real time. Special software displays the name of the visitor as he or she types in a message to all the other visitors, allowing them to 'talk' to each other.

CHCP /ˌsiː aɪtʃ siː ˈpiː/ *noun* (*in MS-DOS and OS/2 operating systems*) a system command that selects which code page to use

CHDIR /ˌsiː aɪtʃ diː aɪ ˈɑː/ *abbr* change directory. ◊ **CD**[1]

cheapernet /ˈtʃiːpənet/ *noun* same as **thin-Ethernet** (*informal*)

check /tʃek/ *noun* **1.** the act of making sure that something is correct **2.** examination ○ *a routine check of the fire equipment* ○ *The auditors carried out checks on the company accounts.* **3.** *US* a mark on paper to show that something is correct ○ *Make a check in the box marked 'R'.* ■ *verb* **1.** to examine or to make sure that something is in good working order ○ *The separate parts of the system were all checked for faults before being packaged.* **2.** *US* to mark with a sign to show that something is correct ○ *Check the box marked 'R'.* (NOTE: The UK term is **tick**.)

'Four bits control three multiplexers within the function unit. The last bit is a check bit to read the block's output.' [*Computing*]

check box /ˈtʃek bɒks/ *noun* a small box displayed with a cross inside it if the option has been selected, or empty if the option is not selected ○ *Select the option by moving the cursor to the check box and pressing the mouse button.*

check character /ˈtʃek ˌkærɪktə/ *noun* an additional character inserted into transmitted data to serve as an error detection check, its value being dependent on the text

check digit /ˈtʃek ˌdɪdʒɪt/ *noun* an additional digit inserted into transmitted text to monitor and correct errors

checking /ˈtʃekɪŋ/ *noun* examination ○ *The maintenance engineer found some defects whilst checking the equipment.*

checkout /ˈtʃekaʊt/ *noun* a place where you pay for the goods you have bought

checksum /ˈtʃek ˌtəʊt(ə)l/, **check total** *noun* a program that checks that data retrieved from memory is correct, summing it and comparing the sum with a stored value ○ *The data must be corrupted if the checksum is different.*

chemical /ˈkemɪk(ə)l/ *adjective* referring to the interaction of substances □ **chemical reaction** interaction between two substances *or* elements ■ *noun* a product resulting from the interaction of other substances or elements

child process /ˈtʃaɪld ˌprəʊses/, **child program** /ˈtʃaɪld ˌprəʊɡræm/ *noun* a routine or program called by another program which remains active while the second program runs

child window /ˈtʃaɪld ˌwɪndəʊ/ *noun* a window within a main window. The smaller window cannot be moved outside the boundary of the main window and is closed when the main window is closed.

chinese /tʃaɪˈniːz/ *noun* a camera movement which consists of a zoom out travel with a pan left or right (*film*)

chip /tʃɪp/ *noun* a device consisting of a small piece of a crystal of a semiconductor onto which are etched or manufactured a number of components such as transistors, resistors and capacitors, which together perform a function

chip set /ˌtʃɪp ˈset/ *noun* a set of chips that together will carry out a function

CHKDSK /ˈtʃekdɪsk/ *noun* (*in MS-DOS*) a system command that runs a check on the status of a disk drive and installed RAM

choke /tʃəʊk/ *noun* ➧ **inductor**

Chooser™ /ˈtʃuːzə/ an operating system utility supplied with the Apple Macintosh that allows a user to select the type of printer, network and other peripherals that are connected

chop /tʃɒp/ ➧ **binary search**

chord keying /ˈkɔːd kiːɪŋ/ *noun* the action of pressing two or more keys at the same time to perform a function

COMMENT: As an example, to access a second window, you may need to press control and F2; pressing shift and character delete keys at the same time will delete a line of text.

chow's foot /ˈtʃaʊz fʊt/ *noun* a metal stand for a camera tripod (*film*)

chroma /ˈkrəʊmə/ *noun* a measure of colour hue and saturation. Also called **chrominance**

chroma key /ˈkrəʊmə kiː/ *noun* (*in video*) a special effect in which an object is photographed against a normally blue background, which is then replaced with another image to give the impression that the object appears against the image. To give the appearance of flying, e.g., record a video sequence of a person against a blue background, then electronically replace this blue colour, the chroma key with footage of sky. ◊ **colour key**

chromatic /krəˈmætɪk/ *adjective* referring to colours

chromaticity /ˌkrəʊməˈtɪsɪti/ *noun* the quality of light according to its most prominent colour and purity

chrominance /ˈkrəʊmɪnəns/ *noun* same as **chroma**

chrominance signal /ˈkrəʊmɪnəns ˌsɪɡn(ə)l/ *noun* the section of a colour monitor signal containing colour hue and saturation information

CIDR /ˌsiː aɪ diː ˈɑː/ *noun* a system of organising IP addresses that is more compact and efficient than the older system, adding a slash and a new IP Prefix number that represents a number of individual addresses. For example, the old system used an IP address such as '194.124.0.0' whereas CIDR would replace this with '194.124.0.0/12'. The IP Prefix number 12 represents 4,096 unique addresses, and the lower the number the more addresses are represented.

CIE /ˌsiː aɪ ˈiː/ *noun* the international group that defines colour and illumination standards. Full form **Commission International de l'Eclairage**

CIF /ˌsiː aɪ ˈef/ *abbr* common intermediate format

CIF videophone /ˌsiː aɪ ef ˈvɪdiəʊfəʊn/ *noun* an ISDN standard for video image transmission over a telephone link which displays colour images at a resolution of

352x288 pixels. This standard uses two ISDN B channels.

CIM /ˌsiː aɪ ˈem/ *noun* **1.** the coordinated use of microfilm for computer data storage and the method of reading the data. Full form **computer input microfilm 2.** the coordinated use of computers in every aspect of design and manufacturing. Full form **computer-integrated manufacturing**

cine- /sɪni/ *prefix* meaning moving pictures or film

cine camera /ˈsɪni ˌkæm(ə)rə/ *noun* a camera that records motion pictures onto a roll of film

cine film /ˈsɪni fɪlm/ *noun* normally refers to 8mm or 16mm photographic film used to record motion pictures with an optional sound track

cinema /ˈsɪnɪmə/ *noun* a building where films are shown to the public

cinema digital sound /ˌsɪnɪmə ˈdɪdʒɪt(ə)l saʊnd/ *noun* full form of **CDS**

Cinemascope™ /ˈsɪnɪməskəʊp/ *noun* the first wide-screen filming system to be extensively used (*film*)

cinematographer /ˌsɪnɪməˈtɒgrəfə/ *noun* the person responsible for lighting and photography on a film set (*film*)

cinematography /ˌsɪnɪməˈtɒgrəfi/ *noun* (*film*) **1.** motion picture photography **2.** special effects giving impression of motion

cine-orientated image /ˌsɪni ˌɔːrientɪd ˈɪmɪdʒ/ *noun* data or graphics on a microfilm where the image is at right angles to the long edge of the roll of film

cine-oriented /ˈsɪni ˌɔːrientɪd/ *adjective* (*in a film or video clip*) referring to an image that is oriented parallel to the outside edge of the medium

cine spool /ˈsɪni spuːl/ *noun* a magnetic tape spool usually made of plastic and not more than 7 inches in width

cipher /ˈsaɪfə/ *noun* a system that transforms a message into an unreadable form with a secret key ○ *Always use a secure cipher when sending data over a telephone line.* (NOTE: The message can be read normally after it has passed through the cipher a second time to decrypt it.)

ciphertext /ˈsaɪfətekst/ *noun* data output from a cipher. Opposite **plaintext**

circuit /ˈsɜːkɪt/ *noun* a connection between the electronic components that perform a function

circuit board /ˈsɜːkɪt bɔːd/ *noun* an insulating board used to hold components which are then connected together electrically to form a circuit

'The biggest shock was to open up the PC and find the motherboard smothered in patch wires (usually a sign that a design fault in the printed circuit board was rectified at the last minute).' [*Computing*]

circuit diagram /ˈsɜːkɪt ˌdaɪəgræm/ *noun* a graphical description of a circuit ○ *The CAD program will plot the circuit diagram rapidly.*

circuitry /ˈsɜːkɪtri/ *noun* a collection of circuits ○ *The circuitry is still too complex.*

circular /ˈsɜːkjʊlə/ *adjective* **1.** which goes round in a circle **2.** sent to many people

circularize /ˈsɜːkjʊləraɪz/ *verb* to send a circular to ○ *The committee has agreed to circularise the members.* ○ *They circularised all their customers with a new list of prices.*

circular reference /ˌsɜːkjʊlə ˈref(ə)rəns/ *noun* (*in a spreadsheet*) an error condition that occurs when two equations in two cells reference each other

circulate /ˈsɜːkjʊˌleɪt/ *verb* **1.** to go round in a circle, and return to the first point **2.** to send information to ○ *They circulated a new list of prices to all their customers.*

circulating /ˈsɜːkjʊleɪtɪŋ/ *adjective* which is moving about freely

COMMENT: Circulating storage devices are not often used now, being slow (serial access) and bulky: typical devices are acoustic or mercury delay lines.

circulation /ˌsɜːkjʊˈleɪʃ(ə)n/ *noun* **1.** movement ○ *The company is trying to improve the circulation of information between departments.* **2.** the number of copies sold ○ *a specialised paper with a circulation of over 10,000* ○ *What is the circulation of this computer magazine?*

circumflex /ˈsɜːkəmfleks/ *noun* a printed accent (like a small 'v' printed upside down) placed above a letter, which may change the pronunciation or distinguish the letter from others

CIS /ˌsiː aɪ ˈes/ *noun* a scanner in which the detectors, a flat bar of light-sensitive diodes, touch the original, without any lens that might distort the image. Full form **contact image sensor**

CISC /ˌsiː aɪ es ˈsiː/ *noun* a type of CPU design whose instruction set contains a number of long, complex instructions that make program writing easier, but reduce execution speed. Full form **complex instruction set computer**. Compare **RISC**

citizens band radio /ˌsɪtɪz(ə)ns bænd ˈreɪdiəʊ/ *noun* a cheap popular system of radio communications, usually between vehicles. Also called **CB radio**

cladding /ˈklædɪŋ/ *noun* protective material surrounding a conducting core ○ *If the cladding is chipped, the fibre-optic cable will not function well.*

claim frame /ˈkleɪm freɪm/ *noun* (*in an FDDI protocol network*) a special frame that is used to determine which station will initialise the network

clamp /klæmp/ *verb* to find the voltage of a signal

clamper /ˈklæmpə/ *noun* a circuit which limits the level of a signal from a scanning head or other input device to a maximum before this is converted to a digital value. Clampers are used to cut out noise and spikes.

clapper /ˈklæpə/ *noun* the mechanical part of a dot matrix printer that drives the printing needles onto the ribbon to print a character on the paper

clapperboard /ˈklæpəbɔːd/ *noun* a board on which is written all relevant information to a shot in a film (*film*)

clarity /ˈklærɪti/ *noun* being clear ○ *The atmospheric conditions affect the clarity of the signal.*

classification /ˌklæsɪfɪˈkeɪʃ(ə)n/ *noun* a way of putting into classes

classify /ˈklæsɪfaɪ/ *verb* to put into classes or under various headings ○ *The diagnostic printouts have been classified under T for test results.*

class interval /ˌklɑːs ˈɪntəv(ə)l/ *noun* the range of values that can be contained in a class

claw /klɔː/ *noun* a mechanism in a camera or projector which moves the film through contact with the holes in the edge of the film (*film*)

clean /kliːn/ *adjective* containing no errors ○ *I'll have to start again – I just erased the only clean copy.* ■ *verb* to make something clean

clean copy /ˌkliːn ˈkɒpi/ *noun* a copy which is ready for keyboarding and does not have many changes to it

clear /klɪə/ *adjective* easily understood ○ *The program manual is not clear on how to copy files.* ■ *verb* **1.** to wipe out or erase or set to zero a computer file or variable or section of memory ○ *Type CLS to clear the screen.* **2.** to release a communications link when transmissions have finished

clearance /ˈklɪərəns/ *noun* authority to access a file ○ *You do not have the required clearance for this processor.*

clear to send /ˌklɪə tə ˈsend/ *noun* full form of **CTS**

click /klɪk/ *noun* **1.** a short duration sound, often used to indicate that a key has been pressed **2.** the act of pressing a mouse button or a key on a keyboard ○ *You move through text and graphics with a click of the button.*

click rate /ˈklɪk reɪt/ *noun* a figure representing the number of times that a particular site in an Internet advertisement is visited, and calculated as a percentage of the number of times that the advertisement is viewed

clicks-and-mortar /ˌklɪks ən ˈmɔːtə/ *noun* referring to businesses that use both the Internet and physical shops to sell their products. Compare **bricks-and-mortar**

click through /ˈklɪk θruː/ *noun* the act of clicking on a banner advertisement and jumping to the advertiser's website

click through rate /ˈklɪk θruː ˌreɪt/ *noun* full form of **CTR**

client /ˈklaɪənt/ *noun* (*in a network*) a workstation or PC or terminal connected to a network that can send instructions to a server and display results

client application /ˌklaɪənt ˌæplɪˈkeɪʃ(ə)n/ *noun* an application that can accept linked or embedded objects from a server application or an application that is used in a client-server system

client area /ˈklaɪənt ˌeəriə/ *noun* (*in a GUI*) an area inside a window that can be used to display graphics or text

client-server architecture /ˌklaɪənt ˌsɜːvə ˈɑːkɪtektʃə/ *noun* a distribution of processing power in which a central server computer carries out the main tasks in response to instructions from terminals or workstations, the results being sent back across the network to be displayed on the terminal that sent the instruction. The client, i.e. the terminal or workstation, does not need to be able to directly access the data stored on the server. nor does it need to carry out a lot of processing.

client-server network /ˌklaɪənt ˈsɜːvə ˌnetwɜːk/ *noun* a method of organising a network in which one central dedicated computer, the server, looks after tasks such as security, user accounts, printing and file sharing, while clients, the terminals or workstations connected to the server, run standard applications

client-side /ˈklaɪənt saɪd/ *adjective* referring to data or a program that runs on the client's computer rather than on the server, e.g. a JavaScript program runs on the user's web browser and is a client side application

clip /klɪp/ *verb* **1.** to select an area of an image that is smaller than the original **2.** to remove the peaks of a waveform ○ *The voltage signal was clipped to prevent excess signal level.*

clip-art /ˈklɪp ɑːt/ *noun* a set of pre-drawn images or drawings that a user can incorporate into a presentation or graphic ○ *We have* *used some clip-art to enhance our presentation.*

clipboard /ˈklɪpˌbɔːd/ *noun* a temporary storage area for data ○ *Copy the text to the clipboard, then paste it back into a new document.*

Clipper chip /ˈklɪpə tʃɪp/ *noun* an electronic component, e.g. an integrated circuit, or chip, that was designed in accordance with the instructions of the US Government to provide a data encryption feature for computers, Internet traffic, telephones, and television programmes. In the original scheme the US Government held the master key to the chip and so could decrypt and read any encrypted messages. This angered many groups concerned with freedom of speech and the US Government has since redesigned the original scheme and suggested an alternative.

clipping /ˈklɪpɪŋ/ *noun* the process of cutting off the outer edges of an image or the highest and lowest parts of a signal

clock /klɒk/ *noun* **1.** a machine which shows the time ○ *The micro has a built-in clock.* **2.** a circuit that generates pulses used to synchronise equipment

clock rate /ˈklɒk reɪt/ *noun* the number of pulses that a clock generates every second

clock speed /ˈklɒk spiːd/ *noun* same as **clock rate**

clogging /ˈklɒɡɪŋ/ *noun* the build up of oxide and binder on a playback head or tape recording which results in drop-outs (*film*)

clone /kləʊn/ *noun* a computer or circuit that behaves in the same way as the original it was copied from ○ *They have copied our new personal computer and brought out a cheaper clone.*

'On the desktop, the IBM/Motorola/Apple triumvirate is planning to energise a worldwide clone industry based on the PowerPC chip.' [*Computing*]

close /kləʊz/ *verb* to shut down access to a file or disk drive

CLOSE /kləʊz/ *noun* (*in a programming language*) a command that means the program has finished accessing a particular file or device

closed captioning /ˌkləʊzd ˈkæpʃənɪŋ/ *noun* a system that transfers text information with a video signal, so that the text data can be decoded and displayed at the bottom of the television screen

closed user group /ˌkləʊzd ˌjuːzə ˈɡruːp/ *noun* full form of **CUG**

close file /ˈkləʊs faɪl/ *noun* to execute a computer instruction to shut down access to a stored file

close menu option /ˌkləʊz ˈmenjuː ˌɒpʃ(ə)n/ *noun* a menu option, normally under the File menu, that will shut the document that is currently open, but will not exit the application. If you have not saved the document, the application will warn you before it closes the document and give you the chance to save any changes.

close up /ˌkləʊz ˈʌp/ *verb* to move pieces of type or typeset words closer together ○ *If we close up the lines, we should save a page.*

close-up /ˈkləʊs ʌp/ *noun* a photograph taken very close to the subject

close-up lens /ˈkləʊs ʌp ˌlenz/ *noun* an extra lens that permits the ordinary lens to focus closer to the subject than normal

close-up shot /ˈkləʊs ʌp ˌʃɒt/ *noun* a camera shot very close to the subject

CLS /ˌsiː el ˈes/ *noun* (*in MS-DOS*) a system command to clear the screen, leaving the system prompt and cursor at the top, left-hand corner of the screen

cluster /ˈklʌstə/ *noun* **1.** one or more sectors on a hard disk that are used to store a file or part of a file **2.** a number of terminals, stations, devices or memory locations, grouped together in one place and controlled by a cluster controller

CLUT /ˌsiː el juː ˈtiː/ *noun* a table of numbers used in Windows and graphics programs to store the range of colours used in an image. Full form **colour look-up table**. ◊ **palette**

CLV /ˌsiː el ˈviː/ *noun* a disk technology in which the disk spins at different speeds according to the track that is being accessed. Full form **constant linear velocity**

CM /ˌsiː ˈem/ *noun* an area of memory whose locations can be directly and immediately addressed by the CPU. Full form **central memory**

C-MAC /ˌsiː em eɪ ˈsiː/ *noun* a new direct-broadcast TV standard using time division multiplexing for signals

CMI *abbr* computer-managed instruction

CMIP /ˌsiː em aɪ ˈpiː/ *noun* a protocol officially adopted by the ISO that is used to carry network management information across a network. Full form **common management information protocol**

CMIP over TCP /ˌsiː em aɪ ˌpiː əʊvə ˌtiː siː ˈpiː/, **CMIS over TCP** full form of **CMOT**

CMIS /ˌsiː em aɪ ˈes/ *noun* a powerful network management system. Full form **common management information specification**

CML *abbr* computer-managed learning

CMOS /ˌsiː em əʊ ˈpiː/ *noun* an integrated circuit design and construction method that uses a pair of complementary p- and n-type transistors. Full form **complementary metal oxide semiconductor**

'Similarly, customers who do not rush to acquire CMOS companion processors for their mainframes will be rewarded with lower prices when they finally do migrate.' [*Computergram*]

COMMENT: The CMOS package uses very low power but is relatively slow and sensitive to static electricity as compared to TTL integrated circuits. Its main use is in portable computers where battery power is being used.

CMOT /ˌsiː em əʊ 'tiː/ *noun* the use of CMIP and CMIS network management protocols to manage gateways in a TCP/IP network. Full form **CMIP over TCP, CMIS over TCP**

CMYK /ˌsiː em waɪ 'keɪ/ *noun* (*in graphics or DTP*) a method of describing a colour by its four component colours. Full form **cyan-magenta-yellow-black**

CNC /ˌsiː en 'siː/ *noun* automatic operation of a machine by computer. Full form **computer numeric control.** ◊ **numerical control**

coat /kəʊt/ *verb* to cover with a layer of liquid □ **coated papers** papers which have been covered with a layer of clay to make them shiny

coating /'kəʊtɪŋ/ *noun* a material covering something ○ *paper which has a coating of clay*

co-axial cable /kəʊks/, **coax** *noun* a cable made up of a central core, surrounded by an insulating layer then a second shielding conductor. Compare **twisted-pair cable** (NOTE: Co-axial cable is used for high frequency, low loss applications including thin Ethernet network cabling and Arcnet network cabling.)

COBOL /'kəʊbɒl/ *noun* a programming language mainly used in business applications. Full form **common ordinary business-oriented language**

cobweb site /'kɒbweb saɪt/ *noun* a website that has not been updated for a long time

code /kəʊd/ *noun* **1.** rules used to convert instructions or data from one form to another **2.** a sequence of computer instructions **3.** a system of signs or numbers or letters which mean something ■ *verb* **1.** to convert instructions or data into another form **2.** to write a program in a programming language

CODEC /'kəʊdek/ *noun* a device which encodes a signal being sent or decodes a signal received. Full form **coder/decoder**

codepage /'kəʊdpeɪdʒ/ *noun* the definition of the character that is produced by each key on the keyboard; in order to use your computer when typing in a different language you need to change the keyboard layout and the font that is used for the characters – both are defined by the codepage

coder /'kəʊdə/ *noun* a device which encodes a signal

coder/decoder /ˌkəʊdə diː'kəʊdə/ *noun* full form of **CODEC**

coding /'kəʊdɪŋ/ *noun* the act of putting a code on something

coercivity /ˌkəʊɜː'sɪvɪti/ *noun* a magnetic field required to remove any flux saturation effects from a material

coherent /kəʊ'hɪərənt/ *adjective* referring to waveforms which are all in phase

coherent bundle /kəʊˌhɪərənt 'bʌnd(ə)l/ *noun* a number of optical fibres, grouped together so that they are all the same length and produce coherent signals from either end

coil /kɔɪl/ *noun* a number of turns of wire ○ *An inductor is made from a coil of wire.*

coincidence circuit /kəʊˌɪnsɪd(ə)ns 'sɜːkɪt/, **coincidence element** /'elɪmənt/ *noun* same as **coincidence gate**

coincidence function /kəʊ'ɪnsɪd(ə)ns ˌfʌŋkʃən/ *noun* same as **AND function**

coincidence gate /kəʊ'ɪnsɪd(ə)ns geɪt/, **coincidence circuit** /kəʊˌɪnsɪd(ə)ns 'sɜːkɪt/, **coincidence element** /kəʊ ˌɪnsɪd(ə)ns 'elɪmənt/ *noun* a gate that produces a logical output depending on various input coincidences. An AND gate requires the coincidence in time of all logically true inputs. ◊ **AND**

coincidence operation /kəʊ 'ɪnsɪd(ə)ns ˌɒpəreɪʃ(ə)n/ *noun* same as **AND operation**

cold /kəʊld/ *adjective* **1.** not hot ○ *The machines work badly in cold weather.* **2.** without being prepared

cold boot /ˌkəʊld 'buːt/ *noun* the act of switching on a computer, or the act of restarting a computer by switching it off and then on again. Compare **warm boot**

coldboot /'kəʊldbuːt/ *verb* to switch on a computer, or to restart a computer by switching it off and then on again. Compare **warm-boot**

cold fault /'kəʊld fɔːlt/ *noun* a computer fault or error that occurs as soon as it is switched on

cold standby /kəʊld 'stændbaɪ/ *noun* a backup system that will allow the equipment to continue running but with the loss of any volatile data. Compare **hot standby, warm standby**

cold start /ˌkəʊld 'stɑːt/ *noun* the act of switching on a computer or to run a program from its original start point

collaboration /kəˌlæbə'reɪʃ(ə)n/ *noun* two or more people working together to produce or use a multimedia application

collate /kə'leɪt/ *verb* **1.** to compare and put items in order **2.** to put signatures in order for sewing and binding

collator /kə'leɪtə/ *noun* a machine which takes sheets or printed signatures and puts them in order for stapling or binding

collision /kə'lɪʒ(ə)n/ *noun* an event that occurs when two electrical signals meet and interfere with each other over a network, normally causing an error

co-location /ˌkəʊ ləʊ'keɪʃ(ə)n/ *noun* an arrangement whereby a computer used as an Internet server is located at a specialist site that is designed to support and maintain servers on behalf of their customers

COMMENT: If you want to set up a website, you might start by renting web space from your ISP or web hosting provider. If your website grows in popularity or requires complex or secure e-commerce facilities, you might find it effective to rent or purchase a server computer dedicated to serving your website – you could locate this server computer anywhere, for example in your office, but you would need to install a high-speed link to the Internet and maintain the computer and its software. A more cost-effective solution is co-location: moving the server to a specialist site, often provided by an ISP, who takes on the job of supporting the high-speed link and the computer.

colon /'kəʊlɒn/ *noun* a printing sign (:) which shows a break in a string of words

colophon /'kɒləfɒn/ *noun* a design or symbol or company name, used on a printed item to show who are the publisher and the printer

colorisation /ˌkʌləraɪ'zeɪʃ(ə)n/ *noun* an electronic process of adding colour to a videotape transfer of a black and white film to be transmitted on television (*film*)

colour /'kʌlə/ *noun* a sensation sensed by the eye, due to its response to various frequencies of light

'...as a minimum, a colour graphics adapter (CGA) is necessary, but for best quality of graphic presentation an enhanced graphics adapter (EGA) should be considered' [*Micro Decision*]

colour balance /'kʌlə ˌbæləns/ *noun* the adjustment of the red, green and blue primary colours to produce a pure white colour. When a colour monitor is configured, a colour sensor is placed on the screen and the red, green and blue electron gun settings are adjusted to produce a pure white colour.

colour depth /'kʌlə depθ/ *noun* the number of different colours that can be displayed by any single pixel in a display, which is determined by the number of colour bits in each pixel

colour display /ˌkʌlə dɪ'spleɪ/ *noun* a display device able to represent characters or graphics in colour

colour key /'kʌlə kiː/ *noun* an image manipulation technique used to superimpose one image on another. It is often used with two video sources to create special effects. One image is photographed against a coloured background, the matte, when then has another image superimposed on it to produce a combined picture. ◊ **chroma key**

colour look-up table /ˌkʌlə 'lʊk ʌp ˌteɪb(ə)l/ *noun* full form of **CLUT**

colour monitor /ˌkʌlə 'mɒnɪtə/ *noun* a screen that has a demodulator that shows information in colour ○ *The colour monitor is great for games.*

colour palette /ˌkʌlə 'pælət/ *noun* the selection of colours that are currently being used in an image

colour printer /ˌkʌlə 'prɪntə/ *noun* a printer that can produce hard copy in colour

colour saturation /ˌkʌlə ˌsætʃə 'reɪʃ(ə)n/ *noun* the purity of a colour signal

colour separation /ˌkʌlə ˌsepə'reɪʃ(ə)n/ *noun* the process of separating a colour image into its constituent colours in order to produce printing plates for colour printing. Full colour printing needs four-colour separation to produce four printing plates for the cyan, magenta, yellow and black inks that together create a colour image.

colour standard /'kʌlə ˌstændəd/ *noun* one of three international standards, NTSC, PAL and SECAM, used to describe how colour TV and video images are displayed and transmitted

colour temperature /'kʌlə ˌtemprɪtʃə/ *noun* the hue or shade of the colour white seen if pure carbon is heated to a particular temperature measured in Kelvin. The standard for many TV and video systems is a colour temperature of 6500K, known as Illuminant D65.

colour tool /'kʌlə tuːl/ *noun* a utility or icon in a graphics or DTP application that allows the user to create custom colours by specifying the CMYK or RGB values and then draw or fill an area with this colour

column /'kɒləm/ *noun* **1.** a series of characters, numbers or lines of text printed one under the other ○ *to add up a column of figures* **2.** a section of printed words in a newspaper or magazine

columnar /kə'lʌmnə/ *adjective* in columns

com /kɒm/ *suffix* a suffix that means that the Internet domain name is a company, usually one based in the USA ○ *www.amazon.com is* *the website address of the US version of the Amazon Internet bookshop.*

COM /ˌsiː əʊ 'em/ *noun* **1.** a standard defined by Microsoft to standardise the way an application can access an object. Full form **Component Object Model** (NOTE: This is a rival standard to CORBA.) **2.** the process of recording the output from a computer directly onto microfilm. Full form **computer output on microfilm**

COM1 /ˌkɒm 'wʌn/ *noun* a name used in PCs to represent the first serial port on the computer. There are normally two serial ports, COM1 and COM2, in a PC, although it can support four. Some PCs have a mouse plugged into the first serial port and the modem plugged into the second port. ◊ **AUX**

coma /'kəʊmə/ *noun* a lens aberration

COMAL /'kəʊbæl/ *noun* a structured programming language similar to BASIC. Full form **common algorithmic language**

comb filter /kəʊm 'fɪltə/ *noun* an electronic device used to separate the luma, Y, and chroma, C, signals from a composite video signal. ◊ **S-Video, Y/C**

combination /ˌkɒmbɪ'neɪʃ(ə)n/ *noun* several things which are joined together; series of numbers which open a lock

combinational /ˌkɒmbɪ'neɪʃ(ə)nəl/ *adjective* which combines a number of separate elements

combine /kəm'baɪn/ *verb* to join together

combi player /'kɒmbi ˌpleɪə/ *noun* a hardware drive that can read two or more different CD-ROM formats

combo box /'kɒmbəʊ bɒks/ *noun* a box that displays a number of different input and output objects

COM file /'kɒm faɪl/ *noun* (*in operating systems for the PC*) a file with the three-letter extension .com to its name that indicates that the file contains a machine code in binary format and so can be executed by the operating system.

comic-strip oriented /ˌkɒmɪk strɪp 'ɔːrientɪd/ *adjective* referring to a film image that is oriented at right angles to the outer edge of the film. Compare **cine-oriented**

Comité Consultatif International Téléphonique et Télégraphique *noun* full form of **CCITT**

comma /'kɒmə/ *noun* a symbol (,) that is often used to separate data or variables or arguments

command /kə'mɑːnd/ *noun* **1.** an electrical pulse or signal that will start or stop a process **2.** a word or phrase which is recognised by a computer system and starts or terminates an action ○ *interrupt command*

COMMAND.COM /kə'mɑːnd kɒm/ *noun* (*in MS-DOS*) a program file that contains the command interpreter for the operating system. This program is always resident in memory and recognises and translates system commands into actions. ○ *MS-DOS will not work because you deleted the COMMAND.COM file by mistake.*

command line interface /kəˌmɑːnd laɪn 'ɪntəfeɪs/ *noun* a user interface in which the user controls the operating system or program by typing in commands; e.g., DOS is a command line interface

command line operating system /kə ˌmɑːnd laɪn 'ɒpəreɪtɪŋ ˌsɪstəm/ *noun* a computer system software that is controlled by a user typing in commands, as in MS-DOS, rather than allowing a user to control the system through images

command prompt /kə'mɑːnd prɒmpt/ *noun* a symbol displayed by the operating system to indicate that a command is expected

comment /'kɒment/ *noun* a helpful note in a program to guide the user ○ *The lack of comments is annoying.*

commentary /'kɒmənt(ə)ri/ *noun* spoken information which describes a film

comment field /'kɒment fiːld/ *noun* a section of a command line in an assembly language program that is not executed, but provides notes and comments

commerce /'kɒmɜːs/ ◆ **e-commerce**

commercial /kə'mɜːʃ(ə)l/ *noun* an advertising film on TV

commercial Internet exchange /kə ˌmɜːʃ(ə)l 'ɪntənet ɪksˌtʃeɪndʒ/ *noun* a connection point for commercial Internet service providers

Commission International de l'Eclairage full form of **CIE**

Commodore Dynamic Total Vision /ˌkɒməˌdɔː daɪˌnæmɪk ˌtəʊt(ə)l 'vɪʒ(ə)n/ *noun* a CD-ROM standard developed by Commodore that combines audio, graphics and text; this standard is mainly intended as an interactive system for home use; the player connects to a television and can also play music CDs. Abbr **CDTV**

common /'kɒmən/ *adjective* **1.** which happens very often ○ *This is a common fault with this printer model.* **2.** belonging to several different people or programs or to everyone

common algorithmic language /ˌkɒmən ˌælgərɪðmɪk 'læŋgwɪdʒ/ *noun* full form of **COMAL**

common gateway interface /ˌkɒmən 'geɪtweɪ ˌɪntəfeɪs/ *noun* full form of **CGI**

common intermediate format /ˌkɒmən ˌɪntəmiːdiət 'fɔːmæt/ *noun* a standard for video images that displays an image 352 pixels wide and 288 pixels high. Abbr **CIF**

common management information protocol /ˌkɒmən ˌmænɪdʒmənt ˌɪnfəˈmeɪʃ(ə)n ˌprəʊtəkɒl/ *noun* full form of **CMIP**

common management information specification /ˌkɒmən ˌmænɪdʒmənt ˌɪnfəˈmeɪʃ(ə)n ˌspesɪfɪkeɪʃ(ə)n/ *noun* full form of **CMIS**

common ordinary business-oriented language /ˌkɒmən ˌɔːd(ə)n(ə)ri ˌbɪznɪs ˌɔːriəntɪd ˈlæŋgwɪdʒ/ *noun* full form of **COBOL**

common real-time applications language /ˌkɒmən ˌrɪəl taɪm ˌæplɪˈkeɪʃ(ə)nz ˌlæŋgwɪdʒ/ *noun* full form of **CORAL**

common user access /ˌkɒmən ˌjuːzə ˈækses/ *noun* full form of **CUA**

communicate /kəˈmjuːnɪˌkeɪt/ *verb* to pass information to someone ○ *He finds it impossible to communicate with his staff.*

communicating applications specification /kəˌmjuːnɪkeɪtɪŋ ˌæplɪkeɪʃ(ə)nz ˌspesɪfɪˈkeɪʃ(ə)n/ *noun* full form of **CAS**

communicating word processor /kə ˌmjuːnɪkeɪtɪŋ ˈwɜːd ˌprəʊsesə/ *noun* a word processor workstation which is able to transmit and receive data

communication /kəˌmjuːnɪˈkeɪʃ(ə)n/ *noun* the passing of information ○ *Communication with the head office has been made easier by the telex.*

communications channel /kəˌmjuːnɪ ˈkeɪʃ(ə)nz ˌtʃæn(ə)l/ *noun* a physical link over which data can be transmitted

communications control unit /kə ˌmjuːnɪkeɪʃ(ə)nz kənˈtrəʊl ˌjuːnɪt/ *noun* an electronic device that controls data transmission and routes in a network

communications link /kəˌmjuːnɪ ˈkeɪʃ(ə)nz lɪŋk/ *noun* the physical path that joins a transmitter to a receiver

communications network /kəˌmjuːnɪ ˈkeɪʃ(ə)nz ˌnetwɜːk/ *noun* a group of devices such as terminals and printers that are interconnected with a central computer, allowing the rapid and simple transfer of data

communications package /kəˌmjuːnɪ ˈkeɪʃ(ə)nz ˌpækɪdʒ/ *noun* a package of software that allows a user to control a modem and use an online service

communications protocol /kəˌmjuːnɪ ˈkeɪʃ(ə)nz ˌprəʊtəʊkɒl/ *noun* the parameters that define how the transfer of information will be controlled ○ *The communications protocol for most dial-up online services is eight-bit words, no stop bit and even parity.*

communications server /kəˌmjuːnɪ ˈkeɪʃ(ə)nz ˌsɜːvə/ *noun* a computer with a modem or fax card attached that allows users on a network to share the use of the modem

communications software /kəˌmjuːnɪ ˈkeɪʃ(ə)nz ˌsɒftweə/, **communications package** /kəˌmjuːnɪˈkeɪʃ(ə)nz ˌpækɪdʒ/ *noun* software that allows a user to control a modem and use an online service

community /kəˈmjuːnɪti/ *noun* a group of people living or working in the same place □ **the local business community** the business people living and working in the area

community antenna television /kə ˌmjuːnɪti ænˌtenə ˌtelɪˈvɪʒ(ə)n/ *noun* a cable television system using a single aerial to pick up television signals and then distribute them over a wide area via cable. Abbr **CATV**

compact /kəmˈpækt/ *adjective* (thing) which does not take up much space

compact disc /ˌkɒmpækt ˈdɪsk/ *noun* a small plastic disc that contains information such as audio signals or data in digital form that can be read by a laser beam. Abbr **CD-I**

compact disc-digital audio /ˌkɒmpækt ˌdɪsk ˌdɪdʒɪt(ə)l ˈɔːdiəʊ/ *noun* a standard that defines how music can be stored in digital form, i.e. as a series of numbers, on a compact disc. Abbr **CD-DA**. Also called **CD-audio**

compact disc erasable /ˌkɒmpækt ˌdɪsk ɪˈreɪzəb(ə)l/ *noun* a format that allows data to be saved to and erased from a compact disc. Abbr **CD-E**

compact disc player /ˌkɒmpækt ˈdɪsk ˌpleɪə/ *noun* a machine that reads the digital data from a CD and converts it back to its original form

compact disc ROM /ˌkɒmpækt ˌdɪsk ˈrɒm/ *noun* same as **CD-ROM** ○ *The compact disc ROM can store as much data as a dozen hard disks.*

compact disc write once /ˌkɒmpækt dɪsk ˌraɪt ˈwʌns/ *noun* CD-ROM disc and drive technology that allows a user to write data to the disc once only. Full form **CD-WO**

companding /kɒmˈpændɪŋ/ *noun* two processes which reduce or compact data before transmission or storage then restore packed data to its original form. Full form **compressing and expanding**

compandor /kɒmˈpændə/ *noun* a device used for companding signals. Full form **compressor/expander**

COMPAQ /ˈkɒmpæk/ a US personal computer company, founded in 1983, that was the first manufacturer to produce a clone to the IBM PC

comparability /ˌkɒmp(ə)rəˈbɪlɪti/ *noun* being able to be compared (NOTE: no plural)

□ **pay comparability** similar pay system in two different companies

comparable /ˈkɒmp(ə)rəb(ə)l/ *adjective* which can be compared ○ *The two sets of figures are not comparable.*

comparator /kəmˈpærətə/ *noun* a logical device whose output is true if there is a difference between two inputs

compare /kəmˈpeə/ *verb* to check the differences between two pieces of information

compare with /kəmˈpeə wɪð/ *verb* to put two things together to see how they differ

comparison /kəmˈpærɪs(ə)n/ *noun* a way of comparing

compatibility /kəmˌpætɪˈbɪlɪti/ *noun* the ability of two hardware or software devices to function together (NOTE: Compatibility of hardware and software, which means that those of one manufacturer or organisation conform to the standards of another, allows programs and hardware to be interchanged without modification.)

> 'The manufacturer claims that this card does not require special drivers on the host machine... and therefore has fewer compatibility problems.' [*Computing*]

compatible /kəmˈpætɪb(ə)l/ *adjective* used to describe two hardware or software devices that function correctly together ■ *noun* a hardware or software device that functions correctly with other equipment ○ *Buy an IBM PC* or *a compatible.*

> '...this was the only piece of software I found that wouldn't work, but it does show that there is no such thing as a totally compatible PC clone' [*Personal Computer World*]

compilation /ˌkɒmpɪˈleɪʃ(ə)n/ *noun* the translation of an encoded source program into machine readable code

> 'This utility divides the compilation of software into pieces and performs the compile in parallel across available machines on the network.' [*Computergram*]

compile /kəmˈpaɪl/ *verb* to convert a high-level language program into a machine code program that can be executed by itself ○ *compiling takes a long time with this old version*

compiler /kəmˌpaɪlə ˈprəʊgræm/, **compiler program** *noun* a piece of software that converts an encoded program into a machine code program ○ *The new compiler has an in-built editor.* Compare **interpreter**

complement /ˈkɒmplɪment/ *noun* an inversion of a binary digit ○ *The complement is found by changing the 1s to 0s and 0s to 1s.* ■ *verb* to invert a binary digit

complementary /ˌkɒmplɪˈment(ə)ri/ *adjective* (two things) that complete each other or go well together

complementary colours /ˌkɒplɪment(ə)ri ˈkʌləz/ *plural noun* colours resulting from subtracting a specific colour from white light, therefore the complementary colour to red is 'minus red', which is cyan (blue-green)

complementary metal oxide semiconductor /ˌkɒmplɪment(ə)ri ˌmet(ə)l ˌɒksaɪd ˈsemikənˌdʌktə/ *noun* full form of **CMOS**

complementation /ˌkɒmplɪmənˈteɪʃ(ə)n/ *noun* a number system used to represent positive and negative numbers

complete /kəmˈpliːt/ *verb* to finish a task ○ *When you have completed the keyboarding, pass the text through the spelling checker.*

completion /kəmˈpliːʃ(ə)n/ *noun* the point at which something is complete ○ *Completion date for the new software package is November 15th.*

complex /ˈkɒmpleks/ *adjective* very complicated or difficult to understand ○ *The complex mathematical formula was difficult to solve.*

complex instruction set computer /ˌkɒmpleks ɪnˌstrʌkʃən ˌset kəmˈpjuːtə/ *noun* full form of **CISC**

complexity /kəmˈpleksɪti/ *noun* being complicated

compliant /kəmˈplaɪənt/ *adjective* that conforms to a particular set of standards ○ *If you want to read PhotoCD compact discs in your computer you must be sure that the CD-ROM drive is PhotoCD* or *CD-ROM XA compliant.*

complicated /ˈkɒmplɪkeɪtɪd/ *adjective* with many different parts or difficult to understand ○ *This program is very complicated.*

component /kəmˈpəʊnənt/ *noun* **1.** a piece of machinery or section which will be put into a final product **2.** an electronic device that produces an electrical signal

Component Object Model /kəmˌpəʊnənt ˈɒbdʒekt ˌmɒd(ə)l/ *noun* full form of **COM**

component video /kəmˈpəʊnənt ˌvɪdiəʊ/ *noun* a method of transmitting video information, used in professional video systems, that has separate signals for the luminance and two chrominance channels to avoid interference

COM port /ˈkɒm pɔːt/ *noun* same as **COM1**

compose /kəmˈpəʊz/ *verb* to arrange the required type, in the correct order, prior to printing □ **composing room** room in a typesetters *or* in a newspaper, where the text is composed by compositors

composite circuit /ˌkɒmpəzɪt 'sɜːkɪt/ *noun* an electronic circuit made up of a number of smaller circuits and components

composite display /ˌkɒmpəzɪt dɪ'spleɪ/ *noun* a video display unit that accepts a single composite video signal and can display an infinite number of colours or shades of grey

composite monitor /ˌkɒmpəzɪt 'mɒnɪtə/ *noun* a colour monitor that receives one video signal from a graphics display adapter, which must then be electronically separated inside the monitor into the red, green and blue colour signals

composite print /'kɒmpəzɪt prɪnt/ *noun* a copy of a film (called the print) that includes both audio and visual effects (*film*)

composite video /ˌkɒmpəzɪt 'vɪdiəʊ/ *noun* a video signal that combines the colour signals and the monochrome signal into one single signal ○ *Most TV set and video players expect a composite video feed.*

composite video signal /ˌkɒmpəzɪt 'vɪdiəʊ ˌsɪgn(ə)l/ *noun* a single television signal containing synchronising pulse and video signal in a modulated form

composition /ˌkɒmpə'zɪʃ(ə)n/ *noun* the process of creating typeset text, either using metal type or by keyboarding on a computer typesetter □ **composition size** printing type size

compositor /kəm'pɒzɪtə/ *noun* a person who sets up the required type prior to printing

compound device /ˌkɒmpaʊnd dɪ'vaɪs/ *noun* a Windows MCI multimedia device that requires a data file

compound document /'kɒmpaʊnd ˌdɒkjʊmənt/ *noun* a document that contains information created by several other applications

compound file /'kɒmpaʊnd faɪl/ *noun* a number of individual files grouped together in one file

compound statement /ˌkɒmpaʊnd 'steɪtmənt/ *noun* a number of program instructions in one line of program ○ *The debugger cannot handle compound statements.*

compress /kəm'pres/ *verb* to squeeze something to fit into a smaller space ○ *Use the archiving program to compress the file.*

compressed video /ˌkɒmprest 'vɪdiəʊ/ *noun* video signals that have been compressed to reduce the data rate required to transmit the information. Whereas a normal television picture is transmitted at around 5090Mbits/second, a compressed video signal can be transmitted at around one tenth of the data rate.

compression /kəm'preʃ(ə)n/ *noun* the process of reducing the size of a file by encoding the data in a more efficient form. For example, if the file contains five letter 'A's in line, which take up five bytes of space, the compression software could encode this to 5A which takes two byes of space.

compression ratio /kəm'preʃ(ə)n ˌreɪʃiəʊ/ *noun* a ratio of the size of an original, uncompressed file to the final, compressed file that has been more efficiently encoded

compressor /kəm'presə/ *noun* **1.** a program or device that provides data compression **2.** an electronic circuit which compresses a signal

comptometer /kɒmp'tɒmɪtə/ *noun* a machine which counts automatically

CompuServe /'kɒmpjuːsɜːv/ an online service provider and information service

computable /kəm'pjuːtəb(ə)l/ *adjective* which can be calculated

computation /ˌkɒmpjʊ'teɪʃ(ə)n/ *noun* a calculation

computational /ˌkɒmpjʊ'teɪʃ(ə)nəl/ *adjective* referring to computation

compute /kəm'pjuːt/ *verb* to calculate or to do calculations (especially when using a computer) ○ *Connect charges were computed on an hourly rate.*

computer /kəm'pjuːtə/ *noun* a machine that receives or stores or processes data very quickly using a program kept in its memory

computer- /kəmpjuːtə/ *prefix* referring to a computer

computer-aided /kəmˌpjuːtə 'eɪdɪd/ *adjective* that uses a computer to make the work easier. Also called **computer-assisted**

computer-aided design /kəmˌpjuːtər ˌeɪdɪd dɪ'zaɪn/ *noun* full form of **CAD**

computer-aided engineering /kəm ˌpjuːtər ˌeɪdɪd ˌendʒɪ'nɪərɪŋ/ *noun* use of a computer to help an engineer solve problems or calculate design or product specifications. Full form of **CAE**

computer-aided instruction /kəm ˌpjuːtər ˌeɪdɪd ɪn'strʌkʃən/ *noun* full form of **CAI**

computer-aided learning /kəm ˌpjuːtər ˌeɪdɪd 'lɜːnɪŋ/ *noun* full form of **CAL**

computer-aided manufacture /kəm ˌpjuːtər ˌeɪdɪd ˌmænjʊ'fæktʃə/ *noun* full form of **CAM**

computer-aided testing /kəmˌpjuːtər ˌeɪdɪd 'testɪŋ/ *noun* full form of **CAT**

computer-aided training /kəmˌpjuːtər ˌeɪdɪd 'treɪnɪŋ/ *noun* full form of **CAT**

computer animation /kəmˌpjuːtə ˌænɪ'meɪʃ(ə)n/ *noun* same as **animation**

computer applications /kəmˌpjuːtə ˌæplɪˈkeɪʃ(ə)nz/ *plural noun* the tasks and uses that a computer can carry out in a particular field or job

computer-assisted /kəmˌpjuːtər əˈsɪstɪd/ *adjective* same as **computer-aided**

computer-assisted design /kəmˌpjuːtər əˌsɪstɪd dɪˈzaɪn/ *noun* full form of **CAD**

computer-assisted engineering /kəmˌpjuːtər əˌsɪstɪd ˌendʒɪˈnɪərɪŋ/ *noun* full form of **CAE**

computer-assisted instruction /kəmˌpjuːtər əˌsɪstɪd ɪnˈstrʌkʃən/ *noun* full form of **CAI**

computer-assisted learning /kəmˌpjuːtər əˌsɪstɪd ˈlɜːnɪŋ/ *noun* full form of **CAL**

computer-assisted manufacture /kəmˌpjuːtər əˌsɪstɪd ˌmænjʊˈfæktʃə/ *noun* full form of **CAM**

computer-assisted testing /kəmˌpjuːtər əˌsɪstɪd ˈtestɪŋ/ *noun* full form of **CAT**

computer-assisted training /kəmˌpjuːtər əˌsɪstɪd ˈtreɪnɪŋ/ *noun* full form of **CAT**

computer-based instruction /kəmˌpjuːtə beɪst ɪnˈstrʌkʃ(ə)n/ *noun* full form of **CBI**

computer-based learning /kəmˌpjuːtə beɪst ɪnˈstrʌkʃ(ə)n/ *noun* full form of **CBL**

computer-based message system /kəmˌpjuːtə beɪst ˈmesɪdʒ ˌsɪstəm/ *noun* full form of **CBMS**

computer-based training /kəmˌpjuːtə beɪst ˈtreɪnɪŋ/ *noun* full form of **CBT**

computer code /kəmˈpjuːtə kəʊd/ *noun* a programming language that consists of commands in binary code that can be directly understood by the central processing unit, without the need for translation

computer conferencing /kəmˌpjuːtə ˈkɒnf(ə)rənsɪŋ/ *noun* the use of a number of computers or terminals connected together to allow a group of users to communicate

computer crime /kəmˈpjuːtə kraɪm/ *noun* theft, fraud or other crimes involving computers

computer dating /kəmˌpjuːtə ˈdeɪtɪŋ/ *noun* the use of a computer to match single people who may want to get married

computer department /kəmˈpjuːtə dɪˌpɑːtmənt/ *noun* a department in a company that manages the company's computers

computer file /kəmˈpjuːtə faɪl/ *noun* a section of information on a computer, e.g. the payroll, list of addresses or customer accounts

computer fraud /kəmˈpjuːtə frɔːd/ *noun* the theft of data, dishonest use of data or other crimes involving computers

computer generation /kəmˌpjuːtə ˌdʒenəˈreɪʃ(ə)n/ *noun* any one in a series of classifications used to define the advances in the field of computing

COMMENT: The development of computers has been divided into a series of 'generations'. The first generation consisted of computers constructed using valves and having limited storage. The second generation of computers were constricted using transistors. The third generation used integrated circuits. The fourth generation, which includes the computers most often used at present, uses low-cost memory and IC packages. The fifth generation comprises future computers using very fast processors, large memory, and allowing human input/output.

computer graphics /kəmˌpjuːtə ˈgræfɪks/ *plural noun* information represented graphically on a computer display

computer graphics metafile /kəmˌpjuːtə ˌgræfɪks ˈmetəfaɪl/ *noun* full form of **CGM**

computer illiterate /kəmˌpjuːtə ɪ ˈlɪtərət/ *adjective* unable to understand computer-related expressions or operations

computer image processing /kəmˌpjuːtə ˈɪmɪdʒ ˌprəʊsesɪŋ/ *noun* the analysis of information in an image, usually by electronic means or using a computer, also used for recognition of objects in an image

computer input microfilm /kəmˌpjuːtə ˌɪnpʊt ˈmaɪkrəʊfɪlm/ *noun* full form of **CIM**

computer-integrated manufacturing /kəmˌpjuːtə ˌɪntɪgreɪtɪd ˌmænjʊˈfæktʃərɪŋ/ *noun* full form of **CIM**

computerisation /kəmˌpjuːtəraɪˈzeɪʃ(ə)n/, **computerization** *noun* the process of introducing a computer system or of changing from a manual to a computer system ○ *Computerisation of the financial sector is proceeding very fast.*

computerise /kəmˈpjuːtəraɪz/, **computerize** *verb* to change from a manual system to one using computers ○ *Our stock control has been completely computerised.*

computer literacy /kəmˌpjuːtə ˈlɪt(ə)rəsi/ *noun* understanding of the basic principles of computers, related expressions and concepts, and the ability to use computers for programming or applications

computer-literate /kəmˌpjuːtə ˈlɪt(ə)rət/ *adjective* able to understand expressions relating to computers and how to use a computer

computer-managed instruction /kəm ˌpjuːtə ˌmænɪdʒd ɪn'strʌkʃən/ *noun* the use of a computer to assist students in learning a subject. Abbr **CMI**

computer-managed learning /kəm ˌpjuːtə ˌmænɪdʒd 'lɜːnɪŋ/ *noun* the use of a computer to teach students and assess their progress. Abbr **CML**

computer network /kəmˌpjuːtə 'netwɜːk/ *noun* the shared use of a series of interconnected computers, peripherals and terminals

computer numerical control /kəm ˌpjuːtə njuːˌmerɪk(ə)l kən'trəʊl/ *noun* same as **numerical control**. full form of **CNC**

computer operator /kəm'pjuːtər ˌɒpəreɪtə/ *noun* a person who operates a computer

computer output on microfilm /kəm ˌpjuːtər ˌaʊtpʊt ɒn 'maɪkrəʊfɪlm/ *noun* full form of **COM**

computer program /kəm'pjuːtə ˌprəʊgræm/ *noun* a series of instructions to a computer, telling it to do a particular piece of work ○ *The user cannot write a computer program with this system.*

computer programmer /kəmˌpjuːtə 'prəʊgræmə/ *noun* a person who writes computer programs

computer-readable /kəmˌpjuːtə 'riːdəb(ə)l/ *adjective* which can be read and understood by a computer ○ *computer-readable codes*

computer science /kəmˌpjuːtə 'saɪəns/ *noun* the scientific study of computers, the organisation of hardware and the development of software

computer setting /kə'mpjuːtə ˌsetɪŋ/ *noun* the process of typesetting using a computerised typesetting machine

computer virus /kəm'pjuːtə ˌvaɪrəs/ *noun* a program which adds itself to an executable file and copies or spreads itself to other executable files each time an infected file is run. A virus can corrupt data, display a message or do nothing.

computing /kəm'pjuːtɪŋ/ *adjective, noun* referring to computers

computing power /kəm'pjuːtɪŋ ˌpaʊə/ *noun* a measure of the speed of a computer and its ability to perform calculations

computing speed /kəm'pjuːtɪŋ spiːd/ *noun* the speed at which a computer calculates

CON /kɒn/ *noun* (*in IBM-PC compatible systems*) a name used to identify the console, i.e. the keyboard and monitor

concatenate /kən'kætəneɪt/ *verb* to join together two or more sets of data

concatenation /kənˌkætə'neɪʃ(ə)n/ *noun* the joining together of two or more sets of data

concatenation operator /kənˌkætə 'neɪʃ(ə)n ˌɒpəreɪtə/ *noun* an instruction that joins two pieces of data or variables together

concave lens /ˌkɒnkeɪv 'lenz/ *noun* a lens that is thinner in the centre than at the edges, bending light out

conceal /kən'siːl/ *verb* to hide information or graphics from a user, or not to display them ○ *The hidden lines are concealed from view with this algorithm.*

concentrate /'kɒnsəntreɪt/ *verb* **1.** to combine a number of lines or circuits or data to take up less space ○ *The concentrated data was transmitted cheaply.* **2.** to focus a beam onto a narrow point

concentrator /'kɒnsəntreɪtə/ *noun* **1.** (*in a Token-Ring network*) a device at the centre of a Token-Ring network, which provides a logical star topology in which nodes are connected to the concentrator, but which connects each arm of the star as a physical ring within the device **2.** (*in an FDDI network*) a node which provides access for one or more stations to the network **3.** (*in an 10Base-T Ethernet network*) the device at the centre of a star-topology 10Base-T Ethernet network that receives signals from one port and regenerates them before sending them out to the other ports **4.** (*in general networking*) a device in which all the cables from nodes are interconnected

conceptual model /kənˌseptʃuəl 'mɒd(ə)l/ *noun* a description of a database or program in terms of the data it contains and its relationships

concertina fold /ˌkɒnsə'tiːnə fəʊld/ *noun* a method of folding continuous paper, one sheet in one direction, the next sheet in the opposite direction, allowing the paper to be fed into a printer continuously with no action on the part of the user. Same as **accordion fold**

concurrency /kən'kʌrənsi/ *noun* data or a resource that is accessed by more than one user or application at a time

concurrent /kən'kʌrənt/ *adjective* almost simultaneous (actions or sets) ○ *Each concurrent process has its own window.*

> 'The system uses parallel-processing technology to allow support for large numbers of concurrent users.' [*Computing*]

concurrently /kən'kʌrəntli/ *adverb* running at almost the same time. ◊ **SISD, SIMD**

condenser lens /kən'densə lenz/ *noun* an optical device, usually made of glass, that concentrates a beam of light onto a certain area

condition /kən'dɪʃ(ə)n/ *verb* to modify data that is to be transmitted so as to meet set parameters ○ *Condition the raw data to a standard format.*

conditional /kən'dɪʃ(ə)n(ə)l/ *adjective* **1.** provided that certain things take place **2.** referring to a process that is dependent on the result of another

conditional jump /kən'dɪʃ(ə)nəl dʒʌmp/ *noun* a programming instruction that provides a jump to a section of a program if a certain condition is met ○ *The conditional branch will select routine one if the response is yes and routine two if no.*

conduct /kən'dʌkt/ *verb* to allow an electrical current to flow through a material ○ *to conduct electricity*

conduction /kən'dʌkʃən/ *noun* the ability of a material to conduct ○ *The conduction of electricity by gold contacts.*

conductive /kən'dʌktɪv/ *adjective* referring to the ability of a material to conduct

conductor /kən'dʌktə/ *noun* a substance such as a metal that conducts electricity ○ *Copper is a good conductor of electricity.* ◊ **semiconductor**

conduit /'kɒndjuɪt/ *noun* a protective pipe or channel for wires or cables ○ *The cables from each terminal are channelled to the computer centre by metal conduit.*

cone /kəʊn/ *noun* the moving section in most loudspeakers

conference /'kɒnf(ə)rəns/ *noun* a meeting of people to discuss problems

conferencing /'kɒnf(ə)rənsɪŋ/ *noun* discussion between remote users using computers linked by a modem or a network

> 'Small organisations and individuals find it convenient to use online services, offering email, conferencing and information services.' [*Computing*]

confidence /'kɒnfɪd(ə)ns/ *noun* feeling sure or being certain ○ *The sales teams do not have much confidence in their manager.* ○ *The board has total confidence in the new system.*

confidence level /'kɒnfɪd(ə)ns ˌlev(ə)l/ *noun* the likelihood that a particular number will lie within a range of values

confident /'kɒnfɪd(ə)nt/ *adjective* certain or sure ○ *I am confident the sales will increase rapidly.* ○ *Are you confident the sales team is capable of handling this product?*

confidential /ˌkɒnfɪ'denʃəl/ *adjective* secret ○ *a confidential report on the new product*

CONFIG.SYS /kən'fɪg sɪs/ *noun* (*in MS-DOS*) a configuration text file that contains commands to set parameters and load driver software. This file is read automatically once the PC is switched on and the operating system has loaded. ○ *If you add a new adapter card to your PC, you will have to add a new command to the CONFIG.SYS file.*

configuration /kənˌfɪgjə'reɪʃ(ə)n/ *noun* the way in which the hardware and software of a computer system are planned and set up

> 'He said only Banyan Vines had the network configuration and administration capabilities required for implementing an international business plan based on client-server computing.' [*Computing*]

configure /kən'fɪgə/ *verb* to select hardware, software and interconnections to make up a special system ○ *This terminal has been configured to display graphics.*

configured-in /kənˌfɪgəd 'ɪn/ *adjective* referring to a device whose configuration state indicates that it is ready and available for use

confirm /kən'fɜːm/ *verb* action to indicate that you agree with a particular action ○ *Click on the OK button to confirm that you want to delete all your files.*

conform /kən'fɔːm/ *verb* to work according to set rules ○ *The software will not run if it does not conform to the operating system standards.*

congestion /kən'dʒestʃən/ *noun* a state that occurs when communication or processing demands are greater than the capacity of a system

connect /kə'nekt/ *verb* to link together two points in a circuit or communications network

connection /kə'nekʃən/ *noun* a link or something which joins

connectivity /ˌkɒnek'tɪvɪti/ *noun* the ability of a device to connect with other devices and transfer information

connector /kə'nektə/ *noun* a physical device with a number of metal contacts that allow devices to be easily linked together ○ *The connector at the end of the cable will fit any standard serial port.*

consecutive /kən'sekjʊtɪv/ *adjective* following one after another ○ *The computer ran three consecutive files.*

consecutively /kə'sekjʊtɪvli/ *adverb* one after the other ○ *The sections of the program run consecutively.*

Conseil Européen pour la Recherche Nucléaire *noun* full form of **CERN**

consistency check /kən'sɪstənsi tʃek/ *noun* a check to make sure that objects, data or items conform to their expected formats

console /'kɒnsəʊl/ *noun* a unit consisting of a keyboard, VDU, and usually a printer, which allows an operator to communicate with a computer system ○ *The console consists of input device such as a keyboard, and an output device such as a printer* or *CRT.* ◊ **CON**

constant /'kɒnstənt/ *noun* an item of data whose value does not change. Opposite **variable** ■ *adjective* which does not change ○ *The disk drive motor spins at a constant velocity.*

constant linear velocity /ˌkɒnstənt ˌlɪniə və'lɒsɪti/ *noun* full form of **CLV**

constrain /kən'streɪn/ *verb* to set limits that define the maximum movement of an object on screen

construct /kən'strʌkt/ *verb* to build or to make (a device or a system)

construction /kən'strʌkʃən/ *noun* the building or making of a system ○ *Construction of the prototype is advancing rapidly.*

consult /kən'sʌlt/ *verb* to ask an expert for advice ○ *He consulted the maintenance manager about the disk fault.*

consultancy /kən'sʌltənsi/ *noun* the act of giving specialist advice ○ *a consultancy firm* ○ *He offers a consultancy service.*

consultant /kən'sʌltənt/ *noun* a specialist who gives advice ○ *They called in a computer consultant to advise them on the system design.*

consumables /kən'sjuːməb(ə)lz/ *plural noun* small cheap extra items required in the day-to-day running of a computer system, e.g. paper and printer ribbons ○ *Put all the printer leads and paper with the other consumables.*

consumer market /kən'sjuːmə ˌmɑːkɪt/ *noun* the potential market for a product that is based on the general public buying advertised products from a shop rather than a specialist or academic market

consumption /kən'sʌmpʃən/ *noun* the act of buying or using goods or services (NOTE: no plural)

contact /'kɒntækt/ *noun* the section of a switch or connector that provides an electrical path when it touches another conductor ○ *The circuit is not working because the contact is dirty.* ■ *verb* to try to call a user or device in a network

contact image sensor /ˌkɒntækt 'ɪmɪdʒ ˌsensə/ *noun* full form of **CIS**

contain /kən'teɪn/ *verb* to hold something inside ○ *Each carton contains two computers and their peripherals.*

container /kən'teɪnə/ *noun* **1.** a box or bottle or can, etc. which can hold goods ○ *The ink is sold in strong metal containers.* ○ *The container burst while it was being loaded.* **2.** a very large metal case of a standard size for loading and carrying goods on trucks, trains and ships ○ *container ship* ○ *container port* ○ *container terminal* ○ *to ship goods in containers* **3.** something that can be set to a value; e.g., a variable is a container, as is an object's colour or position or other properties

containerisation /kənˌteɪnəraɪ'zeɪʃ(ə)n/, **containerization** *noun* the process of putting into containers, or carrying goods in containers

containerize /kən'teɪnəraɪz/ *verb* to put goods into containers; to ship goods in containers

content /'kɒntent/ *noun* information, ideas, text, images or data that form a letter, document, web page, database or book

content-addressable addressing /ˌkɒntent əˌdresəb(ə)l ə'dresɪŋ/ *noun* same as **associative addressing**

contention /kən'tenʃən/ *noun* a situation that occurs when two or more devices are trying to communicate with the same piece of equipment

content provider /'kɒntent prəˌvaɪdə/ *noun* a company that supplies information, e.g. text, news stories, images, video, software, for a publication in a website or other medium

contents /'kɒntents/ *plural noun* things contained or what is inside something ○ *The contents of the bottle poured out onto the computer keyboard.*

context /'kɒntekst/ *noun* words and phrases among which a word is used ○ *The example shows how the word is used in context.*

context-sensitive /ˌkɒntekst 'sensɪtɪv/ *adjective* that relates to the particular context

context-sensitive help /ˌkɒntekst ˌsensɪtɪv 'help/ *noun* a help message that gives useful information about the particular function or part of the program you are in rather than general information about the whole program

context-switching /'kɒntekst ˌswɪtʃɪŋ/ *noun* a process in which several programs are loaded in memory, but only one at a time can be executed

COMMENT: Unlike a true multitasking system which can load several programs into memory and run several programs at once, context-switching only allows one program to be run at a time.

contiguous /kən'tɪgjʊəs/ *adjective* which touches

'If you later edit the file again, some of the new data clusters will not be contiguous with the original clusters but spread around the disk.' [*Computing*]

contiguous graphics /kən,tɪgjʊəs 'græfɪks/ *plural noun* graphic cells or characters which touch each other ○ *Most display units do not provide contiguous graphics: their characters have a small space on each side to improve legibility.*

contingency plan /kən'tɪndʒənsi plæn/ *noun* a secondary plan that will be used if the first fails to work

continual /kən'tɪnjuəl/ *adjective* which happens again and again ○ *The continual system breakdowns have slowed down the processing.*

continually /kən'tɪnjuəli/ *adverb* again and again

continuation /kən,tɪnju'eɪʃ(ə)n/ *noun* the act of continuing

continue /kən'tɪnjuː/ *verb* to go on doing something or to do something which you were doing earlier

continuity /,kɒntɪ'njuːɪti/ *noun* **1.** a clear conduction path between two points **2.** the process of checking that the details of one scene in a film continue into the next scene to be shown, even if the two have been shot at different times

continuous /kən'tɪnjʊəs/ *adjective* with no end or with no breaks; which goes on without stopping

continuously /kən'tɪnjʊəsli/ *adverb* without stopping ○ *The printer overheated after working continuously for five hours.*

continuous tone /kən'tɪnjʊəs təʊn/ *noun* an image such as a photograph that uses all possible values of grey or colours,

contouring /'kɒntʊərɪŋ/ *noun* **1.** (*in a graphics application*) a process that converts a wire-frame drawing into a solid-looking object by adding shadows and texture **2.** (*in a graphics application*) a function that creates realistic-looking ground, e.g. in a virtual-reality system, or a surface

contrast *noun* /'kɒntrɑːst/ **1.** the difference between black and white or between colours ○ *The control allows you to adjust brightness and contrast.* **2.** a control knob on a display that alters the difference between black and white tones or between colours ■ *verb* /kən'trɑːst/ to examine the differences between two sets of information ○ *The old data was contrasted with the latest information.*

contrasting /kən'trɑːstɪŋ/ *adjective* which show a sharp difference ○ *a cover design in contrasting colours*

contrast setting /'kɒntrɑːst ,setɪŋ/ *noun* TV contrast control position

control /kən'trəʊl/ *verb* to be in charge of something or to make sure that something is kept in check ■ *noun* **1.** the process of restricting or checking something or making sure that something is kept in check **2.** conditional program statements **3.** a key on a computer keyboard which sends a control character **4.** power or being able to direct something ○ *The company is under the control of three directors.* ○ *The family lost control of its business.*

controllable /kən'trəʊləb(ə)l/ *adjective* which can be controlled

controller /kən'trəʊlə/ *noun* a hardware or software device that controls a peripheral such as a printer, or that monitors and directs the data transmission over a local area network

'...a printer's controller is the brains of the machine. It translates the signals coming from your computer into printing instructions that result in a hard copy of your electronic document' [*Publish*]

control panel /kən'trəʊl ,pæn(ə)l/ *noun* **1.** a panel with indicators and switches that allows an operator to monitor and control the actions of a computer or peripheral **2.** a utility that displays the user-definable options such as keyboard, country-code and type of mouse

control unit /kən'trəʊl ,juːnɪt/ *noun* the section of the CPU which selects and executes instructions

conventional memory /kən ,venʃ(ə)n(ə)l 'mem(ə)ri/ *noun* (*in an IBM-PC compatible system*) the random access memory region installed in a PC from 0 up to 640Kb. This area of memory can be directly controlled by MS-DOS. Compare **high memory, expanded memory**

convergence /kən'vɜːdʒəns/ *noun* **1.** the combination of two or more different technologies producing a new technology. For example, fax machines are the product of the convergence of telephone, scanning and printing technologies. **2.** (*in a colour monitor*) the accuracy with which the picture beam strikes the three colour dots that form each colour pixel ▶ ◊ **picture beam, pixel**

conversational mode /,kɒnvə 'seɪʃ(ə)n(ə)l məʊd/ *noun* a method of operating that provides immediate responses to a user's input. ◊ **interactive mode**. Compare **batch mode**

conversion /kən'vɜːʃ(ə)n/ *noun* a change from one system to another

conversion tables /kən'vɜːʃ(ə)n ˌteɪb(ə)lz/ *plural noun* a list of source codes or statements and their equivalent in another language or form ○ *Conversion tables may be created and used in conjunction with the customer's data to convert it to our system codes.* Also called **translation tables**

convert /kən'vɜːt/ *verb* to change one thing into another

converter /kən'vɜːtə/ *noun* a device or program that translates data from one form to another ○ *The converter allowed the old data to be used on the new system.*

convertibility /kənˌvɜːtə'bɪləti/ *noun* ability to be changed

convertible /kən'vɜːtəb(ə)l/ *adjective* that can be converted

convertor /kən'vɜːtə/ *noun* another spelling of **converter**

convex lens /ˌkɒnveks 'lenz/ *noun* a lens that is thicker in the centre than the edges, bending light in

convey /kən'veɪ/ *verb* to carry or import information ○ *The chart conveyed the sales problem graphically.*

conveyor /kən'veɪə/ *noun* a method of carrying paper using a moving belt

cookie /'kʊki/ *noun* a tiny file that is stored on your computer when you connect to a remote Internet site using a browser. The cookie is used by the remote site to store information about your options which can then be read when you next visit the site.

cookie file /'kʊki faɪl/ *noun* a file that contains the cookie data supplied by the remote Internet site

cooperative processing /kəʊ ˌɒp(ə)rətɪv 'prəʊsesɪŋ/ *noun* a system in which two or more computers in a distributed network can each execute a part of a program or work on a particular set of data

coordinate /kəʊ'ɔːdɪnət/ *verb* to organise complex tasks, so that they fit together efficiently ○ *She has to coordinate the keyboarding of several parts of a file in six different locations.*

coordination /kəʊˌɔːdɪ'neɪʃ(ə)n/ *noun* the process of organising complex tasks

copperplate printing /ˌkɒpəˌpleɪt 'prɪntɪŋ/ *noun* a printing method that uses a copper plate on which the image is etched

coprocessor /kəʊ'prəʊsesə/ *noun* an extra, specialised processor, e.g. an array or numerical processor, that can work with a main CPU to increase execution speed

> 'Inmos is hiring designers to create highly integrated transputers and co-processors for diverse computer and telecoms systems.' [*Computing*]

copy /'kɒpɪ/ *noun* **1.** a document which looks the same as another; duplicate of an original **2.** a document ■ *verb* to make a second document which is like the first, or to duplicate original data ○ *He copied all the personnel files at night and took them home.*

copy protect /ˌkɒpi prə'tekt/ *noun* a switch that prevents copies of a disk being made

copy protection /'kɒpi prəˌtekʃən/ *noun* the act of preventing copies from being made ○ *A hard disk may crash because of copy protection.*

copyright /'kɒpiraɪt/ *verb* to state the copyright of a written work by printing a copyright notice and publishing the work ■ *adjective* covered by the laws of copyright ○ *It is illegal to take copies of a copyright work.*

copyrighted /'kɒpiraɪtɪd/ *adjective* in copyright

copy typing /'kɒpi ˌtaɪpɪŋ/ *noun* the process of typing documents from handwritten originals, not from dictation (NOTE: no plural)

CORAL /'kɒpi/ *noun* a computer programming language used in a real-time system. Full form **common real-time applications language**

cord /kɔːd/ *noun* a wire used to connect a device to a socket

cordless telephone /ˌkɔːdləs 'telɪfəʊn/ *noun* a telephone which is not connected to a line by a cord, but which uses a radio link

core /kɔː/ *noun* the central conducting section of a cable

coresident /kəʊ'rezɪd(ə)nt/ *adjective* referring to two or more programs that are stored in the main memory at the same time

corona /kə'rəʊnə/ *noun* an electric discharge that is used to charge the toner within a laser printer

corporate video /ˌkɔːp(ə)rət 'vɪdiəʊ/ *noun* a video produced for internal training or as a publicity tool for a company and not intended to be broadcast

correct /kə'rekt/ *adjective* accurate or right ■ *verb* to remove mistakes from something

correction /kə'rekʃ(ə)n/ *noun* the process of making something correct; a change which makes something correct

corrective maintenance /kəˌrektɪv 'meɪntənəns/ *noun* actions to trace, find and repair a fault after it has occurred

correspond /ˌkɒrɪ'spɒnd/ *verb* **1.** □ **to correspond with someone** to write letters to someone **2.** □ **to correspond with something** to fit *or* to match something

correspondence /ˌkɒrɪ'spɒndəns/ *noun* **1.** letters and messages sent from one person to another (NOTE: no plural) □ **business cor-**

respondence letters concerned with a business □ **to be in correspondence with someone** to write letters to someone and receive letters back **2.** the way in which something fits in with something

correspondent /ˌkɒrɪˈspɒndənt/ *noun* **1.** a person who writes letters **2.** a journalist who writes articles for a newspaper on specialist subjects ○ *the computer correspondent* ○ *the 'Times' business correspondent* ○ *He is the Paris correspondent of the 'Telegraph'.*

corrupt /kəˈrʌpt/ *adjective* that contains errors ■ *verb* to introduce errors into data or a program ○ *Power loss during disk access can corrupt the data.*

cost per action /ˌkɒst pɜː ˈækʃən/ full form of **CPA**

co.uk a domain name suffix that indicates a business based in the UK ○ *The Peter Collin Publishing domain name is 'pcp.co.uk'* ◊ **domain**

coulomb /ˈkuːlɒm/ *noun* the SI unit of electrical charge

count /kaʊnt/ *verb* **1.** to add figures together to make a total ○ *He counted up the sales for the six months to December.* **2.** to include ○ *Did you count the sales of software as part of the home sales figures?*

counter /ˈkaʊntə/ *noun* **1.** a device which counts ○ *The loop will repeat itself until the counter reaches 100.* **2.** a register or variable whose contents are increased or decreased by a set amount every time an action occurs ○ *The number of items changed are recorded with the counter.*

counting perforator /ˌkaʊntɪŋ ˈpɜːfəreɪtə/ *noun* a paper tape punch, used in typesetting, that keeps a record of the characters, their widths, etc., to allow justification operations

country file /ˈkʌntri faɪl/ *noun* a file within an operating system that defines the parameters, e.g. character set and keyboard layout, for different countries

couple /ˈkʌp(ə)l/ *verb* to join together ○ *The two systems are coupled together.*

coupler /ˈkʌplə/ *noun* **1.** a mechanical device that is used to connect three or more conductors **2.** a chemical that forms a dye when it reacts with another substance in a copying machine

Courier /ˈkʊriə/ *noun* a fixed-space or monospace typeface

courseware /ˈkɔːsweə/ *noun* the software, manuals and video that make up a training package or CAL product

coverage /ˈkʌv(ə)rɪdʒ/ *noun* the size of the potential audience capable of receiving a broadcast ○ *the company had good media coverage for the launch of its new model* □ **press coverage, media coverage** reports about something in the newspapers *or* on TV, etc. ○ *the company had good media coverage for the launch of its new model*

cp *noun* a UNIX command to make a copy of a file

CPA *noun* the cost of displaying a banner advertisement once to one visitor to a website. Full form **cost per action.** ◊ **banner**

cpi /ˌsiː piː ˈaɪ/ *abbr* characters per inch

CPM *abbr* critical path method

cps /ˌsiː piː ˈes/ *abbr* characters per second

CPU /ˌsiː piː ˈjuː/ *noun* a group of circuits that performs the basic functions of a computer. The CPU is made up of three parts, the control unit, the arithmetic and logic unit and the input/output unit. Full form **central processing unit**

CR *abbr* **1.** card reader **2.** carriage return

crab /kræb/ *verb* move a camera or microphone sideways (*film*)

crane /kreɪn/ *noun* a large camera stand which holds the camera operator and camera (*film*) ◊ **dolly**

crash /kræʃ/ *noun* a failure of a component or a bug in a program during a run, which halts and prevents further use of the system ■ *verb* to come to an sudden stop (*of a computer or program*) ○ *The disk head has crashed and the data may have been lost.*

COMMENT: It is sometimes possible to recover data from a crashed hard disk before reformatting, if the crash was caused by a bad sector on the disk rather than contact between the r/w head and disk surface.

crash-protected /ˈkræʃ prəˌtektɪd/ *adjective* that uses a head protection or data corruption protection system ○ *If the disk is crash-protected, you will never lose your data.*

crawl /krɔːl/ *noun* a mechanical device that moves television or film titles down in front of a camera, to give the impression that they are moving up the screen

crawling title /ˌkrɔːlɪŋ ˈtaɪt(ə)l/ *noun* a line of titles moving across the screen (*film*)

CRC *abbr* **1.** cyclic redundancy check **2.** camera ready copy

create /kriˈeɪt/ *verb* to make ○ *A new file was created on disk to store the document.*

crew /kruː/ *noun* a group of technical staff who work together (as on filming a TV programme, recording an outside broadcast, etc.) ○ *the camera crew had to film all day in the snow*

crispener /ˈkrɪsp(ə)nə/ *noun* an electronic device used to sharpen the edges of objects in an image (*film*)

critical error /ˌkrɪtɪk(ə)l 'erə/ *noun* an error that stops processing or crashes the computer

critical fusion frequency /ˌkrɪtɪk(ə)l 'fjuːʒ(ə)n ˌfriːkwənsi/ *noun* (*on a video, computer or film screen*) the rate of display of frames of graphics or text that makes them appear flicker-free

critical path analysis /ˌkrɪtɪk(ə)l 'pɑːθ əˌnæləsɪs/ *noun* the definition of tasks or jobs and the time each requires arranged in order to achieve certain goals. Also called PERT – Program Evaluation and Review Techniques.

'Surprisingly, critical path analysis and project management, frequently the next career step for engineers, did not seem to warrant a mention.' [*Computing*]

critical path method /ˌkrɪtɪk(ə)l 'pɑːθ ˌmeθəd/ *noun* the use of analysis and the projection of each critical step in a large project to help a management team. Abbr **CPM**

CR/LF *abbr* carriage return/line feed

crop /krɒp/ *verb* **1.** to reduce the size or margins of an image **2.** to cut out a rectangular section of an image

crop mark /'krɒp mɑːk/ *noun* (*in DTP software*) one of the printed marks that show the edge of a page or image and allow it to be cut accurately

cropping /'krɒpɪŋ/ *noun* the removal of areas of artwork or of a photograph which are not needed ○ *The photographs can be edited by cropping, sizing, touching up, etc.*

cross- /krɒs/ *prefix* running from one side to another

cross-platform /ˌkrɒs 'plætfɔːm/ *adjective* available for more than one type of computer or operating system

cross-reference /ˌkrɒs 'ref(ə)rəns/ *noun* a reference in a document to another part of the document ■ *verb* to make a reference to another part of the document ○ *The SI units are cross-referenced to the appendix.*

crosstalk /'krɒstɑːk/ *noun* interference between two communication cables or channels

CRT /ˌsiː ɑː 'tiː/ *noun* a device used for displaying characters, figures or graphical information, similar to a TV set. Full form **cathode ray tube**

COMMENT: CRTs are used in television sets, computer monitors, and VDUs. A CRT consists of a vacuum tube, one end of which is flat and coated with phosphor, the other end containing an electron beam source. Characters *or* graphics are visible when the controllable electron beam strikes the phosphor, causing it to glow.

cruncher, crunching *noun* ♦ **number cruncher, number crunching**

cryogenic memory /ˌkraɪəʊdʒenɪk 'mem(ə)ri/ *noun* a storage medium operating at very low temperatures of around 4°K to use the superconductive properties of a material

cryptanalysis /ˌkrɪptə'næləsɪs/ *noun* the study and methods of breaking ciphers

cryptographic /ˌkrɪptə'græfɪk/ *adjective* referring to cryptography

cryptography /ˌkrɪp'tɒgrəfi/ *noun* the study of encryption and decryption methods and techniques

crystal /'krɪstəl/ *noun* a small slice of quartz crystal which vibrates at a certain frequency, used as a very accurate clock signal for computer or other high precision timing applications

crystal shutter printer /ˌkrɪst(ə)l ˌʃʌtə 'prɪntə/ *noun* a page printer that uses a powerful light controlled by a liquid crystal display to produce an image on a photo-sensitive drum

CSMA-CA /ˌsiː es em siː 'eɪ/ *noun* a method of controlling access to a network not covered by OSI standards, but used in AppleTalk networks. Full form **carrier sense multiple access-collision avoidance**

CSMA-CD /ˌsiː es em siː 'diː/ *noun* a network communications protocol that prevents two sources transmitting at the same time by waiting for a quiet moment, then attempting to transmit. It is used to control data transmission over an Ethernet network. Full form **carrier sense multiple access-collision detection**

CSS *abbr* cascading style sheet

CTM /ˌsiː tiː 'em/ *noun* a method of charging an advertiser for the display of a banner advertisement, where the price covers one thousand visitors clicking on the advertisement and jumping to the advertiser's own website. Full form **click through per thousand**

CTR[1] /kən'trəʊl/ *noun* the number of visitors who click on a banner advertisement on a website and jump to the advertiser's own website. Full form **click through rate**. ◊ **CTM** (NOTE: A click through rate of just a few percent is common, and most advertisers have to pay per thousand impressions of their banner ad.)

CTR[2] /kən'trəʊl/, **CTRL, Ctrl** *noun* the control key, or a key on a computer terminal that sends a control character to the computer when pressed

CTS /ˌsiː tiː 'es/ *noun* an RS232C signal indicating that a line or device is ready for data transmission. Full form **clear to send**

CU *abbr* control unit

CUA *noun* a standard for a user interface, originally developed by IBM, now followed by most software developers. Full form **common user access**

cue /kjuː/ *noun* **1.** a prompt or message displayed on a screen to remind the user that an input is expected **2.** a command or signal for a pre-planned event to commence (*film*)

CUG /ˌsiː juː ˈdʒiː/ *noun* entry to a database or bulletin board system that is restricted to certain known and registered users, usually by means of a password. Full form **closed user group**

cumulative index /ˌkjuːmjʊlətɪv ˈɪndeks/ *noun* an index made up from several different indexes

cumulative trauma disorder /ˌkjuːmjʊlətɪv ˈtrɔːmə dɪsˌɔːdə/ *noun* same as **repetitive strain injury**

current /ˈkʌrənt/ *adjective* referring to the present time ■ *noun* the movement of charge-carrying particles in a conductor

COMMENT: Mains electricity provides a 240v AC supply at 50Hz in the UK and 120v at 60Hz in the USA.

cursor /ˈkɜːsə/ *noun* a marker on a display device which shows where the next character will appear

'Probably the most exciting technology demonstrated was ScreenCam, which allows users to combine voice, cursor movement and on-screen activities into a movie which can be replayed.' [*Computing*]

'...further quick cursor movements are available for editing by combining one of the arrow keys with the control function' [*Personal Computer World*]

COMMENT: Cursors can take several forms, including a square of bright light, a bright underline, or a flashing light.

cursor resource /ˈkɜːsə rɪˌzɔːs/ *noun* an image that is displayed as a cursor (NOTE: Programming languages and authoring tools normally provide a range of different cursor images that a developer can use, for example an egg-timer cursor when waiting or an arrow when pointing.)

custom-built /ˈkʌstəm bɪlt/ *adjective* made specially for one customer

custom colours /ˌkʌstəm ˈkʌləz/ *plural noun* a range of colours in a palette that are used by an image or application. ◊ **system palette**

customer /ˈkʌstəmə/ *noun* a person who buys or uses a computer system or any peripherals

customise /ˈkʌstəmaɪz/, **customize** *verb* to modify a system to the customer's requirements ○ *We used customised computer terminals.* (NOTE: **customises – customising – customised**)

cut /kʌt/ *noun* **1.** the process of removing a piece from a file **2.** a piece removed from a file ■ *verb* to remove sections of text from a file to make it shorter (NOTE: **cutting – cut**)

cut and paste /ˌkʌt ən ˈpeɪst/ *noun* the action of taking a section of text or data from one point and inserting it at another, often used in word-processors and DTP packages for easy page editing

cutaway shot /ˈkʌtəˌweɪ ʃɒt/ *noun* (*film*) **1.** an action shot that is not part of the main action but is connected to it and occurs at the same time **2.** a camera movement away from the principal interest in a television interview, the interviewee, to the interviewer

cut off /ˌkʌt ˈɒf/ *verb* to remove part of something ○ *Six metres of paper were cut off the reel.*

cutoff /ˈkʌtɒf/ *adjective* point at which (something) stops

cutoff frequency /ˈkʌtɒf ˌfriːkwənsi/ *noun* the frequency at which the response of a device drops off

cutter /ˈkʌtə/ *noun* a film editor who decides which scenes are to be kept and in which order, and which are to be discarded (*film*)

cutting /ˈkʌtɪŋ/ *noun* the action of cutting

cutting room /ˈkʌtɪŋ ruːm/ *noun* a room in a film studio where the unedited film is cut and joined together

CWP *abbr* communicating word processor

cXML /ˌsiː eks em ˈel/ *noun* a feature of the XML webpage markup language that provides a standard way of producing pages about products for sale on an online shop (NOTE: The new features allow designers to include information about the product being displayed and how it can be purchased by the viewer.)

cyan /ˈsaɪən/ *noun* the complimentary colour to red, which is blue-green (*film*)

cyan-magenta-yellow-black /ˌsaɪən məˌdʒentə ˈjeləʊ/ *noun* full form of **CMYK**

cyber- /saɪbə/ *prefix* computers and information systems

cyber age /ˈsaɪbə eɪdʒ/ *noun* the present age, considered as a period in which computer technology and electronic communications have become more important and more widely used

cybercafé /ˈsaɪbəˌkæfeɪ/ *noun* a place that provides a shop with terminals connected to the Internet as well as coffee and pastries

cyberlaw /ˈsaɪbəlɔː/ *noun* the set of laws that relate to computers, information systems and networks, considered as a body

cybernetics /ˌsaɪbəˈnetɪks/ *noun* the study of the mechanics of human or electronic machine movements, and the way in which electronic devices can be made to work and imitate human actions

cyberspace /ˈsaɪbəspeɪs/ *noun* the world in which computers and people interact, normally via the Internet

cybersquatting /ˈsaɪbəˌskwɒtɪŋ/ *noun* act by which someone registers a website address, normally a trademark or brand name, then tries to sell the name to the rightful owner (NOTE: Although not yet illegal in most countries, court cases almost always find in favour of the company trying to recover its name. For example if you registered the domain name 'windows.com' then tried to sell this back to Microsoft Corp. you would be guilty of cybersquatting.)

cyberterrorism /ˈsaɪbəˌterərɪz(ə)m/ *noun* terrorist activities that use the Internet to damage complex electronic systems or the data they contain

'There were some instances of war-related hacking over the past few weeks, but nothing that would be considered cyberterrorism.' [*The Guardian*]

cyberwoozling /ˈsaɪbəˌwuːz(ə)lɪŋ/ *noun* the practice of gathering data from the computer of a visitor to a website without his or her knowledge or authorisation

cycle /ˈsaɪk(ə)l/ *noun* **1.** the period of time when something leaves its original position and then returns to it **2.** one completed operation in a repeated process

cyclic /ˈsɪklɪk, ˈsaɪklɪk/ *adjective* that is repeated regularly

cyclic redundancy check /ˌsɪklɪk rɪˈdʌndənsi ˌtʃek/ *noun* an error detection check used in modem communications and many file transfer protocols that looks at one bit in every n bits and compares this with the original to see if an error has occurred in the last n bits. Abbr **CRC**

cyclorama /ˌsaɪkləʊˈrɑːmə/ *noun* a large, curved, white backdrop positioned at the back of a stage or set (*film*)

cylinder /ˈsɪlɪndə/ *noun* **1.** a group of tracks on a disk **2.** the tracks in a multi-disk device that can be accessed without moving the read/write head

cylindrical /sɪˈlɪndrɪk(ə)l/ *adjective* shaped like a cylinder

cypher /ˈsaɪfə/ *noun* another spelling of **cipher**

D

D1 videotape *noun* a 19mm videotape format used for professional, digital recordings

DA *abbr* desk accessory

DAC /ˌdiː eɪ ˈsiː/ *noun* a circuit that outputs an analog signal that is proportional to the input digital number, and so converts a digital input to an analog form ○ *Speech is output from the computer via a D/A converter.* Full form **digital to analog converter**. Also called **D to A converter, d/a converter**

d/a converter /ˌdiː tʊ eɪ kənˈvɜːtə/ *noun* same as **DAC**

DAD *noun* a method of recording sound by converting and storing signals in a digital form on magnetic disk. Full form **digital audio disk**

daemon /ˈdiːmən/ *noun* (*in a UNIX system*) a utility program that performs its job automatically without the knowledge of the user

daisy chain /ˈdeɪzi tʃeɪn/ *noun* a method of connecting equipment with a single cable passing from one machine or device to the next, rather than separate cables to each device

damage /ˈdæmɪdʒ/ *verb* to harm ○ *The faulty read/write head appears to have damaged the disks.*

DAO /ˌdiː eɪ ˈəʊ/ *noun* a programming interface provided with many of Microsoft's database applications that allow the developer to access Jet or ODBC compatible data sources. Full form **data access objects**

darkroom /ˈdɑːkruːm/ *noun* a special room with no light, where photographic film can be developed

dark trace tube /ˌdɑːk ˈtreɪs ˌtjuːb/ *noun* a CRT with a dark image on a bright background

dash /dæʃ/ *noun* a short line in printing

DASH *noun* a sound tape recording system (*film*) Full form **digital audio stationary head**

DAT /ˌdiː eɪ ˈtiː/ *noun* a compact cassette, smaller than an audio cassette, that provides a system of recording sound as digital information onto magnetic tape with very high-quality reproduction. Full form **digital audio tape** (NOTE: It is also used as a high-capacity tape backup system that can store 1.3 GB of data; sound is recorded at a sample rate of either 32, 44.1 or 48 KHz to provide up to two hours of CD-quality sound.)

data /ˈdeɪtə/ *noun* a collection of facts made up of numbers, characters and symbols, stored on a computer in such a way that it can be processed by the computer

COMMENT: Data is different from information in that it is facts stored in machine-readable form. When the facts are processed by the computer into a form that can be understood by people, the data becomes information.

data access objects /ˌdeɪtə ˈækses ˌɒbjekts/ *plural noun* full form of **DAO**

data analysis /ˌdeɪtə əˈnæləsɪs/ *noun* the process of extracting information and results from data

databank /ˈdeɪtəbæŋk/ *noun* **1.** a large amount of data stored in a structured form **2.** a store of personal records in a computer

database /ˈdeɪtəbeɪs/ *noun* an integrated collection of files of data stored in a structured form in a large memory, which can be accessed by one or more users at different terminals

'This information could include hypertext references to information held within a computer database, or spreadsheet formulae.' [*Computing*]

database administrator /ˌdeɪtəbeɪs əd ˈmɪnɪstreɪtə/ *noun* full form of **DBA**

database management system /ˌdeɪtəbeɪs ˈmænɪdʒmənt ˌsɪstəm/, **database manager** /ˌdeɪtəbeɪs ˈmænɪdʒə/ *noun* full form of **DBMS**

database server /ˌdeɪtəbeɪs ˈsɜːvə/ *noun* a piece of database management software that runs on a server computer on a network and is used in a client-server system (NOTE: The user works with client software that formats and displays data that is retrieved by the server software.)

database system /ˈdeɪtəbeɪs ˌsɪstəm/ *noun* a series of programs that allows the user to create, modify, manage and use a database and that often includes features such as a report writer or graphical output of data

data bus connector /ˌdeɪtə ˈbʌs kə ˌnektə/ *noun* full form of **DB connector**

data capture /ˈdeɪtə ˌkæptʃə/ *noun* the act of obtaining data, either by keyboarding or scanning, or often automatically from a recording device or peripheral ○ *In July this year it signed a two-year outsourcing and* *disaster-recovery deal ... for the operation and management of its Birmingham-based data-capture facility. [Computing]*

data carrier detect /ˌdeɪtə ˌkæriə dɪ ˈtekt/ *noun* full form of **DCD**

data cleaning /ˈdeɪtə ˌkliːnɪŋ/ *noun* the process of removing errors from data

data communications /ˌdeɪtə kə ˌmjuːnɪˈkeɪʃ(ə)nz/ *noun* the transmission and reception of data rather than speech or images

data communications equipment /ˌdeɪtə kəˌmjuːnɪˈkeɪʃ(ə)nz ɪˌkwɪpmənt/ *noun* equipment, e.g. a modem, that receives or transmits data. Abbr **DCE**

data compression /ˌdeɪtə kəm ˈpreʃ(ə)n/ *noun* a means of reducing the size of blocks of data by removing spaces, empty sections and unused material

data corruption /ˈdeɪtə kəˌrʌpʃ(ə)n/ *noun* the introduction of errors into data through noise or faulty equipment ○ *Data corruption occurs each time the motor is switched on.*

data delimiter /ˈdeɪtə diːˌlɪmɪtə/ *noun* a special symbol or character that marks the end of a file or data item

data description language /ˌdeɪtə dɪ ˈskrɪpʃən ˌlæŋgwɪdʒ/ *noun* full form of **DDL**

data dictionary/directory /ˌdeɪtə ˌdɪkʃən(ə)ri daɪˈrekt(ə)ri/ *noun* full form of **DD/D**

data element /ˈdeɪtə ˌelɪmənt/ *noun* same as **data item**

data encryption /ˈdeɪtə ɪnˌkrɪpʃ(ə)n/ *noun* the process of encrypting data using a cipher system

data encryption standard /ˌdeɪtə ɪn ˈkrɪpʃən ˌstændəd/ *noun* full form of **DES**

data entry /ˌdeɪtə ˈentri/ *noun* a method of entering data into a system, usually using a keyboard but also direct from disks after data preparation

data error /ˈdeɪtə ˌerə/ *noun* an error due to incorrect or illegal data

data flow diagram /ˈdeɪtə fləʊ ˌdaɪəgræm/ *noun* full form of **DFD**

data format /ˈdeɪtə ˌfɔːmæt/ *noun* the set of rules defining the way in which data is stored or transmitted

datagram /ˈdeɪtəgræm/ *noun* a packet of information in a packet switching system that contains its destination address and route

data independence /ˌdeɪtə ˌɪndɪ ˈpendəns/ *noun* a structure of a database which can be changed without affecting what the user sees

data input /ˌdeɪtə ˈɪnpʊt/ *noun* data transferred into a computer, from an I/O port or peripheral

data input bus /ˌdeɪtə ˈɪnpʊt ˌbʌs/ *noun* full form of **DIB 1**

data integrity /ˌdeɪtə ɪnˈtegrɪti/ *noun* the state of data which has not been corrupted by damage or errors

data item /ˈdeɪtə ˌaɪtəm/ *noun* one unit of data, e.g. the quantity of items in stock, a person's name, age or occupation. Also called **data element**

data link /ˈdeɪtə lɪŋk/ *noun* a connection between two devices to allow the transmission of data

data link layer /ˈdeɪtə lɪŋk ˌleɪə/ *noun* the second layer in the ISO/OSI defined network that sends packets of data to the next link and deals with error correction (NOTE: This layer is normally split into two further sub-layers, medium access control and logical link control (**LLC**).)

data management /ˈdeɪtə ˌmænɪdʒmənt/ *noun* maintenance and upkeep of a database

data migration /ˌdeɪtə maɪˈgreɪʃ(ə)n/ *noun* the process of moving data between a high priority or on-line device to a low-priority or off-line device

data mining /ˈdeɪtə ˌmaɪnɪŋ/ *noun* the task of searching a database in order to find previously unknown patterns and relationships within the data it contains, e.g. searching a retailer's database to find customers who share an interest in a particular activity

> 'Both companies specialise in decision support, statistical analysis and data mining.' [*The Guardian*]

data processing /ˌdeɪtə ˈprəʊsesɪŋ/ *noun* the process of selecting and examining data in a computer to produce information in a special form. Abbr **dp, DP**

data processing manager /ˌdeɪtə ˈprəʊsesɪŋ ˌmænɪdʒə/ *noun* a person who runs a computer department

data projector /ˈdeɪtə prəˌdʒektə/ *noun* a device that uses three large coloured lights, red, green and blue, to project a colour image output from a computer onto a large screen

data protection /ˈdeɪtə prəˌtekʃən/ *noun* the procedure of making sure that data is not copied by an unauthorised user

Data Protection Act /ˌdeɪtə prəˈtekʃən ˌækt/ *noun* a piece of legislation passed in 1984 in the UK that requires any owner of a database that contains personal details to register

data rate /ˈdeɪtə reɪt/ *noun* the maximum rate at which data is processed or transmitted in a synchronous system, usually equal to the system clock rate

data security /'deɪtə sɪˌkjʊərɪti/ *noun* protection of data against corruption or unauthorised users

dataset /'deɪtəset/ *noun US* same as **modem**

data storage /'deɪtə ˌstɔːrɪdʒ/ *noun* a medium able to store data, especially in large quantities

data stream /'deɪtə striːm/ *noun* a set of data transmitted serially one bit or character at a time

data structure /'deɪtə ˌstrʌktʃə/ *noun* a number of related items that are treated as one by the computer (NOTE: For example in an address book record, the name, address, and telephone number form separate entries that would be processed as one by the computer.)

data tablet /'deɪtə ˌtæblət/ *noun* ➧ **graphics tablet**

data terminal equipment /'deɪtə ˌtɜːmɪn(ə)l ɪˌkwɪpmənt/ *noun* full form of **DTE**

data transfer rate /ˌdeɪtə 'trænsfɜː ˌreɪt/ *noun* the rate at which data is moved from one point to another

data transmission /'deɪtə trænz ˌmɪʃ(ə)n/ *noun* the process of sending data from one location to another over a data link

data type /'deɪtə taɪp/ *noun* a category of data which can be stored in a register, e.g. a string or number

data validation /'deɪtə ˌvælɪdeɪʃ(ə)n/ *noun* the process of checking data for errors and relevance in a situation

data warehouse /'deɪtə ˌweəhaʊs/ *noun* a database used for analysing the overall strategy of a business rather than its routine operations

date /deɪt/ *verb* to put a date on a document

day /deɪ/ *noun* the period of work from morning to night □ **to work an eight-hour day** to spend eight hours at work each day □ **day shift** shift which works during the daylight hours such as from 8 a.m. to 5.30 p.m.

dB *abbr* decibel

DBA /ˌdiː biː 'eɪ/ *noun* a person in charge of running and maintaining a database system. Full form **database administrator**

DB connector /ˌdiː biː kə'nektə/ *noun* a D-shape connector normally with two rows of pins used to connect devices that transfer data ○ *The most common DB connectors are DB-9, DB-25 and DB-50 with 9, 25 and 50 connections respectively.* Full form **data bus connector**

DBMS /ˌdiː biː em 'es/ *noun* a series of programs that allow the user to create and modify databases easily. Full form **database management system**. Also called **database manager**

DBS *abbr* direct broadcast satellite

DC *abbr* direct current

DCA /ˌdiː siː 'eɪ/ *noun* a document format defined by IBM that allows documents to be exchanged between computer systems. Full form **document content architecture**

DCC /ˌdiː siː 'siː/ *noun* a magnetic tape in a compact cassette box that is used to store computer data or audio signals in a digital format. Full form **digital compact cassette**

DCD /ˌdiː siː 'diː/ *noun* an RS232C signal from a modem to a computer indicating a carrier is being received ○ *The call is stopped if the software does not receive a DCD signal from the modem.* Full form **data carrier detect**

DCE *abbr* data communications equipment

DCOM /'diː kɒm/ *noun* an enhanced version of the COM specification that allows applications to access objects over a network or over the Internet. Full form **distributed component object model**

DCT *abbr* discrete cosine transform

DD *abbr* double density

DD/D /ˌdiː diː 'diː/ *noun* a piece of software which gives a list of types and forms of data contained in a database. Full form **data dictionary/directory**

DDE /ˌdiː diː 'iː/ *noun* **1.** the keying in of data directly onto disk. Full form **direct data entry 2.** a method in which two active programs can exchange data, one program asking the operating system to create a link between the two programs. Full form **dynamic data exchange**

DDL /ˌdiː diː 'el/ *noun* a part of database system software which describes the structure of the system and data ○ *Many of DDL's advantages come from the fact that it is a second generation language.* Full form **data description language**

DDP /ˌdiː diː 'piː/ *noun* the process of deriving information from data which is kept in different places. Full form **distributed data processing**

DDR *noun* television transmission by satellite (*film*) Full form **direct domestic reception**

dead /ded/ *adjective* **1.** referring to a computer or piece of equipment that does not function **2.** (room or space) that has no acoustical reverberation

deadline /'dedlaɪn/ *noun* date by which something has to be done ○ *we've missed our*

October 1st deadline □ **to meet a deadline** to finish something in time ○ *we've missed our October 1st deadline*

dealer /ˈdiːlə/ *noun* a person who buys and sells ○ *Always buy hardware from a recognised dealer.*

de-bounce /diː ˈbaʊns/ *noun* the process of preventing a single touch on a key from giving multiple key contact

debug /diːˈbʌg/ *verb* to test a program and locate and correct any faults or errors ○ *They spent weeks debugging the system.* (NOTE: **debugging – debugged**)

'Further questions, such as how you debug an application built from multi- sourced software to run on multisourced hardware, must be resolved at this stage.' [*Computing*]

DEBUG /diːˈbʌg/ *noun* an MS-DOS software utility that allows a user to view the contents of binary files and assemble small assembly-language programs

debugger /diːˈbʌgə/ *noun* a piece of software that helps a programmer find faults or errors in a program

decade /ˈdekeɪd/ *noun* a set of ten items or events

decay /dɪˈkeɪ/ *noun* the process of a sound signal fading away ○ *With a short decay, it sounds very sharp.*

decentralised computer network /diː ˌsentrəˌlaɪzd kəmˈpjuːtə/, **decentralized computer network** *noun* a network where the control is shared between several computers

deci- /desi/ *prefix* one tenth of a number

decibel /ˈdesɪbel/ *noun* a unit for measuring the power of a sound or the strength of a signal. Abbr **dB** (NOTE: The decibel scale is logarithmic.)

decimal /ˈdesɪm(ə)l/ *noun* □ **correct to three places of decimals** correct to three figures after the decimal point (e.g. 3.485)

decimalisation /ˌdesɪm(ə)laɪˈzeɪʃ(ə)n/, **decimalization** *noun* the process of changing to a decimal system

decimalise /ˈdesɪm(ə)laɪz/ *verb* to change to a decimal system

decimal point /ˌdesɪm(ə)l ˈpɔɪnt/ *noun* a dot which indicates the division between the whole unit digits and the smaller (fractional) parts of a decimal number (such as 4.75)

decimal system /ˈdesɪm(ə)l ˌsɪstəm/ *noun* a number system using the digits 0 – 9

decimal tabbing /ˌdesɪm(ə)l ˈtæbɪŋ/ *noun* the process of adjusting a column of numbers so that the decimal points are vertically aligned

decimal tab key /ˌdesɪm(ə)l ˈtæb ˌkiː/ *noun* a key for entering decimal numbers, using a word-processor, so that the decimal points are automatically vertically aligned

decipher /dɪˈsaɪfə/ *verb* to convert an encrypted or encoded message (**ciphertext**) into the original message (**plaintext**). Opposite **encipher**

decode /diːˈkəʊd/ *verb* to translate encoded data back to its original form (NOTE: **decodes – decoding – decoded**)

decoder /diːˈkəʊdə/ *noun* a program or device used to convert data into another form

decoding /diˈkəʊdɪŋ/ *noun* the process of converting encoded data back into its original form

decompression /ˌdiːkəmˈpreʃ(ə)n/ *noun* the process of expanding a compressed image or data file so that it can be viewed

decrypt /diːˈkrɪpt/ *verb* to convert encrypted data back into its original form ○ *Decryption is done using hardware to increase speed.*

decryption /diːˈkrɪpʃ(ə)n/ *noun* the converting of encrypted data back into its original form ○ *Decryption is done using hardware to increase speed.*

dedicated /ˈdedɪkeɪtɪd/ *adjective* referring to a program, procedure or system that is reserved for a particular use ○ *There's only one dedicated graphics workstation in this network.*

'The PBX is changing from a dedicated proprietary hardware product into an open application software development platform.' [*Computing*]

deep field /ˌdiːp ˈfiːld/ *noun* a lens or camera that has very close and very distant objects in focus at the same time (*film*) ◊ **deep focus**

deep focus /ˌdiːp ˈfəʊkəs/ *noun* a type of cinematography where objects at a great distance and objects very close to the camera are all in focus (*film*) ◊ **deep field**

de facto standard /ˌdeɪ ˌfæktəʊ ˈstændəd/ *noun* a design, method or system which is so widely used that it has become a standard but has not been officially recognised by any committee

default /dɪˈfɔːlt/ *adjective* a predefined course of action or value that is assumed unless the operator alters it ■ *noun* a value that is used by a program if the user does not make any changes to the settings ○ *An application may ask the user if he wants to install the application to the default, i.e. the C:\APP directory – the user can accept or change this.*

default palette /dɪˌfɔːlt ˈpælət/ *noun* the range of colours used on a particular system if no other is specified (NOTE: A user or application can often change the default palette to create an individual range of colours.)

default rate /dɪˌfɔːlt 'reɪt/ *noun* the baud rate in a modem that is used if no other is selected

default response /dɪˌfɔːlt rɪ'spɒns/ *noun* a value that is used if the user does not enter new data

default value /dɪˌfɔːlt 'væljuː/ *noun* a value which is automatically used by the computer if no other value has been specified ○ *Screen width has a default value of 80.*

'The default values of columns cannot be set in the database schema, so different applications can trash the database.' [*Computing*]

defect /'diːfekt/ *noun* something which is wrong or which stops a machine from working properly ○ *a computer defect* or *a defect in the computer*

defective /dɪ'fektɪv/ *adjective* faulty or not working properly ○ *The machine broke down because of a defective cooling system.*

define /dɪ'faɪn/ *verb* **1.** to assign a value to a variable ○ *All the variables were defined during initialisation.* **2.** to assign the characteristics of processes or data to something (NOTE: **defines – defining – defined**)

definition /ˌdefɪ'nɪʃ(ə)n/ *noun* the ability of a screen to display fine detail

deflect /dɪ'flekt/ *verb* to change the direction of an object or beam

deflection yokes /dɪ'flekʃ(ə)n jəʊkz/ *plural noun* magnetic coils around a cathode ray tube used to control the position of the picture beam on the screen

defocus /di'fəʊkəs/ *verb* to deliberately focus the lens at a point very close to the camera, leaving the background action out-of focus; usually used for special effects

DEFRAG /'diːfræg/ *noun* a defragmentation utility supplied with MS-DOS

defragmentation /ˌdiːfrægmen'teɪʃ(ə)n/ *noun* the reorganisation of files scattered across non-contiguous sectors on a hard disk

COMMENT: When a file is saved to disk, it is not always saved in adjacent sectors, increasing retrieval time. Defragmentation moves files back into adjacent sectors so that the read head does not have to move far across the disk, decreasing retrieval time and thus increasing performance.

degradation /ˌdegrə'deɪʃ(ə)n/ *noun* **1.** the loss of picture or signal quality **2.** the loss of processing capacity because of a malfunction

dejagging /diː'dʒægɪŋ/ *noun* same as **anti-aliasing**

DEL /del/ *noun* an MS-DOS command to delete a file ○ *To delete all files with the extension BAK, use the command DEL *.BAK.* Full form **delete**

delay /dɪ'leɪ/ *noun* time when something is later than planned ○ *There was a delay of thirty seconds before the printer started printing.* ■ *verb* to cause something to have a delay

delete /dɪ'liːt/ *verb* **1.** to cut out words in a document **2.** to remove text, data or a file from a storage device ○ *The word-processor allows us to delete the whole file by pressing this key.* Full form of **DEL** (NOTE: **deletes – deleting – deleted**)

COMMENT: When you delete a file, you are not actually erasing it but making its space on disk available for another file by instructing the operating system to ignore the file by inserting a special code in the file header and deleting the entry from the directory.

deletion /dɪ'liːʃ(ə)n/ *noun* **1.** the making of a cut in a document ○ *The editors asked the author to make several deletions in the last chapter.* **2.** a piece of text removed from a document

delimited-field file /diːˌlɪmɪtd fiːld 'faɪl/ *noun* a data file in which each field is separated by a special character, often a tab character or comma, and each record is separated by a carriage return or a second special character

delimiter /diː'lɪmɪtə/ *noun* **1.** a character or symbol used to indicate to a language or program the start or end of data or a record or information **2.** the boundary between an instruction and its argument

delivery system /dɪˌlɪv(ə)ri 'sɪstəm/ *noun* the combination of hardware and software required to play a particular multimedia title

delta frame /'deltə ˌfreɪm/ *noun* a video frame that contains only the pixel information that has changed since the last frame of the sequence, used to save space when storing video on disk

delta YUV /ˌdeltə ˌwaɪ juː 'viː/ *noun* full form of **DYUV**

demagnetise, demagnetize *verb* to remove stray or unwanted magnetic fields from a disk, tape or recording head (NOTE: **demagnetises – demagnetising – demagnetised**)

demagnetiser, demagnetizer *noun* a device which demagnetises a disk, tape or recording head ○ *He used the demagnetiser to degauss the tape heads.*

demand /dɪ'mɑːnd/ *noun* asking for something to be done ■ *verb* to ask for something and expect to get it ○ *She demanded her money back.*

demand protocol architecture /dɪ ˌmɑːnd ˌprəʊtəkɒl ˈɑːkɪtektʃə/ *noun* full form of **DPA**

demarcation /ˌdiːmɑːˈkeɪʃ(ə)n/ *noun* the process of showing the difference between two areas

demo /ˈdeməʊ/ *noun* same as **demonstration**

democratic network /ˌdeməkrætɪk ˈnetwɜːk/ *noun* a synchronised network in which each station has equal priority

demodulation /diːˌmɒdjuˈleɪʃ(ə)n/ *noun* the recovery of the original signal from a received modulated carrier wave

demodulator /diˈmɒdjʊleɪtə/ *noun* a circuit that recovers a signal from a modulated carrier wave

demonstrate /ˈdemənˌstreɪt/ *verb* to show how something works ○ *He demonstrated the file management program.*

demonstration /ˌdemənˈstreɪʃ(ə)n/ *noun* the act of showing how something works. Also called **demo**

demultiplex /diːˈmʌltɪpleks/ *verb* to split one channel into the original signals that were combined at source

demultiplexor /diːˈmʌltɪpleksə/ *noun* a device that separates out the original multiplexed signals from one channel

denary notation /ˈdiːnəri nəʊˌteɪʃ(ə)n/ *noun* the number system in base ten, using the digits 0 to 9

denial-of-service attack /dɪˌnaɪəl əv ˈsɜːvɪs əˌtæk/ *noun* an illegal action in which a great deal of data is sent to a computer system from many sources at the same in an attempt to overload the system and put it out of action

dense index /ˌdens ˈɪndeks/ *noun* a database index containing an address or entry for every item or entry in the database

densiometer /ˌdensiˈɒmɪtə/ *noun* a photographic device used to measure the density of a photograph

density /ˈdensɪti/ *noun* **1.** the amount of data that can be packed into a space **2.** the amount of light that a photographic negative blocks **3.** the darkness of a printed image or text

> '...diode lasers with shorter wavelengths will make doubling of the bit and track densities possible' [*Byte*]

> COMMENT: Scanner software produces various shades of grey by using different densities or arrangements of black and white dots and/or different size dots.

dependent /dɪˈpendənt/ *adjective* which is variable because of a particular factor ○ *A process that is dependent on the result of another process.*

deposit /dɪˈpɒzɪt/ *noun* **1.** a thin layer of a substance which is put on a surface **2.** a printout of the contents of all or a selected area of memory ■ *verb* to coat a surface with a thin layer of a substance

deposition /ˌdepəˈzɪʃ(ə)n/ *noun* a process by which a surface of a semiconductor is coated with a thin layer of a substance

depth cueing /ˈdepθ ˌkjuːɪŋ/ *noun* (*in graphics*) a method of changing the hue and colour of an object to reflect its depth in a three-dimensional scene

depth of field /ˌdepθ əv ˈfiːld/ *noun* the amount of a scene that will be in focus when photographed with a certain aperture setting

depth of focus /ˌdepθ əv ˈfəʊkəs/ *noun* the position of film behind a camera lens that will result in a sharp image

derive /dɪˈraɪv/ *verb* to come from a source ○ *The results are derived from the raw data.* (NOTE: **derives – deriving – derived**)

DES /ˌdiː iː ˈes/ *noun* a standard developed by the US Government for a high-security block data cipher system. Full form **data encryption standard**. Compare **public key encryption**

descender /dɪˈsendə/ *noun* a part of a printed letter that is below the line

de-scramble /diː ˈskræmb(ə)l/ *verb* to reassemble an original message or signal from its scrambled form

de-scrambler /diː ˈskræmblə/ *noun* a device which changes a scrambled message back to its original, clear form

describe /dɪˈskraɪb/ *verb* to say what someone or something is like ○ *The leaflet describes the services the company can offer.*

description /dɪˈskrɪpʃən/ *noun* words which show what something is like

descriptor /dɪˈskrɪptə/ *noun* a code used to identify a filename or program name or to pass code to a file

design /dɪˈzaɪn/ *noun* the planning or drawing of a product before it is built or manufactured ■ *verb* to plan or to draw something before it is built or manufactured ○ *He designed a new chip factory.*

designer /dɪˈzaɪnə/ *noun* a person who designs ○ *She is the designer of the new computer.*

desk accessory /ˈdesk əkˌsesəri/ *noun* an add-in Apple Mac utility that enhances the system ○ *We have installed several desk accessories that help us manage our fonts.* Abbr **DA**

desktop /ˈdesktɒp/ *adjective* able to be placed on a desk ■ *noun* a GUI workspace that is a graphical representation of a real-life desktop, with icons for telephone, diary, calculator, filing cabinet

COMMENT: A desktop makes it easier for a new user to operate a computer, since he or she does not have to type in commands but instead can point at icons on the desktop using a mouse.

desktop background /ˌdesktɒp ˈbækgraʊnd/ *noun* a pattern or image that is displayed by Windows as a backdrop

desktop icons /ˌdesktɒp ˈaɪkɒnz/ *plural noun* icons that are displayed on the desktop

desktop media /ˌdesktɒp ˈmiːdiə/ *plural noun* a combination of presentation graphics, desktop publishing and multimedia (NOTE: The term was originally used by Apple.)

desktop publishing /ˌdesktɒp ˈpʌblɪʃɪŋ/ *noun* full form of **DTP**

'...desktop publishing or the ability to produce high-quality publications using a minicomputer, essentially boils down to combining words and images on pages' [*Byte*]

Desktop taskbar /ˌdesktɒp ˈtɑːskbɑː/ *noun* a status bar that is normally displayed along the bottom of the screen in Windows 95

desktop video /ˌdesktɒp ˈvɪdiəʊ/ *noun* full form of **DTV**

despatch /dɪˈspætʃ/ *noun* another spelling of **dispatch**

de-spun antenna /ˌdi spʌn ænˈtenə/ *noun* a satellite aerial that always points to the same place on the earth

DESQview™ *noun* software which provides multitasking functionality for an MS-DOS system and allows more than one program to run at the same time

destination /ˌdestɪˈneɪʃ(ə)n/ *noun* a place to which something is sent or to which something is going; location to which a data is sent

destructive cursor /dɪˌstrʌktɪv ˈkɜːsə/ *noun* a cursor that erases the text as it moves over it ○ *Reading the screen becomes difficult without a destructive cursor.*

destructive read /dɪˈstrʌktɪv riːd/ *noun* a read operation in which the stored data is erased as it is retrieved

detail /ˈdiːteɪl/ *noun* a small part of a description ■ *verb* to list in detail ○ *The catalogue details the shipping arrangements for customers.*

detailed /ˈdiːteɪld/ *adjective* in detail

detect /dɪˈtekt/ *verb* to sense something (usually something very slight) ○ *The equipment can detect faint signals from the transducer.*

detection /dɪˈtekʃən/ *noun* the process of detecting something ○ *The detection of the cause of the fault is proving difficult.*

detector /dɪˈtektə/ *noun* a device which can detect

determine /dɪˈtɜːmɪn/ *verb* to fix or to arrange or to decide ○ *to determine prices* or *quantities* ○ *conditions still to be determined*

Deutsche Industrienorm /ˌdɔɪtʃə ˈɪndʊstriːˌnɔːm/ *noun* full form of **DIN**

develop /dɪˈveləp/ *verb* **1.** to plan and produce ○ *to develop a new product* **2.** to apply a chemical process to photographic film and paper to produce an image

developing /dɪˈveləpɪŋ/ *noun* a method by which an invisible image in an exposed photographic film is made permanently visible (*film*)

development /dɪˈveləpmənt/ *noun* the process of planning the production of a new product

development software /dɪˈveləpmənt ˌsɒftweə/ *noun* a suite of programs that helps a programmer write, edit, compile and debug new software

device /dɪˈvaɪs/ *noun* a small useful machine or piece of equipment

'Users in remote locations can share ideas on the Liveboard through the use of a wireless pen-input device and network connections.' [*Computing*]

device driver /dɪˈvaɪs ˌdraɪvə/ *noun* same as **driver**

device handler /dɪˌvaɪs ˈhændlə/ *noun* same as **driver**

device independent bitmap /dɪˌvaɪs ˌɪndɪpendənt ˈbɪtmæp/ *noun* full form of **DIB 2**

devise /dɪˈvaɪz/ *verb* to plan or build a system ○ *They devised a cheap method to avoid the problem.* (NOTE: **devises – devising – devised**)

Dewey decimal classification /ˌdjuːiː ˌdesɪm(ə)l ˌklæsɪfɪˈkeɪʃ(ə)n/ *noun* a library cataloguing system using classes and subclasses that are arranged in groups of ten

DFD /ˌdiː ef ˈdiː/ *noun* a diagram used to describe the movement of data through a system. Full form **data flow diagram**

DGIS /ˌdiː dʒiː aɪ ˈes/ *noun* a standard graphics interface for video adapters, primarily used with the 340x0 range of graphics chips. Full form **direct graphics interface standard**

DHCP /ˌdiː siː eɪtʃ ˈpiː/ *noun* an TCP/IP protocol that is used to assign an Internet address to workstations and servers that are nodes in a network. Full form **dynamic host configuration protocol** (NOTE: A special server running DHCP software manages the process of assigning addresses. A client computer can then ask this server for the address of another node on the network.)

Dhrystone benchmark /ˌdraɪstəʊn ˈbentʃmɑːk/ *noun* a benchmarking system developed to try and measure and compare the performance of computers

DIA/DCA /ˌdiː aɪ eɪ ˌdiː siː ˈeɪ/ *noun* a standard method for the transmission and storage of documents, text and video over networks. It is part of the IBM SNA range of standards. Full form **document interchange architecture/document content architecture**

diagnosis /ˌdaɪəgˈnəʊsɪs/ *noun* the process of finding of a fault or discovering the cause of a fault

diagnostic aid /ˌdaɪəgnɒstɪk ˈeɪd/ *noun* a hardware or software device that helps to find faults

diagnostics /ˌdaɪəgˈnɒstɪks/ *plural noun* functions or tests that help a user find faults in hardware or software

diagonal cut /daɪˈægən(ə)l kʌt/ *noun* a method of joining two pieces of film or magnetic tape together by cutting the ends at an angle so making the join less obvious

diagram /ˈdaɪəˌgræm/ *noun* a drawing which shows something as a plan or a map

diagrammatically /ˌdaɪəgrəˈmætɪkli/ *adverb* using a diagram ○ *The chart shows the sales pattern diagrammatically.*

dial /ˈdaɪəl/ *verb* to call a telephone number on a telephone ○ *to dial a number*

> 'Customers will be able to choose a wide variety of telephony products, from basic auto-dial programs to call-centre applications.' [*Computing*]

dialect /ˈdaɪəlekt/ *noun* a slight variant of a standard language ○ *This manufacturer's dialect of BASIC is a little different to the one I'm used to.*

dialling /ˈdaɪəlɪŋ/ *noun* the act of calling a telephone number. Abbr **IDD** (NOTE: no plural)

> 'Customers will be able to choose a wide variety of telephony products, from basic auto-dial programs to call-centre applications' [*Computing*]

dialling code /ˈdaɪəlɪŋ kəʊd/ *noun* a special series of numbers which you use to make a call to another town or country

dialling tone /ˈdaɪəlɪŋ təʊn/ *noun* a sound made by a telephone that indicates that the telephone system is ready for a number to be dialled

dialogue /ˈdaɪəlɒg/, **dialog** *noun* conversation between people, or an instance of this

dialup *noun* an online information service that is accessed by dialling into the central computer. Also called **dial-up service**

dial-up service /ˌdaɪəl ʌp ˈsɜːvɪs/ *noun* same as **dialup**

DIANE /daɪˈæn/ *abbr* direct information access network for Europe

diaphragm /ˈdaɪəfræm/ *noun* **1.** a thin flexible sheet that vibrates in response to sound waves to create an electrical signal, as in a microphone, or in response to electrical signals to create sound waves, as in a speaker **2.** a mechanical device in a camera that varies the aperture size

diapositive /ˌdaɪəˈpɒzɪtɪv/ *noun* a positive transparency

diary /ˈdaɪəri/ *noun* a book in which you can write notes or appointments for each day of the week

diary management /ˈdaɪəri ˌmænɪdʒmənt/ *noun* a part of an office computer program, which records schedules and appointments

diascope /ˈdaɪəskəʊp/ *noun* a slide projector or device that projects slide images onto a screen

DIB /ˌdiː aɪ ˈbiː/ *noun* **1.** a bus used when transferring data from one section of a computer to another, as between memory and CPU. Full form **data input bus 2.** a file format for a Windows graphics image that consists of a header, colour table and bitmap data. Full form **device independent bitmap** (NOTE: It can be in 1–, 4–, 8– or 24-bit colour resolution.)

dibit /ˈdɪbɪt/ *noun* a digit made up of two binary bits

dichotomising search /daɪ ˈkɒtəmaɪzɪŋ ˌsɜːtʃ/, **dichotomizing search** *noun* same as **binary search**

dichroic /daɪˈkrəʊɪk/ *adjective* referring to a chemical coating on the surface of a lens that reflects selectively different colours of light

dichroic filter /daɪˌkrəʊɪk ˈfɪltə/ *noun* a filter that allows certain wavelengths of light to pass and reflects back those that are not transmitted

dichroic head /daɪˌkrəʊɪk ˈhed/ *noun* a coloured light source that is based on adjustable dichroic filters, generally used with rostrum cameras and enlargers

dictate /dɪkˈteɪt/ *verb* to say something to someone who then writes down your words □ **dictating machine** small tape recorder that is used to record notes *or* letters dictated by someone, which a secretary can play back and type out the text

dictation /dɪkˈteɪʃ(ə)n/ *noun* the act of dictating □ **to take dictation** to write down what someone is saying □ **dictation speed** number of words per minute which a secretary can write down in shorthand

dictionary /ˈdɪkʃən(ə)ri/ *noun* **1.** a book which lists words and meanings. ◊ **spellchecker 2.** a data management structure that allows files to be referenced and sorted. ◊

spellchecker 3. a part of a spelling checker program consisting of a list of correctly spelt words against which the program checks a text (NOTE: The plural is **dictionaries**.)

dielectric /ˌdaɪɪ'lektrɪk/ *noun* insulating material that allows an electric field to pass, but not an electric current

differ /'dɪfə/ *verb* not to be the same as something else ○ *The two products differ considerably.*

difference /'dɪf(ə)rəns/ *noun* the way in which two things are not the same ○ *differences in price* or *price differences* ○ *What is the difference between these two products?*

different /'dɪf(ə)rənt/ *adjective* not the same ○ *Our product range is quite different in design from the Japanese models.*

differential /ˌdɪfə'renʃəl/ *adjective* which shows a difference

DIF file /'dɪf faɪl/ *noun* a file in a de facto standard that defines the way a spreadsheet, its formula and data are stored in a file

diffraction /dɪ'frækʃ(ə)n/ *noun* the bending or spreading of sound waves, radio or light which is caused by contact with objects (*film*)

diffraction lens /ˌdɪfrækʃ(ə)n 'lenz/ *noun* a lens which is used for special effects

diffuse /dɪ'fjuːz/ *verb* to move or insert something over an area or through a substance ○ *The smoke from the faulty machine rapidly diffused through the building.*

diffuser /dɪ'fjuːzə/ *noun* transparent frosted gel or glass which is attached to lamps in order to soften lighting (*film*)

diffusion /dɪ'fjuːʒ(ə)n/ *noun* **1.** a means of transferring doping materials into an integrated circuit substrate **2.** light dispersion

digipulse telephone /ˌdɪdʒipʌls 'telɪfəʊn/ *noun* a push button telephone dialling method using coded pulses

digit /'dɪdʒɪt/ *noun* a symbol or character that represents an integer that is smaller than the radix of the number base used ○ *a phone number with eight digits* or *an eight-digit phone number*

digital /'dɪdʒɪt(ə)l/ *adjective* which represents data or physical quantities in numerical form, especially using a binary system in computer related devices

'Xerox Parc's LCD breakthrough promises the digital equivalent of paper, by producing thin, low-cost flat displays with a 600dpi resolution.' [*Computing*]

digital audio tape /ˌdɪdʒɪt(ə)l 'ɔːdiəʊ ˌteɪp/ *noun* full form of **DAT**

digital camera /ˌdɪdʒɪt(ə)l 'kæm(ə)rə/ *noun* a camera that uses a bank of CCD units to capture an image and store it digitally onto a miniature disk or in RAM in the camera's body

digital cash /ˌdɪdʒɪt(ə)l 'kæʃ/ *noun* a method of paying for goods over the Internet (NOTE: There are several payment systems that use different models including a new bank account for each customer and an electronic purse that carries electronic tokens paid for by a customer.)

digital cassette /ˌdɪdʒɪt(ə)l kə'set/ *noun* a high quality magnetic tape housed in a standard size cassette with write protect tabs and a standard format leader

digital certificate /ˌdɪdʒɪt(ə)l sə'tɪfɪkət/ *noun* ▸ **certificate**

digital channel /ˌdɪdʒɪt(ə)l 'tʃæn(ə)l/ *noun* a communications path that can only transmit data as digital signals. ◊ **ADC** (NOTE: Voice, image, or video signals have to be converted from analog to digital form before they can be transmitted over a digital channel.)

digital compact cassette /ˌdɪdʒɪt(ə)l ˌkɒmpækt kə'set/ *noun* full form of **DCC**

digital computer /ˌdɪdʒɪt(ə)l kəm 'pjuːtə/ *noun* a computer that processes data represented in discrete digital form

digital data /ˌdɪdʒɪt(ə)l 'deɪtə/ *noun* data represented in numerical, especially binary, form

digital display /ˌdɪdʒɪt(ə)l dɪ'spleɪ/ *noun* a video display unit that can only show a fixed number of colours or shades of grey

digital divide /ˌdɪdʒɪt(ə)l dɪ'vaɪd/ *noun* the state of inequality that exists between people who have access to modern information technology and those who do not, since the former have many more opportunities open to them than the latter

digital encryption standard /ˌdɪdʒɪt(ə)l ɪn'krɪpʃən ˌstændəd/ *noun* the standard for encrypting private key data, which uses 56-bit encryption

digital light processing /ˌdɪdʒɪt(ə)l 'laɪt ˌprəʊsesɪŋ/ *noun* full form of **DLP**

digital logic /ˌdɪdʒɪt(ə)l 'lɒdʒɪk/ *noun* the process of applying Boolean algebra to hardware circuits

digitally /'dɪdʒɪt(ə)li/ *adverb* (quantity represented) in digital form ○ *The machine takes digitally recorded data and generates an image.*

digital monitor /ˌdɪdʒɪt(ə)l 'mɒnɪtə/ *noun* a monitor that can only show a fixed number of colours or shades of grey

digital multimeter /ˌdɪdʒɪt(ə)l 'mʌltimiːtə/ *noun* a multimeter that uses a digital readout to indicate voltage, current or impedance levels. Abbr **DMM**

digital nonlinear editing /ˌdɪdʒɪt(ə)l nɒnˌlɪniə 'edɪtɪŋ/ *noun* same as **nonlinear video editing**

digital optical recording /ˌdɪdʒɪt(ə)l ˌɒptɪk(ə)l rɪ'kɔːdɪŋ/ *noun* full form of **DOR**

digital output /ˌdɪdʒɪt(ə)l 'aʊtpʊt/ *noun* computer output in digital form

digital plotter /ˌdɪdʒɪt(ə)l 'plɒtə/ *noun* a plotter whose pen position is controllable in discrete steps, so that drawings in the computer can be output graphically

digital read-out /ˌdɪdʒɪt(ə)l 'riːdaʊt/ *noun* data displayed in numerical form, e.g. numbers on an LCD in a calculator

digital representation /ˌdɪdʒɪt(ə)l ˌreprɪzen'teɪʃ(ə)n/ *noun* data or quantities represented using digits

digital resolution /ˌdɪdʒɪt(ə)l ˌrezə'luːʃ(ə)n/ *noun* **1.** the smallest number that can be represented with one digit **2.** the value assigned to the least significant bit of a word or number

digital signal /ˌdɪdʒɪt(ə)l 'sɪgn(ə)l/ *noun* an electrical signal that has only a number of possible states, as opposed to an analog signal, which is continuously variable

digital signal level one /ˌdɪdʒɪt(ə)l ˌsɪgn(ə)l ˌlev(ə)l 'wʌn/ *noun* full form of **DS-1**

digital signal level zero /ˌdɪdʒɪt(ə)l ˌsɪgn(ə)l ˌlev(ə)l 'zɪərəʊ/ *noun* full form of **DS-0**

digital signalling /ˌdɪdʒɪt(ə)l 'sɪgnəlɪŋ/ *noun* control and dialling codes sent down a telephone line in digital form

digital signal processing /ˌdɪdʒɪt(ə)l 'sɪgn(ə)l ˌprəʊsesɪŋ/ *noun* full form of **DSP**

digital signature /ˌdɪdʒɪt(ə)l 'sɪgnətʃə/ *noun* a unique identification code sent by a terminal or device in digital form

digital speech /ˌdɪdʒɪt(ə)l 'spiːtʃ/ *noun* ◆ **speech synthesis**

digital subscriber line /ˌdɪdʒɪt(ə)l səb 'skraɪbə ˌlaɪn/ *noun* full form of **DSL**

digital switching /ˌdɪdʒɪt(ə)l 'swɪtʃɪŋ/ *noun* the process of operating communications connections and switches only by use of digital signals

digital system /ˌdɪdʒɪt(ə)l 'sɪstəm/ *noun* a system that deals with digital signals

digital theatre system /ˌdɪdʒɪt(ə)l 'θɪətə ˌsɪstəm/ *noun* full form of **DTS**

digital to analog converter /ˌdɪdʒɪt(ə)l tə ˌænəlɒg kən'vɜːtə/ *noun* full form of **DAC**

digital transmission system /ˌdɪdʒɪt(ə)l trænz'mɪʃ(ə)n ˌsɪstəm/ *noun* communication achieved by converting analog signals to a digital form then modulating and transmitting this and finally converting the signal back to analog form at the receiver

digital TV /ˌdɪdʒɪt(ə)l tiː'viː/ *noun* a television that can receive and decode television images and audio sent as digital data, then displayed on a standard screen

digital versatile disc /ˌdɪdʒɪt(ə)l ˌvɜːsətaɪl 'dɪsk/ *noun* full form of **DVD**

digital video /ˌdɪdʒɪt(ə)l 'vɪdiəʊ/ *noun* a video recorded in digital form (NOTE: The output from a video camera is converted to digital form using either a digital camera or a frame grabber. The digital output is then usually compressed before being processed or transmitted or stored on videotape.)

digital videodisc /ˌdɪdʒɪt(ə)l 'vɪdiəʊdɪsk/ *noun* full form of **DVD**

digital video effects /ˌdɪdʒɪt(ə)l 'vɪdiəʊ ɪˌfekts/ *plural noun* full form of **DVE**

digital video interactive /ˌdɪdʒɪt(ə)l ˌvɪdiəʊ ˌɪntər'æktɪv/ *noun* full form of **DV-I**

digital wallet /ˌdɪdʒɪt(ə)l 'wɒlɪt/ *noun* a feature of web browsers that contains a unique personal digital signature and allows the user to pay for goods at online shops in many different ways, including credit card or digital cash (NOTE: A digital wallet makes it simpler and more secure to buy goods from online shops.)

digitise /'dɪdʒɪˌtaɪz/, **digitize** *verb* to change analog movement or signals into a digital form that can be processed by computers ○ *We can digitise your signature to allow it to be printed with any laser printer.* (NOTE: digitises – digitising – digitised)

> 'The contract covers fibre optic cable and Synchronous Digital Hierarchy transmission equipment to be used to digitize the telecommunications network.' [*Computergram*]

digitised photograph /ˌdɪdʒɪˌtaɪzd ˌfəʊtə'grɑːf/, **digitized photograph** *noun* an image or photograph that has been scanned to produce an analog signal which is then converted to digital form and stored or displayed on a computer

digitiser, digitizer *noun* same as **ADC**

digitising pad /'dɪdʒɪtaɪzɪŋ ˌpæd/, **digitising tablet, digitizing pad, digitizing tablet** *noun* a sensitive surface that translates the position of a pen into numerical form, so that drawings can be entered into a computer

digit place /'dɪdʒɪt pleɪs/, **digit position** /ˌdɪdʒɪt pə'zɪʃ(ə)n/ *noun* the position of a digit within a number

DIL /ˌdiː aɪ 'el/ *noun* full form **dual-in-line package**. same as **DIP**

DIM /ˌdiː aɪ 'em/ *noun* software that allows a user to capture, store and index printed text in a digital form. Full form **document im-**

age management (NOTE: It usually works in conjunction with a scanner and a storage medium such as a recordable CD-ROM.)

dimension /daɪ'menʃən/ *noun* a measurement of size ○ *The dimensions of the computer are small enough for it to fit into a case.*

dimensioning /daɪ'menʃənɪŋ/ *noun* the definition of the size of something, especially an array or matrix ○ *Array dimensioning occurs at this line.*

dimmer /'dɪmə/ *noun* an electronic or electrical device which reduces the brightness of lights (*film*)

DIN /ˌdiː aɪ 'en/ *noun* a German industry standards organisation known particularly for specifications for plugs and sockets. Full form **Deutsche Industrienorm**

Dingbat™ /'dɪŋbæt/ *noun* a font that contains stars, bullets, symbols, images and drawings in place of characters ○ *To insert a copyright symbol, use the Dingbat font.*

diode /'daɪəʊd/ *noun* an electronic component that allows an electrical current to pass in one direction and not the other

diopter /daɪ'ɒptə/, **dioptre** *noun* a unit of measurement of the refractive power of a lens

DIP /ˌdiː aɪ 'piː/ *noun* **1.** a standard layout for integrated circuit packages using two parallel rows of connecting pins along each side. Full form **dual-in-line package 2.** software that allows a user to capture, store and index printed text in a digital form

diplex /'dɪpleks/ *noun* the simultaneous transmission of two signals over the same line

DIR /ˌdiː aɪ 'ɑː/ *noun* a MS-DOS system command that displays a list of files stored on a disk. Full form **directory**

direct /daɪ'rekt/ *verb* to manage or to organise ■ *adverb* straight or with no third party involved

direct change-over /daɪˌrekt 'tʃeɪndʒ ˌəʊvə/ *noun* the process of switching from one computer to another in one go

direct current /dɪˌrekt 'kʌrənt/ *noun* a constant value electric current that flows in one direction. Abbr **DC**

direct data entry /daɪˌrekt ˌdeɪtə 'entri/ *noun* full form of **DDE 1**

direct graphics interface standard /daɪˌrekt ˌgræfɪks 'ɪntəfeɪs ˌstændəd/ *noun* full form of **DGIS**

direct image /ˌdaɪrekt 'ɪmɪdʒ/ *noun* an image that is composed directly onto the screen rather than being composed off screen in memory before it is displayed

direct information access network for Europe /daɪˌrekt ˌɪnfəmeɪʃ(ə)n ˌækses ˌnetwɜːk fə 'jʊərəp/ *noun* a package of services offered over the Euronet network. Abbr **DIANE**

direction /daɪ'rekʃən/ *noun* the process of organising or managing ○ *He took over the direction of a software distribution group.* (NOTE: no plural in this meaning)

directional /daɪ'rekʃən(ə)l/ *adjective* which points in a certain direction

directional antenna /daɪˌrekʃ(ə)n(ə)l æn'tenə/ *noun* an aerial that transmits or receives signals from a single direction

directional pattern /daɪˌrekʃ(ə)n(ə)l 'pætən/ *noun* a chart of the response of an aerial or microphone to signals from various directions

directive /daɪ'rektɪv/ *noun* a programming instruction used to control the language translator or compiler

> '...directives are very useful for selecting parts of the code for particular purposes' [*Personal Computer World*]

directly /daɪ'rektli/ *adverb* **1.** immediately **2.** straight or with no third party involved ○ *We deal directly with the manufacturer, without using a wholesaler.*

direct memory access /daɪˌrekt 'mem(ə)ri ˌækses/ *noun* full form of **DMA** ○ *direct memory access transfer between the main memory and the second processor*

directory /daɪ'rekt(ə)ri/ *noun* **1.** a method of organising the files stored on a disk, into groups of files or further sub-directories ○ *The disk directory shows file name, date and time of creation.* **2.** full form of **DIR** (NOTE: The plural is **directories**.)

COMMENT: A directory is best imagined as a folder within a drawer of a filing cabinet: the folder can contain files or other folders.

directory services /daɪ'rekt(ə)ri ˌsɜːvɪsɪz/ *noun* a method of listing all the users and resources linked to a network in a simple and easy-to-access way so that a user can locate another user by name rather than by a complex network address ○ *With directory services installed, it's much easier for our users to find and connect to the shared printers.*

directory website /dəˌrekt(ə)ri 'websaɪt/ *noun* a website that contains a list of other websites, usually organised into sections and often with a search feature (NOTE: Yahoo! (www.yahoo.com) is one of the best-known directories and lists over half a million websites.)

disable /dɪs'eɪb(ə)l/ *verb* to prevent a device or function from operating ○ *He disabled the keyboard to prevent anyone changing the data.*

disassembler /ˌdɪsə'semblə/ *noun* a piece of software that translates a machine code program back into an assembly language form

disc /dɪsk/ *noun* another spelling of **disk** (NOTE: a spelling used only in the context of the **compact disc**, **videodisc**, and digital videodisc)

discard /dɪs'kɑːd/ *verb* to throw out something which is not needed

disclose /dɪs'kləʊz/ *verb* to reveal details of something which were supposed to be secret

disclosure /dɪs'kləʊʒə/ *noun* the act of telling details about something

disconnect /ˌdɪskə'nekt/ *verb* to unplug or break a connection between two devices ○ *Do not forget to disconnect the cable before moving the printer.*

discrete /dɪ'skriːt/ *adjective* referring to values, events, energy or data which occur in small individual units ○ *The data word is made up of discrete bits.*

discrete cosine transform /dɪˌskriːt 'kəʊsaɪn trænsˌfɔːm/ *noun* an algorithm used to encode and compress images. Abbr **DCT**

discrete multi-tone /dɪˌskriːt 'mʌlti ˌtəʊn/ *noun* full form of **DMT**

discretionary /dɪ'skreʃ(ə)n(ə)ri/ *adjective* which can be used if wanted or not used if not wanted

discretionary hyphen /dɪ ˌskreʃ(ə)n(ə)ri 'haɪf(ə)n/ *noun* a marker within a word indicating a position where an end of line hyphen may be inserted if part of the word needs to be carried down to the next line

discussion group /dɪ'skʌʃ(ə)n gruːp/ *noun* a feature of a website that lets any visitor write and post a message on a particular subject, which is displayed to any other visitors, who can then add their comments in reply to the message

dish aerial /'dɪʃ ˌeəriəl/ *noun* a circular concave directional aerial used to pick up long distance transmissions ○ *We use a dish aerial to receive signals from the satellite.*

disjointed /dɪs'dʒɔɪntɪd/ *adjective* (set of information or data) that has no common subject

disk /dɪsk/ *noun* a flat circular plate coated with a substance that is capable of being magnetised. Data is stored on this by magnetising selective sections to represent binary digits. (NOTE: The alternative spelling **disc** is used only in the context of the **compact disc**, **videodisc**, and digital videodisc)

COMMENT: The disk surface is divided into tracks that can be accessed individually; magnetic tapes cannot be accessed in this way.

disk drive /'dɪsk draɪv/ *noun* a device that spins a magnetic disk and controls the position of the read/write head. Also called **disk unit**

diskette /dɪ'sket/ *noun* a light, flexible disk that can store data in a magnetic form, used in most personal computers

diskless /'dɪskləs/ *adjective* which does not use disks for data storage ○ *diskless system* ○ *They want to create a diskless workstation.*

disk operating system /ˌdɪsk 'ɒpəreɪtɪŋ ˌsɪstəm/ *noun* full form of **DOS**

disk unit /dɪsk 'juːnɪt/ *noun* same as **disk drive**

disorderly close-down /dɪsˌɔːdəli 'kləʊz ˌdaʊn/ *noun* a system crash that did not provide enough warning to carry out an orderly close-down

dispatch /dɪ'spætʃ/, **despatch** /dɪ'spætʃ/ *noun* the action of sending material, information or messages to a location

dispenser /dɪ'spensə/ *noun* a device which gives out something □ **cash dispenser** device which gives money when a card is inserted and special instructions keyed in

dispersion /dɪ'spɜːʃ(ə)n/ *noun* a logical function whose output is false if all inputs are true, and true if any input is false

displacement /dɪs'pleɪsmənt/ *noun* an offset used in an indexed address

display /dɪ'spleɪ/ *noun* a device on which information or images can be presented visually

display attribute /dɪ'spleɪ ˌætrɪbjuːt/ *noun* a variable which defines the shape, size or colour of text or graphics displayed

display colour /dɪ'spleɪ ˌkʌlə/ *noun* the colour of characters in a videotext display system

display cycle /dɪ'spleɪ ˌsaɪk(ə)l/ *noun* the set of operations required to display an image on screen

display format /dɪ'spleɪ ˌfɔːmæt/ *noun* the number of characters that can be displayed on a screen, given as row and column lengths

display mode /dɪ'spleɪ məʊd/ *noun* a way of referring to the character set to be used, usually graphics or alphanumerics

display resolution /dɪˌspleɪ ˌrezə'luːʃ(ə)n/ *noun* the number of pixels per unit area that a display can clearly show

display screen /dɪ'spleɪ skriːn/ *noun* the physical part of a VDU, terminal or monitor, which allows the user to see characters or graphics (NOTE: It is usually a cathode ray tube, but sometimes LCD or LED displays are used.)

display space /dɪ'spleɪ speɪs/ *noun* memory or the amount of screen available to show graphics or text

dissolve /dɪ'zɒlv/ *noun* a special effect that is used in presentation graphics software or multimedia to fade out one image and fade in the next

distort /dɪ'stɔːt/ *verb* to introduce unwanted differences between a signal input and output from a device

distortion /dɪ'stɔːʃ(ə)n/ *noun* unwanted differences in a signal before and after it has passed through a piece of equipment

distribute /dɪ'strɪbjuːt/ *verb* to send out data or information to users in a network or system (NOTE: **distributes – distributing – distributed**)

distributed component object model /dɪˌstrɪbjʊtɪd kəmˌpəʊnənt 'ɒbdʒekt ˌmɒd(ə)l/ *noun* full form of **DCOM**

distributed data processing /dɪ ˌstrɪbjʊtɪd 'deɪtə ˌprəʊsesɪŋ/ *noun* full form of **DDP**

distributed processing /dɪˌstrɪbjʊtɪd 'prəʊsesɪŋ/ *noun* a technique to enable processors or computers to share tasks amongst themselves most effectively, in which each processor completes allocated sub-tasks independently and the results are then recombined

distributed system /dɪˌstrɪbjʊtɪd 'sɪstəm/ *noun* a computer system which uses more than one processor in different locations, all connected to a central computer

distribution /ˌdɪstrɪ'bjuːʃ(ə)n/ *noun* the act of sending information out, especially via a network

distributor /dɪ'strɪbjʊtə/ *noun* a company which sells goods for another company which manufactures them ○ *He is the UK distributor for a Japanese software house.*

> 'CORBA sets out a standard for how objects in applications, repositories or class libraries should make requests and receive responses across a distributed computing network' [*Computing*]

dither /'dɪðə/ *verb* **1.** to create a curve or line that looks smoother by adding shaded pixels beside the pixels that make up the image **2.** to create the appearance of a new colour by a pattern of coloured pixels that appear, to the eye, to combine and form a new, composite colour (e.g., a pattern of black and white dots will appear like grey)

DIV *noun* digital satellite data transmission in place of a voice channel. Full form **data in voice**

divergence /daɪ'vɜːdʒəns/ *noun* the failure of light or particle beams to meet at a certain point

diversity /daɪ'vɜːsɪti/ *noun* coming from more than one source; being aimed at more than one use

diverter /daɪ'vɜːtə/ *noun* a circuit or device that redirects a message or signal from one path or route to another

divide /dɪ'vaɪd/ *verb* to cut or to split into parts ○ *In the hyphenation program, long words are automatically divided at the end of lines.*

division /dɪ'vɪʒ(ə)n/ *noun* the act of dividing numbers

DLL /ˌdiː el 'el/ *noun* a library of utility programs that can be called from a main program. Full form **dynamic link library**

DLP /ˌdiː el 'piː/ *noun* a method of projecting an image using an electronic chip that contains thousands of tiny mirrors. Full form **digital light processing**

DMA /ˌdiː em 'eɪ/ *noun* a direct rapid link between a peripheral and a computer's main memory, which avoids accessing routines for each item of data read. Full form **direct memory access**

> 'A 32-bit DMA controller, 16-bit video I/O ports and I/O filters complete the chip.' [*Computing*]

DMM *abbr* digital multimeter

DMT /ˌdiː em 'tiː/ *noun* technology that uses digital signal processors to create sound signals that carry digital video, sound, image and data over cable at high speed. Full form **discrete multi-tone**

DNS /ˌdiː en 'es/ *noun* a distributed database used in an Internet system to map names to addresses. Full form **domain name system** (NOTE: For example you can use the name 'www.bloomsbury.com' to locate the Bloomsbury Publishing website rather than a complex network address (called the IP address).)

DOC *noun* equipment which provides a signal that reinstates lost information on a videotape when it has been temporarily misplaced (*film*) Full form **drop-out compensator**

dock /dɒk/ *verb* to connect a laptop computer to a special docking station on a desk to give it the same resources as a normal desktop

docking station /'dɒkɪŋ ˌsteɪʃ(ə)n/, **docking unit** /'dɒkɪŋ ˌjuːnɪt/ *noun* a special base unit that allows a laptop computer to be inserted into it and provide the same resources as a normal desktop, e.g. mains power, a network adapter, connection to a full-size monitor and extra expansion ports

document /'dɒkjʊmənt/ *noun* a piece of paper with writing on it ■ *verb* /'dɒkjʊ ˌment/ to write a description of a process

documentation /ˌdɒkjʊmen'teɪʃ(ə)n/ *noun* **1.** all documents referring to something ○ *Please send all documentation concerning the product.* **2.** the set of information, notes and diagrams that describe the function, use and operation of a piece of hardware or software

document content architecture /ˌdɒkjʊmənt 'kɒntent ˌɑːkɪtektʃə/ *noun* full form of **DCA**

document image management /ˌdɒkjʊmənt ˌɪmɪdʒ 'mænɪdʒmənt/ *noun* full form of **DIM**

document interchange architecture/document content architecture /ˌdɒkjʊmənt ˌɪntətʃeɪndʒ ˌɑːkɪtektʃə ˌdɒkjʊmənt 'kɒntent ˌɑːkɪtektʃə/ *noun* full form of **DIA/DCA**

document object model /ˌdɒkjʊmənt ˌɒbdʒekt 'mɒd(ə)l/ *noun* full form of **DOM**

Dolby Digital™ /ˌdɒlbi 'dɪdʒɪt(ə)l/ a trade name for a multichannel audio compression and transmission system that uses 5.1 channels

Dolby system™ /'dɒlbi ˌsɪstəm/ a trade name for a system for reducing background noise for recordings

dollar sign /'dɒlə saɪn/ *noun* a printed or written character ($) used in some programming languages to identify a variable as a string type

dolly /'dɒli/ *noun* a moveable stand on which the camera is mounted in order to be able to follow the action (*film*)

dolly pusher /'dɒli ˌpʊʃə/ *noun* a grip who moves the dolly during filming

dolly shot /'dɒli ʃɒt/ *noun* a shot filmed while the camera is moving away from the action

DOM /ˌdiː əʊ 'em/ *noun* a scheme that describes how the different parts of a webpage, the text, images and hyperlinks, are represented. Full form **document object model**

COMMENT: Each item is an object and has a set of attributes that defines how it is displayed and managed by a web browser. Dynamic HTML (DHTML) uses DOM to change how a webpage is displayed by a user's web browser – currently, the Microsoft and Netscape web browsers use different DOM specifications.

domain /dəʊ'meɪn/ *noun* **1.** an area or group of nodes in a network **2.** part of the way of naming users on the Internet in which the domain name is the name of the service provider or company the user works for; in an electronic mail address, the domain name follows the '&' symbol ○ *The Bloomsbury Publishing email address is 'general&bloomsbury.com' where 'general' is the user, 'bloomsbury' is the domain and 'com' is the domain type.*

domain name /dəʊ'meɪn neɪm/ *noun* a unique name that identifies the location of an Internet server or computer on the Internet

COMMENT: The domain name 'bloomsbury.com' is registered to the Bloomsbury Publishing website. The domain name is in a convenient text format, but refers to a physical address that locates the computer that stores the website for the domain name. This physical address is called the IP address and is in the format '194.33.322.22' – the domain name system (DNS) is used to translate the domain name into its correct IP address. The domain name is made up of two or three parts, separated by a 'dot'. There are some global thematic suffixes such as .com (company) and .net (network) which are not restricted by country. For example, 'bloomsbury.com' has the company name 'bloomsbury' followed by the domain type 'com' (for company). There are also country suffixes such as '.au' for Australia, '.cn' for China, '.uk' for the UK and '.de' for Germany, within which each country can have its own private system of domain names. Some of these might look the same as the global thematic suffixes (.net.uk, .org.uk, etc.), but are restricted to the UK, e.g. co.uk, .nhs.uk, .plc.uk and .ltd.uk.

domain name registration /dəʊˌmeɪn neɪm ˌredʒɪ'streɪʃ(ə)n/ *noun* the registration of a domain name with the relevant local registration office. ◊ **DNS**

COMMENT: Before you can use a domain name, you must check that it is available and then fill in an application form with your country's local registration office (your ISP will also be able to help). Domain name management is centred in the USA at the InterNIC organisation; you can also register a domain name directly with the InterNIC using its online order form (www.internic.net). Once the domain name has been approved, it will be assigned a unique IP address that will be used by your ISP to modify the DNS to allow your website to be located by other users.

domain name server /dəʊˌmeɪn neɪm 'sɜːvə/ *noun* a computer on the Internet that stores part or all of the domain name system database

domain name system /dəʊ'meɪn neɪm ˌsɪstəm/ *noun* full form of **DNS**

domestic /də'mestɪk/ *adjective* referring to the home market or the market of the country where the business is based ○ *they produce goods for the domestic market*

domestic satellite /dəˌmestɪk 'sætəlaɪt/ *noun* a satellite used for television or radio transmission, rather than research or military applications

dongle /'dɒŋgl/ *noun* a coded circuit or chip that has to be present in a system before a piece of copyright software will run

DOR /ˌdiː əʊ 'ɑː/ *noun* the recording of signals in binary form as small holes in the surface of an optical or compact disk which can then be read by laser. Full form **digital optical recording**

DOS /dɒs/ *noun* a section of the operating system software, that controls the disk and file access. Full form **disk operating system**

dot /dɒt/ *noun* a small round spot

dot-matrix printer /ˌdɒt 'meɪtrɪks ˌprɪntə/ *noun* a printer in which the characters are made up by a series of closely spaced dots (NOTE: The printer produces a page line by line. Dot-matrix printers can be used either for printing using a ribbon or for thermal or electrostatic printing.)

dots per inch /ˌdɒtz pɜːr 'ɪntʃ/ *plural noun* a standard method used to describe the resolution capabilities of a page printer or scanner ○ *Some laser printers offer high resolution printing: 400 dots per inch.* Abbr **dpi., d.p.i.**

dotted-decimal-notation /ˌdɒtɪd 'desɪm(ə)l/ *noun* a method of writing a domain name, email address or other IP network address using a decimal point, or full stop, to separate the numeric parts of the address (NOTE: For example 'www.bloomsbury.com' is the domain name that can be written in dotted-decimal-notation as '133.223.33.22')

double /'dʌb(ə)l/ *adjective* twice; twice as large; twice the size

double density /ˌdʌb(ə)l 'densəti/ *noun* a system to double the storage capacity of a disk drive by doubling the number of bits which can be put on the disk surface. Abbr **DD**

double sideband /ˌdʌb(ə)l 'saɪdbænd/ *noun* a modulation technique whose frequency spectrum contains two modulated signals above and below the unmodulated carrier frequency

double sideband suppressed carrier (DSBSC) /ˌdʌb(ə)l ˌsaɪdbænd sə ˌpresd 'kæriə/ *noun* a modulation technique that uses two modulated signal sidebands, but no carrier signal

doublet /'dʌblət/ *noun* a word made up of two bits. Also called **dyad**

down /daʊn/ *adjective, adverb* referring to computers or programs that are temporarily not working ○ *The computer system went down twice during the afternoon.* Opposite **up**

download /ˌdaʊn'ləʊd/ *verb* **1.** to load a program or section of data from a remote computer via a telephone line ○ *There is no charge for downloading public domain software from the BBS.* Opposite **upload 2.** to send printer font data stored on a disk to a printer, where it will be stored in temporary memory or RAM **3.** to retrieve a file from a remote computer or online system onto your local computer

'The cards will also download the latest version of the network drivers from the server.' [*Computing*]

downloadable /daʊn'ləʊdəb(ə)l/ *adjective* which can be downloaded

downsize /'daʊnsaɪz/ *verb* to move a company from a computer system based around a central mainframe computer to a networked environment, usually using PCs as workstations, in which the workstations are intelligent ○ *Downsizing is more cost effective and gives more processing power to the end-user.* (NOTE: **downsizes – downsizing – downsized**)

downtime /'daʊn taɪm/, **down time** *noun* a period of time during which a computer system is not working or usable. Opposite **uptime**

downward /'daʊnwəd/ *adjective* towards a lower position

dp, DP *abbr* data processing

DPA /ˌdiː piː 'eɪ/ *noun* a technique of loading protocol stacks in memory only if they are required for a particular session. Full form **demand protocol architecture**

dpi. /ˌdiː piː 'aɪ/, **d.p.i** *abbr* dots per inch ○ *a 300 d.p.i. black and white A4 monitor* ○ *a 300 dpi image scanner.*

COMMENT: 300 d.p.i. is the normal industry standard for a laser printer.

DPM /ˌdiː piː 'em/ *abbr* data processing manager

draft /drɑːft/ *noun* a rough copy of a document before errors have been corrected ■ *verb* to make a rough copy or drawing ○ *He drafted out the details of the program on a piece of paper.*

drag /dræg/ *verb* to move a mouse while holding the button down, so moving an image or icon on screen ○ *You can enlarge a frame by clicking inside its border and dragging to the position wanted.* (NOTE: **dragging – dragged**)

'...press the mouse button and drag the mouse: this produces a dotted rectangle on the screen; you can easily enlarge the frame by dragging from any of the eight black rectangles round the border, showing that it is selected' [*Desktop Publishing*]

drag and drop /ˌdræg ən 'drɒp/ *verb* to drag a section of text or icon or object onto another program icon which starts this program and inserts the data ○ *Drag and drop the document icon onto the word-processor icon and the system will start the program and load the document.*

drag image /ˈdræg ˌɪmɪdʒ/ *noun* the cursor, icon or outline image that is displayed when you drag an object across the screen

drain /dreɪn/ *noun* an electrical current provided by a battery or power supply; connection to a FET ■ *verb* to remove or decrease power or energy from a device such as a battery

DRAM /ˈdiː ræm/ *abbr* dynamic random access memory

draw direct /ˌdrɔː daɪˈrekt/ *noun* the process of drawing an object directly to the screen rather than to an off-screen memory buffer

drawing program /ˈdrɔːɪŋ ˌprəʊgræm/ *noun* a piece of software that allows the user to draw and design on screen

drawing tool /ˈdrɔːɪŋ tuːl/ *noun* any one of a range of functions in a paint program that allows the user to draw (NOTE: Usually displayed as icons in a toolbar, the drawing tools might include a circle-draw, line-draw and freehand drawing tool.)

D-region /diː ˈriːdʒən/ *noun* a section of the ionosphere 50–90km above the earth's surface ○ *The D-region is the main cause of attenuation in transmitted radio signals.*

drill-down /ˌdrɪl ˈdaʊn/ *verb* to work backwards and look at the individual items and formulae that produced the final result

drive /draɪv/ *noun* a part of a computer which operates a disk ■ *verb* to make something such as a disk work ○ *The disk is driven by a motor.*

drive bay /ˈdraɪv beɪ/ *noun* same as **bay**

drive letters /ˈdraɪv ˌletəz/ *noun* a system of letters to identify the different drives that are fitted to the PC

driver /ˈdraɪvə/ *noun* a piece of software that sits between Windows and a peripheral and translates the instructions from Windows into a form that the peripheral can understand. Also called **device driver, device handler**

DRO /ˌdiː ɑːr ˈəʊ/ *noun* a form of storage medium that loses its data after it has been read. Full form **destructive readout**

drop-down list box /ˌdrɒp daʊn ˈlɪst/ *noun* a list of options for an entry that appears when you move the cursor to the entry field

drop-down menu /ˌdrɒp daʊn ˈmenjuː/ *noun* a menu that appears below a menu title when it is selected

drop in /ˌdrɒp ˈɪn/ *noun* a small piece of dirt on a disk or tape surface, which does not allow data to be recorded on that section

drop out /ˌdrɒp ˈaʊt/ *noun* **1.** the failure of a small piece of tape or disk to be correctly magnetised for the accurate storage of data **2.** a short signal loss in a magnetic recording system caused by faults in the magnetic medium or failure in head-to-tape contact

drum /drʌm/ *noun* **1.** an early type of magnetic computer storage **2.** helical scan video tape head assembly **3.** a rotatable cylinder around which film passes in order to ensure steady movement in a photographic sound reproducer

DS-0 /ˌdiː es ˈzɪərəʊ/ *noun* one single circuit in a high-speed T-1 data transmission line, capable of transmitting information in 8-bit frames at a rate of 8,000 frames per second, equal to 64 Kbits/second. Full form **digital signal level zero**

DS-1 /ˌdiː es ˈwʌn/ *noun* a standard that defines the way data is formatted and transmitted over a T-1 line. Full form **digital signal level one**

DSE *abbr* data switching exchange

DSL /ˌdiː es ˈel/ *noun* a system of transmitting data at high speed over standard telephone copper wire. Full form **digital subscriber line**

COMMENT: One of the most popular DSL implementations is the ADSL (asymmetric digital subscriber line) scheme that provides a permanent, high-speed connection to the Internet over standard telephone lines.

DSP /ˌdiː es ˈpiː/ *noun* a special integrated circuit used to manipulate digital signals. Full form **digital signal processing**

D-SUB connector /ˌdiː sʌb kəˈnektə/ *noun* a video connector commonly used on PC monitors to carry all the video signals in one cable

DTC *noun* a videotape recording system which provides two sets of time code information used when editing (*film*) Full form **dual time code.** ◊ **time code**

DTE /ˌdiː tiː ˈiː/ *noun* a device at which a communications path starts or finishes. Full form **data terminal equipment**

DTMF /ˌdiː tiː em ˈef/ *noun* a method of dialling in a telephone system in which each number on the telephone handset generates two tones. Each row and column of the telephone number grid generates a different tone, so each number will send one tone for the corresponding column and another for the row. Full form **dual tone multi-frequency.** Compare **pulse-dialling** (NOTE: If you press number '5' it will send the tone for row two and for column two.)

D to A converter /ˌdiː tʊ ˌeɪ kən'vɜːtə/ *noun* full form **digital to analog converter**. ▶ **DAC**

DTP /ˌdiː tiː 'piː/ *noun* the design, layout and printing of documents using special software, a desktop computer and a printer. Full form **desktop publishing**

DTS /ˌdiː tiː 'es/ *noun* a multichannel audio system. Full form **digital theatre system**

DTV /ˌdiː tiː 'viː/ *noun* a combination of special software and extra hardware that allows a user to edit video on a PC. Full form **desktop video** (NOTE: The hardware connects the PC to a video recorder or camera and captures the video frames. The software can then be used to cut individual frames and rearrange the sequence.)

D-type connector /ˌdiː taɪp kə'nektə/ *noun* a connector that is shaped like an elongated letter D, which prevents the connector from being plugged in upside down ○ *The serial port on a PC uses a 9-pin D-type connector.*

dual /'djuːəl/ *adjective* using two or a pair

dual-in-line package /ˌdjuːəl ɪn laɪn 'pækɪdʒ/ *noun* full form of **DIL, DIP**

dual-scan display /ˌdjuːəl skæn dɪ 'spleɪ/ *noun* a colour LCD screen that updates the image on screen in two passes

dual tone multi-frequency /ˌdjuːəl təʊn ˌmʌlti 'friːkwənsi/ *noun* full form of **DTMF**

dub /dʌb/ *verb* to add sound effects to an animation, multimedia presentation, film or video (NOTE: **dubbing – dubbed**)

dubbing /'dʌbɪŋ/ *noun* **1.** the process of putting together two or more sound records into one combined recording **2.** the process of moving a sound recording from one intermediary to another; e.g. from photographic film to magnetic tape **3.** the process of making a copy, e.g., making a showreel from a group of videotapes **4.** the method of recording new dialogue which is used instead of the original version

duct /dʌkt/ *noun* a pipe containing cables, providing a tidy and protective surrounding for a group of cables

dumb terminal /ˌdʌm 'tɜːmɪn(ə)l/ *noun* a peripheral that can only transmit and receive data from a computer, but is not capable of processing data. Compare **smart terminal**

dummy /'dʌmi/ *noun* an imitation product used to test the reaction of potential customers to its design

dump /dʌmp/ *noun* **1.** data which has been copied from one device to another for storage **2.** the transferring of data to a disk for storage **3.** *US* a printout of the contents of all or selected data in memory

duotone /'djuːəʊtəʊn/ *noun* two-colour reproduction of an image or photograph using only black and either sepia or yellow (*film*)

duplex /'djuːpleks/ *noun* **1.** the simultaneous transmission of two signals on one line. Also called **simultaneous transmission** **2.** a photographic paper that is light sensitive on both sides

duplicate *noun* /'djuːplɪkət/ a copy ■ *verb* /'djuːplɪkeɪt/ to copy

duplicating /'djuːplɪkeɪtɪŋ/ *noun* copying

duplication /ˌdjuːplɪ'keɪʃ(ə)n/ *noun* the copying of documents

duplicator /'djuːplɪkeɪtə/ *noun* a machine which produces multiple copies from a master

durable /'djʊərəb(ə)l/ *adjective* which will not be destroyed easily ○ *durable cartridge*

duration /djʊ'reɪʃ(ə)n/ *noun* the length of time for which something lasts

dustcover /'dʌstkʌvə/ *noun* a protective cover for a machine

duty-rated /'djuːti ˌreɪtɪd/ *adjective* referring to the maximum number of operations that a device can perform in a set time to a certain specification

DUV *noun* data transmission in a frequency range or channel lower than that of a human voice. Full form **data under voice**

DVD /ˌdiː viː 'diː/ *noun* a way of storing over 17Gb of data on a CD-ROM type disc. Full form **digital versatile disc, digital videodisc**

DVD-RAM /ˌdiː viː 'diː ræm/ *noun* a DVD disc drive that allows a user to write, erase and rewrite data onto a DVD disc

DVD-ROM /ˌdiː viː 'diː rɒm/ *noun* a DVD disc drive that can read a DVD disc and provides data transfer rates equal to a standard nine-times CD-ROM

DVD+RW /ˌdiː viː diː plʌs ɑː 'dʌb(ə)l juː/ *noun* a type of rewritable DVD disc that allows a user to store data on the disc (NOTE: The DVD disc offers much greater storage capacity than a standard compact disc of similar size. This standard was developed by Hewlett-Packard, Philips and Sony and has a capacity of 3GB per side.)

DVD-video /ˌdiː viː ˌdiː 'vɪdiəʊ/ *noun* a standard that defines how full-length films can be compressed and stored on a DVD disc and played back on a dedicated player attached to a television set or viewed on a computer fitted with a DVD drive

DVE /ˌdiː viː ˈiː/ *noun* special effects carried out by a PC on a video sequence; e.g., a fade between two sequences or a dissolve. Full form **digital video effects**

DV-I /ˌdiː viː ˈaɪ/ *noun* a system that defines how video and audio signals should be compressed and displayed on a computer. Full form **digital video interactive**

DVI connector /ˌdiː viː ˈaɪ kəˌnektə/ *noun* a connector on a monitor or graphics equipment for video signals (NOTE: DVI-D supports digital video signals, DVI-I supports both analog and digital signals.)

Dvorak keyboard /ˌdvɔːræk ˈkiːbɔːd/ *noun* a keyboard layout that is more efficient to use than a normal QWERTY keyboard layout

dyad /ˈdaɪæd/ *noun* same as **doublet**

dye-polymer recording /ˌdaɪ ˈpɒlɪmə rɪˌkɔːdɪŋ/ *noun* (*in optical disks*) recording method which creates minute changes in a thin layer of dye embedded in the plastic optical disk (NOTE: Dye-polymer recording has one big advantage – that the data stored on the optical disk using this method can be erased.)

dye-sublimation printer /daɪ sʌblɪ ˌmeɪʃ(ə)n ˈprɪntə/ *noun* a high-quality colour printer that produces images by squirting tiny drops of coloured ink onto paper ○ *The new dye-sublimation printer can produce colour images at a resolution of 300 dpi.*

dynamic /daɪˈnæmɪk/ *adjective* referring to data which can change with time

dynamically redefinable character set /daɪˌnæmɪkli riːdɪˌfaɪnəb(ə)l ˈkærɪktə ˌset/ *noun* a computer or videotext character set that can be changed when required

dynamic data exchange /daɪˌnæmɪk ˈdeɪtə ɪksˌtʃeɪndʒ/ *noun* full form of **DDE**

dynamic host configuration protocol /daɪˌnæmɪk həʊst kənˌfɪgjʊˈreɪʃ(ə)n ˌprəʊtəkɒl/ *noun* full form of **DHCP**

dynamic link library /daɪˌnæmɪk ˈlɪŋk ˌlaɪbrəri/ *noun* full form of **DLL**

dynamic multiplexing /daɪˌnæmɪk ˈmʌltɪpleksɪŋ/ *noun* a multiplexing method which allocates time segments to signals according to demand

dynamic random access memory /daɪˌnæmɪk ˌrændəm ˌækses ˈmem(ə)ri/ *noun* abbr **DRAM**

DYUV /ˌdiː waɪ juː ˈviː/ *noun* a digital video encoding technique in which luminance of a pixel is calculated by the RGB input signal, Y0.6G + 0.3R + O.1Babbr of. Full form **delta YUV** (NOTE: From the value of Y it is possible to calculate the values of U and V as UR – Y; VB – Y.)

E

EAN *noun* a numbering system for bar codes, the European version of UPC. Full form **European Article Number**

EAPROM /ˌiː eɪ ˈpiː ˌrɒm/ *noun* a version of EAROM which can be programmed. Full form **electrically alterable programmable read-only memory**

early token release /ˌɜːli ˈtəʊkən rɪˌliːs/ *noun* (*in a Token-Ring or FDDI network*) system that allows two tokens to be present on a ring network, useful when traffic is very busy

EAROM /ˌiː ˈeɪ ˌrɒm/ *noun* a read-only memory chip whose contents can be programmed by applying a certain voltage to a write pin, and can be erased by light or a reverse voltage. Full form **electrically alterable read-only memory**

earth /ɜːθ/ *noun* a connection in a circuit representing zero potential ○ *All loose wires should be tied to earth.* ■ *verb* to connect an electrical device to the earth ○ *All appliances must be earthed.* (NOTE: US English is **ground**)

EAX *abbr* electronic automatic exchange

EBCDIC /ˌiː biː siː diː aɪ ˈsiː/ *noun* an 8-bit binary character coding system used mainly on IBM computers, in which each number represents a different character or symbol. It is similar to the ASCII system. Full form **extended binary coded decimal interchange code**

ebook /ˈiːbʊk/ *noun* an electronic version of a book, in which the text and any pictures are stored in a file format that can then be displayed using special software on a PC or laptop screen or on a dedicated portable or handheld device or PDA. Also called **electronic book**

EBR[1] /ˌiː biː ˈɑː/ *noun* the process of recording the output from a computer directly onto microfilm using an electron beam. Full form **electron beam recording**

EBR[2] /ˌiː biː ˈɑː/ *noun* a transfer system of high quality videotape to film

e-business /ˈiː ˌbɪznəs/ *noun* **1.** a company that does business on the Internet **2.** business activity that is carried out using the Internet

echo /ˈekəʊ/ *noun* the return of a signal back to the source from which it was transmitted (NOTE: The plural is **echoes.**) ■ *verb* to return a received signal along the same transmission path (NOTE: **echoes -echoing – echoed**)

ECL /ˌiː siː ˈel/ *noun* a high-speed logic circuit design using the emitters of the transistors as output connections to other stages. Full form **emitter-coupled logic**

ECMA *abbr* European Computer Manufacturers Association

e-commerce /ˈiː ˌkɒmɜːs/ *noun* the process of buying and selling products on the Internet. Also called **electronic commerce**

EDAC /ˌiː diː eɪ ˈsiː/ *noun* a forward error correction system for data communications. Full form **error detection and correction**

edge detection /ˈedʒ dɪˌtekʃ(ə)n/ *noun* an algorithm and routines used in image recognition to define the edges of an object

EDI /ˌiː diː ˈaɪ/ *noun* a system of sending orders, paying invoices or transferring company information over a network or telephone line using an email system. Full form **electronic data interchange** (NOTE: EDI is often used to send instructions to pay money directly from one company to another, or from one bank to a company.)

edit /ˈedɪt/ *verb* to change, correct and modify text or programs

edit decision list /ˌedɪt dɪˈsɪʒ(ə)n ˌlɪst/ *noun* a method of editing video in which the operator defines the points where he or she would like the video to be edited and then this list of actions is used in an on-line edit suite to carry out the edits automatically. Abbr **EDL**

edition /ɪˈdɪʃ(ə)n/ *noun* all the copies of a book or newspaper printed at one time ○ *The second edition has had some changes to the text.* ○ *Did you see the late edition of the evening paper?*

editorial /ˌedɪˈtɔːriəl/ *adjective* referring to an editor or to editing ■ *noun* a main article in a newspaper, written by the editor

> 'The Smartbook authoring system is a software product that integrates text and fractally compressed images, using any word-processor line editor' [*Computing*]

editorial processing centre /ˌedɪtɔːriəl ˈprəʊsesɪŋ ˌsentə/ *noun* a number of small publishers that share a single computer to provide cheaper computing power

edit window /ˈedɪt ˌwɪndəʊ/ *noun* the area of the screen in which the user can display and edit text or graphics

EDL *abbr* edit decision list

EDLIN /ˌiː diː el aɪ ˈen/ *noun* an MS-DOS system utility that allows a user to make changes to a file on a line-by-line basis

EDO memory /ˌiː diː əʊ ˈmem(ə)ri/ *noun* memory technology that provides better performance by being able to find and read data from a memory location in one operation. Full form **extended data output memory** (NOTE: It can also store the last piece of data that was saved to memory in a cache ready to be read back from memory.)

EDP /ˌiː diː ˈpiː/ *noun* data processing using computers and electronic devices. Full form **electronic data processing**

EDS /ˌiː diː ˈes/ *noun* a disk drive using a removable disk pack as opposed to a fixed disk. Full form **exchangeable disk storage**

EDTV /ˌiː diː tiː ˈviː/ *noun* an enhancement to the NTSC standard for television transmission that offers higher definition and a wide aspect ratio. Full form **extended-definition television** (NOTE: EDTV normally has an aspect ratio of 4:3; if greater than this it is called EDTV-wide.)

educational /ˌedjʊˈkeɪʃ(ə)nəl/ *adjective* referring to education; which is used to teach

educational TV /ˌedjuːkeɪʃənʃ(ə)l tiː ˈviː/ *noun* a television programme that is in some way educational

edutainment /ˌedjʊˈteɪnmənt/ *noun* software that is a cross between entertainment or games software and educational products

EEMS /ˌiː iː em ˈes/ *noun* a development of EMS that is a standard method of expanding the main memory fitted into an IBM PC. Full form **enhanced expanded memory specification**. ◊ **EMS**

EEPROM *abbr* electrically erasable programmable read-only memory

EEROM *abbr* electrically erasable read-only memory

effective /ɪˈfektɪv/ *adjective* which can be used to produce a certain result

effective aperture /ɪˌfektɪv ˈæpətʃə/ *noun* **1.** the received signal power at the output of an aerial **2.** the amount of light allowed through a lens' aperture after taking into account camera faults and lens defects. ◊ **diffusion**

effects track /ɪˈfekts træk/ *noun* a sound track which only contains the audio effects (*film*)

efficiency /ɪˈfɪʃ(ə)nsi/ *noun* working well ○ *He is doubtful about the efficiency of the new networking system.*

efficient /ɪˈfɪʃ(ə)nt/ *adjective* which works well ○ *The program is highly efficient at sorting files.*

efficiently /ɪˈfɪʃ(ə)ntli/ *adverb* in an efficient way ○ *The word-processing package has produced a series of labelled letters very efficiently.*

EFT /ˌiː ef ˈtiː/ *noun* a system in which computers are used to transmit money to and from banks. Full form **electronic funds transfer**

EFTPOS /ˌiː ef ˌtiː piː əʊ ˈes/ *noun* a terminal at a POS that is linked to a central computer which automatically transfers money from the customer's account to the shop's. Full form **electronic funds transfer point-of-sale**

'Alphameric has extended its range specifically for the hospitality market and has developed an eftpos package which allows most credit and debit cards to be processed.' [*Computing*]

EHF *noun* radio frequencies between 30GHz and 300GHz. Full form **extremely high frequency**

EI *noun* the sensitivity of a photographic emulsion (*film*) Full form **exposure index**. ◊ **ASA**

EIA *abbr* Electronics Industry Association

8-bit sample /ˌeɪt bɪt ˈstændəd/ *noun* a single sample of an analogue signal which is stored as an 8-bit number, meaning that it can detect 256 possible levels. ◊ **16-bit sample, 24-bit sample**

eight-inch disk /ˌeɪt ɪntʃ ˈdɪsk/, **8-inch disk** *noun* a high-capacity floppy disk which is eight inches in diameter

eighty-column screen /ˌeɪti ˈkɒləm skriːn/, **80-column screen** *noun* a screen that can display eighty characters horizontally

eighty-track disk /ˌeɪti træk ˈdɪsk/, **80-track disk** *noun* a disk formatted to contain eighty tracks

EIS /ˌiː aɪ ˈes/ *noun* easy-to-use software providing information to a manager or executive about his or her company ○ *The EIS software is very easy to use.* Full form **executive information system**

EISA /ˌiː aɪ es ˈeɪ/ *noun* a group of PC manufacturers who formed an association to promote a 32-bit expansion bus standard as a rival to the MCA bus standard from IBM. Full form **Electronics Industry Standards Association**

COMMENT: The EISA expansion bus standard is backwards compatible with the older ISA standard of expansion cards, but also features 32-bit data path and allows bus mastering.

either-or operation /ˌaɪðə ˈɔː ˌɒpəreɪʃ(ə)n/ *noun* a logical function that produces a true output if any input is true

elapsed time /ɪˌlæpst ˈtaɪm/ *noun* the time taken by the user to carry out a task on a computer

elastic banding /ɪˈlæstɪk bændɪŋ/ *noun* a method of defining the limits of an image on a computer screen by stretching a boundary around it

elastic buffer /ɪˌlæstɪk ˈbʌfə/ *noun* a buffer size that changes according to demand

electret microphone /ɪˌlektrət ˈmaɪkrəfəʊn/ *noun* a reliable, cheap, small and low noise microphone (*film*)

electric /ɪˈlektrɪk/ *adjective* worked by electricity

electrical /ɪˈlektrɪk(ə)l/ *adjective* referring to electricity ○ *The engineers are trying to repair an electrical fault.*

electrically /ɪˈlektrɪk(ə)li/ *adverb* referring to electricity ○ *an electrically-powered motor*

electrically alterable programmable read-only memory /ɪˌlektrɪkli ˌɔːltərəʙ(ə)l ˌprəʊgræməb(ə)l ˌriːd ˌəʊnli ˈmem(ə)ri/ *noun* full form of **EAPROM**

electrically alterable read-only memory /ɪˌlektrɪkli ˌɔːltərəʙ(ə)l ˌriːd ˌəʊnli ˈmem(ə)ri/ *noun* full form of **EAROM**

electrically erasable programmable read-only memory /ɪˌlektrɪkli ɪ ˌreɪzəb(ə)l ˌprəʊgræməb(ə)l ˌriːd ˌəʊnli ˈmem(ə)ri/ *noun* a ROM storage chip which can be programmed and erased using an electrical signal. Abbr **EEPROM**

electrically erasable read-only memory /ɪˌlektrɪkli ɪˌreɪzəb(ə)l ˌriːd ˌəʊnli ˈmem(ə)ri/ *noun* an EAROM memory chip whose contents can be programmed by applying a certain voltage to a write pin, and can be erased by light or a reverse voltage. Abbr **EEROM**

electrician /ɪˌlekˈtrɪʃ(ə)n/ *noun* the person on a set who is responsible for the lighting equipment (*film*)

electricity /ɪˌlekˈtrɪsɪti/ *noun* an electric current used to provide light or heat or power ○ *The electricity was cut off, and the computers crashed.*

electrode /ɪˈlektrəʊd/ *noun* part of an electric circuit or device that collects, controls or emits electrons

electrographic printer /ɪ ˌlektrəʊgræfɪk ˈprɪntə/ *noun* same as **electrostatic printer**

electroluminescence /ˌelektrəʊˌluːmɪ ˈnes(ə)ns/ *noun* light emitted from a phosphor dot when it is struck by an electron or charged particle

electroluminescent /ˌelektrəʊˌluːmɪ ˈnes(ə)nt/ *adjective* capable of emitting light due to electroluminescence ○ *The screen coating is electroluminescent.*

electroluminescing /ˌelektrəʊˌluːmɪ ˈnesɪŋ/ *adjective* emitting light due to electroluminescence

electromagnet /ɪˌlektrəʊˈmægnət/ *noun* a device that consists of a core and a coil of wire that produces a magnetic field when current is passed through the coil

electromagnetic /ɪˌlektrəʊmægˈnetɪk/ *adjective* generating a magnetic field or magnetic effect when supplied with electrical power

electromagnetically /ɪˌlektrəʊmæg ˈnetɪk(ə)li/ *adverb* working due to electromagnetic effects

electromagnetic interference /ɪ ˌlektrəʊmægnetɪk ˌɪntəˈfɪərəns/ *noun* full form of **EMI**

electromagnetic radiation /ɪ ˌlektrəʊmægnetɪk ˌreɪdiˈeɪʃ(ə)n/ *noun* an energy wave consisting of electric and/or magnetic fields

electromechanical switching /ɪ ˌlektrəʊmekænɪk(ə)l ˈswɪtʃɪŋ/ *noun* the connection of two paths by an electrically operated switch or relay

electromotive flow /ɪˌlektrəʊməʊtɪv ˈfləʊ/ *noun* the force of a circuit or system which makes the current flow. The unit of electromotive flow is the volt. (*film*)

electromotive force /ɪˌlektrəʊməʊtɪv ˈfɔːs/ *noun* the difference in electrical potential across a source of electric current. Abbr **EMF**

electron /ɪˈlekˌtrɒn/ *noun* an elementary particle with an elementary negative charge ○ *the electron beam draws the image on the inside of a CRT screen*

electron beam /ɪˈlekˌtrɒn biːm/ *noun* a narrow, focused stream of electrons moving at high speed in the same direction, often in a vacuum ○ *The electron beam draws the image on the inside of a CRT screen.*

electron beam recording /ɪˌlektrɒn ˌbiːm rɪˈkɔːdɪŋ/ *noun* full form of **EBR**

electron flow /ɪˈlektrɒn fləʊ/ *noun* the movement of electrons from one point to another, causing an electrical current

electron gun /ɪˈlekˌtrɒn gʌn/ *noun* a part of a CRT that produces a beam of electrons. Also called **gun**

COMMENT: Black and white monitors have a single beam electron gun, while colour monitors contain three, one for each primary colour (red, green and blue) used.

electronic /ˌelek'trɒnɪk/ *adjective* referring to something which is controlled by or controls electron flow

'...electronic mail is a system which allows computer users to send information to each other via a central computer' [*Which PC?*]

'...electronic publishing will be used for printing on paper, but it can be applied equally to data storage on a database, transmission via telecommunications or for use with visual presentation media such as AV slides or television' [*Electronic Publishing & Print Show*]

electronically /ˌelek'trɒnɪkli/ *adverb* referring to operations using electronic methods ○ *The text is electronically transmitted to an outside typesetter.*

Electronic Arts™ /ˌelektrɒnɪk 'ɑːts/ the largest publisher of interactive software including console games, PC and Macintosh titles

electronic blackboard /ˌelektrɒnɪk 'blækbɔːd/ *noun* a means of transmitting handwritten text and diagrams over a telephone line

electronic book /ˌelektrɒnɪk 'bʊk/ *noun* same as **ebook**

electronic commerce /ˌelektrɒnɪk 'kɒmɜːs/ *noun* same as **e-commerce**

electronic compositor /ˌelektrɒnɪk kəm'pɒzɪtə/ *noun* a computer that allows a user to easily arrange text on screen before it is electronically typeset

electronic data interchange /ˌelektrɒnɪk 'deɪtə ˌɪntətʃeɪndʒ/ *noun* full form of **EDI**

electronic data processing /ˌelektrɒnɪk 'deɪtə ˌprəʊsesɪŋ/ *noun* full form of **EDP**

electronic filing /ˌelektrɒnɪk 'faɪlɪŋ/ *noun* a system of storage of documents which can be easily retrieved

electronic funds transfer /ˌelektrɒnɪk 'fʌndz ˌtrænsfɜː/ *noun* full form of **EFT**

electronic funds transfer point-of-sale /ˌelektrɒnɪk ˌfʌndz ˌtrænsfɜː ˌpɔɪnt əv 'seɪl/ *noun* full form of **EFTPOS**

electronic mail /ˌelɪktrɒnɪk 'meɪl/ *noun* same as **email**

electronic pen /ˌelektrɒnɪk 'pen/ *noun* **1.** a light pen or wand **2.** a stylus used to draw on a graphics tablet ▶ also called **electronic stylus**

electronic point-of-sale /ˌelektrɒnɪk ˌpɔɪnt əv 'seɪl/ *noun* full form of **EPOS**

electronic publishing /ˌelektrɒnɪk 'pʌblɪʃɪŋ/ *noun* **1.** the use of desktop publishing packages and laser printers to produce printed matter **2.** the process of using computers to write and display information, as in viewdata

electronics /ˌelek'trɒnɪks/ *noun* the application of knowledge of electrons and their properties to manufactured products such as computers and telephones ○ *the electronics industry*

Electronics Industry Standards Association /ˌelektrɒnɪks ˌɪndəstri 'stændədz əˌsəʊsieɪʃ(ə)n/ *noun* full form of **EISA**

electronic stylus /ˌelektrɒnɪk 'staɪləs/ *noun* same as **electronic pen**

electronic traffic /ˌelektrɒnɪk 'træfɪk/ *noun* data transmitted in the form of electronic pulses

electronic viewfinder /ˌelektrɒnɪk 'vjuːfaɪndə/ *noun* a miniature cathode ray tube in a television or video camera, that allows the camera operator to see the images being recorded

electrophotographic /ˌelektrəʊˌfəʊtə 'græfɪk/ *adjective* referring to a printing technique used in many laser printers in which a laser beam creates an image on a charged drum (NOTE: The drum then attracts particles of fine black toner to the charged areas and transfers the image to paper which is then passed near a heater to melt the toner onto the paper.)

electro printing /ɪˌlektrəʊ 'prɪntɪŋ/ *noun* transferring sound from an original magnetic track directly to the final copy of the film; this avoids the use of an optical sound track (*film*)

electrostatic /ɪˌlektrəʊ'stætɪk/ *adjective* referring to devices using the properties of static electrical charge

electrostatically /ɪˌlektrəʊ'stætɪkli/ *adverb* using properties of static charge

electrostatic printer /ɪˌlektrəʊstætɪk 'prɪntə/ *noun* a type of printer which forms an image on the paper by charging certain regions to provide character shapes and other images and using ink with an opposite charge which sticks to the paper where required. Also called **electrographic printer**

elegant programming /ˌelɪgənt ˌprəʊ 'græmɪŋ/ *noun* the writing of well-structured programs using the minimum number of instructions

element /'elɪmənt/ *noun* **1.** a small part of an object which is made up of many similar parts **2.** one number or cell of a matrix or array **3.** a coil of resistive wire to which an electric current is applied to generate heat **4.** a substance in which all the atoms have the same number of electrons and charge

elementary /ˌelɪ'ment(ə)ri/ *adjective* made of many similar small sections or objects

elevator /'elɪveɪtə/ *noun* a small, square indicator displayed within a scroll bar that indicates where you are within a long document or image ○ *The user can scroll through the image* or *text by dragging the elevator up* or *down the scroll bar.*

ELF *noun* communications frequencies of less than 100Hz. Full form **extremely low frequency**

eliminate /ɪ'lɪmɪˌneɪt/ *verb* to remove something completely ○ *Using a computer should eliminate all possibility of error in the address system.*

elimination /ɪˌlɪmɪ'neɪʃ(ə)n/ *noun* the removing of something completely

'...pointing with the cursor and pressing the joystick button eliminates use of the keyboard almost entirely' [*Soft*]

elite /ɪ'liːt/ *noun* a typewriter typeface

ellipse /ɪ'lɪps/ *noun* something oval shaped, like an elongated circle

ellipsoidal spotlight /ɪˌlɪpsɔɪd(ə)l 'spɒtlaɪt/ *noun* a spotlight with a sharp beam produced by a spherical lens (*film*)

elliptical cutting /ɪˌlɪptɪk(ə)l 'kʌtɪŋ/, **elliptical editing** /ɪˌlɪptɪk(ə)l 'edɪtɪŋ/ *noun* a film editing process which eliminates much of the action (*film*)

elliptical orbit /ɪˌlɪptɪk(ə)l 'ɔːbɪt/ *noun* the path of a satellite around the earth that is in the shape of an ellipse

ELT *abbr* electronic typewriter

em /em/ *noun* a measure equal to the width of the letter 'm' in a particular font

email /'iː meɪl/, **e-mail** *noun* a system of sending messages to and receiving messages from other users on a network. Also called **electronic mail**

email-enabled application /ˌiːmeɪl ɪn ˌeɪb(ə)ld ˌæplɪ'keɪʃ(ə)n/ *noun* a software application, e.g. a word-processor or spreadsheet, that includes a direct link to an email application to allow a user to send the current document as an email (NOTE: In Microsoft applications, there is a Send option under the File menu that allows a user to send the document using email.)

embedded code /ɪmˌbedɪd 'kəʊd/ *noun* sections or routines written in machine code, inserted into a high-level program to speed up or perform a special function

embedded command /ɪmˌbedɪd kə 'mɑɪnd/ *noun* a printer control command, e.g. one indicating that text should be in italics, inserted into text and used by a word-processor when text formatting

embedded object /ɪmˌbedɪd əb'dʒekt/ *noun* a feature of Windows OLE that allows a file or object, e.g. an image, to be included within another document or file

embedding /ɪm'bedɪŋ/ *noun* (*in Windows*) the act of dragging an object and dropping it into a document or file so that is included within the document

emboldening /ɪm'bɒld(ə)n/ *noun* the process of making a word print in bold type

em dash /'em dæʃ/ *noun* a line as long as an em, used to link two words or parts of words

EMF *abbr* electromotive force

EMI /ˌiː em 'aɪ/ *noun* corruption of data due to nearby electrically generated magnetic fields. Full form **electromagnetic interference**

emission /ɪ'mɪʃ(ə)n/ *noun* the sending out of a signal or radiation, etc. ○ *the emission of the electron beam* ○ *The receiver picked up the radio emission.*

emit /ɪ'mɪt/ *verb* to send out

emitter /ɪ'mɪtə/ *noun* a connection to a bipolar transistor

emitter-coupled logic /ɪˌmɪtə ˌkʌp(ə)ld 'lɒdʒɪk/ *noun* full form of **ECL**

EMMY *noun* the annual prize given by the National Academy of Television, Arts and Sciences for the most outstanding artistic work in each area of film and television (*film*)

emphasis /'emfəsɪs/ *noun* **1.** a filter that helps cut down the background noise and so boost a signal **2.** a special effects function in a paint program that will increase the value of a range of colours so that they appear brighter (NOTE: The plural is **emphases**.)

EMS /ˌiː em 'es/ *noun* a standard in an IBM PC that defines extra memory added above the 640 Kb limit of conventional memory. Full form **expanded memory specification** (NOTE: This memory could only be used by specially written programs.)

emulate /'emjʊˌleɪt/ *verb* to copy or behave like something else ○ *Some laser printers are able to emulate the more popular office printers.* (NOTE: emulates – emulating – emulated)

'...some application programs do not have the right drivers for a laser printer, so look out for laser printers which are able to emulate the more popular office printers' [*Publish*]

emulation /ˌemjʊ'leɪʃ(ə)n/ *noun* behaviour by one computer or printer which is exactly the same as another and which allows the same programs to be run and the same data to be processed

emulator /'emjʊleɪtə/ *noun* a piece of software or hardware that allows a machine to behave like another

'...for an authentic retro coding experience, download an emulator and turn your computer into a virtual BBC Micro.' [*The Guardian*]

emulsion /ɪ'mʌlʃən/ *noun* a light-sensitive coating on photographic film or paper

emulsion laser storage /ɪˌmʌlʃ(ə)n 'leɪzə ˌstɔːrɪdʒ/ *noun* a digital storage technique using a laser to expose light-sensitive material

en /en/ *noun* a unit of measure equal to half the width of an em

enable /ɪn'eɪb(ə)l/ *verb* **1.** to allow something to happen ○ *A spooling program enables editing work to be carried out while printing is going on.* **2.** to use an electronic signal to start a process or access a function on a chip or circuit (NOTE: **enables – enabling – enabled**)

enabled /ɪn'eɪb(ə)ld/ *adjective* referring to a function or menu item that is available to the user ○ *If an option on a menu appears in grey text rather than black, this indicates that these are not enabled and that you cannot use the option.*

encapsulated /ɪn'kæpsjʊleɪtɪd/ *adjective* referring to something contained within another thing

encapsulated PostScript /ɪn ˌkæpsjʊleɪtɪd 'pəʊstskrɪpt/ *noun* a PostScript facility providing commands that describe an image or page contained within a file that can be placed within a graphics or DTP program. Abbr **EPS**

encapsulated PostScript file /ɪn ˌkæpsjʊleɪtɪd 'pəʊstskrɪpt ˌfaɪl/ *noun* a file that contains encapsulated PostScript instructions. Abbr **EPSF**

encapsulation /ɪn'kæpsjʊleɪʃ(ə)n/ *noun* (*in a network*) a system of sending a frame of data in one format within a frame of another format

encipher /ɪn'saɪfə/ *verb* to convert plaintext into a secure coded form by means of a cipher system ○ *Our competitors cannot understand our files – they have all been enciphered.* Opposite **decipher**

enclose /ɪn'kləʊz/ *verb* to surround with something; to put something inside something else

enclosure /ɪn'kləʊʒə/ *noun* a protective casing for equipment

encode /ɪn'kəʊd/ *verb* to apply the rules of a code to a program or data (NOTE: **encodes – encoding – encoded**)

encoder /ɪn'kəʊdə/ *noun* a device that can translate data from one format to another

encoding /ɪn'kəʊdɪŋ/ *noun* the translation of a message or text according to a coding system

encrypt /ɪn'krɪpt/ *verb* to convert plaintext to a secure coded form, using a cipher system ○ *The encrypted text can be sent along ordinary telephone lines, and no one will be able to understand it.*

encryption /ɪn'krɪpʃən/ *noun* the conversion of plaintext to a secure coded form by means of a cipher system

end /end/ *noun* a statement or character to indicate the last word of a source file ■ *verb* to finish or to stop something

en dash /'em dæʃ/ *noun* a line as long as an en, used to link two words or parts of words

ending /'endɪŋ/ *noun* **1.** the action of coming to an end or of stopping something **2.** the end part of something

endless /'endləs/ *adjective* with no end

end of address /ˌend əv ə'dres/ *noun* a transmitted code which indicates that address data has been sent. Abbr **EOA**

end of block /ˌend əv 'blɒk/ *noun* a code which shows that the last byte of a block of data has been sent through a communications link. Abbr **EOB**

end of data /ˌend əv 'deɪtə/ *noun* a code which shows that the end of a stored data file has been reached. Abbr **EOD**

end of document /ˌend əv 'dɒkjʊmənt/ *noun* same as **end of file**

end of file /ˌend əv 'faɪl/ *noun* a marker after the last record in a file. Also called **end of document**. Abbr **EOF**

end of job /ˌend əv 'dʒɒb/ *noun* a code used in batch processing to show that a job has been finished. Abbr **EOJ**

end of message /ˌend əv 'mesɪdʒ/ *noun* a code used to separate the last character of one message from the first of another message. Abbr **EOM**

end of record /ˌend əv 'rekɔːd/ *noun* a code used to show the end of a record. Abbr **EOR**

end of text /ˌend əv 'tekst/ *noun* a code sent after last character of text. Abbr **EOT, ETX**

end of transmission /ˌend əv trænz 'mɪʃ(ə)n/ *noun* a sequence of characters indicating that all the data from a terminal or peripheral has been transmitted. Abbr **EOT**

end user /ˌend 'juːzə/ *noun* a person who will use the device, program or product ○ *The company is creating a computer with a specific end user in mind.*

energy-saving /'enədʒi ˌseɪvɪŋ/ *adjective* which saves energy ○ *The company is introducing energy-saving measures.*

Energy Star /'enədʒi stɑː/ *noun* a standard and logo on a monitor, computer or other electrical device indicating that the product has been specially designed to save electricity

ENG *abbr* electronic news gathering

engaged tone /ɪn'geɪdʒd təʊn/ *noun* the sound made by a telephone showing that the number dialled is busy

engine /'endʒɪn/ *noun* a part of a software package that carries out a particular function ○ *A search engine is the part of a multimedia title that lets a user search for text in a multimedia book.*

enhance /ɪn'hɑːns/ *verb* to make better or clearer

enhanced-definition television /ɪn ˌhɑːnst ˌdefɪnɪʃ(ə)n ˌtelɪ'vɪʒ(ə)n/ *noun* full form of **EDTV**

enhanced dot matrix /ɪnˌhɑːnst ˌdɒt 'meɪtrɪks/ *noun* a clearer character or graphics printout using smaller dots and more dots per inch than standard dot matrix

enhanced expanded memory specification /ɪnˌhɑːnst ɪkˌspændɪd 'mem(ə)ri ˌspesɪfɪkeɪʃ(ə)n/ *noun* full form of **EEMS**

enhanced parallel port /ɪnˌhɑːnst 'pærəlel ˌpɔːt/ *noun* full form of **EPP**

enhanced small device interface /ɪn ˌhɑːnst smɔːl dɪ'vaɪs ˌɪntəfeɪs/ *noun* full form of **ESDI**

enhancement /ɪn'hɑːnsmənt/ *noun* an add-on facility which improves the output or performance of equipment

enlarge /ɪn'lɑːdʒ/ *verb* to make (a photograph) larger

enlargement /ɪn'lɑːdʒmənt/ *noun* **1.** the process of making something larger; a larger version of a photograph **2.** a larger version of a photograph ○ *An enlargement of the photograph was used to provide better detail.* ◊ **blow-up**

enlargement printing /ɪn'lɑːdʒmənt ˌprɪntɪŋ/ *noun* optical printing that enlarges a small frame area, e.g. 16mm to 35mm

ENQ *abbr* enquiry

enquiry /ɪn'kwaɪri/ *noun* **1.** a request for data or information from a device or database **2.** an act of accessing data in a computer memory without changing the data. Abbr **ENQ**

ensure /ɪn'ʃʊə/ *verb* to make sure ○ *Pushing the write-protect tab will ensure that the data on the disk cannot be erased.*

enter /'entə/ *verb* to type in information on a terminal or keyboard. ◊ **carriage return key**

entering /'entərɪŋ/ *noun* the act of typing in data or writing items in a record

enter key /'entə kiː/ *noun* a key pressed to indicate the end of an input or line of text

enterprise network /'entəpraɪz ˌnetwɜːk/ *noun* a network which connects all the workstations or terminals or computers in a company (NOTE: It can be within one building or link several buildings in different countries.)

enterprise software /'entəpraɪz ˌsɒftweə/ *noun* computer software that is designed to integrate and automate all of a company's functions

entity /'entɪti/ *noun* a subject to which the data stored in a file or database refers (NOTE: The plural is **entities**.)

entry /'entri/ *noun* **1.** a single record or data about one action or object in a database or library (NOTE: The plural is **entries**.) **2.** a place where you can enter

entry point /'entri pɔɪnt/ *noun* the address from which a program or subroutine is to be executed

enumerated type /ɪˌnjuːməreɪtɪd 'taɪp/ *noun* data storage or classification using numbers to represent chosen convenient labels

COMMENT: If 'man', 'horse', 'dog', 'cat' are the items of data, stored by the machine simply as 0, 1, 2, 3, they can still be referred to in the program as man, horse etc. to make it easier for the user to recognise them.

envelope /'envələʊp/ *noun* **1.** a transmitted packet of data containing error-detection and control information **2.** (*in multimedia*) the shape of the decay curve of a sound **3.** (*in email*) the data which contains a mail message with the destination address information **4.** a paper packet that contains a letter

envelope feeder /'envələʊp ˌfiːdə/ *noun* a special add-on to a printer used to print on an envelope instead of a sheet of paper

environment /ɪn'vaɪrənmənt/ *noun* **1.** the condition in a computer system of all the registers and memory locations **2.** surroundings or physical conditions **3.** the imaginary space in which a user works when using a computer. This can be changed to suit the user's needs – by defining its characteristics such as colour or wallpaper and by setting up a printer, keyboard and fonts.

EOA *abbr* end of address

EOB *abbr* end of block

EOD /ˌiː əʊ 'diː/ *abbr* end of data

EOF *abbr* end of file

EOJ *abbr* end of job

EOM *abbr* end of message

EOR *abbr* end of record

EOT *abbr* end of text

epidiascope /ˌepɪ'daɪəskəʊp/ *noun* an optical projector which mixes the function of a diascope (a transparency projector) with that of an episcope

episcope /ˈepɪskəʊp/ *noun* a projector that can display opaque material, such as photographs, and documents onto a screen

epitaxial layer /ˌepɪˈtæksiəl ˌleɪə/ *noun* a very thin layer of material or doped semiconductor deposited onto a substrate base

epitaxy /ˈepɪtækis/ *noun* a method of depositing very thin layers of materials onto a base, for use in chip manufacture

EPOS /ˈiːpɒs/ *noun* a system that uses a computer terminal at a point-of-sale site for electronic funds transfer or stock control as well as matters such as product identification. Full form **electronic point-of-sale**

EPP /ˌiː piː ˈpiː/ *noun* a standard that defines the way data can be transferred at high speed through a parallel port connector. Full form **enhanced parallel port**

EPR *noun* a system which ensures consistent frame-frame steadiness in telecine transfer (*film*) Full form **electronic pin registration**

EPROM /ˌiː ˈpiː ˌrɒm/ *abbr* erasable programmable read-only memory

EPS *abbr* encapsulated PostScript

EPSF *abbr* encapsulated PostScript file

equal /ˈiːkwəl/ *adjective* exactly the same ■ *verb* to be the same as ○ *Production this month has equalled our best month ever.*

equalisation /ˌiːkwəlaɪˈzeɪʃən/, **equalization** *noun* the process of making a signal equal (to preset values)

equaliser /ˈiːkwəlaɪzə/, **equalizer** *noun* a device which changes the amplitude of various parts of a signal according to preset values

equalize /ˈiːkwəˌlaɪz/ *verb* to make equal (to preset values) ○ *The received signal was equalised to an optimum shape.*

equally /ˈiːkwəli/ *adverb* in the same way ○ *They were both equally responsible for the successful launch of the new system.*

equate /ɪˈkweɪt/ *verb* to be the same as or to make the same as ○ *The variable was equated to the input data.*

equator /ɪˈkweɪtə/ *noun* an imaginary line running round the middle of the earth

equatorial orbit /ˌekwəˌtɔːriəl ˈɔːbɪt/ *noun* a satellite flight path that follows the earth's equator

equip /ɪˈkwɪp/ *verb* to provide with machinery or equipment

equipment /ɪˈkwɪpmənt/ *noun* machinery and furniture required to make a factory or office work ○ *office equipment* or *business equipment*

equipment failure /ɪˈkwɪpmənt ˌfeɪljə/ *noun* a hardware fault, rather than a software fault

equivalence /ɪˈkwɪvələns/ *noun* **1.** being equivalent **2.** a logical operation that is true if all the inputs are the same

COMMENT: Output is 1 if both inputs are 1 or if both are 0; if the two inputs are different, the output is 0.

erasable /ɪˈreɪzəb(ə)l/ *adjective* which can be erased

erasable memory /ɪˌreɪzəb(ə)l ˈmem(ə)ri/ *noun* same as **erasable storage**

erasable read-only memory /ɪ ˌreɪzəb(ə)l ˌriːd ˌəʊnli ˈmem(ə)ri/ *noun* full form of **EROM**

erasable storage /ɪˌreɪzəb(ə)l ˈstɔːrɪdʒ/ *noun* **1.** a storage medium which can be reused **2.** temporary storage ▶ also called **erasable memory**

erase /ɪˈreɪz/ *verb* **1.** to set all the digits in a storage area to zero **2.** to remove any signal from a magnetic medium (NOTE: **erases – erasing – erased**)

eraser /ɪˈreɪzə/ *noun* a device that erases the contents of something, e.g. a device using UV light to erase an EPROM

eraser tool /ɪˈreɪzə tuːl/ *noun* (*in a graphics program*) function that allows areas of an image to be erased, or set to the background colour. Also called **erase**

ERCC *noun* memory which checks and corrects errors. Full form **error checking and correcting**

ergonomics /ˌɜːgəˈnɒmɪks/ *noun* the science of designing software or hardware so that it is comfortable and safe to use

ergonomist /ɜːˈgɒnəmɪst/ *noun* a scientist who studies people at work and tries to improve their working conditions

EROM /ˈiː rɒm/ *noun* full form **erasable read-only memory**. same as **EAROM**

erratum /eˈrɑːtəm/ *noun* a correction on a separate slip of paper to an error or omission from a document (NOTE: The plural is **errata**.)

error /ˈerə/ *noun* a mistake due to a human operator

'...syntax errors, like omitting a bracket, will produce an error message from the compiler' [*Personal Computer World*]

error detection /ˈerə dɪˌtekʃ(ə)n/ *noun* the process of using special hardware or software to detect errors in a data entry or transmission, then usually to ask for retransmission

error detection and correction /ˌerə dɪˌtekʃən ən kəˈrekʃən/ *noun* full form of **EDAC**

error handling /ˈerə ˌhændlɪŋ/ *noun* same as **exception handling**

error logging /ˈerə ˌlɒgɪŋ/ *noun* the process of recording errors that have occurred ○

Features of the program include error logging.

error message /ˈerə ˌmesɪdʒ/ *noun* a report displayed to the user saying that an error has occurred

error rate /ˈerə reɪt/ *noun* **1.** the number of errors that occur within a certain time **2.** the number of corrupt bits of data in relation to the total transmission length

ESC /ɪˈskeɪp/ *noun* **1.** same as **escape code 2.** same as **escape key**

escape code /ɪˈskeɪp kəʊd/ *noun* a transmitted code sequence which informs the receiver that all following characters represent control actions. Also called **ESC**

escape key /ɪˈskeɪp kiː/ *noun* a key on a keyboard which allows the user to enter escape codes to control the computer's basic modes or actions. Also called **ESC, Esc key**

escapement /ɪˈskeɪpmənt/ *noun* a preset vertical movement of a sheet of paper in a printer

Esc key /ɪˈskeɪp kiː/ *noun* same as **escape key**

ESDI *noun* an interface standard between a CPU and peripherals such as disk drives. Full form **enhanced small device interface.** ◊ **SCSI**

ESS *abbr* electronic switching system

establish /ɪˈstæblɪʃ/ *verb* **1.** to discover and prove something ○ *They established which component was faulty.* **2.** to define the use or value of something

establishing shot /ɪˈstæblɪʃɪŋ ʃɒt/ *noun* an atmospheric long shot that establishes the main location of the film or programme and is generally used in the opening scene (*film*)

etch /etʃ/ *verb* to use an acid to remove selected layers of metal from a metal printing plate or printed circuit board

etch type /ˈetʃ taɪp/ *noun* type for printing produced from an etched plate

Ethernet /ˈiːθənet/ *noun* a standard, IEEE 802.3, defining the protocol and signalling method of a local area network

COMMENT: Ethernet has several implementations: 10Base5 is a bus-based topology running over coaxial cable; 10BaseT uses unshielded-twisted-pair cable in a star-based topology; Ethernet normally has a data transmission rate of 10Mbps.

ETV *abbr* educational TV

Euronet™ /ˈjʊərəʊnet/ *noun* a telephone connected network, covering the EC countries, that provides access to each country's scientific and economic information

European Article Number /ˌjʊərə ˌpiːən ˌɑːtɪk(ə)l ˈnʌmbə/ *noun* full form of **EAN**

evaluate /ɪˈvæljueɪt/ *verb* **1.** to calculate a value or a quantity **2.** to test or try or look at a product before buying it

evaluation /ɪˌvæljuˈeɪʃ(ə)n/ *noun* the action of calculating a value or a quantity

evaluation copy /ɪˌvæljuˈeɪʃ(ə)n ˌkɒpi/ *noun* a demonstration version of a software product that allows a user to try the main functions of a software product before buying it

evaluative abstract /ɪˌvæljuətɪv ˈæbstrækt/ *noun* a library abstract that contains details of the value and usefulness of the document

event /ɪˈvent/ *noun* an action or activity

event-driven /ɪˈvent ˌdrɪv(ə)n/ *adjective* referring to a computer program or process in which each step of the execution relies on external actions

'Forthcoming language extensions will include object-oriented features, including classes with full inheritance, as well as event-driven programming.' [*Computing*]

event handler /ɪˈvent ˌhændlə/ *noun* a routine that responds to an event or message within an object-oriented programming environment ○ *If a user clicks the mouse button this generates a message which can be acted upon by the event handler.*

ewallet /ˈiːˌwɒlət/, **e-wallet** /ˈiː ˌwɒlɪt/ *noun* a feature of web browsers that allows a user to store personal details about his or her credit card, bank account or other ways of paying for goods on the Internet

except /ɪkˈsept/ *preposition, conjunction* not including ○ *All the text has been keyboarded, except the last ten pages.*

exception /ɪkˈsepʃən/ *noun* something which is different from all others in the same category

exceptional /ɪkˈsepʃən(ə)l/ *adjective* not usual or different

exception handling /ɪkˈsepʃ(ə)n ˌhændlɪŋ/ *noun* routines and procedures that diagnose and correct errors or minimise the effects of errors, so that a system will run when an error is detected. Also called **error handling, error management**

excess /ɪkˈses/ *noun* too much of something

excessive /ɪkˈsesɪv/ *adjective* too much or too large ○ *The program used an excessive amount of memory to accomplish the job.*

exchange /ɪksˈtʃeɪndʒ/ *noun* the giving of one thing for another ■ *verb* to swap data between two locations (NOTE: **exchanges – exchanging – exchanged**)

exchangeable /ɪksˈtʃeɪndʒəb(ə)l/ *adjective* which can be exchanged

exchangeable disk storage /ɪks ˌtʃeɪndʒəb(ə)l dɪsk 'stɔːrɪdʒ/ *noun* full form of **EDS**

exclamation mark /ˌekskləˈmeɪʃ(ə)n mɑːk/ *noun* a printed or written sign (!), which shows surprise

exclude /ɪk'skluːd/ *verb* to keep out or not to include

excluding /ɪk'skluːdɪŋ/ *preposition* not including

exclusion /ɪk'skluːʒ(ə)n/ *noun* **1.** the act of not including **2.** restriction of access to a system

exclusive /ɪk'skluːsɪv/ *adjective* which excludes

exe /'eksi/ *noun* an extension to a filename which indicates that the file is a program and can be executed directly by the operating system ○ *In DOS, to start a program type in its EXE file name.*

executable file /'eksɪˌkjuːtəb(ə)l faɪl/ *noun* a file that contains a program rather than data

executable form /'eksɪˌkjuːtəb(ə)l fɔːm/ *noun* a program translated or compiled into a machine code form that a processor can execute

execute /'eksɪˌkjuːt/ *verb* to run or carry out a computer program or process (NOTE: **executes – executing – executed**)

execution /ˌeksɪ'kjuːʃ(ə)n/ *noun* the process of carrying out a computer program or process

execution time /ˌeksɪ'kjuːʃ(ə)n ˌtaɪm/ *noun* **1.** the time taken to run or carry out a program or series of instructions **2.** the time taken for one execution cycle

executive information system /ɪg ˌzekjʊtɪv ɪnfə'meɪʃ(ə)n ˌsɪstəm/ *noun* full form of **EIS**

exhaustive search /ɪg'zɔːstɪv sɜːtʃ/ *noun* a search through every record in a database

EXIT /'eksɪt/ *noun* an MS-DOS system command to stop and leave a child process and return to the parent process

expand /ɪk'spænd/ *verb* to make larger ○ *If you want to hold so much data, you will have to expand the disk capacity.*

expandable /ɪk'spændəb(ə)l/ *adjective* which can be expanded

expanded memory /ɪkˌspændɪd 'mem(ə)ri/ *noun* an extra RAM memory fitted to a computer that is located at an address above 1 Mb

expanded memory specification /ɪk ˌspændɪd 'mem(ə)ri ˌspesɪfɪkeɪʃ(ə)n/ *noun* full form of **EMS**

expansion /ɪk'spænʃən/ *noun* an increase in computing power or storage size

expansion board /ɪk'spænʃən bɔːd/ *noun* a printed circuit board connected to a system to increase its functions or performance. Also called **expansion card**

expansion card /ɪk'spænʃ(ə)n kɑːd/ *noun* same as **expansion board**

expansion slot /ɪk'spænʃ(ə)n slɒt/ *noun* a connector inside a computer into which an expansion board can be plugged ○ *Insert the board in the expansion slot.*

expert /'ekspɜːt/ *noun* a person who knows a lot about something ○ *He is a computer expert.*

expert system /'ekspɜːt ˌsɪstəm/ *noun* ➧ **IKBS**

expiration /ˌekspə'reɪʃ(ə)n/ *noun* coming to an end ◇ **expiration date 1.** last date at which photographic film *or* paper can be used with good results **2.** date when a computer file is no longer protected from deletion by the operating system

expire /ɪk'spaɪə/ *verb* to come to an end or to be no longer valid

explicit reference /ɪkˌsplɪsɪt 'ref(ə)rəns/ *noun* (*within a program or script*) a way of identifying a particular object, e.g. a field or button, by a unique name

Explorer™ /ɪk'splɔːrə/ a program supplied with Windows 95 that lets you manage all the files stored on a disk

exponent /ɪk'spəʊnənt/ *noun* a number indicating the power to which a base a number is to be raised

exponentiation /ˌekspəˌnenʃi'eɪʃ(ə)n/ *noun* the raising of a base number to a certain power

export /ɪk'spɔːt/ *verb* to save data in a different file format from the default

expose /ɪk'spəʊz/ *verb* to allow light to reach photographic film or paper to form an image

exposure /ɪk'spəʊʒə/ *noun* the process of letting light fall on a photographic film to form an image

exposure end point /ɪkˌspəʊʒə 'end ˌpɔɪnt/ *noun* the quantity of light required to produce a certain image density

exposure index /ɪk'spəʊʒə ˌɪndeks/ *noun* the sensitivity of a photographic emulsion

exposure latitude /ɪk'spəʊʒə ˌlætɪtjuːd/ *noun* the extent to which film can be over-exposed or under-exposed and still provide a clear picture

exposure meter /ɪk'spəʊʒə ˌmiːtə/ *noun* a device for measuring the light intensity on or reflected by a scene which is to be filmed

express /ɪk'spres/ *verb* to state or to describe ○ *Express the formula in its simplest form.*

expression /ɪk'spreʃ(ə)n/ *noun* **1.** a mathematical formula or relationship **2.** the definition of a value or variable in a program

extend /ɪk'stend/ *verb* to make longer

extended binary coded decimal interchange code /ɪk,stendɪd ,baɪnəri ,kəʊdɪd ,desɪm(ə)l 'ɪntətʃeɪndʒ ,kəʊd/ *noun* full form of **EBCDIC**

extended character set /ɪk,stendɪd 'kærɪktə ,set/ *noun* a set of 128 special characters that includes accents, graphics and symbols

extended data output memory /ɪk ,stendɪd ,deɪtə 'aʊtpʊt ,mem(ə)ri/ *noun* full form of **EDO memory**

extended-definition television /ɪk ,stendɪd ,defɪnɪʃ(ə)n ,telɪ'vɪʒ(ə)n/ *noun* full form of **EDTV**

extended graphics array /ɪk,stendɪd 'græfɪks ə,reɪ/ *noun* full form of **XGA**

extended memory /ɪk,stendɪd 'mem(ə)ri/ *noun* (*in an IBM PC*) the most popular standard method of adding extra memory above 1 Mb which can be used directly by many operating systems or programs

extensible /ɪk'stensɪb(ə)l/ *adjective* which can be extended

extensible hypertext markup language /ɪk,stensɪb(ə)l ,haɪpətekst 'mɑːkʌp ,læŋgwɪdʒ/ *noun* full form of **XHTML**

extensible markup language /ɪk ,stensɪb(ə)l 'mɑːkʌp ,læŋgwɪdʒ/ *noun* full form of **XML**

extension /ɪk'stenʃən/ *noun* the process of making something longer; something added to something else to make it longer

extent /ɪk'stent/ *noun* the number of pages in a printed document, such as a book ○ *By adding the appendix, we will increase the page extent to 256.*

external /ɪk'stɜːn(ə)l/ *adjective* outside a program or device

external device /ɪk,stɜːn(ə)l dɪ'vaɪs/ *noun* **1.** an item of hardware, e.g. a terminal or printer, which is attached to a main computer **2.** any device that allows communications between the computer and itself but which is not directly operated by the main computer

external disk drive /ɪk,stɜːn(ə)l 'dɪsk ,draɪv/ *noun* a device not built into the computer but added to increase its storage capabilities

extra /'ekstrə/ *noun* an item which is additional to a software or hardware package ○ *The mouse and cabling are sold as extras.*

extract /ɪk'strækt/ *verb* to remove required data or information from a database ○ *We can extract the files required for typesetting.*

extranet /'ekstrənet/ *noun* an intranet that has a connection to the public Internet and allows users to gain access via the Internet (NOTE: It is often used to provide access to people in the company who are working away from the office. Most intranets do not allow access via the public Internet and include security measures that protect against hackers and unauthorised users.)

extrapolation /ɪk,stræpə'leɪʃ(ə)n/ *noun* the process of predicting future quantities or trends by the analysis of current and past data

eyeball /'aɪbɔːl/ *noun* a user of the Internet who visits a particular website or uses a particular product (*slang*)

eye candy /'aɪ ,kændi/ *noun* the decorative elements on a computer screen or a web page that are intended to make it attractive to look at (*informal*)

eye-dropper /'aɪ ,drɒpə/ *noun* a tool in a graphics software application that allows a user to click on a pixel in an image and select the colour of the pixel

eye-lighting /'aɪ ,laɪtɪŋ/ *noun* the process of illuminating a close shot in order to produce a small highlight reflection on the actor's eyeball which causes the eye to sparkle (*film*)

eyepiece /'aɪpiːs/ *noun* a camera viewfinder

eyepiece lens /'aɪpiːs lens/ *noun* a lens in the viewfinder of a camera through which the cameraman looks

eye-strain /'aɪ streɪn/ *noun* pain in the eyes, caused by looking at bright lights or at a VDU for too long

> '...to minimize eye-strain, it is vital to have good lighting conditions with this LCD system' [*Personal Computer World*]

e-zine /'iː ziːn/ *noun* a website that models its contents and layout a printed magazine

F

F *symbol* the hexadecimal number equivalent to decimal number 15

face /feɪs/ *noun* same as **typeface**

facility /fə'sɪlɪti/ *noun* **1.** a mechanism or means allowing something to being done, especially easily ○ *We offer facilities for processing a customer's own disks.* (NOTE: The plural is **facilities**.) **2.** a single large building (*US*) ○ *We have opened our new data processing facility.* **3.** a communications path between two or more locations, with no ancillary line equipment

facsimile /fæk'sɪmɪli/ *noun* an exact copy of an original

facsimile character generator /fæk ˌsɪmɪli 'kærɪktə ˌdʒenəreɪtə/ *noun* a means of displaying characters on a computer screen by copying preprogrammed images from memory

facsimile transmission /fæk'sɪmɪlɪ trænzˌmɪʃ(ə)n/ *noun* full form of **fax**

FACT *noun* an organisation that prevents illegal copying of film and TV material (*film*) Full form **Federation Against Copyright Theft**

factor /'fæktə/ *noun* **1.** something which is important or which has an influence on something else **2.** any number in a multiplication that is the operand

factorise /'fæktəraɪz/, **factorize** *verb* to break down a number into two whole numbers which when multiplied will give the original number ○ *When factorised, 15 gives the factors 1, 15* or *3, 5.* (NOTE: **factorises – factorising – factorised**)

factory /'fækt(ə)ri/ *noun* a building where products are manufactured ○ *computer factory*

fade /feɪd/ *verb* (*of a radio or electrical signal*) to become less strong (NOTE: **fades – fading – faded**)

fade in /ˌfeɪd 'ɪn/ *noun* **1.** an image that starts with a blank screen that gradually shows the image **2.** a sound that starts inaudibly and gradually increases in volume

fade out /ˌfeɪd 'aʊt/ *noun* **1.** an image that gradually changes to a blank screen **2.** a sound that gradually decreases in volume until it is inaudible ■ *verb* to decrease in volume gradually

fader /'feɪdə/ *noun* an instrument which brightens or darkens the picture, or decreases or increases the audio levels (*film*)

fader shutter, fading shutter *noun* a shutter with two blades in a film camera; an adjustable opening can be used to vary the exposure for fade or dissolve effects

fading /'feɪdɪŋ/ *noun* **1.** a variation in strength of radio and television broadcast signals **2.** the process of becoming less dark ○ *When fading occurs turn the density dial on the printer to full black.*

fail /feɪl/ *verb* not to do something which should be done ○ *The company failed to carry out routine maintenance of its equipment.*

fail safe system /'feɪl seɪf ˌsɪstəm/ *noun* a system which has a predetermined state it will go to if a main program or device fails, so avoiding the total catastrophe that a complete system shutdown would produce

> 'The DTI is publishing a new code of best practice which covers hardware reliability and fail-safe software systems.' [*Computing*]

failure /'feɪljə/ *noun* the process of breaking down or stopping; not doing something which should be done

failure rate /'feɪljə reɪt/ *noun* the number of occurrences of a particular type of failure within a specified period of time

fall back routines /'fɔːl bæk ruːˌtiːnz/ *plural noun* routines that are called or procedures which are executed by a user when a machine or system has failed

fall-off /'fɔːl ɒf/ *noun* a gradual decrease in brightness from the centre of a screen to the edges (*film*)

FAM *abbr* fast access memory

family /'fæm(ə)li/ *noun* **1.** a range of different designs of a particular typeface **2.** a range of machines from one manufacturer that are compatible with other products in the same line from the same manufacturer

fan /fæn/ *noun* **1.** a mechanism which circulates air for cooling ○ *If the fan fails, the system will rapidly overheat.* **2.** a spread of data items or devices ■ *verb* **1.** to cool a device by blowing air over it **2.** to spread out a series of items or devices

> 'Intel is investigating other options to solve the Pentium system overheating problems, including selling the chip with its own miniature fan.' [*Computing*]

'...a filtered fan maintains positive air pressure within the cabinet, to keep dust and dirt from entering' [*Personal Computer World*]

fanfold /'fænfəʊld/ *noun* same as **accordion fold**

FAQ /fæk, ˌef eɪ 'kjuː/ *noun* a webpage or help file that contains common questions and their answers related to a particular subject

fascia plate /'feɪʃə pleɪt/ *noun* the front panel on a device ○ *The fascia plate on the disk drive of this model is smaller than those on other models.*

fast /fɑːst/ *adjective* **1.** which moves quickly; which works quickly; (storage or peripheral device) that performs its functions very rapidly ○ *fast program execution* **2.** (photographic lens) with a very wide aperture; highly light-sensitive photographic film

fast access memory /ˌfɑːst ˌækses 'mem(ə)ri/ *noun* abbr **FAM**

FAT /ˌef eɪ 'tiː/ *noun* (*in a PC operating system*) a data file stored on disk that contains the names of each file stored on the disk, together with its starting sector position, date and size. Full form **file allocation table**

fatal error /ˌfeɪt(ə)l 'erə/ *noun* a fault in a program or device that causes the system to crash

FatBits /'fætbɪts/ a MacPaint option which allows a user to edit an image one pixel at a time

father file /'fɑːðə faɪl/ *noun* a backup of the previous version of a file. ◊ **grandfather file, son file**

fault /fɔːlt/ *noun* a situation in which something has gone wrong with software or hardware, causing it to malfunction ○ *The technical staff are trying to correct a programming fault.* ◊ **bug, error**

fault detection /'fɔːlt dɪˌtekʃ(ə)n/ *noun* an automatic process which logically or mathematically determines that a fault exists in a circuit

fault diagnosis /'fɔːlt ˌdaɪəgnəʊsɪs/ *noun* a process by which the cause of a fault is located

fault tolerance /'fɔːlt ˌtɒlərəns/ *noun* the ability of a system to continue functioning even when a fault has occurred

fault-tolerant /ˌfɔːlt 'tɒlərənt/ *adjective* referring to a system or device that is able to continue functioning even when a fault occurs ○ *They market a highly successful range of fault-tolerant minis.*

faulty /'fɔːlti/ *adjective* which does not work properly ○ *There must be a faulty piece of equipment in the system.*

'Hampshire fire brigade is investing £2 million in a command and control system based on the new SeriesFT fault-tolerant Unix machine from Motorola.' [*Computing*]

'...before fault-tolerant systems, users had to rely on cold standby fault tolerance is usually associated with a system's reliability' [*Computer News*]

fax /fæks/, **FAX** *noun* a method of sending and receiving images in digital form over a telephone or radio link (*informal*) ○ *We will send a fax of the design plan.* Full form **facsimile transmission**

fax card /'fæks kɑːd/, **fax adapter** /fæks ə'dæptə/, **fax board** /fæks bɔːd/ *noun* an adapter card which plugs into an expansion slot and allows a computer to send or receive fax data

FCB area of memory (used by the operating system) that contains information about the files in use or those stored on a disk drive. Full form **file control block**

FCC (*film*) *abbr US* Federal Communications Commission ■ *noun* in the printing of film, a control cue device based on the electronic counting of the amount of frames moving through the machine. Full form **frame count cueing**

fd, FD *abbr* **1.** full duplex **2.** floppy disk

FDC /ˌef diː 'siː/ *noun* a combination of hardware and software devices that control and manage the read/write operations of a disk drive from a computer. Full form **floppy disk controller**

FDD *abbr* floppy disk drive

FDDI /ˌef diː diː 'aɪ/ *noun* an ANSI standard for high-speed networks which use fibre optic cable in a dual ring topology, transmitting data at 100 Mbps. Full form **fibre distributed data interface**

FDDI II /ˌef diː diː aɪ 'tuː/ *noun* an enhanced ANSI standard for high-speed networks that uses fibre optic cable and transmits data at 100 Mbps but can also allocate part of the bandwidth to a 64 Kbits/second analog channel for audio or video data. Full form **fibre distributed data interface II**

FDISK /'ef dɪsk/ *noun* an MS-DOS system utility that configures the partitions on a hard disk

fdx, FDX *abbr* full duplex

feasibility /ˌfiːzə'bɪlɪti/ *noun* the likelihood that something will or can be done ○ *He has been asked to report on the feasibility of a project.*

feasibility study /ˌfiːzə'bɪlɪti ˌstʌdi/ *noun* an examination and report into the usefulness and cost of a new product that is being considered for purchase

feature /'fiːtʃə/ *noun* a special function or ability or design of hardware or software

feature film /ˈfiːtʃə fɪlm/ *noun* a commercial, full-length film production to be shown in a cinema; usually ninety minutes in length

FED *abbr* field emission display

Federation Against Copyright Theft /ˌfedəˌreɪʃ(ə)n əˌgenst ˌkɒpiˈraɪt θeft/ *noun* full form of **FACT**

FEDS /ˌef iː diː ˈes/ *noun* a magnetic disk storage system that contains some removable disks such as floppy disks and some fixed or hard disk drives. Full form **fixed and exchangeable disk storage**

feed /fiːd/ *noun* a device which puts something such as paper into and through a machine such as a printer or photocopier ■ *verb* to put something such as paper into and through a machine such as a printer or photocopier ○ *This paper should be manually fed into the printer.* (NOTE: **feeding – fed**)

feedback /ˈfiːdbæk/ *noun* **1.** information from one source which can be used to modify something or provide a constructive criticism of something ○ *We are getting customer feedback on the new system.* **2.** part of an output signal that is fed back to the input and amplified

feeder /ˈfiːdə/ *noun* **1.** a channel that carries signals from one point to another **2.** a mechanism that automatically inserts the paper into a printer

feed horn /ˈfiːd hɔːn/ *noun* a microwave channelling device used to direct transmitted signals

feevee /ˌfiː ˈviː/ *noun US* pay cable, form of cable TV where the viewer pays an extra fee for extra channels (*informal*)

feint /feɪnt/ *noun* very light lines on writing paper

female connector /ˌfiːmeɪl kəˈnektə/ *noun* a connector with female sockets

FEP /ˌef iː ˈpiː/ *noun* a processor placed between an input source and the central computer, whose function is to preprocess received data to relieve the workload of the main computer. Full form **front-end processor**

ferric oxide /ˌferɪk ˈɒksaɪd/, **ferrite** /ˈferaɪt/ *noun* iron oxide used as a tape or disk coating that can be magnetised to store data or signals

ferromagnetic /ˌferəʊmægˈnetɪk/ *adjective* (material) that has a high magnetic permeability

FET /ˌef iː ˈtiː/ *noun* an electronic device that can act as a variable current flow control. Full form **field effect transistor** (NOTE: An external signal varies the resistance of the device and current flow by changing the width of a conducting channel by means of a field. It has three terminals: source, gate and drain.)

fibre distributed data interface /ˌfaɪbə dɪˌstrɪbjʊtɪd ˈdeɪtə ˌɪntəfeɪs/ *noun* full form of **FDDI**

fibre distributed data interface II /ˌfaɪbə dɪˌstrɪbjʊtɪd ˌdeɪtə ˌɪntəfeɪs ˈtuː/ *noun* full form of **FDDI II**

fibre Ethernet /ˌfaɪbə ˈiːθənet/ *noun* a high-speed network that uses optical fibre to link one node to another in a point-to-point topology

fibre optic cable /ˌfaɪbə ˌɒptɪk ˈkeɪb(ə)l/, **fibre optic connection** /ˌfaɪbə ˌɒptɪk kəˈnekʃən/ *noun* a bundle of fine strands of glass or plastic protected by a surrounding material, used for transmission of light signals that carry data at very high speeds

fibre optics /ˌfaɪbə ˈɒptɪks/ *plural noun* the use of thin strands of glass or plastic that can transmit light signals at the speed of light (NOTE: The light or laser signal is pulsed or modulated to represent data being transmitted.)

fibre ribbon /ˌfaɪbə ˈrɪbən/ *noun* a fabric-based ribbon used in printers

fidelity /fɪˈdelɪti/ *noun* the ability of an audio system to reproduce sound correctly. ◊ **hi fi**

field /fiːld/ *noun* **1.** an area of force and energy distribution, caused by magnetic or electric energy sources **2.** a section containing particular data items in a record ○ *The employee record has a field for age.* **3.** a section of an image that is available after the light has passed through the camera and lens. Abbr **FED**

field blanking /ˈfiːld ˌblæŋkɪŋ/ *noun* an interval when television signal field synchronizing pulses are transmitted

field effect transistor /fiːld ɪˈfekt trænˈzɪstə/ *noun* full form of **FET**

field emission display /ˌfiːld ɪˈmɪʃ(ə)n dɪˌspleɪ/ *noun* **1.** a method of producing thin, flat displays for laptop computers in which a miniature colour CRT is located at each pixel point. Abbr **FED** **2.** a method of building up a picture on a television screen

field engineer /ˌfiːld ˌendʒɪˈnɪə/ *noun* an engineer who does not work at one single company, but travels between customers carrying out maintenance on their computers

field fly back /ˌfiːld ˈflaɪ ˌbæk/ *noun* the return of electron beam to the top left hand corner of a screen

field frequency /ˈfiːld ˌfriːkwənsi/ *noun* the number of field scans per second

field label /ˈfiːld ˌleɪb(ə)l/ *noun* a series of characters used to identify a field or its location. Also called **field name**

field length /ˈfiːld leŋθ/ *noun* the number of characters that a field can contain

field marker /ˈfiːld ˌmɑːkə/ *noun* a code used to indicate the end of one field and the start of the next. Also called **field separator**

field name /ˈfiːld neɪm/ *noun* same as **field label**

field programmable device /ˌfiːld ˌprəʊɡræməb(ə)l dɪˈvaɪs/ *noun* same as **PLA**

field programming /ˈfiːld ˌprəʊɡræmɪŋ/ *noun* the writing of data into a PROM

field separator /ˈfiːld ˌsepəreɪtə/ *noun* same as **field marker**

field strength /ˈfiːld streŋθ/ *noun* the amplitude of the magnetic or electric field at one point in that field

field sweep /ˈfiːld swiːp/ *noun* a vertical electron beam movement over a television screen

field sync pulse /ˌfiːld ˈsɪŋk ˌpʌls/ *noun* a pulse in a TV signal that makes sure that the receiver's field sweep is in sync

FIF /ˌef aɪ ˈef/ *noun* a file format used to store graphics images which have been highly compressed using fractals. Full form **fractal image format**

FIFO /ˈfaɪfəʊ/ *noun* a storage read/write method in which the first item stored is the first read. Full form **first in first out**

fifth generation computer /ˌfɪfθ ˌdʒenəreɪʃ(ə)n kəmˈpjuːtə/ *noun* a computer belonging to the next stage of computer system design using fast VLSI circuits and powerful programming languages to allow human interaction

figure /ˈfɪɡə/ *noun* **1.** a printed number **2.** a printed line illustration in a book ○ *See figure 10 for a chart of ASCII codes.*

file /faɪl/ *noun* **1.** documents kept for reference **2.** a section of data on a computer, e.g. payroll, address list or customer accounts, in the form of individual records which may contain data, characters, digits or graphics

'The first problem was solved by configuring a Windows swap file, which I hadn't done before because my 4Mb 486 had never been overloaded.' [*Computing*]

'...the lost file, while inaccessible without a file-recovery utility, remains on disk until new information writes over it' [*Publish*]

file allocation table /ˌfaɪl ˌæləˈkeɪʃ(ə)n ˌteɪb(ə)l/ *noun* full form of **FAT**

file attribute /ˈfaɪl ˌætrɪbjuːt/ *plural noun* a set of data stored with each file which controls particular functions or aspects of the file such as read-only, archived or system file

file deletion /ˈfaɪl dɪˌliːʃ(ə)n/ *noun* the process of erasing a file from storage

file format /ˈfaɪl ˌfɔːmæt/ *noun* a way in which data is stored in a file

file management /ˈfaɪl ˌmænɪdʒmənt/, **file management system** /ˈfaɪl ˌmænɪdʒmənt ˌsɪstəm/ *noun* a section of a DOS that allocates disk space to files, keeping track of the sections and their sector addresses

file manager /ˈfaɪl ˌmænɪdʒə/ *noun* a section of a disk operating system that allocates disk space to files, keeping track of the file sections if it has to be split and their sector addresses

filename /ˈfaɪlneɪm/ *noun* a unique identification code allocated to a program

'...when the filename is entered at the prompt, the operating system looks in the file and executes any instructions stored there' [*PC User*]

filename extension /ˈfaɪlneɪm ɪk ˌstenʃ(ə)n/ *noun* an additional three-character name that is used together with a filename, indicating the type or use of the file

file-recovery utility /ˌfaɪl rɪˈkʌv(ə)ri juː ˌtɪlɪti/ *noun* a piece of software which allows files that have been accidentally deleted or damaged to be read again ○ *A lost file cannot be found without a file-recovery utility.*

file security /ˈfaɪl sɪˌkjʊərɪti/ *noun* hardware or software organisation of a computer system to protect users' files from unauthorised access

file server /ˈfaɪl ˌsɜːvə/ *noun* a computer connected to a network which runs a network operating system software to manage user accounts, file sharing and printer sharing

file sharing /ˈfaɪl ˌʃeərɪŋ/ *noun* a facility allowing one file to be used by two or more users or programs in a network, often using file locking

file storage /ˈfaɪl ˌstɔːrɪdʒ/ *noun* a physical means of preserving data in a file, e.g. a disk drive

file structure /ˈfaɪl ˌstrʌktʃə/ *noun* a way in which a data file is organised

file transfer /ˈfaɪl ˌtrænsfɜː/ *noun* the process of moving a file from one area of memory to another or to another storage device or between computers

file transfer protocol /ˌfaɪl ˈtrænsfɜː ˌprəʊtəkɒl/ *noun* full form of **FTP**

file type /ˈfaɪl taɪp/ *noun* a method of classifying what a file contains ○ *Files with the extension exe are file types that contain program code.*

file update /ˈfaɪl ˌʌpdeɪt/ *noun* **1.** the recent changes or transactions to a file **2.** a new version of software which is sent to users of an existing version

file validation /ˈfaɪl ˌvælɪdeɪʃ(ə)n/ *noun* the process of checking that a file is correct

filing /ˈfaɪlɪŋ/ *noun* **1.** the process of putting documents in order **2.** documents which have to be put in order

filing system /ˈfaɪlɪŋ ˌsɪstəm/ *noun* **1.** a way of putting documents in order for reference **2.** a piece of software which organises files

fill /fɪl/ *verb* **1.** to make something full ○ *The screen was filled with flickering images.* **2.** to put characters into gaps in a field so that there are no spaces left **3.** to draw an enclosed area in one colour or shading

fill light /ˈfɪl laɪt/, **filler** /ˈfɪlə/, **fill-in light** /fɪl ɪn laɪt/ *noun* an additional studio lamp used to provide extra light in shadows (*film*)

film /fɪlm/ *noun* **1.** a transparent strip of plastic, coated with a light-sensitive compound and used to produce photographs with the aid of a camera **2.** a projection at high speed of a series of still images that creates the impression of movement ■ *verb* to expose a photographic film to light by means of a camera, and so to produce images ◇ **film advance 1.** lever on a camera used to wind on a roll of film to the next frame **2.** the distance a phototypesetting machine has to move prior to the next line to be set

film assembly /ˈfɪlm əˌsembli/ *noun* the correct arrangement of photographs or negatives prior to the production of a printing plate

film base /ˈfɪlm beɪs/ *noun* thin transparent roll of plastic used as a supporting material for photographic film

film chain /ˈfɪlm tʃeɪn/ *noun* all the necessary equipment needed when showing film or slides on television, such as a projector, TV camera and synchroniser

film gate /ˈfɪlm geɪt/ *noun* the alliance of the aperture and pressure plates in a camera or a projector to guide the film through, and to also ensure the correct focal distance between the film and the lens

film gauge /ˈfɪlm geɪdʒ/ *noun* the diameter of different types of cinematographic film

filming /ˈfɪlmɪŋ/ *noun* the shooting of a cinema film or TV film ○ *Filming will start next week if the weather is fine.*

film optical scanning device for input into computers /ˌfɪlm ˌɒptɪk(ə)l ˌskænɪŋ dɪˌvaɪs fə ˌɪnpʊt ˌɪntə kəm ˈpjuːtəz/ *noun* full form of **FOSDIC**

film pickup /ˈfɪlm ˌpɪkʌp/ *noun* the transmission of a motion picture film by television by electronically scanning each frame

film projector /ˈslaɪd prəˌdʒektə/, **slide projector** *noun* a mechanical device that displays films or slides on a screen

film recorder /ˈfɪlm rɪˌkɔːdə/ *noun* a device that produces a 35 mm slide from a computer image (NOTE: A film recorder can produce slides at very high resolution, normally around 3,000 lines, by regenerating the image on an internal screen.)

filmsetting /ˈfɪlmˌsetɪŋ/ *noun* the process of photocomposition

film speed /ˈfɪlm spiːd/ *noun* the light sensitivity of photographic film, as determined by ASA or DIN

film strip /ˈfɪlm strɪp/ *noun* a set of related images on a reel of film, usually for educational purposes

filter /ˈfɪltə/ *noun* **1.** an electronic circuit that allows certain frequencies to pass while stopping others **2.** an option in a software application that allows it to import or export a particular foreign file type ○ *Most graphics packages have import filters that will decode TIFF, BMP and PCX file formats.* **3.** optical coloured glass, which stops certain frequencies of light **4.** a pattern of binary digits used to select various bits from a binary word. A one in the filter retains that bit in the source word. ■ *verb* **1.** to remove unwanted elements from a signal or file **2.** to select various bits from a word ○ *Filter the top three bits of the video attribute word.* **3.** to select various records from a database file ○ *We filtered the data to select those customers based in New York.*

final /ˈfaɪn(ə)l/ *adjective* last or coming at the end of a period ○ *to keyboard the final data files*

final cut /ˈfaɪn(ə)l kʌt/ *noun* (*film*) **1.** the original negative when it has been altered to conform with the workprint **2.** the final version of the edited film on which the sound track can now be placed

final trial composite /ˌfaɪn(ə)l ˌtraɪəl ˈkɒmpəzɪt/ *noun* a film containing audio and visual effects; this is the final and approved version of all former trial composites (*film*)

find /faɪnd/ *verb* to get something back which has been lost ○ *It took a lot of time to find the faulty chip.* ■ *noun* a command to locate a piece of information

find and replace /ˌfaɪnd ən rɪˈpleɪs/ *noun* a feature on a word-processor that allows certain words or sections of text to be located and replaced with others

Finder /ˈfaɪndə/ a trade name for a graphical user interface to an Apple Mac allowing a user to view files and folders and start applications using a mouse

fine /faɪn/ *adjective* excellent or of very high quality

fine-tune /ˌfaɪn ˈtjuːn/ *verb* to adjust by small amounts the features or parameters of hardware or software to improve performance ○ *Fine-tuning improved the speed by ten per cent.*

finger /ˈfɪŋɡə/ *noun* a software program on the Internet that will retrieve information about a user based on his or her email address

finish /ˈfɪnɪʃ/ *noun* **1.** the final appearance of something ○ *The product has an attractive finish.* **2.** the end of a process or function ■ *verb* **1.** to do something or to make something completely ○ *The order was finished in time.* **2.** to come to an end ○ *The contract is due to finish next month.*

finished /ˈfɪnɪʃt/ *adjective* which has been completed

firewall /ˈfaɪəwɔːl/ *noun* a hardware or software security system between a server or intranet and the public Internet that allows information to pass out to the Internet but checks any incoming data before passing it on to the private server ○ *We have installed a firewall in our intranet to prevent hackers accessing company data via the Internet link.*

Firewire /ˈfaɪəwaɪə/ a trade name for a high-speed serial interface developed by the Apple Computer Corporation and used to link devices such as a digital camera with the computer. ◊ **USB**

firmware /ˈfɜːmweə/ *noun* a computer program or data that is permanently stored in a hardware memory chip, e.g. a ROM or EPROM. Compare **hardware, software**

first generation computer /ˌfɜːst ˌdʒenəreɪʃ(ə)n kəmˈpjuːtə/ *noun* an original computer made with valve-based electronic technology, started around 1951

first generation image /ˌfɜːst ˌdʒenəreɪʃ(ə)n ˈɪmɪdʒ/ *noun* a master copy of an original image, text or document

first grip /ˌfɜːst ˈɡrɪp/ *noun* on a film set, the principal stagehand who is responsible for the other stagehands (*film*) Also called **key grip**

first in first out /ˌfɜːst ɪn ˌfɜːst ˈaʊt/ *noun* full form of **FIFO**

first party release /ˌfɜːst ˌpɑːti rɪˈliːs/ *noun* the ending of a telephone connection as soon as either party puts his phone down or disconnects his modem

fisheye lens /ˌfɪʃeɪ ˈlenz/ *noun* an extremely wide angle photographic lens that has a field of view of 180 degrees and produces a distorted circular image

fit /fɪt/ *verb* to plot or calculate a curve that most closely approximates a number of points or data (NOTE: fitting – fitted)

fix /fɪks/ *verb* **1.** to make something permanent or to attach something permanently ○ *The computer is fixed to the workstation.* **2.** to mend ○ *The technicians are trying to fix the switchboard.*

fixed and exchangeable disk storage /ˌfɪkst ən ɪksˌtʃeɪndʒəb(ə)l ˈdɪsk ˌstɔːrɪdʒ/ *noun* full form of **FEDS**

fixed disk /ˌfɪkst ˈdɪsk/ *noun* a magnetic disk which cannot be removed from the disk drive

fixed-frequency monitor /ˌfɪkst ˌfriːkwənsi ˈmɒnɪtə/ *noun* a monitor that can only accept one frequency and type of video signal

flag /flæɡ/ *noun* **1.** a way of showing the end of field or of indicating something special in a database ○ *If the result is zero, the zero flag is set.* **2.** a method of reporting the status of a register after a mathematical or logical operation **3.** a square or rectangular opaque sheet which is used to stop light from the camera lens hitting places where it is not needed on the set ■ *verb* to attract the attention of a program while it is running to provide a result, report an action or indicate something special (NOTE: flagging – flagged)

flagging /ˈflæɡɪŋ/ *noun* **1.** the process of putting an indicator against an item so that it can be found later **2.** distortion in a television picture which is created by timing mistakes in a video tape recorder's playback signal

flame /fleɪm/ *verb* send a rude or angry Internet message to a user (NOTE: flames – flaming – flamed)

flare /fleə/ *noun* **1.** an error in which dispersion of light in a lens undesirably brightens the dark areas of an image **2.** areas of film that have been exposed to light on account of the camera not being fully light proof

flared /fleəd/ *adjective* image with unwanted bright spots or lines due to internal lens or camera reflections

flash /flæʃ/ *verb* to switch a light on and off

flashing /ˈflæʃɪŋ/ *noun* a signal sent over a telephone line to get the attention of an operator or user

flash ROM /ˈflæʃ rɒm/ *noun* an electronic memory component that contains data that can normally only be read, but that does allow new data to be stored in the memory using a special electrical signal

flat /flæt/ *adjective* **1.** smooth (surface) **2.** fixed or not changing **3.** lacking contrast (in an image or photograph)

flatbed /ˈflætˌbed/ *adjective* referring to a printing or scanning machine that holds the paper or image on a flat surface while processing ○ *Scanners are either flatbed models or platen type, paper-fed models.*

flatbed scanner /ˌflætbed ˈskænə/ *noun* a device with a flat sheet of glass on which artwork is placed and a scan head that moves below the glass and converts the image into a graphics file

flat file /'flæt faɪl/ *noun* a two-dimensional file of data items

flat file database /ˌflæt faɪl 'deɪtəbeɪs/ *noun* a database program that can only access data stored in one file at a time, not allowing relational data

flat screen /'flæt skriːn/ *noun* a display monitor that has been manufactured with a flat, square-edged front to the monitor

flex /fleks/ *noun* a wire or cable used to connect an appliance to the mains electricity supply (NOTE: no plural: for one item, say **a piece of flex**)

flexibility /ˌfleksɪ'bɪlɪti/ *noun* the ability of hardware or software to adapt to various conditions or tasks

flexible /'fleksɪb(ə)l/ *adjective* which can be altered or changed

flexible machining system /ˌfleksɪb(ə)l mə'ʃiːnɪŋ ˌsɪstəm/ *noun* full form of **FMS 1**

flexible manufacturing system /ˌfleksɪb(ə)l ˌmænjʊ'fæktʃərɪŋ ˌsɪstəm/ *noun* full form of **FMS 2**

flicker /'flɪkə/ *noun* **1.** a computer graphic image whose brightness varies rapidly at a visible rate because of a low image refresh rate or signal corruption **2.** a random variation of brightness in a television picture **3.** an effect that occurs when a frame from a videodisc is frozen and two different pictures are displayed alternately at high speed due to the incorrect field matching **4.** a very short interruption in a film which is caused by a fault in the film projector or by a slow film projector ■ *verb* **1.** to move very slightly ○ *The image flickers when the printer is switched on.* **2.** to vary in brightness rapidly and visibly because of a low image refresh rate or signal corruption

flicker-free /'flɪkə friː/ *adjective* referring to a display that does not flicker

'A CRT (cathode ray tube) monitor paints the screen from top to bottom, and is usually considered 'flicker free' if it refreshes the image 75 times a second, or more' [*The Guardian*]

flier /'flaɪə/ *noun* a small advertising leaflet designed to encourage customers to ask for more information about a product or service

flight simulator /'flaɪt ˌsɪmjʊleɪtə/ *noun* a computer program which allows a user to pilot a plane, showing a realistic control panel and moving scenes, used either as a training programme or a computer game

flip-flop /'flɪp flɒp/ *noun* an electronic circuit or chip whose output can be one of two states determined by one or two inputs, and which can be used to store one bit of digital data. Abbr **FF**

float /fləʊt/ *noun* (*film*) **1.** the slow shake of an image up and down due to faulty synchronisation **2.** overlapping images in multiple exposure rostrum camera work **3.** part of a studio set which can easily be moved into or out of position

floating /'fləʊtɪŋ/ *adjective* referring to a character which is separate from the character it should be attached to

floating point notation /ˌfləʊtɪŋ pɔɪnt nəʊ'teɪʃ(ə)n/ *noun* a numerical notation in which a fractional number is represented with a point after the first digit and a power, so that any number can be stored in a standard form

floating point unit /ˌfləʊtɪŋ pɔɪnt 'juːnɪt/ *noun* a specialised CPU that can process floating point numbers very rapidly ○ *The floating point unit speeds up the processing of the graphics software.* Abbr **FPU**. Also called **floating point processor**

floating window /ˌfləʊtɪŋ 'wɪndəʊ/ *noun* a window that can be moved anywhere on screen

flood /flʌd/, **floodlight** /'flʌdlaɪt/ *noun* a lamp which gives a wide range of light (*film*)

flooding /'flʌdɪŋ/ *noun* a rapid, reliable but not very efficient means of routing packet-switched data, in which each node sends the data received to each of its neighbours

flood track /'flʌd træk/ *noun* the sound track on a photographic film which is not used for sound and reveals the standard maximum width of a picture area (*film*)

floppy disk /ˌflɒpi 'dɪsk/, **floppy** /'flɒpi/ *noun* a secondary storage device in the form of a flat, circular flexible disk onto which data can be stored in a magnetic form. Abbr **FD** (NOTE: The plural of **floppy** is **floppies**.)

COMMENT: Floppy disks are available in various sizes: the commonest are 3.5 inch, 5.25 inch and 8 inch. The size refers to the diameter of the disk inside the sleeve.

floppy disk controller /ˌflɒpi 'dɪsk kənˌtrəʊlə/ *noun* full form of **FDC**

floppy disk drive /ˌflɒpi 'dɪsk ˌdraɪv/ *noun* a disk drive for floppy disks. Abbr **FDD**. Also called **floppy disk unit**

flow /fləʊ/ *noun* a regular movement ○ *Automatic text flow across pages.* ■ *verb* to move smoothly ○ *Work is flowing normally again after the breakdown of the printer.*

flowchart /'fləʊtʃɑːt/ *noun* a diagram showing the arrangement of various work processes as a series of stages

flow control /'fləʊ kənˌtrəʊl/ *noun* management of the flow of data into queues and buffers, to prevent heavy traffic

flow text /ˌfləʊ 'tekst/ *verb* to insert text into a page format in a DTP system (NOTE:

The text fills all the space around pictures, and between set margins.)

fluctuate /ˈflʌktʃueɪt/ *verb* to move up and down ○ *The electric current fluctuates between 1 Amp and 1.3 Amp.*

fluctuating /ˈflʌktjʊeɪtɪŋ/ *adjective* moving up and down ○ *fluctuating signal strength*

fluctuation /ˌflʌktʃuˈeɪʃ(ə)n/ *noun* an up and down movement ○ *Voltage fluctuations can affect the functioning of the computer system.*

fluid head /ˈfluːɪd hed/ *noun* a camera head for a tripod which possesses smooth pan and tilt facilities (*film*)

flush /flʌʃ/ *verb* to clear or erase all the contents of a queue, buffer, file or section of memory ■ *adjective* level or in line with something

fluting /ˈfluːtɪŋ/ *noun* twisting and bending of film edges created by humidity or by winding the film too tightly around a spool (*film*)

flutter /ˈflʌtə/ *noun* the occurrence of fluctuations of tape speed due to mechanical or circuit problems, causing signal distortion ○ *Wow and flutter and common faults on cheap tape recorders.*

flux /flʌks/ *noun* **1.** a measure of magnetic field strength **2.** the amount of reflected light from an object

flux density /ˈflʌks ˌdensəti/ *noun* the intensity of a magnetic flux

fly /flaɪ/ *verb* to move (through the air)

flyback /ˈflaɪbæk/ *noun* an electron picture beam return from the end of a scan to the beginning of the next. Also called **line flyback**

FM *verb* a method of changing the frequency of one signal according to another. Full form **frequency modulation**

COMMENT: FM is often used as a method of representing data through changes in the frequency of a signal (the carrier), and as a method of carrying data over fibre-optic or telephone cables (e.g. many modem standards use FM to transmit data).

FMS /ˌef em ˈes/ *noun* **1.** CNC or control of a machine by a computer. Full form **flexible machining system** **2.** the use of CNC machines, robots and other automated devices in manufacturing. Full form **flexible manufacturing system**

FM synthesiser /ˌef em ˈsɪnθəˌsaɪzə/ *noun* a device or other means for creating sounds by combining base signals of different frequencies (NOTE: Sound cards using an FM synthesiser create sounds of a piano, drum or guitar by combining different frequencies at different levels to recreate the complex sound of a musical instrument.)

FNP *abbr* front-end processor

f-number /ˈef ˌnʌmbə/ *noun* a measurement of the amount of light that an optical lens can collect, measured as the ratio of focal length to maximum aperture

FO *abbr* fibre optics

focal length /ˌfəʊk(ə)l ˈleŋθ/ *noun* the distance between the centre of an optical lens and the focusing plane, when the lens is focused at infinity

focal plane /ˈfəʊk(ə)l pleɪn/ *noun* a plane through the main focus of a camera lens which is at right angles to its optical axis (*film*)

focus /ˈfəʊkəs/ *noun* **1.** a particular window or field that is currently ready to accept a user's command ○ *In Windows, the object that currently has the user's focus has a dotted line around it.* **2.** an image or beam that is clear and well defined ■ *verb* **1.** to adjust a monitor so that the image that is displayed on the screen is sharp and clear **2.** to adjust the focal length of a lens or beam deflection system so that the image or beam is clear and well defined ○ *The camera is focused on the foreground.* ○ *They adjusted the lens position so that the beam focused correctly.*

fog /fɒg/ *noun* an effect on photographic material which has been accidentally exposed to unwanted light, causing a loss of picture contrast

fog filter /ˈfɒg ˌfɪltə/ *noun* a filter placed in front of the camera lens that diffuses the light to produce a softer image; also used to create the impression of fog (*film*)

fogging /ˈfɒgɪŋ/ *noun* a graphic effect that is used to simulate atmospheric fog or haze, used to make a three-dimensional scene more realistic. Also called **haze**

folder /ˈfəʊldə/ *noun* a group of files stored together under a name. ◊ **directory**

folding machine /ˌfəʊldɪŋ məˈʃiːn/ *noun* a machine which automatically folds sheets of paper

folio /ˈfəʊliəʊ/ *noun* a page with a number, especially two facing pages in an account book which have the same number

follow focus /ˌfɒləʊ ˈfəʊkəs/ *verb* to keep an object in focus even if it is moving away from the camera (*film*)

follow spot /ˈfɒləʊ spɒt/ *noun* a very strong spotlight which follows a performer (*film*)

font /fɒnt/ *noun* a set of characters all of the same style, size and typeface. Also called **fount**

'Word Assistant is designed to help wordprocessing users produce better- looking documents. It has style templates and forms providing 25 TrueType fonts, 100 clip-art images and two font utility programs.' [*Computing*]

'...laser printers store fonts in several ways: as resident, cartridge and downloadable fonts' [*Desktop Publishing Today*]

foobar /ˈfuːbɑː/ *noun* a term used by programmers to refer to whatever is being discussed ○ *If a programmer is explaining how a graphic program works, he might refer to an example graphic file that stores the image as 'foobar.gif' – it does not really exist but is just an example.*

foolscap /ˈfuːlskæp/ *noun* a large size of writing paper, longer than A4 (NOTE: no plural) □ **a foolscap envelope** large envelope which takes foolscap paper

foot /fʊt/ *noun* **1.** the bottom part of something ○ *He signed his name at the foot of the letter.* **2.** a measurement of length (= 30cm) ○ *The table is six feet long.* ○ *My office is ten feet by twelve.* **3.** a measurement of length of film which represents a certain number of frames, e.g.: one foot contains 72 frames for Super 8, 40 for 16mm and 16 for 35mm (*film*) (NOTE: The plural is **feet** for (a) and (c). There is no plural for (b). In measurements, **foot** is usually written **ft** or ' after figures: **10ft; 10'**.)

footage /ˈfʊtɪdʒ/ *noun* a measurement of film length in metres or feet (*film*)

footer /ˈfʊtə/, **footing** /ˈfʊtɪŋ/ *noun* a message at the bottom of all the pages in a printed document, e.g. the page number

footnote /ˈfʊtˌnəʊt/ *noun* a note at the bottom of a page, referring to the text above it, usually using a superior number as a reference

footprint /ˈfʊtˌprɪnt/ *noun* **1.** the area covered by a transmitting device such as a satellite or antenna **2.** the area that a computer takes up on a desk

'...signals from satellites in orbit 36,000km above the earth don't care very much whether you are close to an exchange or not....as long as you have a dish within their footprint.' [*The Guardian*]

force /fɔːs/ *noun* strength ■ *verb* to make someone do something ○ *Competition has forced the company to lower its prices.*

forced page break /ˌfɔːst ˈpeɪdʒ ˌbreɪk/ *noun* an embedded code which indicates a new page start

foreground /ˈfɔːgraʊnd/ *noun* **1.** the front part of an illustration, as opposed to the background **2.** a high-priority task done by a computer **3.** the area in a shot which is closest to the camera **4.** an image displayed in front of another image in a video clip. For example, Windows Movie Player displays an object in a high score channel in front of an object in a low score channel. Compare **background**

'This brighter – but still anti-glare – type of screen is especially useful for people using colourful graphic applications, where both the background and foreground are visually important.' [*Computing*]

foreground colour /ˌfɔːgraʊnd ˈkʌlə/ *noun* the colour of characters and text displayed on a screen

foreground mode /ˈfɔːgraʊnd məʊd/ *plural noun* in a computer system in which two modes for program execution are possible, the mode that is for interactive user programs. Compare **background mode**

forelengthen /fɔːˈleŋθən/ *noun* to create an illusion of depth by using a wide angle lens on a camera

foreshorten /fɔːˈʃɔːtən/ *verb* to create an illusion that all objects are very close together by using a long (telephoto) lens on a camera

forest /ˈfɒrɪst/ *noun* a number of interconnected data structure trees

fork /fɔːk/ *noun* (*in an Apple Mac*) a folder that contains system files and information about a file or application

form /fɔːm/ *noun* **1.** a preprinted document with blank spaces where information can be entered ○ *It's been easy to train the operators to use the new software since its display looks like the existing printed forms.* **2.** a graphical display that looks like an existing printed form and is used to enter data into a database **3.** a page of computer stationery **4.** a complete plate or block of type, ready for printing ■ *verb* to create a shape; to construct ○ *The system is formed of five separate modules.*

format /ˈfɔːmæt/ *noun* **1.** a specific method of arranging text or data **2.** the precise syntax of instructions and arguments **3.** the size and shape of a book ○ *The printer can deal with all formats up to quarto.* **4.** the way of arranging a TV programme ■ *verb* to arrange text as it will appear in printed form on paper ○ *Style sheets are used to format documents.*

'As an increasing amount of information within businesses is generated in wordprocessed format, text retrieval tools are becoming a highly attractive pragmatic solution.' [*Computing*]

formatter /ˈfɔːmætə/ *noun* a piece of hardware or software that arranges text or data according to certain rules

formula /ˈfɔːmjʊlə/ *noun* a set of mathematical rules applied to solve a problem (NOTE: The plural is **formulae**.)

formula translator /ˈfɔːmjələ trænsˌleɪtə/ *noun* full form of **FORTRAN**

FORTH /fɔːθ/ *noun* a programming language mainly used in control applications

FORTRAN /ˈfɔːtræn/ *noun* a programming language developed in the first place for scientific use. Full form **formula translator**

forty-track disk /ˌfɔːti træk ˈdɪsk/ *noun* a floppy disk formatted to contain forty tracks of data

forum /ˈfɔːrəm/ *noun* an Internet discussion group for people who share a special interest in something

forward /ˈfɔːwəd/ *adjective* moving in advance or in front ■ *verb* to send an email message that you have received on to another user ○ *I did not know the answer to the question, so I have forwarded your message to my colleague.*

for your information /fə ˌjɔːr ˌɪnfə ˈmeɪʃ(ə)n/ *noun* full form of **FYI**

FOSDIC /ˌef əʊ es diː aɪ ˈsiː/ *noun* a storage device for computer data using microfilm. Full form **film optical scanning device for input into computers**

fount /fɒnt/ *noun* same as **font**

fourcc /ˌfɔː siː ˈsiː/, **four-character code** /ˌfɔː ˌkærɪktə ˈkəʊd/ *noun* a method of identifying the type of data within a RIFF file

4GL *abbr* fourth generation language

Fourier series /ˈfʊriə ˌsɪəriːz/ *noun* a mathematical representation of waveforms by a combination of fundamental and harmonic components of a frequency

fourth generation computer /ˌfɔːθ ˌdʒenəreɪʃ(ə)n kəmˈpjuːtə/ *noun* a computer using technology using LSI circuits, developed around 1970 and still in current use

fourth generation language /ˌfɔːθ ˌdʒenəreɪʃ(ə)n ˈlæŋgwɪdʒ/ *noun* a computer language that is user-friendly and has been designed with the nonexpert in mind. Abbr **4GL**

four-track recorder /ˌfɔː træk rɪˈkɔːdə/ *noun* a tape recorder that is able to record and play back four independent audio tracks at once

FP *abbr* front projection (*film*)

fps *noun* **1.** the number of individual frames of a video sequence that can be displayed each second to give the impression of movement. Full form **frames per second**. ◊ **MPEG 2.** the speed of single frames of a motion picture through a projector or camera every second **3.** the number of television picture frames transmitted per second

COMMENT: To give the impression of smooth continuous video (also called full-motion video), a computer needs to display at least 25 separate frames each second. If the frames are small, there is less data to update; however if the frame is large – e.g. filling a large window – then the computer has to update the hundreds of thousands of pixels that make up each image 25 times per second. To do this needs a fast graphics adapter or special video display hardware

FPU *abbr* floating point unit

FQDN /ˌef kjuː diː ˈen/ *noun* a complete domain name that can be used to identify a server as well as the host, e.g. bloomsbury.com. Full form **fully qualified domain name**

fractal /ˈfrækt(ə)l/ *noun* a geometric shape that repeats itself within itself and always appears the same, however much you magnify the image

fractal compression /ˌfrækt(ə)l kəm ˈpreʃ(ə)n/ *noun* a technique used to compress images

fractal image format /ˌfrækt(ə)l ˈɪmɪdʒ ˌfɔːmæt/ *noun* full form of **FIF**

fraction /ˈfrækʃən/ *noun* **1.** a part of a whole unit, expressed as one figure above another, e.g. 1/4, 1/2, or a figure after a decimal point, e.g. 25. **2.** a mantissa of a floating point number. Also called **fractional part**

fragment /ˈfrægmənt/ *noun* a piece of information that has had to be split up into several smaller units of information before being sent over the Internet. The receiver will re-assemble these units into the correct order.

fragmentation /ˌfrægmənˈteɪʃ(ə)n/ *noun* **1.** (*in main memory*) memory allocation to a number of files, which has resulted in many small, free sections or fragments that are too small to be of any use, but waste a lot of space **2.** (*on a disk drive*) a situation with files stored scattered across non-contiguous sectors on a hard disk

COMMENT: When a file is saved to disk, it is not always saved in adjacent sectors. This will increase the retrieval time. Defragmentation moves files back into adjacent sectors so that the read head does not have to move far across the disk, so it increases performance.

frame /freɪm/ *noun* **1.** a space on magnetic tape for one character code **2.** a packet of transmitted data including control and route information **3.** (*in animation, film or video*) one single image within a sequence of different images that together show movement or animation. Each frame is normally slightly different from the previous one to give the impression of movement. **4.** (*in an HTML webpage*) a set of commands that allow the main window of a browser to be split into separate sections, each of which can be scrolled independently. This allows lots of information to be presented clearly. ◊ **HTML**

5. (*in communications*) a standard unit of information that contains a header with the destination address and sender's address followed by the information and a trailer that contains error detection information **6.** a movable, resizable box that holds text or an image **7.** one screen of data **8.** one individual shot in a film or the area it occupies in the camera lens **9.** one complete image displayed on a television screen (in the US this is made up of 525 lines, in the UK it is 625 lines)

frame-based animation /ˌfreɪm beɪsd ˌænɪˈmeɪʃ(ə)n/ *noun* a series of screens displayed in quick succession, each one slightly different, that gives the impression of movement

frame buffer /ˈfreɪm ˌbʌfə/ *noun* a section of memory used to store an image before it is displayed on screen

frame grabber /ˈfreɪm ˌgræbə/ *noun* a high speed digital sampling circuit that stores a TV picture in memory so that it can then be processed by a computer. Also called **grabber**

'...the frame grabber is distinguished by its ability to acquire a TV image in a single frame interval' [*Electronics & Wireless World*]

frame index /ˈfreɪm ˌɪndeks/ *noun* a counter used by the Microsoft Movie Player software that identifies the current frame of the video

frames per second /ˌfreɪmz pə ˈsekənd/ *noun* full form of **fps**

framework /ˈfreɪmwɜːk/ *noun* the basic structure of a database, process or program ○ *The program framework was designed first.*

framing /ˈfreɪmɪŋ/ *noun* **1.** the positioning of a camera's field of view for a required image **2.** the synchronisation of time division multiplexed frames of data

framing bit /ˈfreɪmɪŋ bɪt/ *noun* a sync bit or transmitted bit used to synchronise devices

framing code /ˈfreɪmɪŋ kəʊd/ *noun* a method of synchronizing a receiver with a broadcast teletext stream of data

free /friː/ *adjective* available for use or not currently being used ■ *verb* to erase, remove or back up programs or files to provide space in memory

freedom /ˈfriːdəm/ *noun* being free to do something without restriction

freedom of information /ˌfriːdəm əv ɪnfəˈmeɪʃ(ə)n/ *noun* the opportunity and ability to examine computer records, either(referring to government activities or about individuals)

freeware /ˈfriːweə/ *noun* software that is in the public domain and can be used by anyone without having to pay

freeze /friːz/ *verb* same as **hang.** ◆ **crash**

freeze frame /ˈfriːz freɪm/ *noun* a video sequence stopped so that only one frame is displayed

frequency /ˈfriːkwənsi/ *noun* a number of cycles or periods of a regular waveform that are repeated per second (NOTE: The plural is **frequencies**.)

frequency equaliser /ˈfriːkwənsi ˌiːkwəlaɪzə/ *noun* a device that changes the amplitude of various frequency components of a signal according to preset values

frequency modulation /ˌfriːkwənsi mɒdjuˈleɪʃ(ə)n/ *noun* full form of **FM**

frequent /ˈfriːkwənt/ *adjective* which comes or goes or takes place often

frequently /ˈfriːkwəntli/ *adverb* often

frequently asked questions /ˌfriːkwənt(ə)li ɑːskd ˈkwestʃənz/ *plural noun* common questions and their answers relating to a particular subject that are contained in a document ○ *The website has a section for FAQ about the new disk drive.* Abbr **FAQ**

friction feed /ˈfrɪkʃ(ə)n fiːd/ *noun* a printer mechanism where the paper is advanced by holding it between two rollers (as opposed to tractor feed)

friendly front end /ˌfrendli ˌfrʌnt ˈend/ *noun* the design of the display of a program that is easy to use and understand

front /frʌnt/ *noun* part of something which faces away from the back ○ *The disks are inserted in slots in the front of the terminal.*

front end /ˌfrʌnt ˈend/ *adjective* **1.** located at the start or most important point of a circuit or network **2.** the visible part of an application that is seen by a user and is used to view and work with information ○ *The program is very easy to use thanks to the uncomplicated front-end.*

front-end processor /ˌfrʌnt end ˈprəʊsesə/ *noun* full form of **FEP**

FSAA *abbr* full scene anti-aliasing

FSK *abbr* frequency shift keying

FTP /ˌef tiː ˈpiː/ *noun* an TCP/IP standard for transferring files between computers; it is a file sharing protocol that operates at layers 5, 6 and 7 of an OSI model network. Full form **file transfer protocol**

full /fʊl/ *adjective* **1.** with as much inside as possible ○ *The disk is full, so the material will have to be stored on another disk.* **2.** complete or including everything

'...transmitter and receiver can be operated independently, making full duplex communication possible' [*Electronics & Power*]

full adder /ˌfʊl ˈædə/ *noun* a binary addition circuit which can produce the sum of two inputs, and can also accept a carry input, producing a carry output if necessary

full duplex /ˌfʊl ˈdjuːpleks/ *noun* data transmission down a channel in two directions simultaneously. Abbr **fd, FD, fdx**

full-motion video /ˌfʊl ˌməʊʃ(ə)n ˈvɪdiəʊ/ *noun* ➧ **fps**

full-motion video adapter /ˌfʊl ˌməʊʃ(ə)n ˈvɪdiəʊ əˌdæptə/ *noun* a computer fitted with a digitising card that is fast enough to capture and display moving video images, at a rate of 25 or 30 frames per second

full scene anti-aliasing /ˌfʊl siːn ˌænti ˈeɪliəsɪŋ/ *noun* a method of anti-aliasing a complete frame of a video or animation rather than just one object, which requires powerful graphics hardware. Abbr **FSAA**

full-screen /ˌfʊl ˈskriːn/ *adjective* referring to a program display that uses all the available screen, and is not displayed within a window

fully /ˈfʊli/ *adverb* completely

fully qualified domain name /ˌfʊli ˌkwɒlɪfaɪd dəʊˈmeɪn ˌneɪm/ *noun* full form of **FQDN**

function /ˈfʌŋkʃən/ *noun* **1.** a mathematical formula in which a result is dependent upon several other numbers **2.** a sequence of computer program instructions in a main program that perform a certain task **3.** a special feature available on a computer or word-processor ○ *The word-processor had a spell-ing-checker function but no built-in text-editing function.* ■ *verb* to operate or perform correctly ○ *The new system has not functioned properly since it was installed.*

functional /ˈfʌŋkʃən(ə)l/ *adjective* which refers to the way something works

functional diagram /ˌfʌŋkʃ(ə)nəl ˈdaɪəgræm/ *noun* a drawing of the internal workings and processes of a machine or piece of software

functional specification /ˌfʌŋkʃ(ə)nəl ˌspesɪfɪˈkeɪʃ(ə)n/ *noun* a specification which defines the results which a program is expected to produce

function key /ˈfʌŋkʃən kiː/ *noun* one of several special keys placed along the top of a PC keyboard that have different uses according to different applications ○ *Tags can be allocated to function keys.*

COMMENT: Function keys often form a separate group of keys on the keyboard, and have specific functions attached to them. They may be labelled F1, F2, and so on. Most applications use the F1 key to display help information and Alt-F4 to quit an application

fuse /fjuːz/ *noun* an electrical protection device consisting of a small piece of metal, which will melt when too much power passes through it

fusion /ˈfjuːʒ(ə)n/ *noun* the process of combining two hardware devices or programs or chemical substances to create a single form

fuzzy logic /ˌfʌzi ˈlɒdʒɪk/, **fuzzy theory** /ˌfʌzi ˈθɪəri/ *noun* a type of logic applied to computer programming, which tries to replicate the reasoning methods of the human brain

FYI /ˌef waɪ ˈaɪ/ *noun* a document file that contains general background information related to the Internet or the TCP/IP protocols. Full form **for your information**. ◊ **RFC** (NOTE: Specific technical information is normally contained in RFC documents.)

G

G *abbr* giga-

COMMENT: In computing G refers to 2^{30}, equal to 1,073,741,824.

gain /geɪn/ *noun* **1.** an increase or enlargement **2.** an amount by which a signal amplitude is changed as it passes through a circuit, usually given as a ratio of output to input amplitude. Opposite **attenuation**

galactic noise /gə'læktɪk nɔɪz/ *noun* random electrical noise which originates from planets and stars in space

galley proofs /'gæli pruːfs/ *plural noun* proofs in the form of long pieces of text, not divided into pages, printed on long pieces of paper

game /geɪm/ *noun* something which is played for enjoyment or relaxation

game console /'geɪm ˌkɒnsəʊl/ *noun* a dedicated computer that is used primarily to play games, designed to connect to a television set rather than a monitor and usually controlled using a gamepad rather than a keyboard and mouse. Also called **games console**

gamepad /'geɪmpæd/ *noun* a device held in the hand to control a computer game

game port /'geɪm pɔːt/ *noun* a connection that allows a joystick to be plugged into a computer

gamma /'gæmə/ *noun* **1.** a unit of magnetic intensity **2.** a measurement of the degree of contrast in a television picture. For television cameras and receivers, the measurement is found from the input and output voltage and the light input or output. **3.** a measure of the contrast of a film emulsion

ganged /gæŋd/ *adjective* referring to mechanically linked devices that are operated by a single action

gap /gæp/ *noun* **1.** a space between recorded data **2.** a space between a read head and the magnetic medium **3.** a method of radio communications using a carrier signal that is switched on and off, as in a telegraphic system

garbage /'gɑːbɪdʒ/ *noun* **1.** a radio interference from adjacent channels **2.** data or information that is no longer required because it is out of date or contains errors

garbage in garbage out /ˌgɑːbɪdʒ ɪn ˌgɑːbɪdʒ 'aʊt/ *noun* full form of **GIGO**

gas discharge display /ˌgæs dɪs ˌtʃɑːdʒ dɪ'spleɪ/, **gas plasma display** /ˌgæs ˌplæzmə dɪ'spleɪ/ *noun* a flat, lightweight display screen that is made of two flat pieces of glass covered with a grid of conductors, separated by a thin layer of a gas which luminesces when one point of the grid is selected by two electric signals. Also called **plasma display**

COMMENT: Mainly used in modern portable computer displays, but the definition is not as good as in cathode ray tube displays.

gate /geɪt/ *noun* **1.** a logical electronic switch whose output depends on the states of the inputs and the type of logical function implemented **2.** a mechanical film or slide frame aligner in a camera or projector **3.** the aperture in which the frame is exposed or projected

gateway /'geɪtweɪ/ *noun* **1.** a device that links two dissimilar networks ○ *We use a gateway to link the LAN to WAN.* **2.** a software protocol translation device that allows users working in one network to access another **3.** a piece of software that allows email messages to be sent via a different route or to another network ○ *To send messages by fax instead of across the network, you'll need to install a fax gateway.*

gateway page /'geɪtweɪ peɪdʒ/ *noun* the first webpage that a visitor to a website sees and the one that contains the key words and phrases that enable a search engine to find it

gauge /geɪdʒ/ *noun* **1.** a device which measures thickness or width **2.** a film or tape diameter, usually described in millimetres ■ *verb* to measure the thickness or width of something

gauss /gaʊs/ *noun* a unit of magnetic induction

gauze /gɔːz/ *noun* a material which is transparent or translucent and is used for special effects (*film*)

Gb *abbr* gigabit

GB *abbr* gigabyte

GDI *abbr* graphics device interface

gel /dʒel/ *noun* a translucent sheet of coloured plastic used to alter the colour characteristics of the source of light (*film*)

gelatin filter /'dʒel ˌfɪltə/, **gel filter** *noun* a sheet of coloured gelatin which is used with a camera to alter the colour of the source light (*film*)

gender changer /'dʒendə ˌtʃeɪndʒə/ *noun* a device for changing a female connection to a male or vice versa (*informal*)

general /'dʒen(ə)rəl/ *adjective* **1.** ordinary or not special **2.** dealing with everything

general packet radio service /ˌdʒen(ə)rəl ˌpækɪt 'reɪdiəʊ ˌsɜːvɪs/ *noun* full form of **GPRS**

general protection fault /ˌdʒen(ə)rəl prə'tekʃən ˌfɔːlt/ *noun* full form of **GPF**

general purpose interface bus /ˌdʒen(ə)rəl ˌpɜːpəs 'ɪntəfeɪs ˌbʌs/ *noun* full form of **GPIB**

generate /'dʒenəˌreɪt/ *verb* to use software or a device to produce codes or a program automatically ○ *to generate an image from digitally recorded data*

generation /ˌdʒenə'reɪʃ(ə)n/ *noun* **1.** the process of producing data or software or programs using a computer ○ *The computer is used in the generation of graphic images.* **2.** the state or age of the technology used in the design of a system **3.** the distance between a file and the original version, used when making backups ○ *The father file is a first generation backup.*

generation loss /ˌdʒenə'reɪʃ(ə)n lɒs/ *noun* degradation of signal quality with each successive recording of a video or audio signal

generator /'dʒenəˌreɪtə/ *noun* a device which generates electricity ○ *The computer centre has its own independent generator, in case of mains power failure.*

generator lock /'dʒenəˌreɪtə lɒk/ *noun* a device that synchronises the timing signals of two video signals from different sources so that they can be successfully combined or mixed. Also called **genlock** (NOTE: It is often used to synchronise the output of a computer's display adapter with an external video source when using the computer to create overlays or titling.)

generic /dʒə'nerɪk/ *adjective* that is compatible with a whole family of hardware or software devices from one manufacturer

genlock /'dʒenlɒk/ *noun* same as **generator lock**

genuine /'dʒenjuɪn/ *adjective* real or correct ○ *Authentication allows the system to recognise that a sender's message is genuine.*

geometric distortion /ˌdʒiːəˌmetrɪk dɪ'stɔːʃ(ə)n/ *noun* linear distortion of a television picture, which can be caused by video tape speed fluctuations

geometry processing /dʒiː'ɒmətri ˌprəʊsesɪŋ/ *noun* a process required to calculate the x, y and z coordinates of a three-dimensional object that is to be displayed on screen ○ *Geometry processing is usually carried out by the CPU* or *by a specialised graphics processor.*

geostationary orbit /ˌdʒiːəʊsteɪʃ(ə)n(ə)ri 'ɔːbɪt/ *noun* a satellite which moves at the same velocity as the earth, so remains above the same area of the earth's surface, and appears stationary when viewed from earth

geostationary satellite /ˌdʒiːəʊ ˌsteɪʃn(ə)ri ˌsætə'laɪt/ *noun* a satellite which moves at the same velocity as the earth, so remains above the same area of the earth's surface, and appears stationary when viewed from the earth

geotargeting /ˌdʒiːəʊ'tɑːgɪtɪŋ/ *noun* a method of analysing what a visitor to your website is viewing or doing and deducing his or her location, then displaying custom content or advertisements accordingly ○ *If a website visitor searches for the weather in Seattle, the intelligent geotargeting software displays banner advertisements from taxi companies in Seattle.*

germanium /dʒɪ'reɪniəm/ *noun* a semiconductor material, used as a substrate in some transistors instead of silicon

get /get/ *noun* an instruction to obtain a record from a file or database

GET method /'get ˌmeθəd/ *noun* (*in HTML for CGI access*) a method of transferring information between a webpage, which uses the HTML form GET command, and a server-based application

ghost /gəʊst/ *noun* **1.** a menu item displayed in grey and not currently available **2.** an effect on a television image in which a weaker copy of the picture is displayed to one side of the main image, caused by signal reflections

ghosting /'gəʊstɪŋ/ *noun* hazy double images appearing in a picture (*film*)

GHz *abbr* gigahertz

GIF /gɪf/ a trade name for a graphics file format of a file containing a bit-mapped image. Full form **graphics interface format**

GIF file /ˌdʒiː aɪ 'ef faɪl/ *noun* graphics file format of a file containing a bit-mapped image

giga- /gɪgə/ *prefix* one thousand million. Abbr **G**

COMMENT: In computing giga refers to 2^{30}, which is equal to 1,073,741,824.

gigabit /'gɪgəbɪt/ *noun* a unit of capacity of a computer local area network, equal to one megabyte of computer information or 1,073,741,824 bits. Abbr **Gb**

gigabyte /'gɪgəbaɪt/ *noun* 10^9 bytes. Abbr **GB**

gigaflop /ˈɡɪɡəflɒp/ *noun* one thousand million floating-point operations per second

gigahertz /ˈɡɪɡəhɜːts/ *noun* a frequency of one thousand million cycles per second. Abbr **GHz**

GIGO /ˈɡaɪɡəʊ/ *noun* the principle that the accuracy and quality of information that is output depends on the quality of the input. Full form **garbage in garbage out**

COMMENT: GIGO is sometimes taken to mean 'garbage in gospel out': i.e. that whatever wrong information is put into a computer, people will always believe that the output results are true.

GINO /ˌdʒiː aɪ en ˈəʊ/ *noun* a graphical control routine written in FORTRAN. Full form **graphical input output**

GKS /ˌdʒiː keɪ ˈes/ *noun* a standard for software command and functions describing graphical input/output to provide the same functions, etc. on any type of hardware. Full form **graphics kernel system**

glare /ɡleə/ *noun* very bright light reflections, especially on a VDU screen ○ *The glare from the screen makes my eyes hurt.*

glitch /ɡlɪtʃ/ *noun* anything which causes the sudden unexpected failure of a computer or equipment (*informal*)

'The programmer was upgrading a verification system at Visa's UK data centre when his work triggered a software glitch causing hundreds of valid cards to be rejected for several hours.' [*Computing*]

global /ˈɡləʊb(ə)l/ *adjective* covering everything

'In an attempt to bring order to an electronic Tower of Babel, pharmaceutical giant Rhone-Poulenc has assembled an X.400-based global messaging network and a patchwork directory system that will be used until a single email system is deployed worldwide.' [*Computing*]

global backup /ˌɡləʊb(ə)l ˈbækʌp/ *noun* **1.** a backup of all data stored on all nodes or workstations connected to a network **2.** a backup of all files on a hard disk or file server

global system for mobile communications /ˌɡləʊb(ə)l ˌsɪstəm fə ˌməʊbaɪl kəˌmjuːnɪˈkeɪʃ(ə)nz/ *noun* full form of **GSM**

glossy /ˈɡlɒsi/ *adjective* shiny (paper) ○ *The illustrations are printed on glossy art paper.* ■ *noun* □ **the glossies** expensive magazines (*informal*)

GND /ˌdʒiː en ˈdiː/ *abbr* ground

go ahead /ˌɡəʊ əˈhed/ *noun* a signal to indicate that a receiver or device is ready to accept information

goal /ɡəʊl/ *noun* **1.** an aim or what you are trying to do **2.** the final state reached when a task has been finished or has produced satisfactory results

gobo /ˈɡəʊbəʊ/ *noun* a moveable opaque shield which is used to hide light between a lamp and a camera lens (*film*)

gold contact /ˌɡəʊld ˈkɒntækt/ *noun* an electrical contact, usually for low-level signals, that is coated with gold to reduce the electrical resistance

golf-ball /ˈɡɒlf bɔːl/ *noun* a metal ball with characters on its surface, which produces printed characters by striking a ribbon onto paper

Google /ˈɡuːɡ(ə)l/ a trade name for a popular search engine

GOSIP /ˈɡɒsɪp/ *noun* a set of standards defined by the US Government to ensure that computers and communications systems can interact. Full form **Government Open Systems Interconnect Profile**

GOSUB /ˈɡəʊsʌb/ *noun* a programming command which executes a routine then returns to the following instruction

GOTO /ˈɡəʊtuː/ *noun* a programming command which instructs a jump to another point or routine in the program ○ *GOTO 105 instructs a jump to line 105.*

COMMENT: GOTO statements are frowned upon by software experts since their use discourages set, structured programming techniques.

go to black /ˌɡəʊ tə ˈblæk/ *verb* to fade gradually from an image to a dark or empty screen

Gouraud shading /ˈɡuːrəʊ ˌʃeɪdɪŋ/ *noun* shading within a three-dimensional scene created by a mathematical equation that is applied to each side of each object and produces a gradual change in colour to give the impression of light and shade

Government Open Systems Interconnect Profile /ˌɡʌv(ə)nmənt ˌəʊpən ˌsɪstəm ˈɪntəkənekt ˌprəʊfaɪl/ *noun* full form of **GOSIP**

GPF /ˌdʒiː piː ˈef/ *noun* an error condition that occurs in Microsoft Windows and causes an application to crash, usually caused by insufficient memory, by using an incompatible peripheral or device driver or by an error in a software program. Full form **general protection fault**

GPIB /ˌdʒiː piː aɪ ˈbiː/ *noun* a standard for an interface bus between a computer and laboratory equipment. Full form **general purpose interface bus**

GPRS /ˌdʒiː piː ɑː ˈes/ *noun* a standard system for wireless radio and mobile telephone communications that is due to replace the existing GSM system. Full form **general packet radio service** (NOTE: GPRS supports high-speed data transfer rates of up to

150Kbps compared to the GSM limit of 9.6Kbps.)

grab /græb/ *verb* to take something and hold it

'...sometimes a program can grab all the available memory, even if it is not going to use it' [*Byte*]

grabber /'græbə/ *noun* same as **frame grabber**

graceful degradation /ˌgreɪsf(ə)l ˌdegrə'deɪʃ(ə)n/ *noun* the process of allowing some parts of a system to continue to function after a part has broken down

grade /greɪd/ *noun* a level or rank ○ *a top-grade computer expert*

grading /'greɪdɪŋ/ *noun* **1.** the process of choosing the colour and density printing values needed for each scene on a negative **2.** (*in the editing of videotapes*) the process of matching colour balance between shots

graduated /'grædʒueɪtɪd/ *adjective* which has a scale or measurements marked on it

graduated filter /ˌgrædʒueɪtɪd 'fɪltə/ *noun* a coloured filter which has a colour on edge and gradually fades into a clear filter on the other side of the filter (*film*)

grain /greɪn/ *noun* the molecular make-up of film emulsion. Fine grain film has very small particles that provide a very sharp, clear image.

graininess /'greɪnɪnəs/ *noun* a collection of visible silver particles which create a granular effect on a film's picture; the more visible the particles are, the grainier the picture

grammage /'græmɪdʒ/ *noun* the weight of paper, calculated as grams per square metre (NOTE: usually shown as **gsm**: *80 gsm paper*)

grammar /'græmə/ *noun* a set of rules for the correct use of a language

grammar checker /'græmə ˌtʃekə/ *noun* a software utility used to check a document or letter to make sure it is grammatically correct

grammatical error /grəˌmætɪk(ə)l 'erə/ *noun* an incorrect use of a computer programming language syntax

grandfather file /'grænfɑːðə faɪl/ *noun* the third most recent version of a backed up file, after father and son files

granularity /ˌgrænjʊ'lærɪti/ *noun* the size of memory segments in a virtual memory system

graph /grɑːf/ *noun* a diagram showing the relationship between two or more variables as a line or series of points

graphic /'græfɪk/ *adjective* referring to representation of information in the form of pictures or plots instead of by text

graphical /'græfɪkl/ *adjective* referring to something represented by graphics

graphical input output /ˌgræfɪkl ˌɪnpʊt 'aʊtpʊt/ *noun* full form of **GINO**

graphically /'græfɪkli/ *adverb* by using pictures ○ *The sales figures are graphically represented as a pie chart.*

graphical user interface /ˌgræfɪkl 'juːzə ˌɪntəfeɪs/ *noun* full form of **GUI**

graphic data /'græfɪk ˌdeɪtə/ *noun* stored data that represents graphical information when displayed on a screen

graphic display /'græfɪk dɪˌpleɪ/ *noun* a computer screen able to present graphical information

graphic display resolution /'græfɪk dɪˌspleɪ ˌrezəluːʃ(ə)n/ *noun* the number of pixels that a computer is able to display on the screen

graphic language /'græfɪk ˌlæŋgwɪdʒ/ *noun* a computer programming language with inbuilt commands that are useful when displaying graphics

graphic object /ˌgræfɪk 'ɒbdʒekt/ *noun* a small graphic image imported from another drawing application and placed on a page (NOTE: In most DTP, paint or drawing packages, the object can be moved, sized and positioned independently from the other elements on the page.)

graphics /'græfɪks/ *noun* pictures or lines which can be drawn on paper or on a screen to represent information ○ *graphics output such as bar charts, pie charts, line drawings, etc.*

graphics accelerator /'græfɪks əkˌseləreɪtə/ *noun* a card that fits inside a computer and uses a dedicated processor chip to speed up the action of drawing lines and images on the screen

graphics adapter /'græfɪks əˌdæptə/ *noun* an electronic device, usually on an expansion card, in a computer that converts software commands into electrical signals that display graphics on a connected monitor ○ *The new graphics adapter is capable of displaying higher resolution graphics.*

graphics character /'græfɪks ˌkærɪktə/ *noun* a preprogrammed shape that can be displayed on a non-graphical screen instead of a character, used extensively in videotext systems to display simple pictures

graphics coprocessor /'græfɪks kəʊˌprəʊsesə/ *noun* same as **graphics processor**

graphics file /'græfɪks faɪl/ *noun* a binary file which contains data describing an image ○ *There are many standards for graphics files including TIFF, IMG and EPS.*

graphics file format /'græfɪks faɪl ˌfɔːmæt/ *noun* a method in which data describing an image is stored

graphics interface format /ˌgræfɪks 'ɪntəfeɪs ˌfɔːmæt/ *noun* full form of **GIF**

graphics kernel system /ˌgræfɪks 'kɜːn(ə)l ˌsɪstəm/ *noun* full form of **GKS**

graphics library /'græfɪks ˌlaɪbr(ə)ri/ *noun* a number of routines stored in a library file that can be added to any user program to simplify the task of writing graphics programs

graphics light pen /ˌgræfɪks 'laɪt ˌpen/ *noun* a high-accuracy light pen used for drawing onto a graphics display screen

graphics mode /'græfɪks məʊd/ *noun* a videotext terminal whose displayed characters are taken from a range of graphics characters instead of text

graphics overlay card /ˌgræfɪks 'əʊvəleɪ ˌkɑːd/ *noun* an expansion card for a PC or Apple Mac that combines generated text or images with an external video source

graphics pad /'græfɪks pæd/ *noun* same as **graphics tablet**

graphics primitive /ˌgræfɪks 'prɪmɪtɪv/ *noun* a basic shape such as an arc, line or filled square that is used to create other shapes or objects

graphics printer /'græfɪks ˌprɪntə/ *noun* a printer capable of printing bit-mapped images

graphics processor /'græfɪks ˌprəʊsesə/ *noun* a secondary processor used to speed up the display of graphics ○ *This graphics adapter has a graphics coprocessor fitted and is much faster.* Also called **graphics coprocessor** (NOTE: It calculates the position of pixels that form a line or shape and display graphic lines or shapes.)

graphics software /'græfɪks ˌsɒftweə/ *noun* prewritten routines which perform standard graphics commands such as line drawing and plotting that can be called from within a program to simplify program writing

graphics tablet /'græfɪks ˌtæblət/ *noun* a flat device which allows a user to input graphical information into a computer by drawing on its surface ○ *It is much easier to draw accurately with a graphics tablet than with a mouse.* Also called **graphics pad**

graphics terminal /'græfɪks ˌtɜːmɪn(ə)l/ *noun* a special terminal with a high-resolution graphic display and graphics tablet or other input device

graphics VDU /ˌgræfɪks ˌviː diː 'juː/ *noun* a special VDU which can display high-resolution or colour graphics as well as text

gray scale /'greɪ skeɪl/ *noun US* another spelling of **grey scale**

greeked /griːkd/ *adjective* (*in a DTP program*) referring to a font with a point size too small to display accurately, shown as a line rather than individual characters

Green Book /ˌgriːn 'bʊk/ *noun* a formal specification for CD-i standard published by Philips

gremlin /'gremlɪn/ *noun* an unexplained fault in a system (*informal*)

grey scale /'greɪ skeɪl/ *noun* **1.** the shades of grey used to measure the correct exposure when filming **2.** the shades which are produced from displaying what should be colour information on a monochrome monitor (NOTE: The US spelling is **gray scale**.)

grid /grɪd/ *noun* a system of numbered squares used to help when drawing

grip /grɪp/ *verb* to hold something tightly ○ *In friction feed, the paper is gripped by the rollers.*

ground /graʊnd/ *noun* an electrical circuit connection to earth or to a point with a zero voltage level. Abbr **GND** (NOTE: **ground** is more common in US English; the British English is **earth**)

ground glass /ˌgraʊnd 'glɑːs/ *noun* a translucent sheet of glass (which has been etched on one side) on which an image is seen in a film camera's viewfinder (*film*)

group /gruːp/ *noun* **1.** a set of computer records containing related information **2.** a six-character word used in telegraphic communications **3.** (*in a GUI*) a collection of icons, of files or programs displayed together in a window ○ *All the icons in this group are to do with painting.* **4.** (*in a network*) a collection of users conveniently identified by one name ○ *The group ACCOUNTS contains all the users who work in the accounts department.* **5.** a collection of objects that can be moved or resized as a single object; (in a GUI) collection of icons of files or programs displayed together in a window ○ *All the icons in this group are to do with painting.* **6.** a single communications channel made up from a number of others that have been multiplexed together ■ *verb* to bring several things together

groupware /'gruːpweə/ *noun* software specially written to be used by a group of people connected to a network and help them carry out a particular task (NOTE: It provides useful functions such as a diary or email that can be accessed by all users.)

gsm, g/m² *noun* a way of showing the weight of paper used in printing ○ *The book is printed on 70 gsm coated paper.* Full form **grams per square metre (per sheet**

GSM /ˌdʒiː es 'em/ *noun* a popular system used for wireless cellular telephone communications throughout Europe, Asia and parts of North America. Full form **global system for mobile communications**. ◊ **GPRS**

COMMENT: The GSM system allows eight calls to share the same radio frequency and carries the digital data that represents voice signals transmitted by each user's telephone. The main drawback of GSM is that it does not offer very fast data transfer rates which has become more important as users want to access the Internet and read email via a mobile telephone connection. GSM provides data transfer at up to 9.6Kbps, but it is due to be replaced by the GPRS system that can support high-speed data transfer at up to 150Kbps.

guarantee /ˌgærən'tiː/ *noun* a legal document promising that a machine will work properly or that an item is of good quality ○ *The system is still under guarantee and will be repaired free of charge.*

guard band /'gɑːd bænd/ *noun* **1.** a section of magnetic tape between two channels recorded on the same tape **2.** the frequency gap between two communication bands to prevent data corruption due to interference between each other

guarding /'gɑːdɪŋ/ *noun* the process of joining a single sheet to a book or magazine

GUI /'guːi/ *noun* an interface between an operating system or program and the user that uses graphics or icons to represent functions or files and allow the software to be controlled more easily. Full form **graphical user interface**. Compare **command line interface**

COMMENT: GUIs normally use a combination of windows, icons, and a mouse to control the operating system. In many GUIs, such as Microsoft Windows and the Apple Mac System, you can control all the functions of the operating system just using the mouse. Icons represent programs and files; instead of entering the file name, you select it by moving a pointer with a mouse.

guide bar /'gaɪd bɑː/ *noun* a special line in a bar code that shows either the start or the finish of the code ○ *The standard guide bars are two thin lines that are a little longer than the coding lines.*

guide path /'gaɪd pɑːθ/ *noun* in audio and video recorders, the posts and mechanical guides that ensure that the tape follows the correct path (*film*)

guide track /'gaɪd træk/ *noun* a sound track of low quality which is recorded with the picture only as a guide for post synchronisation (*film*)

guillotine /'gɪlətiːn/ *noun* an office machine for cutting paper

gulp /gʌlp/ *noun* a group of words, usually two bytes. ◊ **byte, nybble**

gun /gʌn/ *noun* same as **electron gun**

gun microphone /ˌgʌn 'maɪkrəfəʊn/ *noun* a highly directional microphone, also called a rifle microphone, often mounted on a rifle stock that allows it to be easily aimed at the source of the sound (*film*)

gutter /'gʌtə/ *noun* (*in a DTP system*) a blank space or inner margin between two facing pages

G/V *noun* the process of establishing a film or video shot (*film*) Full form **general view**

H

hack /hæk/ *verb* **1.** to experiment and explore computer software and hardware **2.** to break into a computer system for criminal purposes

hacker /ˈhækə/ *noun* a person who hacks

'The two were also charged with offences under the Computer Misuse Act and found guilty of the very actions upon which every hacker is intent.' [*Computing*]

hair in the gate /ˌheər ɪn ðə ˈgeɪt/ *noun* hair-shaped particles visible on the edge of film images after the development process (*film*)

hairline rule /ˈheəlaɪn ruːl/ *noun* (*in a DTP system*) a very thin line

halation /həˈleɪʃ(ə)n/ *noun* a photographic effect seen as a dark region with a very bright surround, caused by pointing the camera into the light

half /hɑːf/ *noun* one of two equal parts ○ *Half the data was lost in transmission.*

half duplex /ˌhɑːf ˈdjuːpleks/ *noun* full form of **HD**

half-intensity /ˌhɑːf ɪnˈtensɪti/ *adjective* referring to a character or graphics display at half the usual display brightness

halftone /ˈhɑːftəʊn/ *adjective* **1.** continuous shading of a printed area **2.** grey shade half way between white and black ■ *noun* a photograph or image that originally had continuous tones, displayed or printed by a computer using groups of dots to represent the tones

halide /ˈheɪlaɪd/ *noun* a silver compound that is used to provide a light-sensitive coating on photographic film and paper

Hall effect /ˈhɔːl ɪˌfekt/ *noun* a description of the effect of a magnetic field on electron flow

halo /ˈheɪləʊ/ *noun* a photographic effect seen as a dark region with a very bright line around it, caused by pointing the camera into the light

halt /hɔːlt/ *noun* a computer instruction to stop a CPU carrying out any further instructions until restarted, or until the program is restarted, usually by external means, e.g. a reset button ■ *verb* to stop ○ *Hitting CTRL S will halt the program.*

Hamming code /ˈhæmɪŋ kəʊd/ *noun* a coding system that uses check bits and checksums to detect and correct errors in transmitted data, mainly used in teletext systems

hand-held /ˈhænd held/ *adjective* which can be held in the hand

'A year ago the hand-held computer business resembled that of PCs a decade ago, with a large number of incompatible models, often software incompatible and using proprietary displays, operating systems and storage media.' [*Computing*]

hand-held computer /ˌhænd held kəmˈpjuːtə/, **hand-held programmable** /ˌhænd held ˈprəʊgræməb(ə)l/ *noun* a very small computer which can be held in the hand, useful for basic information input, when a terminal is not available

hand-held scanner /ˌhænd held ˈskænə/ *noun* a device that is held in your hand and contains a row of photo-electric cells which, when moved over an image, convert it into data which can be manipulated by a computer

H & J /ˌeɪtʃ ənd ˈdʒeɪ/ *noun* the process of justifying lines to a set width, splitting the long words correctly at the end of each line. Full form **hyphenation and justification**

handle /ˈhænd(ə)l/ *noun* **1.** (*in programming*) number used to identify an active file within the program that is accessing the file **2.** (*in a GUI*) a small square displayed that can be dragged to change the shape of a window or graphical object ○ *To stretch the box in the DTP program, select it once to display the handles then drag one handle to change its shape.*

handler /ˈhændlə/ *noun* a part of an operating system software or a special software routine which controls a device or function ○ *The scanner handler routines are supplied on disk.* ◊ **driver**

hand off /ˈhænd ɒf/ *noun* the process of passing control of a communications channel from one transmitter to another

handset /ˈhændset/ *noun* a telephone receiver, with both microphone and loudspeaker. ◊ **acoustic coupler**

handshake /ˈhæn(d)ˌʃeɪk/, **handshaking** *noun* a set of standardised signals between two devices to make sure that the system is working correctly, the equipment is compatible and data transfer is correct (NOTE: Signals would include ready to receive, ready to transmit and data OK.)

handwriting /ˈhændraɪtɪŋ/ *noun* words written by hand ○ *the new PDA has excellent handwriting recognition*

handwriting recognition /ˈhændraɪtɪŋ ˌrekəgnɪʃ(ə)n/ *noun* software that is capable of recognising handwritten text and converting it into ASCII characters ○ *The new PDA has excellent handwriting recognition.*

handwritten /ˌhændˈrɪt(ə)n/ *adjective* written by hand, using a pen or pencil, not typed ○ *The author sent in two hundred pages of handwritten manuscript.*

'...all acquisition, data reduction, processing, and memory circuitry is contained in the single hand-held unit' [*Byte*]

'A year ago the hand-held computer business resembled that of PCs a decade ago, with a large number of incompatible models, often software incompatible and using proprietary displays, operating systems and storage media' [*Computing*]

'...if a line is free, the device waits another 400ms before reserving the line with a quick handshake process' [*Practical Computing*]

handy talkies /ˌhændi ˈtɔːkis/ *plural noun* full form of **HT**

hang /hæŋ/ *verb* to enter an endless loop and not respond to further instruction (NOTE: hung)

hangover /ˈhæŋəʊvə/ *noun* **1.** a sudden tone change on a document that is transmitted over a fax machine as a gradual change, caused by equipment faults **2.** an effect on a TV screen where the previous image can still be seen when the next image appears

hang up /ˌhæŋ ˈʌp/ *verb* to cut off a communications line

hangup /ˈhæŋʌp/ *noun* a sudden stop of a working program, often caused by the CPU executing an illegal instruction or entering an endless loop

hard /hɑːd/ *adjective* **1.** referring to parts of a computer system that cannot be programmed or altered **2.** high contrast (photographic paper or film)

hardbound /ˈhɑːdbaʊnd/ *adjective* (*of a book*) with a hard cased cover, as opposed to a paperback

hard copy /ˌhɑːd ˈkɒpi/ *noun* a printed document or copy of information contained in a computer or system, in a form that is readable. ◊ **soft copy**

hardcover /ˈhɑːdkʌvə/ *noun, adjective* version of a book with a cased binding (as opposed to paperback) ○ *We printed 4,000 copies of the hardcover edition, and 10,000 of the paperback.*

hard disk /ˌhɑːd ˈdɪsk/ *noun* a rigid magnetic disk that is able to store many times more data than a floppy disk, and usually cannot be removed from the disk drive

hard disk drive /ˌhɑːd ˈdɪsk ˌdraɪv/ *noun* a unit used to store and retrieve data from a spinning hard disk on the commands of a computer. Abbr **HDD**. Also called **hard drive**

hard drive /ˈhɑːd draɪv/ *noun* same as **hard disk drive**

hard error /ˌhɑːd ˈerə/ *noun* an error which is permanent in a system

hard hyphen /ˌhɑːd ˈhaɪf(ə)n/ *noun* a hyphen which is always in a word, even if the word is not split (as in co-administrator). ◊ **discretionary hyphen**

hard reset /ˌhɑːd ˈriːset/ *noun* a switch that generates an electrical signal to reset the CPU and all devices, equivalent to turning a computer off and back on again

hard return /ˌhɑːd rɪˈtɜːn/ *noun* a code in a word-processing document that indicates the end of a paragraph or its characteristics

hard-sectoring /ˌhɑːd ˈsektərɪŋ/ *noun* a method of permanently formatting a disk, where each track is split into sectors, sometimes preformatted by a series of punched holes around the central hub, where each hole marks the start of sector

hardware /ˈhɑːdˌweə/ *noun* **1.** the physical units, components, integrated circuits, disks and mechanisms that make up a computer or its peripherals **2.** equipment used on set or location

'Seuqent's Platform division will focus on hardware and software manufacture, procurement and marketing, with the Enterprise division concentrating on services and client-server implementation.' [*Computing*]

hardware compatibility /ˌhɑːdweə kəmˌpætəˈbɪlɪti/ *noun* architecture of two different computers that allows one to run the programs of the other without changing any device drivers or memory locations, or the ability of one to use the add-on boards of the other

hardware configuration /ˌhɑːdweə kənˌfɪgjəˈreɪʃ(ə)n/ *noun* a way in which the hardware of a computer system is connected together

hardware graphics cursor /ˌhɑːdweə ˈgræfɪks ˌkɜːsə/ *noun* an electronic component that is used to calculate the position on screen of a pointer, according to the movement of a mouse, and display the pointer

hardware platform /ˈhɑːdweə ˌplætfɔːm/ *noun* the standard of a particular computer such as IBM PC or Apple Mac

hardware reliability /ˌhɑːdweə rɪˌlaɪəˈbɪlɪti/ *noun* the ability of a piece of hardware to function normally over a period of time

hardwired connection /ˌhɑːdwaɪəd kəˈnekʃ(ə)n/ *noun* **1.** a permanent phone line connection, rather than a plug and socket **2.** a logical function or program, which is built into the hardware, using electronic devices, such as gates, rather than in software

harmonic /hɑːˈmɒnɪk/ *noun* frequency of an order of magnitude greater or smaller than a fundamental

harmonic distortion /ˌhɑːmɒnɪk dɪˈstɔːʃ(ə)n/ *noun* unwanted harmonics produced by a non-linear circuit from an input signal

harmonic telephone ringer /ˌhɑːmɒnɪk ˈtelɪfəʊn ˌrɪŋə/ *noun* a telephone that will only detect a certain range of ringing frequencies, this allows many telephones on a single line to be rung individually

hash /hæʃ/ *verb* to produce a unique number derived from the entry itself, for each entry in a database

hashmark /ˈhæʃmɑːk/, **hash mark** /ˈhæʃ mɑːk/ *noun* a printed sign (#) used as a hard copy marker or as an indicator. Also called **hash**

COMMENT: The US term is **pound sign**. In US usage # means number; #32 = number 32 (e.g. a flat number in a postal address, paragraph number in a text).

hazard /ˈhæzəd/ *noun* a fault in hardware due to incorrect signal timing

haze /heɪz/ *noun* same as **fogging**

haze filter /ˈheɪz ˌfɪltə/, **haze-cutting filter** /ˌheɪz ˌkʌtɪŋ ˈfɪltə/ *noun* a lens filter which cuts out ultraviolet light and reduces haziness (*film*)

HCI *abbr* host controller interface

HD /ˌeɪtʃ ˈdiː/ *noun* data transmission in one direction only, over a bidirectional channel. Full form **half duplex**

HDD *abbr* hard disk drive

HDLC *abbr* high-level data link control

HDTV *abbr* high definition television

HDX *abbr* half duplex

head /hed/ *noun* **1.** data that indicates the start address of a list of items stored in memory **2.** a top edge of a book or of a page **3.** the start of a reel of recording tape **4.** the top part of a device, network or body **5.** an adjustable mounting for a camera on its tripod **6.** the start of a reel of photographic film or recording tape ■ *verb* to be the first item of data in a list ○ *The queue was headed by my file.*

head end /ˈhed end/ *noun* interconnection equipment between an antenna and a cable television network

header /ˈhedə/ *noun* **1.** (*in a local area network*) a packet of data that is sent before a transmission to provide information on destination and routing **2.** information at the beginning of a list of data relating to the rest of the data **3.** a section of words at the top of a page of a document, giving e.g. the title, author's name or page number. Also called **heading**. ◊ **footer**

heading /ˈhedɪŋ/ *noun* **1.** the title or name of a document or file **2.** a header or section of words at the top of each page of a document. Also called **headline 3.** the title for a page within a multimedia book

headlife /ˈhedlaɪf/ *noun* the length of time that a video or tape head can work before being serviced or replaced

headline /ˈhedlaɪn/ *noun* same as **heading**

head wheel /ˈhed wiːl/ *noun* a wheel that keeps video tape in contact with the head

headword /ˈhedwɜːd/ *noun* the main entry word in a printed dictionary

heap /hiːp/ *noun* a temporary data storage area that allows random access. Compare **stack**

heat-absorbing filter /ˌhiːt əbˌzɔːbɪŋ ˈfɪltə/, **heat filter** /ˈhiːt ˌfɪltə/ *noun* a filter that is able to reflect or absorb infrared radiation; used in projectors to reduce the amount of heat on a film

heat-sink /ˈhiːt sɪŋk/ *noun* a metal device used to conduct heat away from an electronic component to prevent damage

helical scan /ˌhelɪk(ə)l ˈskæn/ *noun* a method of storing data on magnetic tape in which the write head stores data in diagonal strips rather than parallel with the tape edge so using the tape area more efficiently and allowing more data to be recorded. It is used most often in video tape recorders.

helios noise /ˈhiːliɒs nɔɪz/ *noun* noise originating from the sun that is picked up by an earth- based antenna when it points in the direction of the sun

help /help/ *noun* **1.** anything which makes it easier to do something ○ *He finds his word-processor a great help in the office.* **2.** a function in a program or system that provides useful information about the program in use ○ *Hit the HELP key if you want information about what to do next.*

COMMENT: Most software applications for IBM PCs have standardised the use of the F1 function key to display help text explaining how something can be done.

help desk /ˈhelp desk/ *noun* a service that provides technical help and support for people using a computer package or network

helper application /ˈhelpə ˌæplɪkeɪʃ(ə)n/ *noun* software which works with a web browser to increase the functionality of the browser ○ *To view Adobe Acrobat* *pages in your web browser you will need to get the Adobe helper application.*

help screen /'help skriːn/ *noun* a display of information about a program or function

hertz /hɜːts/ *noun* an SI unit of frequency, defined as the number of cycles per second of time. Abbr **Hz**

COMMENT: Hertz rate is the frequency at which mains electricity is supplied to the consumer . The hertz rate in the US and Canada is 60; in Europe it is 50.

heterogeneous network /ˌhetərəʊdʒiːniəs 'netwɜːk/ *noun* a computer network joining computers of many different types and makes

heuristic /hjʊə'rɪstɪk/ *adjective* which learns from past experiences ○ *A heuristic program learns from its previous actions and decisions.*

Hewlett Packard /ˌhewlət 'pækɑːd/ manufacturer of computers, test equipment and printers. Abbr **HP**

Hewlett Packard Graphics Language /ˌhewlət ˌpækɑːd 'græfɪks ˌlæŋgwɪdʒ/ a standard set of commands used to describe graphics. Abbr **HPGL**

Hewlett Packard Interface Bus /ˌhewlət ˌpækɑːd 'ɪntəfeɪs bʌs/ a standard method of interfacing peripheral devices or test equipment and computers. Abbr **HPIB**

Hewlett Packard LaserJet /ˌhewlət ˌpækɑːd 'leɪzədʒet/ a trade name for a laser printer manufactured by Hewlett Packard that uses its PCL language to describe a page. Also called **LaserJet**

Hewlett Packard Printer Control Language /ˌhewlət ˌpækɑːd ˌprɪntə kən 'trəʊl ˌlæŋgwɪdʒ/ a standard set of commands developed by Hewlett Packard to allow a software application to control a laser printer's functions. Abbr **HP-PCL**

HF *noun* a radio communications range of frequencies between 3 MHz and 30 MHz. Full form **high frequency**

HFS /ˌeɪtʃ ef 'es/ *noun* (*in an Apple Mac system*) a method used to store and organise files on a disk. Full form **hierarchical filing system**

Hi-8 /ˌhaɪ 'eɪt/ *noun* a video cassette tape format that uses 8mm wide tape; mostly used in camcorders

hidden /'hɪd(ə)n/ *adjective* which cannot be seen

hidden files /'hɪd(ə)n faɪlz/ *plural noun* important system files which are not displayed in a directory listing and cannot normally be read by a user ○ *It allows users to backup* or *restore hidden files independently.*

hidden line algorithm /ˌhɪd(ə)n laɪn 'ælgərɪð(ə)m/ *noun* a mathematical formula that removes hidden lines from a two-dimensional computer image of a 3-D object

hierarchical classification /haɪə ˌrɑːkɪk(ə)l ˌklæsɪfɪ'keɪʃ(ə)n/ *noun* a library classification system where the list of subjects is divided down into more and more selective subsets

hierarchical communications system /ˌhaɪərɑːkɪk(ə)l kəˌmjuːnɪ'keɪʃ(ə)nz ˌsɪstəm/ *noun* a network in which each branch has a number of separate minor branches dividing from it

hierarchical computer network /ˌhaɪərɑːkɪk(ə)l kəm'pjuːtə ˌnetwɜːk/ *noun* a method of allocating control and processing functions in a network to the computers which are most suited to the task

hierarchical database /ˌhaɪərɑːkɪk(ə)l 'deɪtəbeɪs/ *noun* a database in which records can be related to each other in a defined structure

hierarchical directory /ˌhaɪərɑːkɪk(ə)l daɪ'rekt(ə)ri/ *noun* a directory listing of files on a disk, showing the main directory and its files, branches and any sub-directories

hierarchical filing system /ˌhaɪərɑːkɪk(ə)l 'faɪlɪŋ ˌsɪstəm/ *noun* full form of **HFS**

hierarchical routing /ˌhaɪərɑːkɪk(ə)l 'ruːtɪŋ/ *noun* a method of directing network traffic over a complex network by breaking down the structure of the network into separate levels, each level being responsible for directing traffic within its area ○ *The Internet has a three-level hierarchical routing system in which the backbones can direct traffic from one Mid-level to another, the mid-levels can direct traffic from one server site to another and each server site can direct traffic internally.*

hierarchical vector quantisation /ˌhaɪərɑːkɪk(ə)l 'vektə ˌkwɒntaɪzeɪʃ(ə)n/ *noun* full form of **HVQ**

hi fi, hifi *noun* the accurate reproduction of audio signals by equipment such as a record player and amplifier. Full form **high fidelity**

high /haɪ/ *adjective* large or very great

high definition television /ˌhaɪ ˌdefɪnɪʃ(ə)n 'teliˌvɪʒ(ə)n/ *noun* a broadcast television standard that displays images at a different aspect ratio and with much better definition than existing television sets. Abbr **HDTV** (NOTE: There are six standards: all display 16:9 aspect ratio images, three support a resolution of 1920x1080 pixels, three support 1280x720.)

high fidelity /ˌhaɪ fɪ'deləti/ *noun* very good quality sound, usually stereo sound recorded in 16 bits at a sample rate of 44.1 KHz

high fidelity system /ˌhaɪ fɪˈdelɪti ˌsɪstəm/ *noun* high-quality equipment for playing records or compact discs or tapes or for listening to the radio (tape recorder, turntable, amplifier and speakers). ◊ **hi fi**

high-level data link control /ˌhaɪ ˌlev(ə)l ˌdeɪtə lɪŋk kənˈtrəʊl/ *noun* an ISO standard that provides a link-layer protocol and defines how data is formatted before being transmitted over a synchronous network. Abbr **HLDLC**

high-level language /ˌhaɪ ˌlev(ə)l ˈlæŋgwɪdʒ/, **high-level programming language** /ˌhaɪ ˌlev(ə)l ˌprəʊgræmɪŋ ˈlæŋgwɪdʒ/ *noun* a computer programming language which is easy to learn and allows the user to write programs using words and commands that are easy to understand and look like English words. Abbr **HLL** (NOTE: The program is then translated into machine code, with one HLL instruction often representing more than one machine code instruction.)

highlight /ˈhaɪlaɪt/ *verb* **1.** to make part of the text stand out from the rest ○ *The headings are highlighted in bold.* **2.** to select an object or text by dragging the pointer across it; when text is highlighted it normally appears inverted (white on a black background)

high memory /ˌhaɪ ˈmem(ə)ri/ *noun* (*in an IBM PC*) a memory area between 640 Kb and 1 Mb

high memory area /ˌhaɪ ˈmem(ə)ri ˌeəriə/ *noun* (*in an IBM PC*) the first 64 Kb of extended memory above 1 Mb that can be used by MS-DOS programs. Abbr **HMA**

high performance filing system /ˌhaɪ pəˌfɔːməns ˈfaɪlɪŋ ˌsɪstəm/ *noun* full form of **HPFS**

high-resolution /ˌhaɪ ˌrezəˈluːʃ(ə)n/, **high-res** /ˌhaɪ ˈrez/ *noun* the ability to display or detect a very large number of pixels per unit area. Also called **hi-res**

high resolution graphics /ˌhaɪ ˌrezəluːʃ(ə)n ˈgræfɪks/ *noun* full form of **HRG**

high Sierra specification /ˌhaɪ siˌerə ˌspesɪfɪˈkeɪʃ(ə)n/ *noun* an industry standard method of storing data on a CD-ROM disc

high-spec /ˌhaɪ ˈspek/ *plural noun* having a high specification ○ *High-spec cabling needs to be very carefully handled.*

high specification /ˌhaɪ ˌspesɪfɪ ˈkeɪʃ(ə)n/ *noun* a high degree of accuracy or a large number of features

high-speed /ˈhaɪ spiːd/ *adjective* which operates faster than normal data transmission or processing

high-tech /haɪ ˈtek/ *adjective* technologically advanced

highway /ˈhaɪweɪ/ *noun* same as **bus**

hi-res /ˌhaɪ ˈreɪz/ *noun* same as **high-resolution**

hiss /hɪs/ *noun* high-frequency noise mixed with a signal

histogram /ˈhɪstəgræm/ *noun* a graph on which values are represented as vertical or horizontal bars

history /ˈhɪst(ə)ri/ *noun* a feature of some applications that keeps a log of the actions a user has carried out, the places within a hypertext document visited or the sites on the Internet explored

hit /hɪt/ *noun* a successful match or search of a database ■ *verb* to press a key ○ *To save the text, hit ESCAPE S.* (NOTE: hitting – hit)

HLDLC *abbr* high-level data link control

HLL *abbr* high-level language

HMA *abbr* high memory area

HMI *abbr* human-machine interface

HMS time format /ˌeɪtʃ ˌem ˌes taɪm ˈfɔːmæt/ *noun* a system used by MCI to express time in hours, minutes and seconds – normally used only for videodisc devices. ◊ **MCI**

hold /həʊld/ *noun* synchronisation timing pulse for a television time base signal

COMMENT: The hold feature keeps the picture steady and central on the screen. Some televisions have horizontal and vertical hold controls to allow the picture to be moved and set up according to various conditions.

holdup /ˈhɒldʌp/ *noun* **1.** a time period over which power will be supplied by a UPS **2.** a pause in a program or device due to a malfunction

hole /həʊl/ *noun* a punched gap in a punched paper tape or card, representing data

hologram /ˈhɒləˌgræm/ *noun* an imaginary three-dimensional image produced by the interference pattern when a part of a coherent light source, e.g. a laser, is reflected from an object and mixed with the main beam

holograph /ˈhɒləgrɑːf/ *noun* a handwritten manuscript, as written by the author using a pen or pencil, but not typed

holographic image /ˌhɒləgræfɪk ˈɪmɪdʒ/ *noun* a hologram of a three-dimensional object

holographic storage /ˌhɒləgræfɪk ˈstɔːrɪdʒ/ *noun* storage of data as a holographic image which is then read by a bank of photocells and a laser (NOTE: This is a storage medium with massive storage potential.)

holography /hɒˈlɒgrəfi/ *noun* the science and study of holograms and their manufacture

home /həʊm/ *noun* **1.** a place where a person lives **2.** a starting point or the initial point

home banking /ˌhəʊm ˈbæŋkɪŋ/ *noun* a method of examining and carrying out bank transactions in the user's home via a terminal and modem

home computer /ˌhəʊm kəmˈpjuːtə/ *noun* a microcomputer designed for home use, whose applications might include teaching, games, personal finance and word-processing

home consumption /ˌhəʊm kənˈsʌmpʃən/ *noun* the use of something in the home

home key /ˈhəʊm kiː/ *noun* a key on an IBM PC keyboard that moves the cursor to the beginning of a line of text

home page /ˈhəʊm peɪdʒ/ *noun* the opening page of a website

homing /ˈhəʊmɪŋ/ *noun* location of the source of a transmitted signal or data item

homogeneous computer network /ˌhəʊməʊdʒiːniəs kəmˈpjuːtə ˌnetwɜːk/ *noun* a network made up of similar machines that are compatible or from the same manufacturer

homogeneous multiplexing /ˌhəʊməʊdʒiːniəs ˈmʌltɪˌpleksɪŋ/ *noun* a switching multiplexer system in which all the channels contain data using the same protocol and transmission rate

hood /hʊd/ *noun* a cover which protects something

hook /hʊk/ *noun* a point in a program at which a programmer can insert test code or debugging code

hooking /ˈhʊkɪŋ/ *noun* distortion of a video picture caused by tape head timing errors

hop /hɒp/ *noun* the path taken by a packet of data as it moves from one server or router to another

hopper /ˈhɒpə/ *noun* a device which holds punched cards and feeds them into the reader

horizontal /ˌhɒrɪˈzɒnt(ə)l/ *adjective* lying flat or going from side to side, not up and down

horizontal blanking period /ˌhɒrɪzɒnt(ə)l ˈblæŋkɪŋ ˌpɪəriəd/ *noun* the time taken for the picture beam in a monitor to return to the start of the next line from the end of the previous line

horizontal scan frequency /ˌhɒrɪzɒnt(ə)l ˈskæn ˌfriːkwənsi/ *noun* the number of lines on a video display that are refreshed each second

horizontal scrollbar /ˌhɒrɪzɒnt(ə)l ˈskrəʊlbɑː/ *noun* (*in a GUI*) a bar along the bottom of a window that indicates that the page is wider than the window (NOTE: A user can move horizontally across the page by dragging the indicator bar on the scrollbar.)

horizontal scrolling /ˌhɒrɪzɒnt(ə)l ˈskrəʊlɪŋ/ *noun* the process of moving across a page, horizontally

horn /hɔːn/ *noun* a directional radio device with a wider open end leading to a narrow section, used for the reception and transmission of radio waves

host /həʊst/ *noun, adjective* to provide storage space on a server computer where a user can store files or data, often used to store the files required for a website ○ *We chose this company to host our website because it has reliable server computers and high-speed connection to the Internet.*

'...you select fonts manually or through commands sent from the host computer along with the text' [*Byte*]

host address /ˈhəʊst əˌdres/ *noun* same as **Internet address**

host computer /ˌhəʊst kəmˈpjuːtə/ *noun* **1.** the main controlling computer in a multi-user or distributed system **2.** a computer used to write and debug software for another computer, often using a cross compiler **3.** a computer in a network that provides special services or programming languages to all users

'...you select fonts manually or through commands sent from the host computer along with the text' [*Byte*]

hosting service provider /ˈhəʊstɪŋ ˌsɜːvɪs prəˌvaɪdə/ *noun* same as **host service**

host name /ˈhəʊst ˌneɪm/ *noun* a name given to a website on the Internet

host number /ˈhəʊst ˌnʌmbə/ *noun* same as **Internet address**

host service /ˈhəʊst ˌsɜːvɪs/ *noun* a company that provides connections to the Internet and storage space on its computers which can store the files for a user's website ○ *We rent storage space on this host service provider's server for our company website.* ◊ **ISP**. Also called **hosting service provider**

hot key /ˈhɒt kiː/ *noun* a special key or key combination which starts a process or activates a program

hot plugging /ˈhɒt ˌplʌɡɪŋ/ *noun* a feature of a computer that allows a device or peripheral to be plugged in or connected while the computer is working ○ *This server support hot plugging so I can plug in this network card and the operating system software will automatically detect and alter its configuration.* Also called **hot swapping**

hotspot /ˈhɒtspɒt/ *noun* **1.** a special area on an image or display that does something when the cursor is moved onto it ○ *The im-*

age of the trumpet is a hotspot and will play a sound when you move the pointer over it. **2.** a region of high brightness on a film or display screen

hot standby /ˌhɒt ˈstændbaɪ/ *noun* a piece of hardware that is kept operational at all times and is used as backup in case of system failure. Compare **cold standby, warm standby**

hot swapping /ˈhɒt ˌswɒpɪŋ/ *noun* same as **hot plugging**

hotword /ˈhɒtwɜːd/ *noun* a word within displayed text that does something when the cursor is moved onto it or it is selected

house /haʊz/ *noun* a company, especially a publishing company ○ *One of the biggest software houses in the US* ■ *verb* to put a device in a case ○ *The disc is housed in a solid plastic case.*

housekeeping /ˈhaʊsˌkiːpɪŋ/ *noun* tasks that have to be regularly carried out to maintain a computer system, e.g. checking backups and deleting unwanted files

houselights /ˈhaʊslaɪts/ *plural noun* studio lighting, or lights illuminating where the audience is seated (*film*)

housing /ˈhaʊzɪŋ/ *noun* a solid case ○ *The computer housing was damaged when it fell on the floor.*

howler /ˈhaʊlə/ *noun* **1.** a buzzer which indicates to a telephone exchange operator that a user's telephone handset is not on the receiver **2.** a very bad and obvious mistake ○ *What a howler, no wonder your program won't work.*

HP *abbr* Hewlett Packard

HPFS /ˌeɪtʃ piː ef ˈes/ *noun* (*in an OS/2 operating system*) a method of storing file information that is faster and more flexible than MS-DOS FAT. Full form **high performance filing system**

HPGL *abbr* Hewlett Packard Graphics Language

HPIB *abbr* Hewlett Packard Interface Bus

HP-PCL /ˌeɪtʃ ˌpiː ˌpiː siː ˈel/ *abbr* Hewlett Packard Printer Control Language

HRG /ˌeɪtʃ ɑː ˈdʒiː/ *noun* the ability to display a large number of pixels per unit area. Full form **high resolution graphics**

HSV *abbr* hue, saturation and value

HT *plural noun* small portable transceivers. Full form **handy talkies**

HTML /ˌeɪtʃ tiː em ˈel/ *noun* a series of special codes that define the typeface and style that should be used when displaying the text and also allow hypertext links to other parts of the document or to other documents ○ *HTML is used to create documents for the World Wide Web.* Full form **hypertext markup language**

HTTP /ˌeɪtʃ tiː tiː ˈpiː/ *noun* a series of commands used by a browser to ask an Internet web server for information about a webpage. Full form **hypertext transfer protocol**

HTTPd /ˌeɪtʃ tiː tiː piː ˈdiː/ *noun* a server software that carries sends webpage files to a client in response to a request from a user's web browser ○ *When you type a website address into your web browser, this sends a request to the HTTPd server software that replies with the HTML code of a formatted webpage.* Full form **hypertext transfer protocol daemon**

hub /hʌb/ *noun* **1.** the central part of a disk, usually with a hole and ring which the disk drive grips to spin the disk **2.** (*in a star-topology network*) the central ring or wiring cabinet where all circuits meet and form an electrical path for signals **3.** a continuous audible sound of low frequency

hue /hjuː/ *noun* the colour of an image or pixel

hue, saturation and intensity /ˌhjuː ˌsætʃəreɪʃ(ə)n ənd ɪnˈtensɪti/ *noun* a method of defining a colour through its three properties. Abbr **HSI**. Also called **hue, saturation and brightness, hue, saturation and level** (NOTE: Hue is colour defined by its the wavelength; saturation refers to the purity of the colour (where at zero saturation the colour appears white and full saturation is pure colour); and intensity, brightness and level refer to the amount of white.)

hue, saturation and value /ˌhjuː ˌsætʃəreɪʃ(ə)n ənd ˈvæljuː/ *noun* same as **hue, saturation and intensity**. abbr **HSV**

Huffman code /ˈhʌfmən kəʊd/ *noun* a data compression code in which frequent characters occupy less bit space than less frequent ones

huge model /ˌhjuːdʒ ˈmɒd(ə)l/ *noun* (*in programming*) the memory model of an Intel processor that allows data and program code to exceed 64Kb, but the total of both must be less than 1Mb

hum /hʌm/ *noun* a low frequency electrical noise or interference on a signal

human-computer interface /ˌhjuːmən kəmˌpjuːtə ˈɪntəfeɪs/ *noun* abbr **HMI**. same as **human-machine interface**

human-machine interface /ˌhjuːmən məˌʃiːn ˈɪntəfeɪs/ *noun* facilities provided to improve the interaction between a user and a computer system. Abbr **HMI**. Also called **human-computer interface**

hum bars /ˈhʌm bɑːz/ *plural noun* slow-moving horizontal bars on a television picture which are created by the input of an undesirable mains hum into the video signal

hung ◊ **hang**

hunting /ˈhʌntɪŋ/ *noun* **1.** the process of searching out a data record in a file **2.** low-frequency instability of sound or picture created by cyclic variations in tape or film transport speed

HVQ /ˌeɪtʃ viː ˈkjuː/ *noun* a video compression standard which allows colour video images to be transmitted in a bandwidth of 112 Kbps. Full form **hierarchical vector quantisation**

hybrid circuit /ˌhaɪbrɪd ˈsɜːkɪt/ *noun* the connection of a number of different electronic components such as integrated circuits, transistors, resistors and capacitors in a small package, which since the components are not contained in their own protective packages, requires far less space than the individual discrete components

HyperCard /ˈhaɪpəkɑːd/ a trade name for a database system controlled by HyperTalk programming language, used to produce hypertext documents

hyperlink /ˈhaɪpəlɪŋk/ *noun* a word or image or button in a webpage or multimedia title that moves the user to another page when clicked

hypermedia /ˈhaɪpəmiːdiə/ *noun* a hypertext system that is capable of displaying images and sound

HyperTalk /ˈhaɪpətɔːk/ a trade name for a programming language used to control a HyperCard database

HyperTerminal /ˈhaɪpəˌtɜːmɪn(ə)l/ *noun* a communications program that is included with Windows 95 and allows a user to call a remote computer via a modem and transfer files

hypertext /ˈhaɪpətekst/ *noun* **1.** a multimedia system of organising information in which certain words in a document link to other documents and display the text when the word is selected ○ *In this hypertext page, click once on the word 'computer' and it will tell you what a computer is.* **2.** a way of linking one word or image on an Internet page to another page in which clicking on certain words or images moves the user directly to the relevant new page

hypertext markup language /ˌhaɪpətekst ˈmɑːkʌp ˌlæŋgwɪdʒ/ *noun* full form of **HTML**

hypertext transfer protocol /ˌhaɪpətekst ˈtrænsfɜː ˌprəʊtəkɒl/ *noun* full form of **HTTP**

hypertext transfer protocol daemon /ˌhaɪpətekst ˈtrænsfɜː ˌprəʊtəkɒl ˌdiːmən/ *noun* full form of **HTTPd**

hyphen /ˈhaɪf(ə)n/ *noun* a printing sign (-) to show that a word has been split

hyphenated /ˈhaɪfəneɪtɪd/ *adjective* written with a hyphen ○ *The word 'high-level' is usually hyphenated.*

hyphenation /ˌhaɪfəˈneɪʃ(ə)n/ *noun* the splitting of a word at the end of a line, when the word is too long to fit

hyphenation and justification /haɪfə ˌnaɪʃ(ə)n ən ˌdʒʌstɪfɪˈkeɪʃ(ə)n/ *noun* full form of **H & J** ○ *An American hyphenation and justification program will not work with British English spellings.*

Hz *abbr* hertz

I

I750 /ˌaɪ ˌsev(ə)n faɪ ˈəʊ/ *noun* a video processor chip developed by Intel and used to compress and decompress digital video sequences

IAB /ˌaɪ eɪ ˈbiː/ *noun* **1.** an independent committee that is responsible for the design, engineering and management of the Internet. Full form **Internet Activities Board 2.** a group that monitors and manages the development of the Internet. Full form **Internet Architecture Board**

IAM /ˌaɪ eɪ ˈem/ *noun* memory storage that has an access time between that of main memory and a disk based system. Full form **intermediate access memory**

IANA *abbr* Internet Assigned Numbers Authority

I-beam /ˈaɪ biːm/ *noun* a cursor shaped like the letter 'I' used in a GUI to edit text or indicate text operations

IBM /ˌaɪ biː ˈem/ the largest computer company in the world, which developed the first PC based on the Intel processor. Full form **International Business Machines**

IBM-compatible /ˌaɪ biː em kəm ˈpætɪb(ə)l/ *adjective* referring to a personal computer that has hardware and software compatible with the IBM PC regardless of which Intel processor it uses (NOTE: IBM-compatible computers feature an ISA, EISA or MCA expansion bus.)

IC *abbr* integrated circuit

ICE *noun* a communication system (developed by the BBC) which transmits data in the field blanking period. Full form **insertion communication equipment**

ICMP /ˌaɪ ciː em ˈpiː/ *noun* an extension to the Internet Protocol that provides error detection and control messages ○ *The Internet command 'ping' uses ICMP to test if a named node is working correctly.* Full form **Internet control message protocol.** ◊ **IP, PING**

icon /ˈaɪkɒn/, **ikon** *noun* a graphic symbol or small picture displayed on screen, used in an interactive computer system to provide an easy way of identifying a function ○ *The icon for the graphics program is a small picture of a palette.*

> 'Despite (or because of?) the swap file, loading was slow and the hourglass icon of the mouse pointer frequently returned to the arrow symbol well before loading was complete.' [*Computing*]

icon resource /ˈaɪkɒn rɪˌzɔːs/ *noun* a file that contains the bitmap image of an icon, used by a programmer when writing an application

ICQ a software program developed by Mirabilis that supports instant messaging and allows two or more users to send messages to each other via the Internet that are instantly displayed on the other person's screen (NOTE: pronounced 'I-seek-you')

ID *abbr* **1.** identification **2.** identifier

I-D *abbr* Internet-draft

IDA *abbr* integrated digital access

IDD *abbr* international direct dialling

IDE /ˌaɪ diː ˈiː/ *noun* a popular standard for a hard disk drive controller unit that allows data transfer rates up to 4.1MBps and can support two hard disk drives on each controller; enhanced versions of the IDE standard provide more flexibility and speed (also known as AT Attachment – ATA – interface) ○ *IDE drives are fitted to most home PCs.* Full form **integrated drive electronics, integrated device electronics.** ◊ **ATA, SCSI**

ideal /aɪˈdɪəl/ *adjective* perfect or very good for something

ideal format /aɪˌdɪəl ˈfɔːmæt/ *noun* a standard large format for photographic negatives, used mainly in professional equipment

identical /aɪˈdentɪk(ə)l/ *adjective* exactly the same ○ *The two systems use identical software.*

identification /aɪˌdentɪfɪˈkeɪʃ(ə)n/ *noun* a procedure used by a host computer to establish the identity and nature of the calling computer or user. This could be for security and access restriction purposes or to provide transmission protocol information.

identification character /aɪˌdentɪfɪ ˈkeɪʃ(ə)n ˌkærɪktə/ *noun* a single character sent to a host computer to establish the identity and location of a remote computer or terminal

identifier /aɪˈdentɪfaɪə/ *noun* a set of characters used to distinguish between different blocks of data or files. Abbr **ID**

identify /aɪˈdentɪˌfaɪ/ *verb* to establish who someone is or what something is ○ *The user has to identify himself to the system by using a password before access is allowed.*

identity /aɪˈdentɪti/ *noun* who someone or what something is

idiot tape /ˈɪdiət teɪp/ *noun* a tape containing unformatted text, which cannot be typeset until formatting data, such as justification, line width, and page size, has been added by a computer

idle /ˈaɪd(ə)l/ *adjective* referring to a machine, telephone line or device which is not being used, but is ready and waiting to be used

IE *abbr* Internet Explorer

IEC connector /ˌaɪ iː ˈsiː kəˌnektə/ *noun* a standard for a three-pin connector used on sockets that carry mains electricity to the computer ○ *All PCs have a male IEC connector and use a mains lead with a female IEC connector.*

IEEE *abbr US* Institute of Electrical and Electronic Engineers

IESG *noun* a group that reviews Internet standards and manages the IETF. Full form **Internet Engineering Steering Group**

IETF /ˌaɪ iː tiː ˈef/ *noun* a committee that is part of the IAB and determines Internet standards. Full form **Internet Engineering Task Force.** ◊ **IAB**

if /ɪf/ *abbr* intermediate frequency

IFF /ˌaɪ ef ˈef/ *noun* **1.** a standard for compressed files stored on a CD-i. Full form **international file format 2.** a standard that defines how palette data is stored in an Amiga and some graphics programs. Full form **interchange file format**

IF statement /ˈɪf ˌsteɪtmənt/ *noun* a computer programming statement meaning do an action IF a condition is true, and usually followed by THEN

IGMP /ˌaɪ dʒiː em ˈpiː/ *noun* a standard that helps manage how data is transferred during an IP Multicast operation in which one server computer sends each packet of data to several destinations at the same time. Full form **Internet group management protocol** (NOTE: This is useful when broadcasting a lot of data to several different recipients. The IGMP standard is defined in RFC1112.)

ignore /ɪɡˈnɔː/ *verb* not to recognise or not to do what someone says ○ *This command instructs the computer to ignore all punctuation.*

IGP /ˌaɪ dʒiː ˈpiː/ *noun* a protocol that distributes information to gateways, i.e. routers, within a particular network. Full form **interior gateway protocol**

IIL *abbr* integrated injection logic

IIS a piece of web server software developed by Microsoft. Full form **Internet Information Server**

IKBS /ˌaɪ keɪ biː ˈem/ *noun* software that applies the knowledge, advice and rules defined by an expert in a particular field to a user's data to help solve a problem. Full form **intelligent knowledge-based system.** Also called **expert system**

ikon /ˈaɪkɒn/ *noun* another spelling of **icon**

ILF *abbr* infra-low frequency

ILL *abbr* inter-library loan

illegal /ɪˈliːɡ(ə)l/ *adjective* which is against the law

illegally /ɪˈliːɡəli/ *adverb* against the law or against rules ○ *The company has been illegally copying copyright software.*

illegal operation /ɪˌliːɡ(ə)l ˌɒpəˈreɪʃ(ə)n/ *noun* an instruction or process that does not follow the computer system's protocol or language syntax

illegible /ɪˈledʒɪb(ə)l/ *adjective* which cannot be read ○ *If the manuscript is illegible, send it back to the author to have it typed.*

illiterate /ɪˈlɪt(ə)rət/ *adjective* (person) who cannot read

> '...three years ago the number of people who were computer illiterate was much higher than today' [*Minicomputer News*]

illuminance /ɪˈluːmɪnəns/ *noun* a measurement of the amount of light that strikes a surface, measured in lux

illuminate /ɪˈluːmɪneɪt/ *verb* to shine a light on something ○ *The screen is illuminated by a low-power light.*

illumination /ɪˌluːmɪˈneɪʃ(ə)n/ *noun* lighting

illustrate /ˈɪləˌstreɪt/ *verb* to add pictures to a text ○ *The book is illustrated in colour.* ○ *The manual is illustrated with charts and pictures of the networking connections.*

illustration /ˌɪləˈstreɪʃ(ə)n/ *noun* a picture (in a book) ○ *The book has twenty-five pages of full-colour illustrations.*

IMA /ˌaɪ em ˈeɪ/ *noun* a professional organisation that covers subjects including authoring languages, formats and intellectual property. Full form **Interactive Multimedia Association** ■ *abbr* International MIDI Association

iMac /ˌaɪ ˈmæk/ a personal computer developed by Apple Computer Corporation

image /ˈɪmɪdʒ/ *noun* **1.** an exact duplicate of an area of memory **2.** a copy of an original picture or design **3.** a projected picture that is shown when light is shone through a photograph film **4.** a picture displayed on a screen or monitor

image area /ˈɪmɪdʒ ˌeəriə/ *noun* a region of microfilm or display screen on which characters or designs can be displayed

image buffer /ˈɪmɪdʒ ˌbʌfə/ *noun* an area of memory that is used to build up an image before it is transferred to screen

image compression /ˈɪmɪdʒ kəm ˌpreʃ(ə)n/ *noun* the process of compressing the data that forms an image

image degradation /ˈɪmɪdʒ ˌdegrədeɪʃ(ə)n/ *noun* the loss of picture contrast and quality due to signal distortion or bad copying of a video signal

image editing /ˈɪmɪdʒ ˌedɪtɪŋ/ *noun* the process of altering or adjusting an image using a paint package or special image editing program

image editor /ˈɪmɪdʒ ˌedɪtə/ *noun* a piece of software that allows a user to edit, change or create a bitmap image

image enhancement /ˈɪmɪdʒ ɪn ˌhɑːnsmənt/ *noun* the process of adjusting parts of an image using special image processing software to change the brightness or sharpness of an image

imagemap /ˈɪmɪdʒmæp/ *noun* a graphic image that has areas of the image defined as hyperlink hotspots that link to another webpage

image processing /ˈɪmɪdʒ ˌprəʊsesɪŋ/ *noun* the analysis of information contained in an image, usually by electronic means or using a computer which provides the analysis or recognition of objects in the image

image processing software /ˈɪmɪdʒ ˌprəʊsesɪŋ ˌsɒftweə/ *noun* software that allows a user to adjust contrast, colour or brightness levels or apply special effects to a bitmap image

image processor /ˈɪmɪdʒ ˌprəʊsesə/ *noun* an electronic or computer system used for image processing, and to extract information from the image

'The Max FX also acts as a server to a growing number of printers, including a Varityper 5300 with emerald raster image processor and a Canon CLC 500 colour photocopier.' [*Computing*]

image retention /ˈɪmɪdʒ rɪˌtenʃən/ *noun* the time taken for a TV image to disappear after it has been displayed, caused by long persistence phosphor

image scanner /ˈɪmɪdʒ ˌskænə/ *noun* an input device which converts documents or drawings or photographs into a digitised, machine-readable form

image sensor /ˈɪmɪdʒ ˌsensə/ *noun* a photoelectric device which produces a signal related to the amount of light falling on it

image setter /ˈɪmɪdʒ ˌsetə/ *noun* a typesetting device which can process a PostScript page and produce a high-resolution output

image stability /ˈɪmɪdʒ stəˌbɪlɪti/ *noun* the ability of a display screen to provide a flicker-free picture

image storage space /ˌɪmɪdʒ ˈstɔːrɪdʒ ˌspeɪs/ *noun* a region of memory in which a digitised image is stored

image table /ˈɪmɪdʒ ˌteɪb(ə)l/ *noun* each of two bit-mapped tables used to control input and output devices or processes

imaging /ˈɪmɪdʒɪŋ/ *noun* a technique for creating pictures on a screen, in medicine used to provide pictures of sections of the body, using scanners attached to computers

imaging system /ˌɪmɪdʒɪŋ ˈsɪstəm/ *noun* equipment and software used to capture, digitise and compress video or still images

IMAP /ˈaɪmæp/ *noun* a standard that defines how email messages can be accessed and read over a network. Full form **Internet message access protocol**. ◊ **POP 3, SMTP**

COMMENT: This standard (currently at version four) provides an alternative to the common POP 3 standard. The IMAP standard stores a user's messages on a shared server (e.g. at your ISP) and allows a user to connect from any computer and read, send or manage messages. In contrast, the POP 3 protocol downloads all messages from a shared server onto the user's computer. This makes it very difficult for a user to access messages from a different computer, e.g. if you are travelling. Regardless of whether IMAP or POP 3 is used to read messages, the SMTP protocol is normally used to send messages.

IMAX *noun* a wide-screen motion picture system using 70 mm film and having a frame size of 70 multiplied by 46 mm

immunity /ɪˈmjuːnɪti/ *noun* ♦ **interference**

impact /ˈɪmpækt/ *noun* the act of hitting or striking something

'Lexmark is shipping the Wheelwriter family of typewriters that can be connected to a PC using the parallel printer port, making it act like a PC impact printer.' [*Computing*]

impairment scale /ɪmˈpeəmənt skeɪl/ *noun* the scale of the loss of quality in sound or picture reproduction in both film and video. Scale 5 is negligible loss and scale 1 is unacceptable.

impedance /ɪmˈpiːd(ə)ns/ *noun* a measurement of the effect an electrical circuit or cable has on signal current magnitude and phase when a steady voltage is applied. ◊ **ohm**

COMMENT: Network cables need to have the correct impedance for the type of network card installed. 10BaseT unshielded twisted-pair cable normally has an impedance between 100 and105 ohms, while 10Base2 coaxial cable has an impedance of 50 ohms.

impedance mismatch /ɪm'piːd(ə)ns ˌmɪsmætʃ/ *noun* a situation where the impedance of the transmission or receiving end of a system does not match the other, resulting in loss of signal power

implant /ɪm'plɑːnt/ *verb* to fix deeply into something; to bond one substance into another chemically ○ *The dopant is implanted into the substrate.*

implement /'ɪmplɪˌment/ *verb* to carry out or to put something into action

implementation /ˌɪmplɪmən'teɪʃ(ə)n/ *noun* a version of something that works ○ *The latest implementation of the software runs much faster.*

import /ɪm'pɔːt/ *verb* **1.** to bring goods into a country to resell **2.** to bring something in from outside a system ○ *You can import images from the CAD package into the DTP program.* **3.** to convert a file stored in one format to the default format used by a program ○ *Select import if you want to open a TIFF graphics file.*

'At the moment, Acrobat supports only the sending and viewing of documents. There are legal implications associated with allowing users to edit documents in the style of the original application, without having the tool itself on their desks, and there is no import facility back into applications.' [*Computing*]

importation /ˌɪmpɔː'teɪʃ(ə)n/ *noun* the act of importing. Compare **export**

'…text and graphics importation from other systems is possible' [*Publish*]

'At the moment, Acrobat supports only the sending and viewing of documents. There are legal implications associated with allowing users to edit documents in the style of the original application, without having the tool itself on their desks, and there is no import facility back into applications' [*Computing*]

impression /ɪm'preʃ(ə)n/ *noun* the number of books or documents printed all on the same printrun

impression cylinder /ɪm'preʃ(ə)n ˌsɪlɪndə/ *noun* a roller in a printing press that presses the sheets of paper against the inked type

imprint /'ɪmprɪnt/ *noun* the publisher's or printer's name which appears on the title page or in the bibliographical details of a book

imprint position /'ɪmprɪnt pəˌzɪʃ(ə)n/ *noun* on a sheet of paper, place where the next letter or symbol is to be printed

impulse /'ɪmpʌls/ *noun* a voltage pulse which lasts a very short time

impulsive /ɪm'pʌlsɪv/ *adjective* lasting a very short time

IMS *abbr* information management system

inaccuracy /ɪn'ækjʊrəsi/ *noun* a mistake or error ○ *The bibliography is full of inaccuracies.*

inaccurate /ɪn'ækjʊrət/ *adjective* not correct or wrong ○ *He entered an inaccurate password.*

inactive /ɪn'æktɪv/ *adjective* not working or not running

inactive window /ɪnˌæktɪv 'wɪndəʊ/ *noun* (*in a GUI*) a window still displayed, but not currently being used

in-band signalling /ˌɪn bænd 'sɪgn(ə)lɪŋ/ *noun* data transmission in which the signal carrying the data is within the bandwidth of the cable or transmission media

InBox /'ɪnbɒks/ *noun* a feature of the Windows messaging system that can gather together a user's electronic messages including mail sent over the network, fax messages and mail sent over the Internet

inbuilt /'ɪnbɪlt/ *adjective* referring to a feature or device included in a system ○ *This software has inbuilt error correction.*

in camera process /ˌɪn ˌkæm(ə)rə 'prəʊses/ *noun* a type of film processing which takes place inside the camera

incandescence /ˌɪnkæn'des(ə)ns/ *noun* the generation of light by heating a wire in an inert gas (as in a light bulb)

incandescent /ˌɪnkæn'des(ə)nt/ *adjective* shining because of heat produced in an inert gas

incandescent lighting /ˌɪnkændes(ə)nt 'laɪtɪŋ/ *noun* a light using heated tungsten, gas-filled bulbs or tubes instead of bulbs with carbon arcs

incident /'ɪnsɪd(ə)nt/ *noun* light that is reflected from an object (*film*)

in-circuit emulator /ˌɪn ˌsɜːkɪt 'emjʊleɪtə/ *noun* a circuit that emulates a device or integrated circuit and is inserted into a new or faulty circuit to test if it is working correctly ○ *This in-circuit emulator is used to test the floppy disk controller by emulating a disk drive.*

inclined orbit /ɪnˌklaɪnd 'ɔːbɪt/ *noun* orbit that is not polar or equatorial

inclusive /ɪn'kluːsɪv/ *adjective* which counts something in with other things ○ *Prices are inclusive of VAT.*

incoming /'ɪnkʌmɪŋ/ *adjective* which is coming in from outside

incompatible /ˌɪnkəm'pætɪb(ə)l/ *adjective* which cannot work together ○ *They tried to link the two systems, but found they were incompatible.*

incorrect /ˌɪnkə'rekt/ *adjective* not correct or with mistakes ○ *The input data was incorrect, so the output was also incorrect.*

incorrectly /ˌɪnkəˈrektli/ *adverb* not correctly or with mistakes ○ *The data was incorrectly keyboarded.*

increment /ˈɪŋkrɪmənt/ *noun* **1.** the addition of a set number, usually one, to a register, often for counting purposes ○ *An increment is added to the counter each time a pulse is detected.* **2.** the value of the number added to a register ○ *Increase the increment to three.* ■ *verb* **1.** to add something or to increase a number ○ *The counter is incremented each time an instruction is executed.* **2.** to move forward to the next location

incremental backup /ˌɪŋkrɪment(ə)l ˈbækʌp/ *noun* a backup procedure that only backs up the files that have changed since the last backup

incremental plotter /ˌɪŋkrɪment(ə)l ˈplɒtə/ *noun* a graphical output device that can only move in small steps, with input data representing the difference between present position and the position required, so drawing lines and curves as a series of short straight lines

indent *noun* /ˈɪndent/ a space or series of spaces from the left margin, when starting a line of text ■ *verb* /ɪnˈdent/ to start a line of text with a space in from the left margin ○ *The first line of the paragraph is indented two spaces.*

indentation /ˌɪndenˈteɪʃ(ə)n/ *noun* the process of leaving a space at the beginning of a line of text

Indeo /ˈɪndiəʊ/ a trade name for video software technology developed by Intel that allows a computer to store and play back compressed video sequences using software compression techniques

independent /ˌɪndɪˈpendənt/ *adjective* free or not controlled by anyone

independently /ˌɪndɪˈpendəntli/ *adverb* freely or without being controlled or without being connected ○ *In spooling, the printer is acting independently of the keyboard.*

index /ˈɪndeks/ *noun* **1.** a list of items in a computer memory, usually arranged alphabetically **2.** the address to be used that is the result of an offset value added to a start location. ◊ **indexed addressing 3.** a list of terms classified into groups or put in alphabetical order **4.** an alphabetical list printed, usually at the back of a book, giving references to items in the main part of the book **5.** a list of subjects and contents of a book in alphabetical order (usually at the back of a book) **6.** guide marks along the edge of a piece of film or strip of microfilm ■ *verb* to put marks against items so that they will be selected and sorted to form an index

indexed address /ˌɪndeksd əˈdres/ *noun* the address of the location to be accessed, which is found in an index register

indexed addressing /ˌɪndeksd əˈdresɪŋ/ *noun* an addressing mode, in which the storage location to be accessed is made up of a start address and an offset value, which is then added to it to give the address to be used

indexed sequential access method /ˌɪndeks sɪˌkwenʃəl ˈækses ˌmeθəd/ *noun* a data retrieval method using a list containing the address of each stored record, where the list is searched, then the record is retrieved from the address in the list. Abbr **ISAM**

index.html /ˌɪndeks dɒt ˌeɪtʃ tiː em ˈel/ *noun* a filename that is used to store the text and HTML formatting commands for the home page on a website

indexing /ˈɪndeksɪŋ/ *noun* **1.** the use of indexed addressing in software or a computer **2.** the process of building and sorting a list of records **3.** the process of writing an index for a book

index page /ˈɪndeks peɪdʒ/ *noun* **1.** a page of a multimedia book that lists all the other pages within the book and allows a user to locate other pages or areas of interest **2.** the initial opening webpage of a site on the Internet or on a company's intranet

index register /ˈɪndeks ˌredʒɪstə/ *noun* a computer address register that is added to a reference address to provide the location to be accessed. Abbr **IR**

indicate /ˈɪndɪˌkeɪt/ *verb* to show

indication /ˌɪndɪˈkeɪʃ(ə)n/ *noun* a sign or something which shows

indicator /ˈɪndɪˌkeɪtə/ *noun* something which shows the state of a process, usually a light or buzzer

indirect /ˌɪndaɪˈrekt/ *adjective* not direct

induce /ɪnˈdjuːs/ *verb* to generate an electrical current in a coil of wire by electromagnetic effects

inductance /ɪnˈdʌktəns/ *noun* a measurement of the amount of energy a device can store in its magnetic field

induction /ɪnˈdʌkʃən/ *noun* the generation of an electrical current by electromagnetic effects from a nearby source

inductive coordination /ɪnˌdʌktɪv kəʊˌɔːdɪˈneɪʃ(ə)n/ *noun* agreement between electrical power suppliers and communication providers on methods of reducing induced interference

inductor /ɪnˈdʌktə/ *noun* an electrical component consisting of a coil of wire used to introduce inductance effects into a circuit by storing energy in its magnetic field

Industry Standard Architecture /ˌɪndəstri ˌstændəd ˈɑːkɪˌtektʃə/ *noun* full form of **ISA**

inequality operator /ˌɪnɪˈkwɒlɪti ˌɒpəreɪtə/ *noun* a symbol used to indicate that two variables or quantities are not equal ○ *The C programming language uses the symbol '!=' as its inequality operator.*

inert /ɪˈnɜːt/ *adjective* (chemical substance or gas) that does not react with other chemicals

infect /ɪnˈfekt/ *verb* to contaminate a computer system with a virus that is capable of damaging its programs or data

infected computer /ɪnˌfektɪd kəm ˈpjuːtə/ *noun* a computer that carries a virus program

inference /ˈɪnf(ə)rəns/ *noun* **1.** a deduction of results from data according to certain rules **2.** a method of deducing a result about confidential information concerning an individual by using various data related to groups of people

inferior figure /ɪnˌfɪəriə ˈfɪgə/ *noun* any one of the smaller numbers or characters that are printed slightly below normal characters, used in mathematical and chemical formulae. ◊ **subscript, superscript** (NOTE: used with figures and letters: CO_2)

INF file /ˌaɪ en ˈef faɪl/ *noun* a configuration file supplied by a hardware manufacturer to allow Windows to correctly install the device

infinite /ˈɪnfɪnət/ *adjective* with no end

infinity /ɪnˈfɪnɪti/ *noun* **1.** a space or quantity that never ends **2.** the distance of an object from a viewer where beams of light from the object would be seen to be parallel, i.e. very far away **3.** a distance setting on a camera lens beyond which all images are in focus

informatics /ˌɪnfɔːˈmætɪks/ *noun* the science and study of ways and means of information processing and transmission

information /ˌɪnfəˈmeɪʃ(ə)n/ *noun* **1.** knowledge presented to a person in a form which can be understood **2.** data that has been processed or arranged to provide facts which have a meaning

information content /ˌɪnfəˈmeɪʃ(ə)n ˌkɒntent/ *noun* a measurement of the amount of information conveyed by the transmission of a symbol or character, often measured in shannons

information flow control /ˌɪnfə ˈmeɪʃ(ə)n fləʊ kənˌtrəʊl/ *noun* the regulation of access to particular information

information input /ˌɪnfəˈmeɪʃ(ə)n ˌɪnpʊt/ *noun* information received from an input device

information management system /ˌɪnfəmeɪʃ(ə)n ˈmænɪdʒmənt ˌsɪstəm/ *noun* a computer program that allows information to be easily stored, retrieved, searched and updated. Abbr **IMS**

information network /ˌɪnfəˈmeɪʃ(ə)n ˌnetwɜːk/ *noun* a number of databases linked together, usually using telephone lines and modems, allowing a large amount of data to be accessed by a wider number of users

information output /ˌɪnfəmeɪʃ(ə)n ˈaʊtpʊt/ *noun* a display of information on an output device

information processing /ˌɪnfəmeɪʃ(ə)n ˈprəʊsesɪŋ/ *noun* same as **data processing**

information provider /ˌɪnfəˈmeɪʃ(ə)n prəˌvaɪdə/ *noun* a company or user who provides an information source for use in a videotext system, e.g. a company providing weather information or stock market reports. Abbr **ip**

information retrieval /ˌɪnfəmeɪʃ(ə)n rɪ ˈtriːv(ə)l/ *noun* the process of locating quantities of data stored in a database and producing useful information from the data. Abbr **IR**

information storage /ˌɪnfəmeɪʃ(ə)n ˈstɔːrɪdʒ/ *noun* the process of storing data in a form which allows it to be processed at a later date

information storage and retrieval /ˌɪnfəmeɪʃ(ə)n ˌstɔːrɪdʒ ən rɪˈtriːv(ə)l/ *noun* techniques involved in storing information and retrieving data from a store. Abbr **ISR**

information structure /ˌɪnfəˈmeɪʃ(ə)n ˌstrʌktʃə/ *noun* same as **data structure**

information system /ˌɪnfəˈmeɪʃ(ə)n ˌsɪstəm/ *noun* a computer system which provides information according to a user's requests

information technology /ˌɪnfəmeɪʃ(ə)n tekˈnɒlədʒi/ *noun* the technology involved in acquiring, storing, processing, and distributing information by electronic means, including radio, TV, telephone and computers. Abbr **IT**

information theory /ˌɪnfəˈmeɪʃ(ə)n ˌθɪəri/ *noun* the body of formulae and mathematics concerned with data transmission equipment and signals

infra- /ɪnfrə/ *prefix* meaning below or less than. Abbr **ILF**

infra-low frequency /ˌɪnfrə ləʊ ˈfriːkwənsi/ *noun* a range of audio frequencies between 300Hz-3KHz. Abbr **ILF**

infrared /ˌɪnfrəˈred/ *noun* the section of the electromagnetic radiation spectrum extending from visible red to microwaves

infra-red link /ˌɪnfrə red 'lɪŋk/ *noun* a system that allows two computers or a computer and a printer to exchange information using an infrared light beam to carry the data

infrasonic frequency /ˌɪnfrəsɒnɪk 'friːkwənsi/ *noun* a sound wave frequency that is in the range below that audible by the human ear

infrastructure /'ɪnfrəˌstrʌktʃə/ *noun* basic structure or basic services

infringement /ɪn'frɪndʒmənt/ *noun* the act of breaking the law or a rule

inherit /ɪn'herɪt/ *verb* (*in object-oriented programming*) to acquire the characteristics of another class or data type

inheritance /ɪn'herɪt(ə)ns/ *noun* (*in object-oriented programming*) the passing of the characteristics of one class or data type to another, called its descendant

inhibit /ɪn'hɪbɪt/ *verb* to stop a process taking place or to prevent an integrated circuit or gate from operating,, by means of a signal or command

in-house /ˌɪn 'haʊs/ *adverb, adjective* (working) inside a company's building ○ *All the data processing is done in-house.*

INI file /ˌaɪ en 'aɪ faɪl/ *noun* a configuration file used in Windows 3.x and earlier that tells Windows how to load and run an application. (NOTE: The INI file could contain the working directory, user name and user settings.)

initial /ɪ'nɪʃ(ə)l/ *adjective* first or at the beginning ■ *noun* the first letter of a word, especially of a name ○ *What do the initials IBM stand for?*

initialise /ɪ'nɪʃəˌlaɪz/, **initialize** *verb* to set values or parameters or control lines to their initial values, to allow a program or process to be restarted (NOTE: **initialises – initialising – initialised**)

injection laser /ɪnˌdʒekʃən 'leɪzə/ *noun* a solid state laser device used to transmit data as pulses of light down an optic fibre

injection logic /ɪnˌdʒekʃən 'lɒdʒɪk/ *noun* ◆ **integrated injection logic**

ink /ɪŋk/ *noun* **1.** a dark liquid used to mark or write with **2.** colour selected that appears when you paint or draw using a drawing program on a computer ■ *verb* **1.** to draw lines on paper by the use of a plotter device **2.** to apply ink to printing rollers in a printing machine

ink cartridge /'ɪŋk ˌkɑːtrɪdʒ/ *noun* a plastic module that contains ink, for use in a bubble-jet or ink-jet printer

inkie, inky *noun* same as **incandescent lighting** (*informal*)

ink-jet printer /'ɪnk dʒet ˌprɪntə/ *noun* a printer that produces characters by sending a stream of tiny drops of electrically charged ink onto the paper

'...ink-jet printers work by squirting a fine stream of ink onto the paper' [*Personal Computer World*]

inlay /'ɪnleɪ/ *noun* the combination of two television or video signals to produce a single picture

inlay card /ɪn'leɪ kɑːd/ *noun* an identification card inside the box of a CD, DVD or similar recording

in-line /ˌɪn 'laɪn/ *adjective* referring to connection pins on a chip arranged in one or two rows ■ *noun* referring to a graphical image that is part of a webpage ■ *adverb* way in which unsorted or unedited data is processed

inline image /ˌɪnlaɪn 'ɪmɪdʒ/ *noun* a graphical image that is part of a WWW page

inline plug-in /ˌɪnlaɪn 'plʌg ˌɪn/ *noun* ◆ **plug-in**

inner loop /'ɪnə luːp/ *noun* a loop contained inside another loop. ◊ **nested loop**

in phase /ˌɪn 'feɪz/ *adverb* **1.** (two electrical signals) that have no phase difference between them, i.e. there is no delay or a delay of one complete cycle between them **2.** synchronization of film frames and projector shutter timing

input /'ɪnpʊt/ *verb* to transfer data or information from outside a computer to its main memory ○ *The data was input via a modem.* ■ *noun* **1.** the action of inputting information **2.** electrical signals which are applied to relevant circuits to perform the operation ▶ abbr (all senses) **i/p, I/P**

'In fact, the non-Qwerty format of the Maltron keyboard did cause a few gasps when it was first shown to the staff, but within a month all the Maltron users had regained normal input speeds.' [*Computing*]

input-bound /'ɪnpʊt ˌbaʊnd/ *adjective* referring to a program or device that is not running as fast as it could, because it is limited by the input rate from a slower peripheral. Also called **input-limited**

input device /'ɪnpʊt dɪˌvaɪs/ *noun* a device, e.g. a keyboard or bar code reader, that converts actions or information into a form that a computer can understand, and transfers the data to the processor

input-limited /ˌɪnpʊt 'lɪmɪtɪd/ *adjective* same as **input-bound**

input/output /ˌɪnpʊt 'aʊtpʊt/ *noun* full form of **I/O**

input/output device /ˌɪnpʊt 'aʊtpʊt dɪˌvaɪs/ *noun* a peripheral, e.g. such as a terminal in a workstation, that can be used both for inputting and outputting data to a processor

inquiry /ɪn'kwaɪəri/ *noun* another spelling of **enquiry**

insert /ɪn'sɜːt/ *verb* **1.** to put something into something ○ *First insert the system disk in the left slot.* **2.** to add new text inside a word or sentence **3.** to replace a part of an existing recording with inserted material

insertion communication equipment /ɪnˌsɜːʃ(ə)n kəˌmjuːnɪˌkeɪʃ(ə)n ɪ 'kwɪpmənt/ *noun* full form of **ICE**

insertion loss /ɪn'sɜːʃ(ə)n lɒs/ *noun* a weakening of a signal caused by adding a device into an existing channel or circuit

insertion point /ɪn'sɜːʃ(ə)n pɔɪnt/ *noun* the point in a document, indicated by the position of the cursor, where new text typed by the user will be entered

install /ɪn'stɔːl/ *verb* **1.** to put a machine into an office or factory ○ *The system is easy to install and simple to use.* **2.** to set up a new computer system to the user's requirements or to configure a new program to the existing system capabilities

installable device driver /ɪn ˌstɔːləb(ə)l dɪ'vaɪs ˌdraɪvə/ *noun* a device driver that is loaded into memory and remains resident, replacing a similar function built into the operating system

installation /ˌɪnstə'leɪʃ(ə)n/ *noun* **1.** a computer and equipment used for one type of work and processing ○ *The engineers are still testing the new installation.* **2.** the process of setting up a new computer system ○ *The installation of the equipment took only a few hours.*

installation manual /ˌɪnstə'leɪʃ(ə)n ˌmænjʊəl/ *noun* a booklet showing how a system should be installed

install program /'ɪnstɔːl ˌprəʊgræm/ *noun* a piece of software that transfers program code from the distribution disks onto a computer's hard disk and configures the program

instance /'ɪnstəns/ *noun* **1.** (*in object-oriented programming*) an object or duplicate object that has been created **2.** one copy of an application, routine or object ○ *Microsoft Windows will let you run several copies of the same program at the same time.* ○ *Each is called an instance of the original.*

instant jump /'ɪnstənt dʒʌmp/ *noun* (*in a videodisc player*) a hardware feature that allows the player to skip a number of frames, up to 200, in the time it takes to refresh the screen

instant messaging /ˌɪnstənt 'mesɪdʒɪŋ/ *noun* a feature that lets a user type in and exchange messages with one or more other people connected via the Internet. Each of the users in the group runs special software that tells them when a friend or colleague has connected to the Internet and is available to receive messages. Any message that he or she types in is then sent instantly to the other user.

instant replay /ˌɪnstənt riː'pleɪ/ *noun* a feature found in video recording systems that allows the action that has just been recorded to be viewed immediately

instruct /ɪn'strʌkt/ *verb* to tell someone or a computer what to do

instruction /ɪn'strʌkʃən/ *noun* a word used in a programming language that is understood by the computer as a command to carry out a particular action

> 'A Taos kernel, typically 15Kb in size, resides at each processing node to 'translate', non-native instructions – on the fly when needed. This kernel contains the only code which has to be written in the processor's native instruction set.' [*Computing*]

instruction manual /ɪn'strʌkʃən ˌmænjuəl/ *noun* a document describing how to use a system or software

instruction register /ɪn'strʌkʃən ˌredʒɪstə/ *noun* a register in a central processing unit that stores an instruction during decoding and execution operations. Abbr **IR**

instrument /'ɪnstrʊmənt/ *noun* an electronic device that can produce a sound in response to a MIDI note or to a keyboard press

instrumentation /ˌɪnstrʊmen'teɪʃ(ə)n/ *noun* equipment for testing, display or recording signals ○ *We've improved the instrumentation on this model to keep you better informed of the machine's position.*

integer /'ɪntɪdʒə/ *noun* a mathematical term to describe a whole number (NOTE: An integer may be positive or negative or zero.)

integral /ɪntɪgrəl, ɪn'tegəl/ *adjective* referring to an add-on device or special feature that is already built into a system ○ *The integral disk drives and modem reduced desk space.*

integrated /'ɪntɪˌgreɪtɪd/ *adjective* referring to a system containing many peripherals grouped together to provide a neat, complete system

integrated circuit /ˌɪntɪgreɪtɪd 'sɜːkɪt/ *noun* a circuit made up of components all of which are formed on one small piece of semiconductor by means of etching and chemical processes. Abbr **IC** (NOTE: Integrated circuits can be classified as follows: Small Scale Integration (SSI): 1 to 10 components per IC; Medium Scale Integration (MSI): 10 to 100 components per IC; Large Scale Integration (LSI): 100 to 5000 components per IC; Very Large Scale Integration (VLSI): 5,000 to 50,000 components per IC; Ultra Large

Scale Integration (ULSI): over 100,000 components per IC.)

integrated database /ˌɪntɪgreɪtɪd ˈdeɪtəbeɪs/ *noun* a database that is able to provide information for varied requirements without any redundant data

integrated device electronics /ˌɪntɪ ˌgreɪtɪd dɪˌvaɪs ˌelekˈtrɒnɪks/, **integrated drive electronics** /ˌɪntɪˌgreɪtɪd draɪv ˌelek ˈtrɒnɪks/ *noun* full form of **IDE**

integrated injection logic /ˌɪntɪgreɪtɪd ɪnˈdʒekʃən ˌlɒdʒɪk/ *noun* a type of circuit design able to produce very small, low-power components. Abbr **IIL**

integrated modem /ˌɪntɪgreɪtɪd ˈməʊdem/ *noun* a modem that is an internal part of the system

integration /ˌɪntɪˈgreɪʃ(ə)n/ *noun* the process of bringing several operations together ○ *small scale integration (SSI)*

integrity /ɪnˈtegrɪti/ *noun* the reliability of data which is being processed or stored on disk

Intel /ˈɪntel/ the company that developed the first commercially available microprocessor, the 4004, and also developed the range of processors that is used in IBM PCs and compatible computers

Intel Indeo /ˌɪntel ˈɪndiəʊ/ a trade name for software technology developed by Intel that allows a computer to store and play back compressed video sequences using software compression techniques

intelligence /ɪnˈtelɪdʒəns/ *noun* **1.** the ability to reason **2.** the ability of a device to carry out processing or run a program

intelligent /ɪnˈtelɪdʒənt/ *adjective* referring to a machine, program or device that is capable of limited reasoning facilities, giving it human-like responses

intelligent knowledge-based system /ɪnˌtelɪdʒ(ə)nt ˌnɒlɪdʒ beɪsd ˈsɪstəm/ *noun* full form of **IKBS**

intelligent tutoring system /ɪn ˌtelɪdʒ(ə)nt ˈtjuːtərɪŋ ˌsɪstəm/ *noun* a computer-aided learning system that provides responsive and interactive teaching facilities for users

Intel Pentium /ˌɪntel ˈpentiəm/ a trade name for a range of advanced microprocessors that use a 32-bit data bus

INTELSAT /ˈɪntelsæt/ *noun* an international group that deals with the design, construction and allocation of space to various communications satellite projects. Full form **International Telecommunications Satellite Organization**

intensity /ɪnˈtensɪti/ *noun* a measure of the strength of a signal or the brightness of a light source

inter- /ɪntə/ *prefix* between

interact /ˌɪntərˈækt/ *verb* to act on each other

interaction /ˌɪntərˈækʃən/ *noun* the action of two things on each other

interactive /ˌɪntərˈæktɪv/ *adjective* referring to a system or piece of software that allows communication between the user and the computer in conversational mode

> 'Oracle today details its interactive information superhighway aims, endorsed by 17 industry partners. The lynchpin to the announcement will be software based on the Oracle Media Server, a multimedia database designed to run on massively parallel computers.' [*Computing*]

interactive graphics /ˌɪntəræktɪv ˈgræfɪks/ *plural noun* a display system that is able to react to different inputs from the user

interactive media /ˌɪntəræktɪv ˈmiːdiə/ *plural noun* media that provide two-way communications between users and their machines or systems and enable users to control their systems and obtain responses from them in real time

interactive mode /ˌɪntərˈæktɪv ˌməʊd/ *noun* a computer mode that allows the user to enter commands or programs or data and receive immediate responses

Interactive Multimedia Association /ˌɪntəræktɪv ˌmʌltiˈmiːdiə əˌsəʊsieɪʃ(ə)n/ *noun* full form of **IMA**

interactive system /ˌɪntəræktɪv ˈsɪstəm/ *noun* a system which provides an immediate response to the user's commands or programs or data

interactive TV /ˌɪntəræktɪv tiː ˈviː/ *noun* a channel that allows two-way communication between the viewer and the broadcasting station. This feature often allows the user to choose which programme to watch or to respond directly to questions displayed onscreen.

interactive video /ˌɪntəræktɪv ˈvɪdiəʊ/ *noun* full form of **IV**

interactive videotext /ˌɪntəræktɪv ˈvɪdiəʊtekst/ *noun* viewdata service that allows the operator to select pages, display them, ask questions, or use a service such as teleshopping

interactivity /ˌɪntərækˈtɪvɪti/ *noun* two-way communication between users and machines such as computers and television sets, in which the machines provide real-time responses to the inquiries and commands of the users

> '...interactivity is a buzzword you've been hearing a lot lately. Resign yourself to it because you're going to be hearing a lot more of it' [*Music Technology*]

intercarrier noise /ˌɪntəkæriə 'nɔɪz/ *noun* interference caused by two different signal carriers getting mixed ○ *Television intercarrier noise is noticed when the picture and the sound signal carriers clash.*

interchange /'ɪntətʃeɪndʒ/ *noun* the exchange of one thing for another ○ *The machine allows document interchange between it and other machines without reformatting.* ■ *verb* to exchange one thing for another

interchangeable /ˌɪntə'tʃeɪndʒəb(ə)l/ *adjective* which can be exchanged

interchange file format /ˌɪntətʃeɪndʒ 'faɪl ˌfɔːmæt/ *noun* full form of **IFF**

intercharacter spacing /ˌɪntəkærəktə 'speɪsɪŋ/ *noun* a word-processor feature that provides variable spacing between words to create a justified line

intercom /'ɪntəkɒm/ *noun* a short-range voice communications system

interconnect /ˌɪntəkə'nekt/ *verb* to connect together ○ *a series of interconnected terminals*

interconnection /ˌɪntəkə'nekʃən/ *noun* **1.** a section of connecting material between two devices **2.** the connection between a telephone set and a telephone network

interface /'ɪntəfeɪs/ *noun* **1.** the point at which one computer system ends and another begins **2.** a circuit, device or port that allows two or more incompatible units to be linked together in a standard communication system, allowing data to be transferred between them **3.** a section of a program which allows transmission of data to another program ■ *verb* **1.** to modify a device by adding a circuit or connector to allow it to conform to a standard communications system **2.** to connect two or more incompatible devices together with a circuit, in order to allow them to communicate

'The original release of ODBC only included a driver for Microsoft's own SQL Server database. Microsoft has subsequently published the ODBC application program interface enabling third-party vendors to create drivers for other databases and tools.' [*Computing*]

interface card /'ɪntəfeɪs kɑːd/ *noun* an add-on board that allows a computer to interface to certain equipment or conform to a certain standard

interfacing /'ɪntəfeɪsɪŋ/ *noun* hardware or software used to interface two computers, programs or devices

interference /ˌɪntə'fɪərəns/ *noun* **1.** the unwanted addition of signals or noise to a transmitted signal **2.** an effect seen when two signals are added, creating constructive interference when both signals are in phase or destructive interference when they are out of phase

interframe coding /ˌɪntəfreɪm 'kəʊdɪŋ/ *noun* a system for compressing video images, in which only the differences between each frame are recorded

interior gateway protocol /ɪnˌtɪəriə ˌgeɪtweɪ ˌprəʊtəʊ'kɒl/ *noun* full form of **IGP**

interlace /ˌɪntə'leɪs/ *verb* to build up an image on a television screen using two passes to create two picture fields. One displays all the odd-numbered lines, the other all the even-numbered lines. The aim is to reduce the flicker effects on the television picture.

interlaced scanning /ˌɪntəleɪsd 'skænɪŋ/ *noun* a technique for producing an image on a television or computer screen that is clear and correctly aligned in the vertical plane. It involves scanning first all the odd numbered and then all the even numbered lines in the screen image.

interlaced video /ˌɪntəleɪsd 'vɪdiəʊ/ *noun* a video signal made up of two separate fields. This is the normal display mode for home video.

interleave /ˌɪntər'liːv/ *noun* a method of storing data on alternate tracks on a hard disk drive to slow down data transfer rates to match a slower processor ○ *Fast computers run the hard disk with no interleave factor, since they can cope with the fast flow of data to and from the hard disk.*

interleaved /ˌɪntər'liːvd/ *adjective* **1.** referring to sections of two programs executed alternately to give the impression that they are running simultaneously **2.** (thin sheets of paper) which are stuck between the pages of a book ○ *Blank paper was interleaved with the newly printed text to prevent the ink running.*

interleave factor /ˌɪntərˌliːv 'fæktə/ *noun* the ratio of sectors skipped between access operations on a hard disk (NOTE: In a hard disk with an interleave of 3, the first sector is read, then three sectors are skipped and the next sector is read. This is used to allow hard disks with slow access time to store more data on the disk.)

interleaving /ˌɪntər'liːvɪŋ/ *noun* **1.** the technique of dealing with slices or sections of processes alternately, so that they appear to be executed simultaneously **2.** the process of dividing data storage into sections so that each can be accessed separately **3.** the addition of blank paper between printed sheets to prevent the ink from making other sheets dirty

inter-library loan /ɪnˌtɜː ˈlaɪbrəri ləʊn/ *noun* the lending of books or documents from one library to another. Abbr **ILL**

interlinear spacing /ˌɪntəlɪniə ˈspeɪsɪŋ/ *noun* the insertion of spaces between lines of text

interlock /ˌɪntəˈlɒk/ *noun* **1.** a security device that is part of the logon prompt and requires a password **2.** a method of synchronising audio tape with a video or filmed sequence. This can be achieved by using a frame counter or a timer or by running both audio and visual tapes on the same motor. ■ *verb* to prevent a device from performing another task until the present one has been completed

intermediate /ˌɪntəˈmiːdiət/ *adjective* **1.** which is at a stage between two others **2.** widespread term for colour master positives and duplicate negatives which are printed on an integral colour masking film stock

intermediate access memory /ˌɪntəmiːdiət ˌækses ˈmem(ə)ri/ *noun* full form of **IAM**

intermediate frequency /ˌɪntəmiːdiət ˈfriːkwənsi/ *noun* the frequency in a radio receiver to which the incoming received signal is transformed. Abbr **if**

intermittent error /ˌɪntəmɪt(ə)nt ˈerə/ *noun* an error which apparently occurs randomly in a computer or communications system due to a program fault or noise (NOTE: These errors are very difficult to trace and correct due to their apparent random appearance.)

internal /ɪnˈtɜːn(ə)l/ *adjective* which is inside

COMMENT: Many compiled languages are translated to an internal language.

internally stored program /ɪnˌtɜːn(ə)li stɔːd ˈprəʊɡræm/ *noun* a computer program code that is stored in a ROM device in a computer system and does not have to be loaded from backing store

internal memory /ɪnˌtɜːn(ə)l ˈmem(ə)ri/ *noun* storage space that is available within the main computer and is under its direct control. Also called **internal store**

internal modem /ɪnˌtɜːn(ə)l ˌməʊˈdem/ *noun* a modem on an expansion card that fits into an expansion connector and transfers information to the processor through the bus, rather than connecting to a serial port

internal sort /ɪnˈtɜːn(ə)l sɔːt/ *noun* a sorting program using only the main memory of a system

internal store /ɪnˌtɜːn(ə)l ˈstɔː/ *noun* same as **internal memory**

international /ˌɪntəˈnæʃ(ə)nəl/ *adjective* referring to different countries

International Business Machines /ˌɪntənæʃ(ə)nəl ˈbɪznəs məˌʃiːnz/ full form of **IBM**

international direct dialling /ɪntə ˌnæʃ(ə)nəl daɪˌrekt ˈdaɪəlɪŋ kəʊd/ *noun* the process of calling telephone numbers in other countries direct. Abbr **IDD** (NOTE: no plural)

international file format /ˌɪntənæʃ(ə)nəl ˈfaɪl ˌfɔːmæt/ *noun* full form of **IFF**

International MIDI Association /ˌɪntənæʃ(ə)nəl ˈmɪdi əˌsəʊsieɪʃ(ə)n/ *noun* a professional organisation that covers subjects including authoring languages, formats, and intellectual property. Abbr **IMA**

International Standards Organization /ˌɪntənæʃ(ə)nəl ˈstændədz ˌɔːɡənaɪzeɪʃ(ə)n/ *noun* an organisation which creates and regulates standards for many types of computer and networking products. Abbr **ISO**

International Telecommunications Satellite Organization /ˌɪntəˌnæʃ(ə)nəl ˌtelikəˌmjuːnɪˌkeɪʃ(ə)nz ˌsætəˌlaɪt ˌɔːɡənaɪˈzeɪʃ(ə)n/ *noun* full form of **INTELSAT**

inter-negative /ɪnˌtɜː ˈneɡətɪv/ *noun* duplicate colour negative film which is prepared directly from an original colour negative film exposed in the camera (*film*)

Internet /ˈɪntənet/ *noun* an international wide area network that provides file and data transfer, together with electronic mail functions for millions of users around the world. ◊ **HTTP, POP 3, SMTP, World Wide Web**

Internet address /ˈɪntənet əˌdres/ *noun* a unique number that identifies the precise location of a particular node on the Internet The address is a 32-bit number usually written in dotted decimal format, i.e. in the form '123.33.22.32', and it is used by the TCP/IP protocol. A domain name system is used to convert a domain name, e.g. 'bloomsbury.com', into a full Internet address. Also called **IP address**

Internet Architecture Board /ˌɪntənet ˈɑːkɪtektʃə ˌbɔːd/ *noun* full form of **IAB 2** (NOTE: Its members include the IETF and the IRTF.)

Internet Assigned Numbers Authority /ˌɪntənet əˌsaɪnd ˈnʌmbəz ɔːˌθɒrɪti/ *noun* a group that assigns unique identifying numbers to the different protocols and network products used on the Internet. Abbr **IANA**

Internet banking /ˌɪntənet ˈbæŋkɪŋ/ *noun* a system that allows customers to check their bank accounts, pay bills and transfer money by means of the Internet

'...most banks now offer reasonable telephone and Internet banking facilities.' [*The Guardian*]

Internet café /ˈɪntənet ˌkæfeɪ/ *noun* same as **cybercafé**

Internet control message protocol /ˌɪntənet kənˌtrəʊl ˈmesɪdʒ ˌprəʊtəkɒl/ *noun* full form of **ICMP**

Internet-draft /ˈɪntənet drɑːft/ *adjective* referring to draft documents produced by the IETF that often lead to RFCs. Abbr **I-D**

Internet Engineering Steering Group /ˌɪntənet ˌendʒɪnɪərɪŋ ˈstɪərɪŋ gruːp/ *noun* full form of **IESG**

Internet Engineering Task Force /ˌɪntənet ˌendʒɪnɪərɪŋ ˈtɑːsk ˌfɔːs/ *noun* full form of **IETF**

Internet Explorer /ˌɪntənet ɪkˈsplɔːrə/ *noun* a web browser developed by Microsoft which allows a user to view formatted HTML information such as webpages on the Internet. Abbr **IE**

Internet group management protocol /ˌɪntənet gruːp ˈmænɪdʒmənt ˌprəʊtəkɒl/ *noun* full form of **IGMP**

Internet Information Server /ˌɪntənet ˌɪnfəˈmeɪʃ(ə)n ˌsɜːvə/ *noun* full form of **IIS**

Internet merchant account /ˌɪntənet ˈmɜːtʃənt əˌkaʊnt/ *noun* a business bank account that allows the business to accept credit card payments via the Internet. Many businesses have a merchant account, allowing them to accept credit card payments by telephone or mail, but still need a separate IMA to accept payments via the net. Abbr **IMA**

Internet message access protocol /ˌɪntənet ˈmesɪdʒ ˌækses ˌprəʊtəkɒl/ *noun* full form of **IMAP**

Internet number /ˈɪntənet ˌnʌmbə/ *noun* ◆ **Internet address**

Internet protocol /ˌɪntənet ˈprəʊtəkɒl/ *noun* full form of **IP**

Internet relay chat /ˌɪntənet ˌriːleɪ ˈtʃæt/ *noun* a system that allows many users to participate in a chat session in which each user can send messages and sees the text of any other user. Abbr **IRC**

Internet research steering group /ˌɪntənet rɪˌsɜːtʃ ˈstɪərɪŋ gruːp/ *noun* a group that manages the Internet research task force; part of the Internet Society. Abbr **IRSG**

Internet research task force /ˌɪntənet rɪˌsɜːtʃ ˈtɑːsk fɔːs/ *noun* full form of **IRTF**

Internet server application program interface /ˌɪntənet ˌsɜːvə ˌæplɪkeɪʃ(ə)n ˈprəʊgræm ˌɪntəfeɪs/ *noun* full form of **ISAPI**

Internet service provider /ˌɪntənet ˈsɜːvɪs prəˌvaɪdə/ *noun* full form of **ISP**

Internet Society /ˈɪntənet səˌsaɪəti/ *noun* an organisation that has the task of maintaining and enhancing the Internet. It is made up of committees, such as the Internet Advisory Board and the Internet Engineering Task Force, and is not linked to any government or company, so that it provides an independent view of the future of the Internet.

Internet telephony /ˌɪntənet təˈlefəni/ *noun* a system that allows users to make telephone calls using the Internet to carry the voice signals. To make a call, users need a computer with a sound card fitted and a microphone and loudspeaker plugged in, and special software manages the connection and transfers the voice data over the Internet. (NOTE: This system is particularly appealing if you have low-cost dial-up access to the Internet, since it allows you to make long distance calls for the low-price you pay for your Internet connection.)

Internetwork /ˌɪntəˈnetwɜːk/ *noun* a number of networks connected together using bridges or routers to allow users on one network to access any resource on any other of the connected networks

InterNIC *noun* an organisation that was originally responsible for managing the way domain names are registered, assigned and paid for by organisations. Recently, the system has changed to allow a group of companies in different countries to manage the registration and payment process.

interoperability /ˌɪntəˌɒpərəˈbɪlɪti/ *noun* the ability of two devices or computers to exchange information

interpolation /ɪnˌtɜːpəˈleɪʃ(ə)n/ *noun* the calculation of intermediate values between two points

inter-positive /ɪnˌtɜː ˈpɒzɪtɪv/ *noun* positive colour duplicate film made from an original negative (*film*)

interpret /ɪnˈtɜːprɪt/ *verb* to translate what is said in one language into another

interpreter /ɪnˈtɜːprɪtə/ *noun* a piece of software used to translate a user's high-level program into machine code at the time of execution. Compare **compiler** (NOTE: A compiler translates the high-level language into machine code and then executes it, whereas an interpreter makes a translation in real time.)

interrogation /ɪnˌterəˈgeɪʃ(ə)n/ *noun* the act of asking questions

interrupt /ˌɪntəˈrʌpt/ *verb* to stop something happening while it is happening ■ *noun* **1.** the stopping of a transmission as a result of an action at the receiving end of a system **2.** a signal which diverts a central processing unit from one task to another that has higher priority, allowing the CPU to return to the first task later

interrupt request /ˈɪntərʌpt rɪˌkwest/ *noun* a signal from a device that indicates to the CPU that it requires attention. Abbr **IRQ**

interval /ˈɪntəv(ə)l/ *noun* a short pause between two actions ○ *There was an interval between pressing the key and the starting of the printout.*

intervention /ˌɪntəˈvenʃən/ *noun* acting to make a change in a system

interword spacing /ˌɪntəwɜːd ˈspeɪsɪŋ/ *noun* variable spacing between words in a text, used to justify lines

intra /ˈɪntrə/, **intra frame** /ˈɪntrə freɪm/ *noun* a reference frame used to synchronise video data that has been compressed using the MPEG system

intrinsic /ɪnˈtrɪnsɪk/ *adjective* pure (substance) which has had no other chemicals (such as dopants) added ○ *The base material for ICs is an intrinsic semiconductor which is then doped.*

introduce /ˌɪntrəˈdjuːs/ *verb* to put something into something ○ *Errors were introduced into the text at keyboarding.*

intruder /ɪnˈtruːdə/ *noun* a person who is not authorised to use a computer or connect to a network. ◊ **firewall, hacker**

intrusion /ɪnˈtruːʒ(ə)n/ *noun* the action by a telephone operator to allow both parties on each end of the telephone line to hear his or her message

invalid /ˈɪnvəlɪd/ *adjective* not valid ○ *He tried to use an invalid password.*

inverse video /ˌɪnvɜːs ˈvɪdiəʊ/ *noun* a television effect created by swapping the background and foreground text display colours

inversion /ɪnˈvɜːʃ(ə)n/ *noun* **1.** the process of changing over the numbers in a binary word, one to zero and zero to one ○ *The inversion of a binary digit takes place in one's complement.* **2.** the process of changing the logical state of a signal or device to its logical opposite

invert /ˌɪnˈvɜːt/ *verb* to change all binary ones to zeros and zeros to ones

inverter /ɪnˈvɜːtə/ *noun* **1.** a logical gate that provides inversion facilities **2.** a circuit used to provide alternating current supply from a DC battery source

invisible /ɪnˈvɪzɪb(ə)l/ *adjective* visible on a DTP page or graphics layout during the design phase, but not printed

invitation /ˌɪnvɪˈteɪʃ(ə)n/ *noun* action by a processor to contact another device and allow it to send a message

invitation to send /ˌɪnvɪteɪʃ(ə)n tə ˈsend/ *noun* a special character transmitted to indicate to a device that the host computer is willing to receive messages. Abbr **ITS**

invite /ɪnˈvaɪt/ *verb* to ask someone to do something

involve /ɪnˈvɒlv/ *verb* to have to do with; to include (something) in a process ○ *Backing up involves copying current working files onto a separate storage disk.*

I/O /ˌaɪ ˈəʊ/ *noun* the process of receiving or transmitting data between a computer and its peripherals, and other points outside the system. Full form **input/output**

ion /ˈaɪən/ *noun* a charged particle

ion deposition /ˈaɪən ˌdepəzɪʃ(ə)n/ *noun* printing technology that uses a printhead that deposits ions to create a charged image which attracts the toner

ionosphere /aɪˈɒnəsfɪə/ *noun* a layer of charged particles surrounding the earth

ip *abbr* information provider

IP /ˌaɪ ˈpiː/ *noun* one part of the TCP/IP standard that defines how data is transferred over a network. Full form **Internet protocol**

i/p, I/P *abbr* input

IP address /ˌaɪ ˈpiː əˌdres/ *noun* same as **Internet address**

IPng /ˌaɪ piː en ˈdʒiː/ *noun* an upgrade of the Internet Protocol that allows more computers to connect to the Internet and supports more data traffic. Full form **Internet Protocol next generation**

Ipsec /ˌaɪ ˌpiː sɪˈkjʊərəti/, **IP Security** *noun* a set of security protocols that allows information to be transferred securely over the Internet and is used to set up and support secure virtual private networks. The system works with packets of data at the IP layer and supports two types of public-key data encryption. The first, called Transport mode, encrypts the data within a packet, but does not touch the header information, which contains the destination address, subject and source of a packet. The second mode, Tunnel mode, provides a greater level of security by encrypting all of the packet, including the header information.

IP spoofing /ˌaɪ ˌpiː ˈspuːfɪŋ/ *noun* a method of gaining unauthorised access to a computer or network by pretending to be an authorised computer or device (NOTE: Each device on the network has its own unique IP address, and many security systems block or allow access to networks depending on the IP address of the computer that is requesting access. A hacker finds an IP address that is allowed, then modifies the header information in the data packets from his or her own computer to include this IP address. Newer routers and firewalls use a range of techniques to spot this scheme and block the data.)

IR *abbr* **1.** information retrieval **2.** index register **3.** instruction register

IRC *abbr* Internet relay chat

iris /ˈaɪrɪs/ *noun* a small hole in a camera between the lens and the film. The iris is normally variable in size to adjust the amount of light passing through it to the film.

IRQs *abbr* interrupt requests

irretrievable /ˌɪrɪˈtriːvəb(ə)l/ *adjective* which cannot be retrieved ○ *The files are irretrievable since the computer crashed.*

IRSG /ˌaɪ ɑː es ˈdʒiː/ *noun* a group that manages the Internet research task force and is part of the Internet Society. Full form **Internet Research Steering Group**

IRTF /ˌaɪ ɑː tiː ˈef/ *noun* a committee that is part of the IAB and researches new Internet standards before referring them to the IETF for approval. Full form **Internet Research Task Force**

IS *abbr* indexed sequential

ISA /ˈaɪsə/ *noun* a standard used for the 16-bit expansion bus in an IBM PC or compatible. Full form **Industry Standard Architecture**. Compare **EISA, MCA**

ISAM *abbr* indexed sequential access method

ISAPI /ˌaɪ es eɪ aɪ ˈpiː/ *noun* (*on a Windows NT server*) a set of commands and procedures that allow web server software to access other applications on the same server running Windows NT. Full form **Internet server application program interface**

ISBN *abbr* International Standard Book Number

ISDN /ˌaɪ es diː ˈen/ *noun* a method of digital data transmission. It utilises the existing telephone network, but omits the digital/analog conversion required by conventional telephonic equipment; the customer therefore has a fully digital connection. ISDN connections usually provide two 64K bps channels, which can work independently or be combined to achieve transfer speeds of 128K bps. Full form **integrated services digital network**

ISO *abbr* International Standards Organization

ISO 9660 *noun* a standard method of storing files on a CD-ROM, used in many formats including PhotoCD

isolate /ˈaɪsəˌleɪt/ *verb* **1.** to separate something from a system **2.** to insulate (something) electrically

isolation /ˌaɪsəˈleɪʃ(ə)n/ *noun* being isolated

isolator /ˈaɪsəleɪtə/ *noun* a device or material which isolates

isometric view /ˌaɪsəʊˈmetrɪk vjuː/ *noun* (*in graphics*) a drawing that shows all three dimensions of an object in equal proportion ○ *An isometric view does not show any perspective.*

ISO/OSI *abbr* International Standards Organization Open Systems Interconnection

ISO/OSI model /ˌaɪ es əʊ əʊ es ˈaɪ ˌmɒd(ə)l/ *noun* a layered architecture that defines how computers and networks should interact

ISP /ˌaɪ es ˈpiː/ *noun* a company that provides one of the permanent links that make up the Internet and sells connections to private users and companies to allow them to access the Internet. Full form **Internet service provider**

ISR *abbr* information storage and retrieval

ISSN *abbr* International Standard Serial Number

IT *abbr* information technology

italic /ɪˈtælɪk/ *noun* type of character font in which the characters slope to the right ○ *The headline is printed in italic and underlined.*

item /ˈaɪtəm/ *noun* a single thing among many ○ *a data item can be a word* or *a series of figures* or *a record in a file*

iterate /ˈɪtəreɪt/ *noun* a loop or series of instructions in a program which repeat over and over again until the program is completed. Also called **iterative routine**

iteration /ˌɪtəˈreɪʃ(ə)n/ *noun* the repeated application of a program to solve a problem

iterative routine /ˌɪtərətɪv ruːˈtiːn/ *noun* same as **iterate**

ITS *abbr* invitation to send

IV /ˌaɪ ˈviː/ *noun* a system that uses a computer linked to a video disk player to provide processing power and real images or moving pictures. Full form **interactive video** (NOTE: This system is often used in teaching. A student is asked questions, and if he or she answers correctly, the system responds by providing a filmed sequence from the videodisc.)

J

jabber /ˈdʒæbə/ *noun* a continuous random signal transmitted by a faulty adapter card or node on a network

jack /dʒæk/, **jack plug** /ˈdʒæk plʌg/ *noun* a plug which consists of a single pin

jacket /ˈdʒækɪt/ *noun* the cover for a book or disk ○ *The book jacket has the author's name on it.*

jaggies /ˈdʒægiːz/ *plural noun* jagged edges which appear along diagonal or curved lines displayed on a computer screen, caused by the size of each pixel. ◊ **aliasing, anti-aliasing**

JANET /ˈdʒænɪt/ *noun* a wide area network that connects universities and academic establishments. Full form **joint academic network**

jar /dʒɑː/ *verb* to give a sharp shock to a device ○ *You can cause trouble by turning off* or *jarring the PC while the disk read heads are moving.*

Java /ˈdʒɑːvə/ a trade name for a programming language and program definition developed by Sun Microsystems. Java is used to create small applications designed to enhance the functionality of a webpage. It is similar to object-oriented languages such as C++ and can run on any compatible platform. Compare **JavaScript**

Java Beans /ˈdʒɑːvə biːnz/ a trade name for a software system, developed by Sun Microsystems, that provides objects within the Java programming language, and is similar to COM and CORBA and can work with both these standards

Java Database Connectivity /ˌdʒɑːvə ˌdeɪtəbeɪs ˌkɒnekˈtɪvɪti/ a trade name for a set of standard functions that allow a programmer to access a database from within a Java application. Abbr **JDBC**

JavaScript /ˈdʒɑːvəskrɪpt/ a trade name for set of programming commands that can be included within a normal webpage written using HTML commands. When the web browser loads the webpage, it runs the JavaScript commands, normally used to create special effects to a webpage. Compare **HTML, Perl, VBScript**

JCL /ˌdʒaɪ siː ˈel/ *noun* a set of commands that identify, and describe resources required by, a job that a computer has to process. Full form **job control language**

JDBC *abbr* Java Database Connectivity

jet /dʒet/ ◆ **ink-jet printer**

jingle /ˈdʒɪŋg(ə)l/ *noun* a short easily-remembered tune used to advertise a product on television

jitter /ˈdʒɪtə/ *noun* the rapid small up-and-down movement of characters or pixels on a screen displaying image bits in a facsimile transmission ○ *Looking at this screen jitter is giving me a headache.*

job /dʒɒb/ *noun* a task or a number of tasks to be processed as a single unit ○ *The next job to be processed is to sort all the records.*

jobbing printer /ˈdʒɒbɪŋ ˌprɪntə/ *noun* a person who does small printing jobs, such as printing business cards

job control language /ˌdʒɒb kənˈtrəʊl ˌlæŋgwɪdʒ/ *noun* full form of **JCL**

jog /dʒɒg/ *verb* to advance a video tape by one frame at a time

jog/shuttle, jog/shuttle control *noun* a manual control on a video player or camera that allows a user to edit a sequence (NOTE: Jog moves the tape one frame a time, shuttle moves the tape more rapidly.)

join /dʒɔɪn/ *verb* **1.** to link or to put several things together **2.** to combine two or more pieces of information to produce a single unit of information

joint academic network /dʒɔɪnt ˌækəˌdemɪk ˈnetwɜːk/ *noun* full form of **JANET**

Joint Photographic Experts Group /ˌdʒɔɪnt fəʊtəˌgræfɪks ˈekspɜːts gruːp/ *noun* full form of **JPEG**

journal /ˈdʒɜːn(ə)l/ *noun* **1.** a record of all communications to and from a terminal **2.** a list of any changes or updates to a file ○ *The modified records were added to the master file and noted in the journal.*

journal file /ˈdʒɜːn(ə)l faɪl/ *noun* a stored record of every communication between a user and the central computer, used to help retrieve files after a system crash or fault

journalist /ˈdʒɜːn(ə)lɪst/ *noun* a person who writes for a newspaper

joystick /ˈdʒɔɪˌstɪk/ *noun* a device that allows a user to move a cursor around the screen by moving an upright rod connected to an I/O port on the computer

JPEG /ˈdʒeɪ peg/ *noun* a standard that defines a way of storing graphic images in a compressed format in a file on disk. Full form **Joint Photographic Experts Group**

JPEG++ /ˌdʒaɪ peg plʌs ˈplʌs/ *noun* an extension to JPEG that allows parts of an image to be compressed in different ways

JScript /ˈdʒaɪskrɪpt/ a trade name for a version of JavaScript developed by Microsoft

judder /ˈdʒʌdə/ *noun* an unwanted movement in a printing or facsimile machine that results in a distorted picture

jukebox /ˈdʒuːkˌbɒks/ *noun* a CD-ROM drive that can hold several CD-ROM discs and select the correct disc when required

jumbo chip /ˈdʒʌmbəʊ tʃɪp/ *noun* an integrated circuit made using the whole of a semiconductor wafer. ◊ **wafer scale integration**

jump /dʒʌmp/ *noun* a programming command to end one set of instructions and direct the processor to another section of the program ■ *verb* **1.** to direct a CPU to another section of a program **2.** to miss a page or a line or a space when printing ○ *The typewriter jumped two lines.* ○ *The paging system has jumped two folio numbers.*

jump cut /ˌdʒʌmp ˈkʌt/ *verb* to eliminate a part of the continuous action within a scene

jumper /ˈdʒʌmpə/ *noun* a temporary wire connection on a circuit board

jump on zero /ˌdʒʌmp ɒn ˈzɪərəʊ/ *noun* a conditional jump executed if a flag or register is zero

jump out /ˌdʒʌmp ˈaʊt/ *verb* to delete frames in film or video tape editing (*film*)

junction /ˈdʒʌŋkʃən/ *noun* **1.** a connection between wires or cables **2.** a region between two areas of semiconductor which have different doping levels (such as a p-type and n-type area), resulting in a potential difference between them

junk /dʒʌŋk/ *noun* information or hardware which is useless or out of date or non-functional ■ *verb* to make a file or piece of hardware redundant

justification /ˌdʒʌstɪfɪˈkeɪʃ(ə)n/ *noun* the process of moving data bits or characters to the left or right so that the lines have straight margins

justify /ˈdʒʌstɪˌfaɪ/ *verb* **1.** to change the spacing between words or characters in a document so that the left and right margins will be straight **2.** to shift the contents of a computer register by a set amount **3.** to set lines of printed text as wide as possible in a certain page size

K

K /keɪ/ *symbol* kilo

K56flex a trade name for a communications standard developed by Hayes, Pace and other manufacturers for a range of high-speed modems that can transfer data at 56,000 bits per second. ◊ **V series, X2**

Kaleida Labs /kə'laɪdə læbz/ a company formed as a joint venture between Apple and IBM to produce cross-platform multimedia authoring tools

Karnaugh map /'kɑːnəʊ mæp/ *noun* a graphical representation of states and conditions in a logic circuit ○ *The prototype was checked for hazards with a Karnaugh map.*

Kbps /ˌkeɪ biː piː 'es/ *noun* a measure of the amount of data that a device can transfer each second ○ *A fast modem can transfer data at a rate of 56Kbps, whereas an ISDN adapter can transfer data at a rate of 128Kbps.* Full form **kilobits per second**

Kbyte /'keɪ baɪt/ *abbr* kilobyte

Kermit /'kɜːmɪt/ *noun* a file transfer protocol usually used when downloading data with a modem

kern /kɜːn/ *verb* to adjust the space between pairs of letters so that they are printed closer together

kernel /'kɜːn(ə)l/ *noun* the essential instruction routines required as a basis for any operations in a computer system (NOTE: Kernel routines are usually hidden from the user. They are used by the operating system for tasks such as loading a program or displaying text on a screen.)

kerning /'kɜːnɪŋ/ *noun* the slight overlapping of certain printed character areas to prevent large spaces between them, giving a neater appearance

key /kiː/ *noun* **1.** a button on a keyboard that operates a switch ○ *There are 64 keys on the keyboard.* **2.** an important object or group of characters in a computer system, used to represent an instruction or set of data **3.** a special combination of numbers or characters that are used with a cipher to encrypt or decrypt a message ○ *Type this key into the machine, it will decode the last message.* **4.** an identification code or word used for a stored record or data item ○ *We selected all the records with the word 'disk' in their keys.*

keyboard /'kiːbɔːd/ *verb* to enter information by using a keyboard ○ *It was cheaper to have the manuscript keyboarded by another company.*

'...the main QWERTY typing area is in the centre of the keyboard with the 10 function keys on the left' [*Personal Computer World*]

keyboarder /'kiːbɔːdə/ *noun* a person who enters data via a keyboard

keyboarding /'kiːbɔːdɪŋ/ *noun* the action of entering data using a keyboard ○ *The cost of keyboarding is calculated in keystrokes per hour.*

keyboard overlay /'kiːbɔːd ˌəʊvəleɪ/ *noun* a strip of paper that is placed above the keys on a keyboard to indicate their function

keyboard send/receive /ˌkiːbɔːd send rɪ'siːv/ *noun* full form of **KSR**

key combination /'kiː ˌkɒmbɪneɪʃ(ə)n/ *noun* a combination of two or more keys that carry out a function when pressed at the same time

keyed sequential access method /ˌkiːd sɪˌkwenʃəl 'ækses ˌmeθəd/ *noun* full form of **KSAM**

key frame /ˌkiː 'freɪm/ *noun* **1.** a single picture in an animation that describes the main actions in the sequence **2.** (*in a hypertext document*) a page that gives the user a choice of destination **3.** (*in full motion video*) a frame that is recorded in full rather than being compressed or differentially recorded

key grip /ˌkiː 'grɪp/ *noun* same as **first grip** (*film*)

keying /'kiːɪŋ/ *noun* a method of overlaying one particular video signal onto another

key light /'kiː laɪt/ *noun* the main light which projects the most brightness on to the subject being filmed (*film*)

keypad /'kiːˌpæd/ *noun* a group of special keys used for certain applications ○ *You can use the numeric keypad to enter the figures.*

'...it uses a six button keypad to select the devices and functions' [*Byte*]

keystone distortion /ˌkiːstəʊn dɪ 'stɔːʃ(ə)n/ *noun* image distortion in which the vertical lines slant out towards the horizontal edges of the monitor. Also called **trapezoidal distortion**

keystroke /'kiːstrəʊk/ *noun* the action of pressing a key ○ *He keyboards at a rate of 3500 keystrokes per hour.*

key-to-disk /ˌkiː tə ˈdɪsk/ *noun* a system where data is keyed in and stored directly on disk without any processing

keyword /ˈkiːwɜːd/ *noun* **1.** a command word used in a programming language to provide a function ○ *The BASIC keyword PRINT will display text on the screen.* **2.** an important or informative word in a title or document that describes its contents ○ *Computer is a keyword in IT.* **3.** a word which is relevant or important to a text

KHz *abbr* kilohertz

kill /kɪl/ *verb* to erase a file or stop a program during execution

kilo /ˈkɪləʊ/ *prefix* one thousand

kilobit /ˈkɪləbɪt/ *noun* 1,024 bits of data. Abbr **Kb, Kbit**

kilobits per second /ˌkiːləʊ bɪts pɜː ˈsekənd/ *noun* a measure of the amount of data that a device can transfer each second. Abbr **Kbps**

kilobyte /ˈkɪləʊˌbaɪt/ *noun* a unit of measurement for high-capacity storage devices meaning 1,024 bytes of data. Abbr **KB, Kbyte**

kilohertz /ˈkɪləhɜːts/ *noun* a frequency of one thousand cycles per second. Abbr **KHz**

kilo instructions per second /ˌkɪləʊ ɪnˌstrʌkʃənz pɜː ˈsekənd/ *noun* full form of **KIPS**

kilo-ohm /ˈkiːləʊ əʊm/ *noun* one thousand ohms

Kilostream /ˈkɪləstriːm/ a trade name for a leased line connection supplied by British Telecom that provides data transfer rates of 64Kbit per second

kiloword /ˈkɪləwɜːd/ *noun* a unit of measurement of 1,024 computer words

kimball tag /ˈkɪmbɔːl tæg/ *noun* a coded card attached to a product in a shop, containing information about the product that is read by a scanner when the product is sold

kiosk /ˈkiːɒsk/ *noun* a small booth with a screen, a means of user input and a computer, used to provide information for the general public

KIPS /ˌkeɪ aɪ piː ˈes/ *noun* one thousand computer instructions processed every second, used as a measure of computer power. Full form **kilo instructions per second**

kludge, kluge *noun* (*informal*) **1.** a temporary correction made to a badly written or constructed piece of software or to a keyboarding error **2.** hardware which should be used for demonstration purposes only

kluged /kluːdʒd/ *adjective* temporarily repaired

knob /nɒb/ *noun* a round button (such as on a monitor), which can be turned to control some process ○ *Turn the on/off knob.*

knowledge /ˈnəʊ haʊ/ *noun* what is known

knowledge base /ˈnɒlɪdʒ beɪs/ *noun* the computerised data in an expert system that can be used to solve a particular type of problem

knowledge-based system /ˌnɒlɪdʒ beɪst ˈsɪstəm/ *noun* a computer system that applies the stored reactions, instructions and knowledge of experts in a particular field to a problem

knowledge engineering /ˈnɒlɪdʒ ˌendʒɪnɪərɪŋ/ *noun* the process of designing and writing expert computer systems

knowledge industry /ˈnɒlɪdʒ ˌɪndəstri/ *noun* businesses that specialise in data processing or the development and use of information technology

KSAM /ˌkeɪ es eɪ ˈem/ *noun* a file structure that allows data to be accessed using key fields or key field content. Full form **keyed sequential access method**

KSR /ˌkeɪ es ˈɑː/ *noun* a terminal which has a keyboard and monitor, and is linked to a CPU. Full form **keyboard send/receive**. Compare **ASR**

KVA *abbr* kilovolt-ampere output rating

KW *abbr* **1.** kilowatt **2.** kiloword

KWAC /kwæk/ *noun* a library indexing system that uses keywords from the text and title as indexed entries. Full form **keyword and context**

KWIC /kwɪk/ *noun* a library indexing system that uses keywords from the title or text of a book or document as an indexed entry followed by the text it relates to. Full form **keyword in context**

KWOC /kwɒk/ *noun* a library indexing system that indexes books or document titles under any relevant keywords. Full form **keyword out of context**

L

L /el/ *noun* the unit of surface brightness (*film*) Full form **lambert**

L2TP /ˌel tuː tiː ˈpiː/ *noun* a network protocol, an extension to the PPP protocol, that allows the data from small Virtual Private Networks to be transferred over a network such as the public Internet. Full form **layer two tunnelling protocol**. ◊ **tunnelling, PPP, protocol** (NOTE: L2TP operates enclosing the network packets from the Virtual Private Network within a special packet that can then travel over the Internet, a process called tunnelling.)

label /ˈleɪb(ə)l/ *noun* **1.** a word or other symbol used in a computer program to identify a routine or statement ○ *BASIC uses many program labels such as line numbers.* **2.** a character or set of characters used to identify a variable or piece of data or a file **3.** a piece of paper or card attached to something to show instructions for use or an address ■ *verb* to print an address on a label

labelling /ˈleɪb(ə)lɪŋ/ *noun* **1.** the process of putting a label on something ○ *The word-processor has a special utility allowing simple and rapid labelling.* **2.** the process of printing labels

laboratory /ləˈbɒrət(ə)ri/ *noun* a place where scientists work on research and development of new products ○ *The new chip is being developed in the university laboratories.*

lace /leɪs/ *verb* to thread film on to a projector or tape on to a cassette recorder

lag /læg/ *noun* **1.** the time taken for an image to be no longer visible after it has been displayed on a CRT screen (NOTE: Lag is caused by long persistence phosphor.) **2.** the time taken for a signal to pass through a circuit, such that the output is delayed compared to the input ○ *Time lag is noticeable on international phone calls.*

lambert /ˈlæmbət/ *noun* full form of **L**

laminate /ˈlæmɪneɪt/ *verb* to cover a paper with a thin film of plastic, to give it a glossy look ○ *The book has a laminated cover.*

lamp /læmp/ *noun* an electrical component which provides artificial light by heating a thin wire within a glass bulb filled with an inert gas

LAN /læn/, **lan** *noun* a network where the various terminals and equipment are all within a short distance of one another, e.g. in the same building, and can be interconnected by cables. Full form **local area network**

> 'The opportunities to delete and destroy data are far greater on our LAN than in the days when we had a mainframe. PC people are culturally different from mainframe people. You really don't think about security problems when you can physically lock your system up in a closet.' [*Computing*]

landing zone /ˈlændɪŋ zəʊn/ *noun* an area of a hard disk which does not carry data. The head can come into contact with the disk in this area without damaging the disk or data. ◊ **park**

landline /ˈlæn(d)ˌlaɪn/ *noun* a communications link that uses cable to physically and electrically link two devices

landscape /ˈlændskeɪp/ *noun* the orientation of a page or piece of paper where the longest edge is horizontal. Compare **portrait**

language /ˈlæŋgwɪdʒ/ *noun* a system of words or symbols which allows communication with computers, especially one that allows computer instructions to be entered as words which are easy to understand, and then translates them into machine code

> COMMENT: There are three main types of computer languages: machine code, assemble, and high-level language. The more high-level the language is, the easier it is to program and understand, but the slower it is to execute. The following are the commonest high-level languages: ADA, ALGOL, APL, BASIC, C, C++, COBOL, COMAL, CORAL, FORTH, FORTRAN, LISP, LOGO, PASCAL, PL/1, POP-2, PROLOG, and Visual Basic. Assembly language uses mnemonics to represent machine code instructions. Machine code is the lowest level of programming language and consists of basic binary patterns that instruct the processor to perform various tasks.

LAN Manager /ˈlæn ˌmænɪdʒə/ a trade name for a network operating system developed for the PC by Microsoft

LAN server /ˈlæn ˌsɜːvə/ *noun* a computer which runs a network operating system and controls the basic network operations. All the workstations in a LAN are connected to the central network server and users log onto the network server.

LAN Server /ˈlæn ˌsɜːvə/ a trade name for a network operating system for the PC developed by IBM

lap /læp/ *noun* **1.** a person's knees, when he or she is sitting down ○ *He placed the computer on his lap and keyboarded some orders while sitting in his car.* **2.** an overlap of printed colours, which prevents any gaps showing

LAP /ˌel eɪ ˈpiː/ *noun* a CCITT standard protocol used to start and maintain links over an X.25 network. Full form **link access protocol**

lapel microphone /ləˌpel ˈmaɪkrəfəʊn/ *noun* a small microphone that is pinned to the someone's jacket

laptop /ˈlæptɒp/, **laptop computer** /ˌlæptɒp kəmˈpjuːtə/ *noun* a computer that is light enough to carry, but not so small as to fit in a pocket, and that usually consists of a screen, keyboard and disk drive. ◊ **desktop, hand-held computer, PDA**

> 'Michael Business Systems has provided research company BMRB with 240 Toshiba laptop computers in a deal valued at £300,000. The deal includes a three-year maintenance contract.' [*Computing*]

large model /ˌlɑːdʒ ˈmɒd(ə)l/ *noun* (*in an Intel processor*) a memory model in which both code and data can exceed 64Kb in size, but combined size should be less than 1Mb

large-scale /ˈlɑːdʒ skeɪl/ *adjective* working with large amounts of data. Compare **small-scale**

large-scale integration /ˌlɑːdʒ skeɪl ˌɪntɪˈɡreɪʃ(ə)n/ *noun* full form of **LSI**

laser /ˈleɪzə/ *noun* a device that produces coherent light of a single wavelength in a narrow beam, by exciting a material so that it emits photons of light. Full form **light amplification by stimulated emission of radiation**

laser disc /ˈleɪzə dɪsk/ *noun* same as **compact disc**

LaserJet /ˈleɪzədʒet/ same as **Hewlett Packard LaserJet**

laser printer /ˈleɪzə ˌprɪntə/ *noun* a high-resolution computer printer that uses a laser source to print high-quality dot matrix character patterns on paper

LaserWriter /ˈleɪzəraɪtə/ a trade name for a laser printer manufactured by Apple that uses the PostScript page description language

last in first out /ˌlɑːst ɪn ˌfɜːst ˈaʊt/ *adjective* full form of **LIFO** ○ *This computer stack uses a last in first out data retrieval method.*

last in last out /ˌlɑst ɪn lɑːst ˈaʊt/ *adjective* full form of **LILO**

latency /ˈleɪt(ə)nsi/ *noun* a time delay between the moment when an instruction is given to a computer and the execution of the instruction or return of a result, e.g. the delay between a request for data and the data being transferred from memory

latent image /ˌleɪt(ə)nt ˈɪmɪdʒ/ *noun* the recorded invisible image in exposed but undeveloped film

lateral reversal /ˌlæt(ə)rəl rɪˈvɜːs(ə)l/ *noun* the process of creating the mirror image of a picture by swapping left and right

launch /lɔːntʃ/ *noun* the process of putting a new product on the market ○ *The launch of the new PC has been put back six months.* ■ *verb* **1.** to put a new product on the market ○ *The new PC was launched at the Computer Show.* **2.** to start or run a program ○ *You launch the word-processor by double-clicking on this icon.*

launch amplifier /ˈlɔːntʃ ˌæmplɪfaɪə/ *noun* an amplifier used to boost the television signals before they are transmitted over a cable network

launch vehicle /ˈlɔːntʃ ˌviːɪk(ə)l/ *noun* a spacecraft used to transport a satellite from earth into space

layer /ˈleɪə/ *noun* **1.** ISO/OSI standards defining the stages a message has to pass through when being transmitted from one computer to another over a local area network **2.** the division of sections of space at certain distances from the earth into separate regions used for various radio communications. These are: D-Region from 50 – 90km above earth's surface, E-Region from 90 – 150km above earth's surface, F-Region from 150 – 400km above the earth's surface. **3.** a feature of graphics software that provides a stack of separate drawing areas that can be overlaid to produce the final image, or controlled and manipulated independently. It is often used in complex images: e.g., the background might be on layer 1, an image of a house on layer 2 and any special effects on layer 3 – the finished picture is made up of the three layers combined and viewed together.

layered /ˈleɪəd/ *adjective* that consists of layers ○ *The kernel has a layered structure according to user priority.*

layer two tunnelling protocol /ˌleɪə tuː ˈtʌnəlɪŋ ˌprəʊtəkɒl/ *noun* full form of **L2TP**

lay in /ˌleɪ ˈɪn/ *verb* to synchronise a frame of film with the music or sound tracks

lay out /ˌleɪ ˈaʊt/ *verb* to plan and design the positions and sizes of a piece of work to be printed

layout /'leɪaʊt/ *noun* **1.** rules governing the data input and output from a computer **2.** a way of using a sheet of paper. ◊ **landscape, portrait**

LBR *noun* a system for producing characters on a light sensitive film by laser beam directly controlled from a computer. Full form **laser beam recording**

LC circuit /ˌel 'siː ˌsɜːkɪt/ *noun* a simple inductor-capacitor circuit that acts as a filter or oscillator

LCD /ˌel siː 'diː/ *noun* a type of display that uses liquid crystals that turn black when a voltage is applied. LCDs are found in many watches, calculators and other small digital devices. Full form **liquid crystal display**

LCD screen /ˌel siː 'diː skriːn/ *noun* a screen that uses LCD technology to create a thin display and is normally found in laptop computers and flat-screen monitors. Full form **liquid crystal display screen**

LCD shutter printer /ˌel siː ˌdiː 'ʃʌtə/ *noun* a page printer that uses an LCD panel in front of a bright light to describe images onto the photosensitive drum. The LCD panel stops the light passing through, except at pixels that describe the image.

LCP /ˌel siː 'piː/ *noun* rules defining the transmission of data over a channel. Full form **link control procedure**

LDAP /'el dæp/ *noun* a new standard that provides directory services over the Internet; derived from the X.500 standard. LDAP is beginning to be included in many Internet applications and provides a way of organising, locating and using resources on the Internet that are listed within its database. Full form **lightweight directory access protocol**

LDS *noun* a TV signal relay station that transmits signals to another point from which they are distributed over cable. Full form **local distribution service**

lead /liːd/ *noun* **1.** an electrical conducting wire **2.** a thin piece of metal used to give extra space between lines of type before printing

leader /'liːdə/ *noun* **1.** a section of magnetic tape that contains no signal, used at the beginning of the reel for identification and to aid the tape machine to pick up the tape **2.** a row of printed dots

leading /'liːdɪŋ/ *noun* space between lines of printed or displayed text

leading edge /'liːdɪŋ edʒ/ *noun* the first edge of a punched card that enters the card reader

leading zero /ˌliːdɪŋ 'zɪərəʊ/ *noun* the zero digit used to pad out the beginning of a stored number

lead in page /'liːd ɪn ˌpeɪdʒ/ *noun* a videotext page that directs the user to other pages of interest

leaf /liːf/ *noun* **1.** the final node in a tree structure **2.** a page of a book (printed on both sides)

leaflet /'liːflət/ *noun* a small publicity sheet (usually one page folded in half)

leak /liːk/ *noun* a gradual loss of charge from a charged component due to faulty insulation ■ *verb* to lose electric charge gradually ○ *In this circuit, the capacitor charge leaks out at 10% per second.*

leakage /'liːkɪdʒ/ *noun* a loss of signal strength

'...signal leakages in both directions can be a major problem in co-axial cable systems' [*Electronics & Wireless World*]

learning curve /'lɜːnɪŋ kɜːv/ *noun* a graphical description of how someone can acquire knowledge about a product over time

lease /liːs/ *noun* a written contract for letting or renting a piece of equipment for a period against payment of a fee ■ *verb* to allow equipment to be used for a period by another person or organisation in return for a fee

least cost design /ˌliːst kɒst dɪ'zaɪn/ *noun* the best money-saving use of space or components ○ *The budget is only £1000, we need the least cost design for the new circuit.*

least significant bit /ˌliːst sɪgˌnɪfɪkənt 'bɪt/ *noun* full form of **LSB**

least significant digit /ˌliːst sɪg ˌnɪfɪkənt 'dɪdʒɪt/ *noun* full form of **LSD**

leave /liːv/ *verb* □ **leaving files open** a phrase meaning that a file has not been closed or does not contain an end of text marker. This will result in the loss of data since the text will not have been saved.

LED /ˌel iː 'diː/ *noun* a semiconductor diode that emits light when a current is applied. Full form **light-emitting diode** (NOTE: LED displays are used to display small amounts of information, as in pocket calculators, watches, and indicators.)

COMMENT: LED displays are used to display small amounts of information, as in pocket calculators, watches, indicators, etc.

left-click /'left klɪk/ *verb* to press and release the left-hand button on a computer mouse

left-handed mouse /ˌeft ˌhændɪd 'maʊs/ *noun* a mouse that has been configured so that the usual functions of the two buttons are reversed

left justification /ˌleft ˌdʒʌstɪfɪ 'keɪʃ(ə)n/ *noun* the act of making the left-hand margin of the text even

left justify /ˌleft ˈdʒʌstɪfaɪ/ *verb* to make the left-hand margin of the text even

legacy /ˈlegəsi/ *noun* an older technology or a previous version of software or hardware that is still supported in new developments to allow existing applications and hardware to continue to be used

legal /ˈliːg(ə)l/ *adjective* a statement or instruction that is acceptable within language syntax rules

legibility /ˌledʒɪˈbɪlɪti/ *noun* being able to be read ○ *The keyboarders find the manuscript lacks legibility.*

legible /ˈledʒɪb(ə)l/ *adjective* which can be read easily ○ *The manuscript is written in pencil and is hardly legible.*

length /leŋθ/ *noun* the number of data items in a variable or list

lens /lenz/ *noun* an optical system of transparent glass through which light is refracted on curved surfaces to produce photographic images

lens aperture /ˈlenz ˌæpətʃə/ *noun* the opening of a lens system; it may be expressed as a fraction (f)-number, the ratio of focal length to physical opening, or as a measured factor of transmission, T number

lens coating /ˈlenz ˌkəʊtɪŋ/ *noun* a fluoride coating which is used to decrease reflection and to let more light through the lens of the camera

lens flare /ˈlenz fleə/ *noun* a luminous spot which appears on a film image, caused by the lens having received overbright light from a natural or artificial source

lens hood /ˈlenz hʊd/ *noun* an extension of the outer part of lens which prevents unwanted light entering the lens

lens mount /ˈlenz maʊnt/ *noun* a device used to fix a lens to a camera

lens prism /ˈlenz ˌprɪz(ə)m/ *noun* a device which is used for multiple-image photography and is attached to the lens

lens speed /ˈlenz spiːd/ *noun* the maximum aperture of a lens, relating to the amount of light that can enter the lens

lens spotlight /ˈlenz ˌspɒtlaɪt/ *noun* a light whose beam is controlled by a single, sliding lens

lens stop /ˈlenz stɒp/ *noun* lens aperture size

lens turret /ˈlenz ˌtʌrɪt/ *noun* a revolving mounting which carries two or more lenses, making it possible to change lenses very quickly

letter /ˈletə/ *noun* **1.** a piece of writing sent from one person to another or from one company to another, e.g. to give new or information or to send an instructions **2.** a written or printed sign, which goes to make a word (such as A, B, C, etc.) ○ *His name was written in capital letters.*

letterhead /ˈletəhed/ *noun* the name and address of a company printed at the top of the company's notepaper ○ *Business forms and letterheads can now be designed on a PC.*

level /ˈlev(ə)l/ *noun* **1.** the quantity of bits that make up a digital transmitted signal **2.** strength or power of an electrical signal ○ *Turn the sound level down, it's far too loud.*

Level A /ˈlev(ə)l eɪ/ *noun* an ADPCM audio quality level with a 20KHz bandwidth, 38.7KHz sample rate and 8-bit samples

Level B /ˈlev(ə)l biː/ *noun* an ADPCM audio quality level with a 17KHz bandwidth, 38.7KHz sample rate and 8-bit samples

Level C /ˈlev(ə)l siː/ *noun* an ADPCM audio quality level with an 8.5KHz bandwidth, 18.9KHz sample rate and 4-bit samples

lexical analysis /ˌleksɪk(ə)l əˈnæləsɪs/ *noun* a stage in program translation when the compiling or translating software replaces program keywords with machine code instructions

lexicographical order /ˌleksɪkəgræfɪk(ə)l ˈɔːdə/ *noun* the order of items, where the words are listed in the order of the letters of the alphabet, as in a dictionary

LF[1] *abbr* line feed

LF[2] *noun* a range of audio frequencies between 5Hz and 300Hz or range of radio frequencies between 30KHz and 300KHz. Full form **low frequency**

LFE channel /ˌel ef ˈiː ˌtʃæn(ə)l/ *noun* same as **low frequency effects channel**

librarian /laɪˈbreəriən/ *noun* a person who works in a library

> '...a library of popular shapes and images is supplied' [*Practical Computing*]

library /ˈlaɪbrəri/ *noun* **1.** a collection of files, documents, books or records, that can be consulted or borrowed by the public, usually kept in a public place **2.** a collection of things for use on a computer, e.g. programs or diskettes **3.** a collection of routines or instructions used by a computer program

licence /ˈlaɪs(ə)ns/ *noun* a statement of permission that is given by one manufacturer to another and allows the second manufacturer to make copies of the first one's products in return for payment of a fee ○ *The software is manufactured in this country under licence.*

licence agreement /ˈlaɪs(ə)ns əˌgriːmənt/ *noun* a legal document that accompanies any commercial software product and defines how you can use the software and, most importantly, how many people can use the software. Unless you buy a network version of a software product, the licence allows one person to use it. Copying the software is illegal. If you want several people to use the software or if you want to use it on a network, then you need to buy a multi-user licence.

lifetime /ˈlaɪftaɪm/ *noun* the period of time during which a device is useful or not outdated ○ *This new computer has a four-year lifetime.*

LIFO /ˈlaɪfəʊ/ *adjective* used to describe a queue system that reads the last item stored, first ○ *This computer stack uses a LIFO data retrieval method.* Full form **last in first out**. ◊ **FIFO**

lifter /ˈlɪftə/ *noun* a mechanical device that lifts magnetic tape away from the heads when rewinding the tape

light /laɪt/ *noun* energy in the form of electromagnetic effects in the frequency range 400 – 750 nm, which allows a person to see ○ *The VDU should not be placed under a bright light.*

light-emitting diode /ˌlaɪt ɪˌmɪtɪŋ ˈdaɪəʊd/ *noun* full form of **LED**

lighting /ˈlaɪtɪŋ/ *noun* **1.** any regulated illumination of an object or person which is being filmed **2.** the source of this illumination, whether natural or artificial

lighting rig /ˈlaɪtɪŋ rɪg/ *noun* a group of lights and their stands and controls

light pen /ˈlaɪt pen/ *noun* a computer accessory in the shape of a pen that contains a light-sensitive device that can detect pixels on a video screen (NOTE: Light pens are often used with suitable software to draw graphics on a screen or position a cursor.)

light-sensitive /ˌlaɪt ˈsensɪtɪv/ *adjective* which is sensitive to light

light-sensitive device /ˌlaɪt ˌsensɪtɪv dɪˈvaɪs/ *noun* a device (such as a phototransistor) which is sensitive to light, and produces a change in signal strength or resistance

lightweight /ˈlaɪtweɪt/ *adjective* not heavy ○ *A lightweight computer which can easily fit into a suitcase.*

lightweight directory access protocol /ˌlaɪtweɪt daɪˈrekt(ə)ri ˌækses ˌprəʊtəkɒl/ *noun* full form of **LDAP**

LILO /ˈlaɪləʊ/ *adjective* used to describe a data storage method in which the data stored last is retrieved last. Full form **last in last out**

limited distance modem /ˌlɪmɪtɪd ˌdɪstəns ˈməʊdem/ *noun* a data transmission device with a very short range that sends pure digital data rather than data sent on a modulated carrier

limiter /ˈlɪmɪtə/ *noun* a device that removes the part of an input signal that is greater than or less than a predefined limit; used with audio and video signals to prevent overloading an amplifier

limiting resolution /ˌlɪmɪtɪŋ ˌrezəˈluːʃ(ə)n/ *noun* the maximum number of lines that make up an image on a CRT screen

limits /ˈlɪmɪts/ *noun* predefined maximum ranges for numbers in a computer

line /laɪn/ *noun* **1.** a physical connection for data transmission, e.g. a cable between parts of a system or a telephone wire **2.** single long thin mark drawn by a pen or printed on a surface ○ *the printer has difficulty in reproducing very fine lines* **3.** one trace by the electron picture beam on a television screen **4.** row of characters (printed on a page or displayed on a computer screen or printer) ○ *each page has 52 lines of text* **5.** series of characters received as a single input by a computer **6.** one row of commands or arguments in a computer program

> '...straight lines are drawn by clicking the points on the screen where you would like the line to start and finish' [*Personal Computer World*]

linear frame buffer /ˌlɪniə freɪm ˈbʌfə/ *noun* a video memory arranged so that by moving from one address to the next in the buffer you move from one pixel to the one below it on the display

linearity /ˌlɪniˈærɪti/ *noun* the shape of the frequency response curve of a device such as a microphone or A/D converter. If the curve is straight, the device is very accurate, if it is not, the device is introducing frequency distortion.

linear program /ˌlɪniə ˈprəʊgræm/ *noun* a computer program that contains no loops or branches

linear programming /ˌlɪniə ˈprəʊgræmɪŋ/ *noun* a method of mathematically breaking down a problem so that it can be solved by computer

linear video /ˌlɪniə ˈvɪdiəʊ/ *noun* **1.** a continuous playback of a video sequence from videotape **2.** normal video that is played back in a continuous sequence rather than a single frame at a time as in interactive video

linear video editing /ˌlɪniə ˌvɪdiəʊ ˈedɪtɪŋ/ *noun* a video sequence, on videotape, that is edited by inserting or deleting new frames but without changing the order of the frames

line break /ˈlaɪn breɪk/ *noun* the point at which continuous text is split into separate lines

line drawing /ˈlaɪn ˌdrɔːɪŋ/ *noun* an illustration in which objects are drawn using thin lines, without shading or surface texture

line feed /ˈlaɪn fiːd/ *noun* a control on a printer or computer terminal that moves the cursor down by one line. Abbr **LF**

line flyback /ˈlaɪn ˌflaɪbæk/ *noun* same as **flyback**

line frequency /laɪn ˈfriːkwənsi/ *noun* (*in a CRT*) the number of times that the picture beam scans a horizontal row of pixels in a monitor

line of sight /ˌlaɪn əv ˈsaɪt/ *noun* a clear transmission path for radio communications in a straight line

line printer /ˈlaɪn ˌprɪntə/ *noun* a device for printing draft quality information at high speeds, typical output is 200 to 3000 lines per minute (NOTE: Line printers print a whole line at a time, running from right to left and left to right, and are usually dot matrix printers with not very high quality print. Compare page printers, which print a whole page at a time.)

lines per minute /ˌlaɪnz pɜː ˈmɪnət/ *noun* the number of lines printed by a line printer per minute. Abbr **LPM**

line-up /ˈlaɪn ʌp/ *verb* to prepare a camera ready to photograph a scene

link /lɪŋk/ *noun* **1.** a communications path or channel between two components or devices ○ *To transmit faster, you can use the direct link with the mainframe.* **2.** a software routine that allows data transfer between incompatible programs ■ *verb* **1.** to join or interface two pieces of software or hardware **2.** to combine separate routines from different files and library files to create a program **3.** to create an association between two objects in a title, e.g. to link a button to another page in the title that is displayed when the user selects the button ○ *The two computers are linked.*

link access protocol /ˌlɪŋk ˈækses ˌprəʊtəkɒl/ *noun* full form of **LAP**

linkage /ˈlɪŋkɪdʒ/ *noun* the act of linking two things

link control procedure /ˌlɪŋk kənˈtrəʊl prəˌsiːdʒə/ *noun* full form of **LCP**

linked object /ˌlɪŋkd ˈɒbdʒekt/ *noun* one piece of data that is referred to in another file or application

linking /ˈlɪŋkɪŋ/ *noun* the merging of a number of small programs to enable them to run as one unit

Linux /ˈlɪnəks/ a trade name for a version of the UNIX operating system originally developed by Linus Torvalds, who then distributed it free of charge over the Internet. Enthusiasts and other developers have extended and enhanced the software, normally also publishing their software free of charge. Linux is one of the most popular operating systems for developers and people running web-based applications. Unlike many other operating systems, such as Microsoft Windows, the Linux software runs on a range of different types of computer hardware including the PC and Macintosh.

lip sync /ˈlɪp sɪŋk/ *noun* a voice recorded at the same time that a person is filmed to ensure that the movement of the mouth matches the speech (*film*)

liquid crystal display /ˌlɪkwɪd ˌkrɪst(ə)l dɪsˈpleɪ/ *noun* full form of **LCD**

LISP /lɪsp/ *noun* a high-level language used mainly in processing lists of instructions or data and in artificial intelligence work. Full form **list processing**

list /lɪst/ *noun* a series of ordered items of data ■ *verb* to print or display certain items of information

LIST chunk /ˈlɪst ˌtʃʌŋk/ *noun* (*in a RIFF file*) a four-character code LIST that contains a series of subchunks

listing /ˈlɪstɪŋ/ *noun* a display or printed copy of the lines in a program in order

list processing /ˈlɪst ˌprəʊsesɪŋ/ *noun* **1.** the processing of a series of items of data, i.e. such tasks as adding, deleting, sorting or updating entries **2.** full form of **LISP**

listserv /ˈlɪstˌsɜːv/, **listserver** /ˈlɪstsɜːvə/ *noun* a server on the Internet that sends a newsletter or articles to a list of registered users

literacy /ˈlɪt(ə)rəsi/ *noun* the ability to read and write

literal /ˈlɪt(ə)rəl/ *noun* **1.** a computer instruction that contains the actual number or address to be used, rather than a label or its location **2.** a printing error when one character is replaced by another or when two characters are transposed

literate /ˈlɪt(ə)rət/ *adjective* who can read and write

lith film /ˈlɪθ fɪlm/ *noun* high quality and contrast photographic film used in lithographic printing

lithium-Ion battery /ˌlɪθiəm ˈaɪən ˌbæt(ə)ri/ *noun* a type of rechargeable battery that provides high output power in a compact and lightweight unit. This type of battery is often used in mobile telephones, PDAs and lightweight laptop computers.

live /laɪv/ *adjective* action transmitted as it happens rather than being transmitted from a recording

Live3D /ˌlaɪv θriː ˈdiː/ *noun* same as **VRML**

live-on-tape /ˌlaɪv ɒn ˈteɪp/ *noun* action which is recorded without any break, is not edited and is filmed to fit into a particular time frame

live recording /ˌlaɪv rɪˈkɔːdɪŋ/ *noun* an original recording

liveware /ˈlaɪvweə/ *noun* the operators and users of a computer system, as opposed to the hardware and software

LLC /ˌel el ˈsiː/ *abbr* logical link control

LLL *abbr* low-level language

lm *noun* the unit of luminous flux. Full form **lumen**

load /ləʊd/ *noun* **1.** a job or piece of work to be done **2.** impedance presented to a line or device ■ *verb* **1.** to transfer a file or program from disk to main memory **2.** to put something such as a disk into a computer, so that it can be run **3.** to place an impedance or device at the end of a line

'...this windowing system is particularly handy when you want to load or save a file or change directories' [*Byte*]

loader /ˈləʊdə/ *noun* a program which loads another file or program into computer memory

loading /ˈləʊdɪŋ/ *noun* the action of transferring a file or program from disk to memory ○ *Loading can be a long process.*

load point /ˈləʊd pɔɪnt/ *noun* the start of a recording section in a reel of magnetic tape

local /ˈləʊk(ə)l/ *adjective* **1.** referring to a variable or argument that is only used in a certain section of a computer program or structure **2.** referring to a system with limited access

local area network /ˌləʊk(ə)l ˌeəriə ˈnetwɜːk/ *noun* full form of **LAN**

local drive /ˈləʊk(ə)l draɪv/ *noun* a disk drive that is physically attached to a computer, as opposed to a resource that is accessed across a network

local printer /ˌləʊk(ə)l ˈprɪntə/ *noun* a printer physically attached to a computer rather than a shared resource available on a network

LocalTalk /ˈləʊkəltɔːk/ a trade name for a network standard developed by Apple that defines the physical layer, i.e. the cabling system and connectors, used in Apple's AppleTalk network. The network transfers data at 230Kbits/second over unshielded twisted-pair cable.

locate /ləʊˈkeɪt/ *verb* **1.** to place or to set ○ *The computer is located in the main office building.* **2.** to find ○ *Have you managed to locate the programming fault?*

location /ləʊˈkeɪʃ(ə)n/ *noun* **1.** a number or absolute address that specifies the point in memory where a data word can be found and accessed **2.** any setting away from the studio, whether outdoors or indoors, where a film or programme is recorded

lock /lɒk/ *verb* **1.** to prevent access to a system or file **2.** to synchronise two devices or signals, such as two video recorders or two clocks

lockout /ˈlɒkaʊt/ *noun* the process of preventing a user sending messages over a network by continuously transmitting data

lock up /ˌlɒk ˈʌp/ *noun* a faulty operating state of computer that cannot be recovered from without switching off the power

COMMENT: This can be caused by an infinite program loop *or* a deadly embrace.

log /lɒg/ *noun* **1.** a record of computer processing operations **2.** a detailed record of camera and sound-recording operations during filming (*film*)

logarithm /ˈlɒgərɪð(ə)m/ *noun* a mathematical operation that gives the power a number must be raised to, to give the required number ○ *decimal logarithm of 1,000 is 3 (= 10 x 10 x 10)*

logarithmic /ˌlɒgəˈrɪðmɪk/ *adjective* referring to variations in the logarithm of a scale

logarithmic graph /ˌlɒgərɪðmɪk ˈgrɑːf/ *noun* a graph whose axes have a scale that is the logarithm of the linear measurement

log file /ˈlɒg faɪl/ *noun* **1.** a file that contains a record of actions **2.** (*on a web server*) a file that contains details of the visitors to a website, recorded automatically with the visitor's DNS address, the time and the name of the webpage that he or she viewed

logging /ˈlɒgɪŋ/ *noun* an input of data into a system

logging in /ˈlɒgɪŋ ɪn/ *noun* the process of opening operations with a system

logging off /ˈlɒgɪŋ ɒf/ *noun* the process of ending operations with a system

logging on /ˈlɒgɪŋ ɒn/ *noun* same as **logging in**

logging out /ˈlɒgɪŋ aʊt/ *noun* same as **logging off**

logic /ˈlɒdʒɪk/ *noun* **1.** a science which deals with thought and reasoning **2.** a mathematical treatment of formal logic operations such as AND, OR, etc., and their transformation into various circuits. ◊ **Boolean algebra** **3.** a system for deducing results from binary data **4.** the components of a computer or digital system

logical /ˈlɒdʒɪk(ə)l/ *adjective* that uses logic in its operation ○ *Logical reasoning can be simulated by an artificial intelligence machine.*

logical link control /ˌlɒdʒɪk(ə)l ˈlɪŋk kənˌtrəʊl/ *noun* an IEEE 802.2 standard defining the protocol for data-link-level transmissions. Abbr **LLC**. ◊ **data link layer**

logical palette /ˌlɒdʒɪk(ə)l ˈpælət/ *noun* (*in Windows*) a graphics object that includes the colour palette information it requires

logical unit /ˌlɒdʒɪk(ə)l ˈjuːnɪt/ *noun* full form of **LU**

logic-seeking /ˈlɒdʒɪk ˌsiːkɪŋ/ *adjective* referring to a printer that can print the required information with the minimum head movement, detecting ends of lines, justification commands, etc.

login /ˈlɒgɪn/ *verb* to enter various identification data, such as a password, usually by means of a terminal, to the central computer before accessing a program or data (used as a means of making sure that only authorised users can access the computer system)

log in script /ˈlɒg ɪn ˌskrɪpt/ *noun* a series of instructions that are automatically run when you log into a network. For example, if you log into your office network in the morning by typing your name and password, the login script might remind you of important information or just display 'good morning'.

logo /ˈləʊgəʊ/ *noun* a special printed set of characters or symbols used to identify a company or product

LOGO /ˈləʊgəʊ/ *noun* a high-level programming language used mainly for educational purposes, with graphical commands that are easy to use

logoff /lɒgˈɒf/ *verb* same as **logging off**

logon /lɒgˈɒn/ *verb* same as **logging in**

logout /ˈlɒgaʊt/ *noun* same as **logging off**

long filename /ˌlɒŋ ˈfaɪlˌneɪm/ *noun* a feature of Windows 95 that lets a user give files names up to 254 characters in length

long focal-length lens, long lens *noun* ♦ **telephoto lens**

long haul network /ˌlɒŋ hɔːl ˈnetwɜːk/ *noun* a communications network between distant computers that usually uses the public telephone system

long integer /ˌlɒŋ ˈɪntɪdʒə/ *noun* (*in programming languages*) an integer represented by several bytes of data

longitudinal time code /ˌlɒŋgɪtjuːdɪn(ə)l ˈtaɪm kəʊd/ *noun* full form of **LTC**

long persistence phosphor /ˌlɒŋ pə ˌsɪstəns ˈfɒsfə/ *noun* a television screen coating that retains the displayed image for a period of time longer than the refresh rate, so reducing flicker effects

long shot /ˈlɒŋ ʃɒt/ *noun* a photograph of a general view of the setting where the action takes place (*film*)

look-ahead /ˈlʊk əˌhed/ *noun* an action performed by some CPUs that fetch instructions and examine them before they are executed in order to speed up operations

look-up table /ˈlʊk ʌp ˌteɪb(ə)l/ *noun* full form of **LUT** ○ *Look-up tables are preprogrammed then used in processing so saving calculations for each result required.*

'...a lookup table changes a pixel's value based on the values in a table' [*Byte*]

loop /luːp/ *noun* **1.** a procedure or series of instructions in a computer program that are performed again and again until a test shows that a specific condition has been met or until the program is completed **2.** a communications channel that is passed via all receivers and is terminated where it started from **3.** a length of wire coiled in the shape of a circle **4.** a long piece of tape with the two ends joined ■ *verb* to make a piece of wire or tape into a circle

loss /lɒs/ *noun* the power of a signal that is lost when passing through a circuit

lossless compression /ˌlɒsləs kəm ˈpreʃ(ə)nn/ *noun* image compression techniques that can reduce the number of bits used for each pixel in an image, without losing any information or quality. ◊ **Huffman code**

lossy compression /ˌlɒsi kəm ˈpreʃ(ə)n/ *noun* image compression techniques that can reduce the number of bits used for each pixel in an image, but in doing so lose information. ◊ **JPEG**

loudness /ˈlaʊdnəs/ *noun* a volume of a signal which you can hear

loudspeaker /ˌlaʊdˈspiːkə/ *noun* an electromagnetic device that converts electrical signals into audible noise

low angle shot /ˌləʊ ˌæŋg(ə)l ˈʃɒt/ *noun* a camera shot taken from below the subject with the camera tilted up towards subject (*film*)

low band video /ˌləʊ bænd ˈvɪdiəʊ/ *noun* a video tape recording system which is usually used for low-quality home use and does not meet television broadcast standards (*film*)

low contrast /ˌləʊ ˈkɒntrɑːst/ *noun* (*film*) **1.** muted colours in a film **2.** a film which does not have a great contrast between its black and white tones

low contrast filter /ˌləʊ ˌkɒntrɑːst ˈfɪltə/ *noun* a camera lens which mutes colours

low-end /ˌləʊ ˈend/ *adjective* referring to hardware or software that is not very powerful or sophisticated and is designed for beginners

lower case /ˌləʊə ˈkeɪs/ *noun* small characters, e.g. a, b and c, as opposed to upper case, A, B, C

low frequency /ˌləʊ 'friːkwənsi/ *noun* a range of audio frequencies between 5–300Hz or range of radio frequencies between 30–300kHz

low frequency effects channel /ˌləʊ ˌfriːkwənsi ɪ'fekts ˌtʃæn(ə)l/ *noun* a separate audio channel in a multichannel system that provides very low frequency bass sounds. ◊ **Dolby Digital™**. Also called **LFE channel**

low key /ˌləʊ 'kiː/ *noun* (*film*) **1.** pictures in which the lower grey scale tones, or shadowy parts, are emphasised **2.** low lighting of subject

low-level format /ˌləʊ 'lev(ə)l ˌfɔːmæt/ *noun* a process that defines the physical pattern and arrangement of tracks and sectors on a disk

low-level language /ˌləʊ ˌlev(ə)l 'læŋgwɪdʒ/ *noun* a programming language, particular to one system or computer, in which each instruction has a single equivalent machine code instruction, so that programming in it is a long and complex task. Abbr **LLL**

low memory /ˌləʊ 'mem(ə)ri/ *noun* (*in a PC*) available memory locations up to 640Kb. Compare **high memory**

low pass filter /ˌləʊ ˌpɑːs 'fɪltə/ *noun* an electronic circuit that blocks signals above a certain frequency

low-power standby /ˌləʊ 'paʊə ˌstændbaɪ/ *noun* an energy-saving feature of laptop computers and many monitors connected to a desktop

low-priority work /ˌləʊ praɪˌɒrɪti 'wɜːk/ *noun* work that is not particularly important

low-resolution graphics /ˌləʊ ˌrezə ˌluːʃ(ə)n 'græfɪks/, **low-res graphics** /ˌləʊ rez 'græfɪks/ *plural noun* the ability to display character-sized graphic blocks or preset shapes on a screen rather than to create graphics using individual pixels. Compare **high-resolution**

low-speed communications /ˌləʊ spiːd kəˌmjuːnɪ'keɪʃ(ə)nz/ *plural noun* data transmission at less than 2400 bits per second

LPM *abbr* lines per minute

LPT1 /ˌel piː tiː 'wʌnː/ *noun* (*in a PC*) the name given to the first, main parallel printer port in the system

LS *abbr* **1.** long shot **2.** loudspeaker

LSB /ˌel es 'biː/ *noun* a binary digit occupying the right hand position of a word and carrying the least power of two in the word, usually equal to two raised to zero = 1. Full form **least significant bit**

LSD /ˌel es 'diː/ *noun* the digit which occupies the right hand position in a number and so carries least power, being equal to the number radix raised to zero = 1. Full form **least significant digit**

LSI /ˌel es 'aɪ/ *noun* a configuration with between 500 and 10,000 circuits on a single IC. Full form **large-scale integration**

LTC /ˌel tiː 'siː/ *noun* a method of recording a time code signal on a linear audio track along a video tape. The disadvantage of this method is that the code is not readable at slow speeds or when the tape has stopped. Full form **longitudinal time code**

LU /ˌel 'juː/ *noun* a set of protocols developed by IBM to allow communication over an SNA network. LU1, LU2 and LU3 provide control of the session, LU4 supports communication between the devices and LU6.2 is a peer-to-peer protocol. Full form **logical unit**

luma /'luːmə/ *noun* the black and white parts of an image or video signal, represented by the symbol Y. ◊ **S-Video, Y/C**

lumen /'luːmɪn/ *noun* the SI unit of illumination, defined as the amount of flux emitted from a candela into an angle of one steradion

luminance /'luːmɪn(ə)ns/ *noun* the part of a video signal or image that defines the brightness at each point. ◊ **YUV encoding**

luminous flux /'luːmɪnəs flʌks/ *noun* the rate of stream of visible light coming from a source, measured in lumens

lurk /lɜːk/ *verb* to join an online conference, discussion group or chat room and listen to the messages without contributing anything yourself. Most discussion forums do not mind people lurking, since it helps to build confidence in new users and lets them check the content before joining in, however some chat rooms do not approve of lurking and immediately identify anyone joining to discourage people who do not contribute to the forum.

LUT /ˌel juː 'tiː/ *noun* a collection of stored results that can be accessed very rapidly by a program without the need to calculate each result whenever needed. Full form **look-up table**

> '...an image processing system can have three LUTs that map the image memory to the display device' [*Byte*]

lux /lʌks/ *noun* the SI unit of measurement of one lumen per square metre

LV-ROM /ˌel viː 'rɒm/ *noun* a 12-inch diameter optical disc, developed by Philips, that can store both analog video and digital data

M

M *abbr* mega- ■ *noun* **1.** one million **2.** the symbol for 1,048,576, used only in computer and electronic related applications, equal to 2^{20}

Mac /mæk/ *noun* same as **Macintosh**

MAC /ˌem eɪ 'siː/ *noun* a special code transmitted at the same time as a message as proof of its authenticity. Full form **message authentication code** ■ *abbr* medium access control

MacBinary /mæk'baɪnəri/ a trade name for a file storage and transfer system that allows Macintosh files, together with their icons and long file names, to be stored on other computer systems

machine /mə'ʃiːn/ *noun* **1.** a number of separate moving parts or components, acting together to carry out a process **2.** a computer, system or processor made up of various components connected together to provide a function or perform a task

machine address /mə'ʃiːn əˌdres/ *noun* same as **absolute address**

machine code /mə'ʃiːn kəʊd/ *noun* a programming language that consists of commands in binary code that can be directly understood by the central processing unit without the need for translation. Also called **computer code**

Macintosh /'mækɪntɒʃ/ a trade name for a range of personal computers designed by Apple Corporation. The Macintosh uses the Motorola family of processors, the 68000, and offers similar computing power to a PC. The Macintosh is best known for its graphical user interface which allows a user to control the computer using icons and a mouse. ○ *Macintosh computers are not compatible with an IBM PC unless you use special emulation software.* Also called **Mac**

macro /mækrəʊ/ *noun* a program routine or block of instructions identified by a single word or label

macro block /'mækrəʊ blɒk/ *noun* a grid of 16x16 pixels used to analyse and compress video data in the MPEG compression system

macro lens /'mækrəʊ lenz/ *noun* a magnifying lens which is used for close-up shots

Macromedia Director /ˌmækrəʊmiːdiə daɪ'rektə/ a trade name for authoring software for the PC and Macintosh that uses the Lingo scripting language

macro virus /'mækrəʊ ˌvaɪrəs/ *noun* a type of virus that is stored as a macro attached to a document or e-mail message. Most advanced software applications provide a macro language that lets users extend the application and automate features. However, as macro languages become more advanced and powerful, they also provide an opportunity for someone to create a macro that can delete files or corrupt data when run.

COMMENT: A macro virus will run when the document is opened. Some viruses are benign, others carry out malicious damage on your files and data. The virus will also try and spread to other compatible documents and applications on your computer, so that any new documents you create are also infected. Current macro virus attacks have used the macro features of advanced email software to re-send the virus to all the email addresses stored in your email address book. The last major macro virus created so much extra network email traffic on the Internet that many servers were overloaded. The best way to avoid a macro virus is to regularly run virus detection software that can check and remove viruses attached to documents and new email messages.

macrozoom /'mækrəʊzuːm/ *noun* a zoom lens that can focus on very close objects

magazine /ˌmægə'ziːn/ *noun* **1.** a number of pages in a videotext system **2.** a paper, usually with illustrations which comes out regularly, every month or every week ○ *a weekly magazine* ○ *He edits a computer magazine.* **3.** a light-tight film container which is used with a camera, printer or film processing machine

magnet /'mægnɪt/ *noun* something that produces a magnetic field

magnetic /mæg'netɪk/ *adjective* that has a magnetic field associated with it

magnetic ink character recognition /mægˌnetɪk ɪŋk ˌkærɪktə ˌrekəg'nɪʃ(ə)n/ *noun* full form of **MICR**

magnetic tape /mægˌnetɪk 'teɪp/ *noun* a narrow length of thin plastic coated with a magnetic material used to store signals magnetically

COMMENT: Magnetic tape is available on spools of between 200 and 800 metres. The tape is magnetised by the read/write head. Tape is a storage medium that only allows serial access, that is, all the tape has to be read until the required location is found, as opposed to disk storage, which can be accessed randomly.

magneto-optical disc /mæɡˌniːtəʊ ˌɒptɪk(ə)l ˈdɪsk/ *noun* an optical disc that is used in a magneto-optical recording device

magneto-optical recording /mæɡ ˌniːtəʊ ˌɒptɪk(ə)l rɪˈkɔːdɪŋ/ *noun* a method of recording that uses an optical disc covered with a thin layer of magnetic film that is heated by a laser. The particles are then polarised by a weak magnetic field. (NOTE: Magneto-optical discs have very high capacity, over 600MB, and are re-writable.)

magnification /ˌmæɡnɪfɪˈkeɪʃ(ə)n/ *noun* the amount by which something has been made to appear larger ○ *The lens gives a magnification of 10 times.*

magnify /ˈmæɡnɪˌfaɪ/ *verb* to make something appear larger ○ *The photograph has been magnified 200 times.*

magnitude /ˈmæɡnɪtjuːd/ *noun* a level or strength of a signal or variable

mag-opt /ˈmæɡ ɒpt/ *noun* a motion picture print which contains both magnetic and optical sound tracks (*film*)

mag tape /ˈmæɡ teɪp/ *noun* same as **magnetic tape** (*informal*)

mail /meɪl/ *noun* **1.** a system for sending letters and parcels from one place to another **2.** letters sent or received **3.** electronic messages to and from users of a bulletin board or network ■ *verb* to send something by post ○ *to mail a letter*

mail application programming interface /ˌmeɪl ˌæplɪkeɪʃ(ə)n ˈprəʊɡræmɪŋ ˌɪntəfeɪs/ *noun* full form of **MAPI**

mailbox /ˈmeɪlbɒks/, **mail box** /ˈmeɪl bɒks/ *noun* an electronic storage space with an address in which a user's incoming messages are stored

mail-enabled /ˈmeɪl ɪnˌeɪb(ə)ld/ *adjective* referring to an application that has access to an electronic mail system without leaving the application ○ *This word-processor is mail-enabled – you can send messages to other users from within it.*

mail gateway /ˈmeɪl ˌɡeɪtweɪ/ *noun* a software program, or a combination of server and software, that links two different electronic mail systems together so that mail messages can be transferred from one system to another. For example, if you are using Lotus cc:Mail as the electronic mail product within your company, you would need to fit a gateway function to allow messages to be sent to and received by users on the Internet. (NOTE: LAN email systems usually use one of three main standards, MAPI, MHS or VIM, to send mail messages. If you are sending mail from a LAN email system to the Internet, the mail gateway needs to convert this standard to one of the Internet mail standards such as POP3 or SMTP before it can be delivered.)

mailing /ˈmeɪlɪŋ/ *noun* the process of sending something using the post or e-mail

mailing list /ˈmeɪlɪŋ lɪst/ *noun* (*in electronic mail*) list of the e-mail addresses of users who receive information on a regular basis from a company, a person or from other people on the list. An Internet mailing list allows any person whose name and address are on the list to send a message to the list, which will then automatically distribute a copy of this message to all the other people on the list.

mailmerge /ˈmeɪlmɜːdʒ/ *noun* a word-processing program which allows a standard form letter to be printed out to a series of different names and addresses

'Spreadsheet views for data and graphical forms for data entry have been added to the Q&A database, with the traditional reporting, mailmerge, and labels improved through Windows facilities.' [*Computing*]

mail server /ˈmeɪl ˌsɜːvə/ *noun* a computer that stores incoming mail and sends it to the correct user and stores outgoing mail and transfers it to the correct destination server on the Internet

mail transfer agent /ˌmeɪl ˈtrænsfɜː ˌeɪdʒənt/ *noun* a software program that manages the way electronic mail messages are transferred over a network. On computers running the Unix operating system and the Internet the 'sendmail' software is the most popular mail transfer agent. Abbr **MTA**

mail user agent /ˌmeɪl ˈjuːzə ˌeɪdʒənt/ *noun* full form of **MUA**

main /meɪn/ *adjective* most important

mainframe /ˈmeɪnfreɪm kəmˌpjuːtə/, **mainframe computer** /ˌmeɪnfreɪm kəm ˈpjuːtə/ *noun* a large-scale high-power computer system that can handle high-capacity memory and backing storage devices as well as a number of operators simultaneously

mainly /ˈmeɪnli/ *adverb* mostly or usually ○ *Their sales are mainly in the home market.* ○ *We are interested mainly in buying colour printing.*

mains electricity /ˌmeɪns ɪˌlekˈtrɪsəti/ *noun* the normal domestic electricity supply to consumers (NOTE: In the UK this is 240 volts at 50Hz. In the US, it is 110 volts at 60Hz.)

maintain /meɪnˈteɪn/ *verb* to ensure a system is in good condition and functioning correctly

maintainability /ˌmeɪnteɪnəˈbɪlɪti/ *noun* the ability to have repairs carried out quickly and efficiently if a failure occurs

maintenance /ˈmeɪntənəns/ *noun* **1.** the task of keeping a machine in good working condition **2.** tasks carried out in order to keep a system running, e.g. repairing faults and replacing components

maintenance contract /ˈmeɪntənəns ˌkɒntrækt/ *noun* an arrangement with a repair company that provides for regular checks and special repair prices in the event of a fault

maintenance routine /ˈmeɪntənəns ruːˌtiːn/ *noun* a software diagnostic tool used by an engineer during preventative maintenance operations

majuscule /ˈmædʒəskjuːl/ *noun* a capital letter

make directory /ˌmeɪk daɪˈrekt(ə)ri/ *noun* full form of **MD**

male connector /ˌmeɪl kəˈnektə/ *noun* a plug with conducting pins that can be inserted into a female connector to provide an electrical connection

malfunction /mælˈfʌŋkʃən/ *noun* (*of hardware or software*) the fact of not working correctly ○ *The data was lost due to a software malfunction.* ■ *verb* not to work properly ○ *Some of the keys on the keyboard have started to malfunction.*

malfunctioning /mælˈfʌŋkʃənɪŋ/ *adjective* not working properly

MAN /mæn/ *noun* a network extending over a limited geographical area, normally a city. Full form **metropolitan area network**. Compare **LAN, WAN**

manage /ˈmænɪdʒ/ *verb* to direct or to be in charge of something

manageable /ˈmænɪdʒəb(ə)l/ *adjective* that can be dealt with easily ○ *processing problems which are still manageable.*

management /ˈmænɪdʒmənt/ *noun* the act of directing or organising work or a business

management information service /ˌmænɪdʒmənt ˌɪnfəˈmeɪʃ(ə)n ˌsɜːvɪs/ *noun* a department within a company that is responsible for information and data processing. Abbr **MIS** (NOTE: In practice, this department is often responsible for the computer system in a company.)

management information system /ˌmænɪdʒmənt ˌɪnfəˈmeɪʃ(ə)n ˌsɪstəm/ *noun* software that allows managers in a company to access and analyse data. Abbr **MIS**

manager /ˈmænɪdʒə/ *noun* the head of a department in a company ○ *a department manager*

managerial /ˌmænəˈdʒɪəriəl/ *adjective* referring to managers ○ *managerial staff*

Manchester coding /ˈmæntʃestə ˌkɒdɪŋ/ *noun* a method of encoding data and timing signals that is used in communications. The first half of the bit period indicates the value of the bit (1 or 0), and the second half is used as a timing signal.

Mandlebrot set /ˈmænd(ə)lbrɒt set/ *noun* a mathematical equation that is called recursively to generate a set of values. When plotted these form a fractal image. ◊ **fractal**

M and S microphone /ˌem ənd ˈes ˌmaɪkrəfəʊn/ *noun* a combination used for stereo sound recording (*film*) Full form **middle and side microphone**

manipulate /məˈnɪpjʊˌleɪt/ *verb* to move, edit and change text or data ○ *An image processor that captures, displays and manipulates video images.*

manipulation /məˌnɪpjʊˈleɪʃ(ə)n/ *noun* the process of moving or editing or changing text or data ○ *The high-speed database management program allows the manipulation of very large amounts of data.*

man machine interface /ˌmæn məˌʃiːn ˈɪntəfeɪs/ *noun* full form of **MMI**

mantissa /mænˈtɪsə/ *noun* the fractional part of a number ○ *The mantissa of the number 45.897 is 0.897.*

manual /ˈmænjuəl/ *noun* a document containing instructions about the operation of a system or piece of software ○ *The manual is included with the system.* ■ *adjective* done by hand or carried out by the operator without the help of a machine

manually /ˈmænjʊəli/ *adverb* done by hand, not automatically ○ *The paper has to be fed into the printer manually.*

manufacture /ˌmænjʊˈfæktʃə/ *verb* to make in a factory ○ *The company manufactures diskettes and magnetic tape.*

manufacturer /ˌmænjʊˈfæktʃərə/ *noun* a company which manufactures a product ○ *If the system develops a fault it should be returned to the manufacturer for checking.* ○ *The manufacturer guarantees the system for 12 months.*

map /mæp/ *noun* **1.** a diagram representing the internal layout of a computer's memory or communications regions **2.** data that is linked to another set of data **3.** a list of data items or objects within an application or multimedia book ■ *verb* **1.** to display how things are connected or related or derived from one another □ **to map out** to draw or set down the basic way in which something should be done **2.** to retrieve data and display it as a map **3.** to represent a network directory path on a remote computer with a local drive letter, enabling a user to view the contents of the remote directory by simply typing in the drive letter rather than the often long and complex directory path **4.** to represent a network printer connected to another computer on a network with a local printer identifier, so a user can treat the remote network printer as if it is directly connected to their computer **5.** to connect to a disk drive or a printer that is connected to another computer on a network. ◊ **texture mapping 6.** to transform a two-dimensional image into a three-dimensional form that can then be rotated or manipulated **7.** to transfer data from one region of memory to another; e.g., a graphic image is mapped in main memory and on the display **8.** to relate or link one set of data items with another. ◊ **bit-map 9.** (*in an image*) to transform a graphical object from one coordinate system to another so that it can be displayed; e.g., to transform a three-dimensional wire frame model to a solid shaded object. ◊ **texture mapping**

MAPI /ˌem eɪ piː 'aɪ/ *noun* a set of standards, developed by Microsoft, that defines how electronic mail is sent and delivered. Full form **mail application programming interface**

margin /'mɑːdʒɪn/ *noun* **1.** the blank space around a section of printed text **2.** an extra time or space

margination /ˌmɑːdʒɪn'eɪʃ(ə)n/ *noun* the process of giving margins to a printed page

margin of error /ˌmɑːdʒɪn əv 'erə/ *noun* the number of mistakes that is acceptable in a document or in a calculation

mark /mɑːk/ *noun* **1.** a sign put on a page to show something **2.** a transmitted signal that represents a logical one or true condition ■ *verb* to put a mark on something

marker /'mɑːkə/ *noun* a code inserted in a file or text to indicate a special section

mark up /ˌmɑːk 'ʌp/ *verb* to prepare copy for the compositor to set, by showing on the copy the typeface to be used, the line width, and other typesetting instructions

markup language /'mɑːkʌp ˌlæŋgwɪdʒ/ *noun* a computer coding system that gives instructions relating to the layout and style to be used for a document

marquee /mɑː'kiː/ *noun* **1.** (*in graphics*) the area selected by a selection tool **2.** (*in a website*) a piece of text that moves slowly across the screen, used as a special feature of a webpage

mask /mɑːsk/ *noun* **1.** an integrated circuit layout that is used to define the pattern to be etched or doped onto a slice of semiconductor ○ *A mask* or *stencil is used to transfer the transistor design onto silicon.* **2.** a pattern of binary digits used to select various bits from a binary word. A one in the mask retains that bit in the word. **3.** a photographic device used to prevent light reaching selected areas of the film

maskable /'mɑːskəb(ə)l/ *adjective* that can be masked

masking /'mɑːskɪŋ/ *noun* **1.** an operation used to select various bits in a word **2.** the adjustment of the colour balance by matrixing the RGB signals; this method is used to match colour film primaries to the television standard

mass media /ˌmæs 'miːdiə/ *noun* media which aim to reach a large public (such as television, radio, mass-market newspapers)

mass production /ˌmæs prə'dʌkʃən/ *noun* the process of manufacturing large quantities of goods ○ *mass production of monitors*

mass storage /ˌmæs 'stɔːrɪdʒ/ *noun* the storage and retrieval of large amounts of data

master /'mɑːstə/ *adjective* referring to the main or most important device or person in a system ○ *The master computer controls everything else.* ■ *noun* (*film*) a special positive print which is made from an original negative for duplication or protection instead of for projection ■ *adjective* referring to the most up-to-date and correct file ■ *noun* (*film*) **1.** the finished version of any type of programme from which release or show copies will be made **2.** output gain control on an audio mixer or video chain ■ *verb* to learn and understand a language or process ○ *We mastered the new word-processor quite quickly.*

mastering /'mɑːstərɪŋ/ *noun* a process used to convert finished data to a master disc

mat /mæt/ *noun* a plain coloured border that is displayed around an image that is smaller than the window in which it is displayed

match /mætʃ/ *verb* **1.** to search through a database for a similar piece of information **2.** to set a register equal to another

material /mə'tɪəriəl/ *noun* a substance which can be used to make a finished product ○ *Gold is the ideal material for electrical connections.*

math /mæθ/ *noun US* same as **mathematics** (*informal*)

mathematical /ˌmæθə'mætɪk(ə)l/ *adjective* referring to mathematics

mathematical model /ˌmæθəmætɪk(ə)l 'mɒd(ə)l/ *noun* a representation of a system using mathematical ideas and formulae

mathematics /ˌmæθə'mætɪks/ *noun* the study of the relationship between numbers, their manipulation and organisation to (logically) prove facts and theories. ◊ **algebra**. Also called **math**

maths /mæθs/ *noun* same as **mathematics** (*informal*)

maths chip /ˈmæθs ˌtʃɪp/ *noun* a dedicated IC that can be added to a system to carry out mathematical functions far more rapidly than a standard CPU, speeding up the execution of a program

maths coprocessor /ˈmæθs kəʊ ˌprəʊsesə/ *noun* same as **maths chip**

matrix /ˈmeɪtrɪks/ *noun* **1.** an array of numbers or data items arranged in rows and columns **2.** an array of connections between logic gates providing a number of possible logical functions **3.** a pattern of the dots that make up a character on a computer screen, dot-matrix or laser printer **4.** a filmstrip of images which contains dyed emulsion and is combined with two other filmstrips on a film base to create colour film; MATT Character of a non-specular surface which mirrors light equally in all directions (*film*)

matt /mæt/, **matte** *noun* **1.** the addition of an image onto a film of a background **2.** an opaque mask limiting the picture area which is exposed in special effects; the mask can be a cut-out aperture, a high density image on film, or, in video, it may be electronically created in order to blank off the particular signal **3.** a device put before the camera which is used to soften or block light from sections of the action area, or from exposure in the printer ■ *adjective* (print) which is not shiny. ◊ **chroma key**

matte /mæt/ *noun* (*in video or film*) a specified region within an image, which can be coded to appear transparent or opaque. A matte is reveals or masks off part of an image in another plane, and is normally used for special effects in which an object is photographed against a specially coloured background that is then replaced with another image to give the impression that the object appears against that image. ◊ **chroma key**

matte bleed /ˌmæt ˈbliːd/, **matte ride** /ˌmæt ˈraɪd/ *noun* an abnormality in the matte image which causes the matte lines to become visible (*film*)

matter /ˈmætə/ *noun* **1.** a question or problem to be discussed **2.** the main section of text on a page as opposed to titles or headlines

matting /ˈmætɪŋ/ *noun* the process of inserting an image into a background, whether electronically or optically (*film*)

MATV *abbr* master antenna television system

maximise /ˈmæksɪmaɪz/, **maximize** *verb* (*in MS-Windows*) to expand an application icon back to its original display window. Compare **minimise**

maximum /ˈmæksɪməm/ *noun* the highest value used or that is allowed ■ *adjective* the greatest possible or allowable

maximum transmission rate /ˌmæksɪməm trænzˈmɪʃ(ə)n ˌreɪt/ *noun* the greatest amount of data that can be transmitted every second

maximum users /ˌmæksɪməm ˈjuːzəz/ *plural noun* the greatest number of users that a system can support at any one time

Mb *abbr* megabit

MBR /ˌem biː ˈɑː/ *noun* a register in a CPU that temporarily buffers all inputs and outputs. Full form **memory buffer register**

MC *abbr* millicoulomb

MCA /ˌem siː ˈeɪ/ a trade name for the expansion bus within IBM's PS/2 range of personal computers that has taken over from the older ISA/AT bus. MCA is a 32-bit bus that supports bus master devices. Full form **Micro Channel Architecture**

MCGA /ˌem siː dʒiː ˈeɪ/ *noun* a colour graphics adapter standard fitted in low-end IBM PS/2 computers. Full form **multicolour graphics adapter**

MCI /ˌem siː ˈaɪ/ *noun* an interface that allow any program to control a multimedia device such as a sound card or video clip. Full form **media control interface**

MCI device /ˌem siː ˈaɪ dɪˌvaɪs/ *noun* a recognised multimedia device that is installed in a computer with the correct drivers

MD /ˌem ˈdiː/ *noun* a DOS command used to create a new directory on a disk. Full form **make directory**

MDK /ˌem diː ˈkeɪ/ *noun* a product developed by Microsoft that allows developers to produce multimedia applications more easily using the supplied libraries of routines to control video playback, process images and display text. Full form **multimedia developer's kit**

MDRAM /ˌem ˈdiː ræm/ *noun* a type of high-performance memory normally used in video adapter cards to provide fast graphic display. Full form **multibank dynamic random access memory**

mean /miːn/ *noun, adjective* the average value of a set of numbers or values ■ *verb* to signify something ○ *The message DISK FULL means that there is no more room on the disk for further data.*

mean time between failures /ˌmiːn taɪm bɪˌtwiːn ˈfeɪljəz/ *noun* full form of **MTBF**

mean time to failure /ˌmiːn taɪm tə ˈfeɪljə/ *noun* full form of **MTF**

mean time to repair /ˌmiːn ˈtaɪm tə, tʊ/ *noun* full form of **MTTR**

measure /ˈmeʒə/ *noun* **1.** a way of calculating size or quantity **2.** the total width of a printed line of text **3.** a type of action □ **to take measures to prevent something happening** to act to stop something happening □ **safety measures** actions to make sure that something is safe ■ *verb* **1.** to find out the size or quantity of something **2.** to be of a certain size or quantity

measurement /ˈmeʒəmənt/ *noun* a way of judging something ○ *Performance measurement* or *measurement of performance is carried out by running a benchmark program.*

mechanical /mɪˈkænɪk(ə)l/ *adjective* referring to machines

mechanical mouse /mɪˈkænɪk(ə)l maʊs/ *noun* pointing device that is operated by moving it across a flat surface. As the mouse is moved, a ball inside spins and turns two sensors that feed the horizontal and vertical movement back to the computer. Compare **optical mouse**

mechanism /ˈmekəˌnɪz(ə)m/ *noun* a piece of machinery ○ *The printer mechanism is very simple.*

media /ˈmiːdiə/ *plural noun* **1.** physical materials that can be used to store data ○ *Computers can store data on a variety of media, such as disk or CD-ROM.* **2.** the various means of transmitting information, including audio and video, television, radio, newspapers and magazines

media access control /ˌmiːdiə ˈækses kənˌtrəʊl/ *noun* a sublayer within the data-link layer of the OSI network model that provides access to the transmission media. Abbr **MAC**

media control interface /ˌmiːdiə kən ˌtrəʊl ˈɪntəfeɪs/ *noun* full form of **MCI**

Media Player /ˈmiːdiə ˌpleɪə/ a trade name for a Windows utility program that allows a user to control installed multimedia hardware including video disc or audio CDs, or play back multimedia files including sound, animation and video files

MediaServer /ˈmiːdiəˌsɜːvə/ a trade name for a system developed by Netscape to provide audio and video delivery over the Internet

medium /ˈmiːdiəm/ *adjective* middle or average ○ *a medium-sized computer system* ■ *noun* a means of transmitting information (NOTE: The plural is **media** or **mediums**.)

medium access control /ˌmiːdiəm ˌækses kənˈtrəʊl/ *noun* an IEEE 802 standard defining the protocol for data-link-level transmissions. Abbr **MAC**. ◊ **data link layer**

medium frequency /ˌmiːdiəm ˈfriːkwənsi/ *noun* the radio frequency range between 300 to 3000KHz (often referred to as medium wave (MW), especially on radio receivers)

medium scale integration /ˌmiːdiəm skeɪl ˌɪntɪˈgreɪʃ(ə)n/ *noun* an integrated circuit with 10 – 500 components. Abbr **MSI**

medium speed /ˈmiːdiəm spiːd/ *noun* a data communication speed between 2400 and 9600 bits per second (NOTE: Medium speed transmission describes the maximum rate of transfer for a normal voice grade channel.)

medium wave /ˈmiːdiəm weɪv/ *noun* full form of **MW**

meg /meg/ *noun* same as **megabyte** (*informal*) ○ *This computer has a ninety-meg hard disk.*

mega- /megə/ *prefix* one million

megabit /ˈmegəbɪt/ *noun* equal to 1,048,576 bits. Abbr **Mb**

megabits per second /ˌmegəbɪts pɜː ˈsekənd/ *noun* a number of million bits transmitted every second. Abbr **Mbps**

megabyte /ˈmegəbaɪt/ *noun* a measure of the data capacity of a storage device that is equal to 1,048,576 bytes or 2^{20} bytes. Megabytes are used to measure the storage capacity of hard disk drives or main memory (RAM). Abbr **MB**

> 'Doing this reduced a bitmap of my desktop from 2.25 megabytes to a 58K GIF' [*The Guardian*]

mega floating point instructions per second /ˌmegə ˌfləʊtɪŋ pɔɪnt ɪn ˌstrʌkʃənz pɜː sɪˈkɒnd/ *noun* full form of **MFLOPS**

megaflop /ˈmegəflɒp/ *noun* a measure of computing power and speed equal to one million floating point instructions per second. Abbr **MFLOPS**

megahertz /ˈmegəˌhɜːts/ *noun* a measure of frequency equal to one million cycles per second. Abbr **MHz**

megapixel display /ˌmegəpɪks(ə)l dɪ ˈspleɪ/ *noun* a display adapter and monitor that are capable of displaying over one million pixels. This means a resolution of at least 1,024x1,024 pixels.

Megastream /ˈmegəstriːm/ a trade name for a data link provided by British Telecom that offers data transfer at rates up to 8Mbits/second

Mega VGA /ˌmegə viː dʒiː ˈeɪ/ *noun* a 256 colour Super VGA mode with a resolution of 1024x768 that requires one megabyte of video RAM

member /ˈmembə/ *noun* **1.** one object on a page of a multimedia book **2.** an individual record or item in a field

membrane keyboard /ˌmembreɪn ˈkiːbɔːd/ *noun* a keyboard that uses a thin plastic or rubber sheet with key shapes moulded into it. When the user presses on a key, it activates a pressure sensor. (NOTE: The keys in a membrane keyboard have less travel than normal mechanical keys, but since they have no moving parts, they are more robust and reliable.)

memo field /ˈmeməʊ fiːld/ *noun* a field in a database or text window in an application that allows a user to add comments or a memo about the entry

memorise /ˈmeməˌraɪz/, **memorize** *verb* to remember or to retain in the memory

memory /ˈmem(ə)ri/ *noun* storage space in a computer system or medium that is capable of retaining data or instructions

'The lower-power design, together with an additional 8Kb of on-board cache memory, will increase the chip's performance to 75 million instructions per second.' [*Computing*]

'...when a program is loaded into memory, some is used for the code, some for the permanent data, and some is reserved for the stack which grows and shrinks for function calls and local data' [*Personal Computer World*]

memory buffer register /ˈmem(ə)ri ˌbʌfə ˌredʒɪstə/ *noun* full form of **MBR**

memory-intensive software /ˌmem(ə)ri ɪnˌtensɪv ˈsɒftweə/ *noun* software that uses large amounts of RAM or disk storage during run-time, such as programs whose entire code has to be in main memory during execution

memory-resident software /ˌmem(ə)ri ˌrezɪd(ə)nt ˈsɒftweə/ *noun* same as **resident software**

memory stick /ˈmem(ə)ri stɪk/ *noun* a tiny memory expansion device, developed by Sony, that can store up to 128Mb of data, often used in MP3 music players and digital cameras

menu /ˈmenjuː/ *noun* a list of options or programs available to the user

menu-bar /ˈmenjuː bɑː/ *noun* (*in a GUI*) a list of options available to a user which are displayed on a horizontal line along the top of the screen or window. Each menu option activates a pull-down menu.

menu-driven software /ˌmenjuː ˌdrɪv(ə)n ˈsɒftweə/ *noun* a program in which commands or options are selected from a menu by the operator rather than typed in by the user at a prompt

menu item /ˈmenjuː ˌaɪtəm/ *noun* one of the choices in a menu

menu selection /ˈmenjuː sɪˌlekʃən/ *noun* the act of choosing commands from a list of options presented to the operator

menu shortcut /ˌmenjuː ˈʃɔːtkʌt/ *noun* a key combination of two or more keys that is the same are selecting a menu option

merchant account /ˈmɜːtʃənt əˌkaʊnt/ *noun* a bank account that enables its user to deposit payments made by credit card, used especially for trading on the Internet

merge /mɜːdʒ/ *verb* to combine two data files retaining an overall order ○ *The system automatically merges text and illustrations into the document.* (NOTE: **merges – merging – merged**)

merge sort /ˌmɜːdʒ ˈsɔːt/ *noun* a software application in which the sorted files are merged into a new file

mesh /meʃ/ *noun* any system with two or more possible paths at each interconnection

message /ˈmesɪdʒ/ *noun* **1.** a piece of information sent from one person to another **2.** a defined amount of information **3.** a code generated by an action or object and interpreted by another object ○ *If a user presses the mouse button it generates a 'button_down' message that can then be interpreted by a user-interface or program.* **4.** text displayed to a user to report on a condition or program **5.** data that is sent to control an instrument

message authentication code /ˌmesɪdʒ ɔːˌθentɪˈkeɪʃ(ə)n kəʊd/ *noun* full form of **MAC**

message format /ˈmesɪdʒ ˌfɔːmæt/ *noun* a set of predetermined rules defining the coding, size and speed of transmitted messages

messaging /ˈmesɪdʒɪŋ/ *noun* the process of sending a message to other people, e.g. by computer, telephone or pager

metafile /ˈmetəfaɪl/ *noun* **1.** a file that contains other files ○ *The operating system uses a metafile to hold data that defines where each file is stored on disk.* **2.** a file that defines or contains data about other files

metalanguage /ˈmetəˌlæŋgwɪdʒ/ *noun* a language that describes a programming language

meter /ˈmiːtə/ *noun* **1.** a device which counts or records something ○ *an electricity meter* ○ *A meter attached to the photocopier records the number of copies made.* ◊ **multimeter 2.** an icon in the bottom right-hand corner of the status bar that indicates how much power is left in a laptop's battery and whether the laptop is running off battery or mains electricity power ■ *verb* to record and count ○ *The calls from each office are metered by the call logger.*

metropolitan area network /ˌmetrəpɒlɪt(ə)n ˌeəriə ˈnetwɜːk/ *noun* full form of **MAN**

MF *abbr* medium frequency

MFLOPS /'em flɒps/ *noun* a measure of computing speed calculated as the number of floating point instructions that can be processed each second. Full form **mega floating point instructions per second**

MFM /ˌem ef 'em/ *noun* a method of storing data on magnetic media, e.g. a magnetic disk that encodes the data bit according to the state of the previous bit. Full form **modified frequency modulation** (NOTE: MFM is more efficient than FM, but less efficient than RLL encoding.)

MHz *abbr* megahertz

MIC *noun* a device which converts sound to an electrical analogue signal. Full form **microphone**

MICR /ˌem aɪ siː 'ɑː/ *noun* a system that identifies characters by sensing magnetic ink patterns, as used on bank cheques. Full form **magnetic ink character recognition**

Micro Channel Bus /ˌmaɪkrəʊ ˌtʃæn(ə)l 'bʌs/ a proprietary 32-bit expansion bus defined by IBM in its Micro Channel Architecture

microcircuit /'maɪkrəʊˌkɜːkɪt/ *noun* a complex integrated circuit

microcode /'maɪkrəʊkəʊd/ *noun* a set of ALU control instructions implemented as hardwired software

microcomputer /'maɪkrəʊkəmˌpjuːtə/ *noun* a complete small-scale, cheap, low-power computer system based around a microprocessor chip and having limited memory capacity

COMMENT: Microcomputers are particularly used as home computers or as small office computers.

microelectronics /ˌmaɪkrəʊɪlek'trɒnɪks/ *noun* the design and manufacture of electronic circuits with integrated circuits and chips

microfiche /'maɪkrəʊˌfiːʃ/ *noun* a sheet of text and graphics in highly reduced form on a photographic film

microfilm /'maɪkrəʊfɪlm/ *noun* a reel of film containing a sequence of very small images used for document storage ○ *We hold all our records on microfilm.* ■ *verb* to take very small photographs ○ *The 1985 records have been sent away for microfilming.*

microfloppy /'maɪkrəʊˌflɒpi/ *noun* a small size magnetic floppy disk, usually a 3.5 inch disk

microform /'maɪkrəʊfɔːm/ *noun* a medium used for storing information in microimage form

micrographics /'maɪkrəʊˌgræfɪks/ *noun* images and graphics stored as microimages

microimage /'maɪkrəʊˌɪmɪdʒ/ *noun* a graphical image too small to be seen with the naked eye

microinstruction /'maɪkrəʊɪnˌstrʌkʃən/ *noun* a hardwired instruction, part of a microcode, that controls the actions of the ALU in a processor

micron /'maɪkrɒn/ *noun* one millionth of a metre

microphone /'maɪkrəfəʊn/ *noun* a device that converts sound waves into electrical signals

microphotography /ˌmaɪkrəʊfə'tɒgrəfi/ *noun* the photographic production of microimages (too small to be seen with the naked eye)

microprocessor /'maɪkrəʊˌprəʊsesə/ *noun* a set of central processing unit elements, often contained on a single integrated circuit chip, which when combined with other memory and I/O chips will make up a microcomputer

microprocessor unit /'maɪkrəʊ ˌprəʊsesə ˌjuːnɪt/ *noun* a unit containing the main elements of a microprocessor. Abbr **MPU**

microsecond /'maɪkrəʊˌsekənd/ *noun* one millionth of a second

Microsoft /'maɪkrəsɒft/ the biggest developer and publisher of software for the PC and Apple Mac. Microsoft developed the MS-DOS operating system for the IBM PC and later Windows together with a range of application software.

Microsoft Compact Disc Extensions /ˌmaɪkrəsɒft ˌkɒmpækt 'dɪsk ɪkˌstenʃ(ə)nz/ full form of **MSCDEX**

Microsoft Exchange /ˌmaɪkrəsɒft ɪks'tʃeɪndʒ/ a program included with Windows 95 that coordinates the email, fax and network messages sent and received on a PC

Microsoft Exchange Server /ˌmaɪkrəsɒft ɪks'tʃeɪndʒ ˌsɜːvə/ a program that runs on a server under Microsoft Windows NT and provides sophisticated groupware functions using the Exchange client software supplied with Windows 95

Microsoft Internet Explorer /ˌmaɪkrəsɒft ˌɪntənet ɪks'plɔːrə/ ➧ **Internet Explorer**

Microsoft Network /ˌmaɪkrəsɒft 'netwɜːk/ full form of **MSN**

Microsoft Outlook /ˌmaɪkrəsɒft 'aʊtlʊk/ a trade name for an application that provides a range of features to manage email, fax messages, contacts, diary appointments, notes and projects

Microsoft Outlook Express /ˌmaɪkrəsɒft ˌaʊtlʊk ɪk'spres/ a trade name for a free version of Outlook that is normally used for email (NOTE: It has fewer extra features for managing contacts and appointments than Microsoft Outlook.)

Microsoft Windows /ˌmaɪkrəsɒft ˈwɪndəʊz/ same as **Windows**

microwave /ˈmaɪkrəweɪv/ *noun* the radio frequency range from 1 to 3000GHz

microwave communications link /ˌmaɪkrəweɪv kəˌmjuːnɪˈkeɪʃ(ə)nz ˌlɪŋk/ *noun* the use of a microwave beam to transmit data between two points

microwave relay /ˈmaɪkrəʊweɪv ˌriːleɪ/ *noun* radiocommunications equipment used to receive microwave signals, then boost and retransmit them

microwave transmission /ˌmaɪkrəweɪv trænzˈmɪʃ(ə)n/ *noun* communication using modulated microwaves allowing high data rates, used for international telephone and satellite communications

middle and side microphone /ˌmɪd(ə)l ən saɪd ˈmaɪkrəfəʊn/ *noun* full form of **M and S microphone**

MID-F1 /ˌmɪd ef ˈwʌn/ *noun* (*in CD-i*) mid-quality sound at Level B. ◊ **Level B**

MIDI /ˈmɪdi/ *noun* a serial interface that connects electronic instruments. Full form **musical instrument digital interface** (NOTE: The MIDI interface carries signals from a controller or computer that instructs the different instruments to play notes.)

MIDI channel /ˈmɪdi ˌtʃæn(ə)l/ *noun* any one of 15 independent connections that is supported by the MIDI system, allowing 16 different electronic devices to be connected to one main sequencer

MIDI control-change message /ˌmɪdi kənˈtrəʊl tʃeɪndʒ ˌmesɪdʒ/ *noun* a message sent to a synthesiser to control the volume or pitch of a sound or to change the instrument patch used to generate a sound

MIDI device /ˈmɪdi dɪˌvaɪs/ *noun* a device that can receive or send MIDI data

MIDI file /ˈmɪdi faɪl/ *noun* a file format used to store a MIDI song, made up of notes and control-change messages (NOTE: It usually has a MID file extension.)

MIDI time code /ˌmɪdi ˈtaɪm kəʊd/ *noun* full form of **MTC**

mid-user /ˈmɪd ˌjuːzə/ *noun* an operator who retrieves relevant information from a database for a customer or end user

migrate /maɪˈgreɪt/ *verb* to transfer a file from one computer system or database to another (NOTE: **migrates – migrating – migrated**)

migration /maɪˈgreɪʃ(ə)n/ *noun* the process of moving users from one hardware platform to another

millennium bug /mɪˈleniəm bʌg/ *noun* the inability to handle dates later than 1999. This problem, which came to light in the 1990s, affected old hardware and software that stored dates as two digits, with the '19' being assumed. Such dates would not move to '2000' at the turn of the millennium but would revert to '1900', with unpredictable and possibly serious results for the affected systems. In the event, the affected systems were nearly all modified in time. There were very few problems when the year 2000 arrived, and the more apocalyptic predictions did not come to pass.

milli- /mɪlɪ/ *prefix* one thousandth. Abbr **m**

million instructions per second /ˌmɪljən ɪnˌstrʌkʃənz pɜː sɪˈkɒnd/ *noun* full form of **MIPS**

millisecond /ˈmɪlɪˌsekənd/ *noun* one thousandth of a second. Abbr **ms**

MIME /ˌem aɪ em ˈiː/ *noun* a standard that defines a way of sending files using email software. Full form **multipurpose Internet mail extensions**

COMMENT: MIME allows a user to send files over the Internet to another user without having to carry out any other encoding or conversion actions. MIME was developed to get around a problem of many email systems that could only transmit text which is stored in a 7-bit data format; programs, multimedia, graphics and other files are stored using an 8-bit data format.

mini /ˈmɪni/ *noun* same as **minicomputer**

mini- /mɪni/ *prefix* small

minicam /ˈmɪnikæm/ *noun* a hand-held, lightweight video camera (*film*)

minicomputer /ˈmɪnikəmˌpjuːtə/ *noun* a small computer with a greater range of instructions and processing power than a microcomputer but not able to compete with the speed or data-handling capacity of a mainframe computer. Also called **mini**

minidisk /ˈmɪnidɪsk/ *noun* a magnetic disk smaller than the 5.25 inch standard, usually 3.5 inch

minimise /ˈmɪnɪmaɪz/, **minimize** *verb* **1.** to make something as small as possible ○ *We minimised costs by cutting down the number of components.* **2.** (*in Windows*) to shrink an application window to an icon. Compare **maximise** (NOTE: minimises – minimising – minimised)

COMMENT: The application can continue to run in the background. You minimise a window by clicking once on the down arrow in the top right hand corner.

minimum /ˈmɪnɪməm/ *noun* the smallest amount of something (NOTE: The plural is **minimums** or **minima**.)

minmax /ˈmɪnimæks/ *noun* a method used in artificial intelligence to solve problems

minuend /ˈmɪnjuːend/ *noun* a number from which another is subtracted

minus /ˈmaɪnəs/, **minus sign** /ˈmaɪnəs saɪn/ *noun* a printed or written sign, like a small dash, to indicate subtraction or to show a negative value

minuscule /ˈmɪnɪskjuːl/ *noun* a lower case printed character

MIPS /mɪps/ *noun* a measure of processor speed that defines the number of instructions it can carry out per second. Full form **million instructions per second**. Compare **megaflop**

'ICL has staked its claim to the massively parallel market with the launch of the Goldrush MegaServer, providing up to 16,000 Unix MIPS of processing power.' [*Computing*]

mirror /ˈmɪrə/ *verb* **1.** to create an identical copy of something **2.** to duplicate all disk operations onto a second disk drive that can be used if the first breaks down ○ *There's less chance of losing our data now that we have mirrored the server's disk drive.*

'Network-attached storage systems which aim to make it easy to mirror data between units' [*The Guardian*]

mirroring /ˈmɪrərɪŋ/ *noun* the rotation of an image by 180 degrees to produce its mirror image

'...they also offer mirror-disk protection against disk failure, providing automatic backup of a database disks are also mirrored so that the system can continue to run in the event of a disk crash mirroring of the database is handled automatically by systems software' [*Computer News*]

mirror site /ˈmɪrə saɪt/ *noun* an exact copy of a website kept on a different file server so that the main site does not become overloaded and its data is protected against loss if there is a hardware or software failure

MIS *abbr* **1.** management information service **2.** management information system

mismatch /ˈmɪsmætʃ/ *noun* a situation occurring when two things are not correctly matched

mission-critical /ˌmɪʃ(ə)n ˈkrɪtɪk(ə)l/ *adjective* referring to an application or hardware on which a company depends

mix /mɪks/ *noun* **1.** the creative blending together of audio or video sources **2.** a visual effect which is similar to a dissolve ■ *verb* to combine several separate signals into a single signal □ **to mix down** to combine the signals from several sources such as a number of recorded audio tracks *or* instruments into a single signal

mixer /ˈmɪksə/ *noun* an electronic circuit used to combine two or more separate signals into a single output

mixing /ˈmɪksɪŋ/ *noun* **1.** the process of combining several audio signals into a single signal **2.** the process of printing a line of text with several different typefaces

mixing studio /ˈmɪksɪŋ ˌstjuːdiəʊ/ *noun* a room with audio mixers and sound processors used when recording music

MJPEG /ˌem ˈdʒeɪ peg/ *noun* a version of the JPEG image compression system that supports video. Full form **motion JPEG**

MKDIR *abbr* make directory. ◊ **MD**

MKS *noun* a widely used measurement system based on the metre, kilogram and second. Full form **metre kilogram second**. ◊ **SI units**

MMA *abbr* MIDI manufacturers association

MMC /ˌem em ˈsiː/ *noun* a compact memory expansion device that includes digital copyright control features and is often used in MP3 music players and digital cameras. Full form **multimedia card**. Also called **SD card**

MME *abbr* multimedia extensions

MMI /ˌem em ˈaɪ/ *noun* hardware and software designed to make it easier for users to communicate effectively with a machine. Full form **man machine interface**

MMX a trade name for an enhanced Intel processor chip that includes special features and components that are used to improve the performance when dealing with multimedia and communications. Full form **multimedia extensions**

mnemonic /nɪˈmɒnɪk/ *noun* a shortened form of a word or function that is helpful as a reminder, e.g. INCA for increment register A

mnemonic keyboard shortcut /nɪˌmɒnɪk ˌkiːbɔːd ˌʃɔːtˈkʌt/ *noun* a shortcut to a menu option or function by pressing a special key sequence

mobile /ˈməʊbaɪl/ *adjective* **1.** which can move about **2.** meaning a travelling radio base such as a car transceiver (*informal*)

mobile earth terminal /ˌməʊbaɪl ˈɜːθ ˌtɜːmɪn(ə)l/ *noun* satellite communications equipment that is mobile

mobile phone /ˌməʊbaɪl ˈfəʊn/ *noun* a small, portable device that lets someone make and receive telephone calls. Also called **cellular phone**

COMMENT: Older mobile phone standards transmitted the user's voice as an analog radio signal; current phones convert the voice to digital data and transmit this via a radio signal. New mobile phones provide data and messaging services as well as basic telephone functions: some include built-in modems to provide dial-up access to the Internet, many allow text messages to be transmitted to other phone users and some incorporate an electronic diary, organiser and address book. Current mobile telephones transmit information using the GSM, PCS or GPRS standard and can provide basic Internet access using WAP and GPRS.

mobile radiophone /ˌməʊbaɪl ˈreɪdiəʊfəʊn/ *noun* a radio telephone linked to a main telephone system, which uses a network of stations, each covering a certain area, to provide a service over a large area

mobile unit /ˌməʊbaɪl ˈjuːnɪt/ *noun* a complete set of television filming and editing equipment carried in a vehicle (for outside broadcasts)

mock-up /ˈmɒk ʌp/ *noun* a model of a new product for testing or to show to possible customers

MOD /mɒd/ *noun* the remainder after the division of one number by another. Full form **modulus**

modal /ˈməʊd(ə)l/ *adjective* **1.** referring to modes ○ *Dialog boxes are normally modal windows.* **2.** (*in Windows*) referring to a window that is displayed and does not allow a user to do anything outside it

mode /məʊd/ *noun* **1.** a way of doing something **2.** the number of paths taken by light when travelling down an optical fibre **3.** the number that occurs most frequently in a series of samples

'The approach being established by the Jedec committee provides for burst mode data transfer clocked at up to 100MHz.' [*Computing*]

Mode 1 /ˈməʊd wʌn/ *noun* an encoding format used on compact discs that has error-detection and -correction codes

Mode 2 /ˈməʊd tuː/ *noun* an encoding format with two forms, form 1, which is the same as Mode 1, and form 2, which requires no processing and allows data to be sent straight to the output channel

model /ˈmɒd(ə)l/ *noun* **1.** a small copy of something to show what it will look like when finished ○ *He showed us a model of the new computer centre building.* **2.** a style, type or version of a product ○ *The new model B has taken the place of model A.* ■ *adjective* which is a perfect example to be copied ○ *a model agreement* ■ *verb* to make a computerised model of a new product or of a system, e.g. the economic system (NOTE: **modelling – modelled**. The US spellings are **modeling – modeled**.)

modelling /ˈmɒd(ə)lɪŋ/ *noun* **1.** the process of creating computer models **2.** the process of colouring and shading a (normally wire-frame or vecto) graphic object so that it looks solid and real

modem /ˈməʊˌdem/, **MODEM** *noun* a device that allows data to be sent over telephone lines by converting binary signals from a computer into analog sound signals which can be transmitted over a telephone line. Full form **modulator/demodulator**

'AST Research has bundled together a notebook PC with a third-party PCMCIA fax modem technology for a limited-period special offer.' [*Computing*]

COMMENT: The process of converting binary signals to analog is called 'modulation'. When the signal is received, another converter reverses the process (called 'demodulation'). Both parts must be working according to the same standards.

modem standards /ˈməʊdem ˌstændədz/ *plural noun* rules defining transmitting frequencies and other factors which allow different modems to communicate

moderated newsgroup /ˌmɒd(ə)rətɪd ˈnjuːzgruːp/ *noun* a newsgroup in which a moderator reads all the material that has been submitted before it is published in the newsgroup (NOTE: Most newsgroups are not moderated and anyone can write anything. Moderated newsgroups usually have a '-d' after their name.)

moderator /ˈmɒdəˌreɪtə/ *noun* a person responsible for reading messages sent to a mailing list or newsgroup and editing any messages that do not conform to the rules of the list, e.g. by deleting commercial messages

modification /ˌmɒdɪfɪˈkeɪʃ(ə)n/ *noun* a change made to something ○ *The modifications to the system allow it to be run as part of a LAN.*

modifier /ˈmɒdɪˌfaɪə/ *noun* a programming instruction that alters the normal action of a command

modify /ˈmɒdɪˌfaɪ/ *verb* to change something or make something fit a different use ○ *The keyboard was modified for European users.* (NOTE: **modifies – modifying – modified**)

Modula-2 /ˌmɒdjʊlə ˈtuː/ *noun* a high-level programming language derived from Pascal that supports modular programming techniques and data abstraction

modular /ˈmɒdjʊlə/ *adjective* referring to a method of constructing hardware or software products by connecting several smaller blocks together to produce a customised product

modularisation, modularization *noun* the process of designing programs from a set of standard modules

modularity /ˌmɒdjʊˈlærɪti/ *noun* the state or fact of being made up from modules ○ *The modularity of the software* or *hardware allows the system to be changed.*

modular programming /ˌmɒdjʊlə ˈprəʊgræmɪŋ/ *noun* programming with small individually written sections of computer code that can be made to fit into a structured program and can be called up from a main program

modulate /ˈmɒdjʊˌleɪt/ *verb* to change a carrier wave so that it can carry data (NOTE: **modulates – modulating – modulated**)

modulation /ˌmɒdjuˈleɪʃ(ə)n/ *noun* the process of varying a carrier's amplitude or frequency or phase according to an applied signal

modulator /ˈmɒdjʊleɪtə/ *noun* an electronic circuit that varies a carrier signal according to an applied signal

modulator/demodulator /ˌmɒdjʊleɪtə diːˈmɒdjʊleɪtə/ *noun* full form of **modem**

module /ˈmɒdjuːl/ *noun* **1.** a small section of a large program that can, if required, function independently as a program in its own right **2.** a self-contained piece of hardware that can be connected with other modules to form a new system ○ *A multifunction analog interface module includes analog-to-digital and digital-to-analog converters.* **3.** a system for imprinting a signal on a radio frequency carrier (*film*) **4.** a system for producing audio effects where one sound is modulated by another (*film*)

modulo arithmetic /ˈmɒdjuləʊ əˌrɪθmətɪk/ *noun* a branch of arithmetic that uses the remainder of one number when divided by another

modulus /ˈmɒdjʊləs/ *noun* full form of **MOD** ○ *7 mod 3 = 1*

moiré /ˈmwɑːreɪ/ *noun* **1.** picture distortion which is caused by interference beats of similar frequencies **2.** an unwanted watery effect which is created by a set of closely spaced lines which are placed over another set (seen in film or prints). ◊ **screen angle**

moiré effect /ˈmwɑːreɪ ɪˌfekt/ *noun* an interference pattern caused by printing with the wrong screen angle

momentary switch /ˈməʊmənt(ə)ri swɪtʃ/ *noun* a switch that only conducts while it is being pressed

monitor /ˈmɒnɪtə/ *noun* **1.** a VDU used to display high quality text or graphics, generated by a computer **2.** a system that watches for faults or failures in a circuit **3.** a loudspeaker used to listen to the sound signals produced during recording or mixing **4.** a TV screen in a TV studio control room, which shows the image being filmed by one of the cameras **5.** a computer program that allows basic commands to be entered to operate a system, such as load a program, examine the state of devices, etc. ■ *verb* **1.** to check or to examine how something is working ○ *He is monitoring the progress of the trainee programmers.* **2.** to look after and supervise a process or experiment to make sure it is operating correctly ○ *The machine monitors each signal as it is sent out.*

mono- /mɒnəʊ/ *prefix* single or one

monoaural /ˌmɒnəʊˈɔːrəl/ *adjective* having one source of sound or one sound signal. Compare **stereo**

monochromatic light /ˌmɒnəʊkrəmætɪk ˈkʌlə/ *noun* light of a single colour (*film*)

monochrome /ˈmɒnəkrəʊm/ *adjective, noun* referring to an image in one colour, usually shades of grey and black and white

monochrome display adapter /ˌmɒnəkrəʊm dɪˈspleɪ əˌdæptə/ *noun* a video adapter standard used in early PC systems that could display text in 25 lines of 80 columns. Abbr **MDA**

monochrome monitor /ˌmɒnəkrəʊm ˈmɒnɪtə/ *noun* a computer monitor that displays text and graphics in black, white and shades of grey instead of colours

monolithic /ˌ mɒnəˈlɪθɪk/ *adjective* (*of an integrated circuit*) manufactured on a single crystal of semiconductor

monolithic driver /ˌmɒnəlɪθɪk ˈdraɪvə/ *noun* a piece of driver software that has a range of different functions or applications within one program

monomode fibre /ˈmɒnəʊməʊd ˌfaɪbə/ *noun* same as **single mode fibre**

monoprogramming system /ˈmɒnəʊ ˌprəʊgræmɪŋ ˌsɪstəm/ *noun* a computer batch processing system that executes one program at a time. Compare **multi-programming system**

monospaced /ˈmɒnəʊspeɪst/ *adjective* referring to a font in which each character has the same width. Compare **proportionally spaced**

montage /ˈmɒntɑːʒ/ *noun* **1.** a series of quickly changing images, sometimes with general pictures seen simultaneously on the screen **2.** the process of combining several still or video images

Monte Carlo method /ˌmɒnti ˈkɑːləʊ ˌmeθəd/ *noun* a statistical analysis technique

MOO *noun* a virtual space in which participants can discuss a topic online. Full form **multiuser domain, object-oriented**

morphing /ˈmɔːfɪŋ/ *noun* a special effect used in multimedia and games in which one image gradually turns into another

Morse code /ˌmɔːs ˈkəʊd/ *noun* a system of signalling using only two symbols: dots and dashes □ **morse key** switch used to send morse messages by hand

mosaic /məʊ'zeɪɪk/ *noun* **1.** a display character used in videotext systems that is made up of small dots **2.** a light-sensitive surface of a television camera pick-up tube which is scanned by the electron beam

Mosaic /məʊ'zeɪɪk/ a trade name for a popular browser software used to view webpages on the Internet

most significant bit /ˌməʊst sɪg ˌnɪfɪkənt 'bɪt/ *noun* full form of **msb** ○ *The most significant bit in an eight bit binary word represents 128 in decimal notation.*

most significant digit /məʊst sɪg ˌnɪfɪkənt 'dɪdʒɪt/, **most significant character** /məʊst sɪgˌnɪfɪkənt 'kærɪktə/ *noun* full form of **MSD**

motherboard /'mʌðəbɔːd/ *noun* the main printed circuit board of a system, containing most of the components and connections for expansion boards and other features

motion blur /'məʊʃ(ə)n blɜː/ *noun* the blurring of an object that moves too fast to be frozen by the camera

motion control /ˌməʊʃ(ə)n kən'trəʊl/ *noun* a computer that allows a user to control all the aspects of a camera to allow special effects in video or still images

motion JPEG /ˌməʊʃ(ə)n 'dʒeɪ ˌpeg/ *noun* full form of **MJPEG**

motion picture /ˌməʊʃ(ə)n 'pɪktʃə/ *noun* a series of still pictures (each slightly different) which give an object the appearance of motion when projected on to a screen

motion-picture camera /'məʊʃ(ə)n ˌpɪktʃə ˌkæm(ə)rə/ *noun* a box with lens, shutter, viewfinder and film advance system in which motion-picture film is exposed

motion picture experts group /ˌməʊʃ(ə)n ˌpɪktʃə 'ekspɜːts gruːp/ *noun* full form of **MPEG**

motion-picture film /'məʊʃ(ə)n ˌpɪktʃə fɪlm/ *noun* light-sensitive film which is used in a motion picture camera

motor /'məʊtə/ *noun* an electromagnetic machine that converts an electrical supply into (rotary) motion (by means of a magnetic field)

mount /maʊnt/ *verb* **1.** to fix a device or circuit onto a base ○ *The chips are mounted in sockets on the PCB.* **2.** to insert a disk in a disk drive or inform an operating system that a disk drive is ready to be used

mouse /maʊs/ *noun* a small hand-held input device moved on a flat surface to control the position of a cursor on the screen (NOTE: The plural is **mice** or **mouses**.)

'This project has now borne fruit, with the announcement last week of Windots, a project which allows users to 'see' Windows screens in a Braille form of Ascii. Other areas of research include a sound system which allows a sound to 'move', mirroring the movement of a mouse.' [*Computing*]

mouse acceleration /ˌmaʊs əkˌselə 'reɪʃ(ə)n/ *noun* a feature of some mouse driver software that will move the mouse pointer at different speeds according to the speed at which you move the mouse rather than the distance

mouse driver /'maʊs ˌdraɪvə/ *noun* a program which converts positional data sent from a mouse to a standard form of coordinates that can be used by any software

mouse pointer /'maʊs ˌpɔɪntə/ *noun* a small arrow displayed on screen that moves around as the mouse is moved

movable /'muːvəb(ə)l/ *adjective* which can be moved

move /muːv/ *verb* to change the position of something

movement /'muːvmənt/ *noun* the act of changing position or of changing the position of something

movie file /'muːvi faɪl/ *noun* a file stored on disk that contains a series of images that make up an animation or video clip

movie ID /ˌmuːvi ˌaɪ'diː/ *noun* a unique ID number assigned to a movie in Movie Player – each separate instance has a different ID number

Movie Player /ˌmuːvi 'pleɪə/ *noun* a Windows utility that can playback AVI-format video clips or movie files with the MMM extension

Movie Player instance /ˌmuːvi ˌpleɪə 'ɪnstəns/ *noun* one copy of the Movie Player program that is running

Moving Pictures Expert Group /ˌmuːvɪŋ ˌpɪktʃəs 'ekspɜːt ˌgruːp/ *noun* full form of **MPEG**

MP3 /ˌem piː 'θriː/ *noun* a way of encoding digital audio data into a compressed data format that is approximately one twelfth the size of the original without perceptible loss of quality. MP3 files (that normally have the file name extension 'MP3') are now one of the most popular ways of storing and distributing music over the Internet. Because MP3 files are compact and easy to copy, they are relatively quick to download and very easy to distribute – which is causing problems for the original artists who are trying to protect their copyright material. Once you have an MP3 file you can listen to it by opening it and playing it with special software on your computer or by transferring it to a dedicated pocket-sized device that stores the file in its memory, has no moving parts and but can play back CD-quality music. Full form **MPEG audio level 3**

COMMENT: MP3 files, which usually have the file name extension MP3, are now one of the most popular ways of storing and distributing music over the Internet. Because MP3 files are compact and easy to copy, they are relatively quick to download and very easy to distribute, which is causing problems for the original artists who are trying to protect their copyright material. Once you have an MP3 file you can listen to it by opening it and playing it with special software on your computer or by transferring it to a dedicated pocket-sized device that stores the file in its memory, and has no moving parts but that can play back CD-quality music

MPC /ˌem piː ˈsiː/ *noun* an outdated set of minimum requirements for a PC that will allow it to run most multimedia software. Full form **multimedia PC**

MPEG /ˈem peg/ *noun* a group of developers that have defined a series of standards to improve audio and video quality but at the same time increase data compression so that the audio or video information takes less space but retains its quality. Full form **Moving Pictures Expert Group.** ◊ **JPEG** (NOTE: MPEG is often used to compress video clips and its derivative standard MP3 provides one of the most popular ways of compressing and storing audio information, while JPEG provides a popular way to store compressed still images.)

MPEG audio level 3 /ˌem peg ˌɔːdiəʊ ˌlev(ə)l ˈθriː/ *noun* full form of **MP3**

MPPP /ˌem piː piː ˈpiː/ *noun* communications protocol used with ISDN to link the two B-channels in a standard ISDN adapter to create a transmission channel that can transfer data at a higher speed. Full form **multilink point to point protocol**

MPU *abbr* microprocessor unit

ms *abbr* millisecond

msb /ˌem es ˈbiː/, **MSB** *noun* a bit in a word that represents the greatest value or weight, usually the bit furthest to the left. Full form **most significant bit**

MSCDEX /ˌem es siː diː ˈeks/ *noun* driver software installed on a PC to allow DOS and Windows to control a CD-ROM drive. Full form **Microsoft Compact Disc Extensions**

MSD /ˌem es ˈdiː/ *noun* the digit at the far left of a number, which represents the greatest power of the base. Full form **most significant digit**

MS-DOS /ˌem es ˈdɒs/ a trade name for an operating system for the IBM PC range of personal computers that managed data storage onto disks, display output and user input. Windows supports MS-DOS programs through the Command Prompt, which emulates MS-DOS. Full form **Microsoft DOS** (NOTE: MS-DOS is a single-user, single-tasking operating system that is controlled by a command-line interface.)

MSF time format /ˌem es ef ˈtaɪ ˌfɔːmæt/ *noun* a time format that counts frames per second used by MCI, usually used by CD-audio devices, in which there are 75 frames per second

MSI *abbr* medium scale integration

M signal /ˈem ˌsɪgn(ə)l/ *noun* a signal produced from the sum of left and right signals in a stereophonic system

MSN a trade name for an Internet portal. Full form **Microsoft Network**

MS-Windows /ˌem es ˈwɪndəʊz/ same as **Windows**

MSX /ˌem es ˈeks/ *noun* a hardware and software standard for home computers that can use interchangeable software

MTBF /ˌem tiː biː ˈef/ *noun* the average period of time that a piece of equipment will operate between failures. Full form **mean time between failures**

MTC /ˌem tiː ˈsiː/ *noun* a system of messages used to synchronise MIDI sequences with an external device, e.g. an SMPTE time code. Full form **MIDI time code**

MTF /ˌem tiː ˈef/ *noun* the average period of time for which a device will operate, usually continuously, before failing. Full form **mean time to failure**

MTTR /ˌem tiː tiː ˈɑː/ *noun* the average period of time required to repair a faulty piece of equipment. Full form **mean time to repair**

MUA /ˌem juː ˈeɪ/ *noun* software used to create and read email messages that creates a message in the correct format and standard and passes this to the mail transfer agent that is responsible for transferring the message over the network. Full form **mail user agent**

MUD /ˌem tiː ˈeɪ/ *noun* **1.** a virtual online space in which several people can participate in collaborative projects at the same time. Full form **multiuser domain 2.** an adventure game played by multiple users over the Internet. Full form **multiuser dungeon**

multi- /mʌlti/ *prefix* many or more than one ○ *multimegabyte memory card*

multi-access system /ˌmʌltɪ ˌækses ˈsɪstəm/ *noun* a computer system that allows several users to access one file or program at the same time. Also called **multiple access system**

multibank dynamic random access memory /ˌmʌltɪbæŋk daɪˌnæmɪk ˌrændəm ˌækses ˈmem(ə)ri/ *noun* full form of **MDRAM**

multi-board computer /ˌmʌltɪ bɔːd kəm'pjuːtə/ *noun* a computer which has several integrated circuit boards connected with a motherboard

multiburst signal /ˌmʌltɪbɜːst 'sɪgn(ə)l/ *noun* a television test signal

multicast /'mʌltikɑːst/ *verb* to transmit one message to a group of recipients

COMMENT: This could be as simple as sending an email message to a list of email addresses or posting a message to a mailing list. It can also refer to more complex transfers such as a teleconference or videoconference in which several users link together by telephone or video link. A broadcast, in comparison, refers to the process of sending a message to anyone who could receive the message rather than a select group of recipients. Narrowcasting is very similar in concept to a multicasting, but is normally used to refer to the concept, whereas multicasting refers to the technology used.

multicasting /'mʌltikɑːstɪŋ/ *noun* the process of broadcasting to a number of receivers or nodes, with an address in each message to indicate the node required

multichannel /ˌmʌlti'tʃæn(ə)l/ *adjective* with more than one channel

multicolour /ˌmʌlti'kʌlə/ *adjective* with several colours

multicolour graphics adapter /ˌmʌltikʌlə 'græfɪks əˌdæptə/ *noun* full form of **MCGA**

multidimensional /ˌmʌltidaɪ'menʃən(ə)l/ *adjective* with features in more than one dimension

multi-disk /ˌmʌltɪ 'dɪsk/ *adjective* referring to several types of disk

multidrop circuit /'mʌltɪdrɒp ˌsɜːkɪt/ *noun* a network allowing communications between a number of terminals and a central computer, but not directly between terminals

multifrequency /ˌmʌlti'friːkwənsi/ *noun* □ **dual tone, multifrequency (DTMF)** communication signalling system using two different frequencies to transmit binary data

multifunction /ˌmʌltɪ'fʌnkʃən(ə)l/, **multifunctional** *adjective* which has several functions ○ *A multifunction analog interface module includes analog to digital and digital to analog converters.*

multifunctional /ˌmʌltɪ'fʌnkʃən(ə)l/ *adjective* which has several functions ○ *a multifunctional scanner*

multiline /ˌmʌlti'laɪn/ *adjective* in a text box, referring to a display of text broken into several lines rather than as a single continuous line. Also called **multiple line**

multilink system /'mʌltɪlɪŋk ˌsɪstəm/ *noun* a system in which there is more than one connection between two points

multimedia /ˌmʌlti'miːdiə/ *adjective* combining sound, graphics, animation, video and text within an application

'The Oracle Media Server is a multimedia database designed to run on massively parallel computers, running hundreds of transactions per second and managing multiple data types, such as video, audio and text.' [*Computing*]

multimedia card /ˌmʌltimiːdiə 'kɑːd/ *noun* full form of **MMC**

multimedia developer's kit /ˌmʌltimiːdiə dɪ'veləpəz kɪt/ *noun* full form of **MDK**

multimedia extensions /ˌmʌltimiːdiə ɪk'stenʃ(ə)nz/ *plural noun* full form of **MMX**

multimedia PC /ˌmʌltimiːdiə ˌpiː 'siː/ *noun* full form of **MPC**

multimedia-ready /ˌmʌltimiːdiə 'redi/ *adjective* referring to a PC that has all the extra equipment requirement to run most multimedia software

multimeter /'mʌltimiːtə/ *noun* testing equipment that provides an indication of the voltage or current or impedance at a point or of a component. Abbr **AMM**

multimode fibre /ˌmʌltɪməʊd 'faɪbə/ *noun* a commonly used type of optic fibre that uses a glass fibre with a diameter of between 50 and 125 microns and can carry several different frequencies of light with a maximum bandwidth of 2.5 Gbps (NOTE: The disadvantage is that because the fibre is wide, the light disperses quickly and so repeaters need to be installed to boost the signal.)

multipass overlap /ˌmʌltɪpɑːs 'əʊvəlæp/ *noun* a system of producing higher quality print from a dot matrix printer by repeating the line of characters but shifted slightly, so making the dots less noticeable

multi platform /ˌmʌltɪ 'plætˌfɔːm/ *adjective* referring to software that can run on several different hardware platforms

multiple /'mʌltɪp(ə)l/ *adjective* having many parts

multiple access system /ˌmʌltɪp(ə)l 'ækses ˌsɪstəm/ *noun* same as **multi-access system**

multiple base page /ˌmʌltɪp(ə)l beɪs 'peɪdʒ/ *noun* a multi-user system in which each user and the operating system have one page of main memory, which can then call up other pages within main memory

multiple line /ˌmʌltɪp(ə)l 'laɪn/ *adjective* same as **multiline**

multiplex /ˈmʌltɪpleks/ *verb* to combine several messages in the same transmission medium

multiplexing /ˈmʌltɪpleksɪŋ/ *noun* the process of combining several messages in the same transmission medium

multiplexor /ˈmʌltɪpleksə/ *noun* full form of **MUX** ○ *A 4 to 1 multiplexor combines four inputs into a single output.*

multiplication /ˌmʌltɪplɪˈkeɪʃ(ə)n/ *noun* a mathematical operation that adds one number to itself a number of times ○ *The multiplication of 5 and 3 = 15.*

multiply /ˈmʌltɪˌplaɪ/ *verb* to perform the mathematical operation of multiplication (NOTE: **multiplies – multiplying – multiplied**)

multipoint /ˈmʌltipɔɪnt/ *adjective* referring to a connection with several lines, attaching several terminals to a single line to a single computer

multiprocessing system /ˌmʌltɪ ˈprəʊsesɪŋ ˌsɪstəm/ *noun* a system where several processing units work together sharing the same memory

multiprocessor /ˈmʌltiˌprəʊsesə/ *noun* a number of processing units acting together or separately but sharing the same area of memory

multi-programming system /ˌmʌltɪ ˈprəʊgræmɪŋ ˌsɪstəm/ *noun* an operating system used to execute more than one program apparently simultaneously, each program being executed a little at a time. Compare **monoprogramming system**

multipurpose Internet mail extensions /ˌmʌltipɜːpəs ˌɪntənet ˈmeɪl ɪk ˌstenʃ(ə)nz/ *noun* full form of **MIME**

multisession /ˈmʌltɪseʃ(ə)n/ *noun* a CD-ROM which has had data stored onto it at different times (each time is called a session). This normally applies to PhotoCD discs – if the PhotoCD is not full, you can add extra images to it: this is a multisession disc because it contains images added after the first session.

multisession-compatible /ˌmʌltɪseʃ(ə)n kəmˈpætɪb(ə)l/ *adjective* referring to a CD-ROM drive that can read PhotoCD discs or other discs that have been created in several goes

MultiSync™ monitor /ˌmʌltɪsɪŋk ˈmɒnɪtə/ *noun* a monitor which contains circuitry to lock onto the required scanning frequency of any type of graphics card

multitasking /ˈmʌltiˌtɑːskɪŋ/ *noun* the ability of a computer system to run two or more programs at the same time ○ *The system is multi-user and multi-tasking.*

'X is the underlying technology which allows Unix applications to run under a multi-user, multitasking GUI. It has been adopted as the standard for the Common Open Software Environment, proposed recently by top Unix vendors including Digital, IBM and Sun.' [*Computing*]

COMMENT: Few small systems are capable of simultaneous multitasking, since each program would require its own processor. This is overcome by allocating to each program an amount of processing time, executing each a little at a time so that they will appear to run simultaneously due to the speed of the processor and the relatively short gaps between programs.

multi terminal system /ˌmʌltɪ ˌtɜːmɪn(ə)l ˈsɪstəm/ *noun* a system where several terminals are linked to a single CPU

multithreading /ˈmʌltɪθredɪŋ/ *noun* the process of running several different processes in rapid succession within a program (effectively multitasking within a program)

multiuser domain /ˌmʌltijuːzə də ˈmeɪn/ *noun* full form of **MUD**

multiuser domain, object-oriented /ˌmʌltijuːzə dəˌmeɪn ˌɒbdʒekt ˈɔːrientɪd/ *noun* full form of **MOO**

multiuser dungeon /ˌmʌltijuːzə ˈdʌndʒən/ *noun* full form of **MUD**

multiuser program /ˌmʌltijuːzə ˈprəgræm/ *noun* a software diary utility that allows many users to enter appointments and schedule meetings with other users. Also called **network calendar program**

multiuser system /ˌmʌltijuːzə ˈsɪstəm/ *noun* a computer system that can support more than one user at a time ○ *The program runs on a standalone machine* or *a multi-user system.*

multi-window editor /ˌmʌlti ˌwɪndəʊ ˈedɪtə/ *noun* a program used for creating and editing a number of applications programs independently, each in a separate window on screen at the same time

mung up /ˌmʌŋ ˈʌp/ *verb* to distort data or to ruin a file (*informal*)

mush /mʌʃ/ *noun* distortion and loss of signal

mush area /ˈmʌʃ ˌeəriə/ *noun* distortion and loss of signal due to two transmissions interfering

musical instrument digital interface /ˌmjuːzɪk(ə)l ˌɪnstrʊmənt ˌdɪdʒɪt(ə)l ˈɪntəfeɪs/ *noun* full form of **MIDI**

music chip /ˈmjuːzɪk tʃɪp/ *noun* an integrated circuit capable of generating musical sounds and tunes

music track /ˈmjuːzɪk træk/ *noun* a sound track on which is recorded music for a film (*film*)

MUX /ˌem juː 'eks/ *noun* a circuit that combines a number of inputs into a smaller number of outputs. Full form **multiplexor**. Compare **demultiplexor**

MW *abbr* **1.** medium wave **2.** megawatt

My Computer /ˌmaɪ kəm'pjuːtə/ *noun* an icon that is normally in the upper left-hand corner of the screen on a computer running Windows, containing an overview of the PC

N

n *abbr* nano-

NAB /næb/ *noun* a US term used to describe standards specified by this organisation (*film*)

NAB cartridge /ˈnæb ˌkɑːtrɪdʒ/ *noun* an NAB approved continuous loop magnetic tape cartridge which is broadcast standard and is made in three tape capacity sizes

NAB curve /ˈnæb ˌkɜːv/ *noun* the standard for audio playback equalisation

name /neɪm/ *noun* an ordinary word used to identify an address in machine language

name registration /ˈneɪm ˌredʒɪstreɪʃ(ə)n/ *noun* same as **domain name registration**

name resolution /ˈneɪm ˌrezəluːʃ(ə)n/ *noun* the process of converting a domain name into its numerical IP address

name server /ˈneɪm ˌsɜːvə/ *noun* a computer on the Internet that provides a domain name service to any other computer

naming services /ˈneɪmɪŋ ˌsɜːvɪsɪz/ *noun* a method of assigning each user or node or computer on a network a unique name that allows other users to access shared resources even over a wide area network

NAND function /ˈnænd ˌfʌŋkʃ(ə)n/ *noun* a logical function whose output is false if all inputs are true, and true if any input is false

COMMENT: The NAND function is equivalent to an AND function with a NOT function at the output. The output is 0 only if both inputs are 1; if one input is 1 and the other 0, or if both inputs are 0, then the output is 1.

NAND gate /ˈnænd geɪt/ *noun* an electronic circuit that provides a NAND function

nano- /nænəʊ/ *prefix* **1.** one thousand millionth. Abbr **n 2.** *US* one billionth

nanosecond /ˈnænəʊˌsekənd/ *noun* one thousand millionth of a second

Napster /ˈnæpstə/ a trade name for software that allows users to share files, normally MP3-format music files, over the Internet

COMMENT: Napster was originally used to distribute and share MP3 files with a personal recording of a commercial artist in an efficient way. The software, developed by Shawn Fanning, allowed anyone to download music from any another Napster user's computer. Once installed, the free software searches your hard disk for any MP3 music files, then allows other Napster users online to access these files from your hard disk, via the Internet. Because it allows music to be copied and shared very easily, Napster has become unpopular with the recording and music industry and was the subject of a legal case enforcing copyright over the Internet.

narrative /ˈnærətɪv/ *noun* a set of explanatory notes or comments to help a user operate a program

narrow band /ˈnærəʊ bænd/ *noun* a communication method that uses a bandwidth less than that of a voice channel. Abbr **see.** Compare **multicast**

narrow band FM /ˌnærəʊ bænd ˌef ˈem/ *noun* a frequency modulation system using very small bandwidth (with only one pair of sidebands). Abbr **NBFM**

narrow band ISDN /ˌnærəʊ bænd ˌaɪ es diː ˈen/ *noun* the ISDN communications system

narrowcast /ˈnærəʊkɑːst/ *verb* same as **multicast**

NAT /ˌen eɪ ˈtiː/ *noun* a system that allows a local area network to work with two sets of IP addresses for each computer or node in the network. Full form **network address translation**

COMMENT: The first set of addresses is used for internal traffic and the second set (often just one or two addresses) is used for external traffic, for example when accessing resources on the public Internet via a router. This system provides basic security against external attacks, for example using IP spoofing. Its main purpose is that it allows the local area network to use as many IP addresses as are required, but only using a minimal number of public IP addresses, which must be registered and allocated by an organisation such as InterNIC.

National Association of Broadcasters /ˌnæʃ(ə)nəl əˌsəʊsieɪʃ(ə)n əv ˈbrɔːdkɑːstəz/ *noun* full form of **NAB**

National Center for Supercomputing Applications /ˌnæʃ(ə)nəl ˌsentə fə ˈsuːpəkəmˌpjuːtɪŋ ˌæplɪkeɪʃ(ə)nz/ *noun* full form of **NCSA**

National Television System Committee /ˌnæʃ(ə)nəl ˌtelɪˈvɪʒ(ə)n ˌsɪstəm kəˌmɪti/ *noun* full form of **NTSC**

native file format /ˌneɪtɪv ˈfaɪl ˌfɔːmæt/ *noun* a default file format, usually proprietary, that is used by an application to store its data on disk

navigable /ˈnævɪgəb(ə)l/ *adjective* referring to a website that has been designed in such a way that the user can move from one section of the site to another by clicking on highlighted computer links

navigation /ˌnævɪˈgeɪʃ(ə)n/ *noun* the process of moving around a multimedia title using hotspots, buttons and a user interface

NC *abbr* **1.** network computer **2.** numerical control

NCR paper /ˌen siː ˈɑː ˌpeɪpə/ *noun* a special type of paper impregnated with chemicals and used in multipart forms. Full form **no carbon required paper** (NOTE: When NCR paper is printed on by an impact printer, the writing also appears on the sheets below.)

NCSA /ˌen siː es ˈeɪ/ *noun* an organisation that helped define and create the World Wide Web with its Mosaic web browser. Full form **National Center for Supercomputing Applications**

NDIS /ˌen diː eɪ ˈes/ *noun* a standard command interface, defined by Microsoft, between network driver software and NICs. Full form **network driver interface specification**

NDR /ˌen diː ˈɑː/ *noun* a display system that continues to display previous characters when new ones are displayed. Full form **non destructive readout**

near instantaneously compounded audio multiplex /ˌnɪə ˌɪnstənˌteɪniəsli kəmˌpaʊndɪd ˌɔːdiəʊ ˈmʌltɪpleks/ *noun* full form of **NICAM**

negate /nɪˈgeɪt/ *verb* to reverse the sign of a number ○ *If you negate 23.4 the result is –23.4.* (NOTE: **negates – negating – negated**)

negation /nɪˈgeɪʃ(ə)n/ *noun* the reversing of the sign of a number, e.g. from 5 to –5

negation gate /nɪˈgeɪʃ(ə)n geɪt/ *noun* a single input gate whose output is equal to the logical inverse of the input. Also called **NOT gate**

negative /ˈnegətɪv/ *adjective* meaning 'no'

NEQ *abbr* nonequivalence function

nerd /nɜːd/ *noun* a person who is obsessed with computers and rarely talks or thinks about anything that is not technologically exciting (*slang*)

nested loop /ˌnestd ˈluːp/ *noun* a loop inside another loop in the same program

nested macro call /ˌnestɪd ˈmækrəʊ ˌkɔːl/ *noun* a macro called from within another macro

nested structure /ˌnestɪd ˈstrʌktʃə/ *noun* a section of a program in which one control loop or subroutine is used within another

NetBEUI /ˈnet bjuːi/ *noun* an extended version of the NetBIOS network protocol developed by Microsoft, which cannot be routed in a network. Full form **NetBIOS Extended User Interface**

NetBIOS /ˈnet ˌbaɪɒs/ *noun* a commonly used standard set of commands, originally developed by IBM, that allow application programs to carry out basic operations such as file sharing and transferring data between nodes over a network ○ *This software uses NetBIOS calls to manage file sharing.* Full form **Network Basic Input Output System**

NetBIOS Extended User Interface /ˌnet baɪɒs ɪkˌstendɪd ˈjuːzə ˌɪntəfeɪs/ *noun* full form of **NetBEUI**

netiquette /ˈnetɪket/ *noun* a set of unofficial rules that define good manners on the Internet

netphone /ˈnetfəʊn/ *noun* a phone that uses the Internet to make connections and carry voice messages

Netscape /ˈnetskeɪp/ a software company that develops Internet applications

Netscape Navigator /ˌnetskeɪp ˈnævɪgeɪtə/ a trade name for one of the most popular web browsers that provides many features including a news reader and that supports Java applets

NetShow /ˈnetʃəʊ/ a system developed by Microsoft to provide audio and video delivery over the Internet without interruption or glitches in the video sequence

NetWare /ˈnetweə/ a trade name for a network operating system, developed by Novell, that runs on a range of hardware platforms and supports file and print sharing and client-server applications

network /ˈnetwɜːk/ *noun* a system made of a number of points or circuits that are interconnected ■ *verb* to link points together in a network ○ *They run a system of networked micros.*

> 'Asante Technologies has expanded its range of Ethernet-to-LocalTalk converters with the release of AsantePrint 8, which connects up to eight LocalTalk printers, or other LocalTalk devices, to a high-speed Ethernet network.' [*Computing*]

network adapter /ˈnetwɜːk əˌdæptə/ *noun* same as **NIC**

network address /ˈnetwɜːk əˌdres/ *noun* a part of an IP address that defines the main network on which the domain is located (NOTE: For class A networks this is the first byte of the address, for class B networks it is the first two bytes and for class C networks it is the first three bytes. The rest of the IP address forms the host address.)

network address translation /ˌnetwɜːk əˌdres trænsˈleɪʃ(ə)n/ *noun* full form of **NAT**

network administrator /ˌnetwɜːk əd ˈmɪnɪstreɪtə/ *noun* a person who is responsible for looking after a network, with responsibilities including installing, configuring and maintaining the network

network architecture /ˌnetwɜːk ˈɑːkɪtektʃə/ *noun* the way in which a network is constructed, e.g. layers in an OSI system

network calendar program /ˌnetwɜːk ˈkælɪndə ˌprəʊgræm/ *noun* same as **multi-user program**

network computer /ˌnetwɜːk kəm ˈpjuːtə/ *noun* a computer that is designed to run Java programs and access information using a web browser. Abbr **NC**

COMMENT: The network computer has a small desktop box that does not have a floppy disk drive. Instead it downloads any software it requires from a central server. Network computers are simpler and cheaper than current PCs and Apple Mac computers, and are designed to be easier to manage in a large company.

network database /ˌnetwɜːk ˈdeɪtəbeɪs/ *noun* a database structure in which data items can be linked together

network diagram /ˌnetwɜːk ˈdaɪəgræm/ *noun* a graphical representation of the interconnections between points in a network

network directory /ˌnetwɜːk daɪ ˈrekt(ə)ri/ *noun* a directory that is stored on a disk drive on another computer in the network but can be accessed by anyone on the network

network drive /ˈnetwɜːk draɪv/ *noun* a disk drive that is part of another computer on a network but can be used by anyone on the network

network driver interface specification /ˌnetwɜːk ˌdraɪvə ˈɪntəfeɪs ˌspesɪfɪkeɪʃ(ə)n/ *noun* full form of **NDIS**

network file system /ˌnetwɜːk ˈfaɪl ˌsɪstəm/ *noun* a network protocol developed by Sun Microsystems that allows a computer to share its local disk drives with other users on a network and is now used as a standard across most of the Internet. Abbr **NFS**

network hardware /ˌnetwɜːk ˈhɑːdweə/ *noun* same as **networking hardware**

networking /ˈnetwɜːkɪŋ/ *noun* **1.** the working or organisation of a network **2.** the process of interconnecting two or more computers either in the same room or different buildings, in the same town or different towns, allowing them to exchange information **3.** the process of broadcasting a prime-time TV programme over several local stations at the same time

COMMENT: Networking allows a machine with a floppy disk drive to use another PC's hard disk when both machines are linked by a cable and are using networking software.

networking hardware /ˌnetwɜːkɪŋ ˈhɑːdweə/ *noun* the physical links, computers and control equipment that make up a network. Also called **network hardware**

networking software /ˌnetwɜːkɪŋ ˈsɒftweə/ *noun* software that is used to establish the link between a user's program and the network. Also called **network software**

networking specialist /ˈnetwɜːkɪŋ ˌspeʃəlɪst/ *noun* a company or person who specialises in designing and setting up networks ○ *This computer firm is a UK networking specialist.*

network interface card /ˌnetwɜːk ˈɪntəfeɪs ˌkɑːd/ *noun* full form of **NIC**

network management /ˌnetwɜːk ˈmænɪdʒmənt/ *noun* the organisation, planning, running and upkeep of a network

Network Neighborhood /ˌnetwɜːk ˈneɪbəhʊd/ *noun* a Windows 95 utility that allows you to view and manage connections to your computer

network news transfer protocol /ˌnetwɜːk njuːz ˈtrænsfɜː ˌprəʊtəkɒl/ *noun* full form of **NNTP**

network operating system /ˌnetwɜːk ˈɒpəreɪtɪŋ ˌsɪstəm/ *noun* an operating system running on a server computer, usually a dedicated one, that controls access to the network resources, managing network links, printing and users. Abbr **NOS**

network printer /ˌnetwɜːk ˈprɪntə/ *noun* a printer attached to a server or workstation that can be used by any user connected to the network

network protocol /ˌnetwɜːk ˈprəʊtəkɒl/ *noun* a set of handshaking signals that defines how a workstation sends data over a network without clashing with other data transmissions

network redundancy /ˌnetwɜːk rɪ ˈdʌndənsi/ *noun* the existence of extra links between points allowing continued operation in the event of one point failing

network server /ˌnetwɜːk ˈsɜːvə/ *noun* a computer which runs a network operating system and controls the basic network operations (NOTE: All the workstations in a LAN are connected to the central network server and users log onto a network server,)

network software /ˌnetwɜːk ˈsɒftweə/ *noun* same as **networking software**

network topology /ˌnetwɜːk təˈpɒlədʒi/ *noun* the layout of machines in a network, e.g. a star network, ring network or bus network, which will determine what cabling and interfaces are needed and what possibilities the network can offer

neural network /ˌnjʊərəl ˈnetwɜːk/ *noun* a system running an artificial intelligence program that attempts to simulate the way the brain works, how it learns and remembers

neutral /ˈnjuːtrəl/ *adjective* with no state, bias or voltage

new /njuː/ *adjective* recent or not old ○ *They have installed a new computer system.*

newbie /ˈnjuːbi/ *noun* a new user of the Internet (*slang*)

news /njuːz/ *noun* information about things which have happened □ **news agency** office which distributes news to newspapers and television companies □ **newsgroup** collection of articles on the Usenet relating to one particular subject □ **news release** sheet giving information about a new event which is sent to newspapers and TV and radio stations so that they can use it ○ *the company sent out a news release about the new managing director*

newsgroup /ˈnjuːzˌgruːp/ *noun* a feature of the Internet that provides free-for-all discussion forums

newsprint /ˈnjuːzprɪnt/ *noun* mechanical paper used for printing newspapers (NOTE: no plural)

news reader /ˈnjuːz ˌriːdə/ *noun* a piece of software that allows a user to view the list of newsgroups and read the articles posted in each group or submit a new article

new technology /ˌnjuː tekˈnɒlədʒi/ *noun* electronic instruments which have recently been developed

nexus /ˈneksəs/ *noun* a connection point between units in a network

NFS *abbr* network file system

nibble /ˈnɪb(ə)l/ *noun* another spelling of **nybble**

NIC /ˌen aɪ ˈsiː/ *noun* an add-in board that connects a computer to a network. Full form **network interface card**. Also called **network adapter** (NOTE: The board converts the computer's data into electrical signals that are then transmitted along the network cable.)

NICAM /ˈnaɪkæm/ *noun* a digital system used for coding in the television transmission of stereo sound (*film*) Full form **near instantaneously compounded audio multiplex**

Nintendo™ /nɪnˈtendəʊ/ a major video game developer producing both software and hardware consoles

NNTP /ˌen en tiː ˈpiː/ *noun* a standard method of distributing news messages on the Internet, one of the protocols within the TCP/IP protocol suite, that provides a way of creating, reading and distributing messages within newsgroups over the Internet. Full form **network news transfer protocol**

no-break /ˌnəʊ ˈbreɪk/ *adjective* (power supply system) which will not be affected by a power failure. ◊ **UPS**

no carbon required paper /nəʊ ˌkɑːbən rɪˌkwaɪəd ˈpeɪpə/ *noun* full form of **NCR paper**

node /nəʊd/ *noun* an interconnection point in a structure or network ○ *A tree is made of branches that connect together at nodes.*

no-drop image /ˌnəʊ ˈdrɒp ˌɪmɪdʒ/ *noun* (*in a GUI*) an icon image displayed during a drag and drop operation when the pointer is over an object that cannot be the destination object and onto which it cannot be dropped

noise /nɔɪz/ *noun* a random signal present in addition to any wanted signal, caused by static, temperature, power supply, magnetic or electric fields and also from stars and the Sun

nomenclature /nəʊˈmeŋklətʃə/ *noun* a predefined system for assigning words and symbols to represent numbers or terms

nomogram /ˈnɒməgræm/, **nomograph** /ˈnɒməgrɑːf/ *noun* a graphical system for solving one value given two others

non- /nɒn/ *prefix* not

nonaligned /ˌnɒnəˈlaɪnd/ *adjective* referring to two devices which are not correctly positioned in relation to each other, for optimum performance

non breaking space /ˌnɒn ˌbreɪkɪŋ ˈspeɪs/ *noun* (*in word-processing or DTP software*) a space character that prevents two words being separated by a line break

noncompatibility /ˌnɒnkəmˌpætɪˈbɪlɪti/ *noun* inability of two or more pieces of hardware or software to exchange data or use the same peripherals

non-composite video signal /ˌnɒn ˌkɒmpəzɪt ˈvɪdiəʊ ˌsɪgn(ə)l/ *noun* a video signal which has no synchronising signals but contains picture and blanking information

non dedicated server /ˌnɒn ˌdedɪkeɪtɪd ˈsɜːvə/ *noun* a computer that runs a network operating system in the background and can also be used to run normal applications at the same time

non destructive cursor /ˌnɒn dɪˌstrʌktɪv ˈkɜːsə/ *noun* a cursor on a display that does not erase characters already displayed as it passes over them ○ *The screen* *quickly became unreadable when using a non-destructive cursor.*

non destructive readout /ˌnɒn dɪˌstrʌktɪv ˈriːdaʊt/ *noun* full form of **NDR**

nondirectional microphone /ˌnɒndaɪrekʃən(ə)l ˈmaɪkrəfəʊn/ *noun* a microphone which picks up sound equally in every direction (*film*)

nonequivalence function /ˌnɒnɪˈkwɪvələns ˌfʌŋkʃən/ *noun* a logical function in which the output is true if the inputs are not the same, otherwise the output is false. Abbr **NEQ**

nonerasable storage /ˌnɒnɪreɪzəb(ə)l ˈstɔːrɪdʒ/ *noun* a storage medium that cannot be erased and reused

non impact printer /ˌnɒn ɪmˌpækt ˈprɪntə/ *noun* a printer such as an ink-jet printer in which the character form does not hit a ribbon onto the paper

non interlaced /ˌnɒn ˈɪntəleɪsd/ *adjective* (*in a monitor*) referring to a system in which the picture electron beam scans each line of the display once during each refresh cycle (NOTE: The beam in an interlaced display scans every alternate line.)

nonlinear video editing /ˌnɒnlɪniə ˈvɪdiəʊ ˌedɪtɪŋ/ *noun* a method of editing a video sequence in which the video is digitised and stored in a computer and the editor can then cut and move frames in any order before outputting the finished sequence (NOTE: The finished sequence can either be produced directly from the computer output – though this is normally at a lower quality than the original because of compression losses – or the computer can output time code instructions that can be used to edit the original videotape.)

nonprinting code /ˌnɒnprɪntɪŋ ˈkəʊd/ *plural noun* a code that represents an action of the printer rather than a printed character ○ *The line width can be set using one of the non-printing codes, .LW, then a number.*

non scrollable /ˌnɒn ˈskrəʊləb(ə)l/ *adjective* referring to part of the screen display which is always displayed (NOTE: In a WP the text can scroll while instructions are non scrollable.)

non-synchronous sound /ˌnɒn ˌsɪŋkrənəs ˈsaʊnd/, **non-sync sound** *noun* any sound recorded without a camera operating at the same time (*film*)

non volatile memory /ˌnɒn ˌvɒlətaɪl ˈmem(ə)ri/ *noun* a storage medium or memory that retains data even when the power has been switched off ○ *Bubble memory is a non-volatile storage.* Also called **non volatile storage, non volatile store**

non volatile storage /ˌnɒn ˌvɒlətaɪl ˈstɔːrɪdʒ/, **non volatile store** *noun* same as **non volatile memory**

no-op instruction /ˌnəʊ ˈɒp ɪn ˌstrʌkʃ(ə)n/, **no op** /ˌnəʊ ˈɒp/ *noun* an instruction that does not carry out any functions but increments the program counter

no parity /ˌnəʊ ˈpærəti/ *noun* data transmission which does not use a parity bit

NOR function /ˈnɔːr ˌfʌŋkʃən/ *noun* a logical function whose output is false if either input is true

COMMENT: The output is 1 only if both inputs are 0; if the two inputs are different or if both are 1, the output is 0.

NOR gate /ˈnɔːr geɪt/ *noun* an electric circuit or chip which performs a NOR function

normal /ˈnɔːm(ə)l/ *adjective* usual or which happens regularly ○ *The normal procedure is for backup copies to be made at the end of each day's work.*

normal form /ˈnɔːm(ə)l fɔːm/ *noun* a method of structuring information in a database to avoid redundancy and improve storage efficiency

normalisation /ˌnɔːməlaɪˈzeɪʃ(ə)n/, **normalization** *noun* the process of normalising data

normalise /ˈnɔːməˌlaɪz/, **normalize** *verb* **1.** to convert data into a form which can be read by a particular computer system **2.** to store and represent numbers in a pre-agreed form, usually to provide maximum precision ○ *All the new data has been normalised to 10 decimal places.* (NOTE: **normalises – normalising – normalised**)

normalised form /ˈnɔːməlaɪzd fɔːm/ *noun* a floating point number that has been normalised so that its mantissa is within a certain range

normal range /ˈnɔːm(ə)l reɪndʒ/ *noun* the expected range for a result or number (NOTE: Any outside this range are errors.)

NOS *abbr* network operating system

NOT-AND /ˌnɒt ˈænd/ *noun* an equivalent to the NAND function

notation /nəʊˈteɪʃ(ə)n/ *noun* a method of writing or representing numbers

notebook computer /ˌnəʊtbʊk kəmˈpjuːtə/ *noun* a very small portable computer, usually smaller than a laptop computer, that has a small keyboard and display and can be carried easily

NOT function /ˈnɒt ˌfʌŋkʃən/ *noun* a logical inverse function in which the output is true if the input is false

COMMENT: If the input is 1, the output is 0; if the input is 0, the output is 1.

NOT gate /ˈnɒt geɪt/ *noun* same as **negation gate**

notice board /ˈnəʊtɪs bɔːd/ *noun* **1.** a board fixed to a wall where notices can be pinned up **2.** a type of bulletin board on which messages to all users can be left

notification message /ˌnəʊtɪfɪˈkeɪʃ(ə)n ˌmesɪdʒ/ *noun* a message within authoring software to notify other objects that a particular task has been completed ○ *If an object is moved, the application will generate a notification message to tell other processes when it has finished moving the object.*

notify handler /ˈnəʊtɪfaɪ ˌhændlə/ *noun* a series of commands that are executed when a particular notification message is received

Novell /nəʊˈvel/ a large company that produces network software and is best known for its NetWare range of network operating system software that runs on a PC server

ns *abbr* nanosecond

NSFnet /ˌen es ˈef net/ *noun* a wide area network developed by the National Science Foundation to replace ArpaNet as the main US government-funded network linking together universities and research laboratories (NOTE: NSFnet was a crucial stepping-stone in the development history of the Internet. It was closed down in 1995 and replaced by a commercial high-speed network backbone that formed one of the foundations for the current commercial Internet.)

NTFS full form **New Technology File System**

NTSC /ˌen tiː es ˈsiː/ *noun* a US committee that defines standards for television and video. Full form **National Television System Committee**

NuBus /ˈnjuːbʌs/ *noun* a high-speed 96-pin expansion bus used within Apple Mac II computers

null /nʌl/ *adjective* nothing

number /ˈnʌmbə/ *noun* **1.** a representation of a quantity **2.** a written figure ○ *Each piece of hardware has a production number.* ■ *verb* **1.** to put a figure on a document ○ *The pages of the manual are numbered 1 to 196.* **2.** to assign digits to a list of items in an ordered manner

number cruncher /ˈnʌmbə ˌkrʌntʃə/ *noun* a dedicated processor used for high-speed calculations

number crunching /ˈnʌmbə krʌntʃɪŋ/ *noun* the process of performing high-speed calculations ○ *A very powerful processor is needed for graphics applications which require extensive number crunching capabilities.*

numeral /ˈnjuːm(ə)rəl/ *noun* a character or symbol which represents a number

numeric /njuːˈmerɪk/ *adjective* **1.** referring to numbers **2.** which contains only numbers ○ *a numeric field*

numerical /njuːˈmerɪk(ə)l/ *adjective* referring to numbers

numerical analysis /njuːˌmerɪk(ə)l əˈnæləsɪs/ *noun* the study of ways of solving mathematical problems

numerical control /njuːˌmerɪk(ə)l kənˈtrəʊl/ *noun* a machine operated automatically by computer or a set of circuits controlled by stored data. Abbr **NC**

numeric keypad /njuːˌmerɪk ˈkiːpæd/ *noun* a set of ten keys with figures 0–9, included in most computer keyboards as a separate group, used for entering large amounts of data in numeric form. Also called **numeric pad**

numeric pad /njuːˌmerɪk ˈpæd/ *noun* same as **numeric keypad**

Num Lock key /ˈnʌm lɒk ˌkiː/ *noun* (*on a keyboard*) a key that switches the function of a numeric keypad from cursor control to numeric entry

nybble /ˈnɪb(ə)l/, **nibble** *noun* half the length of a standard byte (*informal*)

COMMENT: A nybble is usually 4 bits, but can vary according to different microcomputer.

O

OA *abbr* office automation

object /ˈɒbdʒekt/ *noun* **1.** the data that makes up a particular image or sound **2.** a variable used in an IKBS within a reasoning operation **3.** the data in a statement which is to be operated on by the operator

objective /əbˈdʒektɪv/ *noun* **1.** something which someone tries to do **2.** an optical lens nearest the object viewed **3.** any optical device which has the ability to form images

object language /ˌɒbdʒekt ˈlæŋgwɪdʒ/ *noun* the language of a program after it has been translated. Opposite **source language**

object linking and embedding /ˌɒbdʒekt ˌlɪŋkɪŋ ənd ɪmˈbedɪŋ/ *noun* full form of **OLE**

object linking and embedding 2 /ˌɒbdʒekt ˌlɪŋkɪŋ ənd ɪmˌbedɪŋ ˈtuː/ *noun* full form of **OLE-2**

object-oriented /ˌɒbdʒekt ˈɔːrientɪd/ *adjective* referring to a system or language that uses objects

object-oriented graphics /ˌɒbdʒekt ˌɔːrientɪd ˈgræfɪks/ *plural noun* graphics which use lines and curves, vector definitions, to describe the shapes of the image rather than pixels in a bitmap image ○ *This object-oriented graphics program lets you move shapes around very easily.*

object-oriented language /ˌɒbdʒekt ˌɔːrientɪd ˈlæŋgwɪdʒ/ *noun* a programming language that is used for object-oriented programming, e.g. C++

object-oriented programming /ˌɒbdʒekt ˌɔːrientɪd ˈprəʊgræmɪŋ/ *noun* a method of programming, as in C++, in which each element of the program is treated as an object that can interact with other objects within the program. Abbr **OOP**

Object Request Broker /əbˌdʒekt rɪ ˈkwest ˌbrəʊkə/ *noun* software that links objects together using the CORBA standard. Abbr **ORB**

oblique stroke /əˈbliːk strəʊk/ *noun* a printing sign (/) like stroke sloping to the right

obtain /əbˈteɪn/ *verb* to get or receive something ○ *to obtain data from a storage device*

OCE /ˌəʊ siː ˈiː/ *noun* a set of standards that allow networked Apple Mac users to share objects and files. Full form **open collaboration environment**

OCR /ˌəʊ siː ˈɑː/ *noun* **1.** a device which scans printed or written characters, recognises them and converts them into machine-readable form for processing in a computer. Full form **optical character reader 2.** software or a process that allows printed or written characters to be recognised optically and converted into machine-readable code that can be input into a computer, using an optical character reader. Full form **optical character recognition**

> ‘In 1986, Calera Recognition Systems introduced the first neural-network-based OCR system that could read complex pages containing any mixture of non-decorative fonts without manual training.’ [*Computing*]

COMMENT: There are two OCR fonts in common use: OCR-A, which is easy for scanners to read, and OCR-B, which is easier for people to read than the OCR-A font.

octal /ˈɒkt(ə)l/, **octal notation** /ˌɒkt(ə)l nəʊˈteɪʃ(ə)n/ *noun* a number notation using base 8, with digits 0 to 7

COMMENT: In octal, the digits used are 0 to 7; so decimal 9 is octal 11.

octet /ɒkˈtet/ *noun* a group of eight bits treated as one unit or word. ◊ **byte**

OCX /ˌəʊ siː ˈeks/ *noun* the file extension of an ActiveX component or add-in that is used by an application such as a web browser or custom application running under Windows 95 or 98

ODBC *noun* a software interface that allows an application to access any compatible data source. Full form **open database connectivity** (NOTE: The standard was developed by Microsoft but is used by many different developers as a standard method of providing access to a wide range of databases.)

ODI a trade name for a standard interface, defined by Novell, for an NIC that allows users to have just one network driver that will work with all NICs. Full form **open datalink interface**. Compare **NDIS** (NOTE: The standard also supports more than one protocol, e.g. IPX and NetBEUI.)

OEM /ˌəʊ iː ˈem/ *noun* a company which produces equipment using basic parts made by other manufacturers, and customises the product for a particular application ○ *One OEM supplies the disk drive, another the monitor.* Full form **original equipment manufacturer**

off-cut /ˈɒf kʌt/ *noun* scrap paper that is left when a sheet is trimmed to size

office /ˈɒfɪs/ *noun* a room or building where a company works or where business is done

office automation /ˌɒfɪs ˌɔːtəˈmeɪʃ(ə)n/ *noun* the use of machines and computers to carry out ordinary office tasks. Abbr **OA**

office computer /ˌɒfɪs kəmˈpjuːtə/ *noun* a small computer, sometimes with a hard disk and several terminals, suitable for office use

off-line /ˌɒf ˈlaɪn/ *adverb, adjective* **1.** referring to a processor, printer or terminal that is not connected to a network or central computer, usually temporarily ○ *Before changing the paper in the printer, switch it off-line.* **2.** referring to a peripheral connected to a network but not available for use. Compare **on-line**

off-line editing /ˌɒf laɪn ˈedɪtɪŋ/ *noun* an editing process in which copies of the original sound tape or videotape are used, cut and edited to create an EDL that is then used in an on-line editing suite to automatically assemble all the sectors of the tape according to the instructions in the EDL (NOTE: Off-line editing software allows two or more video clips to be edited and merged with effects.)

off-line newsreader /ˌɒf laɪn ˈnjuːzriːdə/ *noun* a piece of software that allows a user to read newsgroup articles when the computer is not connected to the Internet

off-line printing /ˌɒf laɪn ˈprɪntɪŋ/ *noun* a printout operation that is not supervised by a computer

off-line processing /ˌɒf laɪn ˈprəʊsesɪŋ/ *noun* processing performed by devices not under the control of a central computer

off-line storage /ˌɒf laɪn ˈstɔːrɪdʒ/ *noun* storage that is not currently available for access

offprint /ˈɒfprɪnt/ *noun* a section of a journal reprinted separately

off-scale /ˌɒf ˈskeɪl/ *adverb* outside the area of the standard light point scale of a printer

off screen /ˌɒf ˈskriːn/ *adverb* TV action that is taking place off the screen, outside the viewer's field of vision

off-screen buffer /ˌɒf skriːn ˈbʌfə/ *noun* the area of RAM used to hold an off-screen image before it is displayed on screen

off-screen image /ˌɒf skriːn ˈɪmɪdʒ/ *noun* an image that is first drawn in memory and then is transferred to the display memory to give the impression of fast display action

offset /ˈɒfset/ *noun* positive or negative time displacement in systems using time code synchronisation

ohm /əʊm/ *noun* a unit of measurement of electrical resistance

Ohm's Law /ˈəʊmz lɔː/ *noun* a scientific rule which defines one ohm as: one volt drop across a resistance of one ohm when one amp of current is flowing

OK /ˌəʊ ˈkeɪ/ *noun* used as a prompt in place of 'ready' in some systems

OK button /əʊˈkeɪ ˌbʌt(ə)n/ *noun (in a GUI)* a button with an 'OK' label that is used to start or confirm an action

OLE /ˌəʊ el ˈiː/ *noun (in Microsoft Windows)* a facility for including data formatted in one application within another application; e.g. insertion of an object such as an image or sound into a document or spreadsheet. Full form **object linking and embedding.** ◊ **DDE**

OLE-2 /ˌəʊ el iː ˈtuː/ *noun (in Microsoft Windows)* a facility that extends the functions of OLE to include visual editing to allow the embedded object to be edited without leaving the document in which it is embedded. Full form **object linking and embedding 2** (NOTE: If you insert an image into a document, you can now edit the image without leaving the word-processor. OLE2 also allows applications to exchange information.)

omission factor /əʊˈmɪʃ(ə)n ˌfæktə/ *noun* the number of relevant documents that were missed in a search

omnidirectional /ˌɒmniˈdaɪrekʃən(ə)l/ *adjective* device that can pick up signals from all directions

omnidirectional microphone /ˌɒmnidaɪrekʃən(ə)l ˈmaɪkrəfəʊn/ *noun* a microphone which is able to pick up sound evenly in all directions

OMR /ˌəʊ em ˈɑː/ *noun* **1.** a device that can recognise marks or lines on a special forms such as an order form or a reply to a questionnaire and convert them into a form a computer can process. Full form **optical mark reader** **2.** a process that allows certain marks or lines on special forms such as an order form or a reply to a questionnaire to be recognised by an OMR and input into a computer. Full form **optical mark recognition**

on-board /ˌɒn ˈbɔːd/ *adjective* referring to a feature or circuit which is contained on a motherboard or main PCB

'...the electronic page is converted to a printer-readable video image by the on-board raster image processor the key intelligence features of these laser printers are emulation modes and on-board memory' [*Byte*]

on chip /ˌɒn ˈtʃɪp/ *noun* a circuit constructed on a chip

on-chip /ˌɒn ˈtʃɪp/ *adjective* referring to a circuit constructed on a chip ○ *The processor uses on-chip bootstrap software to allow programs to be loaded rapidly.*

one for one /ˌwʌn fə ˈwʌn/ *noun* a programming language, usually assembler, that produces one machine code instruction for each instruction or command word in the language

COMMENT: Compilers and interpreters are usually used for translating high-level languages that use more than one machine code instruction for each high-level instruction.

100Base-FX *noun* IEEE standard specification for running Ethernet over optical fibre at speeds up to 100Mbps

onion skin architecture /ˈʌnjən skɪn ˌɑːkɪtektʃə/ *noun* a design of a computer system in layers, according to function or priority ○ *The onion skin architecture of this computer is made up of a kernel at the centre, an operating system, a low-level language and then the user's program.*

onion skin language /ˈʌnjən skɪn ˌlæŋgwɪdʒ/ *noun* a database manipulation language that can process hierarchical data structures

online /ɒnˈlaɪn/ *adverb, adjective* referring to a terminal or device connected to and under the control of a central processor ○ *The terminal is online to the mainframe.*

online database /ˌɒnlaɪn ˈdeɪtəbeɪs/ *noun* an interactive search, retrieve and update of database records using an online terminal

online editing /ɒnˌlaɪn ˈedɪtɪŋ/ *noun* the process of creating a finished audio or film sequence from original tape using editing instructions in an EDL list

online help /ˌɒnlaɪn ˈhelp/ *noun* a text screen displayed from within an application that explains how to use the application

online information retrieval /ˌɒnlaɪn ˌɪnfəˈmeɪʃ(ə)n rɪˌtriːvəl/ *noun* a system that allows an operator of an online terminal to access, search and display data held in a main computer

online processing /ˌɒnlaɪn ˈprəʊsesɪŋ/ *noun* processing by devices connected to and under the control of the central computer, during which the user remains in contact with the central computer

online storage /ˌɒnlaɪn ˈstɔːrɪdʒ/ *noun* data storage equipment that is directly controlled by a computer

online transaction processing /ˌɒnlaɪn trænˈzækʃən ˌprəʊsesɪŋ/ *noun* an interactive processing in which a user enters commands and data on a terminal which is linked to a central computer, with results being displayed on the screen

OnNow /ˌɒnˈnaʊ/ *noun* a standard that provides a way of integrating power management and control within all types of computer (NOTE: The main benefit of OnNow is that it allows the development of a computer that is dormant but will be ready to use almost immediately after it has been switched on, unlike current computers that can take a minute to configure and load the operating system.)

on-screen /ˌɒn ˈskriːn/ *adjective* referring to information that is displayed on a computer screen rather than printed out

on-site /ˌɒn ˈsaɪt/ *adjective* located at the place where a particular thing is ○ *The new model has an on-site upgrade facility.*

on the fly /ˌɒn ðə ˈflaɪ/ *adverb* (*to examine and modify data*) during a program run without stopping the run

OOP *abbr* object-oriented programming

o/p, O/P *abbr* output

opacity /əʊˈpæsɪti/ *noun* a measure of how opaque an optical lens is. Opposite **transmittance**

op amp /ˈɒp æmp/ *noun* a versatile electronic component that provides amplification, integration, addition, subtraction and many other functions on signals depending on external components added. Full form **operational amplifier**

opaque /əʊˈpeɪk/ *adjective* will not allow light to pass through it

opaque leader /əʊˌpeɪk ˈliːdə/ *noun* part of a filmstrip which is used as a leader: no image is present

opaque projector /əʊˌpeɪk prəˈdʒektə/ *noun* a device that is able to project an image of an opaque object

op code /ˈɒp kəʊd/ *noun* a part of the machine code instruction that defines the action to be performed. Also called **operation code, order code**

open /ˈəʊpən/ *adjective* **1.** called up and prepared before reading or writing actions can occur ○ *You cannot access the data unless the file is open.* **2.** not closed ■ *verb* **1.** to take the cover off something or to make a door open ○ *Open the disk drive door.* **2.** to call up and prepare a file before accessing, editing or carrying out other transactions on stored records ○ *You cannot access the data unless the file has been opened.*

open access /ˌəʊpən ˈækses/ *noun* a system in which many workstations are available for anyone to use

open architecture /ˌəʊpən ˈɑːkɪtektʃə/ *noun* computer architecture with a published expansion interface that has been designed to allow add-on hardware to be plugged in

open collaboration environment /ˌəʊpən kəˌlæbəˈreɪʃ(ə)n ɪnˌvaɪrənmənt/ *noun* full form of **OCE**

open database connectivity /ˌəʊpən ˌdeɪtəbeɪs ˌkɒnekˈtɪvɪti/ *noun* full form of **ODBC**

open datalink interface /ˌəʊpən ˈdeɪtəlɪŋk ˌɪntəfeɪs/ *noun* full form of **ODI**

open file /ˈəʊpən faɪl/ *noun* a file that can be read from or written to (NOTE: An application opens the file which locates the file on disk and prepares it for an operation.)

open source /ˌəʊpən ˈsɔːs/ *adjective* describes a program for which the source code is freely available and which anyone is legally able to modify and improve

> 'In yet another initiative, aimed at cutting the upfront costs of big IT projects, the OGC is tipping towards a preference for open source software.' [*The Guardian*]

open system /ˈəʊpən ˌsɪstəm/ *noun* a nonproprietary system that is not under the control of one company

open system interconnection /ˌəʊpən ˌsɪstəm ˌɪntəkəˈnekʃ(ə)n/ *noun* full form of **OSI**

open trading protocol /ˌəʊpən ˈtreɪdɪŋ ˌprəʊtəkɒl/ *noun* a standardised computer protocol for transactions involving payments and for methods of payment. Abbr **OTP**

operand /ˈɒpərænd/ *noun* the data in a computer instruction which is to be operated on by the operator ○ *In the instruction ADD 74, the operator ADD will add the operand 74 to the accumulator.*

operate /ˈɒpəreɪt/ *verb* to work or to make a machine work ○ *Do you know how to operate the telephone switchboard?* (NOTE: **operates – operating – operated**)

operation /ˌɒpəˈreɪʃ(ə)n/ *noun* the working of a machine

operational /ˌɒpəˈreɪʃ(ə)nəl/ *adjective* which is working

operational amplifier /ˌɒpəˌreɪʃ(ə)nəl ˌæmplɪˈfaɪə/, **op amp** /ˈɒp æmp/ *noun* a versatile electronic component that provides amplification, integration, addition, subtraction and many other functions on signals depending on external components added

operational information /ˌɒpəˌreɪʃ(ə)nəl ˌɪnfəˈmeɪʃ(ə)n/ *noun* information about the normal operations of a system

operation code /ˌɒpəˈreɪʃ(ə)n kəʊd/ *noun* same as **op code**

operations manual /ˌɒpəˌreɪʃ(ə)nz ˈmænjʊəl/ *noun* same as **instruction manual**

operator /ˈɒpəˌreɪtə/ *noun* **1.** a person who makes a machine or process work ○ *The operator was sitting at his console.* **2.** a character, symbol or word that defines a function or operation ○ *x is the multiplication operator.*

optic /ˈɒptɪk/ *adjective* referring to sight

optical /ˈɒptɪk(ə)l/ *adjective* referring to or making use of light ○ *An optical reader uses a light beam to scan characters.*

optical bar reader /ˌɒptɪk(ə)l ˈbɑː ˌriːdə/ *noun* an optical device that reads data from a bar code

optical character reader /ˌɒptɪk(ə)l ˈkærɪktə ˌriːdə/ *noun* full form of **OCR 1**

optical character recognition /ˌɒptɪk(ə)l ˌkærɪktə ˌrekəgˈnɪʃ(ə)n/ *noun* full form of **OCR 2**

optically /ˈɒptɪk(ə)li/ *adverb* by using an optical device ○ *The text is scanned optically.*

optical mark reader /ˌɒptɪk(ə)l ˈmɑːk ˌriːdə/ *noun* full form of **OMR 1**

optical mark recognition /ˌɒptɪk(ə)l mɑːk ˌrekəgˈnɪʃ(ə)n/ *noun* full form of **OMR 2**

optical mouse /ˈɒptɪk(ə)l maʊs/ *noun* a pointing device that is operated by moving it across a special flat mat; (NOTE: On the mat is printed a grid of lines. As the mouse is moved, two light sensors count the number of lines that have been passed to produce a measure of the distance and direction of travel. An optical mouse has fewer moving parts than a mechanical mouse and so is more reliable, but requires an accurately printed mat.)

optical multiplexing /ˌɒptɪk(ə)l ˈmʌltɪpleksɪŋ/ *noun* the process of sending several light beams down a single path or fibre

optical scanner /ˌɒptɪk(ə)l ˈskænə/ *noun* a piece of equipment that converts an image into electrical signals which can be stored in and displayed on a computer

optics /ˈɒptɪks/ *noun* the science of light and sight

optimisation, optimization *noun* the process of making something work as efficiently as possible

optimise /ˈɒptɪmaɪz/, **optimize** *verb* to make something work as efficiently as possible (NOTE: **optimises – optimising – optimised**)

optimiser /ˈɒptɪmaɪzə/, **optimizer** *noun* a program that adapts another program to run more efficiently

optimising compiler /ˌɒptɪmaɪzɪŋ kəm ˈpaɪlə/ *noun* a compiler that analyses the machine code it produces in order to improve the speed or efficiency of the code

optimum /ˈɒptɪməm/ *adjective* best possible

opt-in mailing list /ˌɒpt ɪn ˈmeɪlɪŋ lɪst/ *noun* a list of email addresses in which each recipient has specifically asked to receive advertising email messages, usually so that he or she can keep up to date with a topic or industry

option /ˈɒpʃən/ *noun* an action which can be chosen ○ *There are usually four options along the top of the screen.*

optional /ˈɒpʃ(ə)n(ə)l/ *adjective* which can be chosen ○ *The system comes with optional 3.5* or *5.25 disk drives.*

optoelectrical /ˌɒptəʊɪˈlektrɪk(ə)l/ *adjective* which converts light to electrical signals or electrical signals into light

optoelectronic /ˌɒptəʊˌelekˈtrɒnɪk/ *adjective* (microelectronic component) that has optoelectrical properties

optoelectronics /ˌɒptəʊˌelekˈtrɒnɪks/ *noun* electronic components that can generate or detect light, such as phototransistors, light-emitting diodes

optomechanical mouse /ˌɒptəʊmɪ ˌkænɪk(ə)l ˈmaʊs/ *noun* same as **mechanical mouse**

OR *noun* a Boolean function that is often used in searches to ask the search engine to find text that contains any of the search words. Compare **AND** (NOTE: For example the phrase 'dog OR cat' will include all documents that contain the words dog or cat.)

Orange Book /ˈɒrɪndʒ bʊk/ *noun* a set of standards published by Philips that define the format for a recordable CD-ROM

orbit /ˈɔːbɪt/ *noun* the path in space that a satellite follows around the earth ■ *verb* to follow a path in space around the earth ○ *The weather satellite orbits the earth every four hours.*

order /ˈɔːdə/ *verb* to sort data according to a key

order code /ˈɔːdə kəʊd/ *noun* same as **op code**

ordered list /ˈɔːdəd lɪst/ *noun* a list of data items which have been sorted into an order

OR function /ˈɔː ˌfʌŋkʃən/ *noun* a logical function that produces a true output if any input is true

COMMENT: The result of the OR function will be 1 if either or both inputs are 1; if both inputs are 0, then the result is 0.

organisation /ˌɔːgənaɪˈzeɪʃ(ə)n/, **organization** *noun* a way of arranging something so that it works efficiently or has a logical structure

organisational /ˌɔːgənaɪˈzeɪʃ(ə)n(ə)l/, **organizational** *adjective* referring to the way in which something is organised

organise /ˈɔːgəˌnaɪz/, **organize** *verb* to arrange something so that it works efficiently or has a logical structure (NOTE: **organises – organising – organised**)

OR gate /ˈɔː geɪt/ *noun* an electronic circuit that provides the OR function

orientated /ˈɔːriənteɪtɪd/ *adjective* aimed towards something

orientation /ˌɔːriənˈteɪʃ(ə)n/ *noun* **1.** the direction or position of an object **2.** (*in word-processing or DTP software*) the direction of a page, either landscape, with long edge horizontal, or portrait, with long edge vertical

origin /ˈɒrɪdʒɪn/ *noun* **1.** the position on a display screen to which all coordinates are referenced, usually the top left hand corner of the screen **2.** a location in memory at which the first instruction of a program is stored

original /əˈrɪdʒən(ə)l/ *adjective* used or made first ■ *noun* **1.** the master data disk, from which a copy can be made **2.** the first document, from which a copy is made ○ *Did you keep the original of the letter?* ○ *The original document is too faint to photocopy well.*

original equipment manufacturer /ə ˌrɪdʒən(ə)l ɪˌkwɪpmənt ˌmænjʊˈfæktʃərə/ *noun* full form of **OEM** ○ *One OEM supplies the disk drive, another the monitor.*

originate /əˈrɪdʒɪneɪt/ *verb* to start or come from a place or source ○ *The data originated from the new computer.* (NOTE: **originates – originating – originated**)

origination /əˌrɪdʒɪˈneɪʃ(ə)n/ *noun* the work involved in creating something

orphan /ˈɔːf(ə)n/ *noun* the first line of a paragraph of text printed alone at the bottom of a column, with the rest of the paragraph at the top of the next column or page. Compare **widow** (NOTE: An orphan makes a page look ugly.)

oscillator /ˈɒsɪˌleɪtə/ *noun* an electronic circuit that produces a pulse or signal at a particular frequency

oscilloscope /ɒˈsɪləskəʊp/ *noun* electronic test equipment that displays on a CRT the size and shape of an electrical signal

OSI /ˌəʊ es ˈaɪ/ *noun* a standard theoretical model of a network that is created from seven different layers each with a different function. This model provides the basis of almost all networks in use. Full form **open system interconnection**. ◊ **ISO/OSI**

outage /ˈaʊtɪdʒ/ *noun* the time during which a system is not operational

outdent /aʊtˈdent/ *verb* to move part of a line of text into the margin. Opposite **indent**

outlet /ˈaʊtlet/ *noun* a connection or point in a circuit or network where a signal or data can be accessed

outline /ˈaʊtlaɪn/ *noun* the main features of something

outline flowchart /ˈaʊt(ə)laɪn ˌfləʊtʃɑːt/ *noun* a flowchart of the main features, steps and decisions in a program or system

outliner /ˈaʊtlaɪnə/ *noun* a utility program used to help a user order sections and subsections of a list of things to do or parts of a project

out of band signalling /ˌaʊt əv ˌbænd ˈsɪɡn(ə)lɪŋ/ *noun* the transmission of signals outside the frequency limits of a normal voice channel

out of phase /ˌaʊt əv ˈfeɪz/ *adverb* situation where a waveform is delayed in comparison to another

out of range /ˌaʊt əv ˈreɪndʒ/ *adjective* referring to a number or quantity that is outside the limits of a system

out-of-sync /ˌaʊt əv ˈsɪŋk/ *adjective* fault when the sound and picture are not synchronised

output /ˈaʊtpʊt/ *noun* **1.** information or data that is transferred from a CPU or the main memory to another device such as a monitor, printer or secondary storage device **2.** the action of transferring information or data from store to a user ▶ abbr **o/p, O/P** ■ *verb* to transfer data from a computer to a monitor or printer ○ *Finished documents can be output to the laser printer.*

outsource /ˈaʊtˌsɔːs/ *verb* to employ another company to manage and support a network for your company

overflow /ˈəʊvəfləʊ/ *noun* **1.** a mathematical result that is greater than the limits of the computer's number storage system **2.** a situation in a network when the number of transmissions is greater than the line capacity and they are transferred by another route ▶ abbr **OV**

overhead /ˈəʊvəhed/ *noun* an extra code that has to be stored to organise the program ○ *The line numbers in a BASIC program are an overhead.*

overheat /ˌəʊvəˈhiːt/ *verb* to become too hot ○ *The system may overheat if the room is not air-conditioned.*

overlap /ˌəʊvəˈlæp/ *noun* **1.** a situation in which one thing covers part of another or two sections of data are placed on top of each other **2.** the continuation of the sound track into the following scene for smooth continuity (*film*) ■ *verb* to cover part of an item with another (NOTE: **overlapping – overlapped**)

overlay /ˈəʊvəleɪ/ *noun* **1.** a small section of a program that is bigger than the main memory capacity of a computer, loaded into memory when required, so that main memory only contains the sections it requires **2.** a device that converts composite video or television signals into a digital format so that they can be displayed on a computer

> 'Many packages also boast useful drawing and overlay facilities which enable the user to annotate specific maps.' [*Computing*]

overlay card /ˈəʊvəleɪ kɑːd/ *noun* same as **video graphics card**

overlay function /ˈəʊvəleɪ ˌfʌŋkʃ(ə)n/ *noun* ◊ **matte, chroma key**

overlaying /ˈəʊvəleɪɪŋ/ *noun* the process of putting an overlay into action

overlay network /ˈəʊvəleɪ ˌnetwɜːk/ *noun* two communications networks that have some common interconnections

overload /ˌəʊvəˈləʊd/ *verb* to demand more than the device is capable of ○ *The computer is overloaded with that amount of processing.*

overmodulation /ˌəʊvəˌmɒdjuˈleɪʃ(ə)n/ *noun* a situation where an amplitude modulated carrier signal is reduced to zero by excessive input signal

overpunching /ˌəʊvəˈpʌntʃɪŋ/ *noun* the process of altering data on a paper tape by punching additional holes

overscan /ˈəʊvəskæn/ *noun* **1.** a faulty or badly adjusted monitor in which the displayed image runs off the edge of the screen **2.** display equipment in which the picture beam scans past the screen boundaries to ensure that the image fills the screen

overstrike /ˈ ʊvəstraɪk/ *verb* to print on top of an existing character to produce a new one

overtones /ˈəʊvətəʊnz/ *noun* ◊ **harmonic**

over-voltage protection /ˌəʊvə ˈvəʊltɪdʒ prəˌtekʃ(ə)n/ *noun* a safety device that prevents a power supply voltage exceeding certain specified limits

overwrite /ˌəʊvəˈraɪt/ *verb* to write data to a location, e.g. memory or disk, and, in doing so, to destroy any data already contained in that location ○ *The latest data input has overwritten the old information.* (NOTE: **overwriting – overwrote – overwritten**)

oxide /ˈɒksaɪd/ *noun* a chemical compound of oxygen

P

p /piː/ *abbr* pico-

P *abbr* peta

PABX *abbr* private automatic branch exchange

pack /pæk/ *verb* **1.** to put things into a container for selling or sending ○ *to pack goods into cartons* **2.** to store a quantity of data in a reduced form, often by representing several characters of data with one stored character

package /ˈpækɪdʒ/ *noun* a group of different items joined together in one deal

package deal /ˌpækɪdʒ ˈdiːl/ *noun* an agreement in which several different items are agreed at the same time ○ *They agreed on a package deal, which involves the development of software, customising hardware, and training staff.*

packaged software /ˌpækɪdʒd ˈsɒftweə/ *noun* same as **software package**

packet /ˈpækɪt/ *noun* a group of data bits which can be transmitted as a group from one node to another over a network

packet Internet groper /ˌpækɪt ˌɪntənet ˈgrəʊpə/ *noun* full form of **PING**

packet switching /ˈpækɪt swɪtʃɪŋ/ *noun* a method of sending data across a WAN in small packets, which are then re-assembled in the correct order at the receiving end

'The network is based on Northern Telecom DPN data switches over which it will offer X.25 packet switching, IBM SNA, and frame-relay transmission.' [*Computing*]

packet switching service /ˈpækɪt ˌswɪtʃɪŋ ˌsɜːvɪs/ *noun* a commercial data transmission service that sends data over its WAN using packet switching. Abbr **PSS**

packing /ˈpækɪŋ/ *noun* **1.** the action of putting goods into boxes and wrapping them for shipping ○ *What is the cost of the packing?* ○ *Packing is included in the price.* **2.** the process of putting large amounts of data into a small area of storage **3.** a material used to protect goods ○ *packed in airtight packing*

pad /pæd/ *noun* a number of keys arranged together ■ *verb* to fill something out and make it bigger or the right size (NOTE: **padding – padded**)

padding /ˈpædɪŋ/ *noun* a character or set of digits added to fill out a string or packet until it is the right length

page /peɪdʒ/ *noun* **1.** a sheet of paper **2.** an amount of text displayed on a computer monitor or screen which would fill a page of paper if printed out or which fills the screen **3.** a section of main store, which contains data or programs ○ *the video adapter uses page-mode RAM to speed up the display* **4.** one side of a printed sheet of paper in a book or newspaper or magazine or catalogue, etc. **5.** a blank area of the screen used as a background for a multimedia book. The design of each page is created by pasting objects, such as windows, buttons, graphic images and text, onto the page. ■ *verb* to make up a text into pages

page addressing /ˈpeɪdʒ əˌdresɪŋ/ *noun* main memory which has been split into blocks, with a unique address allocated to each block of memory which can then be called up and accessed individually, when required

page boundary /ˈpeɪdʒ ˌbaʊnd(ə)ri/ *noun* a point where one page ends and the next starts

page break /ˌpeɪdʒ ˈbreɪk/ *noun* **1.** the point in continuous text at which a page ends and a new page starts **2.** a marker used when word-processing to show where a new page should start

paged address /ˌpeɪdʒd əˈdres/ *noun* (*in a paged-memory scheme*) the actual physical memory address that is calculated from a logical address and its page address

page description language /ˌpeɪdʒ dɪˈskrɪpʃən ˌlæŋgwɪdʒ/ *noun* software that controls a printer's actions to print a page of text to a particular format according to a user's instructions. Abbr **PDL**

page description programming language /ˌpeɪdʒ dɪˌskrɪpʃ(ə)n ˈprəʊgræmɪŋ ˌlæŋgwɪdʒ/ *noun* a programming language that accepts commands to define the size, position and type style for text or graphics on a page

page down key /ˌpeɪdʒ ˈdaʊn ˌkiː/ *noun* a keyboard key that moves the cursor position down by the number of lines on one screen. Abbr **PgDn**

page frame /ˌpeɪdʒ ˈfreɪm/ *noun* a physical address to which a page of virtual or logical memory can be mapped

page image buffer /ˌpeɪdʒ ˈɪmɪdʒ ˌbʌfə/ *noun* memory in a page printer that holds the image as it is built up before it is printed

page impression /ˈpeɪdʒ ɪmˌpreʃ(ə)n/ *noun* a measure used to count how many times a webpage has been displayed to a visitor to a website

page layout /ˈpeɪdʒ ˌleɪaʊt/ *noun* the arrangement of text and pictures within a page of a document ○ *We do all our page layout using desktop publishing software.*

page makeup /ˌpeɪdʒ ˈmeɪkʌp/ *noun* the action of pasting images and text into a page ready for printing

page-mode RAM /ˌpeɪdʒ məʊd ˈræm/ *noun* dynamic RAM designed to access sequential memory locations very quickly ○ *The video adapter uses page-mode RAM to speed up the display.*

page number /ˈpeɪdʒ ˌnʌmbə/ *noun* a unique number assigned to each page within a multimedia application, to be used within hyperlinks and when moving between pages

page orientation /ˈpeɪdʒ ˌɔːriənteɪʃ(ə)n/ *noun* the direction of the long edge of a piece of paper

page preview /ˈpeɪdʒ ˌpriːvjuː/ *noun* (*in WP or DTP software*) a graphical representation of how a page will look when printed, with different type styles, margins and graphics correctly displayed

page proofs /ˈpeɪdʒ pruːfs/ *plural noun* proofs which are divided into pages, but may not have page numbers or headings inserted

page protection /ˈpeɪdʒ prəˌtekʃən/ *noun* the set of software controls used to ensure that pages are not overwritten by accident or copied into a reserved section of memory

pager /ˈpeɪdʒə/ *noun* a small device carried by someone, which allows him to be called from a central office, by using a radio signal

page requests /ˌpeɪdʒ rɪˈkwests/ *plural noun* a measure of the number of pages viewed in a day, providing an indication of the popularity of your website

page setup /ˈpeɪdʒ ˌsetʌp/ *noun* the set of software options that allow a user to set up how the page will look when printed, – usually setting the margins, size of paper, and scaling of a page

pages per minute /ˌpeɪdʒɪz pɜː ˈmɪnət/ *noun* full form of **ppm** ○ *This laser printer can output eight pages per minute.*

page table /ˈpeɪdʒ ˌteɪb(ə)l/ *noun* a list of all the pages and their locations within main memory, used by the operating system when accessing a page

page up key /ˌpeɪdʒ ˈʌp ˌkiː/ *noun* a keyboard key that moves the cursor position up by the number of lines in one screen. Abbr **PgUp**

pagination /ˌpædʒɪˈneɪʃ(ə)n/ *noun* the process of dividing text into pages

paint /peɪnt/ *noun* (*in a graphics program*) colour and pattern used to fill an area ■ *verb* (*in a graphics program*) to fill an enclosed graphics shape with a colour

Paint /ˌpaɪntbrʌʃ ˈpeɪnt/ *noun* an application supplied with Microsoft Windows 3.1x and Windows 95 for creating or editing bitmap images

paint object /ˈpeɪnt ˌɒbdʒekt/ *noun* a bitmap image

paint pots /ˈpeɪnt pɒts/ *plural noun* video controls which are used to change the colour balance in a camera (*film*)

paint program /ˈpeɪnt ˌprəʊɡræm/ *noun* software that allows a user to draw pictures on screen in different colours, with different styles of brush and special effects ○ *I drew a rough of our new logo with this paint program.*

COMMENT: Paint programs normally operate on bitmap images. Drafting or design software normally works with vector-based images.

PAL /ˌpiː eɪ ˈel/ *noun* a standard for television transmission and reception using a 625-line picture transmitted at 25 frames per second;. Full form **phase alternation line** (NOTE: PAL provides a clearer image than NTSC and is used in most of Europe, except for France, which uses SECAM. The US and Japan use NTSC.)

palette /ˈpælət/ *noun* **1.** the range of colours which can be used on a printer or computer display **2.** data structure that defines the colours used in a bitmap image; the palette data defines each colour, the bitmap includes references to the colours in the palette

palette shift /ˈpælət ʃɪft/ *noun* an image displayed using the wrong palette with the unwanted effect that the colours appear distorted

palm computer /ˈpɑːm kəmˌpjuːtə/ *noun* a tiny computer that is about half the size of a paperback book. It does not contain a keyboard, but uses a touch-sensitive screen and character recognition to allow the user to enter information and control applications. Normally used for contact management, calendar and email. One of the most popular products is the 3Com Palm computer that runs its own operating system software and a range of palm computers that can all run the Windows CE operating system software.

palmtop /ˈpɑːmtɒp/ *noun* a personal computer that is small enough to be held in one hand and operated with the other ○ *This palmtop has a tiny keyboard and twenty-line LCD screen.*

PAM *noun* a pulse modulation system in which the height of the pulse varies with the input signal. Full form **pulse amplitude modulation**

pan /pæn/ *verb* **1.** (*in computer graphics*) to smoothly move a viewing window horizontally across an image that is too wide to display all at once **2.** (*in MIDI or sound*) to adjust the balance of a sound between the two stereo channels (NOTE: **panning – panned**) ■ *noun* the rotation of a camera in a horizontal direction in order to film action, subject or background; sometimes used to mean 'follow the action'

pan and tilt head /ˌpæn ən 'tɪlt ˌhed/ *noun* the mount on a tripod for a film or television camera which permits camera movement in both horizontal and vertical directions (*film*)

panchromatic film /ˌpænkrəmætɪk 'fɪlm/, **pan film** /'pæn fɪlm/ *noun* a black and white film which is sensitive to all colours

panel /'pæn(ə)l/ *noun* a flat section of a casing with control knobs or sockets ○ *The socket is on the back panel.*

panorama /ˌpænə'rɑːmə/ *noun* a wide-angle shot which reveals the whole of the scene through a pan shot (*film*)

Pantone Matching System /ˌpæntəʊn 'mætʃɪŋ ˌsɪstəm/ a trade name for a standard method of matching ink colours on screen and on printed output using a book of pre-defined colours. Abbr **PMS**

paper /'peɪpə/ *noun* a thin material used for making books, newspapers or stationery items

paperback /'peɪpəbæk/ *noun* a book which has a paper cover ○ *We are publishing the book as a hardback and as a paperback.*

paperbound /'peɪpəbaʊnd/ *adjective* (*of a book*) bound with a paper cover (as opposed to hardbound)

paper-fed /'peɪpə fed/ *adjective* referring to a device which is activated when paper is introduced into it ○ *a paper-fed scanner*

paperless /'peɪpələs/ *adjective* without using paper

paperless office /ˌpeɪpələs 'ɒfɪs/ *noun* an office which uses computers and other electronic devices for office tasks and avoids the use of paper

> 'Indeed, the concept of the paperless office may have been a direct attack on Xerox and its close ties to the paper document. Yet, as we all know, the paperless office has so far been an empty promise.' [*Computing*]

paper-white monitor /ˌpeɪpə 'waɪt ˌmɒnɪtə/ *noun* a monitor that normally displays black text on a white background, rather than the normal illuminated text on a black background

paragraph /'pærəgrɑːf/ *noun* **1.** (*in a document*) the section of text between two carriage return characters, with a unified subject **2.** (*in a memory map*) a 16-byte section of memory which starts at a hexadecimal address that can be evenly divided by 16

parallel /'pærəlel/ *adjective* **1.** referring to a computer system in which two or more processors operate simultaneously on one or more items of data **2.** referring to two or more bits of a word transmitted over separate lines at the same time

parallel broadcast /ˌpærəlel 'brɔːdkɑːst/ *noun* a broadcast that is transmitted simultaneously by radio or television and over the Internet

parallel input/output /ˌpærəlel ˌɪnpʊt 'aʊtpʊt/ *noun* full form of **PIO**

parallel input/parallel output /ˌpærəlel ˌɪnpʊt ˌpærəlel 'aʊtpʊt/ *noun* full form of **PIPO**

parallel input/serial output /ˌpærəlel ˌɪnpʊt ˌsɪəriəl 'aʊtpʊt/ *noun* full form of **PISO**

parallel running /ˌpærəlel 'rʌnɪŋ/ *noun* the running of an old and a new computer system together to allow the new system to be checked before it becomes the only system used

parameter /pə'ræmɪtə/ *noun* an item of information which defines the limits or actions of something, e.g. a variable, routine or program ○ *The X parameter defines the number of characters displayed across a screen.*

parent directory /'peərənt daɪˌrekt(ə)ri/ *noun* (*in a DOS filing system*) the directory above a subdirectory

parent folder /'peərənt ˌfəʊldə/ *noun* (*in an Apple Mac filing system*) one folder that contains other folders

parent object /'peərənt ˌɒbdʒekt/ *noun* a page that contains the object that is being referenced

parent program /'peərənt ˌprəʊgræm/ *noun* a program that starts another program, a child program, while it is still running (NOTE: Control passes back to the parent program when the child program has finished.)

parity /'pærɪti/ *noun* the fact of being equal

> 'The difference between them is that RAID level one offers mirroring, whereas level five stripes records in parity across the disks in the system.' [*Computing*]

parity bit /'pærɪti bɪt/ *noun* an extra bit added to a data word as a parity checking device

parity check /ˈpærɪti tʃek/ *noun* a method of checking for errors and that transmitted binary data has not been corrupted by adding an extra bit

park /pɑːk/ *verb* to move the read/write head of a hard disk drive over a point on the disk where no data is stored ○ *When parked, the disk head will not damage any data if it touches the disk surface.*

parse /pɑːz/ *verb* to break down high-level language code into its element parts when translating into machine code (NOTE: **parses – parsing – parsed**)

parsing /ˈpɑːzɪŋ/ *noun* an operation to break down high-level language code into its element parts when translating into machine code

part /pɑːt/ *noun* **1.** a section of something **2.** one of a series

particle /ˈpɑːtɪk(ə)l/ *noun* a very small piece of matter

partition /pɑːˈtɪʃ(ə)n/ *noun* an area of a hard disk that is treated as a logical drive and can be accessed as a separate drive ○ *I defined two partitions on this hard disk – called drive C: and D:.* ■ *verb* to divide a hard disk into two or more logical drives that can be accessed as separate drives

parts per quarter note /ˌpɑːts pɜː ˈkɔːtə ˌnəʊt/ *noun* full form of **PPQN**

pascal /ˈpæskəl/ *noun* a unit of pressure

PASCAL /ˈpæskæl/ *noun* a high-level structured programming language used both on micros and for teaching programming

passage /ˈpæsɪdʒ/ *noun* a number of notes that form a small section of a musical score

password /ˈpɑːsˌwɜːd/ *noun* a word or series of characters which identifies a user so that he or she can access a system ○ *The user has to key in the password before he can access the database.*

'...the system's security features let you divide the disk into up to 256 password-protected sections' [*Byte*]

password protection /ˌpɑːswɜːd prəˈtekʃ(ə)n/ *noun* a computer software that requires the user to enter a password before he or she can gain access

paste /peɪst/ *verb* to insert text or graphics that has been copied or cut into a file ○ *Now that I have cut this paragraph from the end of the document, I can paste it in here.* (NOTE: **pastes – pasting – pasted**)

Paste Special /ˌpeɪst ˈspeʃ(ə)l/ *noun* a facility for inserting a special object such as sound, images or data from other applications into a document

patch /pætʃ/ *noun* **1.** a temporary correction made to a program by a user, often on the instructions of the software publisher **2.** a thin piece of translucent film which is used to repair a tear in the film **3.** data that defines a sound in a synthesiser; a patch is also called a program and can be altered by issuing a program-change message

patchboard /ˈpætʃbɔːd/ *noun* same as **plugboard**

patch cord /ˈpætʃ kɔːd/ *noun* a short cable with a connector at each end, used to make an electrical connection on a patch panel

patch panel /ˈpætʃ ˌpæn(ə)l/ *noun* a set of electrical terminals that can be interconnected using short patch cords, allowing quick and simple reconfiguration of a network

path /pɑːθ/ *noun* **1.** a route from one point in a communications network to another **2.** (*in the DOS operating system*) a list of subdirectories in which the operating system should look for a named file

pathname /ˌpɑːθˈneɪm/ *noun* the location of a file with a listing of the subdirectories leading to it ○ *The pathname for the letter file is .DOC.*

pattern /ˈpæt(ə)n/ *noun* a series of regular lines or shapes which are repeated again and again

patterned /ˈpæt(ə)nd/ *adjective* with patterns

pattern palette /ˈpæt(ə)n ˌpælət/ *noun* a range of predefined patterns that can be used to fill an area of an image

pattern recognition /ˌpæt(ə)n ˌrekəgˈnɪʃ(ə)n/ *noun* algorithms or program functions that can identify a shape, e.g. from a video camera

pause control /ˈpɔːz kənˌtrəʊl/ *noun* a tape recorder control which temporarily stops the tape movement; it does not always produce a still frame picture on a video tape recorder (*film*)

pause key /ˈpɔːz kiː/ *noun* a keyboard key that temporarily stops a process, often a scrolling screen display, until the key is pressed a second time

PAX *abbr* private automatic exchange

paycable /ˈpeɪkeɪb(ə)l/ *noun US* a form of cable television where the viewer pays an extra fee for extra channels

payment gateway /ˈpeɪmənt ˌgeɪtweɪ/ *noun* a server or organisation that acts as an interface between the payment systems of the seller and the buyer when payments are made over the Internet

payment gateway certificate authority /ˌpeɪmənt ˌgeɪtweɪ səˈtɪfɪkət ɔːˌθɒrɪti/ *noun* an organisation that issues, renews or cancels the certificates that identify an Internet payment gateway. Abbr **PGCA**

pay TV /ˈpeɪ tiː viː/ *noun* a form of cable television, where the viewer pays for programs or channels watched

PB *abbr* petabyte

PBX *abbr* private branch exchange

PC /ˌpiː ˈsiː/ *noun* a computer that uses an Intel 80x86 processor and is based on the IBM PC-style architecture. Full form **personal computer** (NOTE: PC originally referred to a microcomputer specification with an 8086-based low-power computer.)

PC Card /ˌpiː ˈsiː kɑːd/ *noun* an electronic device, about the same size as a thick credit card, that can be plugged into a PCMCIA adapter to provide a particular function. Also called **PCMCIA card.** ◊ **PCMCIA** (NOTE: For example PC Cards are available that provide a modem, NIC, extra memory and hard disk drive functions.)

PC-compatible /ˌpiː ˌsiː kəmˈpætəb(ə)l/ *adjective* referring to a computer that is compatible with the IBM PC

p-channel metal oxide semiconductor /ˌpiː ˌtʃæn(ə)l ˌmet(ə)l ˌɒksaɪd ˌsemikənˈdʌktə/ *noun* full form of **PMOS**

PCI /ˌpiː siː ˈeɪ/ *noun* a specification produced by Intel defining a type of fast local bus that allows high-speed data transfer between the processor and expansion cards. Full form **peripheral component interconnect**

PCM /ˌpiː siː ˈem/ *noun* **1.** a company that produces add-on boards which are compatible with another manufacturer's computer. Full form **plug-compatible manufacturer** **2.** a way of storing sounds in an accurate, compact format that is used by high-end sound cards. Full form **pulse-code modulation**

PCMCIA /ˌpiː siː em siː aɪ ˈeɪ/ *noun* a specification for add-in expansion cards that are the size of a credit card with a connector at one end ○ *The extra memory is stored on this PCMCIA card and I use it on my laptop.* Full form **Personal Computer Memory Card International Association**

PCMCIA card /ˌpiː siː ˌem ˌsiː aɪ ˈeɪ kɑːd/ *noun* add-in memory or a peripheral which complies with the PCMCIA standard

PCMCIA connector /ˌpiː siː ˌem ˌsiː aɪ ˌeɪ kəˈnektə/ *noun* a 68-pin connector that is inside a PCMCIA slot and on the end of a PCMCIA card

PCMCIA slot /ˌpiː siː ˌem ˌsiː aɪ ˈeɪ slɒt/ *noun* an expansion slot, normally on a laptop, that can accept a PCMCIA expansion card

PC/TV /ˌpiː siː tiː ˈviː/ *noun* a personal computer that can receive, decode and display standard television images

PCU /ˌpiː siː ˈjuː/ *noun* a device used to convert input and output signals and instructions to a form that a peripheral device will understand. Full form **peripheral control unit**

PCX *noun* a standard file format for storing colour graphics images

PCX file /ˌpiː siː eks ˈfaɪl/ *noun* a method of storing a bitmap graphic image file on disk

PD *abbr* public domain

PDA /ˌpiː diː ˈeɪ/ *noun* a lightweight palmtop computer that provides the basic functions of a diary, notepad, address-book and to-do list together with fax or modem communications. Full form **personal digital assistant** (NOTE: Current PDA designs do not have a keyboard, but use a touch-sensitive screen with a pen and handwriting-recognition to control the software.)

PDF /ˌpiː diː ˈef/ *noun* a file format used by Adobe Acrobat. Full form **portable document format**

PDL *abbr* **1.** page description language **2.** program design language

PDM *noun* a pulse modulation system in which the pulse width varies with the magnitude of the input signal. Full form **pulse duration modulation**

PDN *abbr* public data network

peak /piːk/ *noun* the highest point ■ *verb* to reach the highest point

peek /piːk/ *noun* a BASIC computer instruction that allows the user to read the contents of a memory location ○ *You need the instruction PEEK 1452 here to examine the contents of memory location 1452.* Compare **poke**

peer /pɪə/ *noun* each of two similar devices operating on the same network protocol level

peer-to-peer network /ˌpɪə tə ˌpɪə ˈnetwɜːk/ *noun* a local area network, usually using NICs in each computer, that does not use a central dedicated server, but instead each computer in the network shares the jobs ○ *We have linked the four PCs in our small office using a peer-to-peer network.*

pen /pen/ *noun* same as **light pen**

pen computer /ˌpen kəmˈpjuːtə/ *noun* a type of computer that uses a light pen instead of a keyboard for input (NOTE: The computer has a touch-sensitive screen and uses handwriting-recognition software to interpret the commands written on the screen using the light pen.)

pen plotter /ˈpen ˌplɒtə/ *noun* a plotter that uses removable pens to draw an image on paper

Pentium /ˈpentiəm/ a trade name for a range of electronic processor components developed by Intel (NOTE: They are backwards-compatible with the 80x86 family used in IBM PCs. The processor uses a 32-bit address bus and a 64-bit data bus.)

per /pɜː, pə/ *preposition* **1.** at a rate of **2.** out of or for each ○ *The rate of imperfect items is about 25 per 1.000.*

per cent /pə ˈsent/ *adjective, adverb* out of each hundred or for each hundred ○ *what is the increase per cent? fifty per cent of nothing is still nothing* □ **10 per cent** ten in every hundred ○ *what is the increase per cent? fifty per cent of nothing is still nothing*

percentage /pəˈsentɪdʒ/ *noun* an amount shown as part of one hundred □ **percentage increase** increase calculated on the basis of a rate for one hundred □ **percentage point** one per cent

percentile /pəˈsenˌtaɪl/ *noun* one of a series of 99 figures below which a certain percentage of the total falls

per day /pə ˈdeɪ/ *phrase* for each day

perfect /pəˈfekt/ *verb* to make something which is completely correct ○ *He perfected the process for making high grade steel.*

perfect binding /ˌpɜːfɪkt ˈbaɪndɪŋ/ *noun* a method of binding paperback books, where the pages are trimmed at the spine, and glued to the cover

perfect bound /ˌpɜːfekt baʊnd/ *adjective* (*of a book, usually a paperback*) bound without sewing, where the pages are trimmed at the spine and glued to the cover with strong glue

perfectly /ˈpɜːfɪktli/ *adverb* with no mistakes or correctly ○ *She typed the letter perfectly.*

perfector /pəˈfektə/ *noun* a printing machine that prints on both sides of a sheet of paper

perforated tape /ˈpɜːfəˌreɪtɪd teɪp/ *noun* a paper tape or long strip of tape on which data can be recorded in the form of punched holes

perforation /ˌpɜːfəˈreɪʃ(ə)n/ *noun* any one of a line of very small holes in a sheet of paper or continuous stationery, to help when tearing

perforator /ˈpɜːfəreɪtə/ *noun* a machine that punches holes in a paper tape

perform /pəˈfɔːm/ *verb* to do well or badly

performance /pəˈfɔːməns/ *noun* the way in which someone or something works

perigee /ˈperɪdziː/ *noun* the point during the orbit of a satellite when it closest to the earth

period /ˈpɪəriəd/ *noun* **1.** a length of time ○ *for a period of time* or *for a period of months* or *for a six-year period* **2.** a printing sign used at the end of a piece of text, the full stop

periodic /ˌpɪəriˈɒdɪk/, **periodical** /ˌpɪəriˈɒdɪk(ə)l/ *adjective* happening from time to time ○ *a periodic review of the company's performance*

periodically /ˌpɪəriˈɒdɪkli/ *adverb* from time to time

peripheral /pəˈrɪf(ə)rəl/ *adjective* which is not essential ■ *noun* **1.** a piece of computer hardware that is not part of the central processing unit but is controlled by it, e.g. a printer or scanner ○ *Peripherals such as disk drives* or *printers allow data transfer and are controlled by a system, but contain independent circuits for their operation.* Also called **auxiliary device, peripheral unit 2.** any device that allows communication between a system and itself but is not directly operated by the system

peripheral component interconnect /pəˌrɪf(ə)rəl kəmˌpəʊnənt ˈɪntəkənekt/ *noun* full form of **PCI**

peripheral control unit /pəˌrɪf(ə)rəl kənˈtrəʊl ˌjuːnɪt/ *noun* full form of **PCU**

peripheral interface adapter /pəˌrɪf(ə)rəl ˈɪntəfeɪs əˌdæptə/ *noun* full form of **PIA**

peripheral unit /pəˌrɪf(ə)rəl ˈjuːnɪt/ *noun* **1.** an item of hardware such as a terminal, printer or monitor which is attached to a main computer system. Same as **peripheral 2.** any device that allows communication between a system and itself, but is not operated only by the system

Perl /pɜːl/ *noun* an interpreted programming language, usually used under Unix, used to create CGI scripts that can process forms or carry out functions on a web server to enhance a website. Full form **practical extraction and report language**

perlux /ˈpɜːlʌks/ *noun* a material used for a projection screen which is highly reflective and also wide-angle (*film*)

permanent /ˈpɜːmənənt/ *adjective* which will last for a very long time or for ever

permanently /ˈpɜːmənəntli/ *adverb* in a way which will last for a long time or for ever ○ *The production number is permanently engraved on the back of the computer casing.*

permeability /ˌpɜːmiəˈbɪlɪti/ *noun* a measure of the ratio of the magnetic flux in a material to the size of the generating field

permission /pəˈmɪʃ(ə)n/ *noun* authorisation given to a particular user to access a certain shared resource or area of disk ○ *This user cannot access the file on the server because he does not have permission.*

permutation /ˌpɜːmjʊˈteɪʃ(ə)n/ *noun* each of a number of different ways in which something can be arranged ○ *The cipher system is very secure since there are so many possible permutations for the key.*

persistence /pə'sɪstəns/ *noun* the length of time that a CRT will continue to display an image after the picture beam has stopped tracing it on the screen ○ *Slow scan rate monitors need long persistence phosphor to prevent the image flickering.*

person /'pɜːs(ə)n/ *noun* a human being

personal /'pɜːs(ə)n(ə)l/ *adjective* referring to one person

personal computer /ˌpɜːs(ə)n(ə)l kəm 'pjuːtə/ *noun* full form of **PC**

Personal Computer Memory Card International Association /ˌpɜːs(ə)nəl kəmˌpjuːtə ˌmem(ə)ri kɑːd ˌɪntənæʃ(ə)nəl əˌsəʊsi'eɪʃ(ə)n/ *noun* full form of **PCMCIA**

personal digital assistant /ˌpɜːs(ə)n(ə)l ˌdɪdʒɪt(ə)l ə'sɪstənt/ *noun* full form of **PDA**

personal identification device /ˌpɜːs(ə)n(ə)l aɪˌdentɪfɪ'keɪʃ(ə)n dɪˌvaɪs/ *noun* full form of **PID**

personal identification number /ˌpɜːs(ə)n(ə)l aɪˌdentɪfɪ'keɪʃ(ə)n ˌnʌmbə/ *noun* full form of **PIN**

personal information manager /ˌpɜːs(ə)n(ə)l ˌɪnfə'meɪʃ(ə)n ˌmænɪdʒə/ *noun* full form of **PIM**

personalise /'pɜːs(ə)nəlaɪz/, **personalize** *verb* to customise or adapt a product specially for a certain user (NOTE: **personalises – personalising – personalised**)

personnel /ˌpɜːsə'nel/ *noun* staff or all the people working in an office or factory

perspective /pə'spektɪv/ *noun* the appearance of depth in an image in which objects that are further away from the viewer appear smaller

PERT /pɜːt/ *noun* a definition of tasks or jobs and the time each requires, arranged in order to achieve a goal. Full form **program evaluation and review technique**

per week /pə 'wiːk/ *adverb* for each week

per year /pə 'jɪə/ *adverb* for each year

peta /petə/ *prefix* one quadrillion (2^{50}). Abbr **P**

petabyte /'petəbaɪt/ *noun* one quadrillion bytes. Abbr **PB**

pF *noun* the unit of measurement of capacitance equal to one million millionth of a farad. Full form **picofarad**

PFL *abbr* pre-fade listen (*film*)

PgDn /ˌpeɪdʒ 'daʊn/ *abbr* page down key

PGP /ˌpiː dʒiː 'piː/ *noun* an encryption system developed to allow anyone to protect the contents of his or her email messages from unauthorised readers. Full form **pretty good privacy** (NOTE: This system is often used when sending credit card or payment details over the Internet.)

PgUp /ˌpeɪdʒ 'ʌp/ *abbr* page up key

phantom ROM /'fæntəm rɒm/ *noun* a duplicate area of read-only memory that is accessed by a special code

phase /feɪz/ *noun* **1.** one part of a larger process **2.** the coincidence of reference signal and colour burst

phase alternation line /ˌfeɪz ˌɔːltə'neɪʃ(ə)n ˌlaɪn/ *noun* full form of **PAL**

phasing /'feɪzɪŋ/ *noun* (*film*) **1.** two systems or circuits which are adjusted so that they operate in phase **2.** a television and video tape recorder standard alignment process **3.** the loss of quality in transmitted sound when two microphones are placed too near each other

PHIGS /fɪgz/ *noun* a standard application interface between software and a graphics adapter that uses a set of standard commands to draw and manipulate 2D and 3D images. Full form **programmer's hierarchical interactive graphics standard**

phon /fɒn/ *noun* a measure of sound equal to a one thousand Hertz signal at one decibel; zero is just audible to the human ear

phone /fəʊn/ *noun* a telephone or machine used for speaking to someone over a long distance ○ *We had a new phone system installed last week.*

phone back /ˌfəʊn 'bæk/ *verb* to reply by phone ○ *The chairman is in a meeting, can you phone back in about half an hour?* ○ *Mr Smith called while you were out and asked if you would phone him back.*

phoneme /'fəʊniːm/ *noun* one small meaningful sound, several of which may make up a spoken word (NOTE: Phonemes are relevant to the analysis of voice input to recognise words and in the reproduction of speech.)

phonetic /fə'netɪk/ *adjective* referring to phonetics ○ *The pronunciation is indicated in phonetic script.*

phonetics /fə'netɪks/ *noun* written symbols that are used to represent the correct pronunciation of a word

phono connector /ˌfəʊnəʊ kə'nektə/ *noun* a plug and socket standard used to connect audio and video devices. Also called **RCA connector** (NOTE: The male plug has a 1/8-inch metal central core that sticks out from within the centre of an insulated core. If you have fitted a sound card to your PC you will see two phono connectors on the back plate. These let you connect your sound card directly to your CD player or tape recorder.)

phosphor /'fɒsfə/ *noun* a substance that produces light when excited by some form of energy, usually an electron beam, used for coating the inside of a cathode ray tube

COMMENT: A thin layer of phosphor is arranged in a pattern of small dots on the inside of a television screen which produces an image when scanned by the picture beam.

phosphorescence /ˌfɒsfə'res(ə)ns/ *noun* the ability of a material to produce light when excited by some form of energy

photocell /'fəʊtəʊsel/ *noun* an electronic device that produces or varies an electrical signal according to the amount of light shining on it

photocomposition /ˌfəʊtəʊkɒmpə'zɪʃ(ə)n/ *noun* the composition of typeset text direct onto film

photoconductivity /ˌfəʊtəʊkɒndʌk'tɪvɪti/ *noun* a material which varies its resistance according to the amount of light striking it

photoconductor /'fəʊtəʊkənˌdʌktə/ *noun* a photocell whose resistance varies with the amount of light shining on it

photocopier /'fəʊtəʊkɒpiə/ *noun* a machine which makes a copy of a document by photographing and printing it

photocopy /'fəʊtəʊkɒpi/ *noun* a copy of a document made by photographing and printing it ○ *Make six photocopies of the contract.* ■ *verb* to make a copy of a document by photographing and printing it ○ *She photocopied the contract.*

photocopying /'fəʊtəʊkɒpiɪŋ/ *noun* the process of making photocopies (NOTE: no plural) □ **photocopying bureau** office which photocopies documents for companies which do not possess their own photocopiers □ **there is a mass of photocopying to be done** there are many documents waiting to be photocopied

photodigital memory /fəʊtəʊˌdɪdʒɪt(ə)l 'mem(ə)ri/ *noun* a computer memory system that uses a laser to write data onto a piece of film which can then be read many times but not written to again. Also called **WORM**

photodiode /ˌfəʊtəʊ'daɪəʊd/ *noun* an electronic component displaying the electrical properties of a diode but whose resistance varies with the amount of light that shines on it. ◊ **avalanche**

photoelectric /fəʊtəʊɪ'lektrɪk/ *adjective* (material) that generates an electrical signal when light shines on it ○ *The photoelectric cell detects the amount of light passing through the liquid.*

photoelectric cell /ˌfəʊtəʊɪlektrɪk 'sel/ *noun* a component which produces or varies an electrical signal when a light shines on it ○ *The photoelectric cell detects the amount of light passing through the liquid.*

photoelectricity /ˌfəʊtəʊɪˌlek'trɪsɪti/ *noun* the production of an electrical signal from a material that has light shining on it

photoemission /ˌfəʊtəʊɪ'mɪʃ(ə)n/ *noun* a material that emits electrons when light strikes it

photograph /'fəʊtəˌgrɑːf/ *noun* an image formed by light striking a light-sensitive surface, usually coated paper ○ *colour photograph* ○ *black and white photograph* ○ *It's a photograph of the author.* ○ *He took six photographs of the set.* ○ *We will be using a colour photograph of the author on the back of the jacket.*

photographic /ˌfəʊtə'græfɪk/ *adjective* referring to photography or photographs ○ *The copier makes a photographic reproduction of the printed page.*

photographically /ˌfəʊtə'græfɪkli/ *adverb* using photography ○ *The text film can be reproduced photographically.*

photographic film /ˌfəʊtə'græfɪk fɪlm/ *noun* light-sensitive film used in a camera to record images

photographic sound /ˌfəʊtə'græfɪk saʊnd/ *noun* a method of recording and reproducing on film where the sound track takes the form of variations in the density or width of a photographic image (*film*)

photography /fə'tɒgrəfi/ *noun* a method of creating images by exposing light-sensitive paper to light, using a camera

photolithography /ˌfəʊtəʊˌlɪ'θɒgrəfi/ *noun* the process of printing using a lithographic printing plate formed photographically

photomechanical transfer /ˌfəʊtəʊmɪkænɪk(ə)l 'trænsfɜː/ *noun* a system for transferring line drawings and text onto film before printing. Abbr **PMT**

photometer /fəʊ'tɒmɪtə/ *noun* a device which measures the brightness of light (*film*)

photometry /fəʊ'tɒmɪtri/ *noun* study and measurement of light

photon /'fəʊtɒn/ *noun* a packet of electromagnetic radiation

photoprint /'fəʊtəʊprɪnt/ *noun* a final proof

photorealistic /ˌfəʊtəʊriə'lɪstɪk/ *adjective* referring to a computer image that has almost the same quality and clarity as a photograph

photosensitive /ˌfəʊtəʊˈsensɪtɪv/ *adjective* sensitive to light (*film*)

photosensor /ˈfəʊtəʊsensə/ *noun* a component or circuit that can produce a signal related to the amount of light striking it

photostat /ˈfəʊtəʊstæt/ *noun* a type of photocopy ■ *verb* to make a photostat of a document

phototelegraphy /ˌfəʊtətəˈlegrəfi/ *noun* the transmission of images over a telephone line

phototransistor /ˌfəʊtəʊtrænˈzɪstə/ *noun* an electronic component that can detect light and amplify the generated signal or vary a supply according to light intensity

phototypesetter /ˌfəʊtəʊˈtaɪpsetə/ *noun* **1.** a device that can produce very high-resolution text on photosensitive paper or film **2.** a company which specialises in phototypesetting

phototypesetting /ˌfəʊtəʊˈtaɪpsetɪŋ/ *noun* a method of typesetting that creates characters using a computer and exposing a sensitive film in front of a mask containing the required character shape

physical /ˈfɪzɪk(ə)l/ *adjective* real or solid, or which can be touched

physical record /ˌfɪzɪk(ə)l ˈrekɔːd/ *noun* **1.** the maximum unit of data that can be transmitted in a single operation **2.** all the information, including control data, for one record stored in a computer system

PIA /ˌpiː aɪ ˈeɪ/ *noun* a circuit which allows a computer to communicate with a peripheral by providing serial and parallel ports and other handshaking signals required to interface the peripheral. Full form **peripheral interface adapter**

PIC /ˌpiː aɪ ˈsiː/ *noun* an image compression algorithm used in Intel's DVI video system. Full form **picture image compression**

pica /ˈpaɪkə/ *noun* **1.** a method of measurement used in printing and typesetting (equal to twelve point type) **2.** the width of characters in a typeface, usually 12 characters to the inch

PICK /pɪk/ *noun* a multi-user, multitasking operating system that runs on mainframe, mini or PC computers

pickup /ˈpɪkʌp/ *noun* **1.** the arm and cartridge used to playback music from a record **2.** the inserting of a shot in a film **3.** a graph showing the sensitivity of a microphone according to the direction of the source. The two most common patterns are omni-directional (the microphone will pick up sound from any direction) and uni-directional (the microphone is focused and responds to sound from one direction only).

pico- /piːkəʊ/ *prefix* one million millionth of a unit. Abbr **p**

picosecond /ˈpiːkəʊˌsekənd/ *noun* one million millionth of a second. Abbr **pS**

PICS /pɪks/ *noun* a file format used to import a sequence of PICT files on an Apple Mac

PICT /pɪkt/ *noun* a method of storing vector graphic images, developed by Lotus for its 1–2–3 spreadsheet charts and graphs. Full form **PICture**

picture /ˈpɪktʃə/ *noun* a printed or drawn image of an object or scene ○ *This picture shows the new design.* ■ *verb* to visualise an object or scene ○ *Try to picture the layout before starting to draw it in.* (NOTE: **pictures – picturing – pictured**)

PICture /ˈpɪktʃə/ *noun* full form of **PICT**

picture beam /ˈpɪktʃə biːm/ *noun* a moving electron beam in a TV that produces an image on the screen by illuminating the phosphor coating and by varying its intensity according to the received signal

picture element /ˈpɪktʃə ˌelɪmənt/ *noun* same as **pixel**

picture image compression /ˌpɪktʃə ˈɪmɪdʒ kəmˌpreʃ(ə)n/ *noun* full form of **PIC**

picture level benchmark /ˌpɪktʃə ˌlev(ə)l ˈbentʃmɑːk/ *noun* full form of **PLB**

picture object /ˈpɪktʃə ˌɒbdʒekt/ *noun* an image created with a vector drawing package and stored as vectors rather than as a bitmap

picture processing /ˌpɪktʃə ˌprəˈsesɪŋ/ *noun* the analysis of information contained in an image, usually by computer or electronic methods, providing analysis or recognition of objects in the image

picture transmission /ˈpɪktʃə trænz ˌmɪʃ(ə)n/ *noun* the transmission of images over a telephone line

PID /ˌpiː aɪ ˈdiː/ *noun* a device such as a bank card connected with or inserted into a system to identify or provide authorisation for a user. Full form **personal identification device**

piece fraction /ˌpiːs ˈfrækʃən/ *noun* a printed fraction contained in one character space

pie chart /ˈpaɪ tʃɑːt/ *noun* a diagram in which ratios are shown as slices of a circle ○ *The memory allocation is shown on this pie chart.*

piezoelectric /ˌpiːzəʊɪˈlektrɪk/ *adjective* being able to change their electrical properties when a force is applied or to change their physical dimensions when an electrical signal is applied

PIF /ˌpiː aɪ 'ef/ *noun* a Microsoft Windows file that contains the environment settings for a particular program. Full form **program information file**

piggyback /'pɪgibæk/ *verb* to connect two integrated circuits in parallel, one on top of the other to save space ○ *Piggyback those two memory chips to boost the memory capacity.*

piggybacking /'pɪgibækɪŋ/ *noun* the process of using transmitted messages to carry acknowledgements from a message which has been received earlier

pilot /'paɪlət/ *adjective* used as a test, which if successful will then be expanded into a full operation ○ *The company set up a pilot project to see if the proposed manufacturing system was efficient.* ■ *verb* to test something ○ *They are piloting the new system.*

PIM /ˌpiː aɪ 'em/ *noun* a software utility that stores and manages a user's everyday data such as diary, telephone numbers, address book and notes. Full form **personal information manager**

pin /pɪn/ *noun* **1.** one of several short pieces of wire attached to an integrated circuit package that allows the IC to be connected to a circuit board **2.** a short piece of metal, part of a plug which fits into a hole in a socket ○ *Use a three-pin plug to connect the printer to the mains.* **3.** part of a mechanism in a camera or a projector which engages in the perforation hole in order to find the frame

PIN /pɪn/ *noun* a unique sequence of digits that identifies a user to provide authorisation to access a system, often used on automatic cash dispensers or with a PID or password to enter a system. Full form **personal identification number**

pincushion distortion /ˌpɪnkʊʃ(ə)n dɪ'stɔːʃ(ə)n/ *noun* a fault with a monitor that causes the distortion of an image displayed in which the edges curve in towards the centre

pinfeed /'pɪnfiːd/ *noun* same as **tractor feed**

PING /pɪŋ/ *noun* a software utility that will test all the nodes on a network or Internet to ensure that they are working correctly. Full form **packet Internet groper**

pinout /'pɪnaʊt/ *noun* a description of the position of all the pins on an integrated circuit together with their function and signal

PIO /ˌpiː aɪ 'əʊ/ *noun* data input or output from a computer in a parallel form. Full form **parallel input/output.** ◊ **PIPO, PISO**

pipe /paɪp/ *noun* (*in DOS and UNIX*) a symbol, usually (|), that tells the operating system to send the output of one command to another command, instead of displaying it

pipeline /'paɪplaɪn/ *verb* to carry out more than one task at a time: e.g., to compress and store an image on disk as it is being scanned (NOTE: **pipelines – pipelining – pipelined**)

pipelining /ˌpaɪpˌlaɪn 'mem(ə)ri/, **pipeline memory** *noun* a method of executing several instructions in parallel to increase performance (NOTE: Some computers use pipelining to try and boost performance by executing several instructions at once.)

PIPO /ˌpiː aɪ piː 'əʊ/ *noun* a device that can accept and transmit parallel data. Full form **parallel input/parallel output**

piracy /'paɪrəsi/ *noun* the process of copying patented inventions or copyright works

pirate /'paɪrət/ *noun* a person who copies a patented invention or a copyright work and sells it ○ *The company is trying to take the software pirates to court.* ■ *verb* to manufacture copies of an original copyrighted work illegally ○ *a pirated DVD* or *a pirated design* (NOTE: **pirates – pirating – pirated**)

COMMENT: The items most frequently pirated are programs on magnetic disks and tapes, which are relatively simple to copy.

pirate copy /ˌpaɪrət 'kɒpi/ *noun* a copy of software or other copyrighted material which has been made illegally ○ *A pirate copy of a computer program.*

pirate software /ˌpaɪrət 'sɒftweə/ *noun* an illegal copy of a software package

PISO /ˌpiː aɪ es 'əʊ/ *noun* a device that can accept parallel data and transmit serial data. Full form **parallel input/serial output**

pitch /pɪtʃ/ *noun* **1.** the number of characters which will fit into one inch of line, when the characters are typed in single spacing **2.** the actual frequency of a sound **3.** a satellite or antenna movement about the horizontal axis **4.** the standard distance between the leading edges of the perforation holes on a film which is to be used as film stock

pitch scale factor /ˌpɪtʃ 'skeɪl ˌfæktə/ *noun* an instruction to a waveform audio device to change the pitch of the sound by a factor

pix /pɪks/ *plural noun* pictures

pixel /'pɪksəl/ *noun* the smallest single unit or point of a display whose colour or brightness can be controlled. Also called **picture element**

'...adding 40 to each pixel brightens the image and can improve the display's appearance' [*Byte*]

COMMENT: In high resolution display systems the colour or brightness of a single pixel can be controlled; in low resolution systems a group of pixels are controlled at the same time.

pixelated /'pɪksəleɪtɪd/ *adjective* referring to an image on a computer or television screen that is made up of pixels, especially one that is unclear or distorted

pixillation /ˌpɪksəˈleɪʃ(ə)n/ *noun* (*film*) **1.** a film and video visual effect where action is shown as a sequence of stills **2.** an effect in video where the picture is reproduced as a number of enlarged pictures

pix lock /ˈpɪks lɒk/ *noun* the synchronisation of a video playback circuit by an external signal

PLA /ˌpiː el ˈeɪ/ *noun* an integrated circuit that can be permanently programmed to perform logic operations on data using a matrix of links between input and output pins. Full form **programmable logic array**

COMMENT: A PLA consists of a large matrix of paths between input and output pins, with logic gates and a fusible link at each connection point that can be broken or left to conduct when programming to define a function from input to output.

plain old telephone service /ˌpleɪn əʊld ˈtelɪfəʊn ˌsɜːvɪs/ *noun* full form of **POTS**

plaintext /ˌpleɪnˈtekst/ *noun* text or information that has not been encrypted or coded ○ *The messages were sent as plaintext by telephone.* Opposite **ciphertext**

plan /plæn/ *noun* **1.** an organised way of doing something **2.** a drawing which shows how something is arranged or how something will be built ■ *verb* to organise carefully how something should be done (NOTE: **planning – planned**)

PLAN /plæn/ *noun* a low-level programming language

planar /ˈpleɪnə/ *adjective* referring to a method of producing integrated circuits by diffusing chemicals into a slice of silicon to create the different components ■ *noun* referring to graphical objects or images arranged on the same plane

plane /pleɪn/ *noun* one layer of an image that can be manipulated independently within a graphics program

planet /ˈplænɪt/ *noun* a large body in space (such as the earth), moving in orbit round the sun

planetary camera /ˌplænɪt(ə)ri ˈkæm(ə)rə/ *noun* a microfilm camera in which the film and article being photographed are stationary

planner /ˈplænə/ *noun* a software program that allows appointments and important meetings to be recorded and arranged in the most efficient way

planning /ˈplænɪŋ/ *noun* the activity of organising how something should be done ○ *long-term planning* or *short-term planning*

plasma display /ˈplæzmə dɪˌspleɪ/ *noun* same as **gas discharge display**

COMMENT: This is a thin display usually used in small portable computers.

plastic bubble keyboard /ˌplæstɪk ˌbʌb(ə)l ˈkiːbɔːd/ *noun* a keyboard whose keys are small bubbles in a plastic sheet over a contact which when pressed completes a circuit

COMMENT: These are very solid and cheap keyboards but are not ideal for rapid typing.

platform /ˈplætˌfɔːm/ *noun* a standard type of hardware that makes up a particular range of computers ○ *This software will only work on the IBM PC platform.*

platform independence /ˌplætfɔːm ˌɪndɪˈpendəns/ *noun* the fact that software or a network can work with or connect to different types of incompatible hardware

platter /ˈplætə/ *noun* one disk within a hard disk drive

COMMENT: The disks are made of metal or glass and coated with a magnetic compound; each platter has a read/write head that moves across its surface to access stored data.

play back /ˌpleɪ ˈbæk/ *verb* to read data or a signal from a recording ○ *After you have recorded the music, press this button to play it back and hear what it sounds like.*

playback /ˈpleɪbæk/ *noun* recording reproduction; running a multimedia title, viewing a video clip or listening to a recorded sound

playback head /ˈpleɪˌbæk hed/ *noun* a piece of equipment that reads signals recorded on a storage medium and usually converts them to an electrical signal ○ *disk playback head*

playback rate scale factor /ˈpleɪbæk reɪt skeɪl ˌfæktə/ *noun* **1.** (*in waveform audio*) sound played back at a different rate, directed by another application, to create a special effect **2.** (*in video displayed on a computer*) the point at which video playback is no longer smooth and appears jerky because of missed frames

PLB /ˌpiː el ˈbiː/ *noun* benchmark used to measure the performance (not the quality) of a graphics adapter or workstation. Full form **picture level benchmark**

PLD *abbr* programmable logic device

plex database /ˈpleks ˌdeɪtəbeɪs/ *noun* a database structure in which data items can be linked together

plex structure /ˈpleks ˌstrʌktʃə/ *noun* a network structure or data structure in which each node is connected to all the others

PL/M /ˌpiː el ˈem/ *noun* a high level programming language derived for use on microprocessors. Full form **programming language for microprocessors**

plot /plɒt/ *noun* a graph or map ■ *verb* to draw an image (especially a graph) based on information supplied as a series of coordinates

plotter /ˈplɒtə/ *noun* a computer peripheral that draws straight lines between two coordinates

COMMENT: Plotters are used for graph and diagram plotting and can plot curved lines as a number of short straight lines.

plug /plʌg/ *noun* a connector with protruding pins that is inserted into a socket to provide an electrical connection ○ *The printer is supplied with a plug.* ■ *verb* **1.** ○ *No wonder the computer does nothing, you haven't plugged it in at the mains.* □ **plug in** to make an electrical connection by pushing a plug into a socket ○ *No wonder the computer does nothing, you haven't plugged it in at the mains.* **2.** to publicise or to advertise ○ *They ran six commercials plugging holidays in Spain.*

plug and play /ˌplʌg ən ˈpleɪ/ *noun* a facility in PCs that allows a user to plug a new adapter card into their PC without having to configure it or set any switches. Abbr **PNP**

plugboard *noun* a board with a number of sockets connected to devices into which plugs can be inserted to connect various other devices. Also called **patchboard**

plug-compatible manufacturer /ˌplʌg kəmˌpætɪb(ə)l ˌmænjʊˈfæktʃərə/ *noun* full form of **PCM**

plug-in /ˈplʌg ɪn/ *noun* a program that works with a web browser to increase the functionality of the browser. ◊ **browser, helper application**

plug-in unit /ˈplʌg ɪn ˌjuːnɪt/ *noun* a small electronic circuit that can be simply plugged into a system to increase its power

plus /plʌs/, **plus sign** /ˈplʌs saɪn/ *noun* a printed or written sign (+) showing that figures are added or showing a positive value

PLV /ˌpiː el ˈviː/ *noun* the highest-quality video compression algorithm used with DVI full-motion video sequences. Full form **production level video**

PMBX *noun* a small telephone exchange inside a company where all calls coming in or going out have to be placed through the switchboard. Full form **private manual branch exchange**

PMOS /ˈpiː mɒs/ *noun* a metal oxide semiconductor transistor that conducts via a small region of p-type semiconductor. Full form **p-channel metal oxide semiconductor**

PMS /ˌpiː em ˈes/ *abbr* Pantone Matching System

point /pɔɪnt/ *noun* **1.** a measurement system used in typesetting (one point is equal to 0.351 mm) ○ *The text of the book is set in 9 point Times.* ○ *If we increase the point size to 10, will the page extent increase?* (NOTE: usually written **pt** after figures: **10pt Times Bold**) **2.** the exposure increment which is used in a film printing machine; a printer point scale of 1 to 50 is normally used

'...the arrow keys, the spacebar or the mouse are used for pointing, and the enter key or the left mouse button are to pick' [*PC User*]

pointer /ˈpɔɪntə/ *noun* **1.** a variable in a computer program that contains the address to a data item or instruction ○ *Increment the contents of the pointer to the address of the next instruction.* **2.** a graphical symbol used to indicate the position of a cursor on a computer display ○ *Desktop publishing on a PC is greatly helped by the use of a pointer and mouse.*

pointing device /ˈpɔɪntɪŋ dɪˌvaɪs/ *noun* an input device that controls the position of a cursor on screen as it is moved by the user. ◊ **mouse**

point of presence /ˌpɔɪnt əv ˈprezəns/ *noun* full form of **POP**

point-of-sale /ˌpɔɪnt əv ˈseɪl/ *noun* a place in a shop where goods are paid for. Abbr **POS**

point sampling /ˈpɔɪnt ˌsɑːmplɪŋ/ *noun* a method of adding texture and shading to a three-dimensional scene or object, in which the algorithm calculates the perceived depth, position and shade of each point on the image and applies a texture map pixel, or texel, to that point

point size /ˌpɔɪnt ˈsaɪz/ *noun* (*in typography*) a unit of measure equal to 1/72-inch, used to measure type or text

point to point /ˌpɔɪnt tə ˈpɔɪnt/ *noun* **1.** a direct link between two devices **2.** communications network in which every node is directly connected to every other node

point-to-point tunneling protocol /ˌpɔɪnt tə pɔɪnt ˈtʌn(ə)lɪŋ ˌprəʊtəkɒl/ *noun* full form of **PPTP**

poke /pəʊk/ *noun* a computer instruction that modifies an entry in a memory by writing a number to an address in memory ○ *Poke 1423,74 will write the data 74 into location 1423.* Compare **peek**

POL *abbr* problem-orientated language

polar /ˈpəʊlə/ *adjective* referring to poles

polarising filter /ˌpəʊləraɪzɪŋ ˈfɪltə/ *noun* (*film*) **1.** a lens filter which has thousands of tiny lines which allow light of a certain polarity through, reducing glare **2.** a filter which is used to decrease the amount of polarised light passing through the lens by the specific angling of the slits

polarity /pəʊ'lærəti/ *noun* **1.** the definition of direction of flow of flux or current in an object **2.** negative or positive elements in a black and white television image

Polaroid™ /'pəʊlərɔɪd/ *noun* (*film*) **1.** an instant-picture photographic camera **2.** translucent plastic material which is able to polarise visible light

polaroid filter /ˌpəʊlərɔɪd 'fɪltə/ *noun* a photographic filter that only allows light in one plane, vertical or horizontal, to be transmitted

polar orbit /ˌpəʊlə 'ɔːbɪt/ *noun* a satellite flight path that goes over the earth's poles

policy /'pɒlɪsi/ *noun* ➧ **acceptable use policy**

Polish notation /ˌpəʊlɪʃ nəʊ'teɪʃ(ə)n/ *noun* ➧ **reverse Polish notation**

poll /pəʊl/ *verb* (*of a computer*) to determine the state of a peripheral in a network

polling /'pəʊlɪŋ/ *noun* a system of communication between a controlling computer and a number of networked terminals (the computer checks each terminal in turn to see if it is ready to receive or transmit data, and takes the required action)

COMMENT: The polling system differs from other communications systems in that the computer asks the terminals to transmit *or* receive, not the other way round.

polygon /'pɒlɪgən/ *noun* a graphics shape with three or more sides

polygon mesh model /ˌpɒlɪgən 'meʃ ˌmɒd(ə)l/ *noun* same as **wire frame model**

polynomial code /ˌpɒli'nəʊmiəl kəʊd/ *noun* an error detection system that uses a set of mathematical rules applied to the message before it is transmitted and again when it is received to reproduce the original message

pop /pɒp/ *verb* to read and remove the last piece of data from a stack

POP /pɒp/ *noun* telephone access number for a service provider that can be used to connect to the Internet via a modem. Full form **point of presence**

POP 2 /'pɒp tuː/ *noun* a high level programming language used for list processing applications

POP 3 /ˌpɒp 'θriː/ *noun* a system used to transfer electronic mail messages between a user's computer and a server at an ISP

pop-down menu /ˌpɒp daʊn 'menjuː/ *noun* a menu that can be displayed on the screen at any time by pressing the appropriate key, usually displayed over material already on the screen. Also called **pop-up menu**

pop filter /'pɒp ˌfɪltə/ *noun* an electronic circuit used when recording voices to attenuate signals caused by wind or breathing ○ *Every time you say a 'p' you overload the tape recorder, so put this pop filter in to stop it.*

populate /'pɒpjʊleɪt/ *verb* to fill the sockets on a printed circuit board with components

pop-up menu /ˌpɒp ʌp 'menjuː/ *noun* same as **pop-down menu**

pop-up window /ˌpɒp ʌp 'wɪndəʊ/ *noun* a window that can be displayed on the screen at any time on top of anything that is already on the screen

'...you can use a mouse to access pop-up menus and a keyboard for word processing' [*Byte*]

port /pɔːt/ *noun* a socket or physical connection allowing data transfer between a computer's internal communications channel and another external device

portability /ˌpɔːtə'bɪlɪti/ *noun* an extent to which software or hardware can be used on several systems

'...although portability between machines is there in theory, in practice it just isn't that simple' [*Personal Computer World*]

portable /'pɔːtəb(ə)l/ *noun* a compact self-contained computer that can be carried around and used either with a battery pack or mains power supply ■ *adjective* referring to any hardware or software or data files that can used on a range of different computers

portable document format /ˌpɔːtəb(ə)l 'dɒkjʊmənt ˌfɔːmæt/ *noun* full form of **PDF**

portable operating system interface /ˌpɔːtəb(ə)l 'ɒpəreɪtɪŋ ˌsɪstəm ˌɪntəfeɪs/ *noun* full form of **POSIX**

portal /'pɔːt(ə)l/ *noun* a website that provides links to information and other websites

portapack /'pɔːtəpæk/ *noun* a battery-operated, portable video camera and recorder (*film*)

portrait /'pɔːtrɪt/ *adjective* the orientation of a page or piece of paper in which the longest edge is vertical

port replicator /'pɔːt ˌreplɪkeɪtə/ *noun* a version of a docking station that allows a laptop computer to be connected to duplicate the connection ports on the back of the laptop, allowing a user to keep a mouse, power cable, and printer connected to the port replicator and easily insert the laptop to use these ports without having to plug in cables each time the machine is used

POS /pɒz/ *abbr* point-of-sale

positional /pə'zɪʃ(ə)nəl/ *adjective* referring to position

positive /ˈpɒzɪtɪv/ *adjective* **1.** meaning 'yes' **2.** referring to an image that shows objects as they are seen

positive display /ˌpɒzɪtɪv dɪˈspleɪ/ *noun* a display in which the text and graphics are shown as black on a white background to imitate a printed page

positive feedback /ˌpɒzɪtɪv ˈfiːdbæk/ *noun* part of an output signal that is added into the input of a device ○ *Make sure the microphone is not too close to the loudspeaker or positive feedback will occur and you will overload the amplifier.*

positive photoresist /ˌpɒzɪtɪv ˌfəʊtəʊrɪˈzɪst/ *noun* a method of forming photographic images where exposed areas of photoresist are removed, used in making PCBs

POSIX /ˈpɒsɪks/ *noun* the IEEE standard that defines software that can be easily ported between hardware platforms. Full form **portable operating system interface**

post /pəʊst/ *verb* to enter data into a record in a file

poster /ˈpəʊstə/ *noun* a large printed sheet, used to advertise something

posterisation /ˌpəʊstəraɪzeɪʃ(ə)n/ *noun* a special effect in which an image is processed to reduce the number of colours or tones

post-filtering /ˌpəʊst ˈfɪltərɪŋ/ *noun* image processing carried out after the image has been compressed

postfix /ˈpəʊstfɪks/ *noun* a word or letter written after another

postmaster /ˈpəʊstmɑːstə/ *noun* the email address of the person nominally in charge of email within a company

post office protocol /ˈpəʊst ˌɒfɪs ˌprəʊtəkɒl/ *noun* ◊ **POP 3**

postprocessor /ˌpəʊstˈprəʊsesə/ *noun* **1.** a microprocessor that handles semi-processed data from another device **2.** a program that processes data from another program, which has already been processed

post production /ˌpəʊst prəˈdʌkʃən/ *noun* the final editing process of a video or animation in which titles are added and sequences finalised

pot /pɒt/ *abbr* potentiometer

potentiometer /pəˌtenʃiˈɒmɪtə/ *noun* a mechanical variable resistance component consisting of a spindle which is turned to move a contact across a resistance track to vary the resistance of the potentiometer. ◊ **variable resistor**

POTS /pɒts/ *noun* the simplest, standard telephone line without any special features such as call waiting or forwarding, and without high-speed digital access such as ADSL. Full form **plain old telephone service**

power /ˈpaʊə/ *noun* **1.** the unit of energy in electronics equal to the product of voltage and current, measured in watts **2.** a mathematical term describing the number of times a number is to be multiplied by itself ○ *5 to the power 2 is equal to 25.* (NOTE: written as small figures in superscript: **10^5**: say: 'ten to the power five') ■ *verb* to provide electrical or mechanical energy to a device ○ *The monitor is powered from a supply in the main PC.*

power down /ˈpaʊə daʊn/ *verb* to turn off the electricity supply to a computer or other electronic device

powered /ˈpaʊəd/ *adjective* driven by a type of energy or motor ○ *a motor powered by electricity* ○ *a solar-powered calculator*

power user /ˈpaʊə ˌjuːzə/ *noun* a user who needs the latest, fastest model of computer because he or she runs complex or demanding applications

ppm /ˌpiː piː ˈem/ *noun* the number of pages that a printer can print in one minute, used for describing the speed of a printer. Full form **pages per minute**

PPP /ˌpiː piː ˈpiː/ *noun* a protocol that supports a network link over an asynchronous (modem) connection and is normally used to provide data transfer between a user's computer and a remote server on the Internet using the TCP/IP network protocol. Full form **point to point protocol**

PPQN /ˌpiː piː kjuː ˈen/ *noun* the most common time format used with standard MIDI sequences. Full form **parts per quarter note**

PPS *noun* film or video frame speed. Full form **pictures per second**

PPTP /ˌpiː piː tiː ˈpiː/ *noun* a protocol that allows a standard local-area network protocol (such as Novell's IPX or Microsoft's NetBEUI) to be sent over the Internet in a transparent manner without the user or operating system noticing, used by companies that want to use the Internet to connect servers in different offices. Full form **point-to-point tunneling protocol**

practical extraction and report language /ˌpræktɪk(ə)l ɪkˌstrækʃ(ə)n ən rɪ ˈpɔːt ˌlæŋgwɪdʒ/ *noun* full form of **Perl** ○ *If you want to add a search engine to your website, you will need to write a Perl program.*

pre- /priː/ *prefix* before

pre-amplifier /pri ˈæmplɪˌfaɪə/ *noun* an electronic circuit which amplifies a signal to a particular level, before it is fed to an amplifier for output

precede /prɪ'siːd/ *verb* to come before something ○ *This instruction cancels the instruction which precedes it.*

precedence /'presɪd(ə)ns/ *noun* a set of computational rules defining the order in which mathematical operations are calculated

precise /prɪ'saɪs/ *adjective* very exact ○ *The atomic clock will give the precise time of starting the process.*

precision /prɪ'sɪʒ(ə)n/ *noun* the fact that something is very accurate

precompiled code /prikəm,paɪld 'kəʊd/ *noun* a code that is output from a compiler, ready to be executed

predefined /,priːdɪ'faɪnd/ *adjective* which has been defined in advance

predesigned /,priːdɪ'zaɪnd/ *adjective* (*of a graphic material*) provided to the customer already designed ○ *A wide selection of predesigned layouts help you automatically format typical business and technical documents.*

predetermined /,priːdɪ'tɜːmɪnd/ *adjective* which has already been determined

pre-edit /pri 'edɪt/ *verb* to change text before it is run through a machine to make sure it is compatible

pre-emphasise /priː 'emfəsaɪz/ *verb* to boost certain frequencies of a signal before transmission or processing to minimise noise (signals are de-emphasised on reception)

preemptive multitasking /pri,emptɪv 'mʌltitɑːskɪŋ/ *noun* a form of multitasking in which the operating system executes a program for a period of time, then passes control to the next program so preventing any one program using all the processor time

pre-fade listen /,priː feɪd 'lɪs(ə)n/ *noun* a sound desk device which permits channels to be heard before fading up (*film*)

pre-fetch /priː 'fetʃ/ *verb* CPU instructions stored in a short temporary queue before being processed, increasing the speed of execution

pre-filtering /priː'fɪltərɪŋ/ *noun* image processing before the image is compressed (e.g., scaling the image)

prefix /'priː,fɪks/ *noun* **1.** a code, instruction or character at the beginning of a message or instruction **2.** a word attached to the beginning of another word to give it a special meaning

prefix notation /'priːfɪks nəʊ,teɪʃ(ə)n/ *noun* mathematical operations written in a logical way, so that the operator appears before the operands, removing the need for brackets ○ *normal notation: (x-y) + z, but using prefix notation: – xy + z*

pre-flash, pre-fog *noun* the process of exposing film to light before filming so that it has a higher sensitivity to light and reduces contrast (*film*)

preformatted /priː'fɔːmætɪd/ *adjective* which has been formatted already ○ *a preformatted disk*

pre-imaging /pri 'ɪmɪdʒɪŋ/ *noun* the process of generating one frame of an animation or video in a memory buffer before it is transferred on screen for display

premix /'priːmɪks/ *noun* the combination of a number of signals before they have been processed in any way

preparation /,prepə'reɪʃ(ə)n/ *noun* the process of getting something ready

preprinted /priː'prɪntɪd/ *adjective* already printed or printed in advance □ **preprinted form** paper used for printing databases *or* applications programs that already contain some information printed □ **preprinted stationery** computer stationery (such as invoices) which has already been printed with the company's logo and address as well as the blank columns, etc.

preprocess /priː'prəʊses/ *verb* to carry out initial organisation and simple processing of data

preprocessor /priː'prəʊsesə/ *noun* **1.** software that partly processes or prepares data before it is compiled or translated **2.** a small computer that carries out some initial processing of raw data before passing it to the main computer

> '...the C preprocessor is in the first stage of converting a written program into machine instructions the preprocessor can be directed to read in another file before completion, perhaps because the same information is needed in each module of the program' [*Personal Computer World*]

preproduction /,priːprə'dʌkʃən/ *noun* the organisation of the filming or recording of a video or compact disk, taking the form of diagrams and scene descriptions

preprogrammed /priː'prəʊgræmd/ *adjective* referring to a chip that has been programmed in the factory to perform one function

prerecord /,priːrɪ'kɔːd/ *verb* to record something which will be played back later or to record sound effects that are added to a film at a later date ○ *The answerphone plays a prerecorded message.* ■ *noun* a section of text stored in a word-processor system which will be used as the basis for a form letter

pre-roll /'priː rəʊl/ *noun* time needed after having started a telecine, projector or video tape recorder in order to produce steady sound and picture (*film*)

prescan /ˈpriːskæn/ *noun* a feature of many flat-bed scanners that carry out a quick, low-resolution scan to allow you to re-position the original or mark the area that is to be scanned at a higher resolution

presentation graphics /ˌprez(ə)nteɪʃ(ə)n ˈgræfɪks/ *plural noun* graphics used to represent business information or data ○ *The sales for last month looked even better thanks to the use of presentation graphics.*

presentation layer /ˌprez(ə)nˈteɪʃ(ə)n ˌleɪə/ *noun* the sixth ISO/OSI standard network layer that agrees on formats, codes and requests for the start and end of a connection

Presentation Manager /ˌprez(ə)n ˈteɪʃ(ə)n ˌmænɪdʒə/ *noun* a graphical user interface supplied with the OS/2 operating system

presentation software /ˌprez(ə)nteɪʃ(ə)n ˈsɒftweə/ *noun* a software application that allows a user to create a business presentation with graphs, data, text and images

preset /ˌpriːˈset/ *verb* to set something in advance ○ *The printer was preset with new page parameters.*

press /pres/ *verb* to push a key with the fingers ○ *To end the program press ESCAPE.*

press cuttings /ˈpres ˌkʌtɪŋz/ *plural noun* pieces cut from newspapers or magazines which refer to someone or to a company

pressure pad /ˈpreʃə pæd/ *noun* a transducer that converts pressure changes into an electrical signal ○ *The pressure pad under the carpet will set off the burglar alarm if anyone steps on it.*

prestore /priːˈstɔː/ *verb* to store data in memory before it is processed

presynchronisation, presynchronization *noun* the pre-recording of dialogue which is used in synchronisation with lip movements in animation work (*film*)

pretty good privacy /ˌprɪti gʊd ˈprɪvəsi/ *noun* full form of **PGP**

prevent /prɪˈvent/ *verb* to stop something happening ○ *We have changed the passwords to prevent hackers getting into the database.*

preventative /prɪˈventətɪv/, **preventive** /prɪˈventɪv/ *adjective* which tries to stop something happening

prevention /prɪˈvenʃən/ *noun* the process of preventing something happening

preventive maintenance /prɪˌventɪv ˈmeɪntənəns/ *noun* a regular inspection and cleaning of a system to prevent faults occurring

preview /ˈpriːˌvjuː/ *verb* to display text or graphics on a screen as it will appear when it is printed out

previewer /ˈpriːvjuːə/ *noun* a feature that allows a user to see on screen what a page will look like when printed ○ *The built-in previewer allows the user to check for mistakes.*

primarily /ˈpraɪm(ə)rɪli/ *adverb* mainly

primary /ˈpraɪməri/ *adjective* first or basic or most important

prime /praɪm/ *adjective* very important ■ *noun* a number that can only be divided by itself and by one ○ *The number seven is a prime.*

primer /ˈpraɪmə/ *noun* a manual or simple instruction book with instructions and examples to show how a new program or system operates

primitive /ˈprɪmɪtɪv/ *noun* **1.** (*in programming*) a basic routine that can be used to create more complex routines **2.** (*in graphics*) a simple shape such as circle, square, line or curve used to create more complex shapes in a graphics program

print /prɪnt/ *noun* **1.** characters made in ink on paper ○ *The print from the new printer is much clearer than that from old one.* **2.** a positive photographic image in which black is black and white is white. Compare **negative** **3.** an image produced using an etched printing plate ○ *He collects 18th-century prints.* ○ *The office is decorated with Japanese prints.* **4.** a take to be used in the finished film if it is not cut out during the editing process ■ *verb* **1.** to put letters or figures in ink on paper **2.** to put letters or illustrations onto sheets of paper so that they form a book ○ *The book was printed in Hong Kong.* ○ *The book is printing at the moment, so we will have bound copies at the end of the month.* **3.** to write in capital letters ○ *Please print your name and address on the top of the form.*

printed circuit /ˌprɪntɪd ˈsɜːkɪt/, **printed circuit board** *noun* a flat insulating material that has conducting tracks of metal printed or etched onto its surface which complete a circuit when components are mounted on it. Abbr **PCB**

printer /ˈprɪntə/ *noun* **1.** a device that converts input data in an electrical form into a printed readable form. Abbr **PRN** **2.** a person that prints documents or pictures for private customers or other businesses **3.** a company which prints books or newspapers ○ *The book will be sent to the printer next week.* ○ *We are using Japanese printers for some of our magazines.*

printer quality /ˈprɪntə ˌkwɒlɪti/ *noun* the standard of printed text from a particular printer

print format /ˈprɪnt ˌfɔːmæt/ *noun* a way in which text is arranged when printed out, according to embedded codes, used to set features such as margins and headers

printhead /ˈprɪnthed/ *noun* **1.** a row of needles in a dot-matrix printer that produce characters as a series of dots **2.** the metal form of a character that is pressed onto an inked ribbon to print the character on paper

printing /ˈprɪntɪŋ/ *noun* **1.** the action of putting text and graphics onto paper **2.** the number of copies printed at one time ○ *The first printing was 50,000 copies.*

printing negative /ˌprɪntɪŋ ˈnegətɪv/ *noun* a negative copy of an optical sound track on a positive picture print which is used to improve the quality of sound (*film*)

Print Manager /ˈprɪnt ˌmænɪdʒə/ a software utility that is part of Microsoft Windows and is used to manage print queues

printout /ˈprɪntˌaʊt/ *noun* the final printed page

print preview /ˌprɪnt ˈpriːvjuː/ *noun* a function of a software product that lets the user see how a page will appear when printed

print quality /ˈprɪnt ˌkwɒlɪti/ *noun* the quality of the text or graphics printed, normally measured in dots per inch ○ *A desktop printer with a resolution of 600 dpi provides good print quality.*

printrun /ˈprɪntrʌn/ *noun* the number of copies of a book which are printed at one time

Print Screen key /ˌprɪnt ˈskriːn ˌkiː/ *noun* a key in the top right-hand side of the keyboard that sends the characters that are displayed on the screen to the printer

print server /ˈprɪnt ˌsɜːvə/ *noun* a computer in a network which is dedicated to managing print queues and printers

print shop /ˈprɪnt ʃɒp/ *noun* a shop where jobbing printing takes place

printwheel /ˈprɪntwiːl/ *noun* a daisy-wheel or the wheel made up of a number of arms, with a character shape at the end of each arm, used in a daisy-wheel printer

priority /praɪˈɒrɪti/ *noun* the importance of a device or software routine in a computer system ○ *The operating system has priority over the application when disk space is allocated.*

privacy /ˈprɪvəsi/ *noun* the right of an individual to limit the extent of and control the access to the data that is stored about him

privacy of data /ˌprɪvəsi əv ˈdeɪtə/ *noun* the fact that particular data is secret and must not be accessed by users who have not been authorised

privacy of information /ˌprɪvəsi əv ˌɪnfəˈmeɪʃ(ə)n/ *noun* the fact that unauthorised users must not obtain data about private individuals from databases, or that each individual has the right to know what information is being held about him or her on a database

privacy statement /ˈprɪvəsi ˌsteɪtmənt/ *noun* the policy of a company, published on their website, that explains to visitors and customers what the company will or will not do with a customer's personal details

private /ˈpraɪvət/ *adjective* belonging to an individual or to a company, not to the public

private key cryptography /ˌpraɪvət kiː krɪpˈtɒgrəgi/ *noun* a method of encrypting Internet messages that uses a single key both to encode and decode them

privilege /ˈprɪvɪlɪdʒ/ *noun* the status of a user as regards to the type of program he or she can run and the resources he or she can use

privileged account /ˌprɪvəlɪdʒd ə ˈkaʊnt/ *noun* a computer account that allows special programs or access to sensitive system data

PRN /ˌpiː ɑː ˈen/ *noun* an acronym used in MS-DOS to represent the standard printer port. Full form **printer**

problem /ˈprɒbləm/ *noun* a question to which it is difficult to find an answer

problem definition /ˈprɒbləm ˌdefənɪʃ(ə)n/ *noun* the clear explanation, in logical steps, of a problem that is to be solved

problem diagnosis /ˈprɒbləm ˌdaɪəgnəʊsɪs/ *noun* the process of finding the cause of a fault or error and finding the method of repairing it

problem-orientated language /ˌprɒbləm ˌɔːriənteɪtɪd ˈlæŋgwɪdʒ/ *noun* a high-level programming language that allows certain problems to be expressed easily. Abbr **POL**

procedural /prəˈsiːdʒərəl/ *adjective* using a procedure to solve a problem

procedure /prəˈsiːdʒə/ *noun* **1.** a small section of computer instruction code that provides a frequently used function and can be called upon from a main program ○ *This procedure sorts all the files into alphabetical order.* ◊ **subroutine 2.** a method or route used when solving a problem ○ *You should use this procedure to retrieve lost files.*

proceed /prəˈsiːd/ *verb* to move forward ○ *After spellchecking the text, you can proceed to the printing stage.*

process /prəʊˈses/ *noun* a number of tasks that must be carried out to achieve a goal ○

The process of setting up the computer takes a long time. ■ *verb* to carry out a number of tasks to produce a result ○ *We processed the new data.*

process control /ˈprəʊses kənˌtrəʊl/ *noun* the automatic control of a process by a computer

processing /ˈprəʊsesɪŋ/ *noun* **1.** the use of a computer to solve a problem or organise data ○ *Page processing time depends on the complexity of a given page.* ◊ **CPU 2.** the treatment of exposed film with chemicals in order to make the latent image everlastingly visible

processor /ˈprəʊˌsesə/ *noun* a hardware or software device that is able to manipulate or modify data according to instructions

produce /prəˈdjuːs/ *verb* to make or manufacture something

producer /prəˈdjuːsə/ *noun* a person, company or country that manufactures ○ *Country which is a producer of high quality computer equipment.*

product /ˈprɒdʌkt/ *noun* **1.** an item that is made or manufactured **2.** a manufactured item for sale **3.** the result after multiplication

product design /ˈprɒdʌkt dɪˌzaɪn/ *noun* the activity of designing products

product engineer /ˌprɒdʌkt ˌendʒɪˈnɪə/ *noun* an engineer in charge of the equipment for making a product

production /prəˈdʌkʃən/ *noun* **1.** the process of making or manufacturing of goods for sale ○ *Production will probably be held up by industrial action.* **2.** the preparation for broadcast of a programme or advertisement **3.** the complete process of making a film (*film*)

production control /prəˈdʌkʃən kən ˌtrəʊl/ *noun* the control of the manufacturing of a product (using computers)

production level video /prəˌdʌkʃən ˌlev(ə)l ˈvɪdiəʊ/ *noun* full form of **PLV**

production standards /prəˈdʌkʃən ˌstændədz/ *plural noun* the quality of production

product line /ˈprɒdʌkt laɪn/, **product range** /ˈprɒdʌkt reɪndʒ/ *noun* a series of different products made by the same company, which form a group

product range /ˈprɒdʌkt reɪndʒ/ *noun* same as **product line**

professional publishing /prə ˌfeʃ(ə)n(ə)l ˈpʌblɪʃɪŋ/ *noun* publishing books on law, accountancy, and other professions

program /ˈprəʊɡræm/ *noun* **1.** a complete set of instructions which direct a computer to carry out a particular task **2.** data that defines a sound in a synthesiser; a program is also called a patch and can be altered by issuing a program-change message ■ *verb* to write or prepare a set of instructions that direct a computer to perform a certain task

program crash /ˈprəʊɡræm kræʃ/ *noun* an unexpected failure of a program owing to a programming error or a hardware fault ○ *I forgot to insert an important instruction which caused a program to crash, erasing all the files on the disk!*

program design language /ˌprəʊɡræm dɪˈzaɪn ˌlæŋɡwɪdʒ/ *noun* a programming language used to design the structure of a program. Abbr **PDL**

program documentation /ˌprəʊɡræm ˌdɒkjʊmenˈteɪʃ(ə)n/ *noun* a set of instruction notes, examples and tips on how to use a program

program evaluation and review technique /ˌprəʊɡræm ɪˌvæljueɪʃ(ə)n ən rɪˈvjuː tekˌniːk/ *noun* full form of **PERT**

program icon /ˈprəʊɡræm ˌaɪkɒn/ *noun* (*in a GUI*) an icon that represents an executable program file ○ *To run the program, double-click on the program icon.*

program information file /ˌprəʊɡræm ˌɪnfəˈmeɪʃ(ə)n ˌfaɪl/ *noun* full form of **PIF**

programmable /ˈprəʊɡræməb(ə)l/ *adjective* referring to a device that can accept and store instructions then execute them

programmable key /ˌprəʊɡræməb(ə)l ˈkiː/ *noun* a special key on a computer terminal keyboard that can be programmed with various functions or characters

programmable logic array /ˌprəʊɡræməb(ə)l ˌlɒdʒɪk əˈreɪ/ *noun* full form of **PLA**

programmable logic device /ˌprəʊɡræməb(ə)l ˈlɒdʒɪk dɪˌvaɪs/ *noun* full form of **PLD**

programmable memory /ˌprəʊɡræməb(ə)l ˈmem(ə)ri/ *noun* full form of **PROM**

programmable read only memory /ˌprəʊɡræməb(ə)l riːd ˌəʊnli ˈmem(ə)ri/ *noun* full form of **PROM**

Program Manager /ˌprəʊɡræm ˈmænɪdʒə/ *noun* (*in Windows 3.x*) the main part of Windows that the user sees

programmer /ˈprəʊˌɡræmə/ *noun* **1.** a person who is capable of designing and writing a working program ○ *The programmer is still working on the new software.* **2.** a device that allows data to be written into a programmable read only memory

programmer's hierarchical interactive graphics standard /ˌprəʊɡræməz haɪəˌrɑːkɪk(ə)l ɪntərˌæktɪv ˈɡræfɪks ˌstændəd/ *noun* full form of **PHIGS**

programming /ˈprəʊɡræmɪŋ/ *noun* the activity of writing programs for computers

COMMENT: Programming languages are grouped into different levels: the high-level languages such as BASIC and PASCAL are easy to understand and use, but offer slow execution time since each instruction is made up of a number of machine code instructions; low-level languages such as assembler are more complex to read and program in but offer faster execution time.

programming in logic /ˌprəʊɡræmɪŋ ɪn ˈlɒdʒɪk/ *noun* full form of **PROLOG**

programming language for microprocessors /ˌprəʊɡræmɪŋ ˌlæŋɡwɪdʒ fə ˈmaɪkrəɪˌprəʊsesəz/ *noun* full form of **PL/M**

program specification /ˌprəʊɡræm ˌspesɪfɪˈkeɪʃ(ə)n/ *noun* detailed information about a program's abilities, features and methods

program testing /ˈprəʊɡræm ˌtestɪŋ/ *noun* the process of testing a new program with test data to ensure that it functions correctly

progressive scanning /prəʊˌɡresɪv ˈskænɪŋ/ *noun* a method of displaying and transmitting video images in which each line of the image is displayed consecutively, unlike non-interlaced image, which shows alternate lines. ◊ **scan conversion**

project *noun* /ˈprɒdʒekt/ a planned task ○ *His latest project is computerising the sales team.* ■ *verb* /prəˈdʒekt/ to forecast future figures from a set of data ○ *The projected sales of the new PC.*

projection /prəˈdʒekʃən/ *noun* **1.** the forecasting of a situation from a set of data ○ *The projection indicates that sales will increase.* **2.** the process of showing pictures on a screen

projector leader /prəˈdʒektə ˌliːdə/ *noun* a short part of the beginning of a reel of film which allows projectionists to make fast changeovers from one reel to the next when projecting a film

PROLOG /ˈprəʊlɒɡ/ *noun* a high-level programming language using logical operations for artificial intelligence and data retrieval applications. Full form **programming in logic**

PROM /prɒm/ *noun* **1.** read only memory that can be programmed by the user, as distinct from ROM, which is programmed by the manufacturer. Full form **programmable read only memory** **2.** an electronic device in which data can be stored. Full form **programmable memory**

prompt /prɒmpt/ *noun* a message or character displayed to remind the user that an input is expected ○ *The prompt READY indicates that the system is available to receive instructions.*

prompter /ˈprɒmptə/ *noun* the person on a set who gives cues to performers during action filming (*film*) ◊ **cue**

proof /pruːf/ *noun* printed matter from a printer that has to be checked and corrected ■ *verb* to produce proofs of a text

proofer /ˈpruːfə/ *noun* a printer which produces proofs, as opposed to finished printed pages ○ *output devices such as laser proofers and typesetters*

proofing /ˈpruːfɪŋ/ *noun* the process of producing proofs of text which have to be read and corrected

proofread /ˈpruːfriːd/ *verb* to correct spelling and printing errors in a printed text ○ *Has all the text been proofread yet?*

proofreader /ˈpruːfriːdə/ *noun* a person who reads and corrects proofs

propagate /ˈprɒpəˌɡeɪt/ *verb* to travel or spread

propagation delay /ˌprɒpəˈɡeɪʃ(ə)n dɪ ˌleɪ/ *noun* **1.** the time taken for an output to appear in a logic gate after the input is applied **2.** the time taken for a data bit to travel over a network from the source to the destination

properties /ˈprɒpətiz/ *noun* (*in Windows*) the attributes of a file or object

proportionally spaced /prəˌpɔːʃ(ə)nəli ˈspeɪst/ *adjective* referring to a font in which each letter takes a space proportional to the character width. Compare **monospaced**

proprietary file format /prəˌpraɪət(ə)ri ˈfaɪl ˌfɔːmæt/ *noun* a method of storing data devised by a company for its products and incompatible with other products ○ *You cannot read this spreadsheet file because my software saves it in a proprietary file format.*

protect /prəˈtekt/ *verb* to stop something being damaged

protection /prəˈtekʃən/ *noun* the action of protecting something

protective /prəˈtektɪv/ *adjective* designed to protect something ○ *The disks are housed in hard protective cases.*

protocol /ˈprəʊtəkɒl/ *noun* the pre-agreed signals, codes and rules to be used for data exchange between systems

prototype /ˈprəʊtəˌtaɪp/ *noun* the first working model of a device or program, which is then tested and adapted to improve it

prototyping /ˈprəʊtətaɪpɪŋ/ *noun* the process of making a prototype

proxar /ˈprɒksɑː/ *noun* an additional lens which is used in close-up shots to shorten the focal length (*film*)

proxy server /ˌprɒksi ˈsɜːvə/ *noun* a computer that stores copies of files and data normally held on a slow server and so allows users to access files and data quickly. Proxy servers are often used as a firewall between an intranet in a company and the public Internet.

PrtSc /ˌprɪnt ˈskriːn/ *noun* (*on an IBM PC keyboard*) a key that sends the contents of the current screen to the printer. Full form **print screen**

pS /ˌpiː ˈes/ *abbr* picosecond

PSA *noun US* an advertisement for a public service or charity, which is shown on TV, but for which the TV company is not paid. Full form **public service announcement**

pseudo- /sjuːdəʊ/ *prefix* similar to something, but not genuine

pseudo-code /ˈsjuːdəʊ kəʊd/ *noun* English sentence structures, used to describe program instructions that are translated at a later date into machine code

pseudo-digital /ˌsjuːdəʊ ˈdɪdʒɪt(ə)l/ *adjective* referring to modulated analog signals that are produced by a modem and transmitted over telephone lines

pseudo-operation /ˌsjuːdəʊ ˌɒpəˈreɪʃ(ə)n/ *noun* a command in an assembler program that controls the assembler rather than producing machine code

pseudo-random /ˌsjuːdəʊ ˈrændəm/ *noun* a generated sequence that appears random but is repeated over a long period

psophometer /sɒˈfɒmɪtə/ *noun* a meter which measures noise

PSS *abbr* packet switching service

PSTN *abbr* public switched telephone network

PSU /ˌpiː es ˈjuː/ *noun* an electrical circuit that provides certain direct current voltage and current levels from an alternating current source to other electrical circuits. Full form **power supply unit**

> COMMENT: A PSU will regulate, smooth and step down a higher voltage supply for use in small electronic equipment.

public /ˈpʌblɪk/ *adjective* available for anyone to use

publication /ˌpʌblɪˈkeɪʃ(ə)n/ *noun* **1.** the process of making something public ○ *the publication of the report on data protection* ○ *The publication date of the book is November 15th.* **2.** a printed book or leaflet, etc. which is sold to the public or which is given away ○ *Government publications can be bought at special shops.* ○ *The company specialises in publications for the business reader.*

public data network /ˌpʌblɪk ˌdeɪtə ˈnetwɜːk/ *noun* a data transmission service for the public, e.g. the main telephone system in a country. Abbr **PDN**

public domain /ˌpʌblɪk dəʊˈmeɪn/ *noun* the status of documents, text or programs that are not protected by copyright and can be copied by anyone

publicise /ˈpʌblɪsaɪz/, **publicize** *verb* to attract people's attention to a product or service ○ *They are publicising their low prices for computer stationery.* ○ *The new PC has been publicised in the press.*

publicity /pʌˈblɪsɪti/ *noun* the process of attracting the attention of the public to products or services by mentioning them in the media or by advertising them

publicity bureau /pʌˈblɪsɪti ˌbjʊərəʊ/ *noun* an office which organises publicity for companies

publicity campaign /pʌˈblɪsɪti kæmˌpeɪn/ *noun* a period when planned publicity takes place

publicity department /pʌˈblɪsɪti dɪˌpɑːtmənt/ *noun* a department in a company which organises the publicity for the company's products

publicity matter /pʌˈblɪsɪti ˌmætə/ *noun* leaflets or posters, etc., which publicise a product or service

public key cipher system /ˌpʌblɪk kiː ˈsaɪfə ˌsɪstəm/ *noun* a cipher that uses a public key to encrypt messages and a secret key to decrypt them. Conventional cipher systems use one secret key to encrypt and decrypt messages.

public key encryption /ˌpʌblɪk kiː ɪnˈkrɪpʃ(ə)n/ *noun* a method of encrypting data that uses one key to encrypt the data and another different key to decrypt the data

publish /ˈpʌblɪʃ/ *verb* **1.** to produce and sell software **2.** to design, edit and print a text (such as a book or newspaper or catalogue) and sell or give it to the public ○ *The institute has published a list of sales figures for different home computers.* ○ *The company specialises in publishing reference books.* **3.** to share a local resource with other users on a network (such as a file or folder)

publisher /ˈpʌblɪʃə/ *noun* a company which prints books or newspapers and sells or gives them to the public

publishing /ˈpʌblɪʃɪŋ/ *noun* the business of printing books or newspapers and selling them or giving them to the public

> '...desktop publishing or the ability to produce high-quality publications using a minicomputer, essentially boils down to combining words and images on pages' [*Byte*]

pull-down /ˈpʊl daʊn/ *verb* moving film frame to frame in a camera or projector by means of a claw (*film*)

pull-down menu /ˈpʊl daʊn ˌmenjuː/ *noun* a set of options that are displayed below the relevant entry on a menu-bar ○ *The pull-down menu is viewed by clicking on the menu bar at the top of the screen.* Compare **pop-down menu**

pull-up /ˈpʊl ʌp/ *noun* a loop of film used to keep the film flowing steadily through the picture gate over the sound head

pulse /pʌls/ *noun* a short period of a voltage level ■ *verb* to apply a short-duration voltage level to a circuit ○ *We pulsed the input but it still would not work.*

COMMENT: Electric pulse can be used to transmit information, as the binary digits 0 and 1 correspond to 'no pulse' and 'pulse' (the voltage level used to distinguish the binary digits 0 and 1, is often zero and 5 or 12 volts, with the pulse width depending on transmission rate).

pulse-code modulation /ˌpʌls kəʊd ˌmɒdjʊˈleɪʃ(ə)n/ *noun* full form of **PCM**

pulse-dialling /ˈpʌls ˌdaɪəlɪŋ/ *noun* telephone dialling that dials a telephone number by sending a series of pulses along the line ○ *Pulse-dialling takes longer to dial than the newer tone-dialling system.*

punch /pʌntʃ/ *noun* **1.** a device for making holes in punched cards **2.** a mechanism which punches a cue mark in a film leader to show when printing or editorial synchronisation should start **3.** a mechanism which eliminates the splicing noises in prints which are made from an optical sound negative ■ *verb* to make a hole in something

punch-down block /ˌpʌntʃ daʊn ˈblɒk/ *noun* a device used in a local area network to connect UTP cable

punctuation mark /ˌpʌŋktʃuˈeɪʃ(ə)n mɑːk/ *noun* a printing symbol such as a comma or full stop, used for making the meaning of text clear

purge /pɜːdʒ/ *verb* to remove unnecessary or out-of-date data from a file or disk ○ *Each month, I purge the disk of all the old email messages.*

push /pʊʃ/ *verb* to press something or to move something by pressing on it

pushbutton /ˈpʊʃbʌt(ə)n/ *adjective* which works by pressing on a button

push technology /ˈpʊʃ tekˌnɒlədʒi/ *noun* Internet technology that allows subscribers to receive customised information directly

PWM *abbr* pulse width modulation

Q

QAM *abbr* quadrature amplitude modulation

QBE /ˌkjuː biː ˈiː/ *noun* a simple language used to retrieve information from a database management system by, normally, entering a query with known values, which is then matched with the database and used to retrieve the correct data ○ *In most QBE databases, the query form looks like the record format in the database – retrieving data is as easy as filling in a form.* Full form **query by example**

Q Channel /ˈkjuː ˌtʃæn(ə)l/ *noun* (*in a CD audio disc*) one of the eight information channels that holds data identifying the track and the absolute playing time

QL *abbr* query language

qty *abbr* quantity

quad /kwɒd/ *adjective* operating at four times the standard speed, or processing four times the standard amount of data ■ *noun* **1.** a sheet of paper four times as large as a basic sheet **2.** same as **quadruplex**

quadding /ˈkwɒdɪŋ/ *noun* the insertion of spaces into text to fill out a line

quadr- /kwɒdr/ *prefix* four

quadraphony /kwɒˈdrɒfəni/ *noun* a four-channel system of sound (*film*)

quadrature /ˈkwɒdtrətʃə/ *noun* a video playback error due to the heads being wrongly aligned to the edge of the tape

quadrature amplitude modulation /ˌkwɒdtrətʃə ˈæmplɪtjuːd mɒdjuˌleɪʃ(ə)n/ *noun* a data encoding method used by high-speed modems (transmitting at rates above 2,400bps). It combines amplitude modulation and phase modulation to increase the data transmission rate. Abbr **QAM**

quadrature encoding /ˈkwɒdtrətʃə ɪnˌkəʊdɪŋ/ *noun* a system used to determine the direction in which a mouse is being moved. In a mechanical mouse, two sensors send signals that describe its horizontal and vertical movements, these signals being transmitted using quadrature encoding.

quadrophonic /ˌkwɒdrəˈfɒnɪk/ *adjective* (*of an audio music system*) using four speakers

quadruplex /ˈkwɒdrʊpleks/ *noun* **1.** a set of four signals combined into a single one **2.** a four unit video tape recorder which produces video information in continuous almost vertical stripes

quadruplicate /kwɒˈdruːplɪkət/ *noun* ○ *The statements are printed in quadruplicate.* □ **in quadruplicate** with the original and three copies ○ *the statements are printed in quadruplicate* (NOTE: no plural)

quad-speed drive /ˌkwɒd spiːd ˈdraɪv/ *noun* a CD-ROM drive that spins the disc at four times the speed of a single-speed drive, providing higher data throughput of 600Kbps and shorter seek times

quality control /ˈkwɒlɪti kənˌtrəʊl/ *noun* the process of checking that the quality of a product is good

quality of service /ˌkwɒlɪti əv ˈsɜːvɪs/ *noun* the degree to which a network can transfer information without error or fault

Quantel /ˈkwɒntel/ the hardware graphics company that developed Paintbox and Harry production graphics systems

quantifiable /ˈkwɒntɪfaɪəb(ə)l/ *adjective* which can be quantified ○ *The effect of the change in the pricing structure is not quantifiable.*

quantifier /ˈkwɒntɪˌfaɪə/ *noun* a sign or symbol that indicates the quantity or range of a predicate

quantisation, quantization *noun* the conversion of an analog signal to a numerical representation

quantise, quantize *verb* **1.** to convert an analog signal into a numerical representation ○ *The input signal is quantised by an analog to digital converter.* **2.** to process a MIDI file and align all the notes to a regular beat, so removing any timing errors ○ *An analog to digital converter quantises the input signal.*

quantiser, quantizer *noun* a device used to convert an analog input signal to a numerical form, that can be processed by a computer

quantity /ˈkwɒntɪti/ *noun* the amount or number of items ○ *A small quantity of illegal copies of the program have been imported.* ■ *adjective* in large amounts ○ *The company offers a discount for quantity purchases.*

quantum /ˈkwɒntəm/ *noun* (*in communications*) a packet of data that is the result of a signal being quantised

quarter-inch tape /ˌkwɔːtər ɪntʃ ˈteɪp/ *noun* a standard diameter of magnetic tape which is used in tape cartridges and reel-to-reel recorders (*film*)

quartile /ˈkwɔːtaɪl/ *noun* one of three figures below which 25%, 50% or 75% of a total falls

quarto /ˈkwɔːtəʊ/ *noun* a paper size, made when a sheet is folded twice to make eight pages

quasi- /kweɪzaɪ/ *prefix* almost, or similar to

quaternary /ˈkwɔːtɜːnəri/ *adjective* existing as four bits, levels or objects

query /ˈkwɪəri/ *noun* a question ■ *verb* to ask a question about something or to suggest that something may be wrong

query by example /ˌkwɪəri baɪ ɪgˈzɑːmpəl/ *noun* full form of **QBE**

query facility /ˈkwɪəri fəˌsɪlɪti/ *noun* a program, usually a database or retrieval system, that allows the user to ask questions and receive answers or access certain information according to the query

query language /ˈkwɪəri ˌlæŋgwɪdʒ/ *noun* a language in a database management system that allows a database to be searched and queried easily. Abbr **QL**

question /ˈkwestʃ(ə)n/ *noun* **1.** words which need an answer ○ *The managing director refused to answer questions about faulty keyboards.* ○ *The market research team prepared a series of questions to test the public's reactions to colour and price.* **2.** a problem ○ *He raised the question of moving to less expensive offices.* ○ *The main question is that of cost.* ○ *The board discussed the question of launching a new business computer.* ■ *verb* **1.** to ask questions ○ *The police questioned the accounts staff for four hours* ○ *she questioned the chairman on the company's sales in the Far East.* **2.** to query or to suggest that something may be wrong ○ *We all question how accurate the computer printout is.*

question mark /ˈkweʃtʃən mɑːk/ *noun* the character (?) that is often used as a wildcard to indicate that any single character in the position will produce a match ○ *To find all the letters, use the command DIR LETTER?DOC which will list LETTER1.DOC, LETTER2.DOC and LETTER3.DOC.* ◊ **asterisk**

questionnaire /ˌkwestʃəˈneə/ *noun* a printed list of questions, especially used in market research ○ *to send out a questionnaire to test the opinions of users of the system* ○ *to answer* or *to fill in a questionnaire about holidays abroad*

queue /kjuː/ *noun* **1.** a line of people waiting one behind the other ○ *to form a queue* or *to join a queue* **2.** a list of data or tasks that are waiting to be processed, or a series of documents that are dealt with in order ■ *verb* to add more data or tasks to the end of a queue

quick /kwɪk/ *adjective* operating at high speed, or taking little time ○ *The company made a quick recovery.*

QuickDraw /ˈkwɪkdrɔː/ (*in an Apple Macintosh*) a trade name for the graphics routines built into the Macintosh's operating system that control displayed text and images

quickly /ˈkwɪkli/ *adverb* without taking much time

quicksort /ˈkwɪksɔːt/ *noun* a very rapid file sorting and ordering method

QuickTime /ˈkwɪktaɪm/ (*in an Apple Macintosh*) a trade name for the graphics routines built into the Macintosh's operating system that allow windows, boxes and graphic objects, including animation and video files, to be displayed

quit /kwɪt/ *verb* to leave a system or a program ○ *Do not forget to save your text before you quit the system.*

quonking /ˈkwɒnkɪŋ/ *noun* undesired sounds which are picked up by a microphone (*film*)

quotation /kwəʊˈteɪʃ(ə)n/ *noun* part of a text borrowed from another text

quotation marks /kwəʊˈteɪʃ(ə)n mɑːks/ *noun* punctuation marks used for enclosing text to show that it has been quoted from another source

quote /kwəʊt/ *verb* to repeat words used by someone else

quotient /ˈkwəʊʃ(ə)nt/ *noun* the result of one number divided by another

COMMENT: When two numbers are divided, the answer is made up of a quotient and a remainder (the fractional part). 16 divided by 4 is equal to a quotient of 4 and zero remainder; 16 divided by 5 is equal to a quotient of 3 and a remainder of 1.

quoting /ˈkwəʊtɪŋ/ *noun* a feature of many electronic mail applications that allows you to reply to a message and include the text of the original message

QWERTY keyboard /ˌkwɜːti ˈkiːbɔːd/ *noun* a standard English language key layout. The first six letters on the top left row of keys are QWERTY.

R

rack /ræk/ *noun* **1.** a metal supporting frame for electronic circuit boards and peripheral devices such as disk drives **2.** a frame to hold items for display ○ *a display rack* ○ *a rack for holding mag tapes*

racking /ˈrækɪŋ/ *noun* ♦ **framing**

rack mounted /ˈræk ˌmaʊntɪd/ *adjective* referring to a system consisting of removable circuit boards in a supporting frame

radar /ˈreɪdɑː/ *noun* a method of finding the position of objects such as aircraft, by transmitting radio waves which are reflected back if they hit an object and are displayed on a screen

radial transfer /ˌreɪdiəl ˈtrænsfɜː/ *noun* data transfer between two peripherals or programs that are on different layers of a structured system (such as an ISO/OSI system)

radiant /ˈreɪdiənt/ *adjective* which radiates

radiant energy /ˌreɪdiənt ˈenədʒi/ *noun* the amount of energy radiated by an aerial

radiate /ˈreɪdieɪt/ *verb* **1.** to go out in all directions from a central point **2.** to send out rays **3.** to convert electrical signals into travelling electromagnetic waves

radiating element /ˌreɪdieɪtɪŋ ˈelɪmənt/ *noun* a single basic unit of an antenna that radiates signals

radiation /ˌreɪdiˈeɪʃ(ə)n/ *noun* **1.** the sending out of waves of energy from certain substances **2.** the conversion of electrical signals in an antenna into travelling electromagnetic waves

radiator /ˈreɪdieɪtə/ *noun* the single basic unit of an antenna or any device that radiates signals

radio /ˈreɪdiəʊ/ *noun* a medium used for the transmission of speech, sound and data over long distances by radio frequency electromagnetic waves

radio button /ˈreɪdiəʊ ˌbʌt(ə)n/ *noun* (*in a GUI*) a circle displayed beside an option that, when selected, has a dark centre. Only one radio button can be selected at one time.

radiocommunications /ˌreɪdiəʊkəˌmjuːnɪˈkeɪʃ(ə)nz/ *noun* the transmission and reception of sound and data by radio waves

radio frequency /ˈreɪdiəʊ ˌfriːkwənsi/ *noun* full form of **RF**

radix /ˈreɪdɪks/ *noun* the value of the base of the number system being used ○ *The hexadecimal number has a radix of 16.*

ragged /ˈrægɪd/ *adjective* not straight, or with an uneven edge

RAID /reɪd/ *noun* a fast, fault tolerant disk drive system that uses multiple drives which would, typically, each store one byte of a word of data, so allowing the data to be saved faster. Full form **redundant array of inexpensive disks**

> 'A Japanese investor group led by system distributor Technography has pumped $4.2 million (#2.8 million) into US disk manufacturer Storage Computer to help with the development costs of RAID 7 hard disk technology.' [*Computing*]

RAM /ræm/ *noun* memory that allows access to any location in any order, without having to access the rest first. Full form **random access memory**. Compare **sequential access**

> 'The HP Enterprise Desktops have hard-disk capacities of between 260Mb and 1Gb, with RAM ranging from 16Mb up to 128Mb.' [*Computing*]
>
> '...fast memory is RAM that does not have to share bus access with the chip that manages the video display' [*Byte*]

COMMENT: Dynamic RAM, which uses a capacitor to store a bit of data, needs to have each location refreshed from time to time to retain the data, but is very fast and can contain more data per unit area than static RAM, which uses a latch to store the state of a bit. Static RAM, however, has the advantage of not requiring to be refreshed to retain its data, and will keep data for as long as power is supplied.

ramcorder /ˈræmkɔːdə/ *noun* a digital video recorder which stores images as digital data in RAM rather than on film

RAMDAC /ˈræmdæk/ *noun* an electronic component on a video graphics adapter that converts the digital colour signals into electrical signals that are sent to the monitor

R & D *noun* investigation of new products, discoveries and techniques. Full form **research and development**

R & D department /ˌɑːr ən ˈdiː dɪˌpɑːtmənt/ *noun* a department in a company that investigates new products, discoveries and techniques

random /ˈrændəm/ *adjective* not arranged or happening according to a particular order or pattern

random access /ˌrændəm ˈækses/ *noun* the ability to access immediately memory locations in any order ○ *Disk drives are random access, whereas magnetic tape is sequential access memory.*

random access digital to analog converter /ˌrændəm ˌækses ˌdɪdʒɪt(ə)l tə ˌænəlɒg kənˈvɜːtə/ *noun* an electronic component on a video graphics adapter that converts the digital colour signals into electrical signals that are sent to the monitor. Abbr **RAMDAC**

random access memory /ˌrændəm ˈækses ˌmem(ə)ri/ *noun* full form of **RAM**

range /reɪndʒ/ *noun* **1.** a series of items from which the customer can choose ○ *a wide range of products* **2.** a set of allowed values between a maximum and minimum ■ *verb* **1.** to vary or to be different ○ *The company's products range from a cheap laptop micro to a multistation mainframe.* **2.** to put text in order to one side

rank /ræŋk/ *verb* to sort data into an order, usually according to size or importance

raster /ˈræstə/ *noun* a system of scanning the whole of a CRT screen with a picture beam by sweeping across it horizontally, moving down one pixel or line at a time

raster graphics /ˈræstə ˌgræfɪks/ *plural noun* graphics in which the picture is built up in lines across the screen or page

raster image processor /ˌræstə ˈɪmɪdʒ ˌprəʊsesə/ *noun* raster which translates software instructions into an image or complete page which is then printed by the printer ○ *An electronic page can be converted to a printer-readable video image by an on-board raster image processor.* Abbr **RIP**

raster scan /ˈræstə skæn/ *noun* one sweep of the picture beam horizontally across the front of a CRT screen

rate /reɪt/ *noun* the quantity of data or tasks that can be processed in a set time ○ *The processor's instruction execution rate is better than the older version.* ■ *verb* to evaluate how good something is or how large something is

ratings /ˈreɪtɪŋz/ *noun* a calculation of how many people are watching a TV programme

ratings battle, ratings war *noun* a fight between two TV companies to increase their share of the market

ratio /ˈreɪʃiəʊ/ *noun* the proportion of one number to another ○ *The ratio of 10 to 5 is 2:1.*

rational number /ˌræʃ(ə)nəl ˈnʌmbə/ *noun* a number that can be written as the ratio of two whole numbers ○ *24 over 7 is a rational number.*

raw /rɔː/ *adjective* in the original state or not processed

raw data /ˌrɔː ˈdeɪtə/ *noun* pieces of information which have not been input into a computer system

ray /reɪ/ *noun* one line of light or radiation in a beam or from a source ○ *The rays of light pass down the optical fibre.*

ray tracing /reɪ ˈtreɪsɪŋ/ *noun* (*in graphics*) a method of creating life-like computer-generated graphics which correctly show shadows and highlights on an object to suggest the existence of a light source ○ *To generate this picture with ray tracing will take several hours on this powerful PC.*

RCA connector /ˌɑː siː ˈeɪ kəˌnektə/ *noun* same as **phono connector**

RD /ˌɑː ˈdiː/ *noun* (*in DOS*) a command to remove an empty subdirectory. Full form **remove directory**

RDBMS *abbr* relational database management system

reaction /riˈækʃən/ *noun* an action which takes place because of something which has happened earlier

reaction time /riˈækʃən taɪm/ *noun* same as **access time**

read /riːd/ *verb* **1.** to look at printed words and understand them ○ *Conditions of sale are printed in such small characters that they are difficult to read.* **2.** to retrieve data from a storage medium ○ *This instruction reads the first record of a file.*

readable /ˈriːdəb(ə)l/ *adjective* that can be read or understood by someone or by an electronic device ○ *The electronic page is converted to a printer-readable video image.*

reader /ˈriːdə/ *noun* a device that reads data stored on one medium and converts it into another form

reading /ˈriːdɪŋ/ *noun* a note taken of figures or degrees, especially of degrees on a scale

readout /ˈriːdaʊt/ *noun* a display of data ○ *The readout displayed the time.*

read/write cycle /ˌriːd ˈraɪt ˌsaɪk(ə)l/ *noun* a sequence of events used to retrieve and store data

ready /ˈredi/ *adjective* waiting and able to be used ○ *The green light indicates the system is ready for another program.*

Real /rɪəl/ a trade name for a system used to transmit sound and video over the Internet, normally used to transmit live sound, e.g. from a radio station, over the Internet. ◊ **plug-in, streaming data**

real address /ˌrɪəl əˈdres/ *noun* an absolute address that directly accesses a memory location. Compare **paged address**

RealAudio /ˌrɪəl'ɔːdiəʊ/ a trade name for a system used to transmit sound, usually live, over the Internet

realise /'rɪəlaɪz/, **realise the palette** /ˌrɪəlaɪz ðə 'pælət/ *verb* to select a particular set of colours for a 256-colour palette and use this palette when displaying an image, normally by mapping the colours in a logical palette into the system palette

real memory /ˌrɪəl 'mem(ə)ri/ *noun* the actual physical memory that can be addressed by a CPU. Compare **virtual memory**

RealNames /ˌrɪəl'neɪmz/ a system of assigning a trade name or descriptive name to a website address

real number /ˌrɪəl 'nʌmbə/ *noun* (*in computing*) a number that is represented with a fractional part, or a number represented in floating point notation

real time /'rɪəl taɪm/ *noun* the instant nature of the responses of some computer system to events, changes and other stimuli ○ *A navigation system needs to be able to process the position of a ship in real time and take suitable action before it hits a rock.*

'Quotron provides real-time quotes, news and analysis on equity securities through a network of 40,000 terminals to US brokers and investors.' [*Computing*]

'...define a real-time system as any system which is expected to interact with its environment within certain timing constraints' [*British Telecom Technology Journal*]

real-time animation /ˌrɪəl taɪm ˌænɪ'meɪʃ(ə)n/ *noun* an animation in which objects appear to move at the same speed as they would in real life. Real-time animation requires display hardware capable of displaying a sequence with tens of different images every second.

real-time authorisation /ˌrɪəl taɪm ˌɔːθəraɪ'zeɪʃ(ə)n/, **real-time authentication** /ˌrɪəl taɪm ˌɔːθentɪ'keɪʃ(ə)n/ *noun* an online system that can check the authenticity and validity of a customer's credit card within a few seconds, allowing the Internet shop to deliver goods or confirm an order immediately

real-time input /ˌrɪəl taɪm 'ɪnpʊt/ *noun* data input to a system as it happens or is required

real-time system /'rɪəl taɪm ˌsɪstəm/ *noun* a computer system that responds instantly to events, changes and other stimuli ○ *In a real-time system, as you move the joystick left, the image on the screen moves left. If there is a pause for processing it is not a true real-time system.*

real-time video /ˌrɪəl taɪm 'vɪdiəʊ/ *noun* full form of **RTV**

rear projection /ˌrɪə prə'dʒekʃən/ *noun* ♦ **back projection**

reboot /riː'buːt/ *verb* to reload an operating system during a computing session ○ *We rebooted and the files reappeared.* ◊ **boot**

recall /rɪ'kɔːl/ *noun* the process of bringing back text or files from store ■ *verb* /rɪ'kɔːl/ to bring back text or files from store for editing

receipt notification /rɪ'siːt ˌnəʊtɪfɪkeɪʃ(ə)n/ *noun* a feature of many electronic mail applications that will send an automatic message to confirm that the recipient has received the message

receive /rɪ'siːv/ *verb* to accept data from a communications link ○ *The computer received data via the telephone line.*

receive only /rɪˌsiːv 'əʊnli/ *noun* full form of **RO**

receiver /rɪ'siːvə/ *noun* an electronic device that can detect transmitted signals and present them in a suitable form

reception /rɪ'sepʃən/ *noun* the quality of a radio or TV signal received ○ *Signal reception is bad with that aerial.*

re-chargeable /riː 'tʃɑːdʒəb(ə)l/ *adjective* (*of a battery*) which can be charged again with electricity when it is flat

reciprocal link /rɪˌsɪprək(ə)l 'lɪŋk/ *noun* a link connecting two websites and working in both directions so that each site is effectively providing advertising space for the other

recode /riː'kəʊd/ *verb* to code a program which has been coded for one system, so that it will work on another

recognisable /'rekəgnaɪzəb(ə)l/, **recognizable** *adjective* which can be recognised

recognise /'rekəgˌnaɪz/, **recognize** *verb* to see something and remember that it has been seen before ○ *The scanner will recognise most character fonts.*

recognition /ˌrekəg'nɪʃ(ə)n/ *noun* **1.** being able to recognise something **2.** a process that allows something such as letters on a printed text or bars on bar codes to be recognised,

recompile /ˌriːkəm'paɪl/ *verb* to compile a source program again, usually after changes or debugging

reconfiguration /ˌriːkənfɪgə'reɪʃ(ə)n/ *noun* the process of altering the structure of data in a system

reconfigure /ˌriːkən'fɪgə/ *verb* to alter the structure of data in a system ○ *I reconfigured the field structure in the file.* ◊ **configure, set up**

reconnect /ˌriːkə'nekt/ *verb* to connect again ○ *The telephone engineers are trying to reconnect the telephone.*

record *noun* /'rekɔːd/ a set of items of related data ○ *Your record contains several fields that have been grouped together under the one heading.* ■ *verb* /rɪ'kɔːd/ to store data or signals ○ *Record the results in this column.*

recordable CD /rɪˌkɔːdəb(ə)l siː 'diː/ *noun* full form of **CD-R**

recorder /rɪ'kɔːdə/ *noun* equipment able to transfer input signals onto a storage medium

COMMENT: The signal recorded is not always in the same form as the input signal. Many recorders record a modulated carrier signal for better quality. A recorder is usually combined with a suitable playback circuit since the read and write heads are often the same physical device.

recording /rɪ'kɔːdɪŋ/ *noun* **1.** the action of storing signals or data **2.** a signal (especially music) which has been recorded on tape or disk ○ *a new recording of Beethoven's quartets*

recordset /'rekɔːdset/ *noun* a group of records selected from a main database by a filter, search or query

recover /rɪ'kʌvə/ *verb* to get back something which has been lost ○ *It is possible to recover the data but it can take a long time.*

recoverable error /rɪˌkʌv(ə)rəb(ə)l 'erə/ *noun* an error type that allows program execution to be continued after it has occurred

recovery /rɪ'kʌv(ə)ri/ *noun* **1.** the process of returning to normal operating after a fault **2.** the process of getting back something that has been lost ○ *The recovery of lost files can be carried out using the recovery procedure.*

recovery procedure /rɪ'kʌv(ə)ri prə ˌsiːdʒə/ *noun* the processes required to return a system to normal operation after an error

rectangular waveguide /ˌrektæŋgjʊlə 'weɪvgaɪd/ *noun* a microwave channel that is rectangular in cross section

rectifier /'rektɪfaɪə/ *noun* an electronic circuit that converts an alternating current supply into a direct current supply

rectify /'rektɪˌfaɪ/ *verb* **1.** to correct something or to make something right ○ *They had to rectify the error at the printout stage.* **2.** to remove the positive or negative sections of a signal so that it is unipolar

recursion /rɪ'kɜːʒ(ə)n/ *noun* a subroutine in a program that calls itself during execution. Also called **recursive routine**

recursive filtering /rɪˌkɜːsɪv 'fɪlərɪŋ/ *noun* a technique which reduces video noise and defects (*film*)

recursive routine /rɪˌkɜːsɪv 'ruːtiːn/ *noun* same as **recursion**

Recycle Bin /riː'saɪk(ə)l bɪn/ *noun* a folder in Windows 95 where deleted files are automatically stored, with an icon on the Desktop that looks like a wastepaper bin ○ *If you want to delete a file* or *folder, drag it onto the Recycle Bin icon* or *press the Delete key.*

red, green, blue /ˌred griːn 'bluː/ *noun* the three colour picture beams used in a colour TV

COMMENT: There are three colour guns producing red, green, and blue beams acting on groups of three phosphor dots at each pixel location.

red, green, blue display /ˌred griːn 'bluː dɪˌspleɪ/ *noun* full form of **RGB display**

red book audio /ˌred bʊk 'ɔːdiəʊ/ *noun* ◊ **compact disc-digital audio**

redefinable /ˌriːdɪ'faɪnəb(ə)l/ *adjective* which can be redefined

redefine /ˌriːdɪ'faɪn/ *verb* to change the function or value assigned to a variable or object ○ *I have redefined this key to display the figure five when pressed.*

'...one especially useful command lets you redefine the printer's character-translation table' [*Byte*]

redirect /ˌriːdaɪ'rekt/ *verb* **1.** to send a message to its destination by another route **2.** (*in DOS and UNIX operating systems*) to treat the output of one program as input for another program

redirection /ˌriːdaɪ'rekʃən/ *noun* the process of sending a message to its destination by another route ○ *Call forwarding is automatic redirection of calls.*

redliner /'redlaɪnə/ *noun* a feature of workgroup or word-processor software that allows a user to highlight text in a different colour

redo /riː'duː/ *verb* to do something again

redraw /riː'drɔː/ *verb* to draw something again ○ *Can the computer redraw the graphics showing the product from the top view?*

reduce /rɪ'djuːs/ *verb* to make something smaller

reduced instruction set computer /rɪ ˌdjuːst ɪnˌstrʌkʃən set kəm'pjuːtə/ *noun* full form of **RISC**

redundancy /rɪ'dʌndənsi/ *noun* the process of providing extra components in a system in case there is a breakdown

redundant /rɪ'dʌndənt/ *adjective* **1.** referring to data that can be removed without losing any information ○ *The parity bits on the* *received data are redundant and can be removed.* **2.** referring to an extra piece of equipment kept ready for a task in case of faults

redundant array of inexpensive disks /rɪˌdʌndənt əˌreɪ əv ˌɪnɪkspensɪv ˈdɪsks/ *noun* full form of **RAID**

re-entrant program /riː ˌentrənt ˈprəʊɡræm/, **re-entrant code** /kəʊd/, **re-entrant routine** /ruːˈtiːn/ *noun* one program or code shared by many users in a multi-user system. It can be interrupted or called again by another user before it has finished its previous run, and will return to the point at which it was interrupted when it has finished that run.

reference /ˈref(ə)rəns/ *noun* **1.** a value used as a starting point for other values, often zero **2.** the act of mentioning or dealing with something ■ *verb* to access a location in memory ○ *The access time taken to reference an item in memory is short.*

reflect /rɪˈflekt/ *verb* to send back (light or image) from a surface ○ *In a reflex camera, the image is reflected by an inbuilt mirror.*

reflectance /rɪˈflektəns/ *noun* the difference between the amount of light or signal incident and the amount that is reflected back from a surface. Opposite **absorptance**

reflection /rɪˈflekʃən/ *noun* light or an image which is reflected

reflective disk /rɪˈflektɪv dɪsk/ *noun* a videodisc that uses a reflected laser beam to read the data etched into the surface

reformat /ˌriːˈfɔːmæt/ *verb* to format a disk that already contains data, and erasing the data by doing so ○ *Do not reformat your hard disk unless you can't do anything else.*

reformatting /riːˈfɔːmætɪŋ/ *noun* the act of formatting a disk which already contains data ○ *Reformatting destroys all the data on a disk.* ◊ **format**

refract /rɪˈfrækt/ *verb* to change the direction of light as it passes through a material (such as water or glass)

refraction /rɪˈfrækʃən/ *noun* the apparent bending of light or sound that occurs when it travels through a material

refractive index /rɪˌfræktɪv ˈɪndeks/ *noun* a measure of the angle that light is refracted by, as it passes through a material

refresh /rɪˈfreʃ/ *verb* to update regularly the contents of dynamic RAM by reading and rewriting stored data to ensure data is retained ○ *memory refresh signal*

refresh rate /rɪˈfreʃ reɪt/ *noun* the number of times every second that the image on a CRT is redrawn

'Philips autoscan colour monitor, the 4CM6099, has SVGA refresh rates of 72Hz (800 x 600) and EVGA refresh rates of 70Hz (1,024 x 768).' [*Computing*]

regenerate /rɪˈdʒenəˌreɪt/ *verb* **1.** to redraw an image on a screen many times a second so that it remains visible **2.** to receive distorted signals, process and error check them, then retransmit the same data

regeneration /rɪˌgenəˈreɪʃ(ə)n/ *noun* the process of regenerating a signal

regenerator /riːˈdʒenəreɪtə/ *noun* a device used in communications that amplifies or regenerates a received signal and transmits it on. Regenerators are often used to extend the range of a network.

region /ˈriːdʒən/ *noun* a special or reserved area of memory or program or screen

region fill /ˈriːdʒ(ə)n fɪl/ *noun* the process of filling an area of the screen or a graphics shape with a particular colour

register /ˈredʒɪstə/ *noun* **1.** a special location within a CPU that is used to hold data and addresses to be processed in a machine code operation **2.** a reserved memory location used for special storage purposes ■ *verb* **1.** to react to a stimulus **2.** to correctly superimpose two images

Registry /ˈredʒɪstri/ *noun* a database of information about configuration and program settings that forms the basis of Windows

regulate /ˈregjʊleɪt/ *verb* to control a process, usually using sensors and a feedback mechanism

regulation /ˌregjʊˈleɪʃ(ə)n/ *noun* a law or rule, which most people have to obey

regulation line /ˌregjʊleɪʃ(ə)n ˈlaɪn/ *noun* the ability of a power supply to prevent input line changes affecting output supplies

regulation load /ˌregjʊleɪʃ(ə)n ˈləʊd/ *noun* the ability of a power supply to prevent output load changes affecting output supplies

rehyphenation /riːˌhaɪfəˈneɪʃ(ə)n/ *noun* the process of changing the hyphenation of words in a text after it has been put into a new page format or line width

reject /rɪˈdʒekt/ *verb* to refuse to accept something ○ *The computer rejects all incoming data from incompatible sources.*

rejection /rɪˈdʒekʃən/ *noun* the process or fact of refusing to accept something

relational database /rɪˌleɪʃ(ə)n(ə)l ˈdeɪtəbeɪs/, **relational database management system** /rɪˌleɪʃn(ə)l ˌdeɪtəbeɪs ˌmænɪdʒmənt ˈsɪstəm/ *noun* a database in which all the items of data can be interconnected. Data is retrieved by using one item of data to search for a related field. ○ *If you search the relational database for the surname, you can pull out his salary from the related accounts database.* Abbr **RDBMS**

relationship /rɪ'leɪʃ(ə)nʃɪp/ *noun* a way in which two similar things are connected

relative /'relətɪv/ *adjective* compared to something else

relay /'riːleɪ/ *noun* an electromagnetically controlled switch ○ *There is a relay in the circuit.* ■ *verb* to receive data from one source and then retransmit it to another point ○ *All messages are relayed through this small micro.*

release /rɪ'liːs/ *noun* **1.** a version of a product ○ *The latest software is release 5.* **2.** the process of putting a new product on the market ■ *verb* to put a new product on the market

reliability /rɪˌlaɪə'bɪlɪti/ *noun* the ability of a device to function as intended, efficiently and without failure ○ *It has an excellent reliability record.*

reliable /rɪ'laɪəb(ə)l/ *adjective* which can be trusted to work properly ○ *The early versions of the software were not completely reliable.*

relief printing /rɪˌliːf 'prɪntɪŋ/ *noun* a printing process in which the ink is held on a raised image

reload /riː'ləʊd/ *verb* to load something again ○ *We reloaded the program after the crash.* ◊ **load**

relocatable /ˌriːləʊ'keɪtəb(ə)l/ *adjective* which can be moved to another area of memory without affecting its operation

relocate /ˌriːləʊ'keɪt/ *verb* to move data from one area of storage to another ○ *The data is relocated during execution.*

relocation /ˌriːləʊ'keɪʃ(ə)n/ *noun* the process of moving to another area in memory

REM /rem/ *noun* a statement in a BASIC program that is ignored by the interpreter, allowing the programmer to write explanatory notes. Full form **remark**

remainder /rɪ'meɪndə/ *noun* a number equal to the dividend minus the product of the quotient and divider ○ *7 divided by 3 is equal to 2 remainder 1.* Compare **quotient**

remark /rɪ'mɑːk/ *noun* full form of **REM**

remedial maintenance /rɪˌmiːdiəl 'meɪntənəns/ *noun* maintenance to repair faults which have developed in a system

remote /rɪ'məʊt/ *adjective* referring to communications with a computer at a distance from the systems centre ○ *Users can print reports on remote printers.*

remote job entry /rɪˌməʊt dʒɒb 'entri/ *noun* full form of **RJE**

removable /rɪ'muːvəb(ə)l/ *adjective* which can be removed ○ *a removable hard disk*

removal /rɪ'muːv(ə)l/ *noun* the act of taking something away ○ *The removal of this instruction could solve the problem.*

remove /rɪ'muːv/ *verb* to take something away or to move something to another place ○ *The file entry was removed from the floppy disk directory.*

remove directory /rɪˌmuːv daɪ'rekt(ə)ri/ *noun* full form of **RD**

rename /riː'neɪm/ *verb* to give a new name to a file

rendering /'rend(ə)rɪŋ/ *noun* the process of colouring and shading a (normally wireframe or vector object) graphic object so that it looks solid and real

renumber /'riːnʌmbə/ *noun* a feature of some computer languages which allows the programmer to allocate new values to all or some of a program's line numbers

reorganise /riː'ɔːgənaɪz/, **reorganize** *verb* to organise something again or in a different way ○ *Wait while the spelling checker database is being reorganised.*

repaginate /riː'pædʒɪneɪt/ *verb* to change the lengths of pages of text before they are printed ○ *The text was repaginated with a new line width.*

repagination /riːˌpædʒɪ'neɪʃ(ə)n/ *noun* the action of changing pages lengths ○ *The dtp package allows simple repagination.*

repeat /rɪ'piːt/ *verb* to do an action again

repeater /rɪ'piːtə/ *noun* a device used in communications that amplifies or regenerates a received signal and transmits it on. Regenerators are often used to extend the range of a network, while the repeater works at the physical layer of the OSI network model. ◊ **bridge, OSI, router**

repeating group /rɪ'piːtɪŋ gruːp/ *noun* a pattern of data that is duplicated in a bit stream

reperforator /riː'pɜːfəreɪtə/ *noun* a machine that punches paper tape according to received signals

repertoire /'repəˌtwɑː/ *noun* the range of functions of a device or software ○ *The manual describes the full repertoire.*

repetitive letter /rɪˌpetətɪv 'letə/ *noun* a form letter or standard letter into which the details of each addressee are inserted

repetitive strain injury /rɪˌpetɪtɪv 'streɪn ˌɪndʒəri/, **repetitive stress injury** /rɪˌpetɪtɪv stres 'ɪndʒəri/ *noun* pain in the arm, wrist or hands felt by someone who performs the same movement many times over a certain period, as when operating a computer ○ *RSI can be avoided by adjusting your chair so that you do not excessively flex your wrists when typing.* Abbr **RSI**

replace /rɪ'pleɪs/ *verb* **1.** to put something back where it was before **2.** to find a certain item of data and put another in its place. ◊ **search and replace**

replay *noun* /'riːpleɪ/ **1.** the playing back or reading back of data or a signal from a recording **2.** the process of repeating a short section of filmed action, usually in slow motion ○ *The replay clearly showed the winner.* ○ *This video recorder has a replay feature.* ■ *verb* /riː'pleɪ/ to play back something that has been recorded

replenish /rɪ'plenɪʃ/ *verb* to charge a battery with electricity again

replicate /'replɪˌkeɪt/ *verb* to copy something ○ *The routine will replicate your results with very little effort.*

report program generator /rɪ'pɔːt ˌprəʊgræm ˌdʒenəreɪtə/ *noun* a programming language used mainly on personal computers for the preparation of business reports, allowing data in files, databases, etc., to be included. Abbr **RPG**

represent /ˌreprɪ'zent/ *verb* **1.** to act as a symbol for something ○ *The hash sign is used to represent a number in a series.* **2.** to act as a salesperson for a product

representation /ˌreprɪzen'teɪʃ(ə)n/ *noun* the action of representing something

representative /ˌreprɪ'zentətɪv/ *adjective* typical example of something ■ *noun* salesman who represents a company ○ *The representative called yesterday about the order.*

reprint /'riːprɪnt/ *verb* **1.** to print more copies of a document or book **2.** to create a positive film print from a negative ■ *noun* the printing of copies of a book after the first printing ○ *We ordered a 10,000 copy reprint.*

repro /'riːprəʊ/ *noun* finished artwork or camera-ready copy, ready for filming and printing (*informal*)

reproduce /ˌriːprə'djuːs/ *verb* to copy data or text from one material or medium to another similar one

reproduction /ˌriːprə'dʌkʃ(ə)n/ *noun* the action of copying

reprogram /riː'prəʊgræm/ *verb* to alter a program so that it can be run on another type of computer

repro proof /'riːprəʊ pruːf/ *noun* a perfect proof ready to be reproduced

request /rɪ'kwest/ *noun* something that someone asks for ■ *verb* to ask for something

require /rɪ'kwaɪə/ *verb* to need something or to demand something ○ *Delicate computer systems require careful handling.*

required hyphen /rɪˌkwaɪəd 'haɪf(ə)n/ *noun* hyphen which is always in a word, even if the word is not split (as in co-administrator)

requirements /rɪ'kwaɪəmənts/ *plural noun* things which are needed ○ *Memory requirements depend on the application software in use.*

re-route /ˌriː 'ruːt/ *verb* to send something by a different route

rerun /ˌriː'rʌn/ *verb* to run a program or a printing job again

res /rez/ *noun* same as **resolution**

resample /riː'sɑːmp(ə)l/ *verb* to change the number of pixels used to make up an image

resave /riː'seɪv/ *verb* to save a document or file again ○ *It automatically resaves the text.*

rescue dump /'reskjuː dʌmp/ *noun* data automatically saved on disk when a computer fault occurs. The rescue dump describes the state of the system at that time, and is used to help in debugging.

research /rɪ'sɜːtʃ/ *noun* scientific investigation carried out in order to learn new facts about a field of study

research and development /rɪˌsɜːtʃ ən dɪ'veləpmənt/ *noun* full form of **R & D** ○ *The company has spent millions of dollars on R & D.*

reserved character /rɪˌzɜːvd 'kærɪktə/ *noun* a special character which is used by the operating system or which has a particular function to control an operating system and cannot be used for other uses

reserved sector /rɪˌzɜːvd 'sektə/ *noun* the area of disk space that is used only for control data storage

reset /ˌriː'set/ *verb* **1.** to return a system to its initial state, in order to allow a program or process to be started again **2.** to set a register or counter to its initial state ○ *When it reaches 999 this counter resets to zero.* **3.** to set data equal to zero

COMMENT: Hard reset is similar to soft reset but with a few important differences. Hard reset is a switch that directly signals the CPU, while soft reset signals the operating system; hard reset clears all memory contents, while a soft reset does not affect memory contents; hard reset should always reset the system, while a soft reset does not always work if the operating system has been upset in a significant way.

reset-set flip-flop /ˌriːset set 'flɪp ˌflɒp/ *noun* full form of **RS-flip-flop**

reshape handle /'riːʃeɪp ˌhænd(ə)l/ *noun* (*in a GUI*) a small square displayed on a frame around an object or image that a user can select and drag to change the shape of the frame or graphical object

resident /ˈrezɪd(ə)nt/ *adjective* referring to data or a program that is always in a computer

resident fonts /ˌrezɪd(ə)nt ˈfɒnts/ *plural noun* font data which is always present in a printer or device and which does not have to be downloaded

resident software /ˌrezɪd(ə)nt ˈsɒftweə/ *noun* a program that is held permanently in memory (whilst the machine is on)

residual /rɪˈzɪdjuəl/ *adjective* remaining after the rest or the others have disappeared or have been dealt with

resist /rɪˈzɪst/ *verb* to fight against something or to refuse to do something ■ *noun* a substance used to protect a pattern of tracks on a PCB, which is not affected by etching chemicals

resistance /rɪˈzɪstəns/ *noun* a measure of the voltage drop across a component with a current flowing through it. ◊ **Ohm's Law**

resistor /rɪˈzɪstə/ *noun* an electronic component that provides a known resistance. Abbr **RTL**

resistor transistor logic /rɪˌzɪstə træn ˌzɪstə ˈlɒdʒɪk/ *noun* a circuit design method using transistors and resistors. Abbr **RTL**

resolution /ˌrezəˈluːʃ(ə)n/ *noun* **1.** the number of pixels that a screen or printer can display per unit area ○ *The resolution of most personal computer screens is not much more than 70 dpi (dots per inch).* Also called **res 2.** the difference between two levels that can be differentiated in a digitised signal **3.** the degree of accuracy with which something can be measured or timed

'Group IV fax devices can send a grey or colour A4 page in about four seconds, at a maximum resolution of 15.7 lines per millimetre over an Integrated Services Digital Network circuit.' [*Computing*]

resolver /rɪˈzɒlvə/ *noun* a system which regulates the speed of a magnetic film recorder or a tape playback machine (*film*)

resolving power /rɪˈzɒlvɪŋ ˌpaʊə/ *noun* a measurement of the ability of an optical system to detect fine black lines on a white background, given as the number of lines per millimetre

resonance /ˈrez(ə)nəns/ *noun* a situation in which a body oscillates with a very large amplitude because the frequency applied to it is the same as its natural frequency

resource /rɪˈzɔːs/ *noun* a useful device, product, program or graphic object

resource interchange file format /rɪ ˌzɔːs ˌɪntətʃeɪndʒ ˈfaɪl ˌfɔːmæt/ *noun* full form of **RIFF**

resource sharing /rɪˈzɔːs ˌʃeərɪŋ/ *noun* the use of one resource in a network or system by several users

respond /rɪˈspɒnd/ *verb* to reply or to react because of something

response /rɪˈspɒns/ *noun* a reaction caused by something

restart /rɪˈstɑːt/ *verb* to start something again ○ *First try to restart your system.*

rest in proportion /ˌrest ɪn prə ˈpɔːʃ(ə)n/ *noun* full form of **RIP**

restore /rɪˈstɔː/ *verb* to put something back into an earlier state

'...first you have to restore the directory that contains the list of deleted files' [*Personal Computer World*]

restrict /rɪˈstrɪkt/ *verb* to keep something within a certain limit

restriction /rɪˈstrɪkʃ(ə)n/ *noun* something that restricts data flow or access

result code /rɪˈzʌlt kəʊd/ *noun* a message sent from a modem to the local computer indicating the state of the modem

retain /rɪˈteɪn/ *verb* to keep something

retention /rɪˈtenʃ(ə)n/ *noun* the act of keeping something

retouch /riːˈtʌtʃ/ *verb* to change a print or photograph slightly by hand, to make it clearer or to remove any blemishes ○ *I retouched the scratch mark on the last print.* ○ *The artwork for the line drawings needs retouching in places.*

retrain /ˌriːˈtreɪn/ *verb* to re-establish a better quality connection when the quality of a line is very bad

retransmission /ˌriːtrænzˈmɪʃ(ə)n/ *noun* a signal or data that has been retransmitted

retransmit /ˌriːtrænzˈmɪt/ *verb* to transmit again (a received signal)

retrieval /rɪˈtriːv(ə)l/ *noun* the process of searching, locating and recovering information from a file or storage device

retrieve /rɪˈtriːv/ *verb* to extract information from a file or storage device ○ *These are the records retrieved in that search.*

retro- /retrəʊ/ *prefix* relating to an earlier time, state, or stage of development

retrospective parallel running /ˌretrəʊspektɪv ˈpærəlel ˌrʌnɪŋ/ *noun* running a new computer system with old data to check if it is accurate

retrospective search /ˌretrəʊspektɪv ˈsɜːtʃ/ *noun* a search of documents on a certain subject since a certain date

return /rɪˈtɜːn/ *noun* **1.** an instruction that causes program execution to return to the main program from a subroutine ○ *The program is not working because you missed out* *the return instruction at the end of the subroutine.* **2.** a key on a keyboard used to indicate that all the required data has been entered ○ *You type in your name and code number then press return.* **3.** the indication of an end of line (in printing)

return to zero signal /rɪˌtɜːn tə ˈzɪərəʊ ˌsɪgn(ə)l/ *noun* a recording reference mark taken as the level of unmagnetised tape

reveal /rɪˈviːl/ *verb* to display previously hidden information once a condition has been met

reverse /rɪˈvɜːs/ *adjective* going in the opposite direction ■ *verb* to go or travel in the opposite direction

'...the options are listed on the left side of the screen, with active options shown at the top left in reverse video' [*PC User*]

reverse engineering /rɪˌvɜːs ˌendʒɪˈnɪərɪŋ/ *noun* a method of product design in which the finished item is analysed to determine how it should be constructed

reverse Polish notation /rɪˌvɜːs ˌpəʊlɪʃ nəʊˈteɪʃ(ə)n/ *noun* mathematical operations written in a logical way, so that the operator appears after the numbers to be acted upon, removing the need for brackets ○ *Three plus four, minus two is written in RPN as 3 4 + 2 – = 5.* Abbr **RPN**

reverse video /rɪˌvɜːs ˈvɪdiəʊ/ *noun* a screen display mode in which white and black are reversed and colours are complemented

revert /rɪˈvɜːt/ *verb* to return to a normal state ○ *After the rush order, we reverted back to our normal speed.*

review /rɪˈvjuː/ *verb* to see something again, usually in order to check it ○ *The program allows the user to review all wrongly spelled words.*

revise /rɪˈvaɪz/ *verb* to update or correct a version of a document or file ○ *The revised version has no mistakes.*

rewind /ˌriːˈwaɪnd/ *verb* to return a tape or film or counter to its starting point ○ *The tape rewinds onto the spool automatically.*

rewrite *verb* /riːˈraɪt/ to write something again. ◊ **regenerate** ■ *noun* /ˈriːraɪt/ the act of writing something again ○ *The program is in its second rewrite.*

RF, R/F *noun* the electromagnetic spectrum that lies between the frequency range 10KHz and 3000GHz. Full form **radio frequency**

RFC /ˌɑː ef ˈsiː/ *noun* a document that contains information about a proposed new standard and asks users to look at the document and make any comments. Full form **request for comment**

RGB /ˌɑː dʒiː ˈbiː/ *noun* a high-definition monitor system that uses three separate input signals controlling red, green and blue colour picture beams. Full form **red, green, blue**

COMMENT: There are three colour guns producing red, green, and blue beams acting on groups of three phosphor dots at each pixel location.

RGB display /ˌɑː dʒiː ˌbiː dɪˈspleɪ/, **RGB monitor** /ˈmɒnɪtə/ *noun* a monitor that uses RGB

RI *abbr* ring indicator

RIAA curve *noun* standards for recording and equalisation set by the RIAA – Recording Industries Association of America (*film*)

ribbon /ˈrɪbən/ *noun* a long thin flat piece of material

rich text format /ˌrɪtʃ ˈtekst ˌfɔːmæt/ *noun* a way of storing a document that includes all the commands that describe the page, type, font and formatting. Abbr **RTF**

RIFF /rɪf/ *noun* a multimedia data format jointly introduced by IBM and Microsoft that uses tags to identify parts of a multimedia file structure and allows the file to be exchanged between platforms. Full form **resource interchange file format**

RIFF chunk /ˈrɪf tʃʌŋk/ *noun* a chunk with the ID RIFF

RIFF file /ˈrɪf faɪl/ *noun* a file that contains tagged information that complies with the RIFF file format

rifle microphone /ˌraɪf(ə)l ˈmaɪkrəfəʊn/ *noun* a long, highly directional microphone which can pick up sound over a great distance (*film*)

right-click /ˌraɪt ˈklɪk/ *verb* to press and release the right-hand button of a computer mouse

right-click menu /ˌraɪt ˈklɪk ˌmenjuː/ *noun* a small pop-up menu that appears when you click on the right-hand button of a two-button mouse

right-hand button /ˌraɪt hænd ˈbʌt(ə)n/ *noun* a button on the right-hand side of a two or three-button mouse

right justification /ˌraɪt ˌdʒʌstɪfɪˈkeɪʃ(ə)n/ *noun* the process of aligning the text and spacing characters so that the right margin is straight

right justify /ˌraɪt ˈdʒʌstɪˌfaɪ/ *verb* to align the right margin so that the text is straight

rightsizing /ˈraɪt ˌsaɪzɪŋ/ *noun* the process of moving a company's information technology structure to the most cost-effective hardware platform, which in practice often means moving from a mainframe-based network to a PC-based network

rigid /ˈrɪdʒɪd/ *adjective* which cannot easily bend

ring /rɪŋ/ *noun* **1.** a data list whose last entry points back to the first entry **2.** the topology of a network in which the wiring sequentially connects one workstation to another ■ *verb* to telephone

ring counter /ˈrɪŋ ˌkaʊntə/ *noun* an electronic counter in which any overflow from the last digit is fed into the input

ringing /ˈrɪŋɪŋ/ *noun* (*film*) **1.** interference in a television picture **2.** noise caused by an alternating or pulsating current

ring topology network /ˌrɪŋ təˌpɒlədʒi ˈnetwɜːk/ *noun* a type of network in which each terminal is connected one after the other in a circle

RIP *abbr* **1.** raster image processor **2.** routing information protocol

ripple /ˈrɪp(ə)l/ *noun* **1.** a small alternating current voltage apparent on a badly regulated direct current output supply **2.** a visual effect which creates wavy images during film dissolves

ripple-through effect /ˈrɪp(ə)l θruː ɪ ˌfekt/ *noun* (*in a spreadsheet*) the results, changes or errors appearing in a spreadsheet as a result of the value in one cell being changed

RISC /ˌɑː aɪ es ˈsiː/ *noun* a CPU design whose instruction set contains a small number of simple fast-executing instructions, which makes program writing more complex but increases speed. Full form **reduced instruction set computer.** ◊ **WISC**

rise time /ˈraɪz taɪm/ *noun* the time taken for a voltage to increase its amplitude (from 10 to 90 per cent or zero to RMS value of its final amplitude) □ **the circuit has a fast rise time** electronic circuit that is able to handle rapidly changing signals such as very high frequency signals

RJ11 connector *noun* a popular standard of four-wire modular connector

RJ45 connector *noun* a popular name for an eight-pin modular connector used in 10BaseT networks to connect UTP cables

RJE /ˌɑː dʒeɪ ˈiː/ *noun* a batch processing system in which instructions are transmitted to the computer from a remote terminal. Full form **remote job entry**

RLE /ˌɑː el ˈiː/ *noun* a data compression technique that stores any sequence of bits of data with the same value to a single value. Full form **run-length encoding**

RLL encoding /ˌɑː el el ɪnˈkəʊdɪŋ/ *noun* a fast and efficient method of storing data onto a disk in which the changes in a run of data bits is stored. Full form **run-length limited encoding**

rm /ˌɑː ˈem/ *noun* (*in UNIX*) a command to remove an empty subdirectory

RMDIR *abbr* remove directory. Same as **RD**

RMS line current /ˌɑː em es ˈlaɪn ˌkʌrənt/ *noun* the root mean square of the electrical current on a line

RO /ˌɑː ˈəʊ/ *noun* a computer terminal that can only accept and display data, not transmit. Full form **receive only**

roam /rəʊm/ *verb* (*in wireless communications*) to move around freely and still be in contact with a wireless communications transmitter

robot /ˈrəʊˌbɒt/ *noun* **1.** a device that can be programmed to carry out certain manufacturing tasks which are similar to tasks carried out by people **2.** same as **bot**

robotics /rəʊˈbɒtɪks/ *noun* the study of artificial intelligence, programming and building involved with robot construction

robust /rəʊˈbʌst/ *adjective* referring to a system which can resume working after a fault

robustness /rəʊˈbʌstnəs/ *noun* **1.** the strength of a system's casing and its ability to be knocked or dropped ○ *This hard disk is not very robust.* **2.** a system's ability to continue functioning even with errors or faults during a program execution

rock and roll /ˌrɒk ən ˈrəʊl/ *verb* to move backwards and forwards in synchronization during editing

rogue indicator /rəʊg ˈɪndɪˌkeɪtə/ *noun* a special code used only for control applications, e.g. an end of file marker

rogue value /ˌrəʊg ˈvæljuː/ *noun* an item in a list of data which shows that the list is terminated. Also called **terminator**

role indicator /ˈrəʊl ˌɪndɪˌkeɪtə/ *noun* a symbol used to show the role of a index entry in its particular context

roll /rəʊl/ *noun* **1.** a length of film or tape wound around itself ○ *He put a new roll of film into the camera.* **2.** unwanted vertical movement in a picture ■ *verb* **1.** to rotate a device about its axis **2.** to start filming

rollback /ˈrəʊlbæk/ *noun* reloading software after the master software has been corrupted

rolling headers /ˌrəʊlɪŋ ˈhedəs/ *noun* titles or headers of (teletext) pages displayed as they are received

rolling title /ˌrəʊlɪŋ ˈtaɪt(ə)l/ *noun* titles which move vertically up a picture area. ◊ **crawling title**

roll in/roll out /ˌrəʊl ɪn ˌrəʊl ˈaʊt/ *noun* the transfer of one process (in a multiprogramming system) from storage to processor then back once it has had its allocated processing time

rollover /'rəʊləʊvə/ *noun* a keyboard with a small temporary buffer so that it can still transmit correct data when several keys are pressed at once

roll scroll /'rəʊl skrəʊl/ *noun* displayed text that moves up or down the computer screen one line at a time

ROM /rɒm/ *abbr* read only memory

roman /'rəʊmən/ *noun* ordinary typeface, neither italic nor bold ○ *The text is set in Times Roman.*

Roman numerals /ˌrəʊmən 'njuːmərəlz/ *plural noun* numbers represented using the symbols I, V, X, L, C, D and M

romware /'rɒmweə/ *noun* software which is stored in ROM

root /ruːt/ *noun* a fractional power of a number

rotary /'rəʊtəri/ *adjective* which works by turning

rotary camera /ˌrəʊtəri 'kæm(ə)rə/ *noun* a camera able to photograph microfilm as it is moved in front of the lens by moving the film at the same time

rotary erase head /ˌrəʊtəri ɪ'reɪz ˌhed/ *noun* a video tape recorder's erase head

rotary movement /'rəʊtəri ˌmuːvmənt/ *noun* the effect of spinning images on film created by an optical-spin device in an optical printer

rotary press /'rəʊtəri pres/ *noun* a printing press whose printing plate is cylindrical

rotary printer /'rəʊtəri ˌprɪntə/ *noun* a constant contact printing machine where the two films at the time of exposure are transported on a revolving sprocket

rotary shutter, rotating shutter *noun* a rotating camera or projector shutter which intermittently blocks the passage of light as it moves through

rotate /rəʊ'teɪt/ *verb* to move data within a storage location in a circular manner

rotating helical aperture scanner /rəʊˌteɪtɪŋ ˌhelɪk(ə)l 'æpətʃə ˌskænə/ *noun* a type of scanner in which the original image is lit and the reflection sent, through a lens and mirror, through a rotating spiral slit and finally onto a photodetector cell; as the spiral slit turns, it has the effect of moving up the image

rotation /rəʊ'teɪʃ(ə)n/ *noun* the degree to which an object has been rotated

rough copy /ˌrʌf 'kɒpi/ *noun* a draft of a program which, it is expected, will have changes made to it before it is complete

round /raʊnd/ *adjective* in the form of a circle or curve

rounding /'raʊndɪŋ/ *noun* **1.** an approximation of a number to a slightly larger or smaller one of lower precision **2.** the process of giving graphics a smoother look

route /ruːt/ *noun* the path taken by a message between a transmitter and receiver in a network ○ *The route taken was not the most direct since a lot of nodes were busy.*

router /'ruːtɪd/ *noun* **1.** a communications device that receives data packets in a particular protocol and forwards them to their correct location via the most efficient route **2.** (*in a LAN*) a device that connect two or more LANs that use the same protocol and allows data to be transmitted between each network. The router works at the network-layer level of the OSI model. ◊ **bridge, OSI**

routine /ruː'tiːn/ *noun* a number of instructions that perform a particular task, but are not a complete program. They are included as part of a program. ○ *The routine copies the screen display onto a printer.*

'Hewlett-Packard has announced software which aims to reduce PC-network downtime and cut support costs by automating housekeeping routines such as issuing alerts about potential problems.' [*Computing*]

COMMENT: Routines are usually called from a main program to perform a task. Control is then returned to the part of the main program from which the routine was called once that task is complete.

routing /'ruːtɪŋ/ *noun* the process of determining a suitable route for a message through a network ○ *There is a new way of routing data to the central computer.*

routing information protocol /'ruːtɪŋ ˌɪnfəmeɪʃ(ə)n ˌprəʊtəkɒl/ *noun* a protocol used on the Internet to calculate the best route by which to transfer information over the Internet. RIP bases its selection on the distance that each route takes. Abbr **RIP**

row /raʊ/ *noun* **1.** a line of printed or displayed characters ○ *The figures are presented in rows, not in columns.* **2.** a horizontal line on a punched card ○ *Each entry is separated by a row of dots.* **3.** a horizontal set of data elements in an array or matrix

RPG *abbr* report program generator

RS-232C *noun* an EIA approved standard used in serial data transmission, covering voltage and control signals

RS-422 *noun* an EIA approved standard that extends the RS-232's 50ft limit

RS-423 *noun* an EIA approved standard that extends the RS-232's 50ft limit, introduced at the same time as the RS-422 standard, but less widely used

COMMENT: The RS232C has now been superseded by the RS423 and RS422 interface standards, which are similar to the RS232 but allow higher transmission rates.

RSA cipher system /ˌɑːr es eɪ ˈsaɪfə ˌsɪstəm/ *noun* the Rivest, Shamir and Adleman public key cipher system

RS-flip-flop /ˌɑːr es ˈflɪp ˌflɒp/ *noun* electronic bistable device whose output can be changed according to the Reset and Set inputs. Full form **reset-set flip-flop**. ◊ **flip-flop**

RTF *abbr* rich text format

RTL *abbr* resistor transistor logic

RTV /ˌɑː tiː ˈviː/ *noun* real-time video compression used within DVI software to provide usable, but lower-quality, images that are compressed in real-time at 10 frames per second. Full form **real-time video**

rubber banding /ˌrʌbə ˈbændɪŋ/ *noun* ◆ **elastic banding**

rubber numbers /ˌrʌbə ˈnʌmbəs/ *plural noun* identification numbers which are imprinted on developed rush prints and sound records during film editing (*film*)

rubric /ˈruːbrɪk/ *noun* printed headings of a book chapter or section

rule /ruːl/ *noun* **1.** a set of conditions that describe a function ○ *The rule states that you wait for the clear signal before transmitting.* **2.** in printing, a thin line

ruler /ˈruːlə/ *noun* a bar displayed on screen that indicates a unit of measurement, often used in DTP or word-processor software to help with layout

run /rʌn/ *verb* to operate, or to make a device operate ○ *The computer has been running ten hours a day.*

rundown /ˈrʌndaʊn/ *noun* the order in which programme events will be broadcast (*film*)

run-duration /ˈrʌn djʊˌreɪʃ(ə)n/ *noun, adjective* same as **run-time**

run-length encoding /ˌrʌn leŋθ en ˈkəʊdɪŋ/ *noun* full form of **RLE**

run-length limited encoding /ˌrʌn leŋθ ˌlɪmɪtɪd enˈkəʊdɪŋ/ *noun* full form of **RLL encoding**

running head /ˈrʌnɪŋ hed/ *noun* the title line of each page in a document

run off /ˌrʌn ˈɒf/ *noun* an error in positioning of film which causes it to move over a sprocket's teeth and be damaged (*film*)

run on /ˌrʌn ˈɒn/ *verb* **1.** to make text continue without a break ○ *The line can run on to the next without any space.* **2.** to print more copies to add to a print run ○ *We decided to run on 3,000 copies to the first printing.*

run-time /ˈrʌn taɪm/, **run duration** /ˈrʌn djʊˌreɪʃ(ə)n/ *noun* **1.** the period of a time that a program takes to run **2.** the time during which a computer is executing a program ▶ also called **run-duration** ■ *adjective* referring to an operation carried out only when a program is running

rushes /ˈrʌʃɪz/ *plural noun* (*film*) **1.** the initial prints made from a picture or sound negative in order to check the quality **2.** unedited video tape

R/W *abbr* read/write

R/W cycle /ˌɑː ˈdʌb(ə)l juː ˌsaɪ(ə)l/ *abbr* read/write cycle

R/W head /ˌɑː ˈdʌb(ə)l juː ˌhed/ *noun* an electromagnetic device that allows data to be read from or written to a storage medium. Full form **read/write head**

S

S100 bus, S-100 bus *noun* an IEEE-696 standard bus, a popular 8– and 16-bit microcomputer bus using 100 lines and a 100-pin connector. ◊ **bus** (NOTE: say 'S one hundred bus')

SAA a trade name for a standard developed by IBM which defines the look and feel of an application regardless of the hardware platform. SAA defines which keystrokes carry out standard functions, the application's display and how the application interacts with the operating system. Full form **Systems Application Architecture**

SAFE a signature validation technique. Full form **signature analysis using functional analysis**

safe area /ˈseɪf ˌeəriə/ *noun* the area of a TV image that will be seen on a standard television set

safe format /ˌseɪf ˈfɔːmæt/ *noun* a format operation that does not destroy the existing data and allows the data to be recovered in case the wrong disk was formatted

safe mode /ˌseɪf ˈməʊd/ *noun* a special operating mode of Windows 95 that is automatically selected if Windows 95 detects that there is a problem when starting

safety margin /ˈseɪfti ˌmɑːdʒɪn/ *noun* an extra amount of time or space provided so that errors can be absorbed

safety measures /ˈseɪfti ˌmeʒəz/ *plural noun* actions taken to make sure that something is safe

safety net /ˈseɪfti net/ *noun* a software or hardware device that protects the system or files from excessive damage in the event of a system crash ○ *If there is a power failure, we have a safety net in the form of a UPS.*

salami technique /səˈlɑːmi tekˌniːk/ *noun* computer fraud involving many separate small transactions that are difficult to detect and trace

SAM /ˌes eɪ ˈem/ *noun* a type of storage in which a particular data item can only be accessed by reading through all the previous items in the list. Full form **serial-access memory**

COMMENT: Magnetic tape is a form of SAM. You have to go through the whole tape to access one item, while disks provide random access to stored data.

sample /ˈsɑːmpəl/ *noun* a measurement of a signal at a point in time ○ *The sample at three seconds showed an increase.* ■ *verb* to obtain a number of measurements of a signal which can be used to provide information about the signal

sampler /ˈsɑːmplə/ *noun* **1.** an electronic circuit that takes many samples of a signal and stores them for future analysis **2.** an electronic circuit used to record audio signals in digital form and store them to allow future playback

sample rate /ˈsɑːmpəl reɪt/ *noun* a number of measurements of a signal that are recorded every second. A PC sound card normally supports one of the following three standard rates: 11,025, 22,050 and 44,100 samples per second, normally written as 11.025KHz, 22.05KHz and 44.1KHz.

sample size /ˈsɑːmpəl saɪz/ *noun* the size of the word used to measure the level of the signal when it is sampled

sans serif /ˌsænz ˈserɪf/ *noun* a typeface whose letters have no serifs

sapphire /ˈsæfaɪə/ *noun* a blue-coloured precious stone used as a substrate for certain chips

SAS *abbr* single attachment station

satellite /ˈsætəˌlaɪt/ *noun* **1.** a small system that is part of a larger system **2.** a device that orbits the earth receiving, processing and transmitting signals or generating images or data to be transmitted back to earth, such as weather pictures

COMMENT: In a network the floppy disk units are called 'satellites' and the hard disk unit the 'server'. In a star network each satellite is linked individually to a central server.

satellite computer /ˌsætəlaɪt kəm ˈpjuːtə/ *noun* a computer doing various tasks under the control of another computer

saturated colour /ˌsætʃəreɪtɪd ˈkʌlə/ *noun* bright colours such as red and orange that do not reproduce well on video and can cause distortion or can spread over the screen

saturation /ˌsætʃəˈreɪʃ(ə)n/ *noun* a point where a material cannot be further magnetised

save /seɪv/ *verb* to store data or a program on an auxiliary storage device ○ *This WP saves the text every 15 minutes in case of a fault.*

save as /ˈseɪv əz/ *noun* an option in an application that allows the user to save the current work in a file with a different name

SBC /ˌes biː ˈsiː/ *noun* a computer whose main components such as processor, input/output and memory are all contained on one PCB. Full form **single board computer**

SBM /ˌes biː ˈem/ *noun* an extension to the Red Book CD-Audio specification in which studio-quality 20-bit sound samples are stored in the 16-bit data format used by CD-Audio. Full form **super bit mapping**

scalable /ˈskeɪləb(ə)l/ *adjective* referring to fonts used for computer graphics that can be made to appear in a wide range of sizes

scalable font /ˌskeɪləb(ə)l ˈfɒnt/ *noun* a method of describing a font so that it can produce characters of different sizes

scalable software /ˌskeɪləb(ə)l ˈsɒftweə/ *noun* a groupware application that can easily accommodate more users on a network without the need for investment in new software

scalar /ˈskeɪlə/ *noun* a variable that has a single value assigned to it ○ *A scalar has a single magnitude value, a vector has two* or *more positional values.*

scale /skeɪl/ *noun* the ratio of two values

scan /skæn/ *noun* an examination of an image or object or list of items to obtain data describing it ○ *The heat scan of the computer quickly showed which component was overheating.* ■ *verb* **1.** to examine and produce data from the shape or state of an object or drawing or file or list of items ○ *The facsimile machine scans the picture and converts this to digital form before transmission.* **2.** to convert a printed image or photograph into a digital bitmap form (*optical*) **3.** to move a picture beam across a screen, one line at a time, to refresh the image on the CRT **4.** to convert an optical image (from a video camera) into a digital form by examining each pixel on one line of a frame, then moving down one line ○ *The fax machine scans the picture and converts this to digital form before transmission.* ○ *The machine scans at up to 300 dpi resolution.*

scan conversion /ˈskæn kənˌvɜːʃ(ə)n/ *noun* the process of converting an interlaced video signal to a non-interlaced signal or a composite to a separated RGB signal

scan line /ˌskæn ˈlaɪn/ *noun* one of the horizontal lines of phosphor, or phosphor dots, on the inside of a CRT or monitor. The monitor's picture beam sweeps along each scan line to create the image on the screen.

scanner /ˈskænə/ *noun* **1.** a device which scans ○ *A scanner reads the bar-code on the product label using a laser beam and photodiode.* **2.** a device that converts an image or document into graphical data which can be manipulated by a computer

'Ricoh's Fax 300L Computer Link is connected to a PC via a RS232C serial interface, and enables users to send faxes from within Dos and Windows applications without printing a hard copy: It can also act as a scanner for graphics, and a printer for documents.' [*Computing*]

scanner memory /ˈskænə ˌmem(ə)ri/ *noun* the memory area allocated to store images which have been scanned

scanning /ˈskænɪŋ/ *noun* **1.** the action of examining and producing data from the shape of an object or drawing **2.** a method which examines an area line-by-line through the use of an electron beam, and is particularly used in television

COMMENT: A modem with auto-baud scanning can automatically sense which baud rate to operate on and switches automatically to that baud rate.

scanning line /ˈskænɪŋ laɪn/ *noun* a path traced on a CRT screen by the picture beam

scanning rate /ˈskænɪŋ reɪt/ *noun* the time taken to scan one line of a CRT image

scanning resolution /ˈskænɪŋ rezə ˌluːʃ(ə)n/ *noun* the ability of a scanner to distinguish between small points. The usual resolution is 300 dpi.

scanning software /ˈskænɪŋ ˌsɒf(t)weə/ *noun* a dedicated program that controls a scanner and allows certain operations, e.g. rotate, edit or store, to be performed on a scanned image

scanning spot /ˈskænɪŋ spɒt/ *noun* **1.** a small area of an image that is being read by a facsimile machine that moves over the whole image **2.** a small area covered by the picture beam on a TV screen that moves to follow a scanning line to write the whole of an image onto the screen

'...scanning time per page ranged from about 30 seconds to three minutes' [*PC Business World*]

scanning spot beam /ˌskænɪŋ ˈspɒt ˌbiːm/ *noun* a satellite transmission to a number of areas, as the satellite passes over them

SCART connector /ˈskɑːt kəˌnektə/ *noun* a special connector normally used to carry video or audio signals between video equipment

scatter /ˈskætə/ *noun* part of a beam that is deflected or refracted. ◊ **backscatter**

scatter graph /ˈskætə grɑːf/ *noun* individual points or values plotted on a two axis graph

scatter proofs /ˈskætə pruːfs/ *plural noun* proofs not arranged in any order prior to PMT. ◊ **backscatter**

scavenging /ˈskævɪndʒɪŋ/ *noun* the act of searching through and accessing database material without permission

scene /siːn/ *noun* (*film*) **1.** a group of interrelated shots combined into a continuous action **2.** a location for a specific shot or a group of shots

scene sync /ˈsiːn sɪŋk/ *noun* a system which allows both movement of the foreground camera to be synchronised with the mask camera in chroma key, and colour separation overlay special effects (*film*)

schedule /ˈʃedjuːl/ *noun* the order in which tasks are to be done, or the order in which CPU time will be allocated to processes in a multi-user system

scheduled circuits /ˌʃedʒuːld ˈsɜːkɪtz/ *noun* telephone lines for data communications only

scheduler /ˈʃedjuːlə/ *noun* a program that organises the use of a CPU or of peripherals which are shared by several users

scheduling /ˈʃedjuːlɪŋ/ *noun* a method of working that allows several users to share the use of a CPU

schema /ˈskiːmə/ *noun* a graphical description of a process or database structure

schematic /skiˈmætɪk/ *adjective* a diagram showing system components and how they are connected

scissor /ˈsɪzə/ *verb* **1.** to define an area of an image and then cut out this part of the image so it can then be pasted into another image **2.** to define an area of an image and delete any information that is outside this area

scissoring /ˈsɪzərɪŋ/ *noun* **1.** the process of defining an area of an image and then cutting out this part of the image so that it can then be pasted into another image **2.** the process of defining an area of an image and deleting any information that is outside this area

scope /skəʊp/ *noun* **1.** the range of values that a variable can contain **2.** electronic test equipment that displays on a CRT the size and shape of an electrical signal (*informal*) Also called **oscilloscope**

score /skɔː/ *noun* **1.** a list of actions that control how objects or cast members move with time within a presentation **2.** the description of a piece of music using musical notes

scramble /ˈskræmb(ə)l/ *verb* to code speech or data which is transmitted in such a way that it cannot be understood unless it is decoded

scrambler /ˈskræmblə/ *noun* **1.** a device that codes a data stream into a pseudo-random form before transmission to eliminate any series of ones or zeros or alternate ones and zeros that would cause synchronisation problems at the receiver **2.** a device that codes speech or other signals prior to transmission so that someone who is listening in without authorisation cannot understand what is being transmitted (the scrambled signals are de-scrambled on reception to provide the original signals) ○ *He called the President on the scrambler telephone.*

scrapbook /ˈskræpˌbʊk/ *noun* a utility on an Apple Macintosh that stores frequently used graphic images ○ *We store our logo in the scrapbook.*

scrape flutter /ˈskreɪp ˌflʌtə/ *noun* an error in magnetic recording which is caused by the recording tape sticking which produces flutter (*film*)

scratch /skrætʃ/ *noun* **1.** an area of memory or of a file used for the temporary storage of data **2.** a mark on the surface of a disk ○ *This scratch makes the disk unreadable.* ■ *verb* to delete or move an area of memory to provide room for other data

scratch file /ˈskrætʃ faɪl/ *noun* same as **work file**

scratchpad /ˈskrætʃpæd/ *noun* a workspace or area of high speed memory used for temporary storage of data currently in use

> 'Mathcad is described as an easy-to-use 'handy scratch pad for quick number crunching', which is positioned as an alternative to popular spreadsheets.' [*Computing*]

screen /skriːn/ *noun* **1.** a display device capable of showing a quantity of information, such as a CRT or VDU. ◊ **readout 2.** a grid of dots or lines placed between the camera and the artwork, which has the effect of dividing the picture up into small dots, creating an image which can be used for printing **3.** something which protects ■ *verb* **1.** to protect something with a screen ○ *The PSU is screened against interference.* **2.** to select **3.** to display or show information ○ *The film is now being screened.*

screen angle /ˈskriːn ˌæŋɡ(ə)l/ *noun* the angle at which a screen is set before the photograph is taken

screen attribute /ˈskriːn ˌætrɪbjuːt/ *noun* a set of attribute bits which define how each character will be displayed on screen. They set background and foreground colour and bold, italic or underline.

screen buffer /ˈskriːn ˌbʌfə/ *noun* a temporary storage area for characters or graphics before they are displayed

screen capture /ˈskriːn ˌkæptʃə/ *verb* to store the image currently displayed on screen in a file

screen cleaning kit /ˈskriːn ˌkliːnɪŋ ˌkɪt/ *noun* the liquids and cloth which remove any static and dirt from a VDU screen

screen dump /ˈskriːn ˌdʌmp/ *noun* the process of outputting the text or graphics displayed on a screen to a printer

screen editor /ˈskriːn ˌedɪtə/ *noun* software which allows the user to edit text on-screen, with one complete screen of information being displayed at a time

screen format /ˈskriːn ˌfɔːmæt/ *noun* a way in which a screen is laid out

screenful /ˈskriːnfʊl/ *noun* a complete frame of information displayed on a screen

screen grab /ˌskriːn ˈgræb/ *noun* **1.** the process of digitising a single frame from a display or television **2.** the process of capturing what is displayed on a monitor and storing it as a graphics file

screen refresh /ˌskriːn rɪˈfreʃ/ *verb* to update regularly the images on a CRT screen by scanning each pixel with a picture beam to make sure the image is still visible

screen saver /ˈskriːn ˌseɪvə/ *noun* software which, after a pre-determined period of user inactivity, replaces the existing image on screen and displays moving objects to protect against screen burn

screen shot /ˌskriːn ˈʃɒt/ *noun* ➧ **screen capture**

script /skrɪpt/ *noun* **1.** a set of instructions which carry out a function, normally used with a macro language or batch language ○ *I log in automatically using this script with my communications software.* **2.** text which will be spoken by actors in a film or TV programme

scripting language /ˈskrɪptɪŋ ˌlæŋgwɪdʒ/ *noun* a simple programming language (normally proprietary to an application) that allows a user to automate the application's functions ○ *This communications software has a scripting language that lets me dial and log in automatically.*

scriptwriter /ˈskrɪptraɪtə/ *noun* a person who writes film or TV scripts

scroll /skrəʊl/ *verb* to move displayed text vertically up or down the screen, one line or pixel at a time

scroll arrows /ˈskrəʊl ˌærəʊz/ *plural noun* (*in a GUI*) arrows that when clicked, move the contents of the window up or down or sideways

scroll bar /ˈskrəʊl bɑː/ *noun* (*in a GUI*) a bar displayed along the side of a window with a marker which indicates how far you have scrolled ○ *The marker is in the middle of the scroll bar so I know I am in the middle of the document.*

scrub /skrʌb/ *verb* to wipe information off a disk or remove data from store ○ *Scrub all files with the .BAK extension.*

SCSI /ˈskʌzi/ *noun* a standard high-speed parallel interface used to connect computers to peripheral devices (such as disk drives and scanners). Full form **small computer system interface**

'...the system uses SCSI for connecting to the host and ESDI for interconnecting among drives within a multidrive system' [*Byte*]

COMMENT: SCSI is the current standard used to interface high-capacity, high-performance disk drives to computers. Smaller disk drives are connected with an IDE interface, which is slower, but cheaper. SCSI replaced the older ESDI interface and allows several (usually eight) peripherals to be connected, in a daisy-chain, to one controller.

SD *abbr* single density

SD card /ˌes ˈdiː ˌkɑːd/ *noun* same as **MMC**

SDLC /ˌes diː el ˈsiː/ *noun* data transmission protocol most often used in IBM's Systems Network Architecture (SNA). It defines how synchronous data is transmitted. Full form **synchronous data link control**

seal /siːl/ *verb* to close something tightly so that it cannot be opened ○ *The hard disk is in a sealed case.*

seamless integration /ˌsiːmləs ˌɪntɪˈgreɪʃ(ə)n/ *noun* the process of including a new device or software into a system without any problems ○ *It took a lot of careful planning, but we succeeded in a seamless integration of the new application.*

search /sɜːtʃ/ *noun* the process of looking for and identifying a character or word or section of data in a document or file ■ *verb* **1.** to look for an item of data **2.** to move quickly backwards and forwards to different parts of a programme without losing the synchronisation of the sound and picture (*film*)

'...a linear search of 1,000 items takes 500 comparisons to find the target, and 1,000 to report that it isn't present. A binary search of the same set of items takes roughly ten divisions either to find or not to find the target' [*Personal Computer World*]

searchable /ˈsɜːtʃəb(ə)l/ *adjective* able to be accessed by a search facility

search and replace /ˌsɜːtʃ ənd rɪˈpleɪs/ *noun* a feature on word-processors which allows the user to find certain words or phrases, then replace them with another word or phrase

search directory /ˈsɜːtʃ daɪˌrekt(ə)ri/ *noun* a website in which links to information are listed in categories or in alphabetical order

search engine /ˈsɜːtʃ ˌendʒɪn/ *noun* **1.** (*on the Internet*) software that searches a database. ◊ **agent 2.** (*on the Internet*) a website that compiles a list of websites and allows a visitor to find a website by searching for words

searching storage /ˈsɜːtʃɪŋ ˌstɔːrɪdʒ/ *noun* a method of data retrieval that uses part of the data rather than an address to locate the data

SECAM /ˌes iː siː eɪ ˈem/ *noun* a standard for television transmission and reception similar to PAL except that SECAM uses frequency modulation to transmit the chroma signal. SECAM is used in France and Eastern Europe. Full form **Système Electronique Couleur Avec Mémoire**

second /ˈsekənd/ *adjective* (thing) which comes after the first ○ *We have two computers, the second one being used if the first is being repaired.*

secondary /ˈsekənd(ə)ri/ *adjective* second in importance or less important than the first

sector /ˈsektə/ *noun* the smallest area on a magnetic disk which can be addressed by a computer; the disk is divided into concentric tracks, and each track is divided into sectors which, typically, can store 512 bytes of data ■ *verb* to divide a disk into a series of sectors

COMMENT: A disk is divided into many tracks, each of which is then divided into a number of sectors which can hold a certain number of bits.

secured /sɪˈkjʊəd/ *adjective* (*of a file*) protected against accidental writing or deletion or against unauthorised access

Secure Digital Card /sɪˌkjʊə ˌdɪdʒɪt(ə)l ˈkɑːd/ *noun* same as **MMC**

secure electronic transactions /sɪ ˌkjʊə ˌelektrɒnɪk trænzˈækʃənz/ *plural noun* full form of **SET**

secure encryption payment protocol /sɪˌkjʊə ɪnˌkrɪpʃən ˈpeɪmənt ˌprəʊtəkɒl/ *noun* full form of **SEPP**

secure hypertext transfer protocol /sɪˌkjʊə ˌhaɪpətekst ˈtrænsfɜː ˌprəʊtəkɒl/ *noun* full form of **S-HTTP**

secure server /sɪˌkjʊə ˈsɜːvə/ *noun* an Internet server that allows data to be encrypted and thus is suitable for use in e-commerce

secure site /sɪˌkjʊə ˈsaɪt/ *noun* a website that includes features to ensure that any information transferred between the user and the website is encrypted and cannot be read by a hacker. Also called **secure website**

COMMENT: A secure website is usually used in a shopping site to allow a customer to type in their personal details (such as their credit-card number) without risk. Secure websites almost always use a system called SSL (secure sockets layer) that creates a secure channel when you visit the site; when you visit a secure site, the small padlock icon in the status bar at the bottom of your web browser is locked. If the padlock icon is open, this is not a secure site and you should not type in sensitive information, such as a credit-card number.

secure sockets layer /sɪˌkjʊə ˈsɒkɪts ˌleɪə/ *noun* full form of **SSL**

secure system /sɪˌkjʊə ˈsɪstəm/ *noun* a system that cannot be accessed without authorisation

secure transaction technology /sɪ ˌkjʊə trænˈzækʃən tekˌnɒlədʒi/ *noun* full form of **STT**

secure website /sɪˌkjʊə ˈwebsaɪt/ *noun* same as **secure site**

security /sɪˈkjʊərɪti/ *noun* the state of being protected or being secret ○ *The system has been designed to assure the security of the stored data.*

security backup /sɪˈkjʊərɪti ˌbækʌp/ *noun* a copy of a disk, tape or file kept in a safe place in case the working copy is lost or damaged

security check /sɪˈkjʊərɪti tʃek/ *noun* identification of authorised users (by a password) before granting access

Sega™ /ˈseɪɡə/ *noun* a videogame company that develops software and hardware for the console games market; developed the Mega-Drive console

segment /ˈseɡmənt/ *noun* a section of a main program which can be executed in its own right, without the rest of the main program being required ■ *verb* to divide a long program into shorter sections which can then be called up when required. ◊ **overlay**

'...you can also write in smaller program segments. This simplifies debugging and testing' [*Personal Computer World*]

select /sɪˈlekt/ *verb* **1.** to find and retrieve specific information from a database **2.** to position a pointer over an object (such as a button or menu option) and click on the mouse-button

selectable /sɪˈlektəb(ə)l/ *adjective* which can be selected

selectable attributes /sɪˌlektəb(ə)l ˈætrɪbjuːtz/ *plural noun* the attributes of a device which can be chosen by the user

selection /sɪˈlekʃən/ *noun* **1.** the action or process of selecting ○ *Selection of information from a large database may take some time.* **2.** the process of defining an area of an image (often used to cut out an area of the image, or to limit a special effect to an area)

selection tool /sɪˈlekʃən tuːl/ *noun* (*in a paint or drawing program*) an icon in a toolbar that allows a user to select an area of an image which can then be cut, copied or processed in some way

selective /sɪ'lektɪv/ *adjective* which chooses certain items

selective sort /sɪ'lektɪv sɔːt/ *noun* the process of sorting a section of data items into order

selectivity /sɪˌlek'tɪvɪti/ *noun* the ability of a radio receiver to distinguish between two nearby carrier frequencies

selector /sɪ'lektə/ *noun* a mechanical device which allows a user to choose an option or function

self- /self/ *prefix* oneself or itself

self-correcting codes /ˌself kəˌrektɪŋ 'kəʊdz/ *plural noun* a character coding system which is able to detect and correct an error or bad character

self extracting archive /ˌself ɪk ˌstræktɪŋ 'ɑːkaɪv/ *noun* a compressed file that includes the program to de-compress the contents

semi- /semi/ *prefix* half or partly

semicolon /ˌsemi'kəʊlɒn/ *noun* a printed sign (;) which marks the end of a program line or statement in some languages (such as C and Pascal)

semiconductor /ˌsemikən'dʌktə/ *noun* a material with conductive properties between those of a conductor (such as a metal) and an insulator

COMMENT: Semiconductor material such as silicon is used as a base for manufacturing integrated circuits and other solid-state components, usually by depositing various types of doping substances on or into its surface.

sender /'sendə/ *noun* a person who sends a message

Send To command /'send tʊ kəˌmɑːnd/ *noun* a menu command, available from the File menu of Windows applications, that allows a user to send the file or data currently open in the application to another application

sense /sens/ *verb* to examine the state of a device or electronic component ○ *The condition of the switch was sensed by the program.*

sensitive /'sensɪtɪv/ *adjective* which can sense even small changes ○ *The computer is sensitive even to very slight changes in current.*

sensor /'sensə/ *noun* an electronic device which produces an output dependent upon the condition or physical state of a process ○ *The sensor's output varies with temperature.* ◊ **transducer**

sentinel /'sentɪn(ə)l/ *noun* a marker or pointer to a special section of data

separate *adjective* /'sep(ə)rət/ not together ■ *verb* /'sepəreɪt/ to divide

separated graphics /ˌsepəreɪtɪd 'græfɪks/ *plural noun* displayed characters that do not take up the whole of a character matrix, resulting in spaces between them

separator /'sepəˌreɪtə/ *noun* a symbol used to distinguish parts of an instruction line in a program, such as command and argument. ◊ **delimiter**

SEPP /ˌes iː piː 'piː/ *noun* a system developed to provide a secure link between a user's browser and a vendor's Website to allow the user to pay for goods over the Internet. Full form **secure encryption payment protocol**. ◊ **PGP, S-HTTP, SSL, STT**

sequence /'siːkwəns/ *noun* **1.** a number of items or data arranged as a logical, ordered list **2.** a series of musical notes that define a tune **3.** a series of video frames

sequence control register /ˌsiːkwəns kənˌtrəʊl 'redʒɪstə/, **sequence counter** /ˌsiːkwəns 'kaʊntə/ *noun* a CPU register which contains the address of the next instruction to be processed. Abbr **SCR**. Also called **sequence register, instruction address register, instruction counter**

sequenced packet exchange /ˌsiːkwənsd 'pækɪt ɪksˌtʃeɪndʒ/ *noun* full form of **SPX**

sequencer /'siːkwənsə/ *noun* **1.** software that allows a user to compose tunes for MIDI instruments, record notes from instruments and mix together multiple tracks **2.** a hardware device that can record or playback a sequence of MIDI notes

sequence register /'siːkwəns ˌredʒɪstə/ *noun* same as **sequence control register**

sequence shot /'siːkwəns ʃɒt/ *noun* a long shot in which both cameras and actors move about; used to remove the necessity of shooting close-ups when the action is very intense (*film*)

sequential /sɪ'kwenʃ(ə)l/ *adjective* arranged in an ordered manner

sequential access /sɪˌkwenʃ(ə)l 'ækses/ *noun* a method of retrieving data from a storage device by starting at the beginning of the medium and reading each record until the required data is found

COMMENT: A tape storage system uses sequential access, since the tape has to be played through until the section required is found. The access time of sequential access storage is dependent on the position in the file of the data, compared with random access which has the same access time for any piece of data in a list.

sequentially /sɪ'kwenʃəli/ *adverb* (done) one after the other, in sequence

serial /'sɪəriəl/ *adjective* referring to data or instructions which are ordered sequentially (one after the other) and not in parallel

serial-access memory /ˌsɪəriəl ˌækses ˈmem(ə)ri/ *noun* full form of **SAM**

serial data transmission /ˌsɪəriəl ˈdeɪtə trænzˌmɪʃ(ə)n/ *noun* the transmission of the separate bits that make up data words, one at a time down a single line

serial input/output /ˌsɪəriəl ˌɪnpʊt ˈaʊtpʊt/ *noun* full form of **SIO**

serial input/parallel output /ˌsɪəriəl ˌɪnpʊt ˌpærəlel ˈaʊtpʊt/ *noun* a device which can accept serial data and transmit parallel data. Abbr **SIPO**. Also called **serial to parallel converter**

serial input/serial output /ˌsɪəriəl ˌɪnpʊt ˌsɪəriəl ˈaʊtpʊt/ *noun* full form of **SISO**

serially /ˈsɪəriəli/ *adverb* one after the other or in a series ○ *Their transmission rate is 64,000 bits per second through a parallel connection* or *19,200 serially.*

series /ˈsɪəriːz/ *noun* a group of related items ordered sequentially

serif /ˈserɪf/ *noun* a small decorative line attached to parts of characters in certain typefaces

server /ˈsɜːvə/ *noun* a dedicated computer which provides a function to a network

'Sequent Computer Systems' Platform division will focus on hardware and software manufacture, procurement and marketing, with the Enterprise division concentrating on services and server implementation.' [*Computing*]

COMMENT: In a network the hard disk machine is called the 'server' and the floppy disk units the 'satellites'. In a star network each satellite is linked individually to a central server.

server access logs /ˌsɜːvə ˈækses lɒgs/ *plural noun* ➧ **access log**

server farm /ˈsɜːvə fɑːm/ *noun* a business consisting of a group of Internet servers, all of which are linked to one another and are engaged in web hosting

server message block /ˌsɜːvə ˈmesɪdʒ blɒk/ *noun* full form of **SMB**

service /ˈsɜːvɪs/ *verb* to check or repair or maintain a system ○ *The disk drives were serviced yesterday and are working well.*

service contract /ˈsɜːvɪs ˌkɒntrækt/ *noun* an agreement that an engineer will service equipment if it goes wrong

service provider /ˈsɜːvɪs prəˌvaɪdə/ *noun* a company that offers users a connection to the Internet; the service provider has a computer that acts as a domain name server and has a high-speed link to the Internet. It provides modem access to the Internet via point-of-presence telephone numbers. You connect to the Internet by setting up an account with the service provider then dialling into its point-of-presence telephone number with a modem.

services /ˈsɜːvɪsɪz/ *plural noun* **1.** a set of functions provided by a device **2.** (*in an OSI network model*) a set of functions provided by one OSI layer for use by a higher layer

session /ˈseʃ(ə)n/ *noun* **1.** a period of work **2.** the time during which a program or process is running or active **3.** a separate occasion when image data is recorded onto a disc

set /set/ *noun* **1.** a number of related data items **2.** the width of a printed typeface **3.** a radio or television receiver **4.** the physical layout of a stage or filming studio including props and background ■ *verb* **1.** to make one variable equal to a value ○ *We set the right-hand margin at 80 characters.* **2.** to define a parameter value **3.** to give a binary data bit the value of one **4.** to compose a text into typeset characters ○ *The page is set in 12 point Times Roman.* ◊ **typeset**

SET /set/ *plural noun* the standards created by a group of banks and Internet companies that allow users to buy goods over the Internet without risk of hackers. Full form **secure electronic transactions**. Same as **SSL**

setting /ˈsetɪŋ/ *noun* **1.** the action of fixing or arranging something □ **tab settings** preset points along a line, where the printing head *or* cursor will stop for each tabulation command **2.** the action of composing text into typeset characters

set up /ˈset ʌp/ *verb* to configure, initialise, define or start an application or system ○ *The new computer worked well as soon as the engineer had set it up.*

sex changer /ˈseks ˌtʃeɪndʒə/ *noun* a device for changing a female connection to a male or vice versa

sf signalling /ˌes ef ˈsɪgn(ə)lɪŋ/ *noun* same as **single-frequency signalling**

SGML /ˌes dʒiː emˈel/ *noun* a hardware-independent standard which defines how documents should be marked up to indicate bolds, italics, margins and so on. Full form **Standard Generalized Markup Language**

shade /ʃeɪd/ *noun* **1.** a variation in a printed colour due to added black **2.** the quantity of black added to a colour to make it darker

shading /ˈʃeɪdɪŋ/ *noun* **1.** the process of showing darker sections of a line drawing by adding dark colour or by drawing criss-cross lines **2.** the adjustment of contrast in a television picture

shadow /ˈʃædəʊ/ *noun* the area where broadcast signals cannot be received because of an obstacle that blocks the transmission medium ○ *The mountain casts a shadow* *over those houses, so they cannot receive any radio broadcasts.*

shadowmask /ˈʃædəʊmɑːsk/ *noun* a sheet with holes placed just behind the front of a colour monitor screen to separate the three-colour picture beams

shadow memory /ˌʃædəʊ ˈmem(ə)ri/, **shadow page** /ˈʃædəʊ peɪdʒ/ *noun* duplicate memory locations accessed by a special code

shadow ROM /ˈʃædəʊ rɒm/ *noun* read-only shadow memory

shannon /ˈʃænən/ *noun* a measure of the information content of a transmission

Shannon's Law /ˈʃænənz lɔː/ *noun* a law defining the maximum information-carrying capacity of a transmission line

COMMENT: Shannon's Law is defined as B lg(1 + S/N) where B = Bandwidth, lg is logarithm to the base two and S/N is Signal to Noise ratio.

share /ʃeə/ *verb* to own or use something together with someone else ○ *The facility is shared by several independent companies.*

shared access /ˌʃeəd ˈækses/ *noun* the use of a computer or peripheral by more than one person or system

shared file /ˌʃeəd ˈfaɪl/ *noun* a stored file which can be accessed by more than one user or system

shared folder /ˌʃeəd ˈfəʊldə/ *noun* a folder of files stored on a computer's local hard disk drive that can be used (or shared) by other users on the network

shareware /ˈʃeəˌweə/ *noun* software which is available free to try, but if kept the user is expected to pay a fee to the writer (often confused with public domain software which is completely free)

'Bulletin board users know the dangers of 'flaming' (receiving hostile comments following a naive or ridiculous assertion) and of being seen 'troughing' (grabbing every bit of shareware on the network).' [*Computing*]

sheet /ʃiːt/ *noun* a large piece of paper

shelf life /ˈʃelf laɪf/ *noun* the maximum storage time of a product before it is no longer guaranteed good to use ○ *The developer has a shelf life of one year.*

shell /ʃel/ *noun* software which operates between the user and the operating system, often to try and make the operating system more friendly or easier to use

shell out /ˌʃel ˈaʊt/ *verb* (when running an application) to exit to the operating system, whilst the original application is still in memory; the user then returns to the application ○ *I shelled out from the word-processor to check which files were on the floppy, then went back to the program.*

shell script /ˌʃel ˈskrɪpt/ *noun* a scripting language (such as Perl) that is used to create programs that can enhance a website, e.g. to search a site for a key word

shell sort /ˌʃel ˈsɔːt/ *noun* an algorithm for sorting data items, in which items can be moved more than one position per sort action

SHF *abbr* super high frequency

shield /ʃiːld/ *noun* a metal screen connected to earth, used to prevent harmful voltages or interference reaching sensitive electronic equipment ■ *verb* to protect a signal or device from external interference or harmful voltages

shift /ʃɪft/ *verb* **1.** to move a bit or word of data left or right by a certain amount (usually one bit) **2.** to change from one character set to another, allowing other characters (such as capitals) to be used

Shift key /ˈʃɪft kiː/ *noun* the key on a keyboard which switches on secondary functions for keys, such as another character set, by changing the output to upper case

Shockwave /ˈʃɒkweɪv/ a trade name for a system developed by Macromedia that allows web browsers to display complex multimedia effects

shoot /ʃuːt/ *verb* to take a picture or record a video sequence with a camera

shopping agent /ˈʃɒpɪŋ ˌeɪdʒənt/ *noun* a computer program used to browse websites searching for a product or service

shopping basket /ˈʃɒpɪŋ ˌbɑːskɪt/, **shopping cart** /ˈʃɒpɪŋ kɑːt/ *noun* software that runs on a web server and provides an electronic version of a real shopping basket; the software allows a visitor to the website to view items in the catalogue, add items to their shopping basket and then pay for the goods at an electronic checkout. ◊ **real-time authorisation, secure site**

short circuit /ˌʃɔːt ˈsɜːkɪt/ *noun* an electrical connection of very low resistance between two points ■ *verb* to connect two points together with a (very low resistance) link

short-circuited /ˌʃɔːt ˈsɜːkɪt/ *adjective* used to describe two points that are electrically connected, usually accidentally

shortcut /ˈʃɔːtˌkʌt/ *noun* a feature of Windows that allows a user to define an icon that links to another file or application, e.g., you could place shortcut icons on the Windows Desktop to allow you to start an application without using the menu commands. The shortcut has the same icon as the original file but has a tiny arrow in the bottom left-hand corner. It is not a duplicate of the original, rather it is a pointer to the original file.

short message service /ˌʃɔːt ˈmesɪdʒ ˌsɜːvɪs/ *noun* a system that allows short text messages to be sent between and to mobile telephones; the service depends upon the telephone company. Abbr **SMS**

short-run /ˈʃɔːt rʌn/ *adjective* with a printrun of only a few hundred copies ○ *a printer specialising in short-run printing* ○ *The laser printer is good for short-run leaflets.*

short wave /ˈʃɔːt weɪv/ *noun* radio communications frequency below 60 metres

short-wave receiver /ˌʃɔːt weɪv rɪˈsiːvə/ *noun* a radio receiver able to pick up broadcasts on the short wave bands

shot /ʃɒt/ *noun* the continuous recording of action or images by a film camera in a small number of frames

show copy /ˈʃəʊ ˌkɒpi/ *noun* a selected copy of a finished film, video or programme which is to be shown to an audience

show-through /ˈʃəʊ θruː/ *noun* text printed on one side of a piece of paper that can be seen from the other

shrink /ʃrɪŋk/ *verb* to become smaller ○ *The drawing was shrunk to fit the space.* (NOTE: **shrinks – shrank – has shrunk**)

S-HTTP /ˌes ˌeɪtʃ tiː tiː ˈpiː/ *noun* a system developed to provide a secure link between a user's browser and a vendor's Website to allow the user to pay for goods over the Internet. Full form **secure hypertext transfer protocol**. ◊ **PGP, SEPP, SET, SSL, STT**

shut down /ˌʃʌt ˈdaʊn/ *verb* to switch off and stop the functions of a machine or system

shut-off mechanism /ˈʃʌt ɒf ˌmekənɪz(ə)m/ *noun* a device which stops a process in case of fault

COMMENT: Most hard disks have an automatic shut-off mechanism to pull the head back from the read position when the power is turned off.

shutter /ˈʃʌtə/ *noun* **1.** a revolving device which protects a film from light at the aperture in a camera and diminishes the projection light in a projector while the film is moving at the aperture **2.** a device to control intensity of a spotlight

shutter control /ˌʃʌtə kənˈtrəʊl/ *noun* **1.** a device on a camera which diminishes exposure by partly closing the shutter **2.** a camera device which slowly opens and closes the shutter in order to attain fade-in and fade-out effects

shutter speed /ˈʃʌtə spiːd/ *noun* the time span for which a shutter is open during the required frame exposure

shuttle search /ˈʃʌt(ə)l sɜːtʃ/ *noun* the capacity to play back a film, video and audio tape in both directions and to duplicate the picture over a large range of speeds

sideband /ˈsaɪdbænd/ *noun* the frequency band of a modulated signal, a little above or below the carrier frequency

side lobe /ˈsaɪd ləʊb/ *noun* the side sections of an aerial's response pattern

sideways ROM /ˈsaɪdweɪz rɒm/ *noun* software which allows selection of a particular memory bank or ROM device

SIG /sɪɡ/ *noun* a group within a larger club which is interested in a particular aspect of software or hardware ○ *Our local computer club has a SIG for comms and networking.* Full form **special interest group**

sign /saɪn/ *noun* polarity of a number or signal (whether it is positive or negative) ■ *verb* to identify oneself to a computer using a personalised signature

signal /ˈsɪɡn(ə)l/ *noun* **1.** a generated analog or digital waveform used to carry information ○ *The signal received from the computer contained the answer.* **2.** a short message used to carry control codes ■ *verb* to send a message to a computer ○ *Signal to the network that we are busy.*

signalling /ˈsɪɡn(ə)lɪŋ/ *noun* **1.** a method used by a transmitter to warn a receiver that a message is to be sent **2.** a communication to the transmitter about the state of the receiver

signal reflection /ˈsɪɡn(ə)l rɪˌflekʃ(ə)n/ *noun* the amount of transmitted signal that is reflected at the receiver due to an impedance mismatch or fault

signal to noise ratio /ˌsɪɡn(ə)l tə ˈnɔɪz ˌreɪʃiəʊ/ *noun* the difference between the power of the transmitted signal and the noise on the line. Abbr **S/N**

signature /ˈsɪɡnɪtʃə/ *noun* **1.** a special authentication code, such as a password, which a user gives prior to access to a system or prior to the execution of a task (to prove identity) **2.** the name written in a special way by someone ○ *Do you recognise the signature on the cheque?* **3.** a series of printed and folded pages in a book (usually 8, 16 or 32 pages)

significance /sɪɡˈnɪfɪkəns/ *noun* a special meaning

significant /sɪɡˈnɪfɪkənt/ *adjective* which has a special meaning

signify /ˈsɪɡnɪˌfaɪ/ *verb* to mean ○ *A carriage return code signifies the end of an input line.*

silicon /ˈsɪlɪkən/ *noun* an element with semiconductor properties, used in crystal form as a base for IC manufacture

COMMENT: Silicon is used in the electronics industry as a base material for integrated circuits. It is grown as a long crystal which is then sliced into wafers before being etched or treated, producing several hundred chips per wafer. Other materials, such as germanium or gallium arsenide, are also used as a base for ICs.

Silicon Valley /ˌsɪlɪkən ˈvæli/ *noun* an area in California where many US semiconductor device manufacturers are based

SIMD /ˌes aɪ em ˈdiː/ *noun* the architecture of a parallel computer which has a number of ALUs and data buses with one control unit. Full form **single instruction stream multiple data stream**

SIMM /ˌes aɪ em ˈem/ *noun* a small, compact circuit board with an edge connector along one edge that carries densely-packed memory chips ○ *You can expand the main memory of your PC by plugging in two more SIMMs.* Full form **single in-line memory module**

simple device /ˌsɪmp(ə)l dɪˈvaɪs/ *noun* a multimedia device that does not require a data file for playback, such as a CD drive used to play audio CDs

simple mail transfer protocol /ˌsɪmpəl meɪl ˈtrænsfɜː ˌprəʊtəkɒl/ *noun* full form of **SMTP**

simple network management protocol /ˌsɪmpəl ˌnetwɜːk ˈmænɪdʒmənt ˌprəʊtəkɒl/ *noun* a network management system which defines how status data is sent from monitored nodes back to a control station; SNMP is able to work with virtually any type of network hardware and software. Abbr **SNMP**

simplex /ˈsɪmpleks/ *noun* full form of **SPX**. opposite **duplex**

simplify /ˈsɪmplɪˌfaɪ/ *verb* to make something simpler ○ *Function keys simplify program operation.*

simulate /ˈsɪmjʊˌleɪt/ *verb* to copy the behaviour of a system or device with another ○ *This software simulates the action of an aircraft.*

simulation /ˌsɪmjʊˈleɪʃ(ə)n/ *noun* an operation where a computer is made to imitate a real life situation or a machine, and shows how something works or will work in the future ○ *Simulation techniques have reached a high degree of sophistication.*

simulator /ˈsɪmjʊˌleɪtə/ *noun* a device which simulates another system

simulcast /ˈsɪməlkɑːst/ *noun* to broadcast a programme at the same time on both television and radio

simultaneous /ˌsɪm(ə)lˈteɪniəs/ *adjective* which takes place at the same time as something else

simultaneously /ˌsɪm(ə)lˈteɪniəsli/ *adverb* at the same time

simultaneous transmission /ˌsɪm(ə)lteɪniəs trænzˈmɪʃ(ə)n/ *noun* the transmission of data or control codes in two directions at the same time. Same as **duplex**

sin /sɪn/, **sine** *noun* a mathematical function defined as: the sine of an angle (in a right-angled triangle) is equal to the ratio of opposite to hypotenuse sides

sine wave /ˈsaɪn weɪv/ *noun* a waveform that is the sine function with time (classic wave shape, changing between a maximum and minimum with a value of zero at zero time)

single /ˈsɪŋg(ə)l/ *adjective* only one

single attachment station /ˌsɪŋg(ə)l ə ˌtætʃmənt ˈsteɪʃ(ə)n/ *noun* (*in an FDDI network*) a station with only one port through which to attach to the network; SAS stations are connected to the FDDI ring through a concentrator. Abbr **SAS**

single board computer /ˌsɪŋg(ə)l bɔːd kəmˈpjuːtə/ *noun* full form of **SBC**

single-frequency signalling /ˌsɪŋg(ə)l ˈfriːkwənsi ˌsɪgn(ə)lɪŋ/ *noun* the use of various frequency signals to represent different control codes. Also called **sf signalling**

single function software /ˌsɪŋg(ə)l ˈfʌŋkʃən ˌsɒftweə/ *noun* an applications program used for one kind of task only

single in-line memory module /ˌsɪŋg(ə)l ɪn laɪn ˈmem(ə)ri ˌmɒdjuːl/ *noun* full form of **SIMM**

single in-line package /ˌsɪŋg(ə)l ɪn laɪn ˈpækɪdʒ/ *noun* an electronic component which has all its leads on one side of its package. Abbr **SIP**

single instruction stream multiple data stream /ˌsɪŋg(ə)l ɪnˌstrʌkʃən striːm ˌmʌltɪp(ə)l ˈdeɪtə ˌstriːm/ *noun* full form of **SIMD**

single instruction stream single data stream /ˌsɪŋg(ə)l ɪnˌstrʌkʃən striːm ˌsɪŋg(ə)l ˈdeɪtə striːm/ *noun* full form of **SISD**

single mode fibre /ˌsɪŋg(ə)l məʊd ˈfaɪbə/ *noun* an optic fibre that has a very narrow diameter (of 10 microns or less) and is designed to transmit a single light signal over a long distance; this type of fibre has a bandwidth of 5Gbits/second and is normally used for long distance telephone networks

single sideband /ˌsɪŋg(ə)l ˈsaɪdbænd/ *noun* a modulated signal filtered to leave just one sideband, usually the upper (this is very economical on bandwidth but requires more complex circuitry)

single-sided disk /ˌsɪŋg(ə)l ˌsaɪdɪd ˈdɪsk/ *noun* a floppy disk that can only store data on one side, because of the way it is manufactured or formatted. Abbr **SSD**

single-user system /ˌsɪŋg(ə)l ˌjuːzə ˈsɪstəm/ *noun* a computer system which can only be used by a single user at a time (as opposed to a multi-user system)

sink /sɪŋk/ *noun* the receiving end of a communications line. Opposite **source**

sinusoidal /ˌsaɪnəˈsɔɪd(ə)l/ *adjective* waveform or motion that is similar to a sine wave ○ *The carrier has a sinusoidal waveform.*

SIO *abbr* serial input/output

SIP *abbr* single in-line package

siphoning /ˈsaɪfənɪŋ/ *noun* the transmission of a direct broadcast TV programme over a cable network

SISD /ˌes aɪ es ˈdiː/ *noun* the architecture of a serial computer, which has one ALU and data bus, with one control unit. Full form **single instruction stream single data stream**

SISO *abbr* serial input/serial output

site /saɪt/ *noun* a place where something is based

site licence /ˈsaɪt ˌlaɪs(ə)ns/ *noun* a licence between a software publisher and a user which allows any number of users in that site to use the software ○ *We have negotiated a good deal for the site licence for the 1200 employees in our HQ.*

site poll /ˌsaɪt ˈpəʊl/ *verb* to poll all the terminals or devices in a particular location or area. ◊ **polling**

SI units /ˌes ˈaɪ ˌjuːnɪts/ *plural noun* international measurement units such as candela, lumen, and ampere. Full form **Système International units.** ◊ **MKS**

sixteen-bit /ˌsɪksˈtiːn bɪt/ *adjective* (*of a microcomputer system or CPU*) which handles data in sixteen bit words, providing much faster operation than older eight-bit systems

16-bit sample /ˌsɪkstiːn bɪt ˈsɑːmp(ə)l/ *noun* a single sample of an analog signal which is stored as a 16-bit number, meaning that there are 65,536 possible levels. A '16-bit sound card' can sometimes mean that the card generates 16-bit samples, but it can also mean that it generates 8-bit samples, but fits into a 16-bit expansion slot. ◊ **8-bit sample, 24-bit sample**

64-bit /ˌsɪksti ˈfɔː bɪt/ data that is transferred sixty-four bits at a time along sixty-four parallel conductors; in a processor this refers to its ability to manipulate numbers that are sixty-four bits long

size /saɪz/ *noun* the physical dimensions of an image, object or page ■ *verb* to calculate the resources available, and those required, to carry out a particular job

sizing /ˈsaɪzɪŋ/ *noun* the process of reducing or enlarging a picture to fit ○ *Photographs can be edited by cropping, sizing, etc.*

sketch /sketʃ/ *noun* a rough drawing made rapidly ■ *verb* to make a rough rapid drawing

skew /skjuː/ *noun* **1.** the amount by which something is not correctly aligned **2.** a television picture distortion in a zig zag shape which can be caused by a mechanical fault in the video tape motion or tension ■ *verb* to align something incorrectly ○ *This page is badly skewed.*

skip /skɪp/ *verb* **1.** to ignore an instruction in a sequence of instructions ○ *The printer skipped the next three lines of text.* **2.** to transmit radio waves over an abnormally long distance due to the reflective properties of the atmosphere

slashed zero /ˌslæʃd ˈzɪərəʊ/ *noun* a printed or written sign (Ø)

slave /sleɪv/ *noun* **1.** a remote secondary computer or terminal controlled by a central computer **2.** a recorder which dubs playbacks from a master tape; the video tape used for this dubbing process

sleep /sliːp/ *noun* the state of a system that is waiting for a signal (log-on) before doing anything. ◊ **wake**

sleeve /sliːv/ *noun* a paper or plastic cover for a magnetic disk

slew /sluː/ *noun* a rapid movement of paper in a printer, ignoring the normal line advance

slicing /ˈslaɪsɪŋ/ *noun* the process of cutting thin round wafers from a bar of silicon crystal

slide /slaɪd/ *noun* **1.** one image in a presentation or a single frame of positive photographic film **2.** a transparency which is to be projected by transmitted light ■ *verb* to move smoothly across a surface ○ *The disk cover slides on and off easily.*

slide show /ˈslaɪd ʃəʊ/ *noun* a feature of a presentation graphics software in which slides (static images) are displayed in a sequence under the control of the presenter

slip pages /ˈslɪp ˌpeɪdʒɪz/, **slip proofs** /ˈslɪp pruːfs/ *noun* proofs, where each page of text is printed on a separate piece of paper

slot /slɒt/ *noun* a long thin hole ○ *The system disk should be inserted into the left-hand slot on the front of the computer.* ■ *verb* to insert an object into a hole ○ *The disk slots into one of the floppy drive apertures.*

slow motion /ˌsləʊ ˈməʊʃ(ə)n/ *noun* **1.** the playing back of a video tape or disk sequence slower than recorded ○ *The film switched to slow motion.* ○ *Play the film again in slow motion.* **2.** the process of filming with a motion picture camera with the film moving at a more accelerated speed than normal so that when the film is projected at a normal rate, the action seems to be slowed down

slow scan /ˈsləʊ skæn/ *noun* a television transmission and scanning at a slower frame rate than usual

slow scan TV /ˌsləʊ skæn tiː ˈviː/ *noun* a system used to transmit still video frames over a telephone line

SLSI *abbr* super large scale integration

slur /slɜː/ *noun* **1.** a printed image which is blurred because of movement during printing **2.** distortion of voice during transmission

small /smɔːl/ *adjective* not large

small computer system interface /ˌsmɔːl kəmˌpjuːtə ˈsɪstəm ˌɪntəfeɪs/ *noun* full form of **SCSI**

small-scale /ˈsmɔːl skeɪl/ *adjective* working with small amounts of data. Compare **large-scale**

small scale integration /ˌsmɔːl skeɪl ˌɪntɪˈgreɪʃ(ə)n/ *noun* an integrated circuit with 1 to 10 components. Abbr **SSI**

smart /smɑːt/ *adjective* intelligent

smart card /ˈsmɑːt kɑːd/ *noun* a plastic card with a memory and microprocessor device embedded in it, so that it can be used for electronic funds transfer or for identification of the user

smart terminal /ˌsmɑːt ˈtɜːmɪn(ə)l/ *noun* a computer terminal which can process information. Compare **dumb terminal**

SMATV *noun* a distributor of cable or microwave satellite broadcasts to separate viewers from a central antenna. Full form **satellite master antenna television**

SMB /ˌes em ˈbiː/ *noun* a system developed by Microsoft which allows a user to access another computer's files and peripherals over a network as if they were local resources. Full form **server message block**

smiley /ˈsmaɪli/ *noun* a face created with text characters, used to provide the real meaning to an email message; e.g., :-) means laughter or a joke, and :-(means sad

smooth scroll /ˌsmuːð ˈskrəʊl/ *noun* text which is moved up a screen pixel by pixel rather than line by line, which gives a smoother movement

SMPTE /ˌes em piː tiː ˈiː/ *noun* an organisation that defines standards for television production systems; e.g., the SMPTE time code standard is widely used to synchronise audio and video equipment using hours, minutes, seconds, frame data that is stored in an 80-bit word. Full form **Society for Motion Picture and TV Engineers**

SMPTE division type /ˌes em piː tiː ˌiː dɪˈvɪʒ(ə)n ˌtaɪp/ *noun* a timing format which specifies the number of frames per second used, and in which time is shown as hours, minutes, seconds, frames; standard SMPTE division types are 24, 25 and 30 frames per second

SMPTE offset /ˌes em piː tiː iː ˈɒfset/ *noun* a MIDI event that defines when a MIDI file is to be played back

SMPTE time code /ˌes em piː tiː iː ˈtaɪm ˌkəʊd/ *noun* a method of assigning a unique identifying number to each frame in a video sequence

SMS *abbr* short message service

SMT /ˌes em ˈtiː/ *noun* a method of manufacturing circuit boards in which the electronic components are bonded directly onto the surface of the board rather than being inserted into holes and soldered into place ○ *Surface-mount technology is faster and more space-efficient than soldering.* Full form **surface-mount technology**

SMTP /ˌes em tiː ˈpiː/ *noun* a standard protocol which allows electronic mail messages to be transferred from one system to another, normally used as the method of transferring mail from one Internet server to another or to send mail from a computer to a server. Full form **simple mail transfer protocol**. Compare **POP 3**

S/N *abbr* signal to noise ratio

SNA /ˌes en ˈeɪ/ *noun* design methods developed by IBM which define how communications in a network should occur and allow different hardware to communicate. Full form **Systems Network Architecture**

snail mail /ˈsneɪl meɪl/ *noun* a term used to refer to the usually slow postal delivery as opposed to nearly instant electronic mail delivery (*slang*)

snapshot /ˈsnæpˌʃɒt/ *noun* **1.** a recording of all the states of a computer at a particular instant **2.** the process of storing in main memory the contents of a screen full of information at an instant **3.** a personal photograph taken quickly

snapshot dump /ˈsnæpˌʃɒt dʌmp/ *noun* a printout of all the registers and a section of memory at a particular instant, used when debugging a program

snd /saʊnd/ *noun* a filename extension used to indicate a file that contains digitised sound data. Full form **SouND**

SNMP *abbr* simple network management protocol

SNOBOL /ˈsnəʊbɒl/ *noun* a high-level programming language which uses string processing methods. Full form **string orientated symbolic language**

snow /snəʊ/ *noun* interference displayed as flickering white flecks on a monitor

s/n ratio /ˌes 'en ˌreɪʃiəʊ/ *noun* the ratio of the amplitude of the transmitted signal to the noise on the received signal. Full form **signal to noise ratio**

soak /səʊk/ *verb* to run a program or device continuously for a period of time to make sure it functions correctly

Society for Motion Picture and TV Engineers /səˌsaɪəti fə ˌməʊʃ(ə)n ˌpɪktʃə ən ˌtiː 'viː/ *noun* full form of **SMPTE**

socket /'sɒkɪt/ *noun* a device with a set of holes, into which a plug fits

socket driver /'sɒkɪt ˌdraɪvə/ *noun* same as **Winsock**

SOCKS /sɒks/ *noun* a network protocol developed to support the transfer of TCP/IP (Internet) traffic through a proxy server. It is commonly used to provide a way for users on a local area network to access the Internet via a single shared connection.

SOF /ˌes əʊ 'ef/ *noun* an indication of synchronised picture and sound on film. Full form **sound-on-film**

soft /sɒft/ *adjective* **1.** referring to material which loses its magnetic effects when removed from a magnetic field **2.** referring to data which is not permanently stored in hardware. Soft usually refers to data stored on magnetic medium. Compare **hard error 3.** one shape that gradually changes to another

soft copy /ˌsɒft 'kɒpi/ *noun* text listed on screen (as opposed to hard copy on paper). ◊ **hard copy**

soft error /ˌsɒft 'erə/ *noun* a random error caused by software or data errors which is very difficult to trace and identify since it only appears under certain conditions

soft-fail /ˌsɒft 'feɪl/ *adjective* referring to a system which is still partly operational even after a part of the system has failed

soft font /ˌsɒft 'fɒnt/ *noun* fonts or typefaces stored on a disk, which can be downloaded or sent to a printer and stored in temporary memory or RAM

soft goods /'sɒft gʊdz/ *plural noun* software that can be purchased and paid for in an online shop, and which is then downloaded directly onto a computer instead of receiving a CD-ROM sent by post

soft hyphen /ˌsɒft 'haɪf(ə)n/ *noun* same as **discretionary hyphen**

soft keyboard /ˌsɒft 'kiːbɔːd/ *noun* a keyboard where the functions of the keys can be changed by programs

soft keys /ˌsɒft 'kiːz/ *plural noun* keys which can be changed by means of a program

soft reset /ˌsɒft 'riːset/ *noun* an instruction that terminates any program execution and returns the user to the monitor or BIOS

soft-sectored disk /ˌsɒft ˌsektəd 'dɪsk/ *noun* a disk where the sectors are described by an address and start code data written onto it when the disk is formatted

software /'sɒftweə/ *noun* **1.** any program or group of programs which instructs the hardware on how it should perform, including operating systems, word processors and applications programs **2.** films, audio tapes and audio disks that are commercially accessible (NOTE: no plural for **software.** For the plural say **pieces of software.**) **3.** programmes for broadcast which are presented on electronic equipment

software compatible /ˌsɒftweə kəm'pætɪb(ə)l/ *adjective* referring to a computer which will load and run programs written for another computer

software developer /'sɒftweə dɪˌveləpə/ *noun* a person or company which writes software

software development /'sɒftweə dɪˌveləpmənt/ *noun* the processes required to produce working programs from an initial idea

software documentation /ˌsɒftweə ˌdɒkjʊmen'teɪʃ(ə)n/ *noun* information, notes and diagrams describing the function, use and operation of a piece of software

software engineer /'sɒftweə ˌendʒɪnɪə/ *noun* a person who can write working software to fit an application

software engineering /'sɒftweə ˌendʒɪnɪərɪŋ/ *noun* a field of study covering all software-related subjects

software house /'sɒftweə haʊs/ *noun* a company which develops and sells computer programs

software library /'sɒftweə ˌlaɪbrəri/ *noun* a number of specially written routines, stored in a library file which can be inserted into a program, saving time and effort. Abbr **H**

software licence /'sɒftweə ˌlaɪs(ə)ns/ *noun* an agreement between a user and a software house, giving details of the rights of the user to use or copy the software

software life cycle /ˌsɒftweə 'laɪf ˌsaɪk(ə)l/ *noun* the period of time when a piece of software exists, from its initial design to the moment when it becomes out of date

software maintenance /'sɒftweə ˌmeɪntənəns/ *noun* the process of carrying out updates and modifications to a software package to make sure the program is up to date

software-only video playback /ˌsɒftweə ˌəʊnli ˌvɪdiəʊ ˈpleɪbæk/ *noun* the ability to display full-motion video standard on any multimedia computer, without requiring special hardware

software package /ˈsɒftweə ˌpækɪdʒ/ *noun* computer programs and manuals designed for a special purpose

software piracy /ˈsɒftweə ˌpaɪrəsi/ *noun* the illegal copying of software for sale

software quality assurance /ˌsɒftweə ˌkwɒlɪti əˈʃʊərəns/ *noun* the process of making sure that software will perform as intended. Abbr **SQA**

software reliability /ˌsɒftweə rɪˌlaɪə ˈbɪlɪti/ *noun* the ability of a piece of software to perform the task required correctly

software specification /ˌsɒftweə ˌspesɪfɪˈkeɪʃ(ə)n/ *noun* detailed information about a piece of software's abilities, functions and methods

software system /ˈsɒftweə ˌsɪstəm/ *noun* all the programs required for one or more tasks

soft zone /ˌsɒft ˈzəʊn/ *noun* a text area to the left of the right margin in a word-processed document, where if a word does not fit completely, a hyphen is automatically inserted

solar /ˈsəʊlə/ *adjective* referring to the sun

solar cell /ˈsəʊlə sel/ *noun* a component that converts the light of the sun into electrical energy

Solaris™ /səʊˈlɑːrɪs/ a multi-tasking, multiprocessing operating system and system utilities developed by SunSoft for SPARC computers and PCs with a 80386

solarisation /səʊləraɪˈzeɪʃ(ə)n/, **solarization** *noun* **1.** a flare in a film image due to the film having been struck by light during processing **2.** a photographic effect where the picture image colours or tones are reversed, such as normally light areas becoming darker and vice versa; an almost identical effect can be created by video techniques

solar power /ˈsəʊlə ˌpaʊə/ *noun* (electrical) power derived from the sun

solenoid /ˈsɒlənɔɪd/ *noun* a mechanical device operated by an electromagnetic field

solid modelling /ˌsɒlɪd ˈmɒd(ə)lɪŋ/ *noun* a function in a graphics program that creates three-dimensional solid-looking objects by shading

solid-state /ˈsɒlɪd steɪt/ *adjective* referring to semiconductor devices

solution /səˈluːʃ(ə)n/ *noun* **1.** the answer to a problem **2.** a liquid in which certain chemicals have been dissolved

solve /sɒlv/ *verb* to find the answer to a problem

sonar /ˈsəʊnɑː/ *noun* a device that uses sound waves to determine the state and depth of water

son file /ˈsʌn faɪl/ *noun* the latest working version of a file. Compare **father file, grandfather file**

song /sɒŋ/ *noun* a complete musical tune

song key /ˈsɒŋ kiː/ *noun* a musical key used to play a MIDI song

sonic /ˈsɒnɪk/ *adjective* referring to sound; (sound signals) within the human hearing range (20 – 20,000Hz)

sophisticated /səˈfɪstɪkeɪtɪd/ *adjective* technically advanced ○ *A sophisticated desktop publishing program.*

sophistication /səˌfɪstɪˈkeɪʃ(ə)n/ *noun* the state of being technically advanced ○ *The sophistication of the new package is remarkable.*

sort /sɔːt/ *verb* to put data in order, according to a system, on the instructions of the user ○ *To sort addresses into alphabetical order.*

sortkey /ˈsɔːtkiː/, **sort field** /ˈsɔːt fiːld/ *noun* a field in a stored file which is used to sort the file ○ *The orders were sorted according to dates by assigning the date field as the sortkey.*

sound /saʊnd/ *noun* a noise

Sound Blaster /ˈsaʊnd ˌblɑːstə/ a trade name for a type of sound card for PC compatibles developed by Creative Labs that allows sounds to be recorded to disk (using a microphone) and played back

sound capture /ˈsaʊnd ˌkæptʃə/ *noun* the conversion of an analog sound into a digital form that can be used by a computer

sound card /ˌsaʊnd ˈkɑːd/ *noun* an expansion card which produces analog sound signals under the control of a computer ○ *This software lets you create almost any sound – but you can only hear them if you have a sound card fitted.*

sound chip /ˌsaʊnd ˈtʃɪp/ *noun* a device that will generate a sound or tune

sound file /ˌsaʊnd ˈfaɪl/ *noun* a file stored on disk that contains sound data

sound pressure level /ˌsaʊnd ˈpreʃə ˌlev(ə)l/ *noun* full form of **SPL**

soundproof /ˈsaʊndpruːf/ *adjective* which does not allow sound to pass through ○ *The telephone is installed in a soundproof booth.*

Sound Recorder /ˈsaʊnd rɪˌkɔːdə/ a utility included with Microsoft Windows that allows a user to play back digitised sound files or record sound onto disk and carry out very basic editing

source /sɔːs/ *noun* **1.** a point where a transmitted signal enters a network. Opposite **sink 2.** an original or initial point **3.** the name of a terminal on an FET device

source document /'sɔːs ˌdɒkjʊmənt/ *noun* a form or document from which data is extracted prior to entering it into a database

source file /ˌsɔːs 'faɪl/ *noun* a program written in source language, which is then converted to machine code by a compiler

source language /'sɔːs ˌlæŋgwɪdʒ/ *noun* **1.** a language in which a program is originally written **2.** a language of a program prior to translation. Opposite **object language, target language**

space /speɪs/ *noun* **1.** a gap between characters or lines **2.** a transmitted signal representing a binary zero. Opposite **mark** ■ *verb* to spread out text ○ *The line of characters was evenly spaced out across the page.*

space bar /'speɪs bɑː/ *noun* a long bar at the bottom of a keyboard, which inserts a space into the text when pressed

spacing /'speɪsɪŋ/ *noun* the process of putting spaces between characters or lines of printed text ○ *The spacing on some lines is very uneven.*

spam /spæm/ *noun* an article that has been posted to more than one newsgroup, so is likely to contain commercial messages (*slang*)

spam killer /'spæm ˌkɪlə/ *noun* a piece of software that automatically identifies and deals with spam in incoming e-mail

spanning tree /'spænɪŋ triː/ *noun* a method of creating a network topology that does not contain any loops and provides redundancy in case of a network fault or problem

spark printer /'spɑːk ˌprɪntə/ *noun* a thermal printer which produces characters on thermal paper by electric sparks

sparse array /ˌspɑːs ə'reɪ/ *noun* a data matrix structure containing mainly zero or null entries

spatial measurement /ˌspeɪʃ(ə)l 'meʒəmənt/ *noun* a method of allowing a computer to determine the position of a pointer within three dimensions (often using a sensitive glove)

speaker /'spiːkə/ *noun* ➧ **loudspeaker**

spec /spek/ *noun* same as **specifications** (*informal*)

special /'speʃ(ə)l/ *adjective* which is different or not usual

special character /ˌspeʃ(ə)l 'kærɪktə/ *noun* a character which is not a standard one in a certain font (such as a certain accent or a symbol)

special interest group /ˌspeʃ(ə)l 'ɪntrəst ˌgruːp/ *noun* full form of **SIG**

specialise /'speʃəlaɪz/ *verb* to study and be an expert in a subject ○ *He specialises in the design of CAD systems.*

specialist /'speʃəlɪst/ *noun* an expert in a certain field of study ○ *You need a specialist programmer to help devise a new word-processing program.*

specifications /ˌspesɪfɪ'keɪʃ(ə)nz/ *noun* detailed information about what is to be supplied or about a job to be done ○ *high spec cabling needs to be very carefully handled* □ **to work to standard specifications** to work to specifications which are accepted anywhere in the same industry □ **the work is not up to specification, does not meet the customer's specifications** the product was not manufactured in the way which was detailed in the specifications

specific code /spəˌsɪfɪk 'kəʊd/ *noun* a binary code which directly operates the central processing unit, using only absolute addresses and values

specificity /ˌspesɪ'fɪsəti/ *noun* the ratio of non-relevant entries not retrieved to the total number of non-relevant entries contained in a file, database or library

specify /'spesɪˌfaɪ/ *verb* to state clearly what is needed

spectrum /'spektrəm/ *noun* a range of frequencies; range of colours

spectrum analyser /'spektrəm ˌænəlaɪzə/ *noun* electronic test equipment that displays the amplitudes of a number of frequencies in a signal

speech /spiːtʃ/ *noun* the act of speaking or making words with the voice

'...speech conveys information, and the primary task of computer speech processing is the transmission and reception of that information' [*Personal Computer World*]

speech recognition /ˌspiːtʃ ˌrekəg'nɪʃ(ə)n/ *noun* the process of analysing spoken words in such a way that a computer can recognise spoken words and commands

speech synthesis /'spiːtʃ ˌsɪnθəsɪs/ *noun* the production of spoken words by a speech synthesiser

speech synthesiser /'spiːtʃ ˌsɪnθəsaɪzə/ *noun* a device which takes data from a computer and outputs it as spoken words

spellcheck /'speltʃek/ *verb* to check the spelling in a text by comparing it with a dictionary held in the computer

spellchecker /'speltʃekə/, **spelling checker** /ˌspelɪŋ 'tʃekə/ *noun* a dictionary of correctly spelled words, held in a computer, and used to check the spelling of a text ○

The program will be upgraded with a word-processor and a spelling checker.

spherical aberration /ˌsferɪk(ə)l ˌæbəˈreɪʃ(ə)n/, **spherical distortion** *noun* optical distortion causing lines to appear curved

spherical optics /ˌsferɪk(ə)l ˈɒptɪks/ *plural noun* camera or spotlight lenses which have surfaces with different curvatures which are used to create changes in the paths followed by light rays

spherisation /ˌsfɪəraɪˈzeɪʃ(ə)n/ *noun* a special effect provided by a computer graphics program that converts an image into a sphere, or 'wraps' the image over a spherical shape

spider /ˈspaɪdə/ *noun* a program that searches through the millions of pages that make up the world wide web for new information, changes or pages that have been deleted. These changes are then added to a search engine index to ensure that it is always up to date.

spike /spaɪk/ *noun* a very short duration voltage pulse

spill /spɪl/, **spill light** /ˈspɪl laɪt/ *noun* unwanted light created by a diffusion of light along the principal beam of a light source

spillage /ˈspɪlɪdʒ/ *noun* a situation when too much data is being processed and cannot be contained in a buffer

spin /spɪn/ *verb* to turn round fast ○ *The disk was spun by the drive.*

spindle /ˈspɪnd(ə)l/ *noun* an object which grips and spins a disk in the centre hole

spindling /ˈspɪndlɪŋ/ *noun* the process of turning a disk by hand

spine /spaɪn/ *noun* the back edge of the book which is covered by the binding ○ *The author's name and the title usually are shown on the spine as well as on the front cover.*

spirit duplicator /ˌspɪrɪt ˈdjuːplɪkeɪtə/ *noun* a short-run printing method using spirit to transfer ink onto the paper

SPL /ˌes piː ˈel/ *noun* a measure of loudness, in decibels (dB). Full form **sound pressure level**

splash screen /ˈsplæʃ skriːn/ *noun* the initial screen that is displayed for a few seconds when a program is started ○ *The splash screen normally displays the product logo and gives basic copyright information.*

splice /splaɪs/ *verb* to join two lengths of magnetic tape, forming a continuous length

split-field lens /ˌsplɪt fiːld ˈlenz/, **split-focus lens** /ˌsplɪt ˈfəʊkəs ˌlenz/ *noun* a camera lens which is able to achieve perfect focus at two different planes

split-focus shot /ˌsplɪt ˈfəʊkəs ˌʃɒt/ *noun* a shot where the focus of the camera is altered from one plane to another

split screen /ˈsplɪt skriːn/ *noun* **1.** software which can divide the display into two or more independent areas, to display two text files or a graph and a text file ○ *We use split screen mode to show the text being worked on and another text from memory for comparison.* **2.** a shot where two or more images are visible in different areas of the same picture

splitter /ˈsplɪtə/ *noun* a device which allows a number of other a devices to be plugged into one supply or line

spoof /spuːf/ *verb* to send e-mail using a false name or e-mail address

spool /spuːl/ *noun* a reel on which a tape or printer ribbon is wound ■ *verb* to transfer data from a disk to a tape

spooler *noun* a device which holds a tape and which receives information from a disk for storage

spooling /ˈspuːlɪŋ/ *noun* the process of transferring data to a disk from which it can be printed at the normal speed of the printer, leaving the computer available to do something else

spooling device /ˈspuːlɪŋ dɪˌvaɪs/ *noun* same as **spooler**

spot /spɒt/ *noun* a point on a CRT screen that is illuminated by the electron beam

spot beam /ˈspɒt biːm/ *noun* narrow (satellite) antenna coverage of a select region (on earth)

spotting /ˈspuːlɪŋ/ *noun* the retouching, with an opaque substance, of undesirable marks on film which appeared during the developing process

spot wobble /ˈspɒt ˌwɒb(ə)l/ *noun* vertical fluctuation of a television display's scanning beam in order to make the raster spacing less obvious

spreadsheet /ˈspredʃiːt/ *noun* a program which allows calculations to be carried out on several columns of numbers

sprite /spraɪt/ *noun* an object which moves round the screen in computer graphics

sprocket *noun* a wheel with teeth round it which fit into holes in continuous stationery or punched tape

sprocket feed /ˈsprɒkɪt fiːd/ *noun* a paper feed where the printer pulls the paper by turning sprocket wheels which fit into a series of holes along each edge of the sheet. ◊ **tractor feed**

sprocket holes /ˈsprɒkɪt həʊlz/ *plural noun* **1.** a series of small holes on each edge of continuous stationery, which allow the sheet to be pulled through the printer **2.** perforations in the edges of a strip of film

sprocket wheel /ˈsprɒkɪt wiːl/ *noun* same as **sprocket**

spur /spɜː/ *noun* a connection point into a network

spurious data /ˌspjʊəriəs ˈdeɪtə/ *noun* unexpected or unwanted data or an error in a signal, often due to noise

SPX /ˌes piː ˈeks/ a trade name for a network transport protocol developed by Novell and used to carry IPX network traffic. Full form **sequenced packet exchange** ■ *noun* data transmission in only one direction. Full form **simplex**. Opposite **duplex**

spyware /ˈspaɪweə/ *noun* a type of software that can be installed on someone's hard disk without that person's knowledge. It is designed to send back encoded information about the computer owner's identity and the way he or she uses the Internet to the person who installed it.

SQA *abbr* software quality assurance

SQL /ˌes kjuː ˈel/ *noun* a simple, commonly used standard, database programming language that is only used to create queries to retrieve data from the database. Full form **structured query language**

square wave /ˌskweə ˈweɪv/ *noun* a pulse that rises vertically, levels off, then drops vertically; the ideal shape for a digital signal

squeeze /skwiːz/ *noun* the horizontal compression of film images by using an anamorphic lens

squeeze room /ˈskwiːz ruːm/ *noun* a system which alters the shape of a television image for an artistic effect

SSD *abbr* single-sided disk

SSI *abbr* small scale integration

SSL /ˌes es ˈel/ *noun* a protocol designed by Netscape that provides secure communications over the Internet. Full form **secure sockets layer**. ◊ **PGP, SEPP, SET, STT**

ST *noun* a range of personal computers developed by Atari that use the Motorola 68000 series CPU

stabiliser /ˈsteɪbɪlaɪzə/, **stabilizer** *noun* a mount which holds the camera steady

stability /stəˈbɪlɪti/ *noun* the condition of being stable

stable /ˈsteɪb(ə)l/ *adjective* not moving or not changing

stack /stæk/ *noun* temporary storage for data, registers or tasks where items are added and retrieved from the same end of the list. ◊ **LIFO**

stackable hub /ˌstækəb(ə)l ˈhʌb/ *noun* a hub device that has an external connector to allow several devices to be connected together so that network information can pass from one network ring to another

stage /steɪdʒ/ *noun* one of several points in a process ○ *The text is ready for the printing stage.*

staged /steɪdʒd/ *adjective* carried out in stages, one after the other

stage window /ˌsteɪdʒ ˈwɪndəʊ/ *noun* a window in which a video or animation sequence is viewed (normally refers to a window in which a Movie Player sequence is played)

stand-alone /ˈstænd əˌəʊn/, **standalone** *adjective* referring to a device or system that can operate without the need of any other devices ○ *The workstations have been networked together rather than used as standalone systems.* ■ *noun* such a device or system

standard /ˈstændəd/ *adjective* normal or usual

standard document /ˌstændəd ˈdɒkjʊmənt/, **standard form** /ˈstændəd fɔːm/ *noun* a printed document or form which is used many times (with different names and addresses often inserted – as in a form letter)

standard function /ˌstændəd ˈfʌŋkʃən/ *noun* a special feature included as normal in a computer system

Standard Generalized Markup Language /ˌstændəd ˌdʒen(ə)rəlaɪzd ˈmɑːkʌp ˌlæŋgwɪdʒ/ *noun* full form of **SGML**

standardise /ˈstændədaɪz/ *verb* to make a series of things conform to a standard ○ *to standardise control of transmission links*

standard letter /ˌstændəd ˈletə/ *noun* a letter which is sent without any change to the main text, but which is personalised by inserting the names and addresses of different people

standard paragraph /ˌstændəd ˈpærəgrɑːf/ *noun* a printed paragraph which is used many times (with different names and addresses often inserted – as in a form letter)

standards /ˈstændədz/ *plural noun* normal quality or normal conditions which are used to judge other things ○ *this batch of disks is not up to standard* □ **up to standard** of an acceptable quality ○ *this batch of disks is not up to standard*

standards converter /ˈstændədz kən ˌvɜːtə/ *noun* a device to convert received signals conforming to one standard into a different standard

standard text /ˌstændəd ˈtekst/ *noun* a printed text which is used many times (with different names and addresses often inserted – as in a form letter)

standby /ˈstændbaɪ/ *adjective* referring to a device or program that is ready for use in case of failure ■ *noun* such a device or program

standby equipment /ˈstændbaɪ ɪ ˌkwɪpmənt/ *noun* a secondary system identical to the main system, to be used if the main system breaks down

staple /ˈsteɪp(ə)l/ *noun* a bent metal pin which attaches pages together ■ *verb* to attach papers together with a bent metal pin ○ *The booklet is stapled together.* ○ *The collator gathers signatures together before stapling.*

star filter /ˈstɑː ˌfɪltə/ *noun* a filter with an engraved design which creates star effects on strong light sources

star network /ˈstɑː ˌnetwɜːk/ *noun* a network of several machines where each node is linked individually to a central hub. Compare **bus network, ring topology network**

start /stɑːt/ *noun* the beginning or first part

start bit /ˈstɑːt ˌbɪt/ *noun* a transmitted bit used (in asynchronous communications) to indicate the start of a character. Opposite **stop bit**

Start button /ˈstɑːt ˌbʌt(ə)n/ *noun* a button that is normally in the bottom left-hand corner of a Windows 95 Desktop screen and provides a convenient route to the programs and files on the computer

start of text /ˌstɑːt əv ˈtekst/ *noun* a transmitted code indicating the end of control or address information and the start of the message. Abbr **SOT, STX**

start page /ˈstɑːt peɪdʒ/ *noun* the webpage to which a visitor to a website is automatically taken first

startup disk /ˈstɑːtʌp dɪsk/ *noun* a floppy disk which holds the operating system and system configuration files which can, in case of hard disk failure, be used to boot the computer

Startup folder /ˈstɑːtʌp ˌfəʊldə/ *noun* a special folder on a hard disk that contains programs that will be run automatically when the user next starts Windows

startup screen /ˈstɑːtʌp skriːn/ *noun* text or graphics displayed when an application or multimedia book is run

statement /ˈsteɪtmənt/ *noun* **1.** an expression used to convey an instruction or define a process **2.** an instruction in a source language which is translated into several machine code instructions

state-of-the-art /ˌsteɪt əv ði ˈɑːt/ *adjective* very modern or technically as advanced as possible

'...the main PCB is decidedly non-state-of-the-art' [*Personal Computer World*]

static /ˈstætɪk/ *adjective* **1.** referring to data that does not change with time **2.** referring to a system that is not dynamic

COMMENT: Static RAM uses bistable devices such as flip-flops to store data; these take up more space on a chip than the capacitative storage method of dynamic RAM but do not require refreshing.

static object /ˌstætɪk ˈɒbdʒekt/ *noun* an object in an animation or video that does not move within the frame

station /ˈsteɪʃ(ə)n/ *noun* a point in a network or communications system which contains devices to control the input and output of messages, allowing it to be used as a sink or source

stationary /ˈsteɪʃ(ə)n(ə)ri/ *adjective* not moving

stationery /ˈsteɪʃ(ə)n(ə)ri/ *noun* office supplies for writing, especially paper, envelopes, labels, etc.

statistical /stəˈtɪstɪk(ə)l/ *adjective* based on statistics

statistician /ˌstætɪˈstɪʃ(ə)n/ *noun* a person who analyses statistics

statistics /stəˈtɪstɪks/ *noun* the study of facts in the form of figures ■ *plural noun* a collection of numerical data

status /ˈsteɪtəs/ *noun* importance or position of something

status bar /ˈsteɪtəs bɑː/ *noun* a line at the top or bottom of a screen which gives information about the task currently being worked on, e.g. position of cursor, number of lines, filename, time

status line /ˈsteɪtəs laɪn/ *noun* same as **status bar**

ST connector /ˌes tiː kəˈnektə/ *noun* a connector used to terminate optical fibres

STD *abbr* subscriber trunk dialling

STDM *abbr* statistical time division multiplexing

steadicam /ˈstedikæm/ *noun* a device which prevents camera shake and provides smooth action with a hand-held camera

steep learning curve /ˌstiːp ˈlɜːnɪŋ ˌkɜːv/ *noun* **1.** referring to a product that is very difficult to use **2.** such a product

steg analysis /ˈsteg əˌnæləsɪs/ *noun* the process of searching through computerised graphics or music files to find slight changes in the normal patterns that may show the presence of hidden messages

step /step/ *noun* a single unit

step frame /ˈstep freɪm/ *verb* to capture a video sequence one frame at a time, used when the computer is not powerful or fast enough to capture real-time full-motion video

stepper motor, stepping motor *noun* a motor which turns in small steps as instructed by a computer (used in printers, disk drives and robots)

step printing /ˈstep ˌprɪntɪŋ/ *noun* a printing process where the film is exposed one frame at a time

step through /ˈstep θruː/ *noun* a function of a debugger that allows a developer to execute a program one instruction at a time to see where the fault lies

steradion /stəˈreɪdiɒn/ *noun* a unit of solid angle

stereo /ˈsteriəʊ/, **stereophonic** /ˌsteriəˈfɒnɪk/ *adjective* referring to sound recorded onto two separate channels from two separate microphone elements and played back through a pair of headphones or two speakers

stereophony /ˌsteriˈɒfəni/ *noun* sound reproduction using two or more channels to produce a three dimensional effect of sound

stereoscopy /ˌsteriˈɒskəpi/ *noun* a photography system which provides a three dimensional effect

stickiness /ˈstɪkinəs/ *noun* the ability of a website to attract visitors and to keep them interested for a long time

sticky /ˈstɪki/ *adjective* used to describe an Internet site that attracts visitors, especially one that keeps them interested for a long time

still /stɪl/ *noun* a single image or frame within a video or film sequence

still frame /ˈstɪl freɪm/ *noun* an individual film or video tape frame which is continuously reproduced

stochastic model /stəˈkæstɪk ˌmɒd(ə)l/ *noun* a mathematical representation of a system which includes the effects of random actions

stock control program /ˌstɒk kənˈtrəʊl ˌprəʊgræm/ *noun* software designed to help manage stock in a business

stop /stɒp/ *verb* to cease doing something

stop-action photos /ˌstɒp ˌækʃənˈfəʊtəʊz/ *noun* images in which objects have been intermittently filmed one frame at a time so that when they are projected at a normal speed the changes that occur to these objects will be apparent

stop and wait protocol /ˌstɒp ən ˈweɪt ˌprəʊtəkɒl/ *noun* communications protocol in which the transmitter waits for a signal from the receiver that the message was correctly received before transmitting further data

stop bit /ˈstɒp bɪt/ *noun* a transmitted bit used in asynchronous communications to indicate the end of a character. Opposite **start bit**

stop down /ˌstɒp ˈdaʊn/ *verb* to decrease the width of a lens aperture by altering the diaphragm of the iris

stop element /ˈstɒp ˌelɪmənt/ *noun* same as **stop bit**

stop frame /ˈstɒp freɪm/ *noun* ▸ **still frame**

stop motion /ˌstɒp ˈməʊʃ(ə)n/ *noun* the filming, projecting or printing of one frame at a time

storage /ˈstɔːrɪdʒ/ *noun* memory or the part of a computer system in which data or programs are kept for further use

storage device /ˈstɔːrɪdʒ dɪˌvaɪs/ *noun* any device which can store data and then allow it to retrieved when required

storage medium /ˈstɔːrɪdʒ ˌmiːdiəm/ *noun* any physical material that can be used to store data for a computer application

storage tube /ˈstɔːrɪdʒ tjuːb/ *noun* a special CRT used for computer graphics, which retains an image on screen without the need for refresh actions

store /stɔː/ *noun* memory or the part of a computer system in which data or programs are kept for further use ■ *verb* to save data, which can then be used again as necessary ○ *Storing a page of high resolution graphics can require 3Mb.*

COMMENT: Storage devices include hard and floppy disk, RAM, punched paper tape and magnetic tape.

store and forward /ˌstɔː ən ˈfɔəwəd/ *noun* an electronic mail communications system which stores a number of messages before retransmitting them

story board /ˈstɔːri bɔːd/ *noun* a series of pictures or drawings that show how a video or animation progresses

straight cut /ˈstreɪt kʌt/ *noun* the cutting from one shot to another with no intervening visual effect

stray /streɪ/ *adjective* referring to something that has avoided being stopped ○ *The metal screen protects the CPU against stray electromagnetic effects from the PSU.*

streaking /ˈstriːkɪŋ/ *noun* **1.** vertical stripes on a camera pick-up tube which can divide an image light into red-blue-green components without using dichroic mirrors **2.** horizontal television picture distortion

stream /striːm/ *noun* a long flow of serial data

streaming /ˈstriːmɪŋ/ *noun* the process of reading data from a storage device in one continuous operation, without processor intervention

'...the product has 16Mb of memory, 45Mb of Winchester disk storage and 95Mb streaming tape storage' [*Minicomputer News*]

streaming audio /ˌstriːmɪŋ 'ɔːdiəʊ/ *noun* digital audio data that is continuously transmitted (normally over the Internet) using a streaming protocol to provide stereo sound

streaming data /ˌstriːmɪŋ 'deɪtə/, **streaming protocol** *noun* a method of sending a continuous stream of data over the Internet to provide live video or sound transmission

COMMENT: Older methods of sending continuous live data used a standard web server (an HTTP server) to transmit the data. However, an HTTP server is designed to send data when it is ready rather than sending a regular stream of data that is required by multimedia. If you have ever tried to view a video clip over the Internet, you may have encountered this burst-transmission problem: when traffic or server load lightens, you can watch 20 frames per second, when the server is busy, you can watch one frame per minute. To provide a good multimedia server, the data delivery must be regulated and ideally synchronised. There are many different standards used to deliver sound and video over the Internet including Progressive Network's RealAudio, Microsoft's NetShow server, with supports both audio and video, and Netscape's MediaServer. Each of these streaming data technologies allows the user or publisher to limit the delivery of data to a maximum data rate. There are several standard formats used including Microsoft's multimedia delivery format, ASF (active streaming format) and other standards developed by Macromedia, VDOnet, Vivo, and VXtreme.

streaming video /ˌstriːmɪŋ 'vɪdiəʊ/ *noun* video image data that is continuously transmitted (normally over the Internet) using a streaming protocol to provide smooth moving images

strikethrough /'straɪkθruː/ *noun* a horizontal line used for indicating deleted text

string /strɪŋ/ *noun* any series of consecutive alphanumeric characters or words that are manipulated and treated as a single unit by the computer

string orientated symbolic language /ˌstrɪŋ ˌɔːriənteɪtɪd sɪmˌbɒlɪk 'læŋgwɪdʒ/ *noun* full form of **SNOBOL**

stringy floppy /ˌstrɪŋi 'flɒpi/ *noun* same as **tape streamer**

strip /strɪp/ *noun* a long thin piece of material ■ *verb* to remove the control data from a received message, leaving only the relevant information

stripe /straɪp/ *noun* a long thin line of colour

striping /'straɪpɪŋ/ *noun* the process of adding longitudinal time-code to video rushes

strobe /strəʊb/ *verb* to send a pulse, usually on the selection line, of an electronic circuit ■ *noun* the pulse of an electric circuit

strobe lighting /ˌstrəʊb 'laɪtɪŋ/ *noun* electronic flash lighting working at the same rate as a motion picture camera frame, creating sharp images of fast-moving objects

stroboscope /strəʊb/, **strobe** *noun* a light source which produces flashes of light

stroke /strəʊk/ *noun* **1.** the width (in pixels) of a pen or brush used to draw on-screen **2.** a basic curved or straight line that makes up a character

structure /'strʌktʃə/ *noun* a way in which something is organised or formed ■ *verb* to organise or to arrange in a certain way

structured design /ˌstrʌktʃəd dɪ'zaɪn/ *noun* a number of interconnected modules which are intended to solve problems

structured query language /ˌstrʌktʃəd 'kwɪəri ˌlæŋgwɪdʒ/ *noun* full form of **SQL**

STT /ˌes tiː 'tiː/ *noun* a system developed to provide a secure link between a user's browser and a vendor's Website to allow the user to pay for goods over the Internet. Full form **secure transaction technology**. ◊ **PGP, SEPP, SET, S-HTTP, SSL**

stub /stʌb/ *noun* a short program routine which contains comments to describe the executable code that will, eventually, be inserted into the routine

studio /'stjuːdiəʊ/ *noun* a place where a designer draws; a place where recordings take a place; a place where films are made

STX *abbr* start of text

style /staɪl/ *noun* the typeface, font, point size, colour, spacing and margins of text in a formatted document

style sheet /'staɪl ʃiːt/ *noun* **1.** a template which can be preformatted to generate automatically the style or layout of a document such as a manual, book or newsletter **2.** a sheet giving the style which should be followed by an editor

stylus /'staɪləs/ *noun* **1.** a pen-like device which is used in computer graphics systems to dictate cursor position on the screen **2.** (*in a transducer*) a needle which converts signals on an audio record into electrical signals **3.** a transducer that detects data stored on a videodisc

stylus printer /'staɪləs ˌprɪntə/ *noun* ◆ **dot-matrix printer**

sub- /sʌb/ *prefix* less than, less important than or lower than

subdirectory /ˈsʌbdɪˌrekt(ə)ri/ *noun* a directory of disk or tape contents contained within the main directory

'...if you delete a file and then delete the subdirectory where it was located, you cannot restore the file because the directory does not exist' [*Personal Computer World*]

sub-domain /ˈsʌb dəʊˌmeɪn/ *noun* a second level of addressing on the Internet that normally refers to a department name within a larger organisation

subdomain name /ˌsʌbdəˈmeɪn ˌneɪm/ *noun* an organisational name consisting of two or three letters, e.g. ac or .com, that precedes the two-letter country domain name in an Internet address, as in '.com.au', the address for Australian commercial sites.

subjective camera /səbˌdʒektɪv ˈkæm(ə)rə/ *noun* scenes shot from the point of view of the camera in order to intensify audience reaction

submenu /ˈsʌbmenjuː/ *noun* a secondary menu displayed as a choice from a menu

submit button /səbˌmɪt ˈbʌt(ə)n/ *noun* a button displayed on a webpage that sends information entered by a user on a web form to a program running on a web server for processing, e.g., the submit button could be used to start a search query

subnet /ˈsʌbnet/ *noun* a self-contained part of a large network, normally referring to one, independently-managed part of the Internet

subnet address /ˈsʌbnet əˌdres/, **subnet number** /ˈsʌbnet ˌnʌmbə/ *noun* the part of an IP address that identifies a subnet that is connected to a larger network. The first part of the IP address identifies the network, the next part of the IP address identifies the subnet and the last part of the IP address identifies a single host server.

subnet mask /ˈsʌbnet mɑːsk/ *noun* a filter that is used to select the portion of an IP address that contains the subnet address

subnotebook /sʌbˈnəʊtbʊk/ *noun* a very small portable computer, smaller and lighter than a standard full-size notebook or laptop computer. A subnotebook often has a smaller keyboard and display and often only includes a hard disk drive with any floppy disk drive or CD-ROM drive in a separate, external unit that can be plugged in when needed.

subprogram /ˈsʌbprəʊɡræm/ *noun* **1.** a subroutine in a program **2.** a program called up by a main program

subroutine /ˈsʌbruːˌtiːn/ *noun* a section of a program which performs a required function and can be called upon at any time from inside the main program

COMMENT: A subroutine is executed by a call instruction which directs the processor to its address; when finished it returns to the instruction after the call instruction in the main program.

subscriber /səbˈskraɪbə/ *noun* **1.** a person who has a telephone **2.** a person who pays for access to a service such as a BBS

subscript /ˈsʌbskrɪpt/ *noun* a small character which is printed below the line of other characters. ◊ **superscript** (NOTE: used in chemical formulae: CO_2)

subset /ˈsʌbˌset/ *noun* a small set of data items which forms part of a another larger set

substance /ˈsʌbstəns/ *noun* any matter whose properties can be described

substitute /ˈsʌbstɪtjuːt/ *verb* to put something in the place of something else (NOTE: you substitute one thing **for** another)

substitution /ˌsʌbstɪˈtjuːʃ(ə)n/ *noun* the act of replacing something by something else

substrate /ˈsʌbstreɪt/ *noun* a base material on which an integrated circuit is constructed. ◊ **integrated circuit**

subsystem /ˈsʌbsɪstəm/ *noun* one smaller part of a large system

subtitle /ˈsʌbtaɪt(ə)l/ *noun* a caption which is inserted over the filmed action, generally at the bottom of the screen, to provide information, to give a direct translation of dialogue in a foreign language, or as an aid to the hard of hearing

subtotal /ˈsʌbˌtəʊt(ə)l/ *noun* the total at the end of a column, which when added to others makes the grand total

subtractive primaries /səbˌtræktɪv ˈpraɪməriz/ *plural noun* the colours cyan, magenta and yellow

subtrahend /ˈsʌbtrəhend/ *noun* in a subtraction operation, the number to be subtracted from the minuend

subvoice grade channel /ˌsʌbvɔɪs ɡreɪd ˈtʃæn(ə)l/ *noun* a communications channel using frequencies (240 – 300Hz) below a voice channel, used for low speed data transmission

successive /səkˈsesɪv/ *adjective* which follow one after the other ○ *Each successive operation adds further characters to the string.*

suffix notation /ˌsʌfɪks nəʊˈteɪʃ(ə)n/ *noun* mathematical operations written in a logical way, so that the symbol appears after the numbers to be acted upon

suitcase /ˈsuːtkeɪs/ *noun* (*in the Apple Macintosh environment*) an icon which contains a screen font and allows fonts to be easily installed onto the system

suite of programs /ˌswiːt əv ˈprəʊɡræmz/ *noun* **1.** a group of programs which run one after the other ○ *The word-processing system uses a suite of three programs, editor, spelling checker and printing controller.* **2.** a number of programs used for a particular task

summation check /sʌ'meɪʃ(ə)n tʃek/ *noun* an error detection check performed by adding together the characters received and comparing with the required total

sun outage /'sʌn ˌaʊtɪdʒ/ *noun* the length of time during which a satellite does not operate due to the position of the moon or earth, causing a shadow over the satellite's solar cells

super- /suːpə/ *prefix* very good or very powerful

super bit mapping /ˌsuːpə 'bɪt ˌmæpɪŋ/ *noun* full form of **SBM**

supercomputer /ˌsuːpəkəm'pjuːtə/ *noun* a very powerful mainframe computer used for high speed mathematical tasks

super high frequency /ˌsuːpə haɪ 'friːkwənsi/ *noun* the frequency range between 3 – 30GHz. Abbr **SHF**

superimpose /ˌsuːpərɪm'pəʊz/ *verb* **1.** to lay one picture over another so that they both remain visible **2.** to add a graphic or a caption over a picture

superior number /sʊˌpɪəriə 'nʌmbə/ *noun* a superscript figure

super large scale integration /ˌsuːpə ˌlɑːdʒ skeɪl ˌɪntɪ'greɪʃ(ə)n/ *noun* an integrated circuit with more than 100,000 components. Abbr **SLSI**

super master group /ˌsuːpə 'mɑːstə gruːp/ *noun* a collection of 900 voice channels

superscript /'suːpəˌskrɪpt/ *noun* a small character printed higher than the normal line of characters. Compare **subscript** (NOTE: used often in mathematics: **10^5** say: ten to the power five)

supersede /ˌsuːpə'siːd/ *verb* to take the place of something which is older or less useful ○ *The new program supersedes the earlier one, and is much faster.*

superstation /'suːpəˌsteɪʃ(ə)n/ *noun US* a TV system, where a single TV station broadcasts many programmes simultaneously via satellite and cable

superuser /'suːpəˌjuːzə/ *noun* a UNIX user with all access rights, equivalent to an administrator under the Windows system

super VGA /ˌsuːpə viː dʒiː 'eɪ/ *noun* full form of **SVGA**

super VHS /ˌsuːpə ˌviː eɪtʃ 'es/ *noun* full form of **S-VHS**

supervise /'suːpəˌvaɪz/ *verb* to watch carefully to see if work is well done

supervision /ˌsuːpə'vɪʒ(ə)n/ *noun* the act of supervising

supervisor /'suːpəˌvaɪzə/ *noun* **1.** a person who makes sure that equipment is always working correctly **2.** a section of a computer operating system that regulates the use of peripherals and the operations undertaken by the CPU

supervisory /'suːpəvaɪzəri/ *adjective* as a supervisor

supplier /sə'plaɪə/ *noun* a company which supplies something ○ *a supplier of computer parts*

supply /sə'plaɪ/ *noun* the process of providing goods, products or services ○ *The electricity supply has failed.* ■ *verb* to provide something which is needed and for which someone will pay ○ *The computer was supplied by a recognised dealer.*

support /sə'pɔːt/ *verb* to give help to or to help to run ○ *The main computer supports six workstations.*

suppress /sə'pres/ *verb* to remove ○ *The filter is used to suppress the noise due to static interference.*

suppression /sə'preʃ(ə)n/ *noun* the act of suppressing

suppressor /sə'presə/ *noun* a device which suppresses interference

surf /sɜːf/ *verb* to explore a website looking at the webpages in no particular order, but simply moving between pages using the links

surface-mount technology /ˌsɜːfɪs maʊnt tek'nɒlədʒi/ *noun* full form of **SMT**

surge /sɜːdʒ/ *noun* a sudden increase in electrical power in a system, due to a fault, noise or component failure

COMMENT: Power surges can burn out circuits before you have time to pull the plug. A surge protector between your computer and the wall outlet will help prevent damage.

surge protector /'sɜːdʒ prəˌtektə/ *noun* an electronic device which cuts off the power supply to sensitive equipment if it detects a power surge that could cause damage

suspend /sə'spend/ *noun* a command that is used when running Windows on a battery-powered laptop computer to shut down almost all of the electronic components of the laptop

sustain /sə'steɪn/ *verb* to keep a voltage at a certain level for a period of time ■ *noun* the body of a sound signal. Compare **attack, decay**

SVGA /ˌes viː dʒiː 'eɪ/ *noun* an enhancement to the standard VGA graphics display system which allows resolutions of up to 800x600pixels with 16million colours. Full form **super VGA**

S-VHS /ˌes viː eɪtʃ ˈes/ *noun* a high-resolution version of the standard VHS video cassette standard which can record 400 lines of a video signal rather than the usual 260 lines of VHS. Full form **super VHS**

S-Video /ˌes ˈvɪdiəʊ/ *noun* a method of transmitting a video signal in which the luminance and colour components (the luma, Y, and chroma, C) are transmitted over separate wires to improve the quality of the video, used in Hi8, S-VHS and other video formats to provide better quality than composite video. Also called **Y/C video**

SW *abbr* short wave

swap /swɒp/ *noun* same as **swapping** ■ *verb* to stop using one program, put it into store temporarily, run another program, and when that is finished, return to the first one

swap file /ˈswɒp faɪl/ *noun* a file stored on the hard disk used as a temporary storage area for data held in RAM, to provide virtual memory

swapping /ˈswɒpɪŋ/ *noun* (*in a virtual memory system*) an activity in which program data is moved from main memory to disk, while another program is loaded or run. ◊ **virtual memory**. Also called **swap**

sweep /swiːp/ *noun* the movement of the electron beam over the area of a television screen in regular horizontal and vertical steps, producing the image

sweetening /ˈswiːt(ə)nɪŋ/ *noun* **1.** the addition of new sound to a voice track **2.** the addition of sound effects to the visual images **3.** the improvement of the quality of image, colour, etc., through electronic modification

swim /swɪm/ *noun* computer graphics which move slightly due to a faulty display unit

switch /swɪtʃ/ *noun* **1.** (*in some command-line operating systems*) an additional character entered on the same line as the program command, which affects how the program runs **2.** a point in a computer program where control can be passed to one of a number of choices **3.** a mechanical or solid state device that can electrically connect or isolate two or more lines ■ *verb* to connect or disconnect two lines by activating a switch

switchboard /ˈswɪtʃbɔːd/ *noun* a central point in a telephone system, where the lines from various telephone handsets meet, where calls can be directed to any other telephone

switchboard operator /ˈswɪtʃbɔːd ˌɒpəreɪtə/ *noun* a person who works a central telephone switchboard, by connecting incoming and outgoing calls to various lines

switching /ˈswɪtʃɪŋ/ *noun* a constant update of connections between changing sinks and sources in a network

symbol /ˈsɪmbəl/ *noun* a sign or picture which represents something ○ *This language uses the symbol ? to represent the print command.*

symbolic /sɪmˈbɒlɪk/ *adjective* which acts as a symbol or which uses a symbol name or label

sync /sɪŋk/ *noun* **1.** two events or timing signals which happen at the same time **2.** the exact aligning of the sound and picture components of a film so that they coincide

synchronisation /ˌsɪŋkrənaɪˈzeɪʃ(ə)n/ *noun* the action of synchronising two or more devices

synchronise /ˈsɪŋkrəˌnaɪz/ *verb* to make sure that two or more devices or processes are coordinated in time or action

synchroniser /ˈsɪŋkrənaɪzə/ *noun* **1.** a device that will perform a function when it receives a signal from another device **2.** a machine used to edit the sound track and the film at the same time

synchronous /ˈsɪŋkrənəs/ *adjective* which runs in sync with something else (such as a main clock)

synchronous data link control /ˌsɪŋkrənəs ˈdeɪtə lɪŋk kənˌtrəʊl/ *noun* full form of **SDLC**

synonym /ˈsɪnənɪm/ *noun* a word which means the same thing as another word

synonymous /sɪˈnɒnɪməs/ *adjective* meaning the same ○ *The words 'error' and 'mistake' are synonymous.*

syntactic error /sɪnˌtæktɪk ˈerə/ *noun* a programming error in which the program statement does not follow the syntax of the language

syntax /ˈsɪntæks/ *noun* grammatical rules which apply to a programming language

synthesis /ˈsɪnθəsɪs/ *noun* the process of producing something artificially from a number of smaller elements

synthesise /ˈsɪnθəsaɪz/ *verb* to produce something artificially from a number of smaller elements

> '...despite the fact that speech can now be synthesized with very acceptable quality, all it conveys is linguistic information' [*Personal Computer World*]

synthesiser /ˈsɪnθəsaɪzə/ *noun* a device which generates signals, sound or speech

SyQuest /ˈsaɪkwest/ a manufacturer of storage devices, including a range of removable hard disk drives and backup units. ◊ **Zip disk**

system /ˈsɪstəm/ *noun* any group of hardware or software or peripherals, etc., which work together

System 7™ /ˌsɪstəm ˈsev(ə)n/ a version of the operating system for the Apple Macintosh personal computer that introduces multitasking, virtual memory and peer-to-peer file sharing

system administrator /ˌsɪstəm ədˈmɪnɪstreɪtə/ *noun* ➧ **network administrator**

system backup /ˌsɪstəm ˈbækʌp/ *noun* a copy of all the data stored on a computer, server or network

system colours /ˌsɪstəm ˈkʌləz/ *plural noun* same as **default palette**

system crash /ˈsɪstəm kræʃ/ *noun* a situation where the operating system stops working and has to be restarted

system design /ˌsɪstəm dɪˈzaɪn/ *noun* the process of identifying and investigating possible solutions to a problem, and deciding upon the most appropriate system to solve the problem

Système Electronique Couleur Avec Mémoire *noun* full form of **SECAM**

system life cycle /ˌsɪstəm ˈlaɪf ˌsaɪk(ə)l/ *noun* the time when a system exists, between its initial design and its becoming out of date

system manager /ˌsɪstəm ˈmænɪdʒə/ *noun* a person responsible for the computers or network in a company

System Monitor /ˈsɪstəm ˌmɒnɪtə/ *noun* a Windows utility that allows a user to view how the resources on their PC are performing and, if they have shared the device, who else on the network is using the resources

system operator /ˌsɪstəm ˈɒpəreɪtə/ *noun* a person who manages an online bulletin board or maintains a computer network

system palette /ˌsɪstəm ˈpælət/ *noun* the range of colours that are available on a particular operating system and can be shared by all applications

systems analysis /ˈsɪstəmz əˌnæləsɪs/ *noun* **1.** the process of analysing a process or system to see if it could be more efficiently carried out by a computer **2.** the process of examining an existing system with the aim of improving or replacing it

Systems Application Architecture /ˌsɪstəmz ˌæplɪkeɪʃ(ə)n ˈɑːkɪtektʃə/ *noun* full form of **SAA**

system security /ˌsɪstəm sɪˈkjʊərɪti/ *noun* measures, such as password, priority protection, authorisation codes, designed to stop browsers and hackers

Systems Network Architecture /ˌsɪstəmz ˈnetwɜːk ˌɑːkɪtektʃə/ *noun* full form of **SNA**

system software /ˌsɪstəm ˈsɒftweə/ *noun* programs which direct the basic functions, input-output control, etc., of a computer

system specifications /ˌsɪstəm ˌspesɪfɪˈkeɪʃ(ə)nz/ *plural noun* details of hardware and software required to perform certain tasks

system support /ˌsɪstəm səˈpɔːt/ *noun* a group of people who maintain and operate a system

system tray /ˈsɪstəm treɪ/ *noun* (*in Windows*) an area of the taskbar normally in the bottom right-hand corner next to the clock. The system tray displays tiny icons that show which system software programs were run automatically when Windows started and are now running in the background.

T

T *abbr* tera-

T1 committee /ˌtiː ˈwʌn kəˌmɪti/ *noun* an ANSI committee which sets digital communications standards for the US, particularly ISDN services

T1 link /ˌtiː ˈwʌn ˌlɪŋk/ *noun* (*in the US*) a high speed, long distance data transmission link not related to the T1 committee, that can carry data at 1.544Mbits per second

tab /tæb/ *verb* **1.** to tabulate or to arrange text in columns with the cursor automatically running from one column to the next in keyboarding ○ *The list was neatly lined up by tabbing to column 10 at the start of each new line.* **2.** in a GUI, method of moving from one button or field to another without using the mouse, but by pressing the tab key to move the focus

tabbing /ˈtæbɪŋ/ *noun* the movement of the cursor in a word-processing program from one tab stop to the next ○ *Tabbing can be done from inside the program.*

table /ˈteɪb(ə)l/ *noun* a list of data in columns and rows on a printed page or on the screen

table of contents /ˌteɪb(ə)l əv ˈkɒntents/ *noun* **1.** a list of the contents of a book, usually printed at the beginning **2.** data at the start of a disc that describes how many tracks are on the CD, their position and length **3.** a page with a list of the headings of all the other main pages in the title and links so that a user can move to them

tablet /ˈtæblət/ *noun* a graphics pad or flat device which allows a user to input graphical information into a computer by drawing on its surface

tab settings /ˈtæb ˌsetɪŋz/, **tab stops** /ˈtæb stɒps/ *plural noun* preset points along a line, where the printing head or cursor will stop for each tabulation command

tabulate /ˈtæbjʊˌleɪt/ *verb* to arrange text in columns, with the cursor moving to each new column automatically as the text is keyboarded

tabulating /ˈtæbjʊleɪtɪŋ/ *noun* the action of processing punched cards, such as a sorting operation

tabulation /ˌtæbjʊˈleɪʃ(ə)n/ *noun* **1.** arrangement of a table of figures **2.** the process of moving a printing head or cursor a preset distance along a line

tabulator /ˈtæbjʊleɪtə/ *noun* part of a word-processor which automatically sets words or figures into columns

TACS *noun* a UK standard for cellular radio systems. Full form **total access communication system**

tactile /ˈtæktaɪl/ *adjective* using the sense of touch

tag /tæg/ *noun* **1.** one section of a computer instruction **2.** a set of identifying characters attached to a file or item (of data) ○ *Each file has a three letter tag for rapid identification.*

tag image file format /ˌtæg ˌɪmɪdʒ ˈfaɪl ˌfɔːmæt/ *noun* full form of **TIFF**

tail /teɪl/ *noun* **1.** data recognised as the end of a list of data **2.** a control code used to signal the end of a message

take /teɪk/ *noun* a camera shot of an individual piece of action

take-up /ˈteɪk ʌp/ *noun* a device such as a reel on which film or tape is wound from a projector, camera gate or editing machine

take-up reel /ˈteɪk ʌp ˌriːl/ *noun* a reel onto which magnetic tape is collected

talk /tɔːk/ *verb* to speak or to communicate

> '...a variety of technologies exist which allow computers to talk to one another' [*Which PC?*]

talkback /ˈtɔːkbæk/ *noun* speech communications between a control room and a studio

> '...a variety of technologies exist which allow computers to talk to one another' [*Which PC?*]

tape /teɪp/ *noun* a long thin flat piece of material

COMMENT: Cassettes *or* reels of tape are easy to use and cheaper than disks, the cassette casing usually conforming to a standard size. They are less adaptable and only provide sequential access, usually being used for master copies *or* making backups.

tape backup /ˈteɪp ˌbækʌp/ *noun* the process of using (usually magnetic) tape as a medium for storing back-ups from faster main or secondary storage, such as RAM or hard disk

tape drive /ˈteɪp draɪv/ *noun* a mechanism which controls magnetic tape movement over the tape heads ○ *Our new product has a 96MB streaming tape drive.*

tape format /ˈteɪp ˌfɔːmæt/ *noun* a way in which blocks of data, control codes and location data is stored on tape

tape streamer /ˈteɪp ˌstriːmə/ *noun* a device containing a continuous loop of tape, used as backing storage. Also called **stringy floppy**

Targa /ˈtɑːɡə/ *noun* a graphics file format which uses the .TGA extension on a PC, developed by Truevision to store raster graphic images in 16–, 24– and 32-bit colour.

target /ˈtɑːɡɪt/ *noun* a goal which you aim to achieve

targetcast /ˈtɑːɡɪtkɑːst/ *verb* to broadcast a website only to a group of people who are known to be potentially interested in it, and not to everyone on the Internet

target computer /ˌtɑːɡɪt kəmˈpjuːtə/ *noun* a computer on which software is to be run

target disk /ˈtɑːɡɪt dɪsk/ *noun* a disk onto which a file is to be copied

target language /ˈtɑːɡɪt ˌlæŋɡwɪdʒ/ *noun* a language into which a language will be translated from its source language ○ *The target language for this PASCAL program is machine code.* Opposite **source language**

target program /ˌtɑːɡɪt ˈprəʊɡræm/ *noun* an object program or computer program in object code form, produced by a compiler

target window /ˈtɑːɡɪt ˌwɪndəʊ/ *noun* a window in which text or graphics will be displayed

tariff /ˈtærɪf/ *noun* a charge incurred by a user of a communications or computer system ○ *There is a set tariff for logging on, then a rate for every minute of computer time used.*

TASI *noun* a method of using a voice channel for other signals during the gaps and pauses in a normal conversation. Full form **time assigned speech interpolation**

task /tɑːsk/ *noun* a job which is to carried out by a computer

taskbar /ˈtɑːskbɑː/ *noun* a bar that normally runs along the bottom of the screen in Windows and displays the Start button and a list of other programs or windows that are currently active

task management /ˈtɑːsk ˌmænɪdʒmənt/ *noun* system software which controls the use and allocation of resources to programs

task swapping /ˈtɑːsk ˌswɒpɪŋ/ *noun* the process of exchanging one program in memory for another which is temporarily stored on disk. Task switching is not the same as multitasking which can execute several programs at once.

task switching /ˈtɑːsk ˌswɪtʃɪŋ/ *noun* same as **task swapping**

TAT *abbr* turnaround time

TBC *abbr* time-base corrector

T carrier /ˈtiː ˌkæriə/ *noun* a US standard for digital data transmission lines, such as T1, T1C, and corresponding signal standards DS1, DS1C

TCIP *noun* discernable time-code numerals in video-tape editing. Full form **time code in picture**

TCM *abbr* thermal control module

T-commerce /ˌtiː ˈkɒmɜːs/ *noun* a business conducted by means of interactive television

T connector /ˈtiː kəˌnektə/ *noun* a coaxial connector, shaped like the letter ‘T’, which connects two thin coaxial cables using BNC plugs and provides a third connection for another cable or network interface card

TCP /ˌtiː siː ˈpiː/ *noun* standard data transmission protocol that provides full duplex transmission, bundles data into packets and checks for errors. Full form **transmission control protocol**

TCP/IP /ˌtiː siː piː aɪ ˈpiː/ *noun* a data transfer protocol used in networks and communications systems, often used in Unix-based networks. This protocol is used for all communications over the internet. Full form **transmission control protocol/interface program**

TDM /ˌtiː diː ˈem/ *noun* a method of combining several signals into one high-speed transmission carrier, each input signal being sampled in turn and the result transmitted to a the receiver which re-constructs the signals. Full form **time division multiplexing**

TDR /ˌtiː diː ˈɑː/ *noun* a test that identifies where cable faults lie by sending a signal down the cable and measuring how long it takes for the reflection to come back. Full form **time domain reflectometry**

TDS /ˌtiː diː ˈes/ *noun* a computer system that will normally run batch processing tasks until interrupted by a new transaction, at which point it allocates resources to the new transaction. Full form **transaction-driven system**

technical /ˈteknɪk(ə)l/ *adjective* referring to a particular machine or process ○ *The document gives all the technical details on the new computer.*

technically /ˈteknɪkli/ *adverb* in a technical way ○ *Their system is technically far more advanced than ours.*

technical support /ˌteknɪk(ə)l səˈpɔːt/ *noun* a person who provides such advice

technician /tek'nɪʃ(ə)n/ *noun* a person who is specialised in industrial work

technique /tek'niːk/ *noun* a skilled way of doing a job ○ *The company has developed a new technique for processing customers' disks.*

technological /ˌteknə'lɒdʒɪk(ə)l/ *adjective* referring to technology

technology /tek'nɒlədʒi/ *noun* the process of applying scientific knowledge to industrial processes

tel *abbr* telephone

tele- /teli/ *prefix* long distance

telebanking /'teliˌbæŋkɪŋ/ *noun* a system by which an account holder can carry out transactions with his bank via a terminal and communications network

telecommunications /ˌtelikəˌmjuːnɪ'keɪʃ(ə)nz/ *noun* the technology of passing and receiving messages over a distance, as in radio, telephone, telegram, satellite broadcast, etc.

telecommuting /'telikəmjuːtɪŋ/ *noun* the practice of working on a computer in one place (normally from home) that is linked by modem to the company's central office allowing messages and data to be transferred

teleconference /'teliˌkɒnf(ə)rəns/ *noun* a meeting held among people in different locations by means of telecommunications equipment

teleconferencing /'teliˌkɒnf(ə)rənsɪŋ/ *noun* **1.** the process of linking video, audio and computer signals from different locations so that distant people can talk and see each other, as if in a conference room **2.** part of video-conferencing where the image is renewed only at intervals in order to decrease the transmission bandwidth required

telecontrol /'telikənˌtrəʊl/ *noun* the control of a remote device by a telecommunications link

telegram /'telɪgræm/ *noun* a message sent to another country by telegraph ○ *to send an international telegram*

telegraph /'telɪgrɑːf/ *noun* a message transmitted using a telegraphy system ■ *verb* to send a telegram to another person; to send printed or written or drawn material by long-distance telegraphy ○ *They telegraphed their agreement.* ○ *The photographs were telegraphed to New York.*

telegraphic /ˌtelɪ'græfɪk/ *adjective* referring to a telegraph system

telegraphic address /ˌtelɪˌgræfɪk ə'dres/ *noun* a short address to which a telegram is sent

telegraph office /'telɪgrɑːf ˌɒfɪs/ *noun* an office from which telegrams can be sent

telegraphy /tə'legrəfi/ *noun* a system of sending messages along wires using direct current pulses

teleinformatic services /telɪɪnˌfɔːmətɪk 'sɜːvɪsɪz/ *plural noun* any of various data only services, such as telex, facsimile, which use telecommunications

telematics /ˌtelɪ'mætɪks/ *noun* the interaction of all data processing and communications devices

telemessage /'telɪmesɪdʒ/ *noun* a message sent by telephone, and delivered as a card

telemetry /tə'lemɪtri/ *noun* data from remote measuring devices transmitted over a telecommunications link

teleordering /'teliˌɔːdərɪŋ/ *noun* a book ordering system, in which the bookseller's orders are entered into a computer which then puts the order through to the distributor at the end of the day

telephone /'telɪfəʊn/ *noun* a machine used for speaking to someone or communicating with another computer (using modems) over a long distance

telephone line /'telɪfəʊn laɪn/ *noun* a cable used to connect a telephone handset with a central exchange

telephonist /tə'lefənɪst/ *noun* a person who works a telephone switchboard

telephony /tə'lefəni/ *noun* a series of standards that define the way in which computers can work with a telephone system to provide voice-mail, telephone answering, and fax services

telephony application programming interface /təˌlefəni ˌæplɪkeɪʃ(ə)n 'prəʊgræmɪŋ ˌɪntəfeɪs/ *noun* a system developed by Microsoft and Intel that allows a PC to control a single telephone. Abbr **TAPI**

telephony services application programming interface /təˌlefəni ˌsɜːvɪsɪz ˌæplɪkeɪʃ(ə)n 'prəʊgræmɪŋ ˌɪntəfeɪs/ *noun* a system developed by Novell and AT&T that allows a PC to control a PBX telephone exchange. Abbr **TSAPI**

telephoto distortion /ˌtelɪfəʊtəʊ dɪs'tɔːʃ(ə)n/ *noun* the compression result which occurs in shots filmed with a telephoto lens; objects far away from the camera seem to be closer, and a performer's movement towards or away from the camera seems to be slower

telephoto lens /ˌtelɪfəʊtəʊ 'lenz/ *noun* a camera objective lens with long focal length and short back focus. This type of lens gives the impression that an object is closer than it really .is.

teleprinter /'teliˌprɪntə/ *noun* a device that is capable of sending and receiving data from a distant point by means of a telegraphic circuit, and printing out the message on a printer ○ *You can drive a teleprinter from this modified serial port.*

teleprinter interface /'teliprɪntə ˌɪntəfeɪs/ *noun* a terminal interface or hardware and software combination required to control the functions of a terminal

teleprinter roll /'teliprɪntə ˌrəʊl/ *noun* a roll of paper onto which messages are printed

teleprocessing /'teliˌprəʊsesɪŋ/ *noun* the processing of data at a distance (as on a central computer from outside terminals). Abbr **TP**

telerecording /ˌtelɪrɪ'kɔːdɪŋ/ *noun* the transferral of a television or video programme to motion picture film

telesales /'teliˌseɪlz/ *noun* sales made by telephone

teleshopping /'telɪˌʃɒpɪŋ/ *noun* the use of a telephone-based data service such as viewdata to order products from a shop

telesoftware /'teliˌsɒftweə/ *noun* software which is received from a viewdata or teletext service. Abbr **TSW**

teletext /'teliˌtekst/ *noun* a method of transmitting text and information with a normal television signal, usually as a serial bit stream which can be displayed using a special decoder

teletype /'telitaɪp/ *noun* a term used for teleprinter equipment. Abbr **TTY**

teletypesetting /ˌtelɪ'taɪpsetɪŋ/ *noun* a typesetter operated from a punched paper tape

teletypewriter /ˌtelɪ'taɪpraɪtə/ *noun* a keyboard and printer attached to a computer system which can input data either direct or by making punched paper tape

television /ˌtelɪ'vɪʒ(ə)n/ *noun* **1.** a device which can receive (modulated) video signals from a computer or broadcast signals with an aerial and display images on a CRT screen with sound **2.** a system for broadcasting pictures and sound using high-frequency radio waves, captured by a receiver and shown on a screen **3.** the actual broadcasts themselves, or the set on which they are seen ▶ abbr **TV**

television monitor /ˌtelɪ'vɪʒ(ə)n ˌmɒnɪtə/ *noun* a device able to display signals from a computer without sound, but is not able to broadcast signals, usually because there is no demodulator

television receiver/monitor /ˌtelɪvɪʒ(ə)n rɪˌsiːvə 'mɒnɪtə/ *noun* a device able to act as a TV receiver or monitor

television scan /'telɪˌvɪʒ(ə)n skæn/ *noun* a horizontal movement of the picture beam over the screen, producing one line of an image

television tube /'telɪˌvɪʒ(ə)n tjuːb/ *noun* a CRT with electronic devices which provide the line by line horizontal and vertical scanning movement of the picture beam

telex /'teleks/ *noun* a system for sending messages using telephone lines, which are printed out at the receiving end on a special printer ○ *to send information by telex* ○ *The order came by telex.* ■ *verb* to send a message using a teleprinter ○ *Can you telex the Canadian office before they open?* ○ *He telexed the details of the contract to New York.* ◇ **a telex 1.** a machine for sending and receiving telex messages ○ *he sent a telex to his head office* **2.** a message sent by telex ○ *we received his telex this morning*

telnet /'telnet/ *noun* a TCP/IP protocol that allows a user to connect to and control via the Internet a remote computer as if they were there and type in commands as if they were sitting in front of the computer

template /'temˌpleɪt/ *noun* **1.** a plastic or metal sheet with cut-out symbols to help in the drawing of flowcharts and circuit diagrams **2.** (*in text processing*) standard text, such as a standard letter or invoice, into which specific details can be added ○ *a template paragraph command enables the user to specify the number of spaces each paragraph should be indented* **3.** an opaque sheet which is placed in a spotlight and which has been cut into a certain shape in order to produce a patterned shadow

template command /'templeɪt kə ˌmɑːnd/ *noun* a command which allows functions or other commands to be easily set ○ *A template paragraph command enables the user to specify the number of spaces each paragraph should be indented.*

tempo /'tempəʊ/ *noun* **1.** (*in MIDI or music*) the speed at which the notes are played, measured in beats per minute ○ *A typical MIDI tempo is 120 beats per minute.* **2.** (*in a multimedia title*) the speed at which frames are displayed

temporary /'temp(ə)rəri/ *adjective* not permanent

temporary storage /ˌtemp(ə)rəri 'stɔːrɪdʒ/ *noun* storage which is not permanent

temporary swap file /ˌtemp(ə)rəri 'swɒp ˌfaɪl/ *noun* a file on a hard disk which is used by software to store data temporarily or for software that implements virtual memory, such as Microsoft's Windows

10Base2 /ˌten beɪs 'tuː/ *noun* IEEE standard specification for running Ethernet over thin coaxial cable

10Base5 /ˌten beɪs ˈfaɪv/ IEEE standard specification for running Ethernet over thick coaxial cable

10Base-FX *noun* IEEE standard specification for running Ethernet over optical fibre at speeds up to 10Mbps

10BaseT /ˌten beɪs ˈtiː/ *noun* IEEE standard specification for running Ethernet over unshielded twisted pair cable

tera- /terə/ *prefix* 10^{12}; one million million. Abbr **T**

terabyte /ˈterəbaɪt/ *noun* one thousand gigabytes or one million megabytes of data

terahertz /ˈterəhɜːts/ *noun* a frequency of one million million hertz

terminal /ˈtɜːmɪn(ə)l/ *noun* **1.** a device usually made up of a display unit and a keyboard which allows entry and display of information when on-line to a central computer system ○ *The new intelligent terminal has a built-in text editor.* **2.** an electrical connection point **3.** a point in a network where a message can be transmitted or received. ◊ **source, sink**

terminal character set /ˌtɜːmɪn(ə)l ˈkærɪktə ˌset/ *noun* the range of characters available for a particular type of terminal, which might include graphics or customised characters

terminate /ˈtɜːmɪˌneɪt/ *verb* to end

terminate and stay resident program /ˌtɜːmɪneɪt ən steɪ ˈrezɪd(ə)nt ˌprəʊgræm/ *noun* a program which loads itself into main memory and carries out a function when activated ○ *When you hit Ctrl-F5, you will activate the TSR program and it will display your day's diary.* Also called **TSR program**

termination /ˌtɜːmɪˈneɪʃ(ə)n/ *noun* the process of ending or stopping

terminator /ˈtɜːmɪneɪtə/ *noun* **1.** (*in a LAN*) a resistor that fits onto each end of a coaxial cable in a bus network to create an electrical circuit **2.** (*in an SCSI installation*) a resistor that fits onto the last SCSI device in the daisy-chain, creating an electrical circuit **3.** same as **rogue value**

ternary /ˈtɜːnəri/ *adjective* referring to a number system with three possible states

test /test/ *verb* to carry out an examination of a device or program to see if it is working correctly

test data /ˈtest ˌdeɪtə/ *noun* data with known results prepared to allow a new program to be tested

test equipment /ˈtest ɪˌkwɪpmənt/ *noun* special equipment which tests hardware or software

text /tekst/ *noun* a set of alphanumeric characters that convey information

text-editing facilities /ˈtekst ˌedɪtɪŋ fə ˌsɪlɪtiz/ *plural noun* a word-processing system which allows the user to add, delete, move, insert and correct sections of text

text editor /ˈtekst ˌedɪtə/ *noun* same as **screen editor**

text file /ˈtekst faɪl/ *noun* a file that contains text rather than digits or data

text message /ˈtekst ˌmesɪdʒ/ *noun* a message sent in the form of text, especially one that appears on the viewing screen of a mobile phone or pager

text processing /ˈtekst ˌprəʊsesɪŋ/ *noun* the use of a computer to create, store, edit and print or display text

text retrieval /ˈtekst rɪˌtriːv(ə)l/ *noun* an information retrieval system that allows the user to examine complete documents rather than just a reference to a document

textual /ˈtekstʃuəl/ *adjective* referring to text ○ *The editors made several textual changes before the proofs were sent back for correction.*

texture mapping /ˈtekstʃə ˌmæpɪŋ/ *noun* **1.** a special computer graphics effect using algorithms to produce an image that looks like the surface of something such as marble, brick, stone or water **2.** the process of covering one image with another to give the first a texture

text window /ˈtekst ˌwɪndəʊ/ *noun* a window in a graphics system, where the text is held in a small space on the screen before being allocated to a final area

TFT *adjective* a technology used in high-resolution LCD flat-panel screens, in which each pixel is controlled by one or more transistors. Full form **thin film transistor**

TFT display *noun* a computer display that uses TFT technology. Also called **active matrix display**

TFTP /ˌtiː ef tiː ˈpiː/ *noun* a simple form of the standard FTP (file transfer protocol) system, commonly used to load the operating system software onto a diskless workstation from a server when the workstation boots up when it is switched on. Full form **trivial file transfer protocol**. ◊ **FTP**

TFT screen /ˌtiː ef ˈtiː ˌskriːn/ *noun* same as **TFT display**

thaw /θɔː/ *noun* a special effect in which action starts again after a freeze frame effect, especially in a videowall presentation (*film*)

thermal /ˈθɜːm(ə)l/ *adjective* referring to heat

thermal printing /ˌθɜːm(ə)l ˈprɪntɪŋ/ *noun* **1.** a printing system which has a print head with a number of quick-heating elements which work with heat-sensitive paper, or with ordinary paper when using a special ribbon **2.** an imaging system which uses enclosed bubbles in an emulsion

thermal transfer /ˌθɜːm(ə)l trænsˈfɜː/, **thermal wax** /ˈθɜːm(ə)l wæks/, **thermal wax transfer printer** /ˌθɜːm(ə)l wæks ˌtrænsfɜː ˈprɪntə/ *noun* a method of printing where the colours are produced by melting coloured wax onto the paper ○ *Thermal wax transfer technology still provides the best colour representation on paper for PC output.*

thermistor /θɜːˈmɪstə/ *noun* an electronic device whose resistance changes with temperature

thermo-sensitive /ˌθɜːməʊ ˈsensɪtɪv/ *adjective* which is sensitive to heat

thesaurus /θɪˈsɔːrəs/ *noun* a file which contains synonyms that are displayed as alternatives to a misspelt word during a spell-check

thick-Ethernet /ˌθɪk ˈiːθənet/ *noun* a network implemented using thick coaxial cable and transceivers to connect branch cables. ◊ **Ethernet, thin-Ethernet**

thimble printer /ˈθɪmb(ə)l ˌprɪntə/ *noun* a computer printer using a printing head similar to a daisy wheel but shaped like a thimble

thin /θɪn/ *adjective* with only a small distance between two surfaces

thin-Ethernet /ˌθɪn ˈiːθənet/ *noun* the most popular type of Ethernet network implemented using thin coaxial cable and BNC connectors. ◊ **Ethernet, thick-Ethernet** (NOTE: It is limited to distances of around 1000 m)

thin-film transistor /ˌθɪn fɪlm træn ˈzɪstə/ *noun* full form of **TFT**

32-bit /ˈθɜːtiː tuː ˌbɪt/ data that is transferred thirty-two bits at a time along thirty-two parallel conductors; in a processor this refers to its ability to manipulate numbers that are thirty-two bits long

thirty-two bit system /ˌθɜːti tuː ˌbɪt ˈsɪstəm/, **32-bit system** *noun* a microcomputer system or CPU that handles data in 32 bit words

thrashing /ˈθræʃɪŋ/ *noun* **1.** excessive disk activity **2.** a configuration or program fault in a virtual memory system that results in a CPU wasting time moving pages of data between main memory and disk or backing store

thread /θred/ *noun* **1.** a program which consists of many independent smaller sections or beads **2.** the accurate positioning of film or tape in the path of a projector, or another film mechanism for take-up (NOTE: 'thread up' also used in the context of definition (ii))

> 'WigWam makes it easier for a user to follow a thread in a bulletin-board conference topic by ordering responses using a hierarchical indent similar to that found in outline processor.' [*Computing*]

threaded file /ˌθredɪd ˈfaɪl/ *noun* a file in which an entry contains data and an address to the next entry that contains the same data, allowing rapid retrieval of all identical entries

threaded language /ˌθredɪd ˈlæŋgwɪdʒ/ *noun* a programming language which allows many small sections of code to be written then used by a main program

threaded tree /ˌθredɪd ˈtriː/ *noun* a structure in which each node contains a pointer to other nodes

three-colour process /ˌθriː ˌkʌlə ˈprəʊses/ *noun* a process used to convert a colour image into three separate colours (red, blue and yellow)

3D /ˌθriː ˈdiː/ *adjective* referring to an image which has three dimensions (width, breadth and depth), and therefore gives the impression of being solid. Full form **three-dimensional**

three-dimensional /ˌθriː daɪ ˈmenʃ(ə)nəl/ *adjective* full form of **3D**

three input adder /ˌθriː ˌɪnpʊt ˈædə/ *noun* ◆ **full adder**

threshold /ˈθreʃhəʊld/ *noun* a preset level which causes an action if a signal exceeds or drops below it

threshold howl /ˈθreʃhəʊld haʊl/ *noun* acoustic feedback which is created by sound from the loudspeakers re-entering the microphone

throughput /ˈθruːˌpʊt/ *noun* the rate of production by a machine or system, measured as total useful information processed in a set period of time ○ *For this machine throughput is 1.3 inches per second scanning speed.*

through-the-lens focus /ˌθruː ðə ˌlenz ˈfəʊkəs/ *noun* a camera viewfinder which can focus through the camera lens without parallax

thumbnail /ˈθʌmˌneɪl/ *noun* a miniature graphical representation of an image, used as a quick and convenient method of viewing the contents of graphics or DTP files before they are retrieved

TIFF /tɪf/ *noun* standard file format used to store graphic images. Full form **tag image file format**

tilde /ˈtɪldə/ *noun* a printed accent (~), commonly used over the letter 'n' in Spanish, vowels in Portuguese, etc.

tile /taɪl/ *verb* (*in a GUI*) to arrange a group of windows so that they are displayed side by side without overlapping (NOTE: **tiles – tiling – tiled**)

tilt /tɪlt/ *verb* **1.** to sweep a video camera up and down. Compare **pan 2.** to alter the slope of the frequency response in a sound reproducer

tilt and swivel /ˌtɪlt ən ˈswɪv(ə)l/ *adjective* referring to a monitor which is mounted on a pivot so that it can be moved to point in the most convenient direction for the operator

time /taɪm/ *noun* a period expressed in hours, minutes, seconds and related units ■ *verb* to measure the time taken by an operation ○ *If you do not answer this question within one minute, the program times out and moves onto the next question.* (NOTE: **times – timing – timed**) □ **to time out** (*of an event or option*) to become no longer valid after a period of time ○ *If you do not answer this question within one minute, the program times out and moves onto the next question.*

time bomb /ˈtaɪm bɒm/ *noun* a computer virus that is designed to take effect on a particular date or when a computer application is used for a particular length of time

time code /ˈtaɪm kəʊd/ *noun* a sequence of timing information recorded on an audio track in a videotape

time division multiplexing /ˌtaɪm dɪ ˌvɪʒ(ə)n ˈmʌltɪpleksɪŋ/ *noun* full form of **TDM**

time domain reflectometry /ˌtaɪm dəʊ ˌmeɪn ˌriːflekˈtɒmətri/ *noun* full form of **TDR**

time of peak demand /ˌtaɪm əv ˌpiːk dɪ ˈmɑːnd/ *noun* the time when something is being used most

time out /ˌtaɪm ˈaʊt/ *verb* (of an event or option) to become no longer valid after a period of time ○ *If you do not answer this question within one minute, the program times out and moves onto the next question.*

timeout /ˈtaɪmaʊt/ *noun* **1.** a logoff procedure carried out if no data is entered on an online terminal **2.** a period of time reserved for an operation

timer /ˈtaɪmə/ *noun* a device which records the time taken for an operation to be completed

time-sharing /ˈtaɪm ˌʃeərɪŋ/ *noun* an arrangement which allows several independent users to use a computer system or be online at the same time

COMMENT: In time-sharing, each user appears to be using the computer all the time, when in fact each is using the CPU for a short time slice only. The CPU processes one user for a short time then moves on to the next.

time slice /ˈtaɪm slaɪs/ *noun* the amount of time allowed for a single task in a time-sharing system or in multiprogramming

tiny model /ˌtaɪni ˈmɒd(ə)l/ *noun* a memory model of the Intel 80x86 processor family that allows a combined total of 64 Kb for data and code

title /ˈtaɪt(ə)l/ *noun* an identification name given to a file or program or disk

title bar /ˈtaɪt(ə)l bɑː/ *noun* a horizontal bar at the top of a window which displays the title of the window or application

T junction /ˌtiː ˈdʒʌŋkʃ(ə)n/ *noun* a connection at right angles to a cable carrying the main signal or power

TK *abbr* telecine

TMP *noun* the high-speed duplication of a videotape from a master tape. Full form **thermal magnetic duplication**

TMSF time format /ˌtiː em es ef ˈtaɪm ˌfɔːmæt/ *noun* a time format used mainly by audio CD devices to measure time in frames and tracks. Full form **tracks, minutes, seconds, frames time format**

T network /ˈtiː ˌnetwɜːk/ *noun* a simple circuit network with three electronic components connected in the shape of a letter T

T-number /ˈtiː ˌnʌmbə/ *noun* ▸ **T-stop**

toggle /ˈtɒg(ə)l/ *verb* to switch something between two states (NOTE: **toggles – toggling – toggled**)

token /ˈtəʊkən/ *noun* **1.** an internal code which replaces a reserved word or program statement in a high-level language **2.** (*in a local area network*) a control packet which is passed between workstations to control access to the network

token bus network /ˌtəʊkən ˈbʌs ˌnetwɜːk/ *noun* an IEEE 802.4 standard for a local area network formed with a bus-topology cable, in which workstations transfer data by passing a token

token-passing /ˈtəʊkən ˌpɑːsɪŋ/ *noun* a method of controlling access to a local area network by using a token (NOTE: A workstation cannot transmit data until it receives the token.)

Token Ring network /ˈtəʊkən rɪŋ ˌnetwɜːk/ *noun* an IEEE 802.5 standard that uses a token passed from one workstation to the next in a ring network ○ *Token Ring networks are very democratic and retain performance against increasing load.* (NOTE: A workstation can only transmit data if it captures the token. Token Ring networks, although logically rings, are often physically wired in a star topology.)

tone /təʊn/ *noun* **1.** sound at one single frequency **2.** a shade of a colour ○ *The graphics package can give several tones of blue.*

tone dialling /ˈtəʊn ˌdaɪəlɪŋ/ *noun* a method of dialling a telephone number using sounds to represent the digits of the number (NOTE: This method of dialling is the current standard method of dialling numbers and has generally replaced the older pulse dialling system. A Hayes-compatible modem can dial the number '123' using tone dialling with the AT command 'ATDT123' or using pulse dialling with the AT command 'ATDP123')

toner /ˈtəʊnə/ *noun* a finely powdered ink, usually black, that is used in laser printers ○ *If you get toner on your hands, you can only wash it off with cold water.* (NOTE: The toner is transferred onto the paper by electrical charge, then fixed permanently to the paper by heating.)

tone signalling /ˈtəʊn ˌsɪgn(ə)lɪŋ/ *noun* tones used in a telephone network to convey control or address signals

tool /tuːl/ *noun* (*in a graphical front end*) a function accessed from an icon in a toolbar, e.g. a circle-draw option

toolbar /ˈtuːlbɑː/ *noun* a window that contains a range of icons that access tools

Toolbook /ˈtuːlbʊk/ *noun* a multimedia authoring tool developed by Asymetrix which uses the OpenScript script language to control objects and actions

toolbox /ˈtuːlbɒks/ *noun* a set of predefined routines or functions that are used when writing a program

Toolbox /ˈtuːlbɒks/ *noun* (*in an Apple Mac*) a set of utility programs stored in ROM to provide graphic functions

toolkit /ˈtuːlkɪt/ *noun* a series of functions which help a programmer to write or debug programs

tools /tuːlz/ *noun* a set of utility programs such as backup and format in a computer system

top /tɒp/ *noun* a part which is the highest point of something

top-level domain /ˌtɒp ˌlev(ə)l dəʊˈmeɪn/ *noun* the part of an Internet address that identifies an Internet domain, e.g. a two-letter country code or a three-letter code such as .edu for education or .com for commercial when used without a country code.

topology /tɒˈpɒlədʒi/ *noun* a way in which the various elements in a network are interconnected (NOTE: The plural is **topologies**.)

total access communication system /ˌtəʊt(ə)l ˌækses kəˌmjuːnɪˌkeɪʃ(ə)n ˈsɪstəm/ *noun* full form of **TACS**

touch /tʌtʃ/ *verb* to make contact with something with the fingers

touch pad /ˈtʌtʃ pæd/ *noun* a flat device which can sense where on its surface and when it is touched, used to control a cursor position or switch a device on or off

touch screen /ˈtʌtʃ skriːn/ *noun* a computer display which has a grid of infrared transmitters and receivers, positioned on either side of the screen used to control a cursor position (NOTE: When a user wants to make a selection or move the cursor, he or she points to the screen, breaking two of the beams, which gives the position of the pointing finger.)

touch up /ˌtʌtʃ ˈʌp/ *verb* to remove scratches or other marks from a photograph or image

TP *abbr* **1.** teleprocessing **2.** transaction processing

TPI *abbr* tracks per inch

trace /treɪs/ *noun* **1.** a method of verifying that a program is functioning correctly, in which the current status and contents of the registers and variables used are displayed after each instruction step **2.** a cathode ray tube image which is produced by a flowing electronic stream **3.** a function that can take a bitmap image and process it to find the edges of the shapes and so convert these into a vector line image

trace program /ˈtreɪs ˌprəʊgræm/ *noun* a diagnostic program which executes a program that is being debugged, one instruction at a time, displaying the states and registers

traceroute /ˈtreɪsruːt/ *noun* a software utility that finds and displays the route taken for data travelling between a computer and a distant server on the Internet

COMMENT: The display shows the different servers that the data travels through, together with the time taken to travel between each server (called a hop). Traceroute works by sending out a time-to-live (TTL) query data packet to the distant server. It starts by sending out packets with a very low time-to-live, then gradually increases the length of time that the packet can survive until one is returned by the host – this then provides the shortest time it will take to reach the host. If you are trying to view a website you can use traceroute to check which section of the link to the website's server is the slowest. Windows includes a traceroute utility 'tracert'. Click the Start button and select the Run option then type in 'tracert' followed by the domain name of the distant web server, e.g. tracert 'www.bloomsbury.com"

tracing /ˈtreɪsɪŋ/ *noun* a function of a graphics program that takes a bitmap image and processes it to find the edges of the shapes and so convert these into a vector line image that can be more easily manipulated

tracing function /ˌtreɪsɪŋ ˈfʌŋkʃən/ *noun* the function of a graphics program that takes a bitmap image and processes it to find the edges of the shapes and so convert these into a vector line image that can be more easily manipulated

track /træk/ *noun* **1.** any one of a series of thin concentric rings on a magnetic disk which the read/write head accesses and along which the data is stored in separate sectors **2.** a song **3.** a method of separating the notes within a tune either by channel or by part or instrument **4.** a series of instructions that define how an object moves with time ■ *verb* **1.** to follow a path or track correctly ○ *The read head is not tracking the recorded track correctly.* **2.** to move a camera and its mount towards or away from the action, or to follow a moving subject

COMMENT: The first track on a tape is along the edge and the tape may have up to nine different tracks on it, while a disk has many concentric tracks around the central hub. The track and sector addresses are set up during formatting.

trackball /ˈtrækbɔːl/ *noun* a device used to move a cursor on-screen which is controlled by turning a ball contained in a case

tracking /ˈtrækɪŋ/ *noun* **1.** the correct alignment of a read head and the tape in a tape player **2.** degradation of a video clip because the action moves too fast to be accurately captured by the camera

tracks per inch /ˌtræks pɜːr ˈɪntʃ/ *noun* a measure of the number of concentric data tracks on a disk surface per inch. Abbr **TPI**

tractor feed /ˈtræktə fiːd/ *noun* a method of feeding paper into a printer, in which sprocket wheels on the printer connect with the sprocket holes on either edge of the paper to pull the paper through

traffic /ˈtræfɪk/ *noun* the totality of messages and other signals processed by a system or carried by a communications link ○ *Our Ethernet network begins to slow down if the traffic reaches 60 per cent of the bandwidth.*

trail /treɪl/ *noun* a line or route followed by something

trailer /ˈtreɪlə/ *noun* **1.** the final byte of a file containing control or file characteristics **2.** a brief film which advertises a motion picture that is about to be released **3.** a leader or piece of non magnetic tape to the start of a reel of magnetic tape to make loading easier

transaction /trænˈzækʃən/ *noun* a single action which affects a database, e.g. a sale, a change of address or a new customer

transaction processing /trænˈzækʃən ˌprəʊsesɪŋ/ *noun* interactive processing in which a user enters commands and data on a terminal which is linked to a central computer, with results being displayed on-screen. Abbr **TP**

'At present, users implementing client-server strategies are focusing on decision support systems before implementing online transaction processing and other mission-critical applications.' [*Computing*]

transborder data flow /ˌtrænzbɔːdə ˈdeɪtə ˌfləʊ/ *noun* the passing of data from one country to another using communications links such as satellites or land lines

transceiver /trænˈsiːvə/ *noun* a transmitter and receiver, or a device which can both transmit and receive signals, e.g. a terminal or modem

transcoder /trænsˈkəʊdə/ *noun* an electronic device used to convert television signal standards ○ *Use the transcoder to convert PAL to SECAM.*

transcribe /trænˈskraɪb/ *verb* to copy data from one backing storage unit or medium to another (NOTE: **transcribes – transcribing – transcribed**)

transcription /trænˈskrɪpʃən/ *noun* the action of transcribing data

transducer /trænzˈdjuːsə/ *noun* an electronic device which converts signals in one form into signals in another ○ *the pressure transducer converts physical pressure signals into electrical signals*

transfer /ˈtrænsfɜː/ *verb* **1.** to change command or control of something ○ *All processing activities have been transferred to the mainframe.* **2.** to copy a section of memory to another location (NOTE: **transferring – transferred**) ■ *noun* the process of changing command or control

transfer rate /ˈtrænsfɜː reɪt/ *noun* the speed at which data is transferred from backing store to main memory or from one device to another ○ *With a good telephone line, this pair of modems can achieve a transfer rate of 14.4Kbps.*

transform /trænsˈfɔːm/ *verb* to change something from one state to another

transformation /ˌtrænsfəˈmeɪʃ(ə)n/ *noun* the action of changing, or changing something, from one state to another

transformational rules /trænzfə ˈmeɪʃ(ə)n(ə)l ruːlz/ *noun* a set of rules applied to data which is to be transformed into coded form

transformer /trænsˈfɔːmə/ *noun* a device which changes the voltage or current amplitude of an AC signal

transient /'trænziənt/ *adjective* referring to a state or signal which is present for a short period of time

transistor /træn'zɪstə/ *noun* an electronic semiconductor device which can control the current flow in a circuit (NOTE: There are two main types of transistor, bipolar and unipolar.)

transition /træn'zɪʃ(ə)n/ *noun* **1.** a short period of time between two events **2.** the period between two frames in a slide show or animation. The user can normally define how one frame changes to the next.

translate /træns'leɪt/ *verb* **1.** to convert data from one form into another (NOTE: **translates – translating – translated**) **2.** to move an image on screen without rotating it (*graphics*)

translation tables /træns'leɪʃ(ə)n ˌteɪb(ə)lz/ *plural noun* same as **conversion tables**

translator /træns'leɪtə/, **translator program** /træns'leɪtə ˌprəʊgræm/ *noun* a program which translates a high level language program into another language, usually machine code. ◊ **interpreter, compiler**

translucent /træns'luːs(ə)nt/ *adjective* material which allows light to pass through

transmission /trænz'mɪʃ(ə)n/ *noun* the process of sending signals from one device to another

transmission channel /trænz'mɪʃ(ə)n ˌtʃæn(ə)l/ *noun* a physical connection between two points which allows data to be transmitted, e.g. a link between a CPU and a peripheral

transmission control protocol /trænz ˌmɪʃ(ə)n kən'trəʊl ˌprəʊtəkɒl/ *noun* full form of **TCP**

transmission control protocol/interface program /trænzˌmɪʃ(ə)n kən'trəʊl ˌprəʊtəʊkɒl 'ɪntəfeɪs ˌprəʊgræm/ *noun* full form of **TCP/IP**

transmissive disk /trænz'mɪsɪv dɪsk/ *noun* an optical data storage disk in which the reading laser beam shines through the disk to a detector below

transmit /trænz'mɪt/ *verb* to send information from one device to another, using any medium such as radio, cable or wire link (NOTE: **transmitting – transmitted**)

transmittance /trænz'mɪtəns/ *noun* the amount of light transmitted through a material in ratio to the total light incident on the surface of the material

transmitter /trænz'mɪtə/ *noun* a device which will take an input signal, process it, e.g. to modulate or convert it to sound, then transmit it by a medium such as radio or light. Abbr **TX**

transparency /træns'pærənsi/ *noun* **1.** transparent positive film, which can be projected onto a screen or to make film for printing **2.** the amount one image shows of another image beneath it

transparent /træns'pærənt/ *adjective* **1.** referring to an image that shows another image beneath it **2.** referring to a computer program which is not obvious to the user or which cannot be seen by the user when it is running ■ *noun* a device or network that allows signals to pass through it without being altered in any way

transparent GIF /trænsˌpærənt ˌdʒiː aɪ 'ef/ *noun* a graphic image stored in the GIF file format with one colour from the palette assigned as a transparent colour (NOTE: When the image is displayed, any part of the image in this colour will be transparent to allow any image beneath to show through. This feature is used a lot in webpages to place images on a patterned background.)

transphasor /trænz'feɪzə/ *noun* an optical transistor constructed from a crystal which is able to switch a main beam of light according to a smaller input signal

COMMENT: This is used in the latest research for an optical computer that could run at the speed of light.

transponder /træn'spɒndə/ *noun* a communications device that receives and retransmits signals

transport /træns'pɔːt/ *verb* to carry something from one place to another, often in a vehicle

transportable /træns'pɔːtəb(ə)l/ *adjective* which can be carried, though perhaps requiring a vehicle ○ *A transportable computer is not as small as a portable* or *a laptop.*

transposition /ˌtrænspə'zɪʃ(ə)n/ *noun* the process of changing the order of a series of characters (as 'comupter' for 'computer' or '1898' for '1988') ○ *A series of transposition errors caused faulty results.*

transverse mode noise /ˌtrænz'vɜːs məʊd nɔɪz/ *noun* interference which is apparent between power supply lines

trap /træp/ *noun* a device or piece of software or hardware that will catch something such as a variable, fault or value

trapezium distortion /trəˌpiːziəm dɪ 'stɔːʃ(ə)n/ *noun* in a visual or video system, image distortion which produces a rectangular shape

trapezoidal distortion /ˌtræpɪzɔɪdəl dɪs'tɔːʃ(ə)n/ *noun* same as **keystone distortion**

trashcan /'træʃkæn/ *noun* (*in a GUI*) an icon which looks like a dustbin that deletes any file that is dragged onto it

tree of folders /ˌtriː əv 'fəʊldəz/ *noun* a view of all the folders stored on a disk arranged to show folders and subfolders

tremendously high frequency /trɪ ˌmendəsli haɪ 'friːkwənsi/ *noun* the radio frequency between 300GHz and 3000GHz. Abbr **THF**

triad /'traɪæd/ *noun* a triangular shaped grouping of the red, green and blue colour phosphor spots at each pixel location on the screen of a colour RGB monitor

trial /'traɪəl/ *noun* a test for new equipment to see if it works

trials engineer /'traɪəlz ˌendʒɪnɪə/ *noun* a person who designs, runs and analyses trials of new equipment

triangle /'traɪæŋgəl/ *noun* a spreader with three sides for tripod legs (*film*)

triax /'traɪæks/ *noun* a coaxial cable with an additional screen which conveys power and coded commands to a television camera, and also receives the video signal from the camera (*film*) ○ *Triax is used when the camera is far away from the control unit.*

tributary station /ˌtrɪbjʊt(ə)ri 'steɪʃ(ə)n/ *noun* any station on a multilink network other than the main control station

trim /trɪm/ *verb* to cut off the edge of something ○ *The printed pages are trimmed to 198 x 129mm.* ○ *You will need to trim the top part of the photograph to make it fit.*

triniscope /'trɪnɪskəʊp/ *noun* a colour video display system which uses three different cathode ray tubes to produce the red, green and blue images

Trinitron™ /'trɪnɪtrɒn/ *noun* a colour television cathode ray tube which uses striped phosphors and aperture grille

triple standard /ˌtrɪp(ə)l 'stændəd/ *noun* a video tape recorder, television monitor or other apparatus which can receive NTSC, PAL or SECAM standard video signals

trivial file transfer protocol /ˌtrɪviəl 'faɪl ˌtrænsfɜː ˌprəʊtəkɒl/ *noun* full form of **TFTP**

TRL *abbr* transistor-resistor logic

Trojan Horse /'trəʊdʒ(ə)n hɔːs/ *noun* a program inserted into a system by a hacker that will perform a harmless function while copying information held in a classified file into a file with a low priority, which the hacker can then access without the authorised user's knowledge

troposphere /'trɒpəsfiə/ *noun* a region of space extending up to six miles above the earth's surface, causing radio wave scatter. ◊ **ionosphere**

troubleshoot /'trʌb(ə)lʃuːt/ *verb* **1.** to debug computer software **2.** to locate and repair faults in hardware

troubleshooter /'trʌb(ə)lʃuːtə/ *noun* a person who troubleshoots hardware or software (NOTE: **troubleshot**)

trough /trɒf/ *noun* the lowest point in a waveform. Compare **peak**

true /truː/ *adjective* referring to a logical condition representing a non-zero value

TrueType /'truːtaɪp/ a trade name for an outline font technology introduced by Apple and Microsoft as a means of printing exactly what is displayed on screen

truncate /trʌŋ'keɪt/ *verb* **1.** to cut something short **2.** to give an approximate value to a number by reducing it to a certain number of digits ○ *3.5678 truncated to 3.56* (NOTE: **truncates – truncating – truncated**)

truncation /trʌŋ'keɪʃ(ə)n/ *noun* removal of digits from a number so that it is a particular length

trunk /trʌŋk/ *noun* a bus or communication link consisting of wires or leads which connect different parts of a hardware system

trunk call /'trʌŋk kɔːl/ *noun* a long-distance telephone call

trunk exchange /'trʌŋk ɪksˌtʃeɪndʒ/ *noun* a telephone exchange that only handles trunk calls

truth table /'truːθ ˌteɪb(ə)l/ *noun* a method of defining a logic function as the output state for all possible inputs

Tseng Labs /'seŋ læbz/ a manufacturer of chipsets used in graphics adapters

TSR *abbr* terminate and stay resident

T-stop /'tiː stɒp/ *noun* a lens setting which shows the actual light transmission through the lens after being absorbed and reflected (*film*)

TSW *abbr* telesoftware

TTL /ˌtiː tiː 'el/ *noun* the most common family of logic gates and high-speed transistor circuit designs in which the bipolar transistors are directly connected, usually collector to base. Full form **transistor-transistor logic**

tune /tjuːn/ *verb* **1.** to set a system at its optimum point by careful adjustment (NOTE: **tunes – tuning – tuned**) **2.** to adjust a transmitter to the correct frequency **3.** to adjust a radio receiver's frequency until the required station is received clearly

tuner /'tjuːnə/ *noun* an electronic circuit that detects a transmitted television carrier signal at a particular frequency and removes the audio or video information to display on a CRT

tunnelling /ˈtʌn(ə)lɪŋ/ *noun* a method of enclosing a packet of data from one type of network within another packet so that it can be sent over a different, incompatible network

Turing machine /ˈtjʊrɪŋ məˌʃiːn/ *noun* a mathematical model of a device which could read and write data to a controllable tape storage while altering its internal states

Turing test /ˈtjʊrɪŋ test/ *noun* a test to decide if a computer is 'intelligent'

turn /tɜːn/ *verb* ○ *Turn off the power before unplugging the monitor.* □ **turn off** to switch off or disconnect the power supply to a machine ○ *Turn off the power before unplugging the monitor.* □ **turn on** to switch on or connect the power supply to a machine ○ *Turn on the computer and get to work.*

turnaround document /ˈtɜːnəˌraʊnd ˌdɒkjʊmənt/ *noun* a document which is printed out from a computer, sent to a user and returned by the user with new notes or information written on it, which can be read by a document reader

turnaround time /ˈtɜːnəraʊnd ˌtaɪm/ *noun* **1.** the length of time it takes to switch data flow direction in a half duplex system **2.** the time taken to activate a program and produce the result which the user has asked for ▶ abbr **TAT**

turnkey system /ˈtɜːnkiː ˌsɪstəm/ *noun* a complete system which is designed to a customer's needs and is ready to use (NOTE: To operate it, the user only has to switch it on or turn a key.)

turn off /ˌtɜːn ˈɒf/ *verb* to switch off or to disconnect the power supply to a machine ○ *Turn off the power before unplugging the monitor.*

turn on /ˌtɜːn ˈɒn/ *verb* to switch on or to connect the power supply to a machine

turtle /ˈtɜːt(ə)l/ *noun* a device whose movements and position are controllable, used to draw graphics with instructions in the computer language LOGO (NOTE: It is either a device which works on a flat surface (floor turtle) or one which draws on a VDU screen (screen turtle), and is often used as a teaching aid.)

turtle graphics /ˈtɜːt(ə)l ˌɡræfɪks/ *plural noun* graphic images created using a turtle and a series of commands ○ *The charts were prepared using turtle graphics.*

TV /ˌtiː ˈviː/ *abbr* television

TV-out /ˌtiː ˈviː aʊt/ *noun* a connector on a computer or graphics adapter that provides a modulated signal that can be displayed on a standard television or recorded on a video recorder

TVRO *noun* equipment for reception and display without transmission. Full form **television receive only**

TWAIN /tweɪn/ *noun* an application programming interface standard developed by Hewlett-Packard, Logitech, Eastman Kodak, Aldus, and Caere that allows software to control image hardware

tweak /twiːk/ *verb* to make small adjustments to a program or hardware to improve performance

tweening /ˈtwiːnɪŋ/ *noun* (*in computer graphics*) the process of calculating the intermediate images that lead from a starting image to a different finished image ○ *Using tweening, we can show how a frog turns into a princess in five steps.*

tweeter /ˈtwiːtə/ *noun* a small loudspeaker used for high frequency sounds only (*informal*) Compare **woofer**

24/96 /ˌtwenti fɔː ˌnaɪnti ˈsɪks/ a popular standard for high-performance digital audio equipment that provides 24-bit samples and a sample rate of 96KHz

24-bit sample /ˌtwenti fɔː bɪt ˈsɑːmp(ə)l/ *noun* a single sample of an analogue signal which is stored as three bytes (a 24-bit digital number), meaning that there are 16,777,216 possible levels. ◊ **8-bit sample, 16-bit sample**

twisted-pair cable /ˌtwɪstɪd peə ˈkeɪb(ə)l/ *noun* a cable which consists of two insulated copper wires twisted around each other, to reduce induction and so interference

COMMENT: The EIA specifies five levels of cable for different purposes. The Category 1 standard defines an older-style unshielded twisted-pair cable that is formed by loosely twisting two insulated wires together to reduce noise and interference; this type of cable is not suitable for data transmission. The Category 2 (part of the EIA/TIA 568 specification) standard defines a type of unshielded twisted-pair cable that can be used to transmit data at rates up to 4MHz. The Category 3 (part of the EIA/TIA 568 specification) standard defines a type of unshielded twisted-pair cable that can be used to transmit data at rates up to 10MHz; this type of cable is the minimum standard of cable required for a 10BaseT network. The standard suggests that the cable should have three twists per foot of cable. The Category 4 (part of the EIA/TIA 568 specification) standard defines a type of unshielded twisted-pair cable that is the minimum standard of cable required for data transmission rates up to 16Mbs on a Token Ring network. The Category 5 (part of the EIA/TIA 568 specification) standard defines a type of cable that can carry data transmitted at up to 100MHz and is suitable for FDDI over copper wire, 100BaseT or other high-speed networks.

twisted-pair Ethernet /ˌtwɪstɪd peə ˈiːθənet/ *noun* a star-topology network that uses twisted-pair cable and transmits data at 10 Mbps;. Also called **10BaseT**

twitter /ˈtwɪtə/ *noun* video picture distortion which produces a flicker at the horizontal edges of objects

2D /ˌtuː ˈdiː/ an object in a graphic image that has only the appearance of width and height, not depth, so does not look like a solid object

two-dimensional /ˌtuː daɪˈmenʃən(ə)l/ *adjective* which has two dimensions, i.e. flat, with no depth

two-part /ˌtuːˈpɑːt/ *adjective* referring to paper with a top sheet for the original and a second sheet for a copy ○ *two-part invoices*

two-way cable /ˌtuː weɪ ˈkeɪb(ə)l/ *noun US* a system of cable TV, where the viewer can take which programmes he wants by selecting them or where the viewer can respond to broadcast questions by sending his response down the cable

two-way radio /ˌtuː weɪ ˈreɪdiəʊ/ *noun* a radio transmitted and receiver in a single housing, allowing duplex communication with another user

two-wire circuit /ˌtuː ˌwaɪə ˈsɜːkɪt/ *noun* two insulated wires used to carry transmitted and received messages independently

TX *abbr* transmitter

type /taɪp/ *noun* **1.** a sort or category of something **2.** printed characters on a page ○ *they switched to italic type for the heading* **3.** the definition of the processes or sorts of data which a variable in a computer can contain **4.** same as **font 5.** a metal bars with a raised character used for printing ■ *verb* to enter information via a keyboard ○ *I typed in the command again, but it still didn't work.* (NOTE: **types – typing – typed**)

typeface /ˈtaɪpfeɪs/ *noun* a set of characters in a particular design and particular weight ○ *Most of this book is set in the Times typeface.*

typescript /ˈtaɪpskrɪpt/ *noun* a copy of a text written by an author on a typewriter

typeset /ˈtaɪpset/ *verb* to set text in type for printing ○ *In desktop publishing, the finished work should look almost as if it had been typeset.*

typesetter /ˈtaɪpsetə/ *noun* **1.** a machine which produces very high-quality text output using a laser to create an image on photosensitive paper, usually at a resolution of 1275 or 2450 dpi **2.** a person who typesets ○ *the text is ready to be sent to the typesetter*

typesetting /ˈtaɪpsetɪŋ/ *noun* the action of setting text in type ○ *Typesetting costs can be reduced by supplying the typesetter with prekeyed disks.* ◊ **phototypesetting**

type size /ˈtaɪp saɪz/ *noun* the size of a font, measured in points

type style /ˈtaɪp staɪl/ *noun* the weight and angle of a font, e.g. bold or italic

typewriter /ˈtaɪpraɪtə/ *noun* a machine which prints letters or figures on a piece of paper when a key is pressed by striking an inked ribbon onto the paper with a character type

typewriter faces /ˈtaɪpraɪtə ˌfeɪsɪz/ *plural noun* the spacing, size and font of characters available on a typewriter

typewritten /ˈtaɪprɪt(ə)n/ *adjective* written on a typewriter ○ *He sent in a typewritten job application.*

typing /ˈtaɪpɪŋ/ *noun* the process of writing letters with a typewriter (NOTE: no plural)

typing error /ˈtaɪpɪŋ ˌerə/ *noun* a mistake made when using a typewriter

typo /ˈtaɪpəʊ/ *noun* a typographical error which is made while typesetting (*informal*)

typographer /taɪˈpɒɡrəfə/ *noun* a person who designs a section of art or text to be printed

typographic /ˌtaɪpəˈɡræfɪk/, **typographical** /ˌtaɪpəˈɡræfɪk(ə)l/ *adjective* referring to typography or to typesetting ○ *No typographical skills are required for this job.* ○ *A typographical error made while typesetting is called a 'typo'.*

typography /taɪˈpɒɡrəfi/ *noun* the art and methods used in working with type

U

UART /ˈjuːɑːt/ *noun* a chip which converts asynchronous serial bit streams to a parallel form or parallel data to a serial bit stream. Full form **universal asynchronous receiver/transmitter**

U-format cassette /juː ˌfɔːmæt kəˈset/ *noun* a standard size videocassette which uses a three-quarter inch tape for use with the U-Matic system

UHF /ˌjuː eɪtʃ ˈef/ *noun* a range of frequencies normally used to transmit television signals. Full form **ultra high frequency**

ULA /ˌjuː el ˈeɪ/ *noun* a chip containing a number of unconnected logic circuits and gates which can then be connected by a customer to provide a required function. Full form **uncommitted logic array**

Ultimedia /ˌʌltiˈmidiə/ a trade name for a multimedia concept developed by IBM that combines sound, video, images and text, and defines the hardware required to run it

ultra- /ʌltrə/ *prefix* **1.** very large **2.** further than

Ultra ATA /ˌʌltrə eɪ tiː ˈeɪ/ *noun* a version of the AT Attachment hard disk drive interface standard that can support a data transfer rate of up to 33 MBps (NOTE: To manage this high-speed data transfer from the hard disk interface to the rest of your PC, it needs to have a high-speed version of DMA)

ultra high frequency /ˌʌltrə haɪ ˈfriːkwənsi/ *noun* full form of **UHF**

ultrasonic /ˌʌltrəˈsɒnɪk/ *adjective* (sound pressure waves) at a frequency above the audio band (above 20kHz)

U-Matic /juː ˈmætɪk/ *noun* a video tape format, 3/4-inch wide, used for professional video recording

U-Matic SP *noun* an enhanced format of the U-Matic tape standard that offers better quality

UMTS /ˌjuː em tiː ˈes/ *noun* a third generation mobile communication system that supports voice data, and video signals to the handset. Full form **universal mobile telecommunications system**

un- /ʌn/ *prefix* meaning not ○ *the use of a password is to prevent unauthorised access to the data*

unallowable digit /ʌnəˌlaʊəb(ə)l ˈdɪdʒɪt/ *noun* an illegal combination of bits in a word, according to predefined rules

unary operation /ˌjuːnəri ˌɒpəˈreɪʃ(ə)n/ *noun* a computing operation on only one operand, e.g. the logical NOT operation

unattended operation /ˌʌnətendɪd ˌɒpəˈreɪʃ(ə)n/ *noun* an operation that can proceed without the need for a person to supervise

unauthorised /ʌnˈɔːθəraɪzd/, **unauthorized** *adjective* which has not been authorised ○ *The use of a password is to prevent unauthorised access to the data.*

unbundled software /ʌnˌbʌnd(ə)ld ˈsɒftweə/ *noun* software which is not included in the price of the equipment

unclocked /ʌnˈklɒkd/ *adjective* referring to an electronic circuit or flip-flop which changes state as soon as an input changes, not with a clock signal

uncommitted logic array /ˌʌnkəmɪtɪd ˈlɒdʒɪk əˌreɪ/ *noun* full form of **ULA**

unconditional /ˌʌnkənˈdɪʃ(ə)nəl/ *adjective* which does not depend on any condition being met

undelete /ˈʌndɪiːt/ *verb* to restore deleted information or a deleted file ○ *Don't worry, this function will undelete your cuts to the letter.* (NOTE: **undeletes – undeleting – undeleted**)

underflow /ˈʌndəfləʊ/ *noun* the result of a numerical operation that is too small to be represented with the given accuracy of a computer

underline /ˈʌndəlaɪn/ *noun* a line drawn or printed under a piece of text. Also called **underscore** ■ *verb* to print or write a line under a piece of text (NOTE: **underlines – underlining – underlined**)

underscore /ˈʌndəskɔː/ *verb* same as **underline** (NOTE: **underscores – underscoring – underscored**)

undertake /ˌʌndəˈteɪk/ *verb* to agree to do something ○ *He has undertaken to reprogram the whole system.* (NOTE: **undertakes – undertaking – undertook – undertaken**)

undetected /ˌʌndɪˈtektɪd/ *adjective* which has not been detected ○ *The programming error remained undetected for some time.*

undetected error /ˌʌndɪtektɪd ˈerə/ *noun* an error which is not detected by a coding system

undo /ʌn'duː/ *verb* to reverse the previous action, normally an editing command ○ *You've just deleted the paragraph, but you can undo it from the option in the Edit menu.* (NOTE: **undoes – undoing – undid**)

unedited /ʌn'edɪtɪd/ *adjective* which has not been edited

unformatted /ʌn'fɔːmætɪd/ *adjective* **1.** referring to a text file which contains no formatting commands, margins or typographical commands ○ *It is impossible to copy to an unformatted disk.* **2.** referring to a disk which has not been formatted ○ *The cartridge drive provides 12.7Mbyte of unformatted storage.*

ungroup /ʌn'gruːp/ *verb* to convert a single complex object back into a series of separate objects

uni- /juːni/ *prefix* one or single

unidirectional microphone /ˌjuːnidaɪrekʃən(ə)l 'maɪkrəfəʊn/ *noun* a microphone that is most sensitive in one direction only. Compare **omnidirectional**

uniform resource locator /ˌjuːnɪfɔːm rɪ'zɔːs ləʊˌkeɪtə/ *noun* full form of **URL**

uninstall /ˌʌnɪn'stɑːl/ *verb* to remove a piece of software from a computer

uninterruptible power supply /ˌʌnɪntərʌptɪb(ə)l 'paʊə səˌplaɪ/ *noun* full form of **UPS**

unipolar /ˌjuːni'pəʊlə/ *adjective* **1.** (*referring to a transistor*) which can act as a variable current flow control (NOTE: An external signal varies the resistance of the device.) **2.** referring to a transmission system in which a positive voltage pulse and zero volts represents the binary bits 1 and 0

unique /juː'niːk/ *adjective* which is different from everything else ○ *Each separate memory byte has its own unique address.*

unique identifier /juːˌniːk aɪ'dentɪfaɪə/ *noun* a set of characters used to distinguish between different resources in a multimedia book

unit /'juːnɪt/ *noun* **1.** the smallest element **2.** a single machine, possibly with many different parts

universal /ˌjuːnɪ'vɜːs(ə)l/ *adjective* which applies everywhere or which can be used everywhere or used for a number of tasks

universal asynchronous receiver/transmitter /ˌjuːnɪvɜːsəl ˌeɪsɪŋkrənəs rɪˌsiːvə trænz'mɪtə/ *noun* full form of **UART**

universal mobile telecommunications system /ˌjuːnɪvɜːs(ə)l ˌməʊbaɪl ˌtelikəmjuːnɪ'keɪʃ(ə)nz ˌsɪstəm/ *noun* full form of **UMTS**

universal product code /ˌjuːnɪvɜːs(ə)l 'prɒdʌkt ˌkəʊd/ *noun* a standard printed bar coding system used to identify products in a shop using a bar code reader or at a EPOS. Abbr **UPC**

universal resource locator /ˌjuːnɪvɜːs(ə)l rɪ'zɔːs ləʊˌkeɪtə/ *noun* full form of **URL**

universal serial bus /ˌjuːnɪvɜːs(ə)l 'sɪəriəl ˌbʌs/ *noun* full form of **USB**

universal synchronous asynchronous receiver/transmitter /ˌjuːnɪvɜːsəl ˌsɪŋkrənəs ˌeɪsɪŋkrənəs rɪ ˌsiːvə trænz'mɪtə/ *noun* full form of **USART**

UNIX /'juːnɪks/ *noun* a popular multiuser, multitasking operating system developed by AT&T Bell Laboratories to run on almost any computer, from PCs to minicomputers and large mainframes

'Hampshire fire brigade is investing £2 million in a command and control system based on the new SeriesFT fault-tolerant Unix machine from Motorola.' [*Computing*]

unjustified /ʌn'dʒʌstɪfaɪd/ *adjective* referring to text which has not been justified

unlock /ʌn'lɒk/ *verb* to make it possible for other users to write to a file or access a system

unmoderated list /ʌnˌmɒdəreɪtɪd 'lɪst/ *noun* a mailing list that sends any material submitted to the listserv on to all the subscribers without a person reading or checking the content

unmodulated /ʌn'mɒdjʊleɪtɪd/ *adjective* referring to a signal which has not been modulated

unmount /ʌn'maʊnt/ *verb* **1.** to remove a disk from a disk drive **2.** to inform the operating system that a disk drive is no longer in active use

unpack /ʌn'pæk/ *verb* to remove packed data from storage and expand it to its former state ○ *This routine unpacks the archived file.*

unplug /ʌn'plʌg/ *verb* to take a plug out of a socket ○ *Do not move the system without unplugging it.* (NOTE: **unplugging – unplugged**)

unpopulated /ʌn'pɒpjʊleɪtɪd/ *adjective* referring to a printed circuit board which does not yet contain any components or whose sockets are empty

unprotected /ˌʌnprə'tektɪd/ *adjective* referring to data which can be modified and is not protected by a security measure

unrecoverable error /ʌnrɪˌkʌvərəb(ə)l 'erə/ *noun* a computer hardware or software error which causes a program to crash

unshielded twisted-pair cable /ˌʌnʃiːldɪd ˌtwɪstɪd 'peə ˌkeɪb(ə)l/ *noun* full form of **UTP cable**

unsigned /ʌn'saɪnd/ *adjective* referring to a number system which does not represent negative numbers

unsolicited mail /ˌʌnsə'lɪsɪtɪd meɪl/ *noun* an advertising email message that has not been requested. ◊ **spam** (NOTE: Do not send out unsolicited mail to unknown email addresses unless you want to annoy the recipients and damage your company's reputation)

unsorted /ʌn'sɔːtɪd/ *adjective* referring to data which has not been sorted ○ *It took four times as long to search the unsorted file.*

unsqueezed /ʌn'swiːzd/ *adjective* (film print) where the compressed picture of an anamorphic negative has been altered for normal projection

unsubscribe /ˌʌnsəb'skraɪb/ *verb* to cancel a subscription to or registration with something, especially an email mailing list (NOTE: **unsubscribes – unsubscribing – unsubscribed**)

> 'All commercial messages will have to include full details of the sender's name and physical address, as well as an unsubscribe option allowing recipients to stop any further messages.' [*The Guardian*]

unsupported /ˌʌnsə'pɔːtɪd/ *adjective* having no technical support system

unwanted /ʌn'wɒntɪd/ *adjective* which is not needed ○ *Use the global delete command to remove large areas of unwanted text.*

unzip /ʌn'zɪp/ *verb* to restore a compressed computer file to its original size (NOTE: **unzipping – unzipped**)

up /ʌp/ *adverb* referring to a computer or program that is working or running ○ *They must have found the fault – the computer is finally up and running.*

up and down propagation time /ˌʌp ən daʊn ˌprɒpə'geɪʃ(ə)n ˌtaɪm/ *noun* the total length of time that a transmission takes to travel from earth to a satellite and back to an earth station

UPC *abbr* universal product code

update /'ʌpdeɪt/ *noun* **1.** a master file which has been made up -to date by adding new material **2.** a piece of printed information which is an up-to-date revision of earlier information **3.** a new version of a system which is sent to users of the existing system ■ *verb* /ʌp'deɪt/ to change or add to specific data in a master file so as to make the information up -to date ○ *He has the original and updated documents on disks.* (NOTE: **updates – updating – updated**)

up/down counter /ˌʌp 'daʊn ˌkaʊntə/ *noun* an electronic counter which can increment or decrement a counter with each input pulse

upgrade /ʌp'greɪd/ *verb* to make a system more powerful or more up -to date by adding new equipment or facilities ○ *They can upgrade the printer.* (NOTE: **upgrades – upgrading – upgraded**)

upkeep /'ʌpkiːp/ *noun* **1.** the process of keeping data up-to-date ○ *The upkeep of the files means reviewing them every six months.* **2.** the process of keeping devices in working order

uplink /'ʌplɪŋk/ *noun* a transmission link from an earth station to a satellite

upload /'ʌpˌləʊd/ *verb* to transfer data files or programs from a small computer to a main CPU ○ *The user can upload PC data to update mainframe applications.* Opposite **download**

uploading /'ʌpləʊdɪŋ/ *noun* the action of transferring files to a main CPU

uppercase /ˌʌpə'keɪs/ *noun* the style of capital letters and other symbols on a keyboard which are accessed by pressing the shift key

upper memory /ˌʌpə 'mem(ə)ri/ *noun* (*in an IBM PC*) 384 Kb of memory located between the 640 Kb and 1 Mb limits, after the 640 Kb conventional memory but before the high memory areas above the 1 Mb range

UPS /ˌjuː piː 'es/ *noun* a power supply which can continue to provide a regulated supply to equipment even after a mains power failure, using a battery. Full form **uninterruptible power supply**

> 'Magnum Power Systems has launched a new UPS for PCs. The BI-UPS prevents loss of data due to power dips or 'brown-outs' – voltage drops because of circuit overload.' [*Computing*]

uptime, up time *noun* the time during which a device is operational and error-free. Opposite **downtime**

upward compatible /ˌʌpwəd kəm 'pætɪb(ə)l/, **upwards compatible** /ˌʌpwədz kəm'pætɪb(ə)l/ *adjective* referring to hardware or software designed to be compatible either with earlier models or with future models which have not yet been developed

URL /ˌjuː ɑː 'el/ *noun* an Internet system used to standardise the way in which World Wide Web addresses are written. Full form **uniform resource locator**

> COMMENT: It is made up of three parts: the first is the protocol, e.g. HTTP or FTP, then the domain name of the service and finally the directory or file name – 'http://www.bloomsbury.com/index.html'

usability /ˌjuːzəˈbɪlɪti/ *noun* the ease with which hardware or software can be used ○ *We have studied usability tests and found that a GUI is easier for new users than a command line.*

usable /ˈjuːzəb(ə)l/ *adjective* which can be used or which is available for use ○ *The PC has 512K of usable memory.*

USART /ˈjuːzɑːt/ *noun* a chip which can be instructed by a CPU to communicate with asynchronous or synchronous bit streams or parallel data lines. Full form **universal synchronous asynchronous receiver/transmitter**

USASCII /ˌjuː es ˈæskiː/ *abbr* USA standard code for information interchange. ◊ **ASCII**

USB /ˌjuː es ˈbiː/ *noun* a standard defining a high-speed serial interface that transfers data at up to 12Mbps and allows up to 127 compatible peripherals to be connected to a computer. Full form **universal serial bus**. ◊ **Firewire**

use *noun* **1.** the state or fact of being employed for a particular purpose ○ *Sorry, the printer is already in use* □ **in use** already in operation ○ *Sorry, the printer is already in use* **2.** the purpose, value or usefulness of something ○ *What use is an extra disk drive?* ○ *It's no use, I cannot find the error.* ■ *verb* **1.** to operate something or employ something for a particular purpose ○ *If you use the computer for processing the labels, it will be much quicker.* **2.** to consume a resource such as heat or light ○ *It's using too much electricity.*

used /juːzd/ *adjective* which is not new ○ *special offer on used terminals*

Usenet /ˈjuːzˌnet/ *noun* a section of the Internet that provides forums, called newsgroups, in which any user can add a message or comment on any other message

user /ˈjuːzə/ *noun* **1.** a person who uses a computer, machine or software **2.** a keyboard operator

'...the user's guides are designed for people who have never seen a computer, but some sections have been spoiled by careless checking' [*PC User*]

user-definable /ˈjuːzə dɪˌfaɪnəb(ə)l/ *adjective* referring to a feature or section of a program that a user can customise as required ○ *The style sheet contains 125 user-definable symbols.*

user documentation /ˌjuːzə ˌdɒkjʊmenˈteɪʃ(ə)n/ *noun* documentation provided with a program which helps the user run it ○ *Using the package was easy with the excellent user documentation.*

user-friendly /ˌjuːzə ˈfrendli/ *adjective* referring to a language, system or program which is easy to use and interact with

'ModelMaker saves researchers a great deal of time and effort, and provides a highly user-friendly environment using menus and 'buttons', instant output, and instant access to a wide variety of mathematical techniques built into the system.' [*Computing*]

user-friendly software /ˌjuːzə ˌfrendli ˈsɒftweə/ *noun* a program which is easy for a nonexpert to use and interact with

user group /ˈjuːzə gruːp/ *noun* an association or club of users of a particular system or computer ○ *I found how to solve the problem by asking people at the user group meeting.*

user guide /ˈjuːzə gaɪd/ *noun* a manual describing how to use a software package or system

user ID /ˌjuːzə aɪ ˈdiː/ *noun* a unique identification code which allows a computer to recognise a user ○ *If you forget your user ID, you will not be able to log on.*

user interface /ˈjuːzə ˌɪntəfeɪs/ *noun* hardware or software designed to make it easier for a user to communicate with a machine

user level /ˈjuːzə ˌlev(ə)l/ *noun* (*in authoring software*) one of two modes that allows a user to run and interact with a multimedia application but not to modify it in any way

user name /ˈjuːzə neɪm/ *noun* (*in a network or multi-user system*) a name by which a user is known to the system and which opens the correct user account

user-selectable /ˌjuːzə sɪˈlektəb(ə)l/ *adjective* which can be chosen or selected by the user

user's manual /ˈjuːzəz ˌmænjʊəl/ *noun* a booklet showing how a device or system should be used

utility program /juːˈtɪlɪti ˌprəʊgræm/ *noun* a program which is concerned with such routine activities as file searching, copying files, file directories, sorting and debugging and various mathematical functions

UTP cable /ˌjuː tiː ˈpiː ˌkeɪb(ə)l/ *noun* a cable consisting of two insulated copper wires twisted around each other, to reduce induction and so interference. Full form **unshielded twisted-pair cable**

COMMENT: UTP is normally used for telephone cabling, but is also the cabling used in the IEEE 802.3 (10BaseT) standard that defines Ethernet running over UTP at rates of up to 10 Mbits per second. Unlike STP cable, the pair of wires are not wrapped in any other layer.

Uuencoding /ˌjuː juː ɪnˈkəʊdɪŋ/ *noun* a method of converting documents and files to a pseudo-text format that allows them to be transmitted as an email message

COMMENT: This gets around the Internet's inability to transfer messages that are not text. It has now been largely replaced by MIME.

V

V /viː/ *abbr* voltage

V20 *noun* a range of processor chips made by NEC, which are compatible with the Intel 8088 and 8086. Also called **V30**

V30 *noun* ▸ **V20**

V.34 *noun* an outdated full-duplex modem communication standard that can transfer data at up to 28,800 bps. Like V.32, the V.34 standard allows the modem to automatically adjust its speed based on the quality of the telephone line to avoid errors.

vaccine /ˈvæksiːn/ *noun* a software utility used to check a system to see if any viruses are present, and remove any that are found

vacuum /ˈvækjuəm/ *noun* a state with no air

vacuum tube /ˈvækjʊəm tjuːb/ *noun* an electronic current flow control device consisting of a heated cathode and an anode in a sealed glass tube with a vacuum inside it

valid /ˈvælɪd/ *adjective* correct, according to a set of rules

validate /ˈvælɪˌdeɪt/ *verb* to check that an input or data is correct according to a set of rules (NOTE: **validates – validating – validated**)

validation /ˌvælɪˈdeɪʃ(ə)n/ *noun* a check performed to validate data. ◊ **verification**

validity /vəˈlɪdɪti/ *noun* the correctness of an instruction or password

value /ˈvæljuː/ *noun* what something is worth, either in money or as a quantity

value-added /ˌvæljuː ˈædɪd/ *adjective* (with extra benefit for a user

value-added network[1] /ˌvæljuː ˌædɪd ˈnetwɜːk/ *noun* a commercial network which offers information services, e.g. stock prices, weather, email or advice, as well as basic file transfer. Abbr **VAN**

value-added network[2] /ˌvæljuː ˌædɪd ˈnetwɜːk/ *noun* a network where the transmission lines are leased from a public utility such as the telephone service, but where the user can add on private equipment. Abbr **VAN**

value-added reseller[1] /ˌvæljuː ædɪd ˈriːselə/ *noun* a company that buys hardware or software and adds another feature, customises or offers an extra service to attract customers. Abbr **VAR**

value-added reseller[2] /ˌvæljuː ædɪd ˈriːselə/ *noun* a retailer who sells equipment and systems which are specially tailored to certain types of operation. Abbr **VAR**

valve /vælv/ *noun* an electronic current flow control device consisting of a heated cathode and an anode in a sealed glass vacuum tube

VAN /væn/ *abbr* value-added network

V & V /ˌviː ənd ˈviː/ *noun* the process of testing a system to check that it is functioning correctly and that it is suitable for the tasks intended. Full form **verification and validation**

vanishing point perspective /ˈvænɪʃɪŋ pɔɪnt pəˌspektɪv/ *noun* graphics displayed in two dimensions that have the appearance of depth as all lines converge at a vanishing point and objects appear smaller as they are further from the user

vapourware /ˈveɪpəweə/ *noun* products which exist in name only (*informal*)

> ‘Rivals dismissed the initiative as IBM vapourware, designed to protect its installed base of machines running under widely differing operating systems.’ [*Computing*]

VAR *abbr* value-added reseller

variable /ˈveəriəb(ə)l/ *adjective* which is able to change ■ *noun* **1.** a register or storage location which can contain any number or characters and which may vary during the program run. Opposite **constant 2.** a computer program identifier for a variable

variable data rate video /ˌveəriəb(ə)l ˌdeɪtə reɪt ˈvɪdiəʊ/ *noun* full form of **VDRV**

variable resistor /ˌveəriəb(ə)l rɪˈzɪstə/ *noun* a component whose resistance can be changed by turning a knob

varifocal lens /ˌveərifəʊk(ə)l ˈlenz/ *noun* same as **zoom lens** (*see*)

varispeed /ˈveərispiːd/ *noun* a variable speed control on magnetic audio recorders which generally provide a large range; can also be a pitch control

vary /ˈveəri/ *verb* to change, or to change something ○ *The clarity of the signal can vary with the power supply.*

VB *abbr* Visual Basic

Vbox /ˈviːbɒks/ *noun* a device that allows several VCRs, videodiscs and camcorders to be attached and controlled by one unit, developed by Sony. Full form **video box**

VBScript /ˌviː ˈbiː ˌskrɪpt/ *abbr* Visual Basic Script. Compare **JavaScript**

VBX *abbr* Visual Basic Extension (NOTE: Originally developed as a way of adding extra programming features to the Microsoft VB programming language, it is now a standard that can be used by many Windows programming tools; a VBX can be used in 16-bit or 32-bit Windows (versions 3.x or 95) whereas an OCX control will only work with 32-bit Windows (version 95 and later).)

VCPS *abbr* Video Copyright Protection Society

VCR /ˌviː siː ˈɑː/ *noun* a machine that can record analog video signals onto a magnetic cassette tape and play back the tape to display video on a monitor. Full form **video cassette recorder**

COMMENT: The most popular formats are: 1-inch tape, used for studio-quality mastering; 3/4-inch tape, which was widely used but has now been mostly replaced by 1/2-inch tape; 1/2-inch VHS format tape, which was first used only in the home but has now mostly replaced 3/4-inch tape; 1/2-inch Beta format tape, which was the first home VCR format but is no longer used. Some VCRs can be used to store digital data for data backup.

VDRV /ˌviː diː ɑː ˈviː/ *noun* a digital video system that can adjust the amount of data used to represent each different frame and so adjust image quality or stay within bandwidth limits. Full form **variable data rate video**

VDT /ˌviː diː ˈjuː/ *abbr* visual display terminal

VDU *abbr* visual display unit

'...it normally consists of a keyboard to input information and either a printing terminal or a VDU screen to display messages and results' [*Practical Computing*]

'...a VDU is a device used with a computer that displays information in the form of characters and drawings on a screen' [*Electronics & Power*]

vector /ˈvektə/ *noun* **1.** the address which directs a computer to a new memory location **2.** a coordinate that consists of a magnitude and direction **3.** a line which connect points on a cathode ray tube

vectored interrupt /ˌvektəd ˈɪntərʌpt/ *noun* an interrupt signal which directs the processor to a routine at a particular address

vector font /ˈvektə fɒnt/ *noun* the shape of characters within a font that are drawn vector graphics, allowing the characters to be scaled to almost any size without changing the quality

vector graphics /ˈvektə ˌɡræfɪks/, **vector image** /ˌvektə ˈɪmɪdʒ/ *noun* a system of drawing objects using curves and lines. Also called **vector scan**. Compare **bit-mapped graphics**

COMMENT: The images are described by line length and direction from an origin to plot lines and so build up an image rather than a description of each pixel, as in a bitmap. A vector image can be easily and accurately resized with no loss of detail.

vector processor /ˈvektə ˌprəʊsesə/ *noun* a coprocessor that operates on one row or column of an array at a time

vector scan /ˈvektə skæn/ *noun* same as **vector graphics**

vectorscope /ˈvektəskəʊp/ *noun* in television, an oscilloscope to show the form of the chroma signals in colour television systems

'...the great advantage of the vector-scan display is that it requires little memory to store a picture' [*Electronics & Power*]

velocity /vəˈlɒsɪti/ *noun* speed ○ *The disk drive motor spins at a constant velocity.*

vendor /ˈvendə/ *noun* a person who manufactures, sells or supplies hardware or software products

vendor-independent /ˌvendə ˌɪndɪˈpendənt/ *adjective* referring to hardware or software that will work with hardware and software manufactured by other vendors

Venn diagram /ˈven ˌdaɪəɡræm/ *noun* a graphical representation of the relationships between the states in a system or circuit

verification /ˌverɪfɪˈkeɪʃ(ə)n/ *noun* the process of checking that data has been keyboarded correctly or that data transferred from one medium to another has been transferred correctly

verification and validation /ˌverɪfɪkeɪʃ(ə)n ən ˌvælɪˈdeɪʃ(ə)n/ *noun* full form of **V & V**

verifier /ˈverɪfaɪə/ *noun* a special device for verifying input data

verify /ˈverɪˌfaɪ/ *verb* to check that data recorded or entered is correct (NOTE: **verifies – verifying – verifies**)

versamodule eurocard bus /ˌvɜːsəmɒdjuːl ˈjʊərəʊkɑːd ˌbʌs/ *noun* full form of **VME bus**

version /ˈvɜːʃ(ə)n/ *noun* a copy or program or statement which is slightly different from others ○ *The latest version of the software includes an improved graphics routine.*

verso /ˈvɜːsəʊ/ *noun* the left hand page of a book (usually given an even number)

vertical /ˈvɜːtɪk(ə)l/ *adjective* at right angles to the horizontal

vertical format unit /ˌvɜːtɪk(ə)l ˈfɔːmæt ˌjuːnɪt/ *noun* a part of the control system of a printer which governs the vertical format of the document to be printed, e.g. vertical spacing or page length. Abbr **VFU**

vertical interval time code /ˌvɜːtɪk(ə)l ˌɪntəv(ə)l ˈtaɪm ˌkəʊd/ *noun* full form of **VITC**

vertically /ˈvɜːtɪkli/ *adverb* from top to bottom or going up and down at right angles to the horizontal ○ *The page has been justified vertically.*

vertical portal /ˌvɜːtɪk(ə)l ˈpɔːt(ə)l/ *noun* full form of **VORTAL**

vertical scan frequency /ˌvɜːtɪk(ə)l ˈskæn ˌfriːkwənsi/ *noun* the number of times a picture beam in a monitor moves from the last line back up to the first

vertical scrolling /ˌvɜːtɪk(ə)l ˈskrəʊlɪŋ/ *noun* displayed text which moves up or down the computer screen one line at a time

very high frequency /ˌveri haɪ ˈfriːkwənsi/ *noun* the range of radio frequencies between 30–300 MHz. Abbr **VHF**

very large scale integration /ˌveri lɑːdʒ skeɪl ˌɪntɪˈgreɪʃ(ə)n/ *noun* full form of **VLSI**

very low frequency /ˌveri ləʊ ˈfriːkwənsi/ *noun* the range of radio frequencies between 3–30 KHz. Abbr **VLF**

VESA *abbr* Video Electronics Standards Association

VESA local bus /ˌviː iː es eɪ ˈləʊk(ə)l bʌs/ *noun* full form of **VL-bus**

vestigial side band /vesˌtɪdʒiəl ˈsaɪd ˌbænd/ *noun* full form of **VSB**

VFU *abbr* vertical format unit

VFW *abbr* Video for Windows

VGA /ˌviː dʒiː ˈeɪ/ *noun* (*in an IBM PC*) a standard of video adapter developed by IBM that can support a display with a resolution up to 640 x 480 pixels in up to 256 colours, superseded by SVGA

VHF *noun* radio frequency between 30MHz and 300MHZ (used for broadcasting radio and TV programmes). Full form **very high frequency**

VHS *noun* a video cassette tape format, using 1/2-inch wide tape, developed by JVC and now the standard for home and consumer markets. Full form **video home system**

VHS-C /ˌviː eɪtʃ ˈes siː/ *noun* a video cassette system which uses the VHS format

via /ˈvaɪə/ *preposition* going through something or using something to get to a destination ○ *The signals have reached us via satellite.*

VIBGYOR *noun* the colours in the visible spectrum: violet, indigo, blue, green, yellow, orange and red

VidCap /ˈvɪdkæp/ *noun* a utility program used in the Microsoft VFW system to capture a video sequence

video /ˈvɪdiəʊ/ *noun* **1.** text or images or graphics viewed on television or a monitor **2.** an electronic system which records, stores and reproduces visual images

video adapter /ˈvɪdiəʊ əˌdæptə/ *noun* an add-in board which converts data into electrical signals to drive a monitor and display text and graphics. Also called **video board, video controller**

video bandwidth /ˌvɪdiəʊ ˈbændwɪdθ/ *noun* the maximum display resolution, measured in MHz, and calculated by horizontal x vertical resolution x refreshes/sec (NOTE: TV studio recording is limited to 5 MHz; TV broadcasting is limited to 3.58 MHz)

video board /ˈvɪdiəʊ bɔːd/ *noun* same as **video adapter**

video box /ˈvɪdiəʊ bɒks/ *noun* full form of **Vbox**

video buffer /ˈvɪdiəʊ ˌbʌfə/ *noun* memory in a video adapter that is used to store the bitmap of the image being displayed

video capture board /ˌvɪdiəʊ ˈkæptʃə ˌbɔːd/ *noun* a board that plugs into an expansion socket inside a PC and lets a user capture a TV picture and store it in memory so that it can then be processed by a computer

video cassette recorder /ˌvɪdiəʊ kə ˈset rɪˌkɔːdə/ *noun* full form of **VCR**

video-CD /ˌvɪdiəʊ ˌsiː ˈdiː/ *noun* a CD-ROM that stores digital video data conforming to the Philips White Book standard and uses MPEG compression for the full-motion video data

video clip /ˈvɪdiəʊˌklɪp/ *noun* a short video sequence

video codec /ˌvɪdiəʊ ˈkəʊdek/ *noun* an electronic device to convert a video signal to or from a digital form

video compression /ˌvɪdiəʊ kəm ˈpreʃ(ə)n/ *noun* algorithms used to compress analog television signals so that they can be efficiently broadcast over a digital channel

video conferencing /ˈvɪdiəʊ ˌkɒnf(ə)rənsɪŋ/ *noun* the linking of video, audio and computer signals from different locations so that distant people can talk and see each other, as if in a conference room

video controller /ˌvɪdiəʊ kənˈtrəʊlə/ *noun* same as **video adapter**

video digitiser /ˌvɪdiəʊ ˈdɪdʒɪtaɪzə/ *noun* a high-speed digital sampling circuit which stores a TV picture in memory so that it can then be processed by a computer

videodisc /ˈvɪdiəʊdɪsk/ *noun* a read-only optical disc that can store up to two hours of video data, usually used either to store a complete film, as a rival to video cassette, or to use in an interactive system with text, video and still images (NOTE: For interactive use, a videodisc can store 54,000 frames of information. If the videodisc contains a complete film, the data is recorded using a constant linear velocity format; if it is used to store interactive data, it is stored in a constant angular velocity format.)

video display /ˈvɪdiəʊ dɪˌspleɪ/ *noun* a device which can display text or graphical information, e.g. a CRT

video editing /ˌvɪdiəʊ ˈedɪtɪŋ/ *noun* a method of editing a video sequence in which the video is digitised and stored in a computer

video editor /ˈvɪdiəʊ ˌedɪtə/ *noun* a computer that controls two videotape recorders to allow an operator to play back sequences from one and record these on the second machine

Video Electronics Standards Association /ˌvɪdiəʊ elekˌtrɒnɪks ˈstændədz əˌsəʊsieɪʃ(ə)n/ *noun* full form of **VESA**

Video for Windows /ˌvɪdiəʊ fə ˈwɪndəʊz/ a trade name for a set of software drivers and utilities for Microsoft Windows 3.1, developed by Microsoft, that allows AVI-format video files to be played back in a window. Abbr **VFW**

video game /ˈvɪdiəʊ geɪm/ *noun* a game played on a computer, with action shown on a video display

video graphics array /ˌvɪdiəʊ ˈgræfɪks əˌreɪ/ *noun* (*in an IBM PC*) a standard of video adapter developed by IBM that can support a display with a resolution up to 640 x 480 pixels in up to 256 colours, superseded by SVGA. Abbr **VGA**

video graphics card /ˌvɪdiəʊ ˈgræfɪks ˌkɑːd/ *noun* an expansion card that fits into an expansion slot inside a PC and that allows a computer to display both generated text and graphics and moving video images from an external camera or VCR. Also called **overlay card**

video home system /ˌvɪdiəʊ ˈhəʊm ˌsɪstəm/ *noun* full form of **VHS**

video interface chip /ˌvɪdiəʊ ˈɪntəfeɪs ˌtʃɪp/ *noun* a chip which controls a video display allowing information such as text or graphics stored in a computer to be displayed

video lookup table /ˌvɪdiəʊ ˈlʊkʌp ˌteɪb(ə)l/ *noun* a collection of precalculated values of the different colours that are stored in memory and can be examined very quickly to produce an answer without the need to recalculate

video memory /ˌvɪdiəʊ ˈmem(ə)ri/ *noun* a high speed random access memory used to store computer-generated or digitised images

video monitor /ˈvɪdiəʊ ˌmɒnɪtə/ *noun* a device able to display, without sound, signals from a computer

video RAM /ˌvɪdiəʊ ˈræm/ *noun* full form of **VRAM**

video random access memory /ˌvɪdiəʊ ˌrændəm ˌækses ˈmem(ə)ri/, **video RAM** /ˌvɪdiəʊ ˈræm/ *noun* full form of **VRAM**. same as **video memory**

video scanner /ˈvɪdiəʊ ˌskænə/ *noun* a device which allows images of objects or pictures to be entered into a computer ○ *New video scanners are designed to scan three-dimensional objects.*

video server /ˈvɪdiəʊ ˌsɜːvə/ *noun* a dedicated computer on a network used to store video sequences

video signal /ˈvɪdiəʊ ˌsɪgn(ə)l/ *noun* a signal which provides line picture information and synchronisation pulses (*informal*)

video system control architecture /ˌvɪdiəʊ ˌsɪstəm kənˈtrəʊl ˌɑːkɪtektʃə/ *noun* full form of **ViSCA**

video tape /ˈvɪdiəʊ teɪp/ *noun* a magnetic tape on which pictures and sound can be recorded

video tape recorder /ˌvɪdiəʊ ˈteɪp rɪˌkɔːdə/ *noun* full form of **VTR**

video teleconferencing /ˌvɪdiəʊ ˈteliˌkɒnf(ə)rənsɪŋ/ *noun* the linking of computers that can capture and display video so that distant people can talk to and see each other, as if in a conference room

video terminal /ˈvɪdiəʊ ˌtɜːmɪn(ə)l/ *noun* a keyboard with a monitor

videotext /ˈvɪdiəʊtekst/, **videotex** /ˈvɪdiəʊteks/ *noun* a system for transmitting text and displaying it on a screen

COMMENT: This covers information transmitted either by TV signals (teletext) *or* by signals sent down telephone lines (viewdata).

video window /ˈvɪdiəʊ ˌwɪndəʊ/ *noun* a window that displays a moving video image, independent of other displayed material

view /vjuː/ *verb* to look at something, especially something displayed on a screen ○ *The user has to pay a charge for viewing pages on a bulletin board.*

viewdata /ˈvjuːdeɪtə/ *noun* an interactive system for transmitting text or graphics from a database to a user's terminal by telephone lines, providing facilities for information retrieval, transactions, education, games and recreation

COMMENT: The user calls up the page of information required, using the telephone and a modem, as opposed to teletext, where the pages of information are repeated one after the other automatically.

viewer /ˈvjuːə/ *noun* **1.** a utility that allows a user to see what is contained in an image or formatted document file without having to start the program that created it **2.** a device with an eyepiece through which a person can look at film or transparencies **3.** a person who watches television

viewfinder /ˈvjuːfaɪndə/ *noun* the eyepiece in a camera that allows a user to see what is being filmed

viewfinder objective, objective lens *noun* the lens of a visual monitoring viewfinder, in which the picture is formed

vignetting /vɪˈnjetɪŋ/ *noun* the shading of the borders of a picture (*film*)

viral /ˈvaɪrəl/ *adjective* referring to unsolicited emails that automatically forward themselves from one user to another, or to activities that use such emails

viral marketing /ˈvaɪrəl ˌmɑːkɪtɪŋ/ *noun* a form of marketing in which an organisation's customers act as advertisers for its products by spreading knowledge of them to other people, especially over the Internet

virgin /ˈvɜːdʒɪn/ *adjective* referring to a medium that has not been recorded on before

virtual /ˈvɜːtʃuəl/ *adjective* referring to a feature or device which does not actually exist but which is simulated by a computer and can be used by a user as if it did exist

virtual assistant /ˌvɜːtʃuəl əˈsɪst(ə)nt/ *noun* an employee who works as a personal assistant to somebody but does the job from another place solely by using computer and phone links

virtual community /ˌvɜːtʃuəl kə ˈmjuːnɪti/ *noun* a group of people who communicate with each other via the Internet

virtual desktop /ˌvɜːtʃuəl ˈdesktɒp/ *noun* an area that is bigger than the physical limits of the monitor, and which can contain text, images, windows and other facilities. Also called **virtual screen**

virtual device driver /ˌvɜːtʃuəl dɪˈvaɪs ˌdraɪvə/ *noun* full form of **VxD**

virtual machine /ˌvɜːtʃuəl məˈʃiːn/ *noun* a piece of software that allows a Java application to run on a computer. Abbr **VM**

COMMENT: When a developer writes a program in Java, it is compiled to a file format called bytecode (or pseudocode). This file can then be run using another application (the virtual machine) that is specific to the particular computer platform – there are virtual machine applications for PCs, Apple Macs and Sun computers, and each can run the same Java bytecode file, making Java a platform-independent language.

virtual memory /ˌvɜːtʃuəl ˈmem(ə)ri/ *noun* a system of providing extra main memory by using a disk drive as if it were RAM. Also called **virtual storage**

virtual reality /ˌvɜːtʃuəl riˈælɪti/ *noun* full form of **VR** ○ *This new virtual reality software can create a three-dimensional room that you can navigate around.*

'Autodesk suggests that anyone wishing to build Virtual Reality applications with the Cyberspace Developer's Kit should have solid knowledge of programming in C++ along with general knowledge of computer graphics.' [*Computing*]

virtual reality modelling language /ˌvɜːtʃuəl riˌælɪti ˈmɒd(ə)lɪŋ ˌlæŋgwɪdʒ/ *noun* full form of **VRML**

virtual storage /ˌvɜːtʃuəl ˈstɔːrɪdʒ/ *noun* abbr **VS**. same as **virtual memory**

virus /ˈvaɪrəs/ *noun* a program which adds itself to an executable file and copies itself to other executable files each time an infected file is run ○ *If your PC is infected with a virus, your data is at risk.*

COMMENT: Viruses can corrupt data, display a message, or do nothing. They are spread by downloading unchecked files from a bulletin board system or via unregulated networks or by inserting an unchecked floppy disk into your PC – always use a virus detector.

virus checker /ˈvaɪrəs ˌtʃekə/ *noun* a piece of software that is used to try and detect and remove unwanted virus programs from the hard disk of a computer

virus detector /ˈvaɪrəs dɪˌtektə/ *noun* a utility software which checks executable files to see if they contain a known virus

ViSCA /ˈvɪskə/ *noun* a protocol used to synchronise multiple video devices, developed by Sony. Full form **video system control architecture**

visible /ˈvɪzɪb(ə)l/ *adjective* which can be seen

visual /ˈvɪʒʊəl/ *adjective* which can be seen or which is used by sight

Visual Basic /ˌvɪʒʊəl ˈbeɪsɪk/ a trade name for a programming tool, developed by Microsoft, that allows users to create Windows applications very easily. Abbr **VB**

Visual Basic Extension /ˌvɪʒʊəl ˌbeɪsɪk ɪkˈstenʃ(ə)n/ a trade name for a Windows custom software module that adds functionality to another application, similar to the OCX control. Abbr **VBX**

Visual Basic for Applications /ˌvɪʒʊəl ˌbeɪsɪk fər ˌæplɪˈkeɪʃ(ə)nz/ a trade name for a complex macro language developed by Microsoft from its VB programming tool. Abbr **VBA**

Visual Basic Script /ˌvɪʒʊəl ˌbeɪsɪk ˈskrɪpt/ a trade name for a set of programming commands that can be included within a normal webpage, written using HTML commands. Abbr **VBScript**

visual display terminal /ˌvɪzjʊəl dɪ ˈspleɪ ˌtɜːminəl/, **visual display unit** /ˌvɪʒʊəl dɪˈspleɪ ˌjuːnɪt/ *noun* full form of **VDT, VDU**

visualisation /ˌvɪʒuəlaɪˈzeɪʃ(ə)n/, **visualization** *noun* the conversion of numbers or data into a graphical format that can be more easily understood

visualize /ˈvɪʒʊəˌlaɪz/ *verb* to imagine how something will appear, even before it has been created

VITC /ˌviː aɪ tiː ˈsiː/ *noun* a time code recorded onto tape between video frames. Full form **vertical interval time code**

COMMENT: This is preferred to LTC because it does not use the audio track and can be read at slow playback speeds.

VL-bus, VL local bus *noun* a standard defined by the Video Electronics Standards Association which allows up to three special expansion slots that provide direct, bus-master control of the central processor and allow very high speed data transfers between main memory and the expansion card without using the processor ○ *For a high-performance PC, choose one with a VL-bus.* Full form **VESA local bus**

VLF *noun* radio frequency between 30Hz and 30KHz. Full form **very low frequency**

VLSI /ˌviː el es ˈaɪ/ *noun* a system with between 10,000 and 100,000 components on a single IC. Full form **very large scale integration**

VM *abbr* virtual machine

v-mail /ˈviː ˌmeɪl/ *noun* an email message with a video clip as an attachment

VME bus /ˌviː em ˈiː bʌs/ *noun* an expansion bus standard that supports 32-bit data transfer, mostly used in industrial and test equipment. Full form **versamodule eurocard bus**

voice /vɔɪs/ *noun* **1.** the sound of human speech **2.** another name for a note or sound effect (such as a whistle) ○ *Instruments that are multi-voice can play several notes at the same time.*

voice data entry /ˌvɔɪs ˌdeɪtə ˈentri/, **voice data input** /ˌvɔɪs ˌdeɪtə ˈɪnpʊt/ *noun* the input of information into a computer using a speech recognition system and the user's voice

voicemail /ˈvɔɪsmeɪl/ *noun* a computer linked to a telephone exchange that answers a person's telephone when no one is there and allows messages to be recorded, in digital form ○ *I checked my voice mail to see if anyone had left me a message.*

voice-over /ˈvɔɪsˌəʊvə/ *noun* spoken commentary by an actor who does not appear on the screen (as the text of a TV commercial)

voice over Internet protocol /ˌvɔɪs əʊvə ˈɪntənet ˌprəʊtəkɒl/ *noun* full form of **VoIP**

voice-over-the-Net /ˌvɔɪs əʊvə ðə ˈnet/ *adjective* used to describe voice communication using VoIP technology

voice recognition /ˌvɔɪs ˌrekəgˈnɪʃ(ə)n/ *noun* the ability of a computer to recognise certain words in a human voice and provide a suitable response

voice synthesis /ˈvɔɪs ˌsɪnθəsɪs/ *noun* the reproduction of sounds similar to those of the human voice

voice synthesiser /ˈvɔɪs ˌsɪnθəsaɪzə/ *noun* a device which generates sounds which are similar to the human voice

voice unit /ˈvɔɪs ˌjuːnɪt/ *noun* a unit of signal measurement equal to a one millivolt signal across a 600 ohm resistance

'...the technology of voice output is reasonably difficult, but the technology of voice recognition is much more complex' [*Personal Computer World*]

VoIP /vɔɪp/ *noun* a technology that enables voice messages to be sent over the Internet, often at the same time as data in text or other forms. Full form **voice over Internet protocol**

volatile memory /ˌvɒləˌtaɪl ˈmem(ə)ri/, **volatile store** /ˈvɒlətaɪl stɔː/, **volatile dynamic storage** /ˌvɒləˌtaɪl daɪˌnæmɪk ˈstɔːrɪdʒ/ *noun* memory or storage medium which loses data stored in it when the power supply is switched off

volatility /ˌvɒləˈtɪlɪti/ *noun* the number of records that are added or deleted from a computer system compared to the total number in store

volt /vəʊlt/ *noun* an SI unit of electrical potential, defined as voltage across a one ohm resistance when one amp is flowing

voltage /ˈvəʊltɪdʒ/ *noun* an electromotive force expressed in volts. Abbr **V**

COMMENT: Electricity supply can have peaks and troughs of current, depending on the users in the area. Fluctuations in voltage can affect computers; a voltage regulator will provide a steady supply of electricity.

volume /ˈvɒljuːm/ *noun* **1.** a disk or storage device **2.** the total space occupied by data in a storage system

VORTAL /ˈvɔːtəl/ *noun* a portal website that contains information for just one particular industry or interest group. Full form **vertical portal**

COMMENT: General-interest portals such as AOL, Yahoo!, and Excite provide a whole range of general-interest information for users, including news, weather, sports and financial information. An example of a vertical portal is Buzzsaw (www.buzzsaw.com), which provides news and resources for the construction industry.

VR /ˌviː ˈɑː/ *noun* a simulation of a real-life scene or environment by computer. Full form **virtual reality**

VRAM /ˈviː ræm/ *noun* high speed random access memory used to store computer-generated or digitised images. Full form **video random access memory**. Also called **video RAM**

VRML /ˌviː ɑːr em ˈel/ *noun* a system that allows developers to create three-dimensional worlds within a webpage. Full form **virtual reality modelling language**

VS *abbr* virtual storage

VSB /ˌviː es ˈbiː/ *noun* a method of transferring data over coaxial cable, used to modulate and transmit digital television signals. Full form **vestigial side band**

V series /ˈviː ˌsɪəriːz/ *noun* a series of CCITT standards for data transmission using a modem, used in the UK and Europe

VT *abbr* videotape

VT-52 /ˌviː tiː ˌfɪfti ˈtuː/ *noun* a popular standard of a terminal that defines the codes used to display text and graphics

VTR /ˌviː tiː ˈɑː/ *noun* a machine used to record and play back video signals that are stored on open reels of magnetic tape rather than on the sealed, enclosed cassette used by a VCR. Full form **video tape recorder**

VT-terminal emulation /ˌviː tiː ˈtɜːmɪn(ə)l emjuˌleɪʃ(ə)n/ *noun* a standard set of codes developed by Digital Equipment Corporation to control how text and graphics are displayed on its range of terminals

VU *abbr* voice unit

VxD /ˌviː eks ˈdiː/ *noun* a device driver used to control one part of the Windows operating system or to link a peripheral to the Windows operating system. Full form **virtual device driver**

Vxtreme /ˌviː eksˈtriːm/ *noun* a format used to deliver streaming video sequences over the Internet

W

W *abbr* Watt

W3C /ˌdʌb(ə)l juː θriː ˈsiː/ *noun* a group of international industry members that work together to develop common standards for the World Wide Web. Full form **World Wide Web Consortium**

COMMENT: Visit the www.w3.org website for new standards and developments.

wafer /ˈweɪfə/ *noun* a thin round slice of a large single crystal of silicon onto which hundreds of individual integrated circuits are constructed, before being cut into individual chips

wafer scale integration /ˌweɪfə skeɪl ˌɪntɪˈgreɪʃ(ə)n/ *noun* one large chip, the size of a wafer, made up of smaller integrated circuits connected together (NOTE: These are still in the research stage.)

wait condition /ˈweɪt kənˌdɪʃ(ə)n/ *noun* **1.** a state in which a processor is not active, but waiting for input from peripherals **2.** a null instruction which is used to slow down a processor so that slower memory or a peripheral can keep up ▶ also called **wait state**

wait loop /ˈweɪt luːp/ *noun* a processor that repeats one loop of program until some action occurs

wait state /ˈweɪt steɪt/ *noun* same as **wait condition**

wake /weɪk/ *verb* □ **to wake up** to switch on a device or start or initiate a process

wallpaper /ˈwɔːlˌpeɪpə/ *noun* (*in a GUI*) an image or pattern used as a background in a window

WAN /wæn/ *noun* a network in which the various terminals are far apart and linked by radio or satellite. Full form **wide area network**. Opposite **LAN**

wand /wɒnd/ *noun* a bar-code reader or optical device which is held in the hand to read bar codes on products in a store

WAP /wæp/ *noun* **1.** a system that allows a user to access information on an Internet server using a wireless handheld device such as a mobile telephone. Full form **Wireless Application Protocol** **2.** a device that connects to a LAN and allows a computer to access the network using a wireless data transmission ○ *The WAP has an aerial and a built-in hub.* Full form **wireless access point**

COMMENT: WAP can be used over almost all of the current wireless networks, including the popular GSM mobile telephone standard, and can run on almost any operating system or hardware device. A device that supports WAP provides a very simple browser that can display basic graphics and text-based pages of information on a small, monochrome, 6–10 line display, similar to a tiny, simple web page. The user can navigate between pages using two or three buttons on the handheld device or mobile telephone. The arrival of WAP allows users to access email and news-based websites from a mobile telephone, but users have been put off by the very slow speed (no more than 9,600bps) at which data can be transferred over current wireless telephone systems.

WAP markup language /ˌwæp ˈmɑːkʌp ˌlæŋgwɪdʒ/ *noun* full form of **WML**

WAP markup language script /ˌwæp ˌmɑːkʌp ˌlæŋgwɪdʒ ˈskrɪpt/ *noun* same as **WMLScript**

warm /wɔːm/ *verb* □ **to warm up** to allow a machine to stand idle for a time after switching on, to reach the optimum operating conditions

warm boot /ˌwɔːm ˈbuːt/ *noun* the act of restarting a computer without switching it off. Compare **cold boot**

warmboot /ˈwɔːmbuːt/ *verb* to restart a computer without switching it off. Compare **coldboot**

warm standby /ˌwɔːm ˈstændbaɪ/ *noun* a secondary backup device which can be switched into action a short time after the main system fails. Compare **cold standby, hot standby**

warm start /ˌwɔːm ˈstɑːt/ *noun* the process of restarting a program which has stopped, without losing any data. Compare **cold start**

warn /wɔːn/ *verb* to say that something dangerous is about to happen or that there is a possible danger ○ *He warned the keyboarders that the system might become overloaded.* (NOTE: You warn someone **of** something, or **that** something may happen)

warning /ˈwɔːnɪŋ/ *noun* a notice of possible danger ○ *to issue a warning*

warning light /ˈwɔːnɪŋ laɪt/ *noun* a small light which lights up to show that something dangerous may happen ○ *When the warning light on the front panel comes on, switch off the system.*

warrant /ˈwɒrənt/ *verb* to guarantee ○ *All the spare parts are warranted.*

warrantee /ˌwɒrənˈtiː/ *noun* a person who is given a warranty

warrantor /ˌwɒrənˈtɔː/ *noun* a person who gives a warranty

warranty /ˈwɒrənti/ *noun* **1.** a guarantee or legal document which promises that a machine will work properly or that an item is of good quality ○ *The printer is sold with a twelve-month warranty.* ○ *The warranty covers spare parts but not labour costs.* **2.** a promise in a contract

watermark /ˈwɔːtəmɑːk/ *noun* a pattern of bits that is digitally embedded in a data file in order to make it possible to detect unauthorised copies

watt /wɒt/ *noun* an SI unit of measurement of electrical power, defined as power produced when one amp of current flows through a load that has one volt of voltage across it

wave /weɪv/ *noun* a signal motion which rises and falls periodically as it travels through a medium

WAVE /weɪv/ *noun* a standard method of storing an analog signal in digital form under Microsoft Windows. Also called **WAV file** (NOTE: Files have the .WAV extension.)

waveform /ˈweɪvfɔːm/ *noun* the shape of a wave

waveguide /ˈweɪvgaɪd/ *noun* a physical system used to direct waves in a particular direction, usually metal tubes for microwave signals or optical fibres for light signals

wavelength /ˈweɪvˌleŋθ/ *noun* the distance between two adjacent peaks of a wave, equal to the speed divided by the frequency

WAV file /ˈweɪv faɪl/ *noun* same as **WAVE**

WBFM *abbr* wideband frequency modulation

wearable computer /ˌweərəb(ə)l kəmˈpjuːtə/ *noun* a battery-powered computer small enough to be worn on the body

web /web/ *noun* same as **World Wide Web**

web application /ˈweb ˌæplɪkeɪʃ(ə)n/ *noun* a software program that works behind the scenes at a website, runs on a web server and uses the HTTP protocol to deliver information to a user (NOTE: An example is a database of information that can be searched from a webpage or a method of ordering and paying for a product using a webpage.)

WebBot /ˈwebbɒt/ a trade name for a utility used in Microsoft Internet software that helps a user create a particular function in a webpage

web browser /ˈweb ˌbraʊzə/ *noun* same as **browser**

web cam /ˈweb kæm/ *noun* a video camera linked to a website that allows visitors to see live video images of a scene

COMMENT: These devices have become very popular and have been used to display the inside of an office, the view over a city, an office coffee machine, the inside of a bedroom and many other scenes.

webcast /ˈwebkɑːst/ *noun* a broadcast made on the World Wide Web

'It is spending $450m on a community support programme for developers: webcasts, free on-site training, seminars, roadshows and 125 new books.' [*The Guardian*]

web crawler /ˈweb ˌkrɔːlə/ *noun* software that moves over every new webpage on the Internet and produces an index based on the content of the webpages

web designer /ˈweb ðiˌzaɪnə/ *noun* a person who designs websites

weber /ˈveɪbə/ *noun* a unit of magnetic flux (*film*)

weblog /ˈweblɒg/ *noun* a frequently updated personal journal on a website, intended for public viewing

webmaster /ˈwebmɑːstə/ *noun* a person in charge of a website

webpage /ˈwebpeɪdʒ/ *noun* a single file stored on a web server that contains formatted text, graphics and hypertext links to other pages on the Internet or within a website

webpage design software /ˌwebpeɪdʒ dɪˌzaɪn ˈsɒftweə/ *noun* software that provides features that make it easier for a user to create webpages

COMMENT: The design software is similar to desktop publishing software and allows you to drag text and images onto a page, create tables and change the style of text from menu options, without having to edit complex HTML commands.

web portal /ˈweb ˌpɔːt(ə)l/ *noun* a website that provides a wide range of information and resources that include everything a particular user might want from the Internet, on one site

COMMENT: The biggest web portals include AOL, MSN, Yahoo! and Excite, which offer a wide range of general services including news, sports, email, weather, shopping and a search engine.

web ring /ˈweb rɪŋ/ *noun* a series of linked websites that are designed to be visited one after the other until the visitor reaches the first website again

web server /ˈweb ˌsɜːvə/ *noun* a computer that stores the collection of webpages that make up a website

website /ˈwebsaɪt/ *noun* a collection of webpages that are linked and related and can be accessed by a user with a web browser ○ *The Bloomsbury website, http://www.bloomsbury.com, contains information about all the books Bloomsbury publish.*

WebTV /ˌweb tiː ˈviː/ a trade name for a television that also lets a user view webpages

COMMENT: Some TVs include a computer and modem, other systems use an external box that links to the TV and a telephone socket. Some interactive television and cable television installations do not use a telephone socket but instead download and display webpages via the television cable.

webzine /ˈwebziːn/ *noun* same as **e-zine**

weigh /weɪ/ *verb* to have a certain weight ○ *The packet weighs twenty-five grams.*

weighted average /ˌweɪtɪd ˈæv(ə)rɪdʒ/ *noun* an average which is calculated taking several factors into account, giving some more value than others

weighting /ˈweɪtɪŋ/ *noun* the sorting of users, programs or data by their importance or priority

wetware /ˈwetweə/ *noun US* the human brain, intelligence which writes software to be used with hardware (*informal*)

What-You-See-Is-All-You-Get /ˌwɒt juː siː ɪz ˌɔːl juː ˈget/ *noun* full form of **WYSIAYG**

What-You-See-Is-What-You-Get /ˌwɒt juː siː ɪz ˌwɒt juː ˈget/ *noun* full form of **WYSIWYG**

white /waɪt/ *adjective, noun* the colour of snow

COMMENT: With a white writer, the black areas are printed evenly but edges and borders are not so sharp.

White Book /ˈwaɪt bʊk/ *noun* a formal video-CD standard published by Philips and JVC that defines how digital video can be stored on a CD-ROM

white pages /ˌwaɪt ˈpeɪdʒz/ *plural noun* a database of users and their email address stored on the Internet to help other users find an email address

white writer /ˈwaɪt ˌraɪtə/ *noun* a laser printer which directs its laser beam on the points that are not printed. Opposite **black writer**

COMMENT: With a white writer, the black areas are printed evenly but edges and borders are not so sharp.

whois /ˈhuː ɪz/ *noun* an Internet utility that displays information about the owner of a particular domain name

wholesale /ˈhəʊlseɪl/ *noun, adverb* buying goods from manufacturers and selling in large quantities to traders who then sell in smaller quantities to the general public (NOTE: no plural) □ **he buys wholesale and sells retail** he buys goods in bulk at a wholesale discount and then sells in small quantities to the public

wholesale dealer /ˈhəʊlseɪl ˌdiːlə/ *noun* a person who buys in bulk from manufacturers and sells to retailers

wholesaler /ˈhəʊlseɪlə/ *noun* a person who buys goods in bulk from manufacturers and sells them to retailers

wide area network /ˌwaɪd ˌeəriə ˈnetwɜːk/ *noun* full form of **WAN**

wideband /ˈwaɪdbænd/ *noun* same as **broadband**

widescreen /ˈwaɪdskriːn/ *adjective* pictures presented with a larger aspect ratio than 1.4:1

widescreen display /ˌwaɪdskriːn dɪ ˈspleɪ/ *noun* a film, video or TV display with an aspect ratio greater than 1.37, or the same as the full size of a 35 mm film image

widow /ˈwɪdəʊ/ *noun* the first line of a paragraph which is printed by itself at the bottom of a column. Compare **orphan**

width /wɪdθ/ *noun* the size of something from side to side

wild card /ˈwaɪldkɑːd/ *noun* a symbol used when searching for files or data that represents all files ○ *A wild card can be used to find all files names beginning DIC.*

wild track /ˈwaɪld træk/ *noun* sound recorded without a synchronised picture

WIMP /wɪmp/ *noun* a program display which uses graphics or icons to control the software and make it easier to use. Full form **window, icon, mouse, pointer**. ◊ **environment, GUI**. Compare **command line interface**

COMMENT: WIMPs normally use a combination of windows, icons and a mouse to control the operating system. In many GUIs, such as Microsoft Windows, Apple Mac System 7 and DR-GEM, you can control all the functions of the operating system just using the mouse. Icons represent programs and files; instead of entering the file name, you select it by moving a pointer with a mouse.

Winchester disk /draɪv/, **Winchester drive** *noun* a compact high-capacity hard disk which is usually built into a computer system and cannot be removed

window /ˈwɪndəʊ/ *noun* **1.** a reserved section of screen used to display special information, which can be selected and looked at at any time and which overwrites information already on the screen ○ *Several remote sta-*

tions are connected to the network and each has its own window onto the hard disk. **2.** a part of a document currently displayed on a screen ○ *The operating system will allow other programs to be displayed on-screen at the same time in different windows.* **3.** an area of memory or access to a storage device ■ *verb* to set up a section of screen by defining the coordinates of its corners, allowing information to be temporarily displayed and overwriting previous information without altering information in the workspace

'...when an output window overlaps another, the interpreter does not save the contents of the obscured window' [*Personal Computer World*]

window, icon, mouse, pointer /ˌwɪndəʊ ˌaɪkɒn ˌmaʊs ˈpɔɪntə/ *noun* full form of **WIMP**

windowing /ˈwɪndəʊɪŋ/ *noun* **1.** the action of setting up a window to show information on the screen ○ *The network system uses the latest windowing techniques.* **2.** the process of displaying or accessing information via a window

'...windowing facilities make use of virtual screens as well as physical screens' [*Byte*]

'...the network system uses the latest windowing techniques' [*Desktop Publishing*]

'...the functions are integrated via a windowing system with pull-down menus used to select different operations' [*Byte*]

Windows /ˈwɪndəʊz/ a trade name for a family of operating systems developed by Microsoft that interacts with users through a Graphical User Interface. Windows is the operating system used by most of the world's PCs. Also called **Microsoft Windows, MS-Windows**

Windows Explorer /ˌwɪndəʊz ɪk ˈsplɔːrə/ a trade name for a software utility included with Windows that lets a user view the folders and files on the hard disk, floppy disk, CD-ROM and any shared network drives

Windows Internet Naming Service /ˌwɪndəʊz ˌɪntənet ˈneɪmɪŋ ˌsɜːvɪs/ full form of **WINS**

Windows NT /ˌwɪndəʊz en ˈtiː/ a trade name for a high-performance GUI derived from Windows that does not use DOS as an operating system and features 32-bit code

Windows XP /ˌwɪndəʊz eks ˈpiː/ a trade name for a version of the Windows operating system designed for home and business users that provides a 32-bit multitasking operating system with the standard Windows graphical user interface together with improved network and Internet connectivity

windshield /ˈwɪndʃiːld/ *noun* a device which is attached to a microphone in order to reduce wind noise (*film*)

WINS /wɪns/ *noun* a system that works with a network of computers running Windows and provides a database of the IP addresses of each computer on the network. Full form **Windows Internet Naming Service**

COMMENT: This is more difficult than it sounds, since a computer is usually given a different IP address every time it is switched on. The WINS service provides 'name resolution' for Windows networks, DNS provides a similar service for networks with fixed IP addresses, including the public Internet.

Winsock /ˈwɪnsɒk/ *noun* a utility software that is required to control the modem when connecting to the Internet and allows the computer to communicate using the TCP/IP protocol. Also called **socket driver**

wipe /waɪp/ *verb* to clean data from a disk ○ *By reformatting you will wipe the disk clean.* (NOTE: **wipes – wiping – wiped**)

wire /ˈwaɪə/ *noun* a thin metal conductor ■ *verb* to install wiring in something (NOTE: **wires – wiring – wired**)

wire frame model /ˌwaɪə freɪm ˈmɒd(ə)l/ *noun* (*in graphics and CAD*) a method of displaying objects using lines and arcs rather than filled areas. Also called **wire mesh model, stick model**

wireless /ˈwaɪələs/ *noun* a device that can receive radio broadcasts (*old use*) ■ *adjective* communication system that does not require wires to carry signals

wireless access point /ˌwaɪələs ˈækses ˌpɔɪnt/ *noun* full form of **WAP 2**

Wireless Application Protocol /ˌwaɪələs ˌæplɪˈkeɪʃ(ə)n ˌprəʊtəʊkɒl/ *noun* full form of **WAP 1**

wireless LAN /ˌwaɪələs ˈlæn/ *noun* same as **wireless network**

wireless microphone /ˌwaɪələs ˈmaɪkrəfəʊn/ *noun* an audio microphone with a small transmitter attached allowing the transmission of signals without interconnecting wires

wireless modem /ˌwaɪələs ˈməʊdem/ *noun* a modem that can be used with a wireless mobile telephone system (NOTE: A wireless modem normally includes the telephone hardware and an aerial, so does not need to be plugged into a separate mobile telephone.)

wireless network /ˌwaɪələs ˈnetwɜːk/, **wireless LAN** /ˌwaɪələs ˈlæn/ *noun* a network that does not use cable to transmit data between computers, but instead uses radio signals to transmit signals, normally using the 802.11b or 802.11a transmission protocol. Also called **wireless LAN**

wire tap /ˈwaɪə tæp/ *noun* an unauthorised connection to a private communications line in order to listen to conversations or obtain private data

wiring /ˈwaɪərɪŋ/ *noun* a series of wires ○ *The wiring in the system had to be replaced.*

WISC /wɪsk/ *noun* a CPU design that allows a programmer to add extra machine code instructions using microcode, to customise the instruction set. Full form **writable instruction set computer**

wizard /ˈwɪzəd/ *noun* a software utility that helps you create something

WML /ˌdʌb(ə)l juː em ˈel/ *noun* a webpage formatting language that is similar to a very simple version of the standard HTML webpage coding system, but does not include many of the extra features that cannot be displayed on the small screen of a WAP handheld device or navigated with two or three buttons. Full form **WAP markup language**

WMLScript /ˌdʌb(ə)l juː em ˈel ˌskrɪpt/ *noun* a scripting language similar to a very simple version of JavaScript that allows WML webpages to include scripting functions. Full form **WAP markup language script**

woofer /ˈwʊfə/ *noun* a large loudspeaker used to produce low frequency sounds (*informal*)

word /wɜːd/ *noun* **1.** a separate item of language, which is used with others to form speech or writing which can be understood **2.** a separate item of data on a computer, formed of a group of bits, stored in a single location in a memory

word count /ˈwɜːd kaʊnt/ *noun* the number of words in a file or text

WordPad /ˈwɜːdpæd/ a software utility included with versions of Microsoft Windows later than Windows 95 that provides the basic functions of Microsoft Word 6

word-process /ˌwɜːd ˈprəʊses/ *verb* to edit, store and manipulate text using a computer ○ *It is quite easy to read word-processed files.*

word-processing /ˌwɜːd ˈprəʊsesɪŋ/ *noun* the process of using a computer to keyboard, edit and output text, in forms such as letters, labels and address lists ○ *Load the word-processing program before you start keyboarding.* Abbr **WP**

word-processor /ˌwɜːd ˈprəʊˌsesə/ *noun* **1.** a small computer used for word-processing text and documents **2.** a word-processing package or program for a computer which allows the editing and manipulation and output of text, in forms such as letters, labels and address lists

word wrap /ˈwɜːd ræp/ *noun* a system in word-processing in which the operator does not have to indicate the line endings, but can keyboard continuously, leaving the program to insert word breaks and to continue the text on the next line. Also called **wraparound**

work file /ˈwɜːk faɪl/ *noun* a temporary work area which is being used for current work. Also called **scratch file**

workflow /ˈwɜːkfləʊ/ *noun* software designed to improve the flow of electronic documents around an office network, from user to user

workgroup /ˈwɜːkgruːp/ *noun* a small group of users who are working on a project or connected with a local area network

workgroup software /ˈwɜːkgruːp ˌsɒftweə/ *noun* an application designed to be used by many users in a group to improve productivity, e.g. a diary or scheduler

working /ˈwɜːkɪŋ/ *adjective* operating correctly

workload /ˈwɜːkˌləʊd/ *noun* the amount of work which a person or computer has to do ○ *He has difficulty in dealing with his heavy workload.*

workplace /ˈwɜːkpleɪs/ *noun* a place where you work

work print /ˈwɜːk prɪnt/ *noun* a positive print of a film scene which has been selected by the editor (*film*)

work-sharing /ˈwɜːk ˌʃeərɪŋ/ *noun* a system where two part-timers share one job

worksheet /ˈwɜːkˌʃiːt/ *noun* (*in a spreadsheet program*) a two-dimensional matrix of rows and columns that contains cells which can, themselves, contain equations

workspace /ˈwɜːkspeɪs/ *noun* a space on memory which is available for use or is being used currently by an operator

workstation /ˈwɜːkˌsteɪʃ(ə)n/ *noun* a place where a computer user works, with equipment such as a terminal, VDU, printer and modem ○ *The system includes five workstations linked together in a ring topology network.*

> '...an image processing workstation must provide three basic facilities: the means to digitize, display and manipulate the image data' [*Byte*]

world /wɜːld/ *noun* a three-dimensional scene that is displayed on a website and allows a user to move around the scene exploring the objects visible. ◊ **VRML**

World Wide Web /ˌwɜːld ˌwaɪd ˈweb/ *noun* a collection of the millions of websites and webpages that together form the part of the Internet that is most often seen by users. Abbr **www, W3**. Also called **web**

COMMENT: Each website is a collection of webpages containing text, graphics and links to other websites. Each page is created using the HTML language and is viewed by a user with a web browser. Navigating between webpages and websites is called surfing; this requires a computer with a link to the Internet and a web browser to view the webpages stored on the remote web servers. The Internet itself includes email, Usenet and newsgroups as well as websites and webpages.

World Wide Web Consortium /ˌwɜːld waɪd 'web kənˌsɔːtiəm/ *noun* full form of **W3C**

WORM /wɜːm/ *noun* an optical disk storage system that allows the user to write data to the disk once, but the user can then read the data from the disk many times. Full form **write once, read many times memory**

wow /waʊ/ *noun* the fluctuation of the frequency of a recorded signal at playback (usually caused by uneven tape movement)

WP *abbr* word-processing

wraparound /'ræpəˌraʊnd/ *noun* same as **word wrap**

writable instruction set computer /ˌraɪtəb(ə)l ɪnˌstrʌkʃən set kəʊ'pjuːtə/ *noun* full form of **WISC**

write /raɪt/ *verb* **1.** to put words or figures onto paper ○ *She wrote a letter of complaint to the manager.* **2.** to put text or data onto a disk ○ *Access time is the time taken to read from* or *write to a location in memory.* (NOTE: **writes – writing – wrote – written**. You write data **to** a file.)

write black printer /ˌraɪt 'blæk ˌprɪntə/ *noun* a printer in which toner sticks to the points hit by the laser beam when the image drum is scanned. Compare **white writer**

COMMENT: A write black printer produces sharp edges and graphics, but large areas of black are muddy.

write once, read many times memory /ˌraɪt ˌwʌns riːd 'meni ˌtaɪmz ˌmem(ə)ri/ *noun* full form of **WORM**

write-on slides /ˌraɪt ɒn 'slaɪdz/ *plural noun* during a film's production, slides with a matte covering are used, on which information is hand drawn to show the final image

write-permit ring /ˌraɪt pə'mɪt rɪŋ/ *noun* a ring on a reel of magnetic tape which allows the tape to be overwritten or erased

write protect /ˌraɪt prə'tekt/ *verb* to make it impossible to write to a floppy disk or tape by moving a special write-protect tab

writing /'raɪtɪŋ/ *noun* something which has been written

WYSIAYG /'wɪziːeɪg/ *noun* a program in which the output on screen cannot be printed out in any other form, as it contains no hidden print or formatting commands. Full form **What-You-See-Is-All-You-Get**

WYSIWYG /'wɪziːwɪg/ *noun* a program in which the output on the screen is exactly the same as the output on printout, including graphics and special fonts. Full form **What-You-See-Is-What-You-Get**

X

X[1] /eks/ *noun* same as **X-Window System**

'X is the underlying technology which allows Unix applications to run under a multi-user, multitasking GUI. It has been adopted as the standard for the Common Open Software Environment, proposed recently by top Unix vendors including Digital, IBM and Sun.' [*Computing*]

X[2] /eks/ *abbr* extension

X2 *noun* a communications standard developed by US Robotics for its range of high-speed modems that can transfer data at 56,000 bits per second. ◊ **V series**

X.25 *noun* a CCITT standard that defines the connection between a terminal and a packet-switching network

X.400 *noun* a CCITT standard that defines an email transfer method

X.500 *noun* a CCITT standard that defines a method of global naming that allows every user to have a unique identity and allows any user to address an email message to any other user. ◊ **directory services**

XA ♦ **CD-ROM Extended Architecture**

x-axis /ˌeks ˌaʊt 'æksɪs/ *noun* the horizontal axis of a graph

x-coordinate /ˌeks kəʊ'ɔːdɪnət/ *noun* a horizontal axis position coordinate

x direction /ˌeks ˌaʊt dɪ'rekʃ(ə)n/ *noun* a movement horizontally

x distance /ˌeks ˌaʊt 'dɪstəns/ *noun* the distance along an x-axis from an origin

xerographic /ˌzɪərəʊ'græfɪk/ *adjective* referring to xerography

xerographic printer /ˌzɪərəgræfɪk 'prɪntə/ *noun* a printer such as a photocopier in which charged ink is attracted to areas of a charged picture

xerography /zɪə'rɒgrəfi/ *noun* a copying method that relies on ink being attracted to dark regions of a charged picture

Xerox Network System /ˌzɪərɒks 'netwɜːk ˌsɪstəm/ a network protocol developed by Xerox that has provided the basis for the Novell IPX network protocols. Abbr **XNS**

Xerox PARC a Xerox development centre that has developed a wide range of important products including the mouse and GUI

XGA /ˌeks dʒiː 'eɪ/ *noun* a standard for colour video graphics adapter for PCs, developed by IBM, which has a resolution of 1,024 x 768 pixels with 256 colours on an interlaced display. Full form **extended graphics array**

XHTML /ˌeks eɪtʃ tiː em 'el/ *noun* a combination of the HTML and XML webpage markup languages. Full form **extensible hypertext markup language**

COMMENT: XHTML is actually written using the XML language and provides a simpler way of creating webpages that will be displayed in the same way over a wide range of web browser platforms.

XML /ˌeks em 'el/ *noun* a webpage markup language that is a simplified version of the SGML system and allows a designer to create his or her own customised markup tags to improve flexibility. Full form **extensible markup language**

XMODEM /'eks ˌməʊdem/ *noun* a standard file transfer and error-detecting protocol used in asynchronous, modem data transmissions

XMS /ˌeks em 'es/ *noun* a set of rules that define how an MS-DOS program should access extended memory fitted in a PC. Full form **extended memory specification**

XNS *abbr* Xerox Network System

XON/XOFF /ˌeks ɒn eks 'ɒf/ *noun* an asynchronous transmission protocol in which each end can regulate the data flow by transmitting special codes

X/OPEN /ˌeks 'əʊpən/ *noun* a group of vendors that are responsible for promoting open systems

XP *abbr* **1.** Athlon XP **2.** Windows XP

X-ray /'eks ˌreɪ/ *noun* **1.** a ray with a very short length, which is invisible, but can go through soft tissue and register as a photograph on a film **2.** a photograph taken using X-rays ○ *The medical text is illustrated with X-ray photographs.* **3.** a lighting unit that hangs above the set (*film*)

X-ray imaging /'eks reɪ ˌɪmɪdʒɪŋ/ *noun* the process of showing images of the inside of a body using X-rays

X-series /ˌeks ˌaʊt 'sɪəriːz/ *noun* a set of recommendations for data communications over public data networks

X-sheet /'eks ʃiːt/ *noun* written orders for the exposure of animation film

XT /ˌeks 'tiː/ *noun* a trade name for a version of the original IBM PC, developed by IBM, that used an 8088 processor and included a hard disk

X-Window System /ˌeks ˌwɪndəʊ ˈsɪstəm/, **X-Windows** a graphical interface, usually used on Unix workstation computers, made up of a set of API commands and display handling routines that provide a hardware-independent programming interface for applications

'X is the underlying technology which allows Unix applications to run under a multi-user, multitasking GUI. It has been adopted as the standard for the Common Open Software Environment, proposed recently by top Unix vendors including Digital, IBM and Sun.' [*Computing*]

COMMENT: Originally developed for UNIX workstations, it can also run on a PC or minicomputer terminals. The Open Software Foundation has a version of X-Windows called Motif; Sun and Hewlett Packard have a version called OpenLook.

x-y /ˌeks ˈaʊt waɪ/ *noun* the set of coordinates for drawing a graph, where x is the horizontal and y the vertical value

Y

Y *noun* the luminance part of a video image

yaw /jɔː/ *noun* the rotation of satellite about a vertical axis with the earth

y-axis /ˈwaɪ ˌæksɪs/ *noun* the vertical axis of a graph

Y/C /ˌwaɪ ˈsiː/ *noun* two parts of a video signal representing the luminance (Y) and the chrominance (C) parts of the image

Y/C delay /ˌwaɪ ˈsiː dɪˌleɪ/ *noun* an error caused by wrong synchronisation between the luma and chroma signals in a video transmission, seen as a colour halo around objects on the screen

y-coordinate /ˈwaɪ kəʊˌɔːdɪnət/ *noun* the vertical axis position coordinate

Y/C video /ˌwaɪ siː ˈvɪdiəʊ/ *noun* same as **S-Video**

y-direction /ˈwaɪ daɪˌrekʃən/ *noun* a vertical movement

y-distance /ˈwaɪ ˌdɪstəns/ *noun* the distance along a y-axis from an origin

Yellow Book /ˈjeləʊ bʊk/ *noun* a formal specification for CD-ROM published by Philips, which includes data storage formats and has an extension to cover the CD-ROM XA standard

yellow-magenta-cyan-black /ˌjeləʊ məˌdʒentə ˈsaɪən blæk/ *noun* full form of **YMCK**

YMCK /ˌwaɪ em siː ˈkeɪ/ *noun* colour definition based on the four colours used in DTP software when creating separate colour film to use for printing. Full form **yellow-magenta-cyan-black**

YMODEM /ˈwaɪ ˌməʊdem/ *noun* a variation of the XMODEM file transfer protocol that uses 1024-byte blocks and can send multiple files

YUV encoding /ˌwaɪ juː viː ɪnˈkaəʊdɪŋ/ *noun* a video encoding system in which the video luminance (Y) signal is recorded at full bandwidth but the chrominance signals (U&V) are recorded at half their bandwidth

Z

Z *symbol* impedance

Z80 /ˌzed 'eɪti/ *noun* an 8-bit processor developed by Zilog, used in many early popular computers

zap /zæp/ *verb* to wipe off all data currently in the workspace ○ *He pressed CONTROL Z and zapped all the text.* (NOTE: zapping – zapped)

z-axis /'zed ˌæksɪs/ *noun* an axis for depth in a three-dimensional graph or plot

z buffer /'zed ˌbʌfə/ *noun* an area of memory used to store the z-axis information for a graphics object displayed on screen

zero /'zɪərəʊ/ *noun* **1.** the digit 0 ○ *The code for international calls is zero one zero (010).* **2.** the equivalent of logical off or false state (NOTE: The plural is **zeros** or **zeroes**.) ■ *verb* to erase or clear a file or the contents of a programmable device

zero insertion force socket /ˌzɪərəʊ ɪn ˌsɜːʃ(ə)n fɔːs 'sɒkɪt/ *noun* a chip socket that has movable connection terminals, allowing the chip to be inserted without using any force, then a small lever is turned to grip the legs of the chip. Also called **ZIF socket**

zero slot LAN /ˌzɪərəʊ slɒt 'læn/ *noun* a local area network that does not use internal expansion adapters, but instead the serial port or, sometimes, an external pocket network adapters connected to the printer port

zero wait state /ˌzɪərəʊ 'weɪt ˌsteɪt/ *noun* the state of a device (normally processor or memory chips) that is fast enough to run at the same speed as the other components in a computer, so does not have to be artificially slowed down by inserting wait states

ZIF socket /'zɪf ˌsɒkɪt/ *noun* same as **zero insertion force socket**

zine /ziːn/ *noun* a paper, Internet magazine or other periodical published by its author, issued at irregular intervals and usually aimed at specialist readers

ZIP /zɪp/ *noun* a filename extension given to files that contain compressed data, usually generated by the PKZIP shareware utility program

zip code /'zɪp 'kəʊd/ *noun US* letters and numbers used to indicate a town or street in an address on an envelope

Zip disk /'zɪp dɪsk/ *noun* a proprietary type of removable storage device, similar to a removable hard disk drive, manufactured by Iomega Corp. to provide a convenient backup and storage medium with 100 Mb or 1Gb disk capacity.

zip file /'zɪp faɪl/ *noun* a computer file with the extension .zip containing data that has been compressed for storage or transmission.

ZMODEM /'zed ˌməʊdem/ *noun* an enhanced version of the XMODEM file transfer protocol that includes error detection and the ability to restart a transfer where it left off if the connection is cut

zone /zəʊn/ *noun* **1.** a region or part of a screen defined for specialised printing **2.** the division of the area of a television picture raste. Usually, zone 1 is the part held within a circle of 0.8 of picture height, zone 2 is the circle equal to picture width, and zone 3 is the rest of the area outside zone 2.

zoom /zuːm/ *verb* **1.** to enlarge an area of text or graphics to make it easier to work on **2.** to change the focal length of a lens to enlarge the object in the viewfinder

> '...any window can be zoomed to full-screen size by pressing the F-5 function key' [*Byte*]

> '...there are many options to allow you to zoom into an area for precision work' [*Electronics & Wireless World*]

zoomed video port /ˌzuːmd 'vɪdiəʊ ˌpɔːt/ *noun* full form of **ZV Port**

zooming /'zuːmɪŋ/ *noun* the process of enlarging an area of text or graphics ○ *Variable zooming from 25% to 400% of actual size.*

zoom lens /'zuːm lenz/ *noun* a lens whose focal length can be varied to make an object larger in the viewfinder

zoom microphone /ˌzuːm 'maɪkrəfəʊn/ *noun* a microphone which can give a zoom effect by moving towards or away from sound

ZV Port /ˌzed 'viː ˌpɔːt/ *noun* an interface port that allows data to be transferred from a PC Card directly to the computer's video controller without passing through the computer's central processor. Full form **zoomed video port** (NOTE: It is used to allow a laptop computer to display live images from a video camera plugged into the computer's PC Card socket.)

SUPPLEMENTS

HTML codes

The following is a list of the basic HTML codes (or tags) used to format webpages.

<a> ... </a>
creates a hyperlink target or source. For example,

```
<a href="www.bloomsbury.com">link to Bloomsbury</a>
```

will create a hyperlink to the Bloomsbury Publishing Plc webpage.

<address> ... </address>
enclosed text is formatted in smaller typeface as an address

<applet> ... </applet>
defines an applet within the document

<area>
defines the area of a graphic image that will respond to a mouse click using a client-side imagemap

<b> ... </b>
formats enclosed text in a bold typeface

<base>
defines the URL that is added in front of all relative URLs used within the document

<basefont>
defines the point size of the font used to format for the following text

<bgsound>
defines the audio file played as a background sound to the document (used in MS-IE)

<big> ... </big>
formats enclosed text in a bigger typeface

<blockquote> ... </blockquote>
formats the enclosed text as a quotation

<body> ... </body>
defines the start and finish of this document's body text; also used to define a graphic image used as a background, and to set the default colour of the text, hyperlinks and margins for the document

**
**
inserts a line break in the text; the <p> code also inserts a carriage return

<caption> ... </caption>
defines the caption for a table

<center> ... </center>
formats enclosed text to be centered across the line

<cite> ... </cite>
formats enclosed text as a citation

<code> ... </code>
formats enclosed text as program code, normally using the Courier typeface

<col>
defines the properties for a column that has been defined using <colgroup>

HTML codes *continued*

<colgroup>
defines a column

<comment> ... </comment>
defines the enclosed text to be a comment. Only works in MS IE; with any other browser you should use the <!> comment <> tag format

<dd> ... </dd>
defines one element of a definition list

<dfn> ... </dfn>
formats enclosed text as a definition

<dir> ... </dir>
creates a directory list using the <li> to create entries

<div> ... </div>
divides the text within a document and formats each division

<dl> ... </dl>
creates a definition list using the <dd> and <dt> tags to create entries

<dt> ... </dt>
defines the definition part of an entry within a definition list

<em> ... </em>
formats enclosed text with emphasis (similar to bold typeface)

<embed> ... </embed>
points to an object to embed in a document

<font> ... </font>
defines the size, colour and typeface of the font to use for the enclosed text

<form> ... </form>
defines the following tags to be treated as one form; also defines how to process the form and where to send the encoded information

<frame> ... </frame>
defines a frame, including its border, colour, name and text

<frameset> ... </frameset>
defines a collection of frames

<h> ... </h>
defines a pre-set font size, such as <h1> for a large headings, <h4> for small headings

<hr>
breaks the current line of text and inserts a horizontal rule across the page

<html> ... </html>
defines the start and end of the entire html document

<i>... </i>
formats enclosed text using an italic typeface

<iframe> ... </iframe>
defines a floating frame

HTML codes *continued*

<img>
includes an image within a document, also defines a border for the image, size, alternative caption text and whether the image is a video clip

<input type=checkbox>
defines a checkbox button within a form

<input type=file>
defines a file-selection list within a form

<input type=image>
defines an image input element within a form

<input type=password>
defines a text input that displays an asterisk when text is entered

<input type=radio>
defines a radio button within a form

<input type=reset>
defines a button to reset the form's contents

<input type=submit>
defines a button to submit the form's contents to the named process

<input type=text>
defines a text input element to allow users to enter a line of text

<isindex>
defines the html document to be searchable by a defined search engine

<kbd> ... </kbd>
formats enclosed text as a keyboard input

<li> ... </li>
defines an item in a list; the list can be ordered using <ol> or unordered using <ul>

<link>
defines a link within a document header

<listing> ... </listing>
an old tag that is the same as the <pre> tag

<map> ... </map>
defines an image map that contains hotspots

<marquee> ... </marquee>
creates an animated scrolling text line, used in MS-IE

<menu> ... </menu>
defines a menu that has items created using the <li> tag

<meta>
allows the programmer to include extra information about the document

<multicol> ... </multicol>
defines multiple columns within the document; only used in Netscape Navigator

HTML codes *continued*

<nextid>
used by automated html document generators as a reference point within a file

<nobr> ... </nobr>
prevents the browser adding breaks within the enclosed text

<noframes> ... </noframes>
defines content that should be displayed if the browser does not support frames

<noscript> ... </noscript>
defines content that should be used if the browser does not support Java; only used in Netscape Navigator

<object> ... </object>
defines an object, applet or OLE object to be inserted into the document

<ol> ... </ol>
defines the start and end of a numbered list; items are inserted using the <li> tag

<option> ... </option>
defines one option within a <select> tag

<p> ... </p>
defines the start and end of a paragraph

<param> ... </param>
defines the parameters to be passed to an applet or object

<plaintext>
formats the rest of the document as plain text with spaces and breaks

<pre> ... </pre>
formats the enclosed text as plaintext with spaces and breaks

<s> ... </s>
formats enclosed text with a strikethrough (horizontal line)

<samp> ... </samp>
defines enclosed text as an example (sample)

<script> ... </script>
defines the start and end of a script written in a language such as JavaScript or VBScript

<select> ... </select>
defines a list of options within a form, each created using the <option> tag

<small> ... </small>
formats enclosed text in a small type size

<spacer>
inserts a character space within a line of text; only used in Netscape Navigator

<span> ... </span>
define a style sheet that formats text over several tags

<strike> ... </strike>
formats enclosed text with a strikethrough (horizontal line)

HTML codes *continued*

<strong> ... </strong>
formats enclosed text with emphasis, similar to bold typeface

<style> ... </style>
defines a collection of text formatting commands that can be referred to with this style command

_{...}
formats enclosed text as subscript

^{...}
formats enclosed text as superscript

<table> ... </table>
defines a table including border, colour, size and width; columns are added with <td> and rows with <tr>

<tbody>
a group of rows within a table

<td> ... </td>
defines a cell within a table, effectively adds a column to the table

<textarea> ... </textarea>
defines a multiple line text input element for a form

<tfoot>
defines rows within a table that are formatted as a footer to the table

<th> ... </th>
defines the header to each column in a table

<thead>
defines rows within a table that are formatted as a header to the table

<title> ... </title>
defines the title of an html document

<tr> ... </tr>
defines a row of cells within a table

<tt> ... </tt>
formats enclosed text in a monospaced typewriter-style font

<ul> ... </ul>
defines the start and end of a bulleted list of elements; each element is added using <li>

<var> ... </var>
enclosed text is the name of a variable

<wbr>
defines a possible point for a word break within a <nobr> line

<xmp> ... </xmp>
an old tag that formats enclosed text, similar to <pre>

Prefixes

T	tera-	10^{12}
G	giga-	10^{9}
M	mega-	10^{6}
k	kilo-	10^{3}
d	deci-	10^{-1}
c	centi-	10^{-2}
m	milli-	10^{-3}
µ	micro-	10^{-6}
n	nano-	10^{-9}
p	pico-	10^{-12}
f	femto-	10^{-15}
a	atto-	10^{-18}

Symbols

%	per cent
=	equals
≈	approximately equal to
≠	is not equal to
<	is less than
>	is more than
+	plus
-	minus
÷	divided by
x	multiplied by
∴	therefore
&	and

Decimal Conversion Table

	Decimal	BCD	Binary	Octal	Hexadecimal
base	*10*	*2*	*2*	*8*	*16*
	00	0000 0000	0000	00	0
	01	0000 0001	0001	01	1
	02	0000 0010	0010	02	2
	03	0000 0011	0011	03	3
	04	0000 0100	0100	04	4
	05	0000 0101	0101	05	5
	06	0000 0110	0110	06	6
	07	0000 0111	0111	07	7
	08	0000 1000	1000	10	8
	09	0000 1001	1001	11	9
	10	0001 0000	1010	12	A
	11	0001 0001	1011	13	B
	12	0001 0010	1100	14	C
	13	0001 0011	1101	15	D
	14	0001 0100	1110	16	E
	15	0001 0101	1111	17	F

Unicode Characters 0 – 207 in Decimal and Hexadecimal

dec	hex	char	dec	hex	char	dec	hex	char	dec	hex	char
0	0	NUL	52	34	4	104	68	h	156	9C	ST
1	1	SOH	53	35	5	105	69	i	157	9D	OSC
2	2	STX	54	36	6	106	6A	j	158	9E	PM
3	3	ETX	55	37	7	107	6B	k	159	9F	APC
4	4	EOT	56	38	8	108	6C	l	160	A0	NBSP
5	5	ENQ	57	39	9	109	6D	m	161	A1	¡
6	6	ACK	58	3A	:	110	6E	n	162	A2	¢
7	7	BEL	59	3B	;	111	6F	o	163	A3	£
8	8	BS	60	3C	<	112	70	p	164	A4	¤
9	9	HT	61	3D	=	113	71	q	165	A5	¥
10	0A	LF	62	3E	>	114	72	r	166	A6	¦
11	0B	VT	63	3F	?	115	73	s	167	A7	§
12	0C	FF	64	40	@	116	74	t	168	A8	¨
13	0D	CR	65	41	A	117	75	u	169	A9	©
14	0E	SO	66	42	B	118	76	v	170	AA	ª
15	0F	SI	67	43	C	119	77	w	171	AB	«
16	10	DLE	68	44	D	120	78	x	172	AC	¬
17	11	DC1	69	45	E	121	79	y	173	AD	SHY
18	12	DC2	70	46	F	122	7A	z	174	AE	®
19	13	DC3	71	47	G	123	7B	{	175	AF	¯
20	14	DC4	72	48	H	124	7C	|	176	B0	°
21	15	NAK	73	49	I	125	7D	}	177	B1	±
22	16	SYN	74	4A	J	126	7E	~	178	B2	²
23	17	ETB	75	4B	K	127	7F	DEL	179	B3	³
24	18	CAN	76	4C	L	128	80	xxx	180	B4	´
25	19	EM	77	4D	M	129	81	xxx	181	B5	µ
26	1A	SUB	78	4E	N	130	82	BPH	182	B6	¶
27	1B	ESC	79	4F	O	131	83	NBH	183	B7	·
28	1C	FS	80	50	P	132	84	IND	184	B8	¸
29	1D	GS	81	51	Q	133	85	NEL	185	B9	¹
30	1E	RS	82	52	R	134	86	SSA	186	BA	º
31	1F	US	83	53	S	135	87	ESA	187	BB	»
32	20	SP	84	54	T	136	88	HTS	188	BC	¼
33	21	!	85	55	U	137	89	HTJ	189	BD	½
34	22	“	86	56	V	138	8A	VTS	190	BE	¾
35	23	#	87	57	W	139	8B	PLD	191	BF	¿
36	24	$	88	58	X	140	8C	PLU	192	C0	À
37	25	%	89	59	Y	141	8D	RI	193	C1	Á
38	26	&	90	5A	Z	142	8E	SS2	194	C2	Â
39	27	‘	91	5B	[	143	8F	SS3	195	C3	Ã
40	28	(	92	5C	\	144	90	DCS	196	C4	Ä
41	29	)	93	5D	]	145	91	PU1	197	C5	Å
42	2A	*	94	5E	^	146	92	PU2	198	C6	Æ
43	2B	+	95	5F	_	147	93	STS	199	C7	Ç
44	2C	,	96	60		148	94	CCH	200	C8	È
45	2D	-	97	61	a	149	95	MW	201	C9	É
46	2E	.	98	62	b	150	96	SPA	202	CA	Ê
47	2F	/	99	63	c	151	97	EPA	203	CB	Ë
48	30	0	100	64	d	152	98	SOS	204	CC	Ì
49	31	1	101	65	e	153	99	xxx	205	CD	Í
50	32	2	102	66	f	154	9A	SCI	206	CE	Î
51	33	3	103	67	g	155	9B	CSI	207	CF	Ï

Unicode Characters 208 – 255 in Decimal and Hexadecimal

dec	hex	char	dec	hex	char	dec	hex	char	dec	hex	char
208	D0	Đ	220	DC	Ü	232	E8	è	244	F4	ô
209	D1	Ñ	221	DD	Ý	233	E9	é	245	F5	õ
210	D2	Ò	222	DE	Þ	234	EA	ê	246	F6	ö
211	D3	Ó	223	DF	ß	235	EB	ë	247	F7	÷
212	D4	Ô	224	E0	à	236	EC	ì	248	F8	ø
213	D5	Õ	225	E1	á	237	ED	í	249	F9	ù
214	D6	Ö	226	E2	â	238	EE	î	250	FA	ú
215	D7	×	227	E3	ã	239	EF	ï	251	FB	û
216	D8	Ø	228	E4	ä	240	F0	ð	252	FC	ü
217	D9	Ù	229	E5	å	241	F1	ñ	253	FD	ý
218	DA	Ú	230	E6	æ	242	F2	ò	254	FE	þ
219	DB	Û	231	E7	ç	243	F3	ó	255	FF	ÿ

Notes:
1. Characters 0 – 127 form the ASCII character set.
2. Characters 32 – 127 and 160 – 255 are the same in the ANSI character set.

Unicode CO and CI controls

NUL null
SOH start of heading
SOT start of text
ETX end of text
EOT end of transmission
ENQ enquiry
ACK acknowledge
BEL bell
BS backspace
HT horizontal tab
LF line feed
VT vertical tab
FF form feed
CR carriage return
SO shift out
SI shift in
DLE data link escape
DC device control
NAK negative ack.
SYN synchronous idle
ETB end of transmission block
CAN cancel

EM end of medium
SUB substitute
ESC esape
FS file separator
GS group separator
RS record separator
US unit separator
SP space
DEL delete
BPH break permitted here
NBH no break here
IND indent
NEL next line
SSA start of selected area
OSC operating system command
ESA end of selected area
HTS character tabulation set
HTJ character tabulation with justification
VTS line tabulation set
PLD partial line forward
PLU partial line backward

RI reverse line feed
SS2 single shift two
SS3 single shift three
DCS device control string
PU1 private use one
PU2 private use two
STS set tranmit state
CCH cancel character
MW message waiting
SPA start of guarded area
EPA end of guarded area
SOS start of string
SCI single character introducer
CSI control sequence introducer
ST string terminator
PM privacy message
APC application program command
NBSP no-break space
SHY soft hyphen

Logic Function Tables

Written as — **Drawn as** — **logic table**

A

A	A
0	0
1	1

A AND B

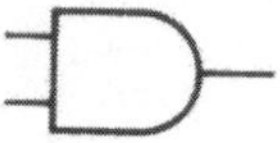

A	B	$A \cdot B$
0	0	0
0	1	0
1	0	0
1	1	1

A OR B

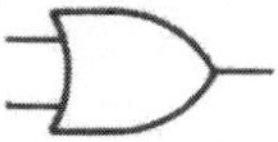

A	B	$A+B$
0	0	0
0	1	1
1	0	1
1	1	1

A EXOR B

A	B	A exor B
0	0	0
0	1	1
1	0	1
1	1	0

NOT A

A	$\overline{A}$
0	1
1	0

A NAND B

A	B	$\overline{A \cdot B}$
0	0	1
0	1	1
1	0	1
1	1	0

A NOR B

A	B	$\overline{A+B}$
0	0	1
0	1	0
1	0	0
1	1	0

A EXNOR B

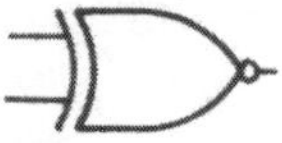

A	B	A exnor B
0	0	1
0	1	0
1	0	0
1	1	1

Printed and bound by CPI Group (UK) Ltd, Croydon, CR0 4YY
11/10/2024
01043550-0004